CASES ON THE
LAW OF CONTRACT

SIXTH EDITION

BY

G. C. CHESHIRE
D.C.L., LL.D., F.B.A.

OF LINCOLN'S INN, BARRISTER
SOMETIME VINERIAN PROFESSOR OF ENGLISH LAW IN THE UNIVERSITY OF
OXFORD AND FELLOW OF ALL SOULS COLLEGE, OXFORD

AND

C. H. S. FIFOOT
M.A., F.B.A.

OF THE MIDDLE TEMPLE, BARRISTER
SOMETIME FELLOW OF HERTFORD COLLEGE, OXFORD

LONDON
BUTTERWORTHS
1973

ENGLAND:	BUTTERWORTH & CO. (PUBLISHERS) LTD. LONDON: 88 Kingsway, WC2B 6AB
AUSTRALIA:	BUTTERWORTHS PTY. LTD. SYDNEY: 586 Pacific Highway, Chatswood, NSW 2067 MELBOURNE: 343 Little Collins Street, 3000 BRISBANE: 240 Queen Street, 4000
CANADA:	BUTTERWORTH & CO. (CANADA) LTD. TORONTO: 14 Curity Avenue, 374
NEW ZEALAND:	BUTTERWORTHS OF NEW ZEALAND LTD. WELLINGTON: 26/28 Waring Taylor Street, 1
SOUTH AFRICA:	BUTTERWORTH & CO. (SOUTH AFRICA) (PTY.) LTD. DURBAN: 152-154 Gale Street

First Published	..	..	..	.. *March,* 1946
Reprinted	..	..	..	*February,* 1948
Second Edition	..	..	..	.. *July,* 1954
Third Edition	..	..	..	.. *April,* 1959
Reprinted	..	..	..	*February,* 1963
Fourth Edition	..	..	..	.. *July,* 1965
Fifth Edition	..	..	..	.. *June,* 1969
Sixth Edition	..	..	..	.. *March,* 1973

ISBN — Casebound: 0 406 56503 1
Limp: 0 406 56504 x

MADE AND PRINTED IN GREAT BRITAIN BY
WILLIAM CLOWES AND SONS LIMITED
LONDON, BECCLES AND COLCHESTER

PREFACE

In this edition we have removed thirteen cases and added fifteen. Among the additions are *Jones* v. *Padavatton*, a useful example of the problems raised by the doubtful intention to create legal relations; *Thornton* v. *Shoe Lane Parking, Ltd.*, a discussion of exemption clauses in a novel setting; *Lewis* v. *Averay*, described by LORD DENNING as likely " to interest students and find its place in the text-books "; and judgments of the House of Lords in *Gallie* v. *Lee* which, by disproving *Howatson* v. *Webb* and over-ruling *Carlisle* and *Cumberland Banking Co.* v. *Bragg*, have made welcome changes in the operation of the plea *non est factum*. We have also set side by side the alternative guiding-lines to the relative importance of contractual terms offered by the Court of Appeal in *Hong Kong Fir Shipping Co. Ltd.* v. *Kawasaki Kisen Kaisha, Ltd.* and *The Mihalis Angelos*.

In the previous edition of this book we had given the text of the Misrepresentation Act, 1967. We have now added that of the Law Reform (Frustrated Contracts) Act, 1943. These statutes have at least two features in common. In each the drafting is in places ambiguous or obscure; and each has tempted surprisingly few litigants to " chance their arm " and thus clarify its meaning.

It is again our grateful duty to repeat our thanks to the Incorporated Council of Law Reporting for England and Wales, and to the proprietors of the All England Law Reports, the Commonwealth Law Reports, the Law Journal Reports and the Law Times Reports, for permission to reprint the statements of fact and the judgments, or parts thereof, in the cases which we have copied from their publications.

We wish also to thank the publishers and the printers for their great help in the preparation of this edition.

G.C.C.
C.H.S.F.

15th January, 1973.

CONTENTS

TABLE OF CASES

A

PAGE

PAGE

Joseph Constantine Steamship Line, Ltd. *v.* Imperial Smelting Corporation Ltd.,
[1942] A.C. 154; [1941] 2 All E.R. 165; 110 L.J.(K.B.) 433; 165 L.T. 27; 57 T.L.R.
485; 46 Com. Cas. 258, H.L. 415, 431
Joseph Evans & Co. *v.* Heathcote. *See* Evans (Joseph) & Co. *v.* Heathcote.
Joynson *v.* Hunt & Son (1905), 93 L.T. 470; 21 T.L.R. 692, C.A. 452

K

Karberg's Case. *See* Metropolitan Coal Consumers' Association, *Re*, Karberg's Case.
Karsales (Harrow), Ltd. *v.* Wallis, [1956] 2 All E.R. 866; [1956] 1 W.L.R. 936; 100 Sol.
Jo. 548, C.A. 100, 101
Kearley *v.* Thomson (1890), 24 Q.B.D. 742; [1890] All E.R. Rep. 1055; 59 L.J. (Q.B.)
288; 63 L.T. 150; 54 J.P. 804; 38 W.R. 614; 6 T.L.R. 267, C.A. 253, 268
Kearney *v.* Whitehaven Colliery Co., [1893] 1 Q.B. 700; [1893] All E.R. Rep. 556; 62
L.J. (M.C.) 129; 68 L.T. 690; 57 J.P. 645; 41 W.R. 594; 9 T.L.R. 402; 4 R. 388,
C.A. 305
Keenan *v.* Handley (1864), 2 De G.J. & Sm. 283; 10 L.T. 800; 28 J.P. 660; 10 Jur. (N.S.)
906; 12 W.R. 1021 351
Keighley, Maxsted & Co. *v.* Durant [1901] A.C. 240; [1900–3] All E.R. Rep. 40; 70
L.J. (K.B.) 662; 84 L.T. 777; 17 T.L.R. 527; 45 Sol. Jo. 536 .. .. **374**
Kekewich *v.* Manning (1851), 1 De G.M. & G. 176; 21 L.J. (Ch.) 577; 18 L.T. (O.S.) 263;
16 Jur. 625 340
Kelly *v.* Solari (1841), 9 M. & W. 54; [1835–42] All E.R. Rep. 320; 11 L.J. (Ex.) 10; 6
Jur. 107 .. .. 501, 504, 505
Kemble *v.* Farren (1829), 6 Bing. 141; [1824–34] All E.R. Rep. 641; 3 Moo. & P. 425; 7
L.J. (O.S.) (C.P.) 258 482
Kendall *v.* Hamilton (1879), 4 App. Cas. 504; [1874–80] All E.R. Rep. 932; 48 L.J.
(Q.B.) 705; 41 L.T. 418; 28 W.R. 97, H.L. 381
Kennedy *v.* Panama, etc. Mail Co. (1867), L.R. 2 Q.B. 580; 8 B. & S. 571; 36 L.J. (Q.B.)
260; 17 L.T. 62; 15 W.R. 1039 122
Keppell *v.* Bailey (1834), 2 My. & K. 517; [1834–34] All E.R. Rep. 10; Coop. *temp.* Brough
298 359
Kerrison *v.* Glyn, Mills, Currie & Co. (1909), 101 L.T. 675; [1911–13] All E.R. Rep. 417;
26 T.L.R. 37; 54 Sol. Jo. 181; 15 Com. Cas. 1; reversed (1910), 102 L.T. 674; 26
T.L.R. 404; 15 Com. Cas. 241, C.A.; (1911), 81 L.J. (K.B.) 465; 105 L.T. 721; 28
T.L.R. 106; 56 Sol. Jo. 139; 17 Com. Cas. 41, H.L. 505
King, *Re, Ex parte* Unity Joint Stock Mutual Banking Association (1858), 3 De G. & J.
63; 27 L.J. (Bcy.) 33; 31 L.T. (O.S.) 242; 4 Jur. (N.S.) 1257; 6 W.R. 640 .. 324, 325, 326
King's Norton Metal Co., Ltd. *v.* Edridge, Merrett & Co., (1897), 14 T.L.R. 98, C.A.: 134, 161
Kirchner & Co. *v.* Gruban, [1909] 1 Ch. 413; [1908–10] All E.R. Rep. 242; 78 L.J. (Ch.)
117; 99 L.T. 932; 53 Sol. Jo. 151 493
Kirton *v.* Eliott (1613), 2 Bulst. 69; *sub nom.* Ketsey's Case, Cro. Jac. 320; *sub nom.*
Keteley's Case, 1 Brownl. 120 323
Kish *v.* Taylor, [1912] A.C. 604; [1911–13] All E.R. Rep. 481; 81 L.J. (K.B.) 1027; 106
L.T. 900; 28 T.L.R. 425; 56 Sol. Jo. 518; 12 Asp. M.L.C. 217; 17 Com. Cas. 355,
H.L. 75
Knightsbridge Estates Trust, Ltd. *v.* Byrne, [1939] Ch. 441; [1938] 4 All E.R. 618; 108
L.J. (Ch.) 105; 160 L.T. 68; 82 Sol. Jo. 989; 55 T.L.R. 196, C.A.; on appeal, [1940]
A.C. 613; [1940] 2 All E.R. 401; 109 L.J. (Ch.) 200; 162 L.T. 388; 56 T.L.R. 652;
84 Sol. Jo. 488, H.L. 286
Koufos *v.* Czarnikow (C.), Ltd. *See* Heron II, The, Koufos *v.* Czarnikow (C.), Ltd.
Krawill Machinery Corporation *v.* Herd (Robert C.) & Co., Inc., [1959] 1 Lloyd's Rep.
305 337
Krell *v.* Henry, [1903] 2 K.B. 740; [1900–3] All E.R. Rep. 20; 72 L.J. (K.B.) 794; 89
L.T. 328; 52 W.R. 246; 19 T.L.R. 711, C.A. 127

L

Lake *v.* Simmons, [1927] A.C. 487; [1927] All E.R. Rep. 49; 96 L.J.K.B. 621; 137
L.T. 233; 43 T.L.R. 417; 71 Sol. Jo. 369; 33 Com. Cas. 16, H.L. 161
Lamb *v.* Vice (1840), 6 M. & W. 467; 8 Dowl. 360; 9 L.J. (Ex.) 177; 4 Jur. 341 .. 342
Lamb (W. T.) & Sons *v.* Goring Brick Co., [1932] 1 K.B. 710; [1931] All E.R. Rep. 314;
101 L.J. (K.B.) 214; 146 L.T. 318; 48 T.L.R. 160; 37 Com. Cas. 73, C.A. .. 283
Langford Property Co., Ltd. *v.* Batten, [1949] 2 All E.R. 422; 65 T.L.R. 577; 93 Sol. Jo.
616, C.A.; reversed, [1951] A.C. 223; [1950] 2 All E.R. 1079; 66 (pt. 2) T.L.R. 958;
94 Sol. Jo. 821, H.L. 133
Lansdown *v.* Lansdown (1730), 2 Jac. & W. 205; Mos. 364.. 135
Law *v.* Hodson (1809), 11 East, 300; 2 Camp. 147 231
Lawford *v.* Billericay Rural Council, [1903] 1 K.B. 772; 72 L.J. (K.B.) 554; 88
L.T. 317; 67 J.P. 245; 51 W.R. 630; 19 T.L.R. 322; 47 Sol. Jo. 366; 1 L.G.R.
535, C.A. 513
Laythoarp *v.* Bryant (1836), 2 Bing. (N.C.) 735; 2 Hodg. 25; 3 Scott, 238; 5 L.J.
(C.P.) 217 5
Leaf *v.* International Galleries, [1950] 2 K.B. 86; [1950] 1 All E.R. 693; 66 (pt. 1)
T.L.R. 1031, C.A. 60, 62, **188**
Leather Cloth Co. *v.* Lorsont (1869), L.R. 9 Eq. 345; 39 L.J. (Ch.) 86; 21 L.T. 661;
34 J.P. 328; 18 W.R. 572 .. .. 282, 290, 291
Ledingham *v.* Bermejo Estancia Co., Ltd., [1947] 1 All E.R. 749 35

THE PHENOMENA OF AGREEMENT

Carlill v. Carbolic Smoke Ball Co.

[1893] 1 Q.B. 256

An offer, to be capable of acceptance, must involve a definite promise by the offeror that he will bind himself if the exact terms specified by him are accepted.

An offer may be made either to a particular person or to the public at large.

If an offer takes the form of a promise in return for an act, the performance of that act is in itself an adequate indication of assent.

APPEAL from a decision of Hawkins, J.[1]

The defendants, who were the proprietors and vendors of a medical preparation called " The Carbolic Smoke Ball," inserted in the *Pall Mall Gazette* of November 13, 1891, and in other newspapers, the following advertisement :

> " 100*l*. reward will be paid by the Carbolic Smoke Ball Company to any person who contracts the increasing epidemic influenza, colds, or any disease caused by taking cold, after having used the ball three times daily for two weeks according to the printed directions supplied with each ball. 1000*l*. is deposited with the Alliance Bank, Regent Street, shewing our sincerity in the matter. During the last epidemic of influenza many thousand carbolic smoke balls were sold as preventives against this disease, and in no ascertained case was the disease contracted by those using the carbolic smoke ball. One carbolic smoke ball will last a family several months, making it the cheapest remedy in the world at the price, 10*s*., post free. The ball can be refilled at a cost of 5*s*. Address, Carbolic Smoke Ball Company, 27, Princes Street, Hanover Square, London."

The plaintiff, a lady, on the faith of this advertisement, bought one of the balls at a chemist's, and used it as directed, three times a day, from November 20, 1891, to January 17, 1892, when she was attacked by influenza. HAWKINS, J., held that she was entitled to recover the 100*l*. The defendants appealed.

LINDLEY, L.J., delivered judgment dismissing the appeal.

BOWEN, L.J. I am of the same opinion. We were asked to say that this document was a contract too vague to be enforced.

The first observation which arises is that the document itself is not a contract at all, it is only an offer made to the public. The defendants contend next, that it is an offer the terms of which are too vague to be treated as a definite offer, inasmuch as there is no limit of time fixed for the catching of the influenza, and it cannot be supposed that the advertisers seriously meant to promise to pay money to every person who catches the influenza at any time after the inhaling of the smoke ball. It was urged also, that if you look at this document you will find much vagueness as to the persons with whom the contract was intended to be made—that, in the first place, its terms are wide enough to include persons who may have used the smoke ball before the advertisement was issued ; at all events, that it is an offer to the world in general, and, also, that it is unreasonable to suppose it to be a definite offer, because nobody in their senses would contract themselves out of the opportunity of checking the experiment which was going to be made at their own expense. It is also contended that the advertisement is

---

[1] [1892] 2 Q. B. 484.

rather in the nature of a puff or a proclamation than a promise or offer intended to mature into a contract when accepted. But the main point seems to be that the vagueness of the document shews that no contract whatever was intended. It seems to me that in order to arrive at a right conclusion we must read this advertisement in its plain meaning, as the public would understand it. It was intended to be issued to the public and to be read by the public. How would an ordinary person reading this document construe it? It was intended unquestionably to have some effect, and I think the effect which it was intended to have, was to make people use the smoke ball, because the suggestions and allegations which it contains are directed immediately to the use of the smoke ball as distinct from the purchase of it. It did not follow that the smoke ball was to be purchased from the defendants directly, or even from agents of theirs directly. The intention was that the circulation of the smoke ball should be promoted, and that the use of it should be increased. The advertisement begins by saying that a reward will be paid by the Carbolic Smoke Ball Company to any person who contracts the increasing epidemic after using the ball. It has been said that the words do not apply only to persons who contract the epidemic after the publication of the advertisement, but include persons who had previously contracted the influenza. I cannot so read the advertisement. It is written in colloquial and popular language, and I think that it is equivalent to this : " 100*l*. will be paid to any person who shall contract the increasing epidemic after having used the carbolic smoke ball three times daily for two weeks." And it seems to me that the way in which the public would read it would be this : that if anybody, after the advertisement was published, used three times daily for two weeks the carbolic smoke ball, and then caught cold, he would be entitled to the reward. Then again it was said : " How long is this protection to endure ? Is it to go on for ever, or for what limit of time ? " I think that there are two constructions of this document, each of which is good sense, and each of which seems to me to satisfy the exigencies of the present action. It may mean that the protection is warranted to last during the epidemic, and it was during the epidemic that the plaintiff contracted the disease. I think, more probably, it means that the smoke ball will be a protection while it is in use. That seems to me the way in which an ordinary person would understand an advertisement about medicine, and about a specific against influenza. It could not be supposed that after you have left off using it you are still to be protected for ever, as if there was to be a stamp set upon your forehead that you were never to catch influenza because you had once used the carbolic smoke ball. I think the immunity is to last during the use of the ball. That is the way in which I should naturally read it, and it seems to me that the subsequent language of the advertisement supports that construction. It says : " During the last epidemic of influenza many thousand carbolic smoke balls were sold, and in no ascertained case was the disease contracted by those using " (not " who had used ") " the carbolic smoke ball," and it concludes with saying that one smoke ball will last a family several months (which imports that it is to be efficacious while it is being used), and that the ball can be refilled at a cost of 5*s*. I, therefore, have myself no hesitation in saying that I think, on the construction of this advertisement, the protection was to enure during the time that the carbolic smoke ball was being used. My brother, the Lord Justice who preceded me, thinks that the contract would be sufficiently definite if you were to read it in the sense that the protection was to be warranted during a reasonable period after use. I have some difficulty myself on that point ; but it is not necessary for me to consider it further, because the disease here was contracted during the use of the carbolic smoke ball.

Was it intended that the 100*l*. should, if the conditions were fulfilled, be paid ? The advertisement says that 1000*l*. is lodged at the bank for the purpose. Therefore, it cannot be said that the statement that 100*l*. would be paid was intended to be a mere puff. I think it was intended to be understood by the public as an offer which was to be acted upon.

But it was said there was no check on the part of the persons who issued the advertisement, and that it would be an insensate thing to promise 100*l*. to a person who used the smoke ball unless you could check or superintend his manner of using it. The answer to that argument seems to me to be that if a person chooses to make extravagant promises of this kind he probably does so because it pays him to make them, and, if he has made them, the extravagance of the promises is no reason in law why he should not be bound by them.

It was also said that the contract is made with all the world—that is, with everybody ; and that you cannot contract with everybody. It is not a contract made with all the world. There is the fallacy of the argument. It is an offer made to all the world ; and why should not an offer be made to all the world which is to ripen into a contract with anybody who comes forward and performs the condition ? It is an offer to become liable to any one who, before it is retracted, performs the condition, and although the offer is made to the world, the contract is made with that limited portion of the public who come forward and perform the condition on the faith of the advertisement. It is not like cases in which you offer to negotiate, or you issue advertisements that you have got a stock of books to sell, or houses to let, in which case there is no offer to be bound by any contract. Such advertisements are offers to negotiate—offers to receive offers—offers to chaffer, as, I think, some learned judge in one of the cases has said. If this is an offer to be bound, then it is a contract the moment the person fulfils the condition. That seems to me to be sense, and it is also the ground on which all these advertisement cases have been decided during the century ; and it cannot be put better than in Willes, J.'s judgment in *Spencer* v. *Harding*[1]. " In the advertisement cases," he says, " there never was any doubt that the advertisement amounted to a promise to pay the money to the person who first gave information. The difficulty suggested was that it was a contract with all the world. But that, of course, was soon overruled. It was an offer to become liable to any person who, before the offer should be retracted, should happen to be the person to fulfil the contract, of which the advertisement was an offer or tender. That is not the sort of difficulty which presents itself here. If the circular had gone on, ' and we undertake to sell to the highest bidder,' the reward cases would have applied, and there would have been a good contract in respect of the persons." As soon as the highest bidder presented himself, says Willes, J., the person who was to hold the *vinculum juris* on the other side of the contract was ascertained, and it became settled.

Then it was said that there was no notification of the acceptance of the contract. One cannot doubt that, as an ordinary rule of law, an acceptance

---

[1] (1870), L. R. 5 C. P. 561, at p. 563.

of an offer made ought to be notified to the person who makes the offer, in order that the two minds may come together. Unless this is done the two minds may be apart, and there is not that consensus which is necessary according to the English Law—I say nothing about the laws of other countries —to make a contract. But there is this clear gloss to be made upon that doctrine, that as notification of acceptance is required for the benefit of the person who makes the offer, the person who makes the offer may dispense with notice to himself if he thinks it desirable to do so, and I suppose there can be no doubt that where a person, in an offer made by him to another person, expressly or impliedly intimates a particular mode of acceptance as sufficient to make the bargain binding, it is only necessary for the other person to whom such offer is made to follow the indicated method of acceptance ; and if the person making the offer expressly or impliedly intimates in his offer that it will be sufficient to act on the proposal without communicating acceptance of it to himself, performance of the condition is a sufficient acceptance without notification.

That seems to me to be the principle which lies at the bottom of the acceptance cases, of which two instances are the well-known judgment of Mellish, L.J., in *Harris's* case[1], and the very instructive judgment of Lord Blackburn in *Brogden* v. *Metropolitan Rail Co.*[2], in which he appears to me to take exactly the line I have indicated.

Now, if that is the law, how are we to find out whether the person who makes the offer does intimate that notification of acceptance will not be necessary in order to constitute a binding bargain ? In many cases you look to the offer itself. In many cases you extract from the character of the transaction that notification is not required, and in the advertisement cases it seems to me to follow as an inference to be drawn from the transaction itself that a person is not to notify his acceptance of the offer before he performs the condition, but that if he performs the condition notification is dispensed with. It seems to me that from the point of view of common sense no other idea could be entertained. If I advertise to the world that my dog is lost, and that anybody who brings the dog to a particular place will be paid some money, are all the police or other persons whose business it is to find lost dogs to be expected to sit down and write me a note saying that they have accepted my proposal ? Why, of course, they at once look after the dog, and as soon as they find the dog they have performed the condition. The essence of the transaction is that the dog should be found, and it is not necessary under such circumstances, as it seems to me, that in order to make the contract binding there should be any notification of acceptance. It follows from the nature of the thing that the performance of the condition is sufficient acceptance without the notification of it, and a person who makes an offer in an advertisement of that kind makes an offer which must be read by the light of that commonsense reflection. He does, therefore, in his offer impliedly indicate that he does not require notification of the acceptance of the offer.

A further argument for the defendants was that this was a *nudum pactum*—that there was no consideration for the promise—that taking the influenza was only a condition, and that the using the smoke ball was only a condition, and that there was no consideration at all ; in fact, that there was no request, express or implied, to use the smoke ball. Now, I will not

---

[1] (1872), 7 Ch. App. 587.   [2] (1877), 2 App. Cas. 666, at p. 691.

enter into an elaborate discussion upon the law as to requests in this kind of contracts. I will simply refer to *Victors* v. *Davies*[1] and Serjeant Manning's note to *Fisher* v. *Pyne*[2], which everybody ought to read who wishes to embark in this controversy. The short answer, to abstain from academical discussion, is, it seems to me, that there is here a request to use involved in the offer. Then as to the alleged want of consideration. The definition of " consideration " given in Selwyn's Nisi Prius, 8th edn., p. 47, which is cited and adopted by Tindal, C.J., in the case of *Laythoarp* v. *Bryant*[3], is this : " Any act of the plaintiff from which the defendant derives a benefit or advantage, or any labour, detriment, or inconvenience sustained by the plaintiff, provided such act is performed or such inconvenience suffered by the plaintiff, with the consent, either express or implied, of the defendant." Can it be said here that if the person who reads this advertisement applies thrice daily, for such time as may seem to him tolerable, the carbolic smoke ball to his nostrils for a whole fortnight, he is doing nothing at all—that it is a mere act which is not to count towards consideration to support a promise (for the law does not require us to measure the adequacy of the consideration). Inconvenience sustained by one party at the request of the other is enough to create a consideration. I think, therefore, that it is consideration enough that the plaintiff took the trouble of using the smoke ball. But I think also that the defendants received a benefit from this user, for the use of the smoke ball was contemplated by the defendants as being indirectly a benefit to them, because the use of the smoke balls would promote their sale.

Then we were pressed with *Gerhard* v. *Bates*[4]. In *Gerhard* v. *Bates*, which arose upon demurrer, the point upon which the action failed was that the plaintiff did not allege that the promise was made to the class of which alone the plaintiff was a member, and that therefore there was no privity between the plaintiffs and the defendant. Then Lord Campbell went on to give a second reason. If his first reason was not enough, and the plaintiff and the defendant there had come together as contracting parties and the only question was consideration, it seems to me Lord Campbell's reasoning would not have been sound. It is only to be supported by reading it as an additional reason for thinking that they had not come into the relation of contracting parties ; but, if so, the language was superfluous. The truth is, that if in that case you had found a contract between the parties there would have been no difficulty about consideration ; but you could not find such a contract. Here, in the same way, if you once made up your mind that there was a promise made to this lady who is the plaintiff, as one of the public—a promise made to her that if she used the smoke ball three times daily for a fortnight and got the influenza, she should have 100*l.*—it seems to me that her using the smoke ball was sufficient consideration. I cannot picture to myself the view of the law on which the contrary could be held when you have once found who are the contracting parties. If I say to a person, " If you use such and such a medicine for a week I will give you 5*l.*," and he uses it, there is ample consideration for the promise.

A. L. SMITH, L.J., delivered judgment to the same effect.

---

[1] (1844), 12 M. & W. 758.
[3] (1836), 3 Scott, 238, at p. 250.
[2] (1840), 1 Man. & G. 265.
[4] (1853), 2 E. & B. 476.

Pharmaceutical Society of Great Britain v. Boots Cash Chemists (Southern), Ltd.

[1952] 2 Q.B. 795

An invitation to treat is not an offer capable of conversion into a contract by acceptance, but represents a process of negotiation that precedes the making of a definite offer. The display of goods in a shop with price attached is only an invitation to treat.

SPECIAL CASE stated by the parties under R.S.C. Ord. 34, r. 1.

The defendants carried on a business comprising the retail sale of drugs at their premises at Edgware, which were entered in the register of premises kept pursuant to section 12 of the Pharmacy and Poisons Act, 1933, from which they regularly sold drugs by retail. The premises comprised a single room so adapted that customers might serve themselves, and the business there was described by a printed notice at the entrance as " Boots Self-Service." On entry each customer passed a barrier where a wire basket was obtained. Beyond the barrier the principal part of the room, which contained accommodation for 60 customers, contained shelves around the wall and on an island fixture in the centre, on which articles were displayed. One part of the room was described by a printed notice as the " Toilet Dept.," and another part as the " Chemists' Dept." On the shelves in the chemists' department drugs, including proprietary medicines, were severally displayed in individual packages or containers with a conspicuous indication of the retail price of each. The drugs and proprietary medicines covered a wide range and one section of the shelves in the chemists' department was devoted exclusively to drugs which were included in or which contained substances included in Part I of the Poisons List referred to in section 17 (1) of the Pharmacy and Poisons Act, 1933; no such drugs were displayed on any shelves outside the section to which a shutter was fitted so that at any time all the articles in that section could be securely inclosed and excluded from display. None of the drugs in that section came within the First Schedule to the Poisons Rules, 1949 (S.I. 1949 No. 539).

The staff employed by the defendants at the premises comprised a manager, a registered pharmacist, three assistants and two cashiers, and during the time that the premises were open for the sale of drugs the manager, the registered pharmacist, and one or more of the assistants were present in the room. Each customer selected from the shelves the article that he wished to buy and placed it in the wire basket; in order to leave the premises the customer had to pass by one of two exits at each of which was a cash desk where a cashier was stationed who scrutinized the articles selected by the customer, assessed the value and accepted payment. The chemists' department was under the personal control of the registered pharmacist, who carried out all his duties at the premises subject to the directions of a superintendent appointed by the defendants in accordance with the provisions of section 9 of the Act. The pharmacist was stationed near the poisons section, where his certificate of registration was conspicuously displayed and was in view of the cash desks. In every case involving the sale of a drug the pharmacist supervised that part of the transaction which took place at the cash desk and was authorized by the defendants to prevent at that stage of the transaction, if he thought fit, any customer from removing any drug from the premises. No steps were taken by the defendants to inform customers before they selected any article which they wished to purchase of the pharmacist's authorization.

On April 13, 1951, at the defendants' premises, two customers, following the procedure outlined above, respectively purchased a bottle containing a medicine known as compound syrup of hypophosphites, containing 0·01% W/V strychnine, and a bottle containing medicine known as famel syrup, containing 0·023% W/V codeine, both of which substances are poisons included in Part I of the Poisons List, but, owing to the small percentages of strychnine and codeine respectively, hypophosphites and famel syrup do not come within the First Schedule to the Poisons Rules, 1949.

The question for the opinion of the court was whether the sales instanced on April 13, 1951, were effected by or under the supervision of a registered pharmacist in accordance with the provisions of section 18 (1) (*a*) (iii) of the Pharmacy and Poisons Act, 1933[1].

. . . . .

LORD GODDARD, C.J. This is a special case stated under Ord. 34, r. 1, by agreement between the parties concerning the application of section 18 of the Pharmacy and Poisons Act, 1933.

[His Lordship stated the facts substantially as set out above and continued:] The question which I have to decide is whether the sale is completed before or after the intending purchaser has passed the scrutiny of the pharmacist and paid his money, or, to put it in another way, whether the offer which initiates the negotiations is an offer by the shopkeeper or an offer by the buyer.

In the well-known case of *Carlill* v. *Carbolic Smoke Ball Co.* the company offered compensation to anybody who, having used a carbolic smoke ball for a certain length of time in a prescribed manner, contracted influenza. One of the inducements held out to people to buy the carbolic smoke ball was the representation that it was a specific against influenza. The plaintiff, who used it according to the prescription which was given, nevertheless, as might have been expected, contracted influenza. She then sued the Carbolic Smoke Ball Co. for, and recovered, the compensation. In the Court of Appeal Bowen, L.J., said[2]: " There can be no doubt that where a person in an offer made by him to another person, expressly or impliedly intimates a particular mode of acceptance as sufficient to make the bargain binding, it is only necessary for the other person to whom such offer is made to follow the indicated method of acceptance; and if the person making the offer, expressly or impliedly intimates in his offer that it will be sufficient to act on the proposal without communicating acceptance of it to himself, performance of the condition is a sufficient acceptance without notification."

Mr. Lloyd-Jones has said that in this case the defendants invite the public to come into their shop and say: " Help yourself to any of these articles, all of which are priced," and that that is an offer by the defendants to sell to any person who comes into the shop any of the articles so priced, which is accepted by any person who helps himself to any one of those articles. Mr. Glyn-Jones, on the other hand, contends that there is nothing revolutionary in this kind of trading, and that it amounts to no more than the

---

[1] Pharmacy and Poisons Act, 1933, s. 18: " (1) . . . it shall not be lawful—(*a*) for a person to sell any poison included in Part I of the Poisons List, unless—(i) he is an authorized seller of poisons; and (ii) the sale is effected on premises duly registered under Part I of this Act; and (iii) the sale is effected by, or under the supervision of, a registered pharmacist."

[2] [1893] 1 Q. B. 256, at p. 269; *supra*, p. 4.

exposure of goods which a shopkeeper sometimes makes either outside or inside his premises, while at the same time he leaves some goods behind the counter.   I think that it is a well-established principle that the mere exposure of goods for sale by a shopkeeper indicates to the public that he is willing to treat but does not amount to an offer to sell.   I do not think I ought to hold that that principle is completely reversed merely because there is a self-service scheme, such as this, in operation.   In my opinion it comes to no more than that the customer is informed that he may himself pick up an article and bring it to the shopkeeper with a view to buying it, and if, but only if, the shopkeeper then expresses his willingness to sell, the contract for sale is completed.   In fact, the offer is an offer to buy, and there is no offer to sell; the customer brings the goods to the shopkeeper to see whether he will sell or not.   In 99 cases out of a 100 he will sell and, if so, he accepts the customer's offer, but he need not do so.   The very fact that the supervising pharmacist is at the place where the money has to be paid is an indication to the purchaser that the shopkeeper may not be willing to complete a contract with anybody who may bring the goods to him.

Ordinary principles of common sense and of commerce must be applied in this matter, and to hold that in the case of self-service shops the exposure of an article is an offer to sell, and that a person can accept the offer by picking up the article, would be contrary to those principles and might entail serious results.   On the customer picking up the article the property would forthwith pass to him and he would be able to insist upon the shopkeeper allowing him to take it away, though in some particular cases the shopkeeper might think that very undesirable.   On the other hand, if a customer had picked up an article, he would never be able to change his mind and to put it back; the shopkeeper could say, " Oh no, the property has passed and you must pay the price."

It seems to me, therefore, that the transaction is in no way different from the normal transaction in a shop in which there is no self-service scheme.   I am quite satisfied it would be wrong to say that the shopkeeper is making an offer to sell every article in the shop to any person who might come in and that that person can insist on buying any article by saying " I accept your offer."   I agree with the illustration put forward during the case of a person who might go into a shop where books are displayed.   In most book-shops customers are invited to go in and pick up books and look at them even if they do not actually buy them.   There is no contract by the shopkeeper to sell until the customer has taken the book to the shopkeeper or his assistant and said " I want to buy this book " and the shopkeeper says " Yes."   That would not prevent the shopkeeper, seeing the book picked up, saying: " I am sorry I cannot let you have that book; it is the only copy I have got and I have already promised it to another customer."   Therefore, in my opinion, the mere fact that a customer picks up a bottle of medicine from the shelves in this case does not amount to an acceptance of an offer to sell.   It is an offer by the customer to buy and there is no sale effected until the buyer's offer to buy is accepted by the acceptance of the price.   The offer, the acceptance of the price, and therefore the sale, take place under the supervision of the pharmacist.   That is sufficient to satisfy the requirements of the section, for by using the words " the sale is effected by, or under the supervision of, a registered pharmacist " the Act envisages that the sale may be effected by someone not a pharmacist.   I think, too, that the sale is effected under his supervision if he is in a position to say " You must not have that; that contains poison," so that in any case, even if I were wrong in the view that I have taken on the question as to when the sale was completed, and it was completed when the customer took the article from the shelf, it would still be effected under the supervision of the pharmacist within the meaning of section 18.

There must, therefore, be judgment for the defendants.

The judgment of LORD GODDARD, C.J., was affirmed by the Court of Appeal: [1953] 1 Q.B. 401[1].

The Crown v. Clarke

[HIGH COURT OF AUSTRALIA]

(1927) 40 Commonwealth Law Reports, 227

Contractual obligations do not arise if services are rendered which in fact fulfil the terms of an offer but are performed in ignorance that the offer exists. There cannot be assent without knowledge of the offer and reliance upon it.

APPEAL from the Supreme Court of Western Australia.

By petition of right under the Crown Suits Act, 1898 (W.A.) Evan Clarke claimed £1,000 from the Crown in the following circumstances:— By proclamation dated 21st May 1926 R. Connell, Commissioner of Police, gave notice that he was authorized by the Government of Western Australia " to offer a reward of one thousand pounds for such information as shall lead to the arrest and conviction of the person or persons who committed the murders " of John Joseph Walsh, inspector of police, and Alexander Henry Pitman, sergeant of police, "and that His Excellency the Governor will be advised to extend a free pardon to any accomplice not being the person who actually committed the murders who shall first give the required information." On 6th June a man named Philip John Treffene and the petitioner were arrested and charged in connection with the murder of Walsh. On 10th June the petitioner, who had seen the proclamation, made a statement to the police: that on 28th April a man named Coulter said to petitioner " ' Pitman and Walsh came on us to-day and Phil shot Pitman before I knew what happened and then I shot Walsh,' and Treffene then spoke and said ' I shot Pitman and I then told Bill I had done my share and he could shoot Walsh; and he did so.' " Coulter was thereupon arrested. Subsequently, on the trial of Treffene and Coulter for the wilful murder of Walsh, the petitioner (who was called as a Crown witness) gave evidence in accordance with his statement. Treffene and Coulter were convicted on that charge. No indictment was presented with reference to the murder of Pitman; and the petitioner was released from custody. After the final determination of the case by the Court of Criminal Appeal the petitioner claimed the reward. The defences set up by the Crown were (*inter alia*) (1) that the petitioner's statement was not made with a view to obtaining the reward; (2) that he gave no information leading to the arrest of the murderers; and (3) that the mere fact that the petitioner gave evidence at the trial which procured the conviction of the two accused for the murder of Walsh did not entitle him to succeed in the action.

The action was heard by McMillan, C.J., who dismissed the petition with costs. His Honour found that Clarke had not acted on the faith of or in

---

[1] See also *Fisher* v. *Bell*, [1961] 1 Q. B. 394; [1960] 3 All E. R. 731, and *Partridge* v. *Crittenden*, [1968] 2 All E. R. 421.

reliance upon the offer made in the proclamation or with any intention of entering into any contract; and he said:—" The inference that the petitioner accepted the contract which would have been drawn from his conduct in giving the information is negatived by the facts and by Clarke's own evidence. He never was and never intended to be an informer. . . . He only told the truth after his arrest in order to save himself from the unfounded charge of murder." From the judgment of the learned Chief Justice the petitioner appealed to the Full Court of the Supreme Court, which, by a majority (Burnside and Draper, JJ., Northmore, J., dissenting), allowed the appeal with costs and ordered that judgment be entered for the petitioner for the sum of £1,000 and costs in the Court below.

From the judgment of the Full Court the Crown now appealed to the High Court.

Isaacs, A.C.J.   This is an appeal from the judgment of the Full Court of Western Australia. Evan Clarke proceeded, by petition of right under the Crown Suits Act, 1898, to sue the Crown for £1,000 promised by proclamation for such information as should lead to the arrest and conviction of the person or persons who committed the murders of two police officers, Walsh and Pitman. The defence was first a comprehensive denial of the petitioner's allegation that on 10th June, 1926, he " gave the said information," and next an affirmative allegation that he made on that date a confession but not with the view of obtaining the reward. The petitioner was thus put to the proof of his case. At the trial the Chief Justice gave judgment for the Crown. In the Full Court, by a majority, the judgment of McMillan, C.J., the trial Judge, was reversed. In the result, two learned Judges thought the Crown should succeed while two others thought Clarke should succeed. The difference of opinion arose with respect to the effect or the accuracy, or both, of the case of *Williams* v. *Carwardine*[1].

The facts of this case, including inferences, are not, as I understand, in dispute. They amount to this: The information for which Clarke claims the reward was given by him when he was under arrest with Treffene on a charge of murder, and was given by him in circumstances which show that in giving the information he was not acting on or in pursuance of or in reliance upon or in return for the consideration contained in the proclamation, but exclusively in order to clear himself from a false charge of murder. In other words, he was acting with reference to a specific criminal charge against himself, and not with reference to a general request by the community for information against other persons. It is true that without his information and evidence no conviction was probable, but it is also abundantly clear that he was not acting for the sake of justice or from any impulse of conscience or because he was asked to do so, but simply and solely on his own initiative, to secure his own safety from the hand of the law and altogether irrespective of the proclamation. He has, in my opinion, neither a legal nor a moral claim to the reward. The learned Chief Justice held that Clarke never accepted or intended to accept the offer in the proclamation, and, unless the mere giving of the information without such intention amounted in law to an acceptance of the offer or to performance of the condition, there was neither " acceptance " nor " performance," and therefore there was no contract. I do not understand either of the learned Judges who formed the majority to controvert this. But they held that *Williams* v. *Carwardine*[1] has stood so

---

[1] (1833), 4 B. & Ad. 621.

long that it should be regarded as accurate, and that, so regarded, it entitled the respondent to judgment. As reported in the four places where it is found[1], it is a difficult case to follow. I cannot help thinking that it is somewhat curtly reported. When the various reports in banc are compared, there are some discrepancies. But two circumstances are important. One is the pregnant question of Denman, C.J., as to the plaintiff's knowledge of the handbill. The question appears in the reports in *Carrington and Payne*[2] and in *Nevile and Manning*[3], but is omitted from the report in *Barnewall and Adolphus*. The other circumstance is the stress placed on motive. The Lord Chief Justice clearly attached importance to the answer given to his question. He, doubtless, finally drew the inference that, having knowledge of the request in the handbill, the plaintiff at last determined to accede, and did accede, to that request, and so acted in response to it, although moved thereto by the incentive supplied by her stings of conscience. Making allowance for what is in all probability an abridged report of what was actually said, I cannot help thinking, on the whole, that not only Denman, C.J., but also some at least of the other members of the Court considered that the motive of the informant was not inconsistent with, and did not in that case displace, the *prima facie* inference arising from the fact of knowledge of the request and the giving of the information it sought. Motive, though not to be confused with intention, is very often strong evidence of that state of mind, both in civil and criminal matters. The evidentiary force of motive in the circumstances of *Williams* v. *Carwardine* is no criterion of its force in the circumstances of any other case, and it can never usurp the legal place of intention. If the decision in *Williams* v. *Carwardine*[4] went no further than I have said, it is in line with the acknowledged and settled theories of contract. If it goes so far as is contended for by the respondent, I am of opinion that it is opposed to unimpeachable authority, and I agree with the suggestion of Sir Frederick Pollock, in the preface to Vol. 38 of the Revised Reports, that it should be disregarded. It is unquestionable—putting aside what are called formal contracts or quasi-contracts—that to create a contractual obligation there must be both offer and acceptance. It is the union of these which constitutes the binding tie, the *obligatio*. The present type of case is no exception. It is not true to say that since such an offer calls for information of a certain description, then, provided only information of that description is in fact given, the informant is entitled to the reward. That is not true unless the word " given " is interpreted as " given in exchange for the offer "—in other words, given in performance of the bargain which is contemplated by the offer and of which the offer is intended to form part. Performance in that case is the implied method of acceptance, and it simultaneously effects the double purpose of acceptance and performance. But acceptance is essential to contractual obligation, because without it there is no agreement, and in the absence of agreement, actual or imputed, there can be no contract. Lord Kinnear in *Jackson* v. *Broatch*[5] said: " It is an excellent definition of a contract that it is an agreement which produces an obligation."

That acceptance is necessary in a case of this kind is recognized in *General Accident Fire and Life Assurance Corporation* v. *Robertson*[6], a case

---

[1] (1833), 4 B. & Ad. 621; 5 C. & P. 566.
[3] (1833), 1 N. & M., at 419.
[5] (1900), 37 S. L. R. 707, at p. 714.
[2] (1833), 5 C. & P., at 574.
[4] (1833), 4 B. & Ad. 621.
[6] [1909] A. C. 404, at p. 411.

sufficiently analogous to be illustrative here, though of course the mode of acceptance was very different. That difference constantly arises because the offeror may always prescribe the method of acceptance. In *Attorney-General for Trinidad* v. *Bourne*[1] the method was to tender payment of the balance of a price. In other cases it may be the posting of a letter, or the despatch of goods, or anything stipulated expressly or by implication, even by hanging out a flag, as suggested by Bramwell, L.J., in *Household Fire Insurance Co.* v. *Grant*.[2] The method indicated by the offeror may be one which either does or does not involve communication to him of the acceptance in order to form the contract and create the obligation; however necessary information of the fact may be required before default in payment, that is, in performance by the offeror, can arise. In *Carlill* v. *Carbolic Smoke Ball Co.*[3] Lindley, L.J., thus states what he thinks, and what I respectfully accept as the true view in a case of that kind, which is in this respect the same as the present case: " The person who makes the offer shows by his language and from the nature of the transaction that he does not expect and does not require notice of the acceptance, apart from notice of the performance." As the learned Lord Justice said higher on the page:[3] " the performance of the conditions is the acceptance of the offer." But the words " performance of the conditions " have reference to the offer, and are senseless without such reference. That this is the opinion of the Lord Justice is evident from his own words[4]: " the person who acts upon this advertisement and accepts the offer." Bowen, L.J., also said[5] that it was " an offer which was to be acted upon," and[6] that it was "sufficient to act upon the proposal without communicating acceptance." That is what the Lord Justice means when he speaks of performing the condition " on the faith of the advertisement."[6] Similarly, in *Offord* v. *Davies*[7] Erle, C.J., speaking of what he called a promise to guarantee repayment of discounts, said:—" This promise by itself creates no obligation. It is in effect conditioned to be binding if the plaintiff acts upon it, either to the benefit of the defendants, or to the detriment of himself. But until the condition has been at least in part fulfilled, the defendants have the power of revoking it."

The controlling principle, then, is that to establish the *consensus* without which no true contract can exist, acceptance is as essential as offer, even in a case of the present class where the same act is at once sufficient for both acceptance and performance. But acceptance and performance of condition, as shown by the judicial reasoning quoted, involve that the person accepting and performing must act on the offer.

I may here refer to a weighty American authority, that of Shaw, C.J., in *Loring* v. *City of Boston*[8]. At p. 411 the learned Chief Justice said of an action to recover a reward offered for the conviction of an incendiary:— " There is now no question of the correctness of the legal principle on which this action is founded. The offer of a reward for the detection of an offender, the recovery of property, and the like, is an offer or proposal, which anyone, capable of performing the service, may accept at any time before it is revoked, and perform the service; and such offer on one side, and acceptance and performance . . . on the other, is a valid contract made on good consideration, which the law will enforce." In the case then before the Court the

---

[1] (1895), A. C. 83, at p. 88.
[3] (1893), 1 Q. B. 256, at p. 262.
[5] (1893), 1 Q. B., at 268.
[7] (1862), 12 C. B. N. S. 748, at p. 757.

[2] (1879), 4 Ex. D. 216, at p. 233.
[4] (1893), 1 Q. B., at 264.
[6] (1893), 1 Q. B., at 269.
[8] (1844), 7 Metc. 409.

offer was published more than three years before the information relied on was given, and in the circumstances the Court held the offer had ceased to operate. The important matter, however, is that the Court, in nonsuiting the plaintiff, said: " We are therefore of opinion, that the offer of the City had ceased before the plaintiffs accepted and acted upon it as such, and that consequently no contract existed upon which this action, founded on an alleged express promise, can be maintained." The reasoning quoted seems to me to be as exact and as modern as that in *Carlill's* case[1], and to be hardly capable of advantageous alteration.

Instances easily suggest themselves where precisely the same act done with reference to an offer would be performance of the condition, but done with reference to a totally distinct object would not be such a performance. An offer of £100 to any person who should swim a hundred yards in the harbour on the first day of the year, would be met by voluntarily performing the feat with reference to the offer, but would not in my opinion be satisfied by a person who was accidentally or maliciously thrown overboard on that date and swam the distance simply to save his life, without any thought of the offer. The offeror might or might not feel morally impelled to give the sum in such a case, but would be under no contractual obligation to do so.

We have had cited to us the case of *Fitch* v. *Snedaker*,[2] decided in 1868. As is seen, it was twenty-four years later than the judgment of Shaw, C.J. It was there held in a case of the present type that, in order to create a contract, there must be both offer and consent to the offer, that motive inducing consent may be immaterial but the consent is vital. Clerke, J.[3], held that as no part of the plaintiff's conduct was " in reference to " the reward—since it was prior to the offer—he could not succeed. Woodruff, J., said[4] that the plaintiff did not " act in any sense of reliance " on the offer, and added: " An offer cannot become a contract unless acted upon or assented to." In 1873, in *Howland* v. *Lounds*[5], the case of *Fitch* v. *Snedaker* was affirmed by the Commissioners of Appeal. In 1875, in *Shuey* v. *United States*[6], Strong, J., speaking for the Supreme Court of the United States, said that an offer of a reward for the apprehension of a man was revocable " at any time before it was accepted, and before anything had been done in reliance upon it." These last-mentioned cases are entirely consonant with and illustrative of the general principles so clearly stated by Shaw, C.J., in *Loring* v. *City of Boston*[7], and by the Court of Appeal in *Carlill's* case[8]. In Holmes on the Common Law the learned author, writing in 1881, says, at pp. 293, 294: " The root of the whole matter is the relation of reciprocal conventional inducement, each for the other, between consideration and promise." As to the reward cases, he says, with reference to something being done in ignorance of the offer:—" In such a case the reward cannot be claimed, because the alleged consideration has not been furnished on the faith of the offer. The tendered promise has not induced the furnishing of the consideration." The learned author also applied the term motive when it is the " conventional " motive, and not merely the independent motive of the person doing the act, as equivalent to acting on the faith of the offer. That may or may not be accurate; but it is not a necessary part of the problem with which we are concerned.

---

[1] (1893), 1 Q. B. 256.
[3] (1868), 38 N. Y., at 249.
[5] (1873), 51 N. Y. 604.
[7] (1844), 7 Metc. 409.

[2] (1868), 38 N. Y. 248.
[4] (1868), 38 N. Y., at 252.
[6] (1875), 92 U. S. 73, 76.
[8] (1893), 1 Q. B. 256.

On the question of fact whether Clarke, making his statement of 10th June, acted upon the offer in the proclamation, the learned Chief Justice, who saw and heard him give his testimony, answered that question in the negative. Reading the notes of the trial, which apparently are to some extent abbreviated, and reading also the statement itself, so far from finding anything which would lead me, with all the disadvantages of an appellate Court, to reverse that finding, I quite agree with it. The learned Judges of the Full Court do not appear to have thought differently on that point.

The appeal should, in my opinion, for the reasons stated, be allowed.

HIGGINS and STARKE, JJ., delivered judgments to the same effect.

Henthorn v. Fraser
[1892] 2 Ch. 27

An unconditional offer remains capable of acceptance until the offeree is made aware of its withdrawal.

Where the parties must, from the context, have reasonably assumed that the post might be used as a means of communicating the acceptance of an offer, the acceptance is complete as soon as it is posted.

The plaintiff brought this action in the Court of the County Palatine for specific performance. The Vice-Chancellor dismissed the action, and the plaintiff appealed. The facts appear from the judgment of Lord Herschell.

LORD HERSCHELL :—This is an action for the specific performance of a contract to sell to the plaintiff certain house property situate in Flamank Street, Birkenhead. The action was tried before the Vice-Chancellor of the County Palatine of Lancashire, who gave judgment for the defendants. On July 7, 1891, the secretary of the building society whom the defendants represent handed to the plaintiff, in the office of the society at Liverpool, a letter in these terms:—

" I hereby give you the refusal of the Flamank Street property at £750 for fourteen days."

It appears that the plaintiff had been for some time in negotiation for the property, and had on two previous occasions made offers for the purchase of it, which were not accepted by the society. These offers were made by means of letters, written by the secretary in the office of the society, and signed by the plaintiff there. The plaintiff resided in Birkenhead, and he took away with him to that town the letter of the 7th of July containing the offer of the society. On the 8th of July a letter was posted in Birkenhead at 3.50 p.m., written by his solicitor, accepting on his behalf the offer to sell the property at £750. This letter was not received at the defendants' office until 8.30 p.m., after office hours, the office being closed at 6 o'clock. On the same day a letter was addressed to the plaintiff by the secretary of the building society in these terms:—

" Please take notice that my letter to you of the 7th inst., giving you the option of purchasing the property, Flamank Street, Birkenhead, for £750, in fourteen days, is withdrawn and the offer cancelled."

This letter was posted in Liverpool between 12 and 1 p.m., and was received in Birkenhead at 5.30 p.m. It will thus be seen that it was received before the plaintiff's letter of acceptance had reached Liverpool, but after it had been posted. One other fact only need be stated. On the 8th of July the secretary of the building society sold the same premises to Mr. Miller for the sum of £760, but the receipt for the deposit paid in respect of the purchase stated that it was subject to being able to withdraw the letter to Mr. Henthorn giving him fourteen days' option of purchase.

If the acceptance by the plaintiff of the defendants' offer is to be treated as complete at the time the letter containing it was posted, I can entertain no doubt that the society's attempted revocation of the offer was wholly ineffectual. I think that a person who has made an offer must be considered as continuously making it until he has brought to the knowledge of the person to whom it was made that it is withdrawn. This seems to me to be in accordance with the reasoning of the Court of King's Bench in the case of *Adams* v. *Lindsell*[1], which was approved by the Lord Chancellor in *Dunlop* v. *Higgins*[2], and also with the opinion of Lord Justice Mellish in *Harris's* case[3]. The very point was decided in the case of *Byrne* v. *Van Tienhoven*[4] by Lord Justice Lindley, and his decision was subsequently followed by Mr. Justice Lush. The grounds upon which it has been held that the acceptance of an offer is complete when it is posted have, I think, no application to the revocation or modification of an offer. These can be no more effectual than the offer itself, unless brought to the mind of the person to whom the offer is made. But it is contended on behalf of the defendants that the acceptance was complete only when received by them and not on the letter being posted. It cannot, of course, be denied, after the decision in *Dunlop* v. *Higgins*[5] in the House of Lords, that, where an offer has been made through the medium of the post, the contract is complete as soon as the acceptance of the offer is posted, but the decision is said to be inapplicable here, inasmuch as the letter containing the offer was not sent by post to *Birkenhead*, but handed to the plaintiff in the defendants' office at *Liverpool*. The question therefore arises in what circumstances the acceptance of an offer is to be regarded as complete as soon as it is posted. In the case of the *Household Fire and Carriage Accident Insurance Co.* v. *Grant*[6], Lord Justice Baggallay said[7]: " I think that the principle established in *Dunlop* v. *Higgins* is limited in its application to cases in which by reason of general usage, or of the relations between the parties to any particular transactions, or of the terms in which the offer is made, the acceptance of such offer by a letter through the post is expressly or impliedly authorized." And in the same case Lord Justice Thesiger based his judgment[8] on the defendant having made an application for shares under circumstances " from which it must be implied that he authorized the company, in the event of their allotting to him the shares applied for, to send the notice of allotment by post." The facts of that case were that the defendant had, in *Swansea*, where he resided, handed a letter of application to an agent of the company, their place of business being situate in London. It was from these circumstances that the Lords Justices implied an authority to the company to accept the defendant's offer to take shares through the medium of the post. Applying the law thus laid down by the Court of Appeal, I think in the present case an authority to accept by post must be implied. Although the plaintiff received the offer at the defendants' office in Liverpool, he resided in another town, and it must have been in contemplation that he would take the offer, which by its terms was to remain open for some days, with him to his place of residence, and those who made the offer must have known that it would be according to the ordinary usages of mankind that if he

---

[1] (1818), 1 B. & Ald. 681. [2] (1848), 1 H. L. Cas. 381, at p. 399. [3] (1872), 7 Ch. App. 587.
[4] (1880), 5 C. P. D. 344. [5] (1848), 1 H. L. Cas. 381. [6] (1879), 4 Ex. D. 216.
[7] *Ibid.*, 227. [8] *Ibid.*, 218.

accepted it he should communicate his acceptance by means of the post.
I am not sure that I should myself have regarded the doctrine that an
acceptance is complete as soon as the letter containing it is posted as resting
upon an implied authority by the person making the offer to the person
receiving it to accept by those means. It strikes me as somewhat artificial
to speak of the person to whom the offer is made as having the implied
authority of the other party to send his acceptance by post. He needs no
authority to transmit the acceptance through any particular channel ; he
may select what means he pleases, the Post Office no less than any other.
The only effect of the supposed authority is to make the acceptance complete
so soon as it is posted, and authority will obviously be implied only when
the tribunal considers that it is a case in which this result ought to be reached.
I should prefer to state the rule thus : Where the circumstances are such
that it must have been within the contemplation of the parties, that, according
to the ordinary usages of mankind, the post might be used as a means of
communicating the acceptance of an offer, the acceptance is complete as
soon as it is posted. It matters not in which way the proposition be stated,
the present case is in either view within it. The learned Vice-Chancellor
appears to have based his decision to some extent on the fact that before the
acceptance was posted the defendants had sold the property to another
person. The case of *Dickinson* v. *Dodds*[1] was relied upon in support of
that defence. In that case, however, the plaintiff knew of the subsequent
sale before he accepted the offer, which, in my judgment, distinguishes it
entirely from the present case. For the reasons I have given, I think the
judgment must be reversed and the usual decree for specific performance
made. The respondents must pay the costs of the appeal and of the action.

LINDLEY and KAY, L.JJ., delivered judgments to the same effect.

Entores, Ltd. v. Miles Far East Corporation

[1955] 2 Q.B. 327

"The ordinary rule of law, to which the special considerations governing
contracts by post are exceptions, is that the acceptance of an offer must be
communicated to the offeror, and the place where the contract is made is
the place where the offeror receives the notification of the acceptance by the
offeree " (BIRKETT, L.J., at p. 335).

The question in this case was whether the contract between the English
plaintiffs and the New York defendants was made in England. If so, the
court in its discretion might permit the writ of summons to be served on the
defendants in New York under the terms of R.S.C., Ord. 11, r. 1 (e). The
master gave leave for the writ to be served, and his decision was approved
by DONOVAN, J. The defendants now appealed to the Court of Appeal.

DENNING, L.J. This is an application for leave to serve notice of a
writ out of the jurisdiction. The grounds are that the action is brought to
recover damages for breach of a contract made within the jurisdiction or by
implication to be governed by English law.

The plaintiffs are an English company. The defendants are an American
corporation with agents all over the world, including a Dutch company in
Amsterdam. The plaintiffs say that the contract was made by Telex
between the Dutch company in Amsterdam and the English company in

---

[1] (1876), 2 Ch. D. 463.

London. Communications by Telex are comparatively new. Each company has a teleprinter machine in its office; and each has a Telex number like a telephone number. When one company wishes to send a message to the other, it gets the Post Office to connect up the machines. Then a clerk at one end taps the message on to his machine just as if it were a typewriter, and it is instantaneously passed to the machine at the other end, which automatically types the message on to paper at that end.

The relevant Telex messages in this case were as follows: September 8, 1954: Dutch company:

" Offer for account our associates Miles Far East Corporation Tokyo up to 400 tons Japanese cathodes sterling 240 longton c.i.f. shipment Mitsui Line September 28 or October 10 payment by letter of credit. Your reply Telex Amsterdam 12174 or phone 31490 before 4 p.m. invited."

English company:

" Accept 100 longtons cathodes Japanese shipment latest October 10 sterling £239 10s. longton c.i.f. London/Rotterdam payment letter of credit stop please confirm latest tomorrow."

Dutch company:

" We received O.K. Thank you."

September 9, 1954: English company:

" Regarding our telephone conversation a few minutes ago we note that there is a query on the acceptance of our bid for 100 tons payment in sterling and you are ascertaining that your Tokyo office will confirm the price to be longton we therefore await to hear from you further."

September 10, 1954: English company:

" Is the price for the sterling cathodes understood to be for longton by Japan as you were going to find this out yesterday ? "

Dutch company:

" Yes, price £239 10s. for longton."

At that step there was a completed contract by which the defendants agreed to supply 100 tons of cathodes at a price of £239 10s. a ton. The offer was sent by Telex from England offering to pay £239 10s. a ton for 100 tons, and accepted by Telex from Holland. The question for our determination is where was the contract made ?

When a contract is made by post it is clear law throughout the common law countries that the acceptance is complete as soon as the letter is put into the post box, and that is the place where the contract is made. But there is no clear rule about contracts made by telephone or by Telex. Communications by these means are virtually instantaneous and stand on a different footing.

The problem can only be solved by going in stages. Let me first consider a case where two people make a contract by word of mouth in the presence of one another. Suppose, for instance, that I shout an offer to a man across a river or a courtyard but I do not hear his reply because it is drowned by an aircraft flying overhead. There is no contract at that moment. If he wishes to make a contract, he must wait till the aircraft is gone and then shout back his acceptance so that I can hear what he says. Not until I have his answer am I bound. I do not agree with the observations of Hill, J., in *Newcomb* v. *De Roos*.[1]

---

[1] (1859) 2 E. & E. 271.

Now take a case where two people make a contract by telephone. Suppose, for instance, that I make an offer to a man by telephone and, in the middle of his reply, the line goes " dead " so that I do not hear his words of acceptance. There is no contract at that moment. The other man may not know the precise moment when the line failed. But he will know that the telephone conversation was abruptly broken off, because people usually say something to signify the end of the conversation. If he wishes to make a contract, he must therefore get through again so as to make sure that I heard. Suppose next, that the line does not go dead, but it is nevertheless so indistinct that I do not catch what he says and I ask him to repeat it. He then repeats it and I hear his acceptance. The contract is made, not on the first time when I do not hear, but only the second time when I do hear. If he does not repeat it, there is no contract. The contract is only complete when I have his answer accepting the offer.

Lastly, take the Telex. Suppose a clerk in a London office taps out on the teleprinter an offer which is immediately recorded on a teleprinter in a Manchester office, and a clerk at that end taps out an acceptance. If the line goes dead in the middle of the sentence of acceptance, the teleprinter motor will stop. There is then obviously no contract. The clerk at Manchester must get through again and send his complete sentence. But it may happen that the line does not go dead, yet the message does not get through to London. Thus the clerk at Manchester may tap out his message of acceptance and it will not be recorded in London because the ink at the London end fails, or something of that kind. In that case, the Manchester clerk will not know of the failure but the London clerk will know of it and will immediately send back a message " not receiving." Then, when the fault is rectified, the Manchester clerk will repeat his message. Only then is there a contract. If he does not repeat it, there is no contract. It is not until his message is received that the contract is complete.

In all the instances I have taken so far, the man who sends the message of acceptance knows that it has not been received or he has reason to know it. So he must repeat it. But, suppose that he does not know that his message did not get home. He thinks it has. This may happen if the listener on the telephone does not catch the words of acceptance, but nevertheless does not trouble to ask for them to be repeated: or the ink on the teleprinter fails at the receiving end, but the clerk does not ask for the message to be repeated: so that the man who sends an acceptance reasonably believes that his message has been received. The offeror in such circumstances is clearly bound, because he will be estopped from saying that he did not receive the message of acceptance. It is his own fault that he did not get it. But if there should be a case where the offeror without any fault on his part does not receive the message of acceptance—yet the sender of it reasonably believes it has got home when it has not—then I think there is no contract.

My conclusion is, that the rule about instantaneous communications between the parties is different from the rule about the post. The contract is only complete when the acceptance is received by the offeror, and the contract is made at the place where the acceptance is received.

In a matter of this kind, however, it is very important that the countries of the world should have the same rule. I find that most of the European countries have substantially the same rule as that I have stated. Indeed, they apply it to contracts by post as well as instantaneous communications. But in the United States of America it appears as if instantaneous communications are treated in the same way as postal communications. In view of this divergence, I think that we must consider the matter on principle: and so considered, I have come to the view I have stated, and I am glad to see that Professor Winfield in this country (55 Law Quarterly Review, 514), and Professor Williston in the United States of America (Contracts, § 82, p. 239), take the same view.

Applying the principles which I have stated, I think that the contract in this case was made in London where the acceptance was received. It was, therefore, a proper case for service out of the jurisdiction.

Apart from the contract by Telex, the plaintiffs put the case in another way. They say that the contract by Telex was varied by letter posted in Holland and accepted by conduct in England, and that this amounted to a new contract made in England. The Dutch company on September 11, 1954, wrote a letter to the English company saying:

> " We confirm having sold to you for account of our associates in Tokyo: 100 metric tons electrolitic copper in cathodes: £239 10s. for longton c.i.f. U.K./Continental main ports: prompt shipment from a Japanese port after receipt of export licence: payment by irrevocable and transferable letter of credit to be opened in favour of Miles Far East Corporation with a first class Tokyo Bank. The respective import licences to be sent directly without delay to Miles Far East Corporation."

The variations consisted in the ports of delivery, the provisions of import licence and so forth. The English company say that they accepted the variations by dispatching from London the import licence and giving instructions in London for the opening of the letter of credit, and that this was an acceptance by conduct which was complete as soon as the acts were done in London.

I am not sure that this argument about variations is correct. It may well be that the contract is made at the place where first completed, not at the place where the variations are agreed. But whether this be so or not, I think the variations were accepted by conduct in London and were therefore made in England. Both the original contract and ensuing variations were made in England and leave can properly be given for service out of the jurisdiction.

I am inclined to think also that the contract is by implication to be governed by English law, because England is the place with which it has the closest connection.

I think that the decisions of the master and the judge were right, and I would dismiss the appeal.

PARKER, L.J. I have come to the same conclusion, and would only add a few words on the basis that the contract sued on is that created by the Telex messages. As was said by Lindley, L.J., in *Carlill* v. *Carbolic Smoke Ball Co.*[1]: " Unquestionably, as a general proposition, when an offer is made, it is necessary in order to make a binding contract, not only that it should be accepted, but that the acceptance should be notified." In the same case Bowen, L.J., said[2]: " One cannot doubt that, as an ordinary rule of law, an acceptance of an offer made ought to be notified to the person who makes the offer, in order that the two minds may come together. Unless this is done the two minds may be apart, and there is not that consensus

---

[1] [1893] 1 Q. B. 256, at. p. 262.   [2] [1893] 1 Q. B. 256, at p. 269.

which is necessary according to English law—I say nothing about the laws of other countries—to make a contract." Accordingly, as a general rule, a binding contract is made at the place where the offeror receives notification of the acceptance, that is where the offeror is.

Since, however, the requirement as to actual notification of the acceptance is for the benefit of the offeror, he may waive it and agree to the substitution for that requirement of some other conduct by the acceptor. He may do so expressly, as in the advertisement cases, by intimating that he is content with the performance of a condition. Again, he may do so impliedly by indicating a contemplated method of acceptance, for example, by post or telegram. In such a case he does not expressly dispense with actual notification, but he is held to have done so impliedly on grounds of expediency. Thus, in *Adams* v. *Lindsell*[1], the court pointed out that unless this were so " no contract could ever be completed by the post. For if the defendants were not bound by their offer when accepted by the plaintiffs till the answer was received, then the plaintiffs ought not to be bound till after they had received the notification that the defendants had received their answer and assented to it. And so it might go on *ad infinitum*." Again, in *Dunlop* v. *Higgins*[2], Lord Cottenham, L.C., pointed out that " Common sense tells us that transactions cannot go on without such a rule "; and in *In re Imperial Land Co. of Marseilles* (*Harris's* case[3]), Mellish, L.J., referred to the mischievous consequences which would follow in commerce if no such rule was adopted. To the same effect is the judgment of Thesiger, L.J., in *Household Fire Insurance Co.* v. *Grant*[4], in which he points out that where the parties are at a distance the balance of convenience dictates that the contract shall be deemed complete when the acceptance is handed to the Post Office.

Where, however, the parties are in each other's presence or, though separated in space, communication between them is, in effect, instantaneous, there is no need for any such rule of convenience. To hold otherwise would leave no room for the operation of the general rule that notification of the acceptance must be received. An acceptor could say: " I spoke the words of acceptance in your presence, albeit softly, and it matters not that you did not hear me "; or, " I telephoned to you and accepted, and it matters not that the telephone went dead and you did not get my message." Though in both these cases the acceptor was using the contemplated or, indeed, the expressly indicated mode of communication, there is no room for any implication that the offeror waived actual notification of the acceptance. It follows that I cannot agree with the observations of Hill, J., in *Newcomb* v. *De Roos*[5].

So far as Telex messages are concerned, though the dispatch and receipt of a message are not completely instantaneous, the parties are to all intents and purposes in each other's presence just as if they were in telephonic communication, and I can see no reason for departing from the general rule that there is no binding contract until notice of the acceptance is received by the offeror. That being so, and since the offer—a counter-offer—was made by the plaintiffs in London, and notification of the acceptance was received by them in London, the contract resulting therefrom was made in London. I would accordingly dismiss the appeal.

BIRKETT, L.J., delivered judgment to the same effect.

---

[1] (1818), 1 B. & Ald. 681, at p. 683.   [2] (1848), 1 H. L. C. 381, at p. 400.
[3] (1872), 7 Ch. App. 587, at p. 594.   [4] (1879), 4 Ex. D. 216.   [5] (1859), 2 E. & E. 271.

Webster v. Higgin

[1948] 2 All E.R. 127

Collateral Contracts. " It is evident, both on principle and on authority, that there may be a contract the consideration for which is the making of some other contract. ' If you will make such and such a contract I will give you one hundred pounds' is in every sense of the word a complete legal contract. It is collateral to the main contract, but each has an independent existence, and they do not differ in respect of their possessing to the full the character and status of a contract ": *per* Lord Moulton in *Heilbut, Symons & Co.* v. *Buckleton*, [1913] A.C. 30, 47.

APPEAL by the plaintiff from an order of His Honour Judge Stewart, made at Leeds County Court, and dated Oct. 22, 1947, whereby, in an action for the return of a motor car bought on hire purchase terms and for the balance of instalments due, the learned judge rescinded the agreement and ordered repayment of the deposit and instalments paid, on the ground that a representation of " roadworthiness " which induced the defendant to purchase the car amounted to a condition precedent and it had not been fulfilled. The appeal was dismissed, but on the ground that what was offered was a collateral guarantee, and, on the undertaking of the defendant to return the car and of the plaintiff that he would no longer regard the hire purchase agreement as being on foot for any purpose, the order for repayment of deposit and instalments was affirmed. The facts appear in the judgment.

Stanley-Price for the plaintiff.
Hurwitz for the defendant.

LORD GREENE, M.R.: The plaintiff is a garage proprietor and part of his business consists in dealing in second-hand cars, among other ways, by means of contracts of hire purchase. The defendant, having been attracted by one of the plaintiff's advertisements, discussed with the plaintiff's foreman the purchase of a car described as a 1933 Hillman 10 horse power car. They discussed it on a hire purchase basis, but at that stage no terms of any hire purchase agreement were gone into, much less agreed. In the result, the defendant, who was not acquainted with motor cars beyond being able to drive them, without examining the car in question and without even having the engine started up, signed a document on the invitation of the plaintiff's foreman. That document is called an order form. It is a printed form with the plaintiff's name printed on it as a heading. It purports to be addressed to him, and by it a proposing purchaser says: " I hereby accept your offer to sell and order from you on the terms and conditions following and overleaf." There are a number of headings dealing with various things. The car, with its colour and upholstery, is described, the price, such matters as the licence and insurance which are to be paid for, and the date for delivery are specified. The document ends by having written in, apparently by the plaintiff, " H.P. Form "—*i.e.*, hire purchase form—" to be signed May 14." It is clear that the only form of purchase which the parties at this stage were contemplating was one by way of hire purchase. The hire purchase form referred to in this " order form " is not in any way identified, and it is not suggested that the words ought to be construed as referring to some particular kind of form. The position, therefore, was that no contract came into existence by the signature on this order form by the defendant for the simple reason that it was a document which contemplated the execution of a definite contractual document, namely, a hire purchase agreement, the terms of which had never been agreed, save in so far as certain matters are referred to, such as the amount of the deposit, the period and the instalment. That, of course, is insufficient to constitute a contract because hire purchase agreements contain a large number of clauses which are not in any sense uniform. Variations are to be found, and the forms which are commonly adopted have varied from time to time. It seems to me, therefore, that this document was in no sense a contractual document.

The importance of it lies in this. On the back of it are set out what are called " Terms and Conditions." The relevant condition is condition 4:

> " The purchaser acknowledges that he has not been induced to enter into this purchase by any representation as to quality, fitness for any purpose, performance or otherwise of the goods other than the representation contained, if the goods be not new, in the written description entered on this order form."

If that had been a contractual document, I could have understood the argument that the purchaser was binding himself in the terms of condition 4, whatever those words may mean, and that he would have so bound himself even if he had not read it; but it was not a contractual document, and before it was signed something had happened which is, to my mind, of crucial importance and was obviously so regarded by the learned county court judge. In the course of a conversation which the defendant had with the plaintiff's foreman, whose authority is not in any way in dispute, the foreman said: " If you buy the Hillman 10 we will guarantee that it is in good condition and that you will have no trouble with it." Those words in the context are obviously an offer of a collateral guarantee. It is a guarantee to the defendant that, if he will enter into a contract of purchase, the guarantee will be given to him. I may say at once that that guarantee was broken as completely and thoroughly as any guarantee can possibly be broken. The evidence relating to the inside of that motor car, given by an expert whose testimony was accepted by the county court judge, amounted to a most deplorable description of what in effect was nothing but a mass of second-hand and dilapidated ironmongery.

If the order form, to which I have just referred, was not contractual, what was it? Reliance is placed on the fact that the defendant signed it. The evidence was that, although he had it in his hand, he did not read it, and that was accepted by the judge. The position at that moment, if correctly analysed, appears to me to have been this. The foreman offers a guarantee. He obtains the signature of the purchaser to a document which I cannot help thinking both parties thought, but, in my view, wrongly thought, was contractual. That document contained a condition which is said to amount to a statement that no guarantee is given. If the document was not contractual, it was nothing more than what I may call a warning. Putting the warning into words it would be this: " I, the foreman, offer you a guarantee, but I warn you that that guarantee has no effect whatsoever." That is what is said to be the construction of condition 4 of that document. If it was a warning, it could only be effective if it was brought clearly to the attention of the person to be warned. He should have been warned that he could place no reliance whatsoever on the clear guarantee offered by the foreman, and merely because he signed at the foot of that document without ever reading that part, or having his attention called to it, does not, to my mind, make it possible to suggest that there is anything in that document which precludes him from relying on the clear guarantee on the faith of which he was negotiating. At a subsequent date the hire purchase agreement was signed, and, in my view, the signature on that hire purchase agreement was the act by which the defendant accepted the offer of a guarantee. The guarantee was: " If you buy this car, I will guarantee it." He bought the car when he put his signature to the hire purchase agreement, for I do not think he bought it before that date in the sense of being contractually bound to take it. It is said, however, that when the defendant signed the hire purchase agreement, the collateral offer of a guarantee which he accepted by signing that agreement was entirely abrogated and nullified by a term in the agreement itself.

We, therefore, have this curious position, analysing the words again: " If you, the purchaser, will sign this contract which contains an exclusion of every guarantee, I will guarantee the car." Of course, that is nonsense, but parties often make nonsensical arrangements. If the contract meant that, we should be bound to give it that meaning, but, whether or not it has that effect must, in my opinion, be a pure question of construction of the contract. The relevant clause in the contract, cl. 5, was in these words:

> The hirer is deemed to have examined (or caused to be examined) the vehicle prior to this agreement and satisfied himself as to its condition, and no warranty, condition, description or representation on the part of the owner as to the state or quality of the vehicle is given or implied . . .

I pause there for a moment. To succeed the plaintiff must satisfy us that those words not merely exclude the giving of any warranty in the contract of sale itself, but that they are sufficient to exclude the operation of a warranty which was given in consideration of the purchaser entering into the contract. In my opinion, that is not the true construction of those words. It is to be noted that the words are " no warranty . . . is given or implied." What is the meaning of the present tense there ? Is it to be read not only as incorporating something that is given or implied by or in this agreement, but also as extending to something which was given, it may be weeks, and, indeed, on the evidence some fortnight, before the agreement was signed ? According to the plaintiff the present tense—" is given or implied "—has a meaning which it will not bear in the context. If the words had been, not merely " no warranty is given or implied," but " any warranty given collateral to this agreement is hereby extinguished," the position, no doubt, would have been different. If words to that effect had been given, the result would, as I have said, been farcical because the guarantee would then be offered in consideration of the purchaser signing a document by which he agreed that the guarantee should be of no value whatsoever. It seems to me that to produce such a result very clear words are wanted, and I do not find them in what I have read. The agreement continues:

> . . . any statutory or other warranty, condition, description or representation whether express or implied as to the state, quality, fitness or roadworthiness being hereby expressly excluded . . .

Again, I read those words as meaning a representation expressed in the document or implied from something in the document. The word " being " is, I think, important because it is the common way and the proper way of giving a definition or an elaboration of something that has already been said. If it was intended to carry the matter further, it would have been in the form of a separate sentence and not in the form of a present participle. If that be right, those words do not add anything to the exclusion by the earlier part of the clause of any representation which is given or implied in the document. The words of the clause are not sufficiently clear to abrogate a separate collateral agreement constituted by an offer of a guarantee and its acceptance by the signing of this document by the purchaser. It appears to me that on the evidence the proper and, indeed, the only conclusion to which the county court judge ought to have come was that there was a collateral guarantee which was broken and that there was nothing in the hire purchase agreement or in the order form to exclude or abrogate that guarantee. That is a question of law with which this court is competent to deal. There are no matters of fact in the judgment of the learned judge which are contrary to the conclusions which I have indicated. The question turns, in my opinion, on the proper conclusion of law to be drawn from the facts found by the county court judge and the true construction of the relevant documents read in the light of such circumstances as are relevant on a question of construction. On that basis, in my opinion, the appeal should be dismissed.

WROTTESLEY and EVERSHED, L. JJ., agreed in dismissing the appeal.

Shanklin Pier, Ltd. v. Detel Products, Ltd.
[1951] 2 All E.R. 471

The parties to a " collateral " contract need not be the same as those to the "main" contract.

McNAIR, J., read the following judgment: This case raises an interesting and comparatively novel question whether or not an enforceable warranty can arise as between parties other than parties to the main contract for the sale of the article in respect of which the warranty is alleged to have been given.

The plaintiffs, Shanklin Pier, Ltd., are and were at all material times, the owners of a pier at Shanklin, in the Isle of Wight, which, during the war, was partly demolished and allowed to fall into disrepair. In or about July, 1946, they had in mind to have this pier repaired and re-painted, and for this purpose they entered into a contract with their contractors, George M. Carter (Erectors), Ltd., to have the necessary repairs effected and to have the whole pier re-painted with two coats of bitumastic or bituminous paint. Under this contract they had the right to vary the specification. In these circumstances, their claim in this action against the defendants, Detel Products, Ltd., is that, in consideration of their specifying that their contractors should use for re-painting the pier two coats of a paint known as " D.M.U.", manufactured by the defendants, the defendants warranted that the D.M.U. paint would be suitable for re-painting the pier, would give a surface impervious to dampness, would prevent corrosion and the creeping of rust, and would have a life of seven to ten years. They further say that, in reliance on this warranty, they duly specified that their contractors should use D.M.U. paint for re-painting the pier in lieu of the bituminous paint originally specified, and that their contractors bought quantities of the paint from the defendants and used it on the pier, that contrary to the warranty the paint was not suitable for re-painting the pier or for the protection of the pier from damp or corrosion or rust, and that its life was of a very short duration, with the result that the plaintiffs were put to extra expense amounting to £4,127 10s. The defence, stated broadly, is that no such warranty was ever given, and that, if given, it would give rise to no cause of action between these parties. Accordingly, the first question which I have to determine is whether any such warranty was ever given.

[His Lordship reviewed the evidence and continued :] In the result, I am satisfied that, if a direct contract of purchase and sale of the D.M.U. had then been made between the plaintiffs and the defendants, the correct conclusion on the facts would have been that the defendants gave to the plaintiffs the warranties substantially in the form alleged in the statement of claim. In reaching this conclusion, I adopt the principle, stated by Holt, C.J., in *Crosse* v. *Gardner*[1] and *Medina* v. *Stoughton*[2], that an affirmation at the time of sale is a warranty, provided it appear on evidence to have been so intended. Before considering the question of law resulting from this finding, I can state the remainder of the narrative briefly. On the faith of these warranties, the plaintiffs in due course caused the specification in the original contract to be amended by the substitution of two coats of D.M.U. without any superimposed decoration or finishing paint, in lieu of the two coats of bituminous paint originally specified, having obtained from their contractors estimates of the extra cost involved. The necessary D.M.U. was purchased by the contractors, and, as the repairs were completed and the old work was prepared for re-painting, the D.M.U. was applied and the property in the D.M.U. then, if not before, passed to the plaintiffs. Within a short time it proved to be unsatisfactory, and it was decided to carry out an extensive process of flame cleaning of the old parts of the structure at a cost of £4,127 10s., in order to remove all traces of bitumen. Notwithstanding this additional expenditure, the paint proved to be a complete failure.

Counsel for the defendants submitted that in law a warranty can give rise to no enforceable cause of action except between the same parties as the parties to the main contract in relation to which the warranty is given. In principle, this submission seems to me to be unsound. If, as is elementary, the consideration for the warranty in the usual case is the entering into of the main contract in relation to which the warranty is given, I see no reason why there may not be an enforceable warranty between A and B supported by the consideration that B should cause C to enter into a contract with A or that B should do some other act for the benefit of A. In support of this proposition, however, counsel for the defendants relied on the decision of the Court of Appeal in *Drury* v. *Victor Buckland, Ltd.*[3], and, particularly, on the judgment of Scott, L.J.

In that case the plaintiff, who had been approached by an agent of the defendants, dealers in refrigerating machines, agreed to purchase such a machine. As she was unable or unwilling to pay forthwith the whole of the purchase price, the deal was put through by the defendants selling the machine to a finance company who in turn entered into a hire-purchase agreement with the plaintiff, under which she eventually, when the whole of the hire-purchase instalments had been paid, acquired title to the machine. The machine proving unsatisfactory, the plaintiff sued the defendants, claiming damages for breach of the implied warranty or condition under s. 14 (1) of the Sale of Goods Act, 1893. This claim failed, Scott, L.J., saying;

" It was a sale by the Buckland company to the hire-purchase company. The property passed to them on the terms that they would get paid by the hire-purchase company . . . Therefore, the claim against them . . . for breach of warranty is a cause of action unsupported by any contract of sale which would carry it . . ."[4]

---

[1] (1688), Carth. 190.   [2] (1700), Salk. 210.
[3] [1941] 1 All E.R. 269.   [4] *Ibid.,* at p. 273.

This judgment can readily be understood in relation to its subject-matter, namely, an implied statutory condition or warranty arising out of a contract of sale, and one can well understand its being said that, as there is no contract of sale between the plaintiff and defendants, no implied warranty or condition can arise between them, but I do not read it as affording any support for the wider proposition for which counsel for the defendants here contended.

The same view of the effect of this judgment as I have indicated was, I think, taken by Jones, J., in *Brown* v. *Sheen and Richmond Car Sales, Ltd.*[1] The learned judge there entered judgment against a motor car dealer on an express oral warranty given in relation to the purchase of a car, the transaction, as in *Drury* v. *Victor Buckland, Ltd.*[2] being carried through with the assistance of a finance company. Counsel for the defendants sought to distinguish that case on the ground that in the statement of facts it is stated that " the plaintiff agreed to buy " the motor car from the defendants, but the pleadings in the case, which I have examined, lend no support to the suggestion that there was in any legal sense any agreement to sell between the plaintiff and the defendants. The judgment of Hilbery, J., in *Parker* v. *Oloxo, Ltd. and Senior*[3], also, I think, negatives the defendants' submission in this case. Accordingly, in my judgment, the plaintiffs are entitled to recover against the defendants £4,127 10s., as damages for breach of the express warranties alleged.[4]

---

[1] [1950] 1 All E.R. 1102.
[2] [1941] 1 All E.R. 269.
[3] [1937] 3 All E.R. 524.
[4] The word " warranty " is ambiguous and may be used to denote a minor as opposed to a major term in a contract. It may seem inappropriate in the present context where the court constructs an independent contract, one side of which is the undertaking in question. But, if the language is unhappy, it is clear that the courts may, and do, construct, from the fact and circumstances of a case, a " collateral " contract.

CONSIDERATION

Thomas v. Thomas

(1842), 2 Q.B. 851

The requirement of consideration, vital to the English conception of contract, is not satisfied by a purely moral obligation, nor is it synonymous with motive. It is the price paid by one party for the promise of the other; and it must move from the promisee. But the courts will not ask if the price is adequate: this is for the parties themselves to decide.

The plaintiff was the widow of John Thomas who owned seven houses in Merthyr Tydvil. On the evening before he died he expressed orally his wish that his wife should have the house in which he was living. He left a will of which his brothers, Benjamin and Samuel, were executors. The will made no mention of the testator's wish that his wife should be given the house in question. The executors knew of it, and a few days after the testator's death they agreed that the plaintiff, so long as she remained a widow, should live in the house; provided (a) that she paid One Pound each year towards the ground rent, and (b) that she kept the house in good repair.

The plaintiff remained in possession of the house until the death of Samuel Thomas. The defendant, the surviving executor, then turned her out of her possession; and she sued him for breach of contract. A verdict was found for the plaintiff; and this was upheld by the Court of Queen's Bench. During the argument in this court, counsel suggested that consideration should be defined as the motive for which the promise was made. " What is meant by the consideration for a promise but the cause or inducement for making it? " The court rejected this suggestion, but upheld the verdict for the plaintiff.

LORD DENMAN, C.J.—There is nothing in this case but a great deal of ingenuity and a little wilful blindness to the actual terms of the instrument itself. The stipulation for the payment towards the ground rent is not a mere proviso but an express agreement; and shows a sufficient legal consideration quite independent of the moral feeling which disposed the executors to enter into such a contract.

PATTESON, J.—It would be giving to *causa* too large a construction if we were to adopt the view urged by counsel: it would be confounding consideration with motive. Motive is not the same thing with consideration. Consideration means something which is of some value in the eye of the law, moving from the plaintiff. It may be some benefit to the defendant or some detriment to the plaintiff; but at all events it must be moving from the plaintiff.[1] Now that which is suggested as the consideration here, a pious respect for the wishes of the testator, does not in any way move from the plaintiff. It moves from the testator, and therefore, legally speaking, it forms no part of the consideration. Then it is said that, if that be so, there is no consideration at all: it is a mere voluntary gift. But when we look at the agreement we find that this is not a mere proviso that the donee shall take a gift with its burdens. It is an express agreement to pay what seems to be a

---

[1] In the nineteenth century the antithesis of benefit and detriment offered a favourite definition of consideration. Later opinion has preferred the definition given by Sir Frederick Pollock: " An act or forbearance of one party, or the promise thereof, is the price for which the promise of the other is bought, and the promise thus given for value is enforceable ". See Pollock, *The Principles of Contract*, 13th edn., p. 133. This definition was adopted by Lord Dunedin in *Dunlop Pneumatic Tyre Co., Ltd.* v. *Selfridge*; [1915] A.C. 847, at p. 855.

fresh apportionment of a ground rent, which is made payable not to a superior landlord but to the executors. So this rent is clearly not something incident to the assignment of the house; for in that case, instead of being payable to the executors, it would have been payable to the landlord. Then, as to the repairs: these houses may possibly be held under a lease containing covenants to repair. But we know nothing about it. For anything that appears, the liability to repair is first created by this instrument.

Judgment for the plaintiff

FOAKES *v.* BEER

CENTRAL LONDON PROPERTY TRUST, LTD. *v.* HIGH TREES HOUSE, LTD.

COMBE *v.* COMBE

If A is under a contractual obligation to B and performs or promises to perform part of that obligation in return for B's promise to forego the balance, such performance or promise on A's part is not consideration for B's promise; for A is doing or promising no more than he was already obliged to do.

But if B now sues A on the original contract, A may use B's promise as a defence to the action provided that A can show (1) that he has acted or omitted to act in reliance upon B's promise; (2) that by this act or omission he has altered his position for the worse; (3) that it is inequitable to allow B to sue on the original obligation.[1] This equitable doctrine, foreshadowed by Lord Cairns in *Hughes* v. *Metropolitan Rail Co.*[2] may be described either as " promissory estoppel " in contrast to an estoppel based on a misrepresentation of fact, or as " quasi-estoppel ", a judicial invention devised on the analogy of estoppel. It may " afford a defence against the enforcement of otherwise enforceable rights; it cannot create a cause of action ": *per* Buckley, J. in *Beesley* v. *Hallwood Estates, Ltd.*, [1960] 2 All E.R. 314, 324.

Foakes v. Beer

(1884), 9 App. Cas. 605

APPEAL from an order of the Court of Appeal.[3]

On August 11, 1875, the respondent recovered judgment against the appellant for £2,077 17s. 2d. for debt and £13 1s. 10d. for costs. On December 21, 1876, a memorandum of agreement was made and signed by the appellant and respondent in the following terms :

" Whereas the said John Weston Foakes is indebted to the said Julia Beer, and she has obtained a judgment in Her Majesty's High Court of Justice, Exchequer Division, for the sum of £2,090 19s. And whereas the said John Weston Foakes has requested the said Julia Beer to give him time in which to pay such judgment, which she has agreed to do on the following conditions. Now this agreement witnesseth that in consideration of the said John Weston Foakes paying to the said Julia Beer on the signing of this agreement the sum of £500, the receipt whereof she doth hereby acknowledge in part satisfaction of the said judgment debt of £2,090 19s., and on condition of his paying her or her executors, administrators, assigns or nominee the sum of £150 on the 1st day of July and the 1st day of January or within one calendar month after each of the said days respectively in every year until the whole of the said sum of £2,090 19s. shall have been fully paid and satisfied, the first of such payments to be made on the 1st day of July next, then she the said Julia Beer hereby undertakes and agrees that she, her executors, administrators or assigns, will not take any proceedings whatever on the said judgment."

---

[1] Thus, if A has himself been guilty of unconscionable conduct, the court will not allow the equity to be pleaded. See *D and C. Builders, Ltd.* v. *Rees, infra*, p. 38.

[2] (1877), 2 App. Cas. 439, at p. 448: see *infra*, p. 40.

[3] (1883), 11 Q.B.D. 221.

The respondent having in June, 1882, taken out a summons for leave to proceed on the judgment, an issue was directed to be tried between the respondent as plaintiff and the appellant as defendant whether any and what amount was on July 1, 1882, due upon the judgment.

At the trial of the issue before Cave, J., it was proved that the whole sum of £2,090 19s. had been paid by instalments, but the respondent claimed interest. The jury under his Lordship's direction found that the appellant had paid all the sums which by the agreement of December 21, 1876, he undertook to pay and within the times therein specified. Cave, J., was of opinion that whether the judgment was satisfied or not, the respondent was, by reason of the agreement, not entitled to issue execution for any sum on the judgment.

The Queen's Bench Division (Watkin Williams and Mathew, JJ.) discharged an order for a new trial on the ground of misdirection.

The Court of Appeal (Brett, M.R., Lindley and Fry, L.JJ.) reversed that decision and entered judgment for the respondent for the interest due, with costs.

EARL OF SELBORNE, L.C. :—My Lords, upon the construction of the agreement of December 21, 1876, I cannot differ from the conclusion in which both the Courts below were agreed. If the operative part could properly be controlled by the recitals, I think there would be much reason to say that the only thing contemplated by the recitals was giving time for payment, without any relinquishment, on the part of the judgment creditor, of any portion of the amount recoverable (whether for principal or for interest) under the judgment. But the agreement of the judgment creditor, which follows the recitals, is that she " will not take any proceedings whatever on the judgment," if a certain condition is fulfilled. What is that condition ? Payment of the sum of £150 in every half year, " until the whole of said sum of £2,090 19s." (the aggregate amount of the principal debt and costs, for which judgment had been entered) " shall have been fully paid and satisfied." A particular " sum " is here mentioned, which does not include the interest then due, or future interest. Whatever was meant to be payable at all, under this agreement, was clearly to be payable by half-yearly instalments of £150 each ; any other construction must necessarily make the conditional promise nugatory. But to say that the half-yearly payments were to continue till the whole sum of £2,090 19s., " and interest thereon," should have been fully paid and satisfied, would be to introduce very important words into the agreement, which are not there, and of which I cannot say that they are necessarily implied. Although, therefore, I may (as indeed I do) very much doubt whether the effect of the agreement, as a conditional waiver of the interest to which she was by law entitled under the judgment, was really present to the mind of the judgment creditor, still I cannot deny that it might have that effect, if capable of being legally enforced.

But the question remains, whether the agreement is capable of being legally enforced. Not being under seal, it cannot be legally enforced against the respondent, unless she received consideration for it from the appellant, or unless, though without consideration, it operates by way of accord and satisfaction, so as to extinguish the claim for interest. What is the consideration ? On the fact of the agreement none is expressed, except a present payment of £500, on account and in part of the larger debt then due and payable by law under the judgment. The appellant did not contract to pay the future instalments of £150 each, at the time therein mentioned ;

much less did he give any new security, in the shape of negotiable paper, or in any other form. The promise *de futuro* was only that of the respondent, that if the half-yearly payments of £150 each were regularly paid, she would " take no proceedings whatever on the judgment." No doubt if the appellant had been under no antecedent obligation to pay the whole debt, his fulfilment of the condition might have imported some consideration on his part for that promise. But he was under the antecedent obligation ; and payment at those deferred dates, by the forbearance and indulgence of the creditor, of the residue of the principal debt and costs, could not (in my opinion) be a consideration for the relinquishment of interest and discharge of the judgment, unless the payment of the £500, at the time of signing the agreement, was such a consideration. As to accord and satisfaction, in point of fact there could be no complete satisfaction, so long as any future instalments remained payable ; and I do not see how any mere payments on account could operate in law as a satisfaction *ad interim*, conditionally upon other payments being afterwards duly made, unless there was a consideration sufficient to support the agreement while still unexecuted. Nor was anything, in fact, done by the respondent in this case, on the receipt of the last payment, which could be tantamount to an acquittance, if the agreement did not previously bind her.

The question, therefore, is nakedly raised by this appeal, whether your Lordships are now prepared, not only to overrule, as contrary to law, the doctrine stated by Sir Edward Coke to have been laid down by all the judges of the Common Pleas in *Pinnel's* case[1] in 1602, and repeated in his note to Littleton, section 344[2], but to treat a prospective agreement, not under seal, for satisfaction of a debt, by a series of payments on account to a total amount less than the whole debt, as binding in law, provided those payments are regularly made ; the case not being one of a composition with a common debtor, agreed to, *inter se*, by several creditors. I prefer so to state the question instead of treating it (as it was put at the Bar) as depending on the authority of the case of *Cumber* v. *Wane*[3], decided in 1718. It may well be that distinctions, which in later cases have been held sufficient to exclude the application of that doctrine, existed and were improperly disregarded in *Cumber* v. *Wane* ; and yet that the doctrine itself may be law, rightly recognized in *Cumber* v. *Wane*, and not really contradicted by any later authorities. And this appears to me to be the true state of the case. The doctrine itself, as laid down by Sir Edward Coke, may have been criticized as questionable in principle by some persons whose opinions are entitled to respect, but it has never been judicially overruled ; on the contrary I think it has always, since the sixteenth century, been accepted as law. If so, I cannot think that your Lordships would do right, if you were now to reverse, as erroneous, a judgment of the Court of Appeal, proceeding upon a doctrine which has been accepted as part of the law of England for 280 years.

The doctrine, as stated in *Pinnel's* case[1], is " that payment of a lesser sum on that day " (it would of course be the same after the day), " in satisfaction of a greater, cannot be any satisfaction for the whole, because it appears to the Judges, that by no possibility a lesser sum can be a satisfaction to the plaintiff for a greater sum." As stated in Coke Littleton, 212(b), it is, " where the condition is for payment of £20, the obligor or feoffor cannot at the time appointed pay a lesser sum in satisfaction of the whole, because

---

[1] (1602), 5 Co. Rep. 117a.   [2] Co. Litt. 212b.   [3] (1718), 1 Stra. 426.

it is apparent that a lesser sum of money cannot be a satisfaction of a greater ; " adding (what is beyond controversy), that an acquittance under seal, in full satisfaction of the whole, would (under like circumstances) be valid and binding.

The distinction between the effect of a deed under seal, and that of an agreement by parol, or by writing not under seal, may seem arbitrary, but it is established in our law ; nor is it really unreasonable or practically inconvenient that the law should require particular solemnities to give to a gratuitous contract the force of a binding obligation. If the question be (as, in the actual state of the law, I think it is), whether consideration is, or is not, given in a case of this kind, by the debtor who pays down part of the debt presently due from him, for a promise by the creditor to relinquish, after certain further payments on account, the residue of the debt, I cannot say that I think consideration is given, in the sense in which I have always under-stood that word as used in our law. It might be (and indeed I think it would be) an improvement in our law, if a release or acquittance of the whole debt, on payment of any sum which the creditor might be content to receive by way of accord and satisfaction (though less than the whole), were held to be, generally, binding, though not under seal ; nor should I be unwilling to see equal force given to a prospective agreement, like the present, in writing though not under seal ; but I think it impossible, without refinements which practically alter the sense of the word, to treat such a release or acquittance as supported by any new consideration proceeding from the debtor. All the authorities subsequent to *Cumber* v. *Wane*[1], which were relied upon by the appellant at your Lordships' Bar (such as *Sibree* v. *Tripp*[2], *Curlewis* v. *Clark*[3], *and Goddard* v. *O'Brien*[4]) have proceeded upon the distinction that, by giving negotiable paper or otherwise, there has been some new consideration for a new agreement, distinct from mere money payments in or towards discharge of the original liability. I think it unnecessary to go through those cases, or to examine the particular grounds on which each of them was decided. There are no such facts in the case now before your Lordships.[5] What is called " any benefit, or even any legal possibility of benefit," in Mr. Smith's notes to *Cumber* v. *Wane*[1], is not (as I conceive) that sort of benefit which a creditor may derive from getting payment of part of the money due to him from a debtor who might otherwise keep him at arm's length, or possibly become insolvent, but is some inde-pendent benefit, actual or contingent, of a kind which might in law be a good and valuable consideration for any other sort of agreement not under seal.

My conclusion is, that the order appealed from should be affirmed, and the appeal dismissed, with costs, and I so move your Lordships.

LORDS WATSON and FITZGERALD delivered judgments to the same effect. LORD BLACKBURN had at first prepared a dissenting judgment, but concluded by " assenting to the judgment proposed, though it was not that which he had originally thought proper."[6]

---

[1] Stra. 426. See also 1 Sm. L. C. 8th Ed. 366.   [2] (1846), 15 M. & W. 23.
[3] (1849), 3 Exch. 375.   [4] (1882), 9 Q. B. D. 37.
[5] See *D. & C. Builders, Ltd.* v. *Rees*, [1965] 3 All E. R. 837, *infra*, p. 38.
[6] (1884), 9 App. Cas., at 622–3.

Central London Property Trust, Ltd. v. High Trees House, Ltd.

[1947] K.B. 130

ACTION tried by DENNING, J.

By a lease under seal made on September 24, 1937, the plaintiffs, Central London Property Trust, Ltd., granted to the defendants, High Trees House, Ltd., a subsidiary of the plaintiff company, a tenancy of a block of flats for the term of ninety-nine years from September 29, 1937, at a ground rent of 2,500*l.* a year. The block of flats was a new one and had not been fully occupied at the beginning of the war owing to the absence of people from London. With war conditions prevailing, it was apparent to those responsible that the rent reserved under the lease could not be paid out of the profits of the flats and, accordingly, discussions took place between the directors of the two companies concerned, which were closely associated, and an arrangement was made between them which was put into writing. On January 3, 1940, the plaintiffs wrote to the defendants in these terms, " we confirm the arrangement made between us by which the ground rent should be reduced as from the commencement of the lease to 1,250*l.* per annum," and on April 2, 1940, a confirmatory resolution to the same effect was passed by the plaintiff company. On March 20, 1941, a receiver was appointed by the debenture holders of the plaintiffs and on his death on February 28, 1944, his place was taken by his partner. The defendants paid the reduced rent from 1941 down to the beginning of 1945 by which time all the flats in the block were fully let, and continued to pay it thereafter. In September, 1945, the then receiver of the plaintiff company looked into the matter of the lease and ascertained that the rent actually reserved by it was 2,500*l.* On September 21, 1945, he wrote to the defendants saying that rent must be paid at the full rate and claiming that arrears amounting to 7,916*l.* were due. Subsequently, he instituted the present friendly proceedings to test the legal position in regard to the rate at which rent was payable. In the action the plaintiffs sought to recover 625*l.*, being the amount represented by the difference between rent at the rate of 2,500*l.* and 1,250*l.* per annum for the quarters ending September 29, and December 25, 1945. By their defence the defendants pleaded (1) that the letter of January 3, 1940, constituted an agreement that the rent reserved should be 1,250*l.* only, and that such agreement related to the whole term of the lease; (2) they pleaded in the alternative that the plaintiff company were estopped from alleging that the rent exceeded 1,250*l.* per annum; and (3) as a further alternative, that by failing to demand rent in excess of 1,250*l.* before their letter of September 21, 1945 (received by the defendants on September 24), they had waived their rights in respect of any rent, in excess of that at the rate of 1,250*l.*, which had accrued up to September 24, 1945.

.   .   .   .   .

DENNING, J., stated the facts and continued: If I were to consider this matter without regard to recent developments in the law, there is no doubt that had the plaintiffs claimed it, they would have been entitled to recover ground rent at the rate of 2,500*l.* a year from the beginning of the term, since the lease under which it was payable was a lease under seal which, according to the old common law, could not be varied by an agreement by parol (whether in writing or not), but only by deed. Equity, however, stepped in, and said that if there has been a variation of a deed by a simple contract (which in the case of a lease required to be in writing would have to be evidenced by writing), the courts may give effect to it as is shown in *Berry* v. *Berry*[1]. That equitable doctrine, however, could hardly apply in the present case because the variation here might be said to have been made without consideration. With regard to estoppel, the representation made in relation to reducing the rent, was not a representation of an existing fact. It was a representation, in effect, as to the future, namely, that payment of the rent would not be enforced at the full rate but only at the reduced rate. Such a representation would not give rise to an estoppel, because, as was said in *Jorden* v. *Money*[2], a representation as to the future must be embodied as a contract or be nothing.

But what is the position in view of developments in the law in recent years? The law has not been standing still since *Jorden* v. *Money*[2]. There has been a series of decisions over the last fifty years which, although they are said to be cases of estoppel, are not really such. They are cases in which a promise was made which was intended to create legal relations and which, to the knowledge of the person making the promise, was going to be acted on by the person to whom it was made, and which was in fact so acted on. In such cases the courts have said that the promise must be honoured. The cases to which I particularly desire to refer are: *Fenner* v. *Blake*[3], *In re Wickham*,[4] *Re William Porter & Co. Ltd.*[5] and *Buttery* v. *Pickard*[6]. As I have said they are not cases of estoppel in the strict sense. They are really promises—promises intended to be binding, intended to be acted on, and in fact acted on. *Jorden* v. *Money*[7] can be distinguished, because there the promisor made it clear that she did not intend to be legally bound, whereas in the cases to which I refer the proper inference was that the promisor did intend to be bound. In each case the court held the promise to be binding on the party making it, even though under the old common law it might be difficult to find any consideration for it. The courts have not gone so far as to give a cause of action in damages for the breach of such a promise, but they have refused to allow the party making it to act inconsistently with it. It is in that sense, and that sense only, that such a promise gives rise to an estoppel. The decisions are a natural result of the fusion of law and equity: for the cases of *Hughes* v. *Metropolitan Rail. Co.*[8], *Birmingham and District Land Co.* v. *London and North Western Rail. Co.*[9] and *Salisbury (Marquess)* v. *Gilmore*[10], afford a sufficient basis for saying that a party would not be allowed in equity to go back on such a promise. In my opinion, the time has now come for the validity of such a promise to be recognized. The logical consequence, no doubt is that a promise to accept a smaller sum in discharge of a larger sum, if acted upon, is binding notwithstanding the absence of consideration: and if the fusion of law and equity leads to this result, so much the better. That aspect was not considered in *Foakes* v. *Beer*[11]. At this time of day, however, when law and equity have been joined together for over seventy years, principles must be reconsidered in the light of their combined effect. It is to be noticed that in the Sixth Interim Report of the Law Revision Committee, pars. 35, 40, it is recommended that such a promise as that to which I have referred, should be enforceable in law even though no consideration for it has been given by the promisee. It seems to me that, to the extent I

---

[1] [1929] 2 K. B. 316.
[2] (1854), 5 H. L. Cas. 185.
[3] [1900] 1 Q. B. 426.
[4] (1917), 34 T. L. R. 158.
[5] [1937] 2 All E. R. 361. [6] [1946] W. N. 25.
[7] (1854), 5 H. L. Cas. 185.
[8] (1877), 2 App. Cas. 439, at p. 448.
[9] (1888), 40 Ch. D. 268, at p. 286.
[10] [1942] 2 K. B. 38, at p. 51.
[11] (1884), 9 App. Cas. 605.

have mentioned, that result has now been achieved by the decisions of the courts.

I am satisfied that a promise such as that to which I have referred is binding and the only question remaining for my consideration is the scope of the promise in the present case. I am satisfied on all the evidence that the promise here was that the ground rent should be reduced to 1,250*l.* a year as a temporary expedient while the block of flats was not fully, or substantially fully let, owing to the conditions prevailing. That means that the reduction in the rent applied throughout the years down to the end of 1944, but early in 1945 it is plain that the flats were fully let, and, indeed, the rents received from them (many of them not being affected by the Rent Restrictions Acts) were increased beyond the figure at which it was originally contemplated that they would be let. At all events the rent from them must have been very considerable. I find that the conditions prevailing at the time when the reduction in rent was made, had completely passed away by the early months of 1945. I am satisfied that the promise was understood by all parties only to apply under the conditions prevailing at the time when it was made, namely, when the flats were only partially let, and that it did not extend any further than that. When the flats became fully let, early in 1945, the reduction ceased to apply.

In those circumstances, under the law as I hold it, it seems to me that rent is payable at the full rate for the quarters ending September 29 and December 25, 1945.

If the case had been one of estoppel, it might be said that in any event the estoppel would cease when the conditions to which the representation applied came to an end, or it also might be said that it would only come to an end on notice. In either case it is only a way of ascertaining what is the scope of the representation. I prefer to apply the principle that a promise intended to be binding, intended to be acted on and in fact acted on, is binding so far as its terms properly apply. Here it was binding as covering the period down to the early part of 1945, and as from that time full rent is payable.

I therefore give judgment for the plaintiff company for the amount claimed.

Combe v. Combe

[1951] 2 K.B. 215

APPEAL from Byrne, J.

The parties, a husband and wife, were married in 1915, but separated in 1939. On February 1, 1943, on the wife's petition, a decree nisi of divorce was pronounced. On February 9, 1943, the wife's solicitor wrote to the husband's solicitor: " With regard to permanent maintenance, we understand that your client is prepared to make her an allowance of 100*l.* per year, free of income tax." On February 19, 1943, the husband's solicitor replied that the husband had " agreed to allow your client 100*l.* per annum, free of tax." On August 11, 1943, the decree was made absolute. The wife's solicitor wrote for the first instalment of 25*l.* on August 26, and asking that future instalments should be paid on November 11, February 11, May 11, and August 11. The husband, himself, replied that he could not be expected to pay in advance. In fact, he never made any payment. The wife pressed for payment but made no application to the Divorce Court for maintenance.

She had an income of between 700*l*. and 800*l*. a year. Her husband had only 650*l*. a year.

On July 28, 1950, the wife brought an action in the King's Bench Division claiming from her husband 675*l*., being arrears of payment at the rate of 100*l*. per year for six and three-quarter years. Byrne, J., held that the first three quarterly instalments of 25*l*. were barred by the Limitation Act, 1939, but gave judgment for the wife for 600*l*. He held on the authority of *Gaisberg* v. *Storr*[1] that there was no consideration for the husband's promise to pay his wife 100*l*., but nevertheless he held that the promise was enforceable on the principle stated in *Central London Property Trust, Ltd.* v. *High Trees House, Ltd.*[2] and *Robertson* v. *Minister of Pensions*[3], because it was an unequivocal acceptance of liability, intended to be binding, intended to be acted on and, in fact, acted on.

The husband appealed.

DENNING, L.J. [after stating the facts:] Much as I am inclined to favour the principle stated in the *High Trees* case[4], it is important that it should not be stretched too far, lest it should be endangered. That principle does not create new causes of action where none existed before. It only prevents a party from insisting upon his strict legal rights, when it would be unjust to allow him to enforce them, having regard to the dealings which have taken place between the parties. That is the way it was put in *Hughes* v. *Metropolitan Rail. Co.*[5], the case in the House of Lords in which the principle was first stated, and in *Birmingham, etc., Land Co.* v. *London and North-Western Rail. Co.*[6], the case in the Court of Appeal where the principle was enlarged. It is also implicit in all the modern cases in which the principle has been developed. Sometimes it is a plaintiff who is not allowed to insist on his strict legal rights. Thus, a creditor is not allowed to enforce a debt which he has deliberately agreed to waive, if the debtor has carried on business or in some other way changed his position in reliance on the waiver: *Re William Porter & Co., Ltd.*[7]; *Buttery* v. *Pickard*[8]; the *High Trees* case[4]; and *Ledingham* v. *Bermejo Estancia Co., Ltd.*[9] A landlord, who has told his tenant that he can live in his cottage rent free for the rest of his life, is not allowed to go back on it, if the tenant stays in the house on that footing: *Foster* v. *Robinson*[10]. On other occasions it is a defendant who is not allowed to insist on his strict legal rights. His conduct may be such as to debar him from relying on some condition, denying some allegation, or taking some other point in answer to the claim. Thus a government department, which had accepted a disease as due to war service, were not allowed afterwards to say it was not, seeing that the soldier, in reliance on the assurance, had abstained from getting further evidence about it: *Robertson* v. *Minister of Pensions*[11]. A buyer who had waived the contract date for delivery was not allowed afterwards to set up the stipulated time as an answer to the seller: *Charles Rickards, Ltd.* v. *Oppenheim*[12]. A tenant who had encroached on an adjoining building, asserting that it was comprised in the lease, was not allowed afterwards to say that it was not included in the lease: *J. F. Perrott & Co., Ltd.* v. *Cohen*[13]. A tenant who had lived in a house rent-free by permission of his

[1] [1950] 1 K. B. 107; [1950] 2 All E.R. 411.   [2] [1947] K. B. 130.
[3] [1949] 1 K. B. 227; [1948] 2 All E.R. 767.   [4] [1947] K. B. 130.
[5] (1877), 2 App. Cas. 439, at p. 448.   [6] (1888), 40 Ch. D. 268, at p. 286.
[7] [1937] 2 All E. R. 361.   [8] [1946] W. N. 25.   [9] [1947] 1 All E. R. 749.
[10] [1951] 1 K. B. 149, at p. 156.   [11] [1949] 1 K. B. 227.
[12] [1950] 1 K. B. 616. at pp. 621–23.   [13] [1951] 1 K. B. 705.

landlord, thereby asserting that his original tenancy had ended, was not afterwards allowed to say that his original tenancy continued: *Foster* v. *Robinson*[1]. In none of these cases was the defendant sued on the promise, assurance, or assertion as a cause of action in itself: he was sued for some other cause, for example, a pension or a breach of contract, and the promise, assurance, or assertion only played a supplementary rôle—an important rôle, no doubt, but still a supplementary rôle. That is, I think, its true function. It may be part of a cause of action, but not a cause of action in itself.

The principle, as I understand it, is that, where one party has, by his words or conduct, made to the other a promise or assurance which was intended to affect the legal relations between them and to be acted on accordingly, then, once the other party has taken him at his word and acted on it, the one who gave the promise or assurance cannot afterwards be allowed to revert to the previous legal relations as if no such promise or assurance had been made by him, but he must accept their legal relations subject to the qualification which he himself has so introduced, even though it is not supported in point of law by any consideration but only by his word.

Seeing that the principle never stands alone as giving a cause of action in itself, it can never do away with the necessity of consideration when that is an essential part of the cause of action. The doctrine of consideration is too firmly fixed to be overthrown by a side-wind. Its ill-effects have been largely mitigated of late, but it still remains a cardinal necessity of the formation of a contract, though not of its modification or discharge. I fear that it was my failure to make this clear which misled Byrne, J., in the present case. He held that the wife could sue on the husband's promise as a separate and independent cause of action by itself, although, as he held, there was no consideration for it. That is not correct. The wife can only enforce it if there was consideration for it. That is, therefore, the real question in the case: was there sufficient consideration to support the promise?

If it were suggested that, in return for the husband's promise, the wife expressly or impliedly promised to forbear from applying to the court for maintenance—that is, a promise in return for a promise—there would clearly be no consideration, because the wife's promise was not binding on her and was therefore worth nothing. Notwithstanding her promise, she could always apply to the Divorce Court for maintenance—maybe only with leave—and no agreement by her could take away that right: *Hyman* v. *Hyman*[2], as interpreted by this court in *Gaisberg* v. *Storr*[3].

There was, however, clearly no promise by the wife, express or implied, to forbear from applying to the court. All that happened was that she did in fact forbear—that is, she did an act in return for a promise. Is that sufficient consideration? Unilateral promises of this kind have long been enforced, so long as the act or forbearance is done on the faith of the promise and at the request of the promisor, express or implied. The act done is then in itself sufficient consideration for the promise, even though it arises *ex post facto*, as Parker, J., pointed out in *Wigan* v. *English and Scottish Law Life Assurance Association*[4]. If the findings of Byrne, J., were accepted, they would be sufficient to bring this principle into play. His finding that the husband's promise was intended to be binding, intended to be acted upon, and was, in fact, acted on—although expressed to be a finding on the *High*

---

[1] [1951] 1 K. B. 149, at p. 156.   [2] [1929] A. C. 601.
[3] [1950] 1 K. B. 107.   [4] [1909] 1 Ch. 291, at p. 298.

Trees principle—is equivalent to a finding that there was consideration within this long settled rule, because it comes to the same thing expressed in different words: see *Oliver* v. *Davis*[1]. But my difficulty is to accept the finding of Byrne, J., that the promise was " intended to be acted upon." I cannot find any evidence of any intention by the husband that the wife should forbear from applying to the court for maintenance, or, in other words, any request by the husband, express or implied, that the wife should so forbear. He left her to apply if she wished to do so. She did not do so, and I am not surprised, because it is very unlikely that the Divorce Court would have then made any order in her favour, seeing that she had a bigger income than her husband. Her forbearance was not intended by him, nor was it done at his request. It was therefore no consideration.

It may be that the wife has suffered some detriment because, after forbearing to apply to the court for seven years, she might not now be given leave to apply: *Scott* v. *Scott*[2]. The court is, however, nowadays much more ready to give leave than it used to be (see *Fisher* v. *Fisher*[3] and *Hasting* v. *Hasting*)[4], and I should have thought that, if she fell on hard times, she would still obtain leave. Assuming, however, that she has suffered some detriment by her forbearance, nevertheless, as the forbearance was not at the husband's request, it is no consideration. In *Scott* v. *Scott*, where a maintenance agreement was made during divorce proceedings, Scrutton, L.J., did say that he had no doubt about there being consideration for it[5], but this must now be taken to be erroneous, having regard to *Hyman* v. *Hyman*[6] and *Gaisberg* v. *Storr*[7].

The doctrine of consideration is sometimes said to work injustice, but I see none in this case, nor was there any in *Oliver* v. *Davis*[8] or *Gaisberg* v. *Storr*[7]. I do not think it would be right for this wife, who is better off than her husband, to take no action for six or seven years and then come down on him for the whole 600*l.*

The truth is that in these maintenance cases the real remedy of the wife is, not by action in the King's Bench Division, but by application in the Divorce Court. I have always understood that no agreement for maintenance, which is made in the course of divorce proceedings prior to decree absolute, is valid unless it is sanctioned by the court. Indeed, I said so in *Emanuel* v. *Emanuel*[9]. I know that such agreements are often made, but their only valid purpose is to serve as a basis for a consent application to the court. The reason why such agreements are invalid, unless approved, is because they are so apt to be collusive. Some wives are tempted to stipulate for extortionate maintenance as the price of giving the husband his freedom. It is to remove this temptation that the sanction of the court is required. It would be a great pity if this salutary requirement could be evaded by taking action in the King's Bench Division. The Divorce Court can order the husband to pay whatever maintenance is just. Moreover, if justice so requires, it can make the order retrospective to decree absolute. That is the proper remedy of the wife here, and I do not think she has a right to any other.

For these reasons I think the appeal should be allowed.

BIRKETT, L.J., and ASQUITH, L.J., also delivered judgments allowing the appeal.

---

[1] [1949] 2 K. B. 727.   [2] [1921] P. 107.   [3] [1942] P. 101.
[4] [1948] P. 68.   [5] [1921] P. 107, at p. 127.   [6] [1929] A. C. 601.
[7] [1950] 1 K. B. 107.   [8] [1949] 2 K. B. 727.   [9] [1946] P. 115.

D. & C. Builders, Ltd. v. Rees

[1965] 3 All E. R. 837

" Where a debtor's own cheque for a lesser amount than he indisputably owes to his creditor is accepted by the creditor in full satisfaction of the debt, the creditor is to be regarded, in any case where he has not required the payment to be made by cheque rather than in cash, as having received the cheque merely as conditional payment of part of what he was entitled to receive : he is free in law, if not in good commercial conscience, to insist on payment of the balance of the amount due to him from the debtor " (WINN, L.J., *infra*, pp. 45–46).

The creditor will be barred by the doctrine of promissory or quasi-estoppel from enforcing his legal rights only where it would be inequitable for him to insist upon them.

APPEAL.

This was an appeal of the defendant from a judgment of His Honour Judge Trapnell given on May 5, 1965, at Shoreditch County Court holding, on a preliminary point, that acceptance by the plaintiff company of a cheque for £300 in settlement of a debt of £482 13s. 1d. did not discharge the debt, and that the plaintiff company was entitled to recover the balance. The defendant appealed.

LORD DENNING, M.R.: D. & C. Builders, Ltd. (" the plaintiffs ") are a little company. " D " stands for Mr. Donaldson, a decorator, " C " for Mr. Casey, a plumber. They are jobbing builders. The defendant, Mr. Rees, has a shop where he sells builders' materials.

In the spring of 1964 the defendant employed the plaintiffs to do work at his premises, 218, Brick Lane. The plaintiffs did the work and rendered accounts in May and June, which came to £746 13s. 1d. altogether. The defendant paid £250 on account. In addition the plaintiffs made an allowance of £14 off the bill. So in July, 1964, there was owing to the plaintiffs the sum of £482 13s. 1d. At this stage there was no dispute as to the work done. But the defendant did not pay.

On August 31, 1964, the plaintiffs wrote asking the defendant to pay the remainder of the bill. He did not reply. On October 19, 1964, they wrote again, pointing out that the " outstanding account of £480 is well overdue ". Still the defendant did not reply. He did not write or telephone for more than three weeks. Then on Friday, November 13, 1964, the defendant was ill with influenza. His wife telephoned the plaintiffs. She spoke to Mr. Casey. She began to make complaints about the work : and then said : " My husband will offer you £300 in settlement. That is all you'll get. It is to be in satisfaction." Mr. Casey said he would have to discuss it with Mr. Donaldson. The two of them talked it over. Their company was in desperate financial straits. If they did not have the £300, they would be in a state of bankruptcy. So they decided to accept the £300 and see what they could do about the rest afterwards. Thereupon Mr. Donaldson telephoned to the defendant's wife. He said to her : " £300 will not even clear our commitments on the job. We will accept £300 and give you a year to find the balance." She said : " No, we will never have enough money to pay the balance. £300 is better than nothing." He said : " We have no choice but to accept." She said : " Would you like the money by cash or by cheque. If it is cash, you can have it on Monday. If by cheque, you can have it tomorrow (Saturday)." On Saturday, November 14, 1964, Mr. Casey went to collect the money. He took with him a receipt prepared on the company's paper with the simple words : " Received the sum of £300 from Mr. Rees."

She gave him a cheque for £300 and asked for a receipt. She insisted that the words " in completion of the account " be added. Mr. Casey did as she asked. He added the words to the receipt. So she had the clean receipt: " Received the sum of £300 from Mr. Rees in completion of the account. Paid, M. Casey." Mr. Casey gave in evidence his reason for giving it: " If I did not have the £300 the company would have gone bankrupt. The only reason we took it was to save the company. She knew the position we were in."

The plaintiffs were so worried about their position that they went to their solicitors. Within a few days, on November 23, 1964, the solicitors wrote complaining that the defendant had " extricated a receipt of some sort or other " from them. They said that they were treating the £300 as a payment on account. On November 28, 1964, the defendant replied alleging bad workmanship. He also set up the receipt which Mr. Casey gave to his wife, adding: " I assure you she had no gun on her." The plaintiffs brought this action for the balance. The defendant set up a defence of bad workmanship and also that there was a binding settlement. The question of settlement was tried as a preliminary issue. The judge made these findings:

> " I concluded that by the middle of August the sum due to the plaintiffs was ascertained and not then in dispute. I also concluded that there was no consideration to support the agreement of November 13 and 14. It was a case of agreeing to take a lesser sum, when a larger sum was already due to the plaintiffs. It was not a case of agreeing to take a cheque for a smaller account instead of receiving cash for a larger account. The payment by cheque was an incidental arrangement."

The judge decided, therefore, the preliminary issue in favour of the plaintiffs. The defendant appeals to this court. He says that there was here an accord and satisfaction—an *accord* when the plaintiffs agreed, however reluctantly, to accept £300 in settlement of the account—and *satisfaction* when they accepted the cheque for £300 and it was duly honoured. The defendant relies on the cases of *Sibree* v. *Tripp*[1] and *Goddard* v. *O'Brien*[2], as authorities in his favour.

This case is of some consequence: for it is a daily occurrence that a merchant or tradesman, who is owed a sum of money, is asked to take less. The debtor says he is in difficulties. He offers a lesser sum in settlement, cash down. He says he cannot pay more. The creditor is considerate. He accepts the proffered sum and forgives him the rest of the debt. The question arises: is the settlement binding on the creditor? The answer is that, in point of law, the creditor is not bound by the settlement. He can the next day sue the debtor for the balance, and get judgment. The law was so stated in 1602 by Lord Coke in *Pinnel's Case*[3]—and accepted in 1884 by the House of Lords in *Foakes* v. *Beer*[4].

Now, suppose that the debtor, instead of paying the lesser sum in cash, pays it by cheque. He makes out a cheque for the amount. The creditor accepts the cheque and cashes it. Is the position any different? I think not. No sensible distinction can be taken between payment of a lesser sum by cash and payment of it by cheque. The cheque, when given, is conditional payment. When honoured, it is actual payment. It is then just the same as cash. If a creditor is not bound when he receives payment by cash, he should not be

---

[1] (1846), 15 M. & W. 23.   [2] (1882), 9 Q. B. D. 37.
[3] (1602), 5 Co. Rep. 117a.
[4] (1884), 9 App. Cas. 605 ;[1881–85] All E.R. Rep. 106.

bound when he receives payment by cheque. This view is supported by the leading case of *Cumber* v. *Wane*[1], which has suffered many vicissitudes but was, I think, rightly decided in point of law.

The case of *Sibree* v. *Tripp*[2] is easily distinguishable. There the plaintiffs brought an action for £500. It was settled by the defendant giving three promissory notes amounting in all to £250. Those promissory notes were given on a new contract, in substitution for the debt sued for, and not as conditional payment. The plaintiff's only remedy thenceforward was on the notes and not on the debt. The case of *Goddard* v. *O'Brien*[3] is not so easily distinguishable. There a creditor was owed £125 for some slates. He met the debtor and agreed to accept £100 in discharge of it. The debtor gave a cheque for £100. The creditor gave a written receipt " in settlement on the said cheque being honoured ". The cheque was clearly given by way of conditional payment. It was honoured. The creditor sued the debtor for the balance of £25. He lost, because the £100 was paid by cheque and not by cash. The decision was criticised by Fletcher Moulton, L.J., in *Hirachand Punamchand* v. *Temple*[4], and by the editors of Smith's Leading Cases (13th Edn.), Vol. I, p. 380. It was, I think, wrongly decided. In point of law payment of a lesser sum, whether by cash or by cheque, is not discharge of a greater sum.

This doctrine of the common law has come under heavy fire. It was ridiculed by Sir George Jessel, M.R., in *Couldery* v. *Bartrum*[5]. It was held to be mistaken by Lord Blackburn in *Foakes* v. *Beer*[6]. It was condemned by the Law Revision Committee in their Sixth Interim Report (Comd. 5449), para. 20 and para. 22. But a remedy has been found. The harshness of the common law has been relieved. Equity has stretched out a merciful hand to help the debtor. The courts have invoked the broad principle stated by Lord Cairns, L.C., in *Hughes* v. *Metropolitan Ry. Co.*[7] :

> " . . . it is the first principle upon which all courts of equity proceed if parties, who have entered into definite and distinct terms involving certain legal results . . . afterwards by their own act, or with their own consent, enter upon a course of negotiation which has the effect of leading one of the parties to suppose that *the strict rights arising under the contract will not be enforced*, or will be kept in suspense, or held in abeyance, that the person who otherwise might have enforced those rights *will not be allowed to enforce them where it would be inequitable, having regard to the dealings which have taken place between the parties.*"

It is worth noticing that the principle may be applied, not only so as to suspend strict legal rights, but also so as to preclude the enforcement of them.

This principle has been applied to cases where a creditor agrees to accept a lesser sum in discharge of a greater. So much so that we can now say that, when a creditor and a debtor enter on a course of negotiation, which leads the debtor to suppose that, on payment of the lesser sum, the creditor will not enforce payment of the balance, and on the faith thereof the debtor pays the lesser sum and the creditor accepts it as satisfaction : then the creditor will not be allowed to enforce payment of the balance when it would be inequitable to do so. This was well illustrated during the last war. Tenants went away to escape the bombs and left their houses unoccupied. The landlords accepted a reduced rent for the time they were empty. It was held that the landlords could not afterwards turn round and sue for the balance: see

---

[1] (1721), 1 Stra. 426.   [2] (1846), 15 M. & W. 23.   [3] (1882), 9 Q.B.D. 37.
[4] [1911] 2 K.B. 330 at p. 340, *infra*, p. 48.   [5] (1881), 19 Ch.D. 394 at p. 399.
[6] (1884), 9 App. Cas. at p. 622; [1881–85] All E.R. Rep. at p. 115.
[7] (1877), 2 App. Cas. 439 at p. 448; [1874–80] All E.R. Rep. 187 at p. 191.

Central London Property Trust, Ltd. v. *High Trees House, Ltd.*[1] This caused at the time some eyebrows to be raised in high places. But they have been lowered since. The solution was so obviously just that no one could well gainsay it.

In applying this principle, however, we must note the qualification. The creditor is barred from his legal rights only when it would be *inequitable* for him to insist on them. Where there has been a *true accord*, under which the creditor voluntarily agrees to accept a lesser sum in satisfaction, and the debtor *acts on* that accord by paying the lesser sum and the creditor accepts it, then it is inequitable for the creditor afterwards to insist on the balance. But he is not bound unless there has been truly an accord between them.

In the present case, on the facts as found by the judge, it seems to me that there was no true accord. The debtor's wife held the creditor to ransom. The creditor was in need of money to meet his own commitments, and she knew it. When the creditor asked for payment of the £480 due to him, she said to him in effect: " We cannot pay you the £480. But we will pay you £300 if you will accept it in settlement. If you do not accept it on those terms, you will get nothing. £300 is better than nothing." She had no right to say any such thing. She could properly have said: " We cannot pay you more than £300. Please accept it on account." But she had no right to insist on his taking it in settlement. When she said: " We will pay you nothing unless you accept £300 in settlement ", she was putting undue pressure on the creditor. She was making a threat to break the contract (by paying nothing) and she was doing it so as to compel the creditor to do what he was unwilling to do (to accept £300 in settlement): and she succeeded. He complied with her demand. That was on recent authority a case of intimidation (see *Rookes* v. *Barnard*[2] and *J. T. Stratford & Son, Ltd.* v. *Lindley*).[3] In these circumstances there was no true accord so as to found a defence of accord and satisfaction (see *Day* v. *McLea*[4]). There is also no equity in the defendant to warrant any departure from the due course of law. No person can insist on a settlement procured by intimidation.

In my opinion there is no reason in law or equity why the creditor should not enforce the full amount of the debt due to him. I would, therefore, dismiss this appeal.

DANCKWERTS, L.J.: I agree with the judgment of Lord Denning, M.R. *Foakes* v. *Beer*[5], applying the decision in *Pinnel's Case*[6], settled definitely the rule of law that payment of a lesser sum than the amount of a debt due cannot be a satisfaction of the debt, unless there is some benefit to the creditor added so that there is an accord and satisfaction.

In *Foakes* v. *Beer*[7], the Earl of Selborne, L.C., while approving *Cumber* v. *Wane*[8] did not overrule the cases which appear to differ from *Cumber* v. *Wane*[8], saying:

" All the authorities subsequent to *Cumber* v. *Wane*[8], which were relied upon by the appellant, such as *Sibree* v. *Tripp*[9], *Curlewis* v. *Clark*[10] and *Goddard*

---

[1] [1947] K.B. 130; [1956] 1 All E.R. 256.
[2] [1964] A.C. 1129; [1964] 1 All E.R. 367.
[3] [1965] A.C. 269 at pp. 283, 284; [1964] 2 All E.R. 209 at p. 216.
[4] (1889) 22 Q.B.D. 610.
[5] (1884), 9 App. Cas. 605; [1881–85] All E.R. Rep. 106.
[6] (1602), 5 Co. Rep. 117a.
[7] (1884), 9 App. Cas. at p. 613; [1881–85] All E.R. Rep. at p. 111.
[8] (1721), 1 Stra. 426.   [9] (1846), 15 M. & W. 23.   [10] (1849), 3 Exch. 375.

v. *O'Brien*[1], have proceeded upon the distinction, that, by giving negotiable paper or otherwise, there had been some new consideration for a new agreement, distinct from mere money payments in or towards discharge of the original liability."

Lord Selborne was distinguishing those cases from the case before the House.

The giving of a cheque of the debtor, however, for a smaller amount than the sum due is very different from "the gift of a horse, hawk, or robe, etc." mentioned in *Pinnel's Case*[2]. I accept that the cheque of some other person than the debtor, in appropriate circumstances, may be the basis of an accord and satisfaction, but I cannot see how in the year 1965 the debtor's own cheque for a smaller sum can be better than payment of the whole amount of the debt in cash. The cheque is only conditional payment, it may be difficult to cash, or it may be returned by the bank with the letters "R.D." on it, unpaid. I think that *Goddard* v. *O'Brien*[3] either was wrongly decided or should not be followed in the circumstances of today.

I agree also that, in the circumstances of the present case, there was no true accord. Mr. and Mrs. Rees really behaved very badly. They knew of the plaintiffs' financial difficulties and used their awkward situation to intimidate them. The plaintiffs did not wish to accept the sum of £300 in discharge of the debt of £482, but were desperate to get some money. It would appear also that the defendant and his wife misled the plaintiffs as to their own financial position. Mr. Rees, in his evidence, said: "In June (1964) I could have paid £700 odd. I could have settled the whole bill." There is no evidence that by August, or even by November, their financial situation had deteriorated so that they could not pay the £482. Nor does it appear that their position was altered to their detriment by reason of the receipt given by the plaintiffs. The receipt was given on November 14 1964. On November 23, 1964, the plaintiffs' solicitors wrote a letter making it clear that the payment of £300 was being treated as a payment on account. I cannot see any ground in this case for treating the payment as a satisfaction on equitable principles.

In my view the county court judge was right in applying the rule in *Foakes* v. *Beer*[4], and I would dismiss the appeal.

WINN, L.J., stated the facts and continued:

The question to be decided may be stated thus. Did the defendant's agreement to give his own cheque for £300 in full settlement of his existing debt to the plaintiffs of £482 13s. 1d. and the plaintiff's agreement to accept it in full payment of that debt, followed by delivery and due payment of such a cheque, constitute a valid accord and satisfaction discharging the debt in law?

Apart altogether from any decided cases bearing on the matter, there might be a good deal to be said, as a matter of policy, in favour of holding any creditor bound by his promise to discharge a debtor on his paying some amount less than the debt due: some judges no doubt so thought when they held readily that acceptance by the creditor of something of a different nature from that to which he was entitled was a satisfaction of the liability (cf. *Pinnel's Case*[5], *Smith* v. *Trowsdale*[6], *Cooper* v. *Parker*[7]). A like approach might at some time in the past have been adopted by the courts to all serious assurances of agreement, but as English law developed, it does not now permit

---

[1] (1882), 9 Q.B.D. 37.   [2] (1602), 5 Co. Rep. 117a.   [3] (1882), 9 Q.B.D. 37.
[4] (1884), 9 App. Cas. 605; [1881–85] All E.R. Rep. 106.
[5] (1602), 5 Co. Rep. 117a.   [6] (1854), 3 E. & B. 83.   [7] (1855), 15 C.B. 882.

in general of such treatment of mere promises. In the more specific field of discharge of monetary debt there has been some conflict of judicial opinion.

Where a cheque for a smaller sum than the amount due is drawn by a person other than the debtor and delivered in satisfaction of his debt, it is clear that the debt is discharged if the cheque be accepted on that basis and duly paid (cf. *Hirachand Punamchand* v. *Temple*[1]).

In the instant case the debtor's own cheque was accepted, though not stipulated for by the creditor, as the equivalent of cash, conditionally of course on its being duly paid on presentation : such is the modern usage in respect of payments of money due, common, though not yet universal, in domestic no less than commercial transactions. This court must now decide the effect of that transaction. Had this case arisen in 1883 it would have fallen to be determined in favour of the defendant by force of the decision of a Divisional Court of two judges, Grove, J., and Huddleston, B., in *Goddard* v. *O'Brien*[2], in which the case of *Cumber* v. *Wane*[3] was distinguished and not followed.

Goddard's case[2] came to be decided on a Case Stated by the judge of the Southwark County Court in which it was set out that the defendant in the action was indebted to the plaintiffs in the sum of £125 odd for billiard table slates sold and delivered by them to him. A representative of the plaintiffs agreed with the defendant to accept the sum of £100 in discharge of the said debt of £125 odd and thereupon the defendant gave to the plaintiffs a cheque for £100 payable on demand and the plaintiffs gave him a receipt stating that the cheque was taken " in settlement of account of £127 7s. 9d. on said cheque being honoured ". The cheque was duly honoured. No other consideration was given by the defendant or received by the plaintiffs in satisfaction of the said debt. The county court judge held that there had been a good accord and satisfaction by reason of the cheque being a negotiable security. The question for the opinion of the court was whether he was right in so ruling. Grove, J., and Huddleston, B., were of the opinion that he was right. Grove, J., said[4] :

> " The difficulty arose from the rule laid down in *Cumber* v. *Wane*[5]. But that doctrine has been much qualified, and I am not sure that it has not been overruled."

He referred to the case of *Sibree* v. *Tripp*[6] and treated it as " a direct authority that the giving of a negotiable security is not within the rule of *Cumber* v. *Wane*[4] ". Huddleston, B., was also of the opinion that[7] " the doctrine of *Cumber* v. *Wane*[5] if not actually overruled, has been very much qualified ". He approved the terms of a note in Smith's Leading Cases (8th Edn.), p. 366, which was in the following terms :

> " The general doctrine in *Cumber* v. *Wane*[5], and the reason of all the exceptions and distinctions which have been engrafted on it, may perhaps be summed up as follows, viz., that a creditor cannot bind himself by a simple agreement to accept a smaller sum in lieu of an ascertained debt of a larger amount, such an agreement being nudum pactum. But if there be any benefit or even any legal possibility of benefit to the creditor thrown in, that additional weight will turn the scale, and render the consideration sufficient to support the agreement."

I interpose the comment that I find it impossible in the instant case to visualise any benefit or legal possibility of benefit to the builders which might

---

[1] [1911] 2 K.B. 330, *infra*, p. 46.   [2] (1882), 9 Q.B.D. 37.
[3] (1721), 1 Stra. 426.   [4] (1882), 9 Q.B.D. at p. 39.
[5] (1721), 1 Stra. 426.   [6] (1846), 15 M. & W. 23.
[7] (1882), 9 Q.B.D. at p. 40.

derive from the receipt of the defendant's cheque for £300 instead of the same amount of cash.

Only two years after the decision in *Goddard's* case[1] the House of Lords, in the case of *Foakes* v. *Beer*[2], had to consider the effect of an agreement between a judgment debtor and a judgment creditor that in consideration of the debtor paying down part of the judgment debt and costs and paying the residue by instalments, the creditor would not take any proceedings on the judgment. The House held this to be a nudum pactum, being without consideration, and that it did not prevent the creditor after payment of the whole debt and costs from proceeding to enforce payment of interest on the judgment. *Pinnel's* case[3] and *Cumber* v. *Wane*[4] were expressly followed. The Earl of Selborne, L.C., said[5]:

"The question, therefore, is nakedly raised by this appeal whether your lordships are now prepared, not only to overrule as contrary to law, the doctrine stated by Sir Edward Coke to have been laid down by all the judges of the Common Pleas in *Pinnel's Case*[3] in 1602, and repeated in his note to Littleton, s. 344 (Co. Litt. 212b), but to treat a prospective agreement, not under seal, for satisfaction of a debt by a series of payments on account to a total amount less than the whole debt, as binding in law, provided those payments are regularly made; the case not being one of a composition with a common debtor, agreed to, *inter se*, by several creditors."

Pausing there, it may be observed that Lord Selborne was considering in this passage the nature and effect of such an agreement rather than the effect of its performance as a satisfaction. He went on to say[6]:

"It may well be that distinctions, which in later cases have been held sufficient to exclude the application of that doctrine [of *Cumber* v. *Wane*[4]] existed and were improperly disregarded in *Cumber* v. *Wane*[4]; and yet that the doctrine itself may be law, rightly recognised in *Cumber* v. *Wane*[4] and not really contradicted by any later authorities; and this appears to me to be the true state of the case."

Lord Selborne then stated his understanding of the doctrine to which he was referring, as stated in *Pinnel's* case[3], to be[7]

"that payment of a lesser sum on the day [it would of course be the same after the day] in satisfaction of a greater, cannot be any satisfaction for the whole, because it appears to the judges that by no possibility a lesser sum can be a satisfaction to the plaintiff for a greater sum."

He further said:

"If the question be . . . whether consideration is, or is not, given in a case of this kind by the debtor who pays down part of the debt presently due from him, for a promise by the creditor to relinquish, after certain further payments on account, the residue of the debt, I cannot say that I think consideration is given, in the sense in which I have always understood that word as used in our law. It might be (and indeed I think it would be) an improvement in our law, if a release or acquittance of the whole debt on payment of any sum which the creditor might be content to receive by way of accord and satisfaction, though less than the whole, were held to be generally binding, though not under seal . . . but I think it impossible . . . to treat such a release or acquittance as supported by any new consideration proceeding from the debtor. All the authorities subsequent to *Cumber* v. *Wane*[8] . . . such as *Sibree* v. *Tripp*[9], *Curlewis* v. *Clark*[10] and *Goddard* v. *O'Brien*[11], have proceeded upon the distinc-

[1] (1882), 9 Q.B.D. 37.   [2] (1884), 9 App. Cas. 605; [1881–85] All E.R. Rep. 106.
[3] (1602), 5 Co. Rep. 117a.   [4] (1721), 1 Stra. 426.
[5] (1884), 9 App. Cas. at p. 612; [1881–85] All E.R. Rep. at p. 110.
[6] (1884), 9 App. Cas. at p. 612; [1881–85 All E.R. Rep. at p. 110.
[7] (1884), 9 App. Cas. at p. 613; [1881–85] All E.R. Rep. at pp. 110, 111.
[8] (1721), 1 Stra. 426.   [9] (1846), 15 M. & W. 23.
[10] (1849), 3 Exch. 375.   [11] (1882), 9 Q.B.D. 37.

tion that, by giving negotiable paper or otherwise, there had been some new consideration for a new agreement, distinct from mere money payments in or towards discharge of the original liability."

It is clear that this speech did not deal with the effect of the giving of any cheque or negotiable instrument in respect of part of the debt due since it left any case involving such an element on one side: on the other hand, it did go a long way to restore the authority of *Pinnel's* case[1] and *Cumber* v. *Wane*[2].

It is further to be noted that Lord Selborne in the last passage quoted emphasised the need for consideration to support the accord and he said further[3]:

> "What is called ' any benefit, or even any legal possibility of benefit ' in Mr. Smith's notes to *Cumber* v. *Wane*[4] (Smith, L.C., 8th Edn. p. 366) is not, as I conceive, that sort of benefit which a creditor may derive from getting payment of part of the money due to him from a debtor who might otherwise keep him at arm's length, or possibly become insolvent, but is some independent benefit, actual or contingent, of a kind which might in law be a good and valuable consideration for any other sort of agreement not under seal."

Lord Blackburn made it clear in his speech that he had felt hesitation in concurring as he did in the decision because he felt convinced that[5]

> " . . . all men of business, whether merchants or tradesmen, do every day recognise and act on the ground that prompt payment of a part of their demand may be more beneficial to them than it would be to insist on their rights and enforce payment of the whole."

He remarked obiter that[6] " if it had been a promissory note . . . the authorities are that it would have been a good satisfaction ".

In 1911 in the case already referred to of *Punamchand* Fletcher Moulton, L.J., said[7]:

> " I have grave doubts whether *Goddard* v. *O'Brien*[8] was rightly decided because, when the facts are looked at, it appears that the cheque was there given, not in substitution for the debt, but only as conditional payment of the amount, so that the case really stood on the same footing as payment of a less amount in discharge of a greater."

Farwell, L.J., in the same case said[9], referring to the case of *Day* v. *McLea*[10]:

> " In that case, there being no consideration for the discharge of the balance of the debt, it was held that the creditor could retain the money, and sue for the balance."

In my judgment it is an essential element of a valid accord and satisfaction that the agreement which constitutes the accord should itself be binding in law, and I do not think that any such agreement can be so binding unless it is either made under seal or supported by consideration. Satisfaction, viz., performance, of an agreement or accord does not provide retroactive validity to the accord, but depends for its effect on the legal validity of the accord as a binding contract at the time when it is made: this I think is apparent when it is remembered that, albeit rarely, existing obligations of debt may be replaced effectively by a contractually binding substitution of a new obligation.

In my judgment this court should now decline to follow the decision in *Goddard* v. *O'Brien*[11] and should hold that where a debtor's own cheque for a

---

[1] (1602), 5 Co. Rep. 117a. [2] (1846), 15 M. & W. 23.
[3] (1884), 9 App. Cas. at pp. 613, 614; [1881–85] All E.R. Rep. at p. 111.
[4] (1721), 1 Stra. 426.
[5] (1884), 9 App. Cas. at p. 622; [1881–85] All E.R. Rep. at p. 115.
[6] (1884), 9 App. Cas. at p. 615; [1881–85] All E.R. Rep. at p. 112.
[7] [1911] 2 K.B. at p. 340.
[8] (1882), 9 Q.B.D. 37 [9] [1911] 2 K.B. at p. 342.
[10] (1889), 22 Q.B.D. 610. [11] (1882), 9 Q.B.D. 37.

lesser amount than he indisputably owes to his creditor is accepted by the creditor in full satisfaction of the debt, the creditor is to be regarded, in any case where he has not required the payment to be made by cheque rather than in cash, as having received the cheque merely as conditional payment of part of what he was entitled to receive: he is free in law, if not in good commercial conscience, to insist on payment of the balance of the amount due to him from the debtor.

I would dismiss this appeal.

Hirachand Punamchand v. Temple
[1911] 2 K.B. 330

If a creditor accepts part payment by a third party in satisfaction of money due to him by a debtor, he cannot afterwards sue the debtor for the balance of the debt.

The plaintiffs were money-lenders carrying on business in India. They lent money to the defendant, an army officer in India, who gave them a promissory note for the amount lent together with interest. They also lent a further sum of money on the security of a bond. They failed to obtain repayment from the defendant, and applied to Sir Richard Temple, the defendant's father, resident in England. After some correspondence Sir Richard's solicitor sent to the plaintiffs a draft for an amount less than that of the debt. The plaintiffs, though they realised that this was an offer to settle their claim, cashed the draft, kept the money and now sued the defendants for the balance of the debt.

SCRUTTON, J. gave judgment for the plaintiffs for the amount claimed. The defendant appealed.

Before the Court of Appeal, counsel for the defendant argued that on the authorities the creditors could not sue for the balance of the debt, though it might be a little doubtful on the cases on what ground this conclusion rests. In *Welby* v. *Drake*[1] Lord Tenterden seems to have put it upon the ground that such an action, being a fraud on the father, is an abuse of the process of the Court. In *Cook* v. *Lister*[2] Willes, J., said, " if a debtor pays a portion of the debt, it does not inure as a discharge of the whole, though so agreed, but, if a stranger pays a part of the debt in discharge of the whole, the debt is gone, because it would be a fraud on the stranger to proceed. So, in the case of a composition made with a body of creditors, the assent to receive the composition discharges the debt, because otherwise fraud would be committed against the rest of the creditors." It seems, however, clear that, whatever the ground may be, there is under such circumstances a defence to the action. *Day* v. *McLea*[3] was treated by the learned judge as an authority in favour of the plaintiffs, but in that case the cheque was sent by the debtor himself, and it was held on the facts that the cheque was not received by the plaintiffs in satisfaction of the debt. That decision is no authority for a case in which a smaller sum is sent by a third party and received by the creditor in satisfaction of the debt.

Counsel for the plaintiff said that in substance the defence set up was one of accord and satisfaction. In the cases which have been cited for the defendant, it is clear that the creditors had agreed to take the amount paid in

---

[1] (1825), 1 C. & P. 557.   [2] (1863), 13 C. B. N. S. 543, 594.
[3] (1889), 22 Q. B. D. 610.

satisfaction of the debt. In the absence of any such agreement the payment of the smaller sum by the father cannot amount to an accord and satisfaction. The fact that the plaintiffs' action in taking the money and afterwards suing the son, may have been wrong as against the father, but cannot afford a defence to the son. It is *res inter alios acta* as between the plaintiffs and the son. [They cited *Goddard* v. *O'Brien*[1]]

The Court of Appeal gave judgment for the defendant and allowed the appeal.

FLETCHER MOULTON, L.J. I think that the plaintiffs' action fails, and that this appeal should be allowed. The facts of this case are such that this result may be arrived at by more than one course of reasoning. I am clearly of opinion that there must be taken to have been an agreement between the plaintiffs and Sir Richard Temple, by which the plaintiffs agreed to accept the money sent by him in satisfaction of the note. No oral testimony was given at the trial, but the facts of the case appear clearly from the correspondence. In the first letter the plaintiffs applied to Sir Richard Temple, the father, in respect of his son's account with them. Then comes a letter from the father's solicitors, in which they offer the plaintiffs a certain sum in settlement of the plaintiffs' two claims against the son, one of which was on a bond and the other on the promissory note. In answer to this letter, two separate letters were written by the plaintiffs, one with regard to the bond, and the other with regard to the note. I need only refer to the latter, as the purport of the two, *mutatis mutandis*, is the same. The plaintiffs in that letter say : " We shall be glad if you will let us know the amount for which Sir Richard Temple is prepared to settle this debt due from his son." Therefore it is clear that the plaintiffs realized that the father was proposing to settle the whole claim on the note, and that they accordingly asked the amount he was prepared to give. The father's solicitors wrote in answer one letter dealing with both claims. In the paragraph relating to the promissory note, they say :

> "Our instructions are, therefore, to pay you Rs. 500 in respect of the principal and Rs. 150 in respect of the one year's interest, making together Rs. 650. We enclose draft by the National Bank of India on the Bank of Bombay, Poona, in your favour for this amount, and shall be glad to receive the promissory note in exchange."

It is perfectly clear from the previous correspondence that this was an offer made for the full settlement of the claim. The plaintiffs, with knowledge that this was the money of the father, sent to them in full settlement of the claim, took the draft, and cashed it, and kept the money. They must be taken to have known that they could only do this rightly, if they agreed to the terms that it should be in full settlement of the debt. Their action was inconsistent with the duty of an honest man, unless, at the time when they took the money, they accepted the terms on which it was offered. They must have known that they could only possess themselves of this money honestly by accepting those terms, and, knowing that, they possessed themselves of it. That appears to me to be overwhelming evidence of an acceptance by them of the proposal made to them by the father. It is

---

[1] (1832), 9 Q.B.D. 37. " Accord and satisfaction is the purchase of a release from an obligation by means of any valuable consideration not being the actual performance of the obligation itself. The accord is the agreement by which the obligation is discharged. The satisfaction is the consideration which makes the agreement operative ": *British Russian Gazette and Trade Outlook, Ltd.* v. *Associated Newspapers, Ltd.*, [1933] 2 K.B. 616, at pp. 643–644.

contended that we ought to come to the contrary conclusion by reason of the letters subsequently written by them on December 31, by which, after pocketing the money which they must have known to be offered in settlement of the debt, they endeavoured to get payment of the debt in full from the defendant's father. We are asked to allow those letters to override the overwhelming evidence of acceptance by them of the father's offer which is afforded by their conduct. I decline to accept the conclusion of fact suggested by the plaintiffs that they dishonestly possessed themselves of the father's money, and shall presume that they did so honestly, and therefore that they accepted it in settlement of their claim against the son on the promissory note.

These being the facts, we have to consider how they affect the debt on the note in point of law. I am of opinion that by that transaction between the plaintiffs and Sir Richard Temple the debt on the promissory note became extinct. I agree with the view expressed by Willes, J., in *Cook* v. *Lister*[1]. The effect of such an agreement between a creditor and a third party with regard to the debt is to render it impossible for the creditor afterwards to sue the debtor for it. The way in which this is worked out in law may be that it would be an abuse of the process of the Court to allow the creditor under such circumstances to sue, or it may be, and I prefer that view, that there is an extinction of the debt; but, whichever way it is put, it comes to the same thing, namely that, after acceptance by the creditor of a sum offered by a third party in settlement of the claim against the debtor, the creditor cannot maintain an action for the balance. That being my view, namely, that either the debt is extinguished, or that the Court will not allow the creditor to assert his claim, I will only say a few words upon two of the cases which have been cited on the subject. By the decision in *Foakes* v. *Beer*[2] the old doctrine that a debtor cannot discharge himself from his debt by payment of an amount smaller than that of the debt was recognized by the House of Lords as law of such old standing that it could not be challenged. This fully explains the decision in *Day* v. *McLea*[3], where a debtor sent a cheque to his creditor for an amount smaller than the debt, stating that it was in settlement of the debt. It was accepted, and yet it was held that there was no settlement. I have grave doubts whether *Goddard* v. *O'Brien*[4] was rightly decided, because, when the facts are looked at, it appears that the cheque was there given, not in substitution for the debt, but only as conditional payment of the amount, so that the case really stood on the same footing as payment of a less amount in discharge of a greater. But in the present case we are dealing with the question of the effect of money paid by a third person. In such a case there is no difference between payment of the total amount and payment of a portion of it only, so long as it is paid in settlement of the debt. If a third person steps in and gives a consideration for the discharge of the debtor, it does not matter whether he does it in meal or in malt, or what proportion the amount given bears to the amount of the debt. Here the money was paid by a third person, and I have no doubt that, upon the acceptance of that money by the plaintiffs with full knowledge of the terms on which it was offered, the debt was absolutely extinguished.

VAUGHAN WILLIAMS and FARWELL, L.JJ., also gave judgment for the defendant.

---

[1] (1863), 13 C.B.N.S. 543.
[3] (1889), 22 Q.B.D. 610.
[2] (1884), 9 App. Cas. 605. *Supra*, p. 28.
[4] (1882), 9 Q.B.D. 37. *Supra*, pp. 45–46.

INTENTION TO CREATE LEGAL RELATIONS

Jones *v.* Padavatton

Edwards *v.* Skyways, Ltd.

Even where there is a concluded agreement supported by consideration, the agreement may not be a contract because there is no intention to create legal relations. Such cases may be divided into two classes: (1) Social, family or other domestic agreements, where the presence or absence of an intention to create legal relations depends upon the inference to be drawn by the court from the language of the parties and the circumstances of the case; (2) Commercial agreements where an intention to create legal relations is presumed. This presumption may be rebutted, but the onus of rebutting is heavy and will be discharged only by clear language.

Jones v. Padavatton
[1969] 2 All E.R. 616

DANCKWERTS, L.J. This is an action between the mother and the daughter, and one which is really deplorable. The points of difference between the two parties appear to be comparatively small, and it is distressing that they could not settle their differences amicably and avoid the bitterness and expense which is involved in this dispute carried as far as this court. Both the mother and the daughter come from Trinidad and appear to be of East Indian descent. At the opening of the story in 1961–62 the mother was resident in Trinidad. The daughter (who had been married to, and divorced from, a Mr. Wyatt) was living in a flat in Washington, D.C. in the United States, and was employed at a satisfactory salary, with pension rights, in the Indian embassy in Washington. She had one child by her marriage, a boy called Tommy. She had been on a holiday with her mother to England in 1957.

A suggestion was made that she might go to England in order to read for the Bar in England and, if she became a qualified barrister, then to go to Trinidad and practise as a lawyer there. There is a dispute as to which of the two parties initiated the idea, but the daughter gave evidence very strongly suggesting that it was the mother's idea. She points to her very satisfactory job with the Indian embassy in Washington and her flat, and claims to have been unwilling to go to England, and to have been induced by extreme pressure. The mother intimated that, if the daughter would go and read for the Bar as suggested, she would provide maintenance for her at the rate of $200 a month. Unfortunately, the mother (Mrs. Jones) was thinking in West Indian dollars in which $200 were equal to £42 a month, and the daughter, living in Washington, was thinking in United States dollars, in which $200 were equal to £70. The two were plainly not *ad idem* then, but the daughter, when she received only £42 per month, seems to have accepted that sum without anything much in the way of protest.

Anyhow, the daughter was entered with Lincoln's Inn as a student, and the necessary fees were paid by a Mr. Agimudie, a lawyer in Trinidad, as the mother's agent. Mr. Agimudie in a contemporary letter assured the daughter that, of course, maintenance would be provided for her. So the daughter went to England in November 1962 and entered on her studies for the Bar. She took her son, Tommy, with her. The precise terms of the arrangement between the mother and the daughter were difficult to discover completely. There is no doubt that the daughter gave consideration for a promise by her

49

mother to provide maintenance at the rate of £42 per month so long as she was reading for the Bar in England by giving up her job and her other advantages in Washington, and by reading for the Bar. But various incidental matters appear never to have been thought out at all. There were no terms recorded in writing, no sort of businesslike statement of the parties' respective obligation, not even of how long the mother was to go on paying if the studies were prolonged or unsuccessful. In fact the daughter has passed all the examinations in Part I except one, but Part II is still to be taken.

The question therefore arises whether any binding legal contract was intended, or whether this was simply a family arrangement in which one member of the family relies on a promise given by another person and trusts that person to carry out the promise. But such an arrangement is not intended to create actionable legal rights. The situation so far has been called " step one ". But in 1964 a new element was introduced. The daughter was experiencing some discomfort in England. She, with Tommy, was occupying one room in Acton, for which she had to pay £6 17s. 6d. per week. In 1964 the mother made a proposal that she should buy a house in London of some size so that the daughter and Tommy could live in a room or in rooms in the house, and the rest of the house could be let off to tenants, and the rents would cover expenses and provide maintenance for the daughter and Tommy in place of the £42 a month. It is not clear whether the mother had in mind a profitable investment in England, or wished to avoid the inconvenience of remitting £42 a month to England, or whether she simply had in mind the difficulties that her daughter was experiencing.

At any rate, a house, no. 181, Highbury Quadrant, was found, which was conveyed into the mother's name. The price was £6,000 and moneys were provided by the mother in several sums for this. But there were also expenses of the purchase, as well as other expenses, and furniture, as it was desirable that the tenancies should be of furnished rooms. The money provided by the mother was insufficient to provide for all these things; until furniture was provided, there could be no tenants. The purchase was completed in December, 1964, and the daughter and Tommy went into occupation on January 31, 1965. Somehow money was found to buy furniture, and tenants began to arrive in February, 1965. The daughter had a power of attorney from her mother. There was, of course, no written agreement, and lots of incidental matters remained open: In what order were the rents to be applied; were outgoings to be paid first, or did the daughter's maintenance come first? There was a doubt whether the daughter's rights were confined to one room, or could she occupy several? In fact she occupied not only one room but also a kitchen, and a so-called store room where various things were stored, but Tommy slept there. This has been called " step two ". The question again arises: Was there any legally binding contract, or was it just an informal family arrangement?

The daughter had been married on January 6, 1965, to a Mr. Padavatton, who is a lecturer at the London School of Economics, I understand, but it is not clear what part he has played in these matters. The new arrangement, or the varied old arrangement, whatever it may be, continued until November 1967. The mother, who had also visited England in 1963, came again to England in August, 1967. The mother, it should be observed, has never received any money from the rents of the house, and she was paying substantial interest on a mortgage on property in Trinidad by which she had raised money for the purchase of the house. There was a most peculiar incident when, on the mother's arrival in England, she was driven to the house by Mr. Rawlins, her solicitor, and could not get in. But nothing really depends on that.

The mother, who had complained that she could not get any accounts from her daughter, had consulted English solicitors, and before this a summons by the mother against the daughter had been taken out claiming possession of the house, and particulars of claim were delivered dated July 4, 1967. Of course, the house is the property of the mother. The mother had given notice to quit on March 20, 1967. A defence and counterclaim dated August 11, 1967, had been delivered, which was amended on February 21, 1968. In these are set out the daughter's version of the arrangements made between the parties, and she counterclaims £1,655 16s. 9d., which the daughter claims she has paid in respect of the house, and ought to be reimbursed to her. On January 11, 1968, the learned county court judge decided against the mother and dismissed the claim for possession. He gave judgment on the counterclaim in favour of the daughter and referred the matter to the registrar. I do not find the grounds of the learned county court judge's decision easy to understand. He regarded both mother and daughter as very respectable witnesses, and he accepted the daughter's story in regard to the arrangements between them.

Before us a great deal of time was spent on discussions as to what were the terms of the arrangements between the parties and it seemed to me that the further the discussions went, the more obscure and uncertain the terms alleged became. The acceptable duration of the daughter's studies was not finally settled, I think. There was a lack of evidence on the matter, and the members of the court were induced to supply suggestions based on their personal knowledge. At any rate, two questions emerged for argument: (i) Were the arrangements (such as they were) intended to produce legally binding agreements, or were they simply family arrangements depending for their fulfilment on good faith and trust, and not legally enforceable by legal proceedings? (ii) Were the arrangements made so obscure and uncertain that, though intended to be legally binding, a court could not enforce them?

Counsel for the daughter argued strenuously for the view that the parties intended to create legally binding contracts. He relied on the old case of *Shadwell* v. *Shadwell*[1] and *Parker* v. *Clark*[2]. Counsel for the mother argued for the contrary view that there were no binding obligations, and that if there were they were too uncertain for the court to enforce. His stand-by was *Balfour* v. *Balfour*[3] The principles involved are very well discussed in *Cheshire and Fifoot on Contract* (8th Edn.), at pp. 97–98. Of course, there is no difficulty, if they so intend, in members of families entering into legally binding contracts in regard to family affairs. A competent equity draftsman would, if properly instructed, have no difficulty in drafting such a contract. But there is possibly in family affairs a presumption against such an intention (which, of course, can be rebutted). I would refer to ATKIN, L.J.'s magnificent exposition in regard to such arrangements in *Balfour* v. *Balfour*[4].

There is no doubt that this case is a most difficult one, but I have reached a conclusion that the present case is one of those family arrangements which depend on the good faith of the promises which are made and are not intended to be rigid, binding agreements. *Balfour* v. *Balfour*[3] was a case of

---

[1] (1860), 9 C.B.N.S. 159. [2] [1960] 1 All E.R. 93; [1960] 1 W.L.R. 286.
[3] [1919] 2 K.B. 571; [1918–19] All E.R. Rep. 860.
[4] [1919] 2 K.B. at pp. 578–580; [1918–19] All E.R. Rep. at pp. 864, 865.

husband and wife, but there is no doubt that the same principles apply to dealings between other relations, such as father and son and daughter and mother. This, indeed, seems to me a compelling case. The mother and the daughter seem to have been on very good terms before 1967. The mother was arranging for a career for the daughter which she hoped would lead to success. This involved a visit to England in conditions which could not be wholly foreseen. What was required was an arrangement which was to be financed by the mother and was such as would be adaptable to circumstances, as it in fact was. The operation about the house was, in my view, not a completely fresh arrangement, but an adaptation of the mother's financial assistance to the daughter due to the situation which was found to exist in England. It was not a stiff contractual operation any more than the original arrangement.

In the result, of course, on this view, the daughter cannot resist the mother's rights as the owner of the house to the possession of which the mother is entitled. What the position is as regards the counterclaim is another matter. It may be, at least in honesty, that the daughter should be reimbursed for the expenditure which she had incurred. In my opinion, therefore, the appeal should be allowed.

SALMON, L.J. I agree with the conclusion at which DANCKWERTS, L.J., has arrived, but I have reached it by a different route. The first point to be decided is whether or not there was ever a legally binding agreement between the mother and the daughter in relation to the daughter's reading for the Bar in England. The daughter alleges that there was such an agreement, and the mother denies it. She says that there was nothing but a loose family arrangement which had no legal effect. The onus is clearly on the daughter. There is no dispute that the parties entered into some sort of arrangement. It really depends on: (a) whether the parties intended it to be legally binding: and (b) if so, whether it was sufficiently certain to be enforceable.

Did the parties intend the arrangement to be legally binding? This question has to be solved by applying what is sometimes (although perhaps unfortunately) called an objective test. The court has to consider what the parties said and wrote in the light of all the surrounding circumstances, and then decide whether the true inference is that the ordinary man and woman, speaking or writing thus in such circumstances, would have intended to create a legally binding agreement.

Counsel for the mother has said, quite rightly, that as a rule when arrangements are made between close relations, for example, between husband and wife, parent and child or uncle and nephew in relation to an allowance, there is a presumption against an intention of creating any legal relationship. This is not a presumption of law, but of fact. It derives from experience of life and human nature which shows that in such circumstances men and women usually do not intend to create legal rights and obligations, but intend to rely solely on family ties of mutual trust and affection. This has all been explained by ATKIN, L.J., in his celebrated judgment in *Balfour* v. *Balfour*[1]. There may, however, be circumstances in which this presumption, like all other presumptions of fact, can be rebutted. Counsel for the daughter has drawn our attention to two cases, in which it was, *Shadwell* v. *Shadwell*[2], and *Parker* v. *Clark*[3]. The former was a curious case. It was decided by

---

[1] [1919] 2 K.B. 571 at pp. 578–580; [1918–19] All E.R. Rep. 860 at pp. 864, 865.
[2] (1860), 9 C.B.N.S. 159.
[3] [1960] 1 All E.R. 93; [1960] 1 W.L.R. 286.

ERLE, C.J., and KEATING, J. (BYLES, J., dissenting) on a pleading point, and depended largely on the true construction of a letter written by an uncle to his nephew. I confess that I should have decided it without hesitation in accordance with the views of BYLES, J. But this is of no consequence. *Shadwell* v. *Shadwell*[1] laid down no principle of law relevant to what we have to decide; it merely illustrated what could never, I think, be seriously doubted, viz., that there may be circumstances in which arrangements between close relatives are intended to have the force of law.

In the present case the learned county court judge, having had the advantage of seeing the mother and the daughter in the witness box, entirely accepted the daughter's version of the facts. He came to the conclusion that on these very special facts the true inference must be that the arrangement between the parties prior to the daughter's leaving Washington were intended by both to have contractual force. On the facts as found by the learned county court judge this was entirely different from the ordinary case of a mother promising her daughter an allowance whilst the daughter read for the Bar, or a father promising his son an allowance at university if the son passed the necessary examinations to gain admission. The daughter here was 34 years of age in 1962. She had left Trinidad and settled in Washington as long ago as 1949. In Washington she had a comfortable flat and was employed as an assistant accountant in the Indian embassy at a salary of $500 a month (over £2,000 a year). This employment carried a pension. She had a son of seven years of age who was an American citizen, and had, of course, already begun his education. There were obviously solid reasons for her staying where she was. For some years prior to 1962, however, the mother, who lived in Trinidad, had been trying hard to persuade her to throw up all that she had achieved in Washington and go to London to read for the Bar. The mother would have been very proud to have a barrister for a daughter. She also thought that her plan was in the interest of her grandson, to whom she was much attached. She envisaged that, after the daughter had been called to the Bar, she would practise in Trinidad and thereafter presumably she (the mother) would be able to see much more of the daughter than formerly. The daughter was naturally loath to leave Washington, and did not regard the mother's suggestion as feasible. The mother, however, eventually persuaded the daughter to do as she wished by promising her that, if she threw up her excellent position in Washington and came to study for the Bar in England, she would pay her daughter an allowance of $200 a month until she had completed her studies. The mother's attorney in Trinidad wrote to the daughter to confirm this. I cannot think that either intended that if, after the daughter had been in London, say, for six months, the mother dishonoured her promise and left her daughter destitute, the daughter would have no legal redress.

In the very special circumstances of this case, I consider that the true inference must be that neither the mother nor the daughter could have intended that the daughter should have no legal right to receive, and the mother no legal obligation to pay, the allowance of $200 a month.

The point was made by counsel for the mother that the parties cannot have had a contractual intention since it would be unthinkable for the daughter to be able to sue the mother if the mother fell on hard times. I am afraid that I am not impressed by this point. The evidence which the learned

---

[1] (1860), 9 C.B.N.S. 159.

county court judge accepted showed that the mother was a woman of some substance, and prior to the agreement had assured the daughter that there would be no difficulty in finding the money. The fact that, if contrary to everyone's expectation the mother had lost her money, the daughter would have been unlikely to sue her throws no light on whether the parties had an intention to contract. The fact that a contracting party is in some circumstances unlikely to extract his pound of flesh does not mean that he has no right to it. Even today sometimes people forbear from mercy to enforce their undoubted legal rights.

The next point made by counsel for the mother was that the arrangements between the mother and the daughter in 1962 were too uncertain to constitute a binding contract. It is true that the mother said $200 a month without stipulating whether she meant West Indian or United States dollars. Obviously she meant West Indian dollars. The daughter says that she thought her mother meant United States dollars. This point does not, however, appear to have given rise to any difficulty. For two years from November, 1962, until December, 1964, the mother regularly paid her daughter £42, the equivalent of $ (West Indian) 200, a month, and the daughter accepted this sum without demur. Then it is said on the mother's behalf that the daughter's obligations are not sufficiently stated. I think that they are plain, to leave Washington, with all that entailed, come to London and genuinely study for the Bar there. If the daughter threw up her studies for the Bar, maybe the mother could not have recovered damages, but she would have been relieved of any obligation to continue the allowance.

Then again it is said that the duration of the agreement was not specified. No doubt, but I see no difficulty in implying the usual term that it was to last for a reasonable time. The parties cannot have contemplated that the daughter should go on studying for the Bar and draw the allowance until she was seventy, nor on the other hand that the mother could have discontinued the allowance if the daughter did not pass her examinations within, say, 18 months. The promise was to pay the allowance until the daughter's studies were completed, and to my mind there was a clear implication that they were to be completed within a reasonable time. Studies are completed either by the student being called to the Bar or giving up the unequal struggle against the examiners. It may not be easy to decide, especially when there is such a paucity of evidence, what is a reasonable time. The daughter, however, was a well-educated intelligent woman capable of earning the equivalent of over £2,000 a year in Washington. It is true that she had a young son to look after, and may well (as the learned judge thought) have been hampered to some extent by the worry of this litigation. But, making all allowance for these factors and any other distraction, I cannot think that a reasonable time could possibly exceed five years from November, 1962, the date when she began her studies.

It follows, therefore, that on no view can she now in November, 1968, be entitled to anything further under the contract which the learned county court judge, rightly I think, held that she made with the mother in 1962. She has some of Part 1 of the Bar examination still to pass, and necessarily the final has not yet even been attempted.

During a visit to England in 1964 the mother found that her daughter was living in one room in Acton costing £6 17s. 6d. a week. This rent represented about three-quarters of the daughter's total income. The mother therefore hit on the idea of buying a house in London in which the

daughter could live more comfortably and cheaply than in Acton. The rest
of the house was to be let off in furnished rooms or flats and after paying the
outgoings the daughter was to pay herself the maintenance and remit any
balance that there might be to her mother in Trinidad. This scheme, so long
as it lasted, provided a convenient method of paying the £42 a month due
under the 1962 agreement. Accordingly, the mother acquired no. 181,
Highbury Quadrant for £6,000 or so in December, 1964. The daughter
moved in in the following month, furnished and equipped the house largely
by hire-purchase, and tenants began to arrive in February, 1965.

The learned county court judge has concluded that in December, 1964,
the original contract between the mother and the daughter was varied, or a
new contract was entered into whereby the daughter acquired the right to
stay on in the mother's house indefinitely, whether the mother liked it or
not. I am afraid that I cannot accept this conclusion. It was for the daughter
to make out such a variation or new contract. In my view she totally failed
to do so.

There is no evidence that the mother bargained away her right to dispose
of her house, or to evict the daughter (who was a mere licensee) whenever she
wished to do so. The evidence shows that all the arrangements in relation
to the house were very vague and made without any contractual intent. By
this arrangement the mother was trying primarily to help the daughter, and
also perhaps to make a reasonable investment for herself. When the mother
brought the arrangement to an end (as she was entitled to do at any time) she
would, of course, have to go on paying £42 a month as long as the 1962
agreement lasted. There is no evidence to suggest that the mother intended
the daughter ever to have more than the equivalent of $ (West Indian) 200 a
month after December, 1964. Nothing was said as to how much the daughter
might pay herself, out of the rents, for maintenance. Certainly she would
have to debit herself with some reasonable figure in respect of her accommodation, no doubt something less than £6 17s. 6d. a week that she had been
spending in Acton, but not less, I should think, than about £5 a week. This
would leave about £22 a month to be deducted from the rents for maintenance up till November, 1967, when in my view the 1962 agreement ran
out. In fact for nearly four years, that is, from December, 1964, until today,
the mother had not received a penny from the daughter in respect of no. 181,
Highbury Quadrant nor, in spite of repeated requests, any proper accounts.

I am not at all surprised that the mother's patience became exhausted in
March, 1967, when she gave notice determining her daughter's licence to
remain in the house. The daughter ignored the notice and has continued in
occupation with her husband and son, apparently with the intention of doing
so indefinitely. She is still there. She seems to take the view (as does the
learned county court judge) that she has a legal claim on the mother to house
her and contribute to her support and that of her son and husband, perhaps
in perpetuity. In this she is mistaken, and so in my judgment is the learned
county court judge. The mother began this action for possession of no. 181,
Highbury Quadrant in 1967. For the reasons I have indicated, there is in
my view no defence to the action, and I would accordingly allow the appeal.

The learned county court judge has referred the counterclaim. If this
reference is pursued, it will involve an account being meticulously taken of all
receipts and expenditure from December, 1964, until the date on which the
daughter yields up possession. This will certainly result in a great waste of
time and money, and can only exacerbate ill-feeling between the mother and

the daughter. With a little goodwill and good sense on both sides, this could and should be avoided by reaching a reasonable compromise on the figures. I can but express the hope that this may be done, for it would clearly be to the mutual benefit of both parties.

FENTON ATKINSON, L.J., also gave judgment allowing the appeal, but preferred the *ratio decidendi* stated by DANCKWERTS, L.J.

Edwards v. Skyways, Ltd.

[1964] 1 All E.R. 494

The plaintiff was employed by the defendants as an aircraft pilot. In January, 1962, the defendants told him that they must reduce their staff and gave him three months' notice to terminate his employment. By his contract he was a member of the defendants' contributing pension scheme and was thereby entitled, on leaving their service before retirement age, to choose one of two options: (*a*) to withdraw his own contributions to the fund, (*b*) to take the right to a paid-up pension payable at the age of fifty. He was a member of the British Air Line Pilots Association. Their officials, acting as the plaintiff's agents, had a meeting with the defendants; and it was agreed that, if the plaintiff chose option (*a*), the defendants would make him an "*ex gratia* payment" equivalent or approximating to the defendants' contributions to the pension fund. The plaintiff, relying on this agreement, chose option (*a*). The defendants paid him the amount of his own contributions, but refused to make the "*ex gratia* payment". The plaintiff sued the defendants for breach of contract.

MEGAW, J., gave judgment for the plaintiff. After stating the facts, he said:

The defendant company admit, as I understand it, that at the meeting a promise was made on their behalf with their authority, although the actual word "promise" was not used. In the defence it was pleaded that no consideration moved from the plaintiff. That plea was expressly abandoned at the hearing. It was conceded that there was consideration. The defendant company admit that it was their intention to carry out their promise when they made it, and that the plaintiff's representatives, and the plaintiff himself, believed, and acted in the belief, that the promise would be fulfilled. Everyone, at the end of the meeting, believed that there was an agreement which would be carried out. But the defendant company say that the promise and the agreement have no legal effect, because there was no intention to enter into legal relations in respect of the promised payment.

It is clear from such cases as *Rose and Frank Co.* v. *J. R. Crompton & Bros., Ltd.*[1] and *Balfour* v. *Balfour*[2], that there are cases in which English law recognises that an agreement, in other respects duly made, does not give rise to legal rights, because the parties have not intended that their legal relations should be affected. Where the subject-matter of the agreement is some domestic or social relationship or transaction, as in *Balfour* v. *Balfour*[3], the law will often deny legal consequences to the agreement, because of the very nature of the subject-matter. Where the subject-matter of the agreement is not domestic or social, but is related to business affairs, the parties may, by

---

[1] [1923] 2 K.B. 261; [1924] All E.R. Rep. 245.
[2] [1919] 2 K.B. 571; [1918–19] All E.R. Rep. 860.
[3] [1919] 2 K.B. 571; [1918–19] All E.R. Rep. 860.

using clear words, show that their intention is to make the transaction binding in honour only, and not in law; and the courts will give effect to the expressed intention. Scrutton, L.J., expressed it thus, in *Rose and Frank Co.* v. *J. R. Crompton & Bros. Ltd.*[1]:

> " It is quite possible for parties to come to an agreement by accepting a proposal with the result that the agreement concluded does not give rise to legal relations. The reason of this is that the parties do not intend that their agreement shall give rise to legal relations. This intention may be implied from the subject-matter of the agreement, but it may also be expressed by the parties. In social and family relations such an intention is readily implied, while in business matters the opposite results would ordinarily follow. But I can see no reason why, even in business matters, the parties should not intend to rely on each other's good faith and honour, and to exclude all idea of settling disputes by any outside intervention with the accompanying necessity of expressing themselves so precisely that outsiders may have no difficulty in understanding what they mean. If they clearly express such an intention I can see no reason in public policy why effect should not be given to their intention."

In the same case, Atkin, L.J., said[2]:

> " To create a contract there must be a common intention of the parties to enter into legal obligations, mutually communicated expressly or impliedly. Such an intention ordinarily will be inferred when parties enter into an agreement which in other respects conforms to the rules of law as to the formation of contracts. It may be negatived impliedly by the nature of the agreed promise or promises, as in the case of offer and acceptance of hospitality, or of some agreements made in the course of family life between members of a family as in *Balfour* v. *Balfour*[3]. If the intention may be negatived impliedly it may be negatived expressly."

In the present case, the subject-matter of the agreement is business relations, not social or domestic matters. There was a meeting of minds—an intention to agree. There was, admittedly, consideration for the defendant company's promise. I accept the propositions of counsel for the plaintiff that in a case of this nature the onus is on the party who asserts that no legal effect was intended, and the onus is a heavy one. Counsel for the plaintiff also submitted, with the support of the well-known textbooks on the law of contract (Anson, and Cheshire and Fifoot), that the test of intention to create or not to create legal relations is " objective ". I am not sure that I know what that means in this context. I do, however, think that there are grave difficulties in trying to apply a test as to the actual intention or understanding or knowledge of the parties; especially where the alleged agreement is arrived at between a limited liability company and a trade association; and especially where it is arrived at at a meeting attended by five or six representatives on each side. Whose knowledge, understanding or intention is relevant? But if it be the " objective " test of the reasonable man, what background knowledge is to be imputed to the reasonable man, when the background knowledge of the ten or twelve persons who took part in arriving at the decision no doubt varied greatly between one another? However that may be, the defendant company say, first, as I understand it, that the mere use of the phrase " *ex gratia* " by itself, as a part of the promise to pay, shows that the parties contemplated that the promise, when accepted, should have no binding force in law. They say, secondly, that even if their first proposition is not correct as a general proposition, nevertheless here there was certain

---

[1] [1923] 2 K.B. at p. 288; [1924] All E.R. Rep. at pp. 249, 250.
[2] [1923] 2 K.B. at p. 293; [1924] All E.R. Rep. at p. 252.
[3] [1919] 2 K.B. 571; [1918–19] All E.R. Rep. 860.

background knowledge, present in the minds of everyone, which gave unambiguous significance to "*ex gratia*" as excluding legal relationship.

As to the first proposition, the words "*ex gratia*" do not, in my judgment, carry a necessary, or even a probable, implication that the agreement is to be without legal effect. It is, I think, common experience amongst practitioners of the law that litigation or threatened litigation is frequently compromised on the terms that one party shall make to the other a payment described in express terms as "*ex gratia*" or "without admission of liability". The two phrases are, I think, synonymous. No one would imagine that a settlement, so made, is unenforceable at law. The words "*ex gratia*" or "without admission of liability" are used simply to indicate—it may be as a matter of *amour propre*, or it may be to avoid a precedent in subsequent cases—that the party agreeing to pay does not admit any pre-existing liability on his part; but he is certainly not seeking to preclude the legal enforceability of the settlement itself by describing the contemplated payments as "*ex gratia*". So here, there are obvious reasons why the phrase might have been used by the defendant company in just such a way. They might have desired to avoid conceding that any such payment was due under the employers' contract of service. They might have wished—perhaps ironically in the event—to show, by using the phrase, their generosity in making a payment beyond what was required by the contract of service. I see nothing in the mere use of the words "*ex gratia*", unless in the circumstances some very special meaning has to be given to them, to warrant the conclusion that this promise, duly made and accepted, for valid consideration, was not intended by the parties to be enforceable in law.

The defendant company's second proposition seeks to show that in the circumstances here the words "*ex gratia*" had a special meaning. What is said is this: When a payment such as this is made by an employer to a dismissed employee the question whether it is subject to income tax in the hands of the recipient is important; it was understood by the defendant company and by the association, and by all their respective representatives at the meeting, that if the company's payment were made as the result of a legally binding obligation, it would be taxable in the hands of the recipient; whereas, if it were to be made without legal obligation on the part of the company, it would not be taxable. (It was not argued before me whether this assertion is right or wrong in law. It was said by the defendant company that that was quite immaterial; what was material was that the parties so believed.) Thus, it is said, the phrase "*ex gratia*" was used, and was understood by all present to be used, deliberately and advisedly as a formula to achieve that there would be no binding legal obligation on the company to pay, and hence to save the recipient from a tax liability. It is said that the offer was accepted by the association with full knowledge and understanding of these matters. Hence, it is said, the agreement by tacit consent, a consent evidenced by the use of the words "*ex gratia*" against this background of common understanding, was an agreement from which legal sanction and consequences were excluded. In my judgment, that submission also fails because the evidence falls far short of showing that this supposed background of avoidance of tax liability was present as an important element in the minds of all, or indeed any, of the persons who attended the meeting of February 8, 1962, or, if this be something different, in the minds of the defendant company or of the association; or that they all, or any of them, directed their minds to the significance of the words "*ex gratia*" which is now suggested on behalf of the defendant company. The question of tax liability, and the possible influence thereon of the use of the words " *ex gratia* ", may indeed have been present in some degree, and as one element, in the minds of some of the persons present at the meeting. That, however, is far from sufficient to establish that the parties—both of them—affirmatively intended not to enter into legal relations in respect of the defendant company's promise to pay.

Lastly, the defendant company say that, even if the agreement were otherwise in all respects a binding agreement, it is not enforceable because its terms are too vague. This is founded on the submission that the precise words used by Mr. Davies at the meeting were " approximating to "; that these precise words are a part of the agreement; that they leave a discretion to the defendant company; that therefore there is no enforceable agreement, and they can refuse to pay anything. I have already indicated my conclusion on the evidence as to what was indeed agreed at the end of the meeting. If this be right, there is nothing in this point. Even if it were wrong, I do not think that English law provides that in such circumstances the plaintiff would be entitled to nothing. At most " approximating to ", if that were the contractual term, would on the evidence connote a rounding off of a few pounds downwards to a round figure. If a contract for the sale of goods is valid and binding when it provides for " about 1000 tons in seller's option ", or " 1000 tons, up to ten per cent. more or less in buyer's option ", it would seem hard to justify treating such a contract as this as a nullity, and I do not think that the law so requires.

Judgment for the plaintiff.

THE CONTENTS OF THE CONTRACT

TERMS AND MERE REPRESENTATIONS

A statement made by one party to the other may be a term of the contract or a " mere representation ". If it is the former, it creates an obligation for whose breach an action for damages lies at common law. If it is the latter, no action lies for damages at common law in the absence of fraud.[1] Whether it is the one or the other depends upon the intention of the parties as inferred by the courts. Did both parties intend that a statement, made either at the time of the bargain or at some earlier moment, should take its place as a term in the contract? The question has given rise to differences of judicial opinion upon the facts of any particular case.

Oscar Chess, Ltd. v. Williams

[1957] 1 All E.R. 325

APPEAL.

This was an appeal by the defendant from an order made by His Honour Judge Rowe Harding at Neath and Port Talbot County Court on July 17, 1956, awarding £115 damages to the plaintiffs against the defendant for breach of a warranty that a second-hand Morris 10 h.p. saloon motor car sold by the defendant to the plaintiffs was a 1948 model, whereas it was in fact a 1939 model.

The facts are stated in the judgments of Denning and Morris, L.JJ.

B. M. Rees for the defendant.

W. N. Francis for the plaintiffs.   Cur. adv. vult.

Nov. 13.   The following judgments were read.

DENNING, L. J.: In March, 1954, a Mrs. Williams, of 13, Victoria Terrace, Port Talbot, acquired a second-hand Morris car, index number ECO 503. She acquired it on the footing that it was a 1948 model at a price of £300. The transaction was put through on hire-purchase from British Wagon Co. The registration book showed that it was first registered on Apr. 13, 1948, with five changes of ownership between 1948 and 1954. During the next fourteen months the car was used a good deal by her son, Mr. W. V. R. Williams [referred to hereinafter as " the defendant "], and he often gave lifts to Mr. Ladd, a motor salesman, employed by Oscar Chess, Ltd., known as the Motor House, Port Talbot [and referred to hereinafter as " the plaintiffs "]. Mr. Ladd lived at 18, Victoria Terrace, a few doors away from the defendant. Mr. Ladd thought that the car looked like a 1948 model. In May, 1955, the defendant told Mr. Ladd that he wanted to get a new Hillman Minx car for £650 and offered the Morris car in part exchange. The defendant described the Morris car as a 1948 10 h.p. Morris and produced the registration book for it. Mr. Ladd checked up in the book the date 1948 as the date of first registration. He looked up " Glass's Guide ", a book which gives current prices for second-hand cars according to the year of manufacture, and said that he would make an allowance of £290 for the Morris car. This allowance of £290 was the factor

---

[1] Rescission of the contract on the ground of misrepresentation is a possibility: *Leaf* v. *International Galleries*, [1950] 2 K.B. 86; [1950] 1 All E.R. 693, *infra*, p. 188, See also Misrepresentation Act, 1967, s. 2, *infra*, p. 194.

which made the transaction possible. If the defendant had not got this allowance, he would not have gone through with the transaction at all. The plaintiffs were, no doubt, ready to give him this good allowance because they would get a substantial profit on the sale of the Hillman car.

The transaction went through accordingly. The plaintiffs sold the new Hillman Minx car for £650 to a finance company who let it on hire-purchase terms to the defendant. The plaintiffs took the Morris car in part exchange, but, to do so, they had first to pay the outstanding £50 to the British Wagon Co. They charged that sum to the defendant. They then took the Morris car, allowing £290 for it, which sum they credited to the finance company who bought the Hillman car. Eight months later the plaintiffs discovered that the Morris car was made, not in 1948, as they thought, but in 1939. They discovered this by taking the chassis and engine numbers and sending those numbers to Morris Motors, Ltd., who looked up their card index and found that the car left the factory on Feb. 3, 1939. Strange to relate, the style and finish of Morris cars had not been changed between 1939 and 1948. Outwardly a 1948 model looked the same as a 1939 model, but the price was of course very different. If the plaintiffs had known that it was a 1939 model they would have given only £175 for it, and not £290. In describing it as a 1948 Morris, the defendant was perfectly innocent. He honestly believed it was a 1948 model, and so, no doubt, did the previous sellers. Someone far back in 1948 must have fraudulently altered the log-book, but he cannot be traced now.

In these circumstances the plaintiffs claim as damages from the defendant the sum of £115, the difference in value between a 1939 Morris car and a 1948 Morris car. The question depends on whether the defendant gave a binding promise to Mr. Ladd that the car was made in 1948. The evidence on this point was very short. Mr. Ladd said in examination in chief: " He offered me a 1948 10 h.p. Morris in part exchange. He produced the registration book." In cross-examination he said:

" I had often had lifts in the defendant's car. I thought it looked like a 1948 model. I checked up in the registration book."

Mr. Ladd's evidence was accepted. Indeed, the defendant did not go into the witness-box to contradict it. On those simple facts counsel for the plaintiffs submitted to the judge that the defendant's representation that the car was a 1948 model was an essential term of the contract, that is, a condition. Alternatively, he submitted that the representation was a warranty, intended as such. The judge found that it was a condition. He said that the allowance of £290 was made by Mr. Ladd " on the assumption that the Morris was a 1948 model," and that

" . . . this assumption was fundamental to the contract, a condition which, if not satisfied, would have caused him to rescind the contract if he had known it to be unsatisfied before the property in the Morris car passed to his principals."

Thereupon the judge awarded £115 to the plaintiffs and did not go on to consider the alternative claim on a warranty.

I entirely agree with the judge that both parties assumed that the Morris car was a 1948 model and that this assumption was fundamental to the contract. This does not prove, however, that the representation was a term of the contract. The assumption was based by both of them on the date given in the registration book as the date of first registration. They both believed that the car was a 1948 model, whereas it was only a 1939 one. They were both mistaken and their mistake was of fundamental importance.

The effect of such a mistake is this: It does not make the contract a nullity from the beginning, but it does in some circumstances enable the contract to be set aside in equity. If the buyer had come promptly, he might have succeeded in getting the whole transaction set aside in equity on the ground of this mistake (see *Solle* v. *Butcher*[1], but he did not do so and it is now too late for him to do it (see *Leaf* v. *International Galleries*[2]). His only remedy is in damages, and to recover these he must prove a warranty.

In saying that he must prove a warranty, I use the word " warranty " in its ordinary English meaning to denote a binding promise. Everyone knows what a man means when he says, " I guarantee it," or " I warrant it," or " I give you my word on it." He means that he binds himself to it. That is the meaning which it has borne in English law for three hundred years from the leading case of *Chandelor* v. *Lopus*[3] onwards. During the last hundred years, however, the lawyers have come to use the word " warranty " in another sense. They use it to denote a subsidiary term in a contract as distinct from a vital term which they call a " condition." In so doing they depart from the ordinary meaning, not only of the word " warranty," but also of the word " condition." There is no harm in their doing this, so long as they confine this technical use to its proper sphere, namely, to distinguish between a vital term, the breach of which gives the right to treat the contract as at an end, and a subsidiary term which does not. The trouble comes, however, when one person uses the word " warranty " in its ordinary meaning and another uses it in its technical meaning. When Holt, C. J., made his famous ruling that " An affirmation at the time of the sale is a warranty, provided it appear on evidence to be so intended,"[4] he used the word " warranty " in its ordinary English meaning of a binding promise. When Viscount Haldane, L.C., and Lord Moulton in 1913, in *Heilbut, Symons & Co.* v. *Buckleton*[5] adopted this ruling (ibid., at pp. 38, 49), they used the word likewise in its ordinary meaning. These different uses of the word seem to have been the source of confusion in the present case. The judge did not ask himself, " Was the representation (that the car was a 1948 Morris car) intended to be a warranty ? " He asked himself, " Was it fundamental to the contract ? " He answered it by saying that it was fundamental, and, therefore, it was a condition and not a warranty. By concentrating on whether it was fundamental, he seems to me to have missed the crucial point in the case which is whether it was a term of the contract at all. The crucial question is: Was it a binding promise or only an innocent misrepresentation ? The technical distinction between a " condition " and a " warranty " is quite immaterial in this case, because it is far too late for the buyer to reject the car. He can, at best, only claim damages. The material distinction here is between a statement which is a term of the contract and a statement which is only an innocent misrepresentation. This distinction is best expressed by the ruling of Holt, C. J., " Was it intended as a warranty or not ? ", using

---

[1] [1950] 1 K. B. 671; [1949] 2 All E. R. 1107, *infra*, p. 131.
[2] [1950] 2 K. B. 86; [1950] 1 All E. R. 693, *infra*, p. 188.
[3] (1603), Cro. Jac. 4.
[4] The words quoted, which were ascribed by Lord Moulton ([1913] A. C. at p. 49) to Holt, C.J., appear in the judgment of Buller, J., in *Pasley* v. *Freeman* ((1789), 3 Term. Rep. 51 at p. 57; 100 E. R. 450 at p. 453), where he said: " . . . it was rightly held by Holt, C.J., [in *Crosse* v. *Gardner* (1688), Carth. 90; and *Medina* v. *Stoughton* (1700), 1 Salk. 210; and has been uniformly adopted ever since, that an affirmation at the time of a sale is a warranty, provided it appear on evidence to have been so intended."
[5] [1913] A. C. 30.

the word " warranty " there in its ordinary English meaning: because it gives the exact shade of meaning that is required.   It is something to which a man must be taken to bind himself.

In applying this test, however, some misunderstanding has arisen by the use of the word " intended."   It is sometimes supposed that the tribunal must look into the minds of the parties to see what they themselves intended. That is a mistake.   Lord Moulton made it quite clear, in *Heilbut, Symons &* *Co.* v. *Buckleton*[1], that " The intention of the parties can only be deduced from the totality of the evidence . . . ."   The question whether a warranty was intended depends on the conduct of the parties, on their words and behaviour, rather than on their thoughts.   If an intelligent bystander would reasonably infer that a warranty was intended, that will suffice.   And this, when the facts are not in dispute, is a question of law.   That is shown by *Heilbut, Symons & Co.* v. *Buckleton* itself, where the House of Lords upset the jury's finding of a warranty.

It is instructive to take some recent instances to show how the courts have approached this question.   When the seller states a fact which is or should be within his own knowledge and of which the buyer is ignorant, intending that the buyer should act on it and he does so, it is easy to infer a warranty; see *Couchman* v. *Hill*[2], where a farmer stated that a heifer was unserved, and *Harling* v. *Eddy*[3], where he stated that there was nothing wrong with her.   So also if the seller makes a promise about something which is or should be within his own control; see *Birch* v. *Paramount Estates, Ltd.*[4], decided on Oct. 2, 1956, in this court, where the seller stated that the house would be as good as the show house.   If, however, the seller, when he states a fact, makes it clear that he has no knowledge of his own but has got his imformation elsewhere, and is merely passing it on, it is not so easy to imply a warranty.   Such a case was *Routledge* v. *McKay*[5], where the seller stated that a motor cycle combination was a 1942 model, and pointed to the corroboration of that statement to be found in the registration book, and it was held that there was no warranty.

Turning now to the present case, much depends on the precise words that were used.   If the seller says: " I believe the car is a 1948 Morris.   Here is the registration book to prove it," there is clearly no warranty.   It is a statement of belief, not a contractual promise.   If, however, the seller says: " I guarantee that it is a 1948 Morris.   This is borne out by the registration book, but you need not rely solely on that.   I give you my own guarantee that it is," there is clearly a warranty.   The seller is making himself contractually responsible, even though the registration book is wrong.

In this case much reliance was placed by the judge on the fact that the buyer looked up " Glass's Guide " and paid £290 on the footing that the car was a 1948 model, but that fact seems to me to be neutral.   Both sides believed the car to have been made in 1948 and in that belief the buyer paid £290.   That belief can be just as firmly based on the buyer's own inspection of the log-book as on a contractual warranty by the seller.

Once that fact is put on one side, I ask myself: What is the proper inference from the known facts ?   It must have been obvious to both that the seller had himself no personal knowledge of the year when the car was made.

---

[1] [1913] A.C. 30, at p. 51.   [2] [1947] K. B. 554; [1947] 1 All E. R. 103.
[3] [1951] 2 K. B. 739; [1951] 2 All E. R. 212.   [4] (1956), 16 Estates Gazette 396.
                              [5] [1954] 1 All E.R. 855.

He only became owner after a great number of changes. He must have been relying on the registration book. It is unlikely that such a person would warrant the year of manufacture. The most that he would do would be to state his belief, and then produce the registration book in verification of it. In these circumstances the intelligent bystander would, I suggest, say that the seller did not intend to bind himself so as to warrant that the car was a 1948 model. If the seller was asked to pledge himself to it, he would at once have said " I cannot do that. I have only the log-book to go by, the same as you."

The judge seems to have thought that there was a difference between written contracts and oral contracts. He thought that the reason why the buyer failed in *Heilbut, Symons & Co.* v. *Buckleton* and *Routledge* v. *McKay* was because the sales were afterwards recorded in writing, and the written contracts contained no reference to the representation. I agree that that was an important factor in those cases. If an oral representation is afterwards recorded in writing, it is good evidence that it was intended as a warranty. If it is not put into writing, it is evidence against a warranty being intended; but it is by no means decisive. There have been many cases, such as *Birch* v. *Paramount Estates, Ltd.*, where the courts have found an oral warranty collateral to a written contract. When, however, the purchase is not recorded in writing at all, it must not be supposed that every representation made in the course of the dealing is to be treated as a warranty. The question then is still: Was it intended as a warranty? In the leading case of *Chandelor* v. *Lopus* in 1603 a man by word of mouth sold a precious stone for £100 affirming it to be a bezoar stone whereas it was not. The declaration averred that the seller *affirmed* it to be a bezoar stone, but did not aver that he *warranted* it to be so. The declaration was held to be ill because (Cro. Jac. at p. 4): " . . . the bare affirmation that it was a bezoar-stone, without warranting it to be so, is no cause of action . . . " That has been the law from that day to this and it was emphatically re-affirmed by the House of Lords in *Heilbut, Symons & Co.* v. *Buckleton*[1].

One final word. It seems to me clear that the plaintiffs, the motor dealers who bought the car, relied on the year stated in the log-book. If they had wished to make sure of it, they could have checked it then and there, by taking the engine number and chassis number and writing to the makers. They did not do so at the time, but only eight months later. They are experts, and, as they did not make that check at the time, I do not think that they should now be allowed to recover against the innocent seller who produced to them all the evidence which he had, namely, the registration book. I agree that it is hard on the plaintiffs to have paid more than the car is worth, but it would be equally hard on the seller to make him pay the difference. He would never have bought the Hillman car unless he had received the allowance of £290 for the Morris car. The best course in all these cases would be to " shunt " the difference down the train of innocent sellers until one reached the rogue who perpetrated the fraud; but he can rarely be traced, or if he can, he rarely has the money to pay the damages. Therefore, one is left to decide between a number of innocent people who is to bear the loss. That can only be done by applying the law about representations and warranties as we know it, and that is what I have tried to do. If the rogue can be traced, he can be sued by whosoever has suffered the

---

[1] [1913] A. C. 30, at p. 50.

loss: but, if he cannot be traced, the loss must lie where it falls. It should not be inflicted on innocent sellers, who sold the car many months, perhaps many years before, and have forgotten all about it and have conducted their affairs on the basis that the transaction was concluded. Such a seller would not be able to recollect after all this length of time the exact words which he used, such as whether he said " I believe it is a 1948 model," or " I warrant it is a 1948 model." The right course is to let the buyer set aside the transaction if he finds out the mistake quickly and comes promptly before other interests have irretrievably intervened, otherwise the loss must lie where it falls: and that is, I think, the course prescribed by law. I would allow this appeal accordingly.

HODSON, L.J. delivered judgment to the same effect, allowing the appeal.

MORRIS, L.J.: In June, 1955, the defendant acquired a new Hillman motor car belonging to the plaintiffs who took a Morris 10 h.p. saloon motor car in part exchange. The form which the transaction took in reference to the Hillman car was that it was sold by the plaintiffs to a hire-purchase company, from whom the defendant then hired it. The Morris car was, in fact, being hired by the defendant from a hire-purchase company, but could become the property of the defendant on payment of £50. The defendant said to the plaintiffs that the Morris car was a 1948 model. On the basis that it was, the allowance in respect of it was computed by reference to a well-known guide recording basic prices of second-hand cars in normal condition for their age. The appropriate figure for the particular 1948 model was shown in the guide as £295. The allowance made to the defendant was £290. The plaintiffs paid £50 to the hire-purchase company from whom the defendant was hiring the Morris car and credited the defendant with the balance of £240. The result of this was that the defendant sold the Morris car to the plaintiffs for £290.

In fact, the Morris car was not a 1948 model, but was a 1939 model, and if the plaintiffs had known this they would not have paid more than £175 for it. When in January, 1956, they discovered that the Morris car was a 1939 model, they not unnaturally claimed £115 from the defendant. Without any fault on their part they had, in effect, paid the defendant £115 too much. In these circumstances it might have been expected that the defendant would voluntarily have reimbursed the plaintiffs, unless there were some difficulties that prevented him. He did not recoup the plaintiffs, however, and they brought an action. Their case was that it was an express term of the contract that the Morris car was a 1948 model. They said that the term was a condition or, in the alternative, a warranty, and that, in the events which had happened, they were entitled to claim damages for breach of warranty.

The statement that the defendant made was that the Morris car was a 1948 model. This was a definite and unqualified statement. It was of this nature because the defendant did not doubt it. It was not a mere expression of tentative or qualified belief. At the hearing it was proved that it was a 1939 model. The defendant did not give evidence. The plaintiffs did not in any way suggest that the defendant had not honestly believed what he had said and they very fairly admitted that the defendant would not have embarked on the new transaction had he not been able to get £290 for his Morris car.

The defendant handed over the registration book of the Morris car which stated that it was first registered in 1948. In the absence of evidence it must remain a matter of speculation why the registration book referable to a 1939 car should record that the first registration was in 1948. It is possible that a 1939 car was first registered in 1948, but this seems very unlikely. In correspondence it was stated on behalf of the defendant that the car had been bought by the defendant's mother in March, 1954. She paid £300 for it—being £10 more than the amount allowed to the defendant for it fourteen months later. Her name is recorded in the book. It is, I think, only reasonable for a purchaser of a car who received a registration book which showed a first registration in 1948 to have believed that the car was a 1948 car. There was evidence, which the learned judge accepted, that the "styling " of a 10 h.p. Morris car had not changed between 1939 and 1948 " so that mere inspection of the car even by a man with knowledge of motor cars would not have indicated that the car in question was of earlier manufacture than 1948."

The case can be approached, and has at all times been approached, on the basis that all concerned honestly believed that the car was a 1948 car. The plaintiffs' representative had often had lifts in the defendant's car and thought that it looked like a 1948 model. It cannot be denied, therefore, that he fully accepted and acted on the statement made to him that the car was a 1948 model. Furthermore, he was handed the registration book and from that he checked that the car was a 1948 model. In strictness, the book only showed that the date of first registration was in 1948, but any dealer in cars would, I think, regard that as confirmation of what he had been told. There was nothing at all to put him on notice that the car was a 1939 model and, indeed, it is not suggested that there was. He believed that the car was a 1948 model and it was because he so believed that he agreed the allowance in the sum of £290. Had he not so believed, he would never have allowed £290. Everything, therefore, points to the importance of the statement that the car was a 1948 model: the statement was amply corroborated when the registration book was handed over for the plaintiffs' representative to see. The learned judge held that the defendant knew that the plaintiffs' representative proceeded to calculate what allowance he would make for the car on the basis that it was a 1948 car.

The only point taken on behalf of the defendant was that the statement which was made did not form a part of the contract. The learned judge rejected this. He held that it was not only a term but an essential term. In my judgment he was correct. The statement that the car was a 1948 car was not a mere representation in respect of the subject-matter of the contract: the statement was adopted as the foundation of the contract which they made. The promise to pay £290 for that particular car (a figure arrived at by reference to the value of 1948 cars) was the counterpart of a term of the contract that that particular car was a 1948 model.

The learned judge held that, if the plaintiffs had discovered after the making of the contract but before property in the car had passed that it was a 1939 car, they could have refused to go on with the transaction: that they could have refused for the reason that it was a condition of the contract that the car was a 1948 model. The learned judge expressed himself as follows:

" Although it appeared that the plaintiffs' agent had often had a lift in the defendant's car (more strictly, the car let on hire-purchase terms to the defendant's mother), the actual transaction, on the evidence, appeared to me to be a sale by description of the car, described as a 1948 10 h.p. Morris car, as part of the larger and somewhat more complex transaction of letting a new Hillman Minx to the defendant on hire-purchase terms, making him an allowance of

£290, the value to the plaintiffs of the said 10 h.p. Morris car, on the assumption that it was a 1948 model.

"Mr. Ladd satisfied me that this assumption was fundamental to the contract, a condition which, if not satisfied, would have caused him to rescind the contract if he had known it to be unsatisfied before the property in the Morris car passed to his principals. The defendant did not elect to give evidence, but Mr. Ladd told me that, for the purpose of calculating the allowance he would give the defendant, he used ' Glass's Guide,' a well-known reference book published monthly in the motor trade, giving the average second-hand price paid by dealers for cars according to the year of manufacture. I have no doubt the defendant knew that Mr. Ladd was calculating the allowance he would make for the car on the basis that it was a 1948 car, and it was never suggested in cross-examination that he did not. There was no suggestion that the defendant's statement that the car was a 1948 model was made otherwise than in good faith, but, so far as Mr. Ladd was concerned, that statement was fundamental, according to his evidence; and apart from Mr. Benjamin's cross-examination to elicit that the defendant had given Mr. Ladd lifts in the car, it was not suggested that Mr. Ladd did otherwise then rely on the defendant's statement as to the year of manufacture, corroborated by the evidence of the registration book, and the documents of the previous hire-purchase transaction relating to the same vehicle."

The plaintiffs do not allege that there was any collateral oral warranty. They submit that the statement of the defendant was not something detached from the contract, but was a part of the contract and was in legal terminology a condition. In my judgment, it was a stipulation of the contract which was a condition. But by the time that the plaintiffs ascertained that the car was a 1939 car, it was too late for them to take any other course than to treat the breach of condition as a breach of warranty (see Sale of Goods Act, 1893, s.11). On this basis the learned judge held that the plaintiffs were relegated to a right to claim damages, which he assessed at £115, being the difference between the value which the car would have had if it had been a 1948 car and its actual true value, which he found was £175.

In deciding the case the learned judge applied his mind to the tests laid down in *Heilbut, Symons & Co.* v. *Buckleton*[1]. In his speech in that case Lord Moulton spoke of the importance of maintaining in its full integrity the principle that a person is not liable in damages for an innocent misrepresentation and made it clear[2] that it would be wrong to say that, merely because a representation is made in the course of a dealing and before completion of a bargain, the representation amounts to a warranty. He approved[3] the statement of Holt, C.J., that an affirmation at the time of a sale is a warranty, provided that it appears on the evidence to have been so intended. The intention of the parties is to be deduced from the totality of the evidence[4].

In coming to his conclusion that what the defendant said about the car being a 1948 model was in this case a part of the contract, the learned judge distinguished *Routledge* v. *McKay*[5] which was one in which the principles laid down in *Heilbut, Symons & Co.* v. *Buckleton* were applied to the facts of that case. There was a sale of a motor cycle by the fifth party to the fourth party and a later claim for damages for breach of a warranty that the cycle was a 1942 model. There was a first meeting between the parties. In answer to a question the fifth party said that the cycle was a 1942 model and pointed to the corroboration of that statement to be found in the registration book. There was a second meeting when the two parties signed a written

---

[1] [1913] A. C. 30.   [2] *Ibid.*, at 50.   [3] *Ibid.*, at 49.   [4] *Ibid.*, at 51.
[5] [1954] 1 All E. R. 855.

contract. The contract made no mention of the cycle being a 1942 model. It was, in fact, a 1930 model. As to the written contract it was held[1] that prima facie it recorded what the parties intended to agree when the actual transaction of sale took place and, as a matter of construction, that it would be extremely difficult to say that such an agreement was consistent with a warranty being given at the same time and so as to be intended to form a part of the bargain then made. There was no statement as to the age of the cycle made at the time of the written contract. It was, therefore, held that there was no warranty given as part of the actual bargain. It was then considered whether the statement previously made during the first meeting was a representation or a warranty, and it was held that the statement then made (at a time when there was no agreement between the parties) was not contractual and that nothing more was intended than a mere representation.

Sir Raymond Evershed, M.R., in his judgment, said[2]:

> " This written memorandum represents prima facie the record of what the parties intended to agree when the actual transaction took place. Counsel for the fifth party contended that the terms of it necessarily exclude any warranty, that is to say, any collateral bargain, either contemporary or earlier in date. I am not sure that I would go so far as that. But I think that as a matter of construction it would be difficult to say that such an agreement was consistent with a warranty being given at the same time so as to be intended to form a part of the bargain then made. I think, with counsel for the fifth party, that the last words ' It is understood that when the £30 is paid . . . this transaction is closed ' would make such a contention difficult. But I will assume that the warranty was given, not when the bargain was struck but on Oct. 23, 1949, on which date alone, according to the evidence, any representation about the date of the motor cycle combination was made at all.
>   " If that representation is to be a warranty it has to be contractual in form. In other words, so far as I can see, once the existence of a warranty as part of the actual bargain is excluded, it must be a separate contract, and the overwhelming difficulty which faces the fourth party is that when the representation was made there was then no bargain, and it is, therefore, in my view, impossible to say that it could have been collateral to some other contract. Even apart from that, it seems to me that on the evidence there is nothing to support the conclusion, as a matter of law and bearing in mind Lord Moulton's observations, that in answering the question posed about the date of the motor cycle combination there was anything more intended than a mere representation."

The learned judge in the present case considered *Routledge* v. *McKay* and correctly distinguished it from the present one. In the present case there was not, as in *Routledge* v. *McKay*, an antecedent statement and then a later written contract which omitted any incorporation of or reference to the statement. *Routledge* v. *McKay* is distinguishable on three grounds. In the present case there was a statement made at the time of the transaction: there was no written contract: and, in so far as there was a document brought into existence, the document consisted of an invoice addressed to the defendant which recorded the complete transaction and which expressly described the car for which an allowance of £290 was being made as a " 1948 Morris 10 saloon." The statement made which described the Morris car was, therefore, an integral part of the contract. It was, I consider, a condition of the contract, on which the plaintiffs contracted: compare *Bannerman* v. *White*[3]. In *Couchman* v. *Hill*[4] a statement was made that a heifer was " unserved". There was in that case a discussion whether the description " unserved "

[1] [1954] 1 All E.R. at p. 859.
[3] (1861), 10 C. B. N. S. 844.
[2] [1954] 1 All E. R. at p. 859.
[4] [1947] K. B. 554; [1947] 1 All E. R. 103.

constituted a warranty or a condition. In his judgment, with which the other members of the court concurred, Scott, L.J., said[1]:

" . . . as a matter of law I think every item in a description which constitutes a substantial ingredient in the ' identity ' of the thing sold is a condition, although every such condition can be waived by the purchaser who thereon becomes entitled to treat it as a warranty and recover damages. I think there was here an unqualified condition which, on its breach, the plaintiff was entitled to treat as a warranty and recover the damages claimed."

In the present case, on a consideration of the evidence which he heard, the learned judge came to the conclusion that the statement which he held to have been made by the defendant at the time of the making of the contract was a statement made contractually. It seems to me that the totality of the evidence points to that view. The statement related to a vitally important matter: it described the subject-matter of the contract then being made and directed the parties to, and was the basis of, their agreement as to the price to be paid or credited to the defendant. In the language of Scott, L.J., it seems to me that the statement made by the defendant was " an item in [the] description " of what was being sold and that it constituted a substantial ingredient in the identity of the things sold. It is with diffidence that I arrive at a conclusion differing from that of my Lords, but I cannot see that the learned judge in any way misdirected himself or misapplied any principle of law, and I see no reason for disturbing his conclusion.

Appeal allowed. Leave to appeal to the House of Lords refused

---

[1] [1947] 1 All E. R. at 105.

RELATIVE IMPORTANCE OF CONTRACTUAL TERMS

HONG KONG FIR SHIPPING CO., LTD *v.* KAWASAKI KISEN KAISHA, LTD.

THE MIHALIS ANGELOS

The obligations created by a contract will not all be of equal weight. Unless the parties have set their own value upon its terms, the courts must determine their relative importance. There is no sure criterion by which this question may be decided. There are, however, potential guiding-lines. Two possibilities have been discussed by the Court of Appeal in recent years.

(1) The courts may concentrate on the effect of the breach rather than on the quality of the term broken. On this assumption the question should not be whether the term as drafted is itself more or less important, but whether its breach produces more or less serious results (*Hong Kong Fir Shipping Co. Ltd.* v. *Kawasaki Kisen Kaisha, Ltd.*).

(2) The courts, on the other hand, may approach the problem by construing the contract in question as at the time of its making and thus inferring the probable intention of the parties. If this view is preferred, the distinction will be made, not between the more or less serious effect of a breach, but between major and minor terms as they stand in the contract (*The Mihalis Angelos*).

The House of Lords has yet to choose between these two lines of approach.

Hong Kong Fir Shipping Co. Ltd. v. Kawasaki Kisen Kaisha, Ltd.

[1962] 1 All E.R. 474

By a time charter dated December 26, 1956, it was mutually agreed between the owners of the vessel Hong Kong Fir, classed Lloyd's 100 A1, and the charterers that (cl. 1) the owners would let and the charterers hire the vessel for twenty-four months from the date of her delivery to the charterers at Liverpool " she being in every way fitted for ordinary cargo service ", and that (cl. 3) the owners would " maintain her in a thoroughly efficient state in hull and machinery during service ". Under the charter, hire was payable at the rate of 47*s*. per ton, but it was provided that no hire should be paid for time lost exceeding twenty-four hours in carrying out repairs to the vessel and that such off-hire periods might at the charterers' option be added to the charter time. The vessel was delivered to the charterers at Liverpool on February 13, 1957, and on the same day she sailed for Newport News, U.S.A., to load a cargo of coal which she was to carry to Osaka. When she was delivered to the charterers at Liverpool, her engine-room was undermanned and her engine-room staff incompetent, although the owners knew that the vessel's machinery was very old and, therefore, required an ample and efficient engine-room staff to maintain it. During the voyage to Osaka, the vessel was off hire for repairs to her engines for a total period of about five weeks, and when she arrived at Osaka, on May 25, 1957, it was found that the engines were in a very bad state and that it would take a further fifteen weeks to make the vessel seaworthy. The condition of the engines at Osaka was due mainly to the inefficiency of the engine-room staff on the voyage from Liverpool. By September 15, 1957, the vessel had been made seaworthy in every respect and then had an efficient and adequate engine-room staff; at that date she was still available to the charterers for seventeen months. In mid-June, there had been a steep fall in freight rates from 47s. to 24s. per ton, and by mid-August the rates had dropped again to 13s. 6d. per ton. On June 6 and September 11, 1957, the charterers had written to the owners repudiating the charter. In an action by the owners for wrongful repudiation, the trial judge found that the owners were in breach of cl. 1 of the charter in delivering a vessel that was unseaworthy with regard to her engine-room staff, and were also in breach of clause 3 in negligently failing to maintain the vessel in an efficient state, but that in June there were no reasonable grounds for thinking that the owners were unable to make the vessel seaworthy by mid-September at the latest. The charterers contended that the owners' breaches of charter entitled them to repudiate the charter, alternatively that the charter had been frustrated. At first instance SALMON, J. held that the charterers were not entitled to repudiate the charter. The charterers appealed, but their appeal was dismissed by the Court of Appeal.

DIPLOCK, L.J. The contract, the familiar Baltime 1939 Charter, and the facts on which this case turns have been already stated in the judgment of SELLERS, L.J., who has also referred to many of the relevant cases. With his analysis of the cases, as with the clear and careful judgment of SALMON, J.[1] I am in agreement, and I desire to add only some general observations on the legal questions which this case involves.

Every synallagmatic contract contains in it the seeds of the problem: in what event will a party be relieved of his undertaking to do that which he has agreed to do but has not yet done? The contract may itself expressly define some of these events, as in the cancellation clause in a charterparty, but, human prescience being limited, it seldom does so exhaustively and often fails to do so at all. In some classes of contracts, such as sale of goods, marine insurance, contracts of affreightment evidenced by bills of lading and those between parties to bills of exchange, Parliament has defined by statute some of the events not provided for expressly in individual contracts of that class; but, where an event occurs the occurrence of which neither the parties nor Parliament have expressly stated will discharge one of the parties from further performance of his undertakings, it is for the court to determine whether the event has had this effect or not. The test whether an event has this effect or not has been stated in a number of metaphors all of which I think amount to the same thing: does the occurrence of the event deprive the party who has further undertakings still to perform of substantially the whole benefit which it was the intention of the parties as expressed in the contract that he should obtain as the consideration for performing those under-takings? This test is applicable whether or not the event occurs as a result of the default of one of the parties to the contract, but the consequences of the event are different in the two cases. Where the event occurs as a result of the default of one party, the party in default cannot rely on it as relieving him-self of the performance of any further undertakings on his part, and the innocent party, although entitled to, need not treat the event as relieving him of the performance of his own undertakings. This is only a specific applica-tion of the fundamental legal and moral rule that a man should not be allowed to take advantage of his own wrong. Where the event occurs as a result of the default of neither party, each is relieved of the further performance of his own

---

[1] [1962] 2 Q.B. 26; [1961] 2 All E.R. 257.

undertakings, and their rights in respect of undertakings previously performed are now regulated by the Law Reform (Frustrated Contracts) Act, 1943.

This branch of the common law has reached its present stage by the normal process of historical growth, and the fallacy in counsel for the charterers' contention that a different test is applicable when the event occurs as a result of the default of one party from that applicable in cases of frustration where the event occurs as a result of the default of neither party arises, in my view, from a failure to view the cases in their historical context. The problem is this. When will a party to a contract be relieved of his undertaking to do that which he has agreed to do but has not yet done? This has exercised the English courts for centuries, probably ever since assumpsit emerged as a form of action distinct from covenant and debt, and long before even the earliest cases which we have been invited to examine; but, until the rigour of the rule in *Paradine* v. *Jane*[1] was mitigated in the middle of the last century by the classic judgments of BLACKBURN, J., in *Taylor* v. *Caldwell*[2], and BRAMWELL, B., in *Jackson* v. *Union Marine Insurance Co.*[3], it was in general only events resulting from one party's failure to perform his contractual obligations which were regarded as capable of relieving the other party from continuing to perform that which he had undertaken to do.

In the earlier cases before the Common Law Procedure Act, 1852, the problem tends to be obscured to modern readers by the rules of pleading peculiar to the relevant forms of action—covenant, debt and assumpsit, and the nomenclature adopted in the judgments, which were mainly on demurrer, reflects this. It was early recognised that contractual undertakings were of two different kinds: those collateral to the main purpose of the parties as expressed in the contract, and those which were mutually dependent so that the non-performance of an undertaking of this class was an event which excused the other party from the performance of his corresponding undertakings. In the nomenclature of the eighteenth and early ninteenth centuries, undertakings of the latter class were called " conditions precedent ", and a plaintiff under the rules of pleading had to aver specially in his declaration his performance or readiness and willingness to perform all those contractual undertakings on his part which constituted conditions precedent to the defendant's undertaking for non-performance of which the action was brought. In the earliest cases, such as *Pordage* v. *Cole*[4] and *Thorpe* v. *Thorpe*[5], the question whether an undertaking was a condition precedent appears to have turned on the verbal niceties of the particular phrases used in the written contract, and it was not until 1779 that LORD MANSFIELD, in the case which is a legal landmark, *Boone* v. *Eyre*[6], swept away these arid technicalities. He said:

> " The distinction is very clear, where mutual covenants go to the whole of the consideration on both sides, they are mutual conditions, the one precedent to the other. But where they go only to a part, where a breach may be paid for in damages, there the defendant has a remedy on his covenant, and shall not plead it as a condition precedent."

This, too, was a judgment on demurrer, but the principle was the same when the substance of the matter was in issue. Other phrases expressing the same idea were used by other judges in the cases which have already been cited by

---

[1] (1647), Aleyn, 26.
[2] (1863), 3 B. & S. 826.
[3] (1874), L.R. 10 C.P. 125.
[4] (1669), 1 Wms. Saund. 319.
[5] (1701), 12 Mod. Rep. 455.
[6] (1779), 1 Hy. Bl. at p. 273 n.

SELLERS, L.J.[1], and I would only add to his comments on them that, when it is borne in mind that, until the latter half of the nineteenth century, the only event that could be relied on to excuse performance by one party of his undertakings was a default by the other party, no importance can be attached to the fact that, in occasional cases, and there may be others besides *Freeman* v. *Taylor*[2], the court has referred to the object or purpose of the party not in default rather than to the object or purpose of the contract. The relevant object or purpose of the party not in default is that on which there has been a consensus *ad idem* of both parties as expressed in the words which they have used in their contract construed in the light of the surrounding circumstances.

The fact that the emphasis in the earlier cases was on the breach by one party to the contract of his contractual undertakings, for this was the commonest circumstance in which the question arose, tended to obscure the fact that it was really the event resulting from the breach which relieved the other party of further performance of his obligations. But the principle was applied early in the nineteenth century and without analysis to cases where the event relied on was one brought about by a party to a contract before the time for performance of his undertakings arose, but which would make it impossible to perform those obligations when the time to do so did arrive: for example, *Short* v. *Stone*[3]; *Ford* v. *Tiley*[4]; *Bowdell* v. *Parsons*[5]. It was not, however, until *Jackson* v. *Union Marine Insurance Co.*[6], that it was recognised that it was the happening of the event and not the fact that the event was the result of a breach by one party of his contractual obligations that relieved the other party from further performance of his obligations. BRAMWELL, B., said[7]:

> ". . . there are the cases which hold that, where the shipowner has not merely broken his contract, but so broken it that the condition precedent is not performed, the charterer is discharged. . . . Why? Not merely because the contract is broken. If it is not a condition precedent, what matters is whether it is unperformed with or without excuse? Not arriving with due diligence, or at a day named, is the subject of a cross-action only. But, not arriving in time for the voyage contemplated, but at such a time that it is frustrated, is not only a breach of contract, but discharges the charterer. And so it should, though he has such an excuse that no action lies."

Once it is appreciated that it is the event and not the fact that the event is a result of a breach of contract which relieves the party not in default of further performance of his obligations, two consequences follow: (i) The test whether the event relied on has this consequence is the same whether the event is the result of the other party's breach of contract or not, as DEVLIN, J., pointed out in *Universal Cargo Carriers Corporation* v. *Citati*[8]. (ii) The question whether an event which is the result of the other party's breach of contract has this consequence cannot be answered by treating all contractual undertakings as falling into one of two separate categories: " conditions ", the breach of which gives rise to an event which relieves the party not in default of further performance of his obligations, and " warranties ", the breach of which does not give rise to such an event. Lawyers tend to speak of this classification as if it were comprehensive, partly for the historical reasons which I have already mentioned, and partly because Parliament

---

[1] [1962] 1 All E.R. at p. 480.
[2] (1831), 8 Bing. 124.
[3] (1846), 8 Q.B. 358.
[4] (1827), 6 B. & C. 325.
[5] (1808), 10 East, 359.
[6] (1874), L.R. 10 C.P. 125.
[7] (1874), L.R. 10 C.P. at p. 147.
[8] [1957] 2 Q.B. at p. 434; [1957] 2 All E.R. at p. 83.

itself adopted it in the Sale of Goods Act, 1893, as respects a number of implied terms in contracts for the sale of goods and has in that Act used the expressions " condition " and " warranty " with that meaning. But it is by no means true of contractual undertakings in general at common law.

No doubt there are many simple contractual undertakings, sometimes express, but more often because of their very simplicity (" It goes without saying ") to be implied, of which it can be predicated that every breach of such an undertaking must give rise to an event which will deprive the party not in default of substantially the whole benefit which it was intended that he should obtain from the contract. And such a stipulation, unless the parties have agreed that breach of it shall not entitle the non-defaulting party to treat the contract as repudiated, is a " condition ". So, too, there may be other simple contractual undertakings of which it can be predicated that *no* breach can give rise to an event which will deprive the party not in default of substantially the whole benefit which it was intended that he should obtain from the contract; and such a stipulation, unless the parties have agreed that breach of it shall entitle the non-defaulting party to treat the contract as repudiated, is a " warranty ". There are, however, many contractual undertakings of a more complex character which cannot be categorised as being " conditions " or " warranties " if the late nineteenth century meaning adopted in the Sale of Goods Act, 1893, and used by BOWEN, L.J., in *Bentsen* v. *Taylor, Sons & Co.* (2),[1], be given to those terms. Of such undertakings, all that can be predicated is that some breaches will, and others will not, give rise to an event which will deprive the party not in default of substantially the whole benefit which it was intended that he should obtain from the contract; and the legal consequences of a breach of such an undertaking, unless provided for expressly in the contract, depend on the nature of the event to which the breach gives rise and do not follow automatically from a prior classification of the undertaking as a " condition " or " warranty ". For instance, to take the example of BRAMWELL, B., in *Jackson* v. *Union Marine Insurance Co*[2], by itself breach of an undertaking by a shipowner to sail with all possible dispatch to a named port does not necessarily relieve the charterer of further performance of his obligation under the charterparty, but, if the breach is so prolonged that the contemplated voyage is frustrated, it does have this effect.

In 1874, when the doctrine of frustration was being foaled by " impossibility of performance " out of " condition precedent ", it is not suprising that the explanation given by BRAMWELL, B., should give full credit to the dam by suggesting that in addition to the express *warranty* to sail with all possible dispatch there was an implied *condition precedent* that the ship should arrive at the named port in time for the voyage contemplated. In *Jackson* v. *Union Marine Insurance Co.*[3], there was no breach of the express warranty; but, if there had been, to engraft the implied condition on the express warranty would have been merely a more complicated way of saying that a breach of a shipowner's undertaking to sail with all possible dispatch may, but will not necessarily, give rise to an event which will deprive the charterer of substantially the whole benefit which it was intended that he should obtain from the charter. Now that the doctrine of frustration has matured and flourished for nearly a century and the old technicalities of pleading " conditions precedent " are more than a century out of date, it does not clarify, but on the contrary obscures, the modern principle of law where such an

---

[1] [1893] 2 Q.B. at p. 280.   [2] (1874), L.R. 10 C.P. at p. 142.   [3] (1874), L.R. 10 C.P. 125.

event *has* occurred as a result of a breach of an express stipulation in a contract, to continue to add the now unnecessary colophon

> " therefore it was an implied *condition* of the contract that a particular kind of breach of an express *warranty* should not occur."

The common law evolves not merely by breeding new principles but also, when they are fully grown, by burying their ancestors.

As my brethren have already pointed out, the shipowner's undertaking to tender a seaworthy ship has, as a result of numerous decisions as to what can amount to " unseaworthiness ", become one of the most complex of contractual undertakings. It embraces obligations with respect to every part of the hull and machinery, stores and equipment and the crew itself. It can be broken by the presence of trivial defects easily and rapidly remediable as well as by defects which must inevitably result in a total loss of the vessel. Consequently, the problem in this case is, in my view, neither solved nor soluble by debating whether the owner's express or implied undertaking to tender a seaworthy ship is a " condition " or a " warranty ". It is, like so many other contractual terms, an undertaking one breach of which may give rise to an event which relieves the charterer of further performance of his undertakings if he so elects, and another breach of which may not give rise to such an event but entitle him only to monetary compensation in the form of damages. It is, with all deference to counsel for the charterers' skilful argument, by no means surprising that, among the many hundreds of previous cases about the shipowner's undertaking to deliver a seaworthy ship, there is none where it was found profitable to discuss in the judgments the question whether that undertaking is a " condition " or a " warranty ". The true answer, as I have already indicated, is that it is neither, but one of that large class of contractual undertakings, one breach of which may have the same effect as that ascribed to a breach of " condition " under the Sale of Goods Act, 1893, and a different breach of which may have only the same effect as that ascribed to a breach of " warranty " under that Act. The cases referred to by SELLERS, L.J., illustrate this, and I would only add that, in the *dictum* which he cites from *Kish* v. *Taylor*[1], it seems to me from the sentence which immediately follows it as from the actual decision in the case and the whole tenor of LORD ATKINSON's speech itself that the word " will " was intended to be " may ".

What the learned judge had to do in the present case as in any other case where one party to a contract relies on a breach by the other party as giving him a right to elect to rescind the contract, was to look at the events which had occurred as a result of the breach at the time at which the charterers purported to rescind the charterparty, and to decide whether the occurrence of those events deprived the charterers of substantially the whole benefit which it was the intention of the parties as expressed in the charterparty that the charterers should obtain from the further performance of their own contractual undertakings. One turns, therefore, to the contract, the Baltime 1939 Charter. Clause 13, the " due diligence " clause, which exempts the shipowners from responsibility for delay or loss or damage to goods on board due to unseaworthiness, unless such delay or loss or damage has been caused by want of due diligence of the owners in making the vessel seaworthy and fitted for the voyage, is in itself sufficient to show that the mere occurrence of the

---

[1] [1912] A.C. at p. 617; 12 Asp. M.L.C. at p. 220.

events that the vessel was in some respect unseaworthy when tendered, or that such unseaworthiness had caused some delay in performance of the charter-party, would not deprive the charterer of the whole benefit which it was the intention of the parties he should obtain from the performance of his obliga-tions under the contract. He undertakes to continue to perform his obliga-tions notwithstanding the occurrence of such events if they fall short of frustration of the contract and even deprives himself of any remedy in damages unless such events are the consequence of want of due diligence on the part of the ship-owner.

The question which the learned judge had to ask himself was, as he rightly decided, whether or not, at the date when the charterers purported to rescind the contract, namely June 6, 1957, or when the owners purported to accept such rescission, namely August 8, 1957, the delay which had already occurred as a result of the incompetence of the engine-room staff, and the delay which was likely to occur in repairing the engines of the vessel, and the conduct of the owners by that date in taking steps to remedy these two matters, were, when taken together, such as to deprive the charterers of substantially the whole benefit which it was the intention of the parties they should obtain from further use of the vessel under the charterparty. In my view, in his judgment—on which I would not seek to improve—the learned judge took into account and gave due weight to all the relevant considerations and arrived at the right answer for the right reasons.

SELLERS, L.J. and UPJOHN, L.J. delivered judgment to the same effect, dismissing the appeal.

The Mihalis Angelos

[1970] 3 All E.R. 125

The facts were thus stated by LORD DENNING, M.R. The material facts are these. On 25 May, 1965, the owners let the vessel Mihalis Angelos to the charterers for a voyage from Haiphong, in North Vietnam, to Hamburg, or other port in Europe. In cl.1 of the charterparty the owners said that she was " expected ready to load under this charter about July 1, 1965 ". The vessel was to proceed to Haiphong and then load a cargo of apatite and carry it to Europe. There was a cancelling clause in case the vessel was not ready to load by July 20, 1965.

The owners were quite wrong in saying that she was " expected to load on July 1 " at Haiphong. They had no reasonable grounds for any such expectation. On May 25, 1965, the date of the charter, the vessel was in the Pacific on her way to Hong Kong. She was not expecting to reach Hong Kong until June 25 or 26. She would need 14 days to discharge, thus taking it to July 9 or 10. She would take two days from Hong Kong to Haiphong. So she could not reasonably be expected to arrive at Haiphong until July 13 or 14. Yet the shipowners, quite wrongly, said that she was expected to arrive on July 1. In point of fact, she made up time across the Pacific, and arrived at Hong Kong on June 23; but the discharge at Hong Kong was unexpectedly prolonged. She did not complete it until July 23. Meanwhile, however, the charterers had their own troubles. They discovered that there was no apatite ore available at Haiphong. They thought that it was due to the war in North Vietnam. It was said that the Americans had bombed the railway line to the port. On July 17, 1965, the charterers cancelled the contract as a case of *force majeure*. The shipowners accepted this information as a repudiation of the contract. They did not charter the vessel to anyone else. Instead they sold her on July 29, as she lay in Hong Kong.

The arbitrators found that if the ship, after discharge at Hong Kong, had proceeded to Haiphong, the charterers would, beyond doubt, have cancelled the charter on the ground that the ship had missed her cancelling date. So the owners, in fact, lost nothing; but they claimed damages on the footing that they lost the charter on July 17 and were entitled to £4,000 damages. The arbitrators rejected this claim. On a special case stated by them MOCATTA, J. set aside their award and gave the owners £4,000. The charterers appealed against this judgment. The Court of Appeal allowed this appeal and restored the arbitrators' award.

MEGAW, L.J. As a result of the admirable clarity and precision of the arbitrators' award, there is no doubt or ambiguity about the facts relevant to this appeal. They may be summarised as follows: the charterers and the owners made a contract in the form of a charterparty on May 25, 1965. By that charter, the owners agreed that the vessel " now trading and expected ready to load under this charter about July 1, 1965 ", should proceed to Haiphong, in North Vietnam, and there load 9,500 tons of a mineral called apatite and should carry that cargo to a port in northern Europe. It was provided that lay days should not commence before July 1, 1965. The first sentence of the cancelling clause, cl. 11, reads:

> " Should the vessel not be ready to load (whether in berth or not) on or before the 20th July 65 Charterers have the option of cancelling this contract, such option to be declared, if demanded, at least 48 hours before vessel's expected arrival at port of loading."

On May 25, 1965, the date of the charter, the owners could not reasonably have estimated that the vessel could or would arrive at Haiphong about July 1, 1965. The arbitrators have expressly so found, and that finding of fact is binding and conclusive. The vessel in fact reached Hong Kong on June 23, but the time of discharge of cargo there, which could have been expected to take 14 days, was substantially and unexpectedly prolonged. Discharge at Hong Kong ended on July 23, 1965.

Meanwhile other events had happened which have led to this litigation. The charterers found, possibly because of warlike activities in and over North Vietnam, that the intended cargo of apatite was not going to be available at Haiphong. On July 17, 1965, the charterers, through their agents, informed the owners, through their agents, that they cancelled the charterparty. They gave as their reason " *force majeure* ". The owners, rightly as is now accepted, denied that the charterers were entitled to cancel the charterparty for " *force majeure* ", whether or not that phrase meant, or was intended to include, frustration of the contract. There was, it is now accepted, no case of frustration. The owners treated the charterers' intimation of cancellation as being a wrongful repudiation of the contract, and on the same day notified the charterers of their acceptance of it as terminating the contract, leaving the owners, so they claimed, with the right to recover damages because of the alleged wrongful repudiation by the charterers. The owners sold the vessel in Hong Kong. They were however, able to provide evidence which satisfied the arbitrators that, if instead of selling the vessel, the owners had sought to employ the vessel on a substituted voyage to a north European port, in place of the cancelled charterparty voyage, the owners would, as a result of the prevailing freight market, have suffered a loss of profit of £4,000 on that notional substituted voyage, as compared with the profit obtainable on the voyage which the charterers had refused to carry out. The only other finding of fact of the arbitrators to which reference need be made is this:

> " We find that if the ship, after discharge at Hong Kong, had proceeded to Haiphong, the Charterers would beyond doubt (there having, on this assumption, been none of this business of anticipatory repudiation) have cancelled the charter, on the ground that the ship had missed her cancelling date."

The owners dispute the relevance of that finding. If relevant, its conclusiveness as a finding of fact by the arbitrators cannot be disputed.

Three issues of law have been argued on this appeal.

The first is whether the charterers were entitled to treat the breach by the owners, now conclusively established by the arbitrators' findings of fact, of the contractual term contained in the words, " expected ready to load under this charter about July 1, 1965 ", as putting an end to their, and the owners', future obligations under the charter. Of course, before the breach could produce that result, the charterers had to notify the owners that they, the charterers, were treating the contract as at an end. But it has been accepted, for the purposes of this case, that such a notification by the charterers would not be ineffective merely because it was accompanied by a statement of the wrong reason, if in fact there was then in existence a right reason. Hence the charterers' notification of July 17, 1965, would be effective, despite the fact that the purported cancellation was expressed to be on the basis of " *force majeure* ", if in fact the owners' breach of the " expected ready to load " term of the charter entitled the charterers to treat the contract as terminated. If so, there could be no question of a wrongful repudiation by the charterers or of any damages being payable by them to the owners, as was claimed in the arbitration. Therefore the crucial question on the first issue is whether the charterers were entitled, because of that breach, to treat the charterparty as at an end.

It is not disputed that when a charter includes the words: " expected ready to load . . ." a contractual obligation on the part of the shipowner is involved. It is not an obligation that the vessel will be ready to load on the stated date, nor about the stated date, if the date is qualified, as here, by " about ". The owner is not in breach merely because the vessel arrives much later, or indeed does not arrive at all. The owner is not undertaking that there will be no unexpected delay, but he is undertaking that he honestly and on reasonable grounds believes, at the time of the contract, that the date named is the date when the vessel will be ready to load. Therefore in order to establish a breach of that obligation the charterer has the burden of showing that the owner's contractually expressed expectation was not his honest expectation, or, at least, that the owner did not have reasonable grounds for it.

In my judgment, such a term in a charterparty ought to be regarded as being a condition of the contract, in the old sense of the word " condition ", i.e. that when it has been broken, the other party can, if he wishes, by intimation to the party in breach, elect to be released from performance of his further obligations under the contract; and that he can validly do so without having to establish that, on the facts of the particular case, the breach has produced serious consequences which can be treated as " going to the root of the contract " or as being " fundamental ", or whatever other metaphor may be thought appropriate for a frustration case.

I reach that conclusion for four interrelated reasons. First, it tends towards certainty in the law. One of the essential elements of law is some measure of uniformity. One of the important elements of the law is predictability. At any rate in commercial law, there are obvious and substantial advantages in having, where possible, a firm and definite rule for a particular class of legal relationship, e.g. as here, the legal categorisation of a particular, definable type of contractual clause in common use. It is surely much better, both for shipowners and charterers (and, incidentally, for their advisers) when a contractual obligation of this nature is under consideration, and still more when they are faced with the necessity for an urgent decision as to the effects of a suspected breach of it, to be able to say categorically: " If a breach is proved, then the charterer can put an end to the contract ", rather than that they should be left to ponder whether or not the courts would be likely, in the particular case, when the evidence had been heard, to decide that in the particular circumstances the breach was or was not such as to go to the root of the contract. Where justice does not require greater flexibility, there is everything to be said for, and nothing against, a degree of rigidity in legal principle.

Secondly, it would, in my opinion, only be in the rarest case, if ever, that a shipowner could legitimately feel that he had suffered an injustice by reason of the law having given to a charterer the right to put an end to the contract because of the breach by the shipowner of a clause such as this. If a shipowner has chosen to assert contractually, but dishonestly or without reasonable grounds, that he expects his vessel to be ready to load on such and such a date, wherein does the grievance lie?

Thirdly, it is, as Mocatta, J. held[1], clearly established by authority binding on this court that where a clause " expected ready to load " is included in a contract for the sale of goods to be carried by sea, that clause is a condition, in the sense that any breach of it enables the buyer to reject the goods without having to show that the dishonest or unreasonable expectation of the seller has in fact been prejudicial to the buyer. The judgment of Bankes, L.J. in which Warrington and Atkin, L.JJ. concurred, in *Finnish Government (Ministry of Food)* v. *H. Ford & Co., Ltd*[2] is in point. The clause there was " Steamers expected ready to load February and/or March 1920 ". Bankes, L.J. said[3]:

"I come to the conclusion therefore that this clause is one containing a contract. It is a contract which is in its nature a condition . . ."

That authority is not only binding in this court, but is, I think, completely and desirably in conformity with the line of cases which have decided—and the law in that respect is now accepted as being beyond dispute—that a statement in a contract of sale as to the loading period is a condition in the sense which I have indicated. If the contract says " loading to be during July ", the buyer can reject the goods if the loading was not complete until midday on August, 1. He is not limited to claiming damages; he is not obliged to show that he has suffered any damage.

It would, in my judgment, produce an undesirable anomaly in our commercial law if such a clause—" expected ready to load "—were to be held to

---

[1] [1970] 1 All E.R. at p. 677, [1970] 2 W.L.R. at p. 915.
[2] (1921) 6 Lloyd L.R. 188.
[3] (1921), 6 Lloyd L.R. at p. 189.

have a materially different legal effect where it is contained in a charterparty from that which it has when it is contained in a sale of goods contract. True, in the latter case the relevant " expectation " is that of the seller of the goods, who may himself be the charterer; whereas in the former case the relevant " expectation " is that of the shipowner. But I do not see that that fact is sufficient to warrant the making of a distinction between the two. True, also, as was stressed by counsel for the owners, the charterparty will almost invariably include a cancelling clause; and it is argued that the fact justifies the drawing of a distinction. Again, I think not, for various reasons. One of them is that the date before which the cancelling clause cannot be exercised (this involves the argument for the owners on the second issue, to be considered hereafter) is itself normally fixed by reference to the date of expected readiness to load, and on the assumption that this is an honest and reasonable expectation.

The fourth reason why I think that the clause should be regarded as being a condition when it is found in a charterparty is that that view was the view of Scrutton, L.J. so expressed in his capacity as the author of Scrutton on Charterparties. The 10th edition of the work, for which the Lord Justice was personally responsible, contained the same expression of opinion as is still to be found in the 17th edition[1] as follows:

"A ship was chartered ' expected to be at X about the 15th December . . . shall with all convenient speed sail to X '. The ship was in fact then on such a voyage that she could not complete it and be at X by December 15th. *Submitted.* that the charterer was entitled to throw up the charter".

In the footnote to that passage reference is made to, amongst other cases, *Corkling* v. *Massey*[2] The facts in the passage are the facts of *Corkling* v. *Massey*[2]. In *Corkling* v. *Massey*[2] the question whether the clause operated as a condition was left undecided by a Divisional Court. Scrutton, L.J.[3] in the sentence: " *Submitted . . .*", indicated how he would have decided it.

Mocatta, J. reached a different conclusion on this issue because, I think, he considered that some observations of Upjohn, L.J. in *Hong Kong Fir Shipping Co., Ltd.* v. *Kawasaki Kisen Kaisha, Ltd*[4], with a citation from the judgment of Bramwell, B. in *Tarrabochia* v. *Hickie*[5], were at least persuasive authority in that direction. Those observations were very general in their effect. I do not think, myself, that Upjohn, L.J. would have intended that they should be treated as derogatory from the principle applicable to the present type of case to be deduced from a passage in the judgment of the Exchequer Chamber in *Behn* v. *Burness*[6] which Edmund Davies, L.J. cited in his judgment and which I need not, therefore, repeat. It is true that that case was concerned with the words " now in the port of Amsterdam ". But in my opinion the principle stated is applicable.

If this first issue be decided, as I think it should be decided, in favour of the charterers, then the appeal succeeds and the other two issues do not need to be decided. Nevertheless, as they were argued fully, it seems desirable that they should be determined by this court.

The second issue is a question of construction of the cancelling clause, cl. 11. The charterers say that even if they were wrong on the first issue, they were entitled, on July 17, 1965, to exercise their option under cl. 11 to cancel the charterparty. True, they purported to cancel because of "*force majeure*";

---

[1] Page 79, case 4.   [2] (1873), L.R. 8 C.P. 395.
[3] Scrutton on Charterparties, 17th Edn., p. 79, case 4.
[4] [1962] 2 Q.B. 26 at p. 63; [1962] 1 All E.R. 474 at p. 483.
[5] (1856), 1 H. & N. 183 at p. 188.   [6] (1863), 3 B. & S. 751 at p. 759.

but the fact that they gave the wrong reason is, they say, not relevant. The owners say that the charterers cannot rely on clause 11 for two reasons. First, the clause by its terms does not permit of the exercise of the option before July 20; secondly, the purported cancellation of the contract could not be treated as an exercise of the option under clause 11 since the charterers expressed their notification of purported cancellation as being on a wholly different ground. We do not have the advantage of the views of Mocatta, J. or of the arbitrators on this issue, since the charterers reserved their argument below and adduced it for the first time in this court. Their reason for taking that course was that there are decisions, or *dicta*, adverse to them by Pearson, J. in *The Helvetia-S*[1], and by Roskill, J. in *The Madeleine*[2].

Respectfully disagreeing on this issue with Lord Denning, M.R., I am comforted by finding myself in agreement with Edmund Davies, L.J. I am of opinion that the first answer given by the owners must be right. If it were wrong, the second answer would not avail the owners. The construction of the clause proposed in the first answer, accords with the view expressed in the cases I have mentioned, which, whether they be *dicta* or more than *dicta*, are, I respectfully think, right. There is nothing in the different wording of the clauses in those two cases which affects the applicability of the reasoning to the present clause.

The owners' proposition is quite simple. The clause begins with the words: " Should the vessel not be ready to load . . on or before July 20, 65 . . ." Those words govern and control the clause. The charterers are given an option, for their own benefit. This option is exercisable, and exercisable only, when the condition is fulfilled, namely, that on July 20, the vessel is not ready to load.

The charterers' contention is that the opening words should be interpreted as though they read: " Should the vessel not be ready to load, or should she be *in such a position that she will not be ready to load*, on or before 20th July 1956 . . ." On July 17, the vessel was still unloading at Hong Kong. There was no possibility, as is now known, of her being able to reach Haiphong by July 20. Hence the charterers (although in fact it did not occur to them to do so) could lawfully have exercised their option under this clause, although July 20 had not yet come. It might perhaps be permissible to give the charterers' construction to the words of the clause, although I think that it would properly be described as a bold construction, if so to do would make the clause a substantially more sensible instrument for carrying out the general purpose for which it was introduced; but I think that counsel for the owners is right in his submission that the bold construction—the reading in of the words which are not there—does not have that effect. It involves reading in also a thought which was not present to the minds of the parties and which in my view is not necessary to give the clause sensible legal and practical effect. If the charterers are confident that the vessel is going to miss her cancelling date, and for some reason are minded to put an end to the charterparty before that date has arrived, there is nothing whatever to prevent them from asking the owners to agree that the charterparty should be cancelled. That does not require cl. 11. If the owners do agree, cl. 11 neither helps nor hinders. There is no need to read into it words that are not there to achieve that which can be achieved by mutual consent. If the owners do not agree, is there any possible advantage to the charterers in

---

[1] [1960] 1 Lloyd's Rep. 540 at p. 551. [2] [1967] 2 Lloyd's Rep. 224 at p. 241.

reading these suggested words into the clause? In the absence of agreement by the owners, the charterers are no better off as a result of the rewriting of the clause. Without any forced construction of the clause, the charterers can, if they are confident of the non-arrival of the vessel by the cancelling date, go ahead and make whatever arrangements they wish in anticipation of exercising their option under the clause when the cancelling date arrives. Of course, if they prove wrong in their forecast of the vessel's arrival, and if the vessel in fact, after all, makes the cancelling date, the charterers will be in trouble if they have already made other arrangements. But that is not a good ground for giving a bold interpretation to the clause. It is really in only a very odd and exceptional case, such as the present, that the suggested extension of meaning could be of any importance; and here, if it were important, it would only be of importance because the charterers misinterpreted their rights under other provisions of the charterparty. No conceivable harm would have been done to them if they had waited until July 20 and then invoked the cancelling clause. The bold construction is called for by the charterers, not because the natural construction leads to practical difficulty, but in order to try to save themselves from the consequences of their own error.

I think that the owners are right in the second issue.

The third issue is as to damages, assuming that there was, as I think there was not, a breach of contract by the charterers. The owners suffered no loss. The arbitrators held that their entitlement was nominal damages only. Long before the arbitration took place, the charterers had tendered £5 to the owners in full settlement of their claim. The arbitrators expressed their conclusion in this way in the award:

> " 29. We think the right view is that when a contract is repudiated, the repudiation accepted, the innocent party can truly say the contract is at an end: its performance is no longer binding but it (or its ghosts) must survive as the datum line for measuring the damages: the innocent party is entitled to be put, financially, in the same position as, but in no better position than, that in which he would have been if the contract had not been repudiated but had come on for performance: and his claim for damages must be based on that method of performing the contract which would have been least profitable to him.
> " 30. We find that if the ship, after discharge at Hong Kong, had proceeded to Haiphong, the Charterers would beyond doubt (there having, on this assumption, been none of this business of anticipatory repudiation) have cancelled the charter, on the ground that the ship had missed her cancelling date.
> " 31. We hold in those circumstances that the Owners are only entitled to be put in the position of having their ship on a charter, which, as soon as she got to Haiphong, could legally have been, and would have been, cancelled: and are entitled to nominal damages accordingly and no more."

In my judgment, the arbitrators' conclusion is right, as are also their reasons.

The contrary view was put forward in a most attractive argument by counsel for the owners. It was an argument which persuaded Mocatta, J. reluctantly to the conclusion that the law is such as to require the award of £4,000 damages in a case such as this, even though not one penny of damage was suffered. When a logical argument leads to such a conclusion, one is bound to consider whether the premise is sound. The premise here, based on some passages in the judgment of Cockburn, C.J. in *Frost* v. *Knight*[1] and on the judgment of Devlin, J. in *Universal Cargo Carriers Corpn* v. *Citati*[2], is that

---

[1] (1872), L.R. 7 Exch. 111, [1861–73] All E.R. Rep. 221.
[2] [1957] 2 Q.B. 401; [1957] 2 All E.R. 70.

where there is an anticipatory breach of contract the law assumes that, when the time for performance of the contract by the shipowners would have come, the repudiator will commit a breach of the contract. The law assumes that there will be a breach. Hence it is not open to the repudiator to say that no breach would then have taken place, although there is a term of the contract which provides that, in the events which would necessarily have happened, he would have been excused further performance under a term of the contract. It would follow that if a contract of sale provided for the delivery of a maximum of 5,000 tons and a minimum of 1,000 tons, the seller, having committed an anticipatory repudiation which had been duly accepted, would be liable for damages on the minimum quantity of 1,000 tons only; whereas if the option were for the seller to deliver no goods at all in certain events, which events, it could be proved, were at the date of the repudiation bound to happen, the seller would be liable for damages on the basis of non-delivery of the whole 5,000 tons.

In my view, where there is an anticipatory breach of contract, the breach is the repudiation once it has been accepted, and the other party is entitled to recover by way of damages the true value of the contractual rights which he has thereby lost, subject to his duty to mitigate. If the contractual rights which he has lost were capable by the terms of the contract of being rendered either less valuable or valueless in certain events, and if it can be shown that those events were, at the date of acceptance of the repudiation, predestined to happen, then in my view the damages which he can recover are not more than the true value, if any, of the rights which he has lost, having regard to those predestined events.

I would allow the appeal. In the absence of agreement between the parties, I would remit the matter to the arbitrators as they request, so that they can bring the matter to finality.

EXCLUDING AND LIMITING TERMS

CHAPELTON *v*. BARRY URBAN DISTRICT COUNCIL

L'ESTRANGE *v*. F. GRAUCOB, LTD.

McCUTCHEON *v*. DAVID MacBRAYNE, LTD.

THORNTON *v*. SHOE LANE PARKING, LTD.

One party to a contract may insert a term excluding or limiting liability which would otherwise be his. Such terms have long been discussed by the courts, and certain conclusions may be drawn.

(1) The document in which the term appears must be an integral part of the contract.

(2) If such a document is signed by the party against whom the excluding or limiting term is designed, it is irrelevant, in the absence of fraud or misrepresentation, whether that party has read it or has otherwise been given notice of it.

(3) If the document is not so signed, it is a question of fact, to be decided upon the circumstances of each case, whether the party relying on the terms has done what is reasonably sufficient to give notice of it to the other party. Such notice must be given before the contract is made.

(4) If a party relies on a previous course of dealing between himself and the other party to the contract, such a course must be consistent.

(5) If there is doubt as to the meaning of the excluding or limiting term, the ambiguity will be resolved against the party who relies on it[1].

Chapelton v. Barry Urban District Council
[1940] 1 K.B. 532

APPEAL from a decision of the judge of the Cardiff and Barry County Court in favour of the defendants.

SLESSER, L.J. This appeal arises out of action brought by Mr. David Chapelton against the Barry Urban District Council, and it raises a question of some importance to the very large number of people who are in the habit of using deck chairs to sit by the seaside at holiday resorts.

On June 3, 1939, Mr. Chapelton went on to the beach at a place called Cold Knap, which is within the area of the Barry Urban District Council, and wished to sit down in a deck chair. On the beach, by the side of a café, was a pile of deck chairs belonging to the defendants, and by the side of the deck chairs there was a notice put up in these terms: " Barry Urban District Council. Cold Knap. Hire of chairs, 2*d*. per session of 3 hours." Then followed words which said that the public were respectfully requested to obtain tickets for their chairs from the chair attendants, and that those tickets must be retained for inspection.

Mr. Chapelton, having taken two chairs from the attendant, one for himself and one for a Miss Andrews, who was with him, received two tickets from the attendant, glanced at them, and slipped them into his pocket. He

---

[1] It should be observed that a stranger to the contract may not rely upon any excluding or limiting term: see *infra*, p. 333.

said in the court below that he had no idea that there were any conditions on those tickets and that he did not know anything about what was on the back of them.   He took the chairs to the beach and put them up in the ordinary way, setting them up firmly on a flat part of the beach, but when he sat down he had the misfortune to go through the canvas, and, unfortunately, had a bad jar, the result of which was that he suffered injury and had to see a doctor, and in respect of that he brought his action.

The learned county court judge has found that if he had been satisfied that the plaintiff had had a valid legal claim, he would have awarded him the sum of 50l. in addition to the special damages claimed.

The learned county court judge also found that the accident to the plaintiff was due to the negligence on the part of the defendants in providing a chair for him which was unfit for its use and gave way in the manner which I have stated.   But he nevertheless found in favour of the defendants by reason of the fact that on the ticket which was handed to Mr. Chapelton when he took the chair appeared these words: " Available for 3 hours. Time expires where indicated by cut-off and should be retained and shown on request.   The Council will not be liable for any accident or damage arising from hire of chair."

As I read the learned county court judge's judgment, he said that the plaintiff had sufficient notice of the special contract printed on the ticket and was, accordingly, bound thereby—that is to say, as I understand it, that the learned county court judge has treated this case as a case similar to the many cases which have been tried in reference to conditions printed on tickets, and more particularly, on railway tickets—and he came to the conclusion that the local authority made an offer to hire out this chair to Mr. Chapelton only on certain conditions which appear on the ticket, namely, that they, the council, would not be responsible for any accident which arose from the use of the chair, and they say that Mr. Chapelton hired the chair on the basis that that was one of the terms of the contract between him and themselves, the local authority.

Questions of this sort are always questions of difficulty and are very often largely questions of fact.   In the class of case where it is said that there is a term in the contract freeing railway companies, or other providers of facilities, from liabilities which they would otherwise incur at common law, it is a question as to how far that condition has been made a term of the contract and whether it has been sufficiently brought to the notice of the person entering into the contract with the railway company, or other body, and there is a large number of authorities on that point.   In my view, however, the present case does not come within that category at all.   I think that the contract here, as appears from a consideration of all the circum- stances, was this: The local authority offered to hire chairs to persons to sit upon on the beach, and there was a pile of chairs there standing ready for use by any one who wished to use them, and the conditions on which they offered persons the use of those chairs were stated in the notice which was put up by the pile of chairs, namely, that the sum charged for the hire of a chair was 2d. per session of three hours.   I think that was the whole of the offer which the local authority made in this case.   They said, in effect: " We offer to provide you with a chair, and if you accept that offer and sit in the chair, you will have to pay for that privilege 2d. per session of three hours."

I think that Mr. Chapelton, in common with other persons who used these chairs, when he took the chair from the pile (which happened to be handed to him by an attendant, but which, I suppose, he might have taken from the pile of chairs himself if the attendant had been going on his rounds collecting money, or was otherwise away) simply thought that he was liable to pay 2*d.* for the use of the chair. No suggestion of any restriction of the council's liability appeared in the notice which was near the pile of chairs. That, I think, is the proper view to take of the nature of the contract in this case. Then the notice contained these further words: " The public are respectfully requested to obtain tickets properly issued from the automatic punch in their presence from the Chair Attendants." The very language of that " respectful request " shows clearly, to my mind, that for the convenience of the local authority the public were asked to obtain from the chair attendants tickets, which were mere vouchers or receipts showing how long a person hiring a chair is entitled to use that chair. It is wrong, I think, to look at the circumstance that the plaintiff obtained his receipt at the same time as he took his chair as being in any way a modification of the contract which I have indicated. This was a general offer to the general public, and I think it is right to say that one must take into account here that there was no reason why anybody taking one of these chairs should necessarily obtain a receipt at the moment he took his chair—and, indeed, the notice is inconsistent with that, because it " respectfully requests " the public to obtain receipts for their money. It may be that somebody might sit in one of these chairs for one hour, or two hours, or, if the holiday resort was a very popular one, for a longer time, before the attendant came round for his money, or it may be that the attendant would not come to him at all for payment for the chair, in which case I take it there would be an obligation upon the person who used the chair to search out the attendant, like a debtor searching for his creditor, in order to pay him the sum of 2*d.* for the use of the chair and to obtain a receipt for the 2*d.* paid.

I think the learned county court judge has misunderstood the nature of this agreement. I do not think that the notice excluding liability was a term of the contract at all, and I find it unnecessary to refer to the different authorities which were cited to us, save that I would mention a passage in the judgment of Mellish, L.J., in *Parker* v. *South Eastern Ry. Co.*[1], where he points out that it may be that a receipt or ticket may not contain terms of the contract at all, but may be a mere voucher, where he says: " For instance, if a person driving through a turnpike-gate received a ticket upon paying the toll, he might reasonably assume that the object of the ticket was that by producing it he might be free from paying toll at some other turnpike-gate, and might put it in his pocket unread." I think the object of the giving and the taking of this ticket was that the person taking it might have evidence at hand by which he could show that the obligation he was under to pay 2*d.* for the use of the chair for three hours had been duly discharged, and I think it is altogether inconsistent, in the absence of any qualification of liability in the notice put up near the pile of chairs, to attempt to read into it the qualification contended for. In my opinion, this ticket is no more than a receipt, and is quite different from a railway ticket which contains upon it the terms upon which a railway company agrees to carry the passenger. This, therefore, is not a question of fact for the learned county court judge. I think the learned county court judge as a matter of law has misconstrued this contract, and

---

[1] (1877), 2 C. P. D. 416, at p. 422.

looking at all the circumstances of the case, has assumed that this condition on the ticket, or the terms upon which the ticket was issued, has disentitled the plaintiff to recover. The class of case which Sankey, L.J., dealt with in *Thompson* v. *London, Midland and Scottish Ry. Co.*[1], which seems to have influenced the learned county court judge in his decision, is entirely different from that which we have to consider in the present appeal.

This appeal should be allowed.

MACKINNON and GODDARD, L.JJ., delivered judgments to the same effect.

L'Estrange v. F. Graucob, Ltd.

[1934] 2 K.B. 394

SCRUTTON, L.J. In this case the plaintiff commenced proceedings against the defendants in the county court, her claim being for 9*l.* 1*s.* as money received by the defendants to the use of the plaintiff as part of the consideration for the delivery of an automatic slot machine pursuant to a contract in writing dated February 7, 1933, which consideration was alleged to have wholly failed by reason of the fact that the machine was delivered in a condition unfit for the purpose for which it was intended. The only document which corresponds to the contract there mentioned is a long document on brown paper headed " Sales Agreement." By their defence the defendants denied that the machine was delivered in a condition unfit for the purpose intended, and denied that the sum claimed was payable to the plaintiff; and they counterclaimed for the balance of the price of the machine. Just before the trial the plaintiff amended her claim by adding a count for breach of an implied warranty that the machine was reasonably fit for the purpose for which it was sold; though she still claimed only 9*l.* 1*s.* There the pleadings stopped. At the trial, as the judge has stated in his judgment, the plaintiff's claim was put in three different ways : total failure of consideration; breach of implied conditions going to the root of the contract; and breach of warranty. The defendants pleaded : no total failure of consideration; no implied conditions; and that no action would lie for breach of implied warranty, as the agreement expressly provided for the exclusion of all implied warranties. To this last defence the plaintiff contended that she was induced to sign the contract by the misrepresentation that it was an order form, and that at the time when she signed she knew nothing of the conditions.

The county court judge has given judgment for the plaintiff for 70*l.*, though there is no claim by the plaintiff for that sum; and he has given judgment for the defendants on the counterclaim for 71*l.* 18*s.* 6*d.*, the balance of the price.

As to the defence that no action would lie for breach of implied warranty, the defendants relied upon the following clause in the contract : " This agreement contains all the terms and conditions under which I agree to purchase the machine specified above and any express or implied condition, statement, or warranty, statutory or otherwise not stated herein is hereby excluded." A clause of that sort has been before the Courts for some time. The first reported case in which it made its appearance seems to be *Wallis,*

Son & Wells v. *Pratt & Haynes*[1], where the exclusion clause mentioned only
" warranty " and it was held that it did not exclude conditions.   In the
more recent case of *Andrews Brothers (Bournemouth), Ltd.* v. *Singer & Co.*[2],
where the draftsman had put into the contract of sale a clause which excluded
only implied conditions, warranties and liabilities it was held that the clause
did not apply to an express term describing the article, and did not exempt
the seller from liability where he delivered an article of a different description.   The clause here in question would seem to have been intended
to go further than any of the previous clauses and to include all terms
denoting collateral stipulations, in order to avoid the result of these decisions.

    The main question raised in the present case is whether that clause
formed part of the contract.   If it did, it clearly excluded any condition
or warranty.

    In the course of the argument in the county court reference was made
to the railway passenger and cloak-room ticket cases, such as *Richardson,
Spence & Co.* v. *Rowntree*[3].   In that case Lord Herschell, L.C., laid down
the law applicable to these cases and stated the three questions which should
there be left to the jury.   In the present case the learned judge asked himself
the three questions appropriate to these cases, and in answering them has
found as facts : (i) that the plaintiff knew that there was printed material
on the document which she signed, (ii) that she did not know that the
document contained conditions relating to the contract, and (iii) that the
defendants did not do what was reasonably sufficient to bring these conditions
to the notice of the plaintiff.

    The present case is not a ticket case, and it is distinguishable from the
ticket cases.   In *Parker* v. *South Eastern Ry. Co.*[4] Mellish, L.J., laid down
in a few sentences the law which is applicable to this case.   He there said[5] :
" In an ordinary case, where an action is brought on a written agreement
which is signed by the defendant, the agreement is proved by proving his
signature, and, in the absence of fraud, it is wholly immaterial that he has
not read the agreement and does not know its contents."   Having said that,
he goes on to deal with the ticket cases, where there is no signature to the
contractual document, the document being simply handed by the one party
to the other[3] : " The parties may, however, reduce their agreement into
writing, so that the writing constitutes the sole evidence of the agreement,
without signing it ; but in that case there must be evidence independently
of the agreement itself to prove that the defendant has assented to it.   In
that case, also, if it is proved that the defendant has assented to the writing
constituting the agreement between the parties, it is, in the absence of fraud,
immaterial that the defendant had not read the agreement and did not know
its contents."   In cases in which the contract is contained in a railway
ticket or other unsigned document, it is necessary to prove that an alleged
party was aware, or ought to have been aware, of its terms and conditions.
These cases have no application when the document has been signed.   When
a document containing contractual terms is signed, then, in the absence of
fraud, or, I will add, misrepresentation[6], the party signing it is bound, and
it is wholly immaterial whether he has read the document or not.

---

[1] [1911] A. C. 394.   [2] [1934] 1 K. B. 17.
[3] [1894] A. C. 217.   [4] (1877), 2 C. P. D. 416.   [5] *Ibid.*, 421.
[6] See *Curtis* v. *Chemical Cleaning and Dyeing Co.*, [1951] 1 K.B. 805; and Misrepresentation Act, 1967, s. 3, *infra*, p. 195.

The plaintiff contended at the trial that she was induced by misrepresentation to sign the contract without knowing its terms, and that on that ground they are not binding upon her. The learned judge in his judgment makes no mention of that contention of the plaintiff, and he pronounces no findings as to the alleged misrepresentation. There is a further difficulty. Fraud is not mentioned in the pleadings, and I strongly object to deal with allegations of fraud where fraud is not expressly pleaded. I have read the evidence with care, and it contains no material upon which fraud could be found. The plaintiff no doubt alleged that the defendants' agent represented to her that the document which was given her to be signed was an order form, but according to the defendants' evidence no such statement was made to her by the agent. Moreover, whether the plaintiff was or was not told that the document was an order form, it was in fact an order form, and an order form is a contractual document. It may be either an acceptance or a proposal which may be accepted, but it always contains some contractual terms. There is no evidence that the plaintiff was induced to sign the contract by misrepresentation.

In this case the plaintiff has signed a document headed " Sales Agreement," which she admits had to do with an intended purchase, and which contained a clause excluding all conditions and warranties. That being so, the plaintiff, having put her signature to the document and not having been induced to do so by any fraud or misrepresentation, cannot be heard to say that she is not bound by the terms of the document because she has not read them.

The county court judge has given judgment for the defendants on the counterclaim for the balance of the price, 71*l*. 18*s*. 6*d*. I do not see how he could have done that unless he found that the contract included the clause in small print providing that, if any instalment of the price should not be duly paid, all the remaining instalments should fall due for immediate payment. That judgment on the counterclaim must stand. As to the claim, judgment was given for the plaintiff for 70*l*. for breach of an implied warranty, though only 9*l*. 1*s*. was claimed. Such a judgment could not have been given even in the High Court without an amendment of the claim. But even if there had been an amendment, the further difficulty would have remained that the signed document contained a clause excluding any implied condition or warranty. If the view which I have expressed as to the effect of a signed document is correct, the plaintiff has no ground of claim, and the judgment in her favour cannot stand. In my opinion, the judgment for the plaintiff on the claim should be set aside and judgment entered for the defendants on the claim ; and the judgment for the defendants on the counterclaim should stand.

MAUGHAM, L.J., delivered judgment to the same effect.

McCutcheon v. David MacBrayne, Ltd.

[1964] 1 All E.R. 430

This was an appeal by Alexander McCutcheon from an interlocutor of the Second Division of the Court of Session (The Lord Justice-Clerk (Lord Grant), Lord Mackintosh and Lord Strachan), dated November 7, 1962, recalling an interlocutor of the Lord Ordinary (Lord Walker), dated March 23,

1962, decreeing in favour of the present appellant for the sum of £480 against the respondents, David MacBrayne, Ltd., being the value of a motor car which was lost through the admitted negligence of the respondents when it was being shipped in the respondents' vessel " Lochiel " from the Isle of Islay to the mainland.

LORD REID: My Lords, the appellant is a farm grieve in Islay. While on the mainland in October, 1960, he asked his brother-in-law, Mr. McSporran, a farmer in Islay, to have his car sent by the respondents to West Loch Tarbert. Mr. McSporran took the car to Port Askaig. He found in the respondents' office there the purser of their vessel " Lochiel ", who quoted the freight for a return journey for the car. He paid the money, obtained a receipt and delivered the car to the respondents. It was shipped on the " Lochiel " but the vessel never reached West Loch Tarbert. She sank owing to negligent navigation by the respondents' servants, and the car was a total loss. The appellant sues for its value, agreed at £480.

The question is, what was the contract between the parties? The contract was an oral one. No document was signed or changed hands until the contract was completed. I agree with the unanimous view of the learned judges of the Court of Session[1] that the terms of the receipt which was made out by the purser and handed to Mr. McSporran after he paid the freight cannot be regarded as terms of the contract. So the case is not one of the familiar ticket cases where the question is whether conditions endorsed on or referred to in a ticket or other document handed to the consignor in making the contract are binding on the consignor. If conditions, not mentioned when this contract was made, are to be added to or regarded as part of this contract it must be for some reason different from those principles which are now well settled in ticket cases. If this oral contract stands unqualified there can be no doubt that the respondents are liable for the damage caused by the negligence of their servants.

The respondents' case is that their elaborate printed conditions form part of this contract. If they do, then admittedly they exclude liability in this case. I think that I can fairly summarise the evidence on this matter. The respondents exhibit copies of these conditions in their office, but neither the appellant nor his agent Mr. McSporran had read these notices, and I agree that they can play no part in the decision of this case. The respondents' practice was to require consignors to sign risk notes, which included these conditions, before accepting any goods for carriage, but on this occasion no risk note was signed. The respondents' clerkess, knowing that Mr. McSporran was bringing the car for shipment, made out a risk note for his signature, but when he arrived she was not there and he dealt with the purser of the " Lochiel ", who was in the office. He asked for a return passage for the car. The purser quoted a charge of some £6. He paid that sum and then the purser made out and gave him a receipt which he put in his pocket without looking at it. He then delivered the car. The purser forgot to ask him to sign the risk note. The Lord Ordinary believed the evidence of Mr. McSporran and the appellant. Mr. McSporran had consigned goods of various kinds on a number of previous occasions. He said

---

[1] 1962 S.C. 506. The freight invoice contained a printed statement, or heading, " Passengers, Passengers' luggage, Goods and Live Stock, are carried subject to the conditions specified on the company's sailing bills, notices and announcements ". By signing a " risk note " a consignor undertook to be bound by the respondents' conditions, which were printed on it.

that sometimes he had signed a note, sometimes he had not. On one occasion he had sent his own car. A risk note for that consignment was produced signed by him. He had never read the risk notes signed by him. He says— " I sort of just signed it at the time as a matter of form ". He admitted that he knew that he was signing in connexion with some conditions, but he did not know what they were. In particular, he did not know that he was agreeing to send the goods at owner's risk. The appellant had consigned goods on four previous occasions. On three of them he was acting on behalf of his employer. On the other occasion he had sent his own car. Each time he had signed a risk note. He also admitted that he knew that there were conditions, but said that he did not know what they were.

The respondents contend that, by reason of the knowledge thus gained by the appellant and his agent in these previous transactions, the appellant is bound by their conditions. But this case differs essentially from the ticket cases. There, the carrier in making the contract hands over a document containing or referring to conditions which he intends to be part of the contract. So if the consignor or passenger, when accepting the document, knows or ought as a reasonable man to know that that is the carrier's intention, he can hardly deny that the conditions are part of the contract, or claim, in the absence of special circumstances, to be in a better position than he would be if he had read the document. But here, in making the contract neither party referred to, or indeed had in mind, any additional terms, and the contract was complete and fully effective without any additional terms. If it could be said that when making the contract Mr. McSporran knew that the respondents always required a risk note to be signed and knew that the purser was simply forgetting to put it before him for signature, then it might be said that neither he nor his principal could take advantage of the error of the other party of which he was aware. But counsel frankly admitted that he could not put his case as high as that. The only other ground on which it would seem possible to import these conditions is that based on a course of dealing. If two parties have made a series of similar contracts each containing certain conditions, and then they make another without expressly referring to those conditions it may be that those conditions ought to be implied. If the officious bystander had asked them whether they had intended to leave out the conditions this time, both must, as honest men, have said " of course not ". But again the facts here will not support that ground. According to Mr. McSporran, there had been no consistent course of dealing; sometimes he was asked to sign and sometimes not. And, moreover, he did not know what the conditions were. This time he was offered an oral contract without any reference to conditions, and he accepted the offer in good faith.

The respondents also rely on the appellant's previous knowledge. I doubt whether it is possible to spell out a course of dealing in his case. In all but one of the previous cases he had been acting on behalf of his employer in sending a different kind of goods and he did not know that the respondents always sought to insist on excluding liability for their own negligence. So it cannot be said that, when he asked his agent to make a contract for him, he knew that this or, indeed, any other special term would be included in it. He left his agent a free hand to contract, and I see nothing to prevent him from taking advantage of the contract which his agent in fact made.

" The judicial task is not to discover the actual intentions of each party:

it is to decide what each was reasonably entitled to conclude from the attitude of the other."[1]

In this case I do not think that either party was reasonably bound or entitled to conclude from the attitude of the other as known to him that these conditions were intended by the other party to be part of this contract. I would therefore allow the appeal and restore the interlocutor of the Lord Ordinary.[2]

LORD HODSON: My Lords, the decision of the Second Division of the Inner House in favour of the respondents seems to me to involve an extension of the application of the doctrine of " course of dealing " which is not warranted by the facts of this case. Assuming in favour of the respondents that the experience of the appellant and his brother-in-law, who acted as his agent, would establish that on previous occasions the respondents' " risk note " embodying conditions absolving them from the consequences of negligence had been regularly signed, this does not establish that the legal situation was the same on October 8, 1960, when the appellant's car was shipped by his brother-in-law on his behalf without the risk note being signed. No question of fraud or mistake arises, and the only question is whether in some way the respondents can establish their immunity by incorporating in the contract of carriage the conditions which were present on earlier transactions but absent on the relevant occasion. The course of dealing on earlier occasions is often relevant in determining contractual relations, but does not assist when, as here, there was on the part of the respondents a departure from an earlier course in that they omitted to ask the appellant's agent to sign the document by which they would have obtained protection.

If the only question had been whether the appellant or his agent had notice of the conditions sought to be imposed, the observations of Baggallay, L.J., in *Parker* v. *South Eastern Ry. Co.*[3] would be material. That case, affirmed in *Hood* v. *Anchor Line (Henderson Brothers), Ltd.*[4], established that the appropriate questions for the jury in a ticket case were: (1) Did the passenger know that there was printing on the railway ticket? (2) Did he know that the ticket contained or referred to conditions? and (3) Did the railway company do what was reasonable in the way of notifying prospective passengers of the existence of conditions and where their terms might be considered? It was in this connexion that Baggallay, L.J., after stating the liability of the company in the conduct of their cloakroom business as bailees for reward in the absence of a special contract constituted by the delivery and acceptance of a ticket or otherwise, proceeded to say[3]:

> " The question then remains whether the plaintiffs were respectively aware, or ought to be treated as aware, of the intention of the company thus to modify the effect of the ordinary contract. Now as regards each of the plaintiffs, if at the time when he accepted the ticket, he, either by actual examination of it, or by reason of previous experience, or from any other cause, was aware of the terms or purport or effect of the endorsed conditions, it can hardly be doubted that he became bound by them."

These observations do not assist the respondents. No effort was made to get the risk note signed, or otherwise to make the conditions therein contained a term of the contract of carriage. In short, the respondents did not seek to impose any conditions. This is a vital distinction between this case and

---

[1] *Law of Contract* by William M. Gloag at p. 7.   [2] 1962 S.C. 506.
[3] (1877), 2 C.P.D. 416 at p. 425.
[4] [1918] A.C. 837; [1918–19] All E.R. Rep. 98.

Parker's case[1], and a decision in favour of the respondents would involve an extension and expansion of what was said by Baggallay, L.J.[2] which seems to me to be unsupported by authority and undesirable on principle.

The law as it stands appears hard on the holders of tickets who, unless they are exceptional persons, will not take pains to make an examination of a ticket offered to them to see if any conditions are imposed. It would be scarcely tolerable to take the further step of treating a contracting party as if he had signed and so bound himself by the terms of a document with conditions embodied in it, when, as here, he has done no such thing but may be supposed, having regard to his previous experience, to have been willing to sign what was put before him if he had been asked. The respondents seek to have the interlocutor appealed against affirmed on two other grounds both of which were rejected in the Scottish courts. First, they claim that the freight invoice, on which the receipt was placed acknowledging the payment of £6 5s., was a contract document containing a sufficient reference to the conditions and was accepted by the appellant's agent on his behalf and the appellant was therefore bound by them. In the second place, they claim that, by posting four copies of the conditions on the Port Askaig Pier and three copies on board their vessel " Lochiel ", they took sufficient steps to give notice of the conditions so as to bind the appellant. The receipt was handed over, as the Lord Justice-Clerk pointed out[3], after the contract was completed and cannot be treated as an offer. It played no part in the formation of the contract and there was no reason to suppose that it referred to conditions. On both these grounds I agree with the learned judges in the Scottish courts that the respondents failed to show that they did what was reasonably sufficient to bring to the notice of the appellant or his agent the conditions on which they found.

I would allow the appeal.

Thornton v. Shoe Lane Parking, Ltd.

[1971] 1 All E. R. 686

LORD DENNING, M.R.: In 1964 Mr. Thornton, the plaintiff, who was a free-lance trumpeter of the highest quality, had an engagement with the BBC at Farringdon Hall. He drove to the City in his motor car and went to park it at a multi-storey automatic car park. It had been open a few months. He had never gone there before. There was a notice on the outside headed " Shoe Lane Parking ". It gave the parking charges, 5s. for two hours, 7s. 6d. for three hours, and so forth; and at the bottom: " ALL CARS PARKED AT OWNERS RISK ". The plaintiff drove up to the entrance. There was not a man in attendance. There was a traffic light which showed red. As he drove in and got to the appropriate place, the traffic light turned green and a ticket was pushed out from the machine. The plaintiff took it. He drove on into the garage. The motor car was taken up by mechanical means to a floor above. The plaintiff left it there and went off to keep his appointment with the BBC. Three hours later he came back. He went to the office and paid the charge

---

[1] (1877), 2 C.P.D. 416.   [2] (1877), 2 C.P.D. at p. 425.
[3] 1962 S.C. at p. 514. The Lord Justice-Clerk (LORD GRANT) went on to say that, having regard to the nature of the document, it was not a document which the plaintiff's agent could reasonably have been expected to scan in order to ascertain what conditions, if any, applied to the contract.

for the time that the car was there. His car was brought down from the upper floor. He went to put his belongings into the boot of the car; but unfortunately there was an accident. The plaintiff was severely injured. The judge has found it was half his own fault, but half the fault of Shoe Lane Parking Ltd, the defendants. The judge awarded him £3,637 6s. 11d.

On this appeal the defendants do not contest the judge's findings about the accident. They acknowledge that they were at fault, but they claim that they are protected by some exempting conditions. They rely on the ticket which was issued to the plaintiff by the machine. They say that it was a contractual document and that it incorporated a condition which exempts them from liability to him. The ticket was headed " Shoe Lane Parking ". Just below there was a " box " in which was automatically recorded the time when the car went into the garage. There was a notice alongside: " Please present this ticket to cashier to claim your car." Just below the time, there was some small print in the left hand corner which said: " This ticket is issued subject to the conditions of issue as displayed on the premises." That is all.

The plaintiff says that he looked at the ticket to see the time on it, and put it in his pocket. He could see there was printing on the ticket, but he did not read it. He only read the time. He did not read the words which said that the ticket was issued subject to the conditions as displayed on the premises. If the plaintiff had read those words on the ticket and had looked round the premises to see where the conditions were displayed, he would have had to have driven his car on into the garage and walked round. Then he would have found, on a pillar opposite the ticket machine, a set of printed conditions in a panel. He would also have found, in the paying office (to be visited when coming back for the car) two more panels containing the printed conditions. If he had the time to read the conditions—it would take him a very considerable time—he would read this:

" Conditions

" The following are the conditions upon which alone motor vehicles are accepted for parking:—

" 1. The customer agrees to pay the charges of [the defendants] . . .

" 2. The Customer is deemed to be fully insured at all times against all risks (including, without prejudice to the generality of the foregoing, fire, damage and theft, whether due to the negligence of others or not) and the [defendants] shall not be responsible or liable for any loss or misdelivery of or damages of whatever kind to the Customer's motor vehicle, or any articles carried therein or thereon or of or to any accessories carried thereon or therein, or *injury to the Customer* or any other person *occurring when the Customer's motor vehicle is in the Parking Building howsoever that loss, misdelivery, damage or injury shall be caused* and it is agreed and understood that the Customer's motor vehicle is parked and permitted by the [defendants] to be parked in the Parking Building in accordance with this Licence entirely at the Customer's risk . . ."

There is a lot more. I have only read about one-tenth of the conditions. The important thing to notice is that the defendants seek by this condition to exempt themselves from liability, not only for damage to the car, but also for injury to the customer howsoever caused. The condition talks about insurance. It is well known that the customer is usually insured against damage to the car; but he is not insured against damage to himself. If the condition is incorporated into the contract of parking, it means that the plaintiff will be unable to recover any damages for his personal injuries which were caused by the negligence of the company.

We have been referred to the ticket cases of former times from *Parker* v. *South Eastern Rail Co*[1] to *McCutcheon* v. *David MacBrayne Ltd*[2]. They were concerned with railways, steamships and cloakrooms where booking clerks issued tickets to customers who took them away without reading them. In those cases the issue of the ticket was regarded as an *offer* by the company. If the customer took it and retained it without objection, his act was regarded as an *acceptance* of the offer: see *Watkins* v. *Rymill*[3] and *Thompson* v. *London Midland and Scottish Rail Co*[4]. These cases were based on the theory that the customer, on being handed the ticket, could refuse it and decline to enter into a contract on those terms. He could ask for his money back. That theory was, of course, a fiction. No customer in a thousand ever read the conditions. If he had stopped to do so, he would have missed the train or the boat.

None of those cases has any application to a ticket which is issued by an automatic machine. The customer pays his money and gets a ticket. He cannot refuse it. He cannot get his money back. He may protest to the machine, even swear at it; but it will remain unmoved. He is committed beyond recall. He was committed at the very moment when he put his money into the machine. The contract was concluded at that time. It can be translated into offer and acceptance in this way. The offer is made when the proprietor of the machine holds it out as being ready to receive the money. The acceptance takes place when the customer puts his money into the slot. The terms of the offer are contained in the notice placed on or near the machine stating what is offered for the money. The customer is bound by those terms as long as they are sufficiently brought to his notice beforehand, but not otherwise. He is not bound by the terms printed on the ticket if they differ from the notice, because the ticket comes too late. The contract has already been made: see *Olley* v. *Marlborough Court Ltd*[5]. The ticket is no more than a voucher or receipt for the money that has been paid (as in the deckchair case, *Chapelton* v. *Barry Urban District Council*[6]), on terms which have been offered and accepted before the ticket is issued. In the present case the offer was contained in the notice at the entrance giving the charges for garaging and saying " at owners risk ", i.e. at the risk of the owner so far as damage to the car was concerned. The offer was accepted when the plaintiff drove up to the entrance and, by the movement of his car, turned the light from red to green, and the ticket was thrust at him. The contract was then concluded, and it could not be altered by any words printed on the ticket itself. In particular, it could not be altered so as to exempt the company from liability for personal injury due to their negligence.

Assuming, however, that an automatic machine is a booking clerk in disguise, so that the old fashioned ticket cases still apply to it, we then have to go back to the three questions put by Mellish, L.J. in *Parker* v. *South Eastern Rail Co*[7], subject to this qualification: Mellish, L.J. used the word " conditions " in the plural, whereas it would be more apt to use the word " condition " in the singular, as indeed Mellish, L.J. himself did at the end of

---

[1] (1877), 2 C.P.D. 416; [1874–80] All E.R. Rep. 166.
[2] [1964] 1 All E.R. 430; [1964] 1 W.L.R. 125.
[3] (1883), 10 Q.B.D. 178 at p. 188.
[4] [1930] 1 K.B. 41 at p. 47, [1929] All E.R. Rep. 474 at p. 478.
[5] [1949] 1 K.B. 532; [1949] 1 All E.R. 127.
[6] [1940] 1 K.B. 532; [1940] 1 All E.R. 356.
[7] (1877), 2 C.P.D. at p. 423; [1874–80] All E.R. Rep. at p. 170.

his judgment[1]. After all, the only condition that matters for this purpose is the exempting condition. It is no use telling the customer that the ticket is issued subject to some " conditions " or other, without more; for he may reasonably regard " conditions " in general as merely regulatory, and not as taking away his rights, unless the exempting condition is drawn specifically to his attention. (Alternatively, if the plural " conditions " is used, it would be better prefaced with the word " exempting ", because the exempting conditions are the only conditions that matter for this purpose.) Telescoping the three questions, they come to this: the customer is bound by the exempting condition if he knows that the ticket is issued subject to it; or, if the company did what was reasonably sufficient to give him notice of it. Counsel for the defendants admitted here that the defendants did not do what was reasonably sufficient to give the plaintiff notice of the exempting condition. That admission was properly made. I do not pause to enquire whether the exempting condition is void for unreasonableness. All I say is that it is so wide and so destructive of rights that the court should not hold any man bound by it unless it is drawn to his attention in the most explicit way. It is an instance of what I had in mind in *J. Spurling, Ltd.* v. *Bradshaw*[2]. In order to give sufficient notice, it would need to be printed in red ink with a red hand pointing to it, or something equally startling.

However, although reasonable notice of it was not given, counsel for the defendants said that this case came within the second question propounded by Mellish, L.J. namely that the plaintiff " knew or believed that the writing contained conditions ". There was no finding to that effect. The burden was on the defendants to prove it, and they did not do so. Certainly there was no evidence that the plaintiff knew of this exempting condition. He is not, therefore, bound by it. Counsel for the defendants relied on a case in this court last year, *Mendelssohn* v. *Normand, Ltd.*[3] Mr. Mendelsshon parked his car in the Cumberland Garage at Marble Arch and was given a ticket which contained an exempting condition. There was no discussion as to whether the condition formed part of the contract. It was conceded that it did. That is shown by the report.[4] Yet the garage company were not entitled to rely on the exempting condition for the reasons there given. That case does not touch the present, where the whole question is whether the exempting condition formed part of the contract. I do not think it did. The plaintiff did not know of the condition, and the defendants did not do what was reasonably sufficient to give him notice of it.

I do not think the defendants can escape liability by reason of the exempting condition. I would, therefore, dismiss the appeal.

MEGAW, L.J. and SIR GORDON WILLMER agreed with LORD DENNING that the appeal should be dismissed. But MEGAW, L.J., at p. 690, preferred to " reserve a final view on the question at what precise moment of time the contract was concluded ".

---

[1] (1877), 2 C.P.D. at p. 424, [1874–80] All E.R. Rep. at p. 170.
[2] [1956] 2 All E.R. 121 at p. 125, [1956] 1 W.L.R. 461 at p. 466.
[3] [1970] 1 Q.B. 177; [1969] 2 All E.R. 1215.
[4] [1970] 1 Q.B. at p. 180.

FUNDAMENTAL BREACH

Suisse Atlantique Société d'Armement Maritime S.A. v. N.V. Rotterdamsche Kolen Centrale

Alexander v. Railway Executive

" There is a rule of construction that normally an exception or exclusion clause or similar provision in a contract shall be construed as not applying to a situation created by a fundamental breach of contract: " *U.G.S. Finance, Ltd.* v. *National Mortgage Bank of Greece and National Bank of Greece, S.A.,* [1964] 1 Lloyd's Rep. 446, per Pearson, L.J. at p. 453.

A rule of construction, as opposed to a rule of law, exists to give effect to the intention of the parties, as inferred from the terms and circumstances of the contract. To discover such intention two rules of construction have special relevance. (1) Any ambiguity must be read against the party responsible for it. (2) The contract must be read as a whole, and particular terms construed in the sense most consistent with its general purport.

Suisse Atlantique Société d'Armement Maritime S.A. v. N.V. Rotterdamsche Kolen Centrale.

[1966] 2 All E.R. 61

[The plaintiffs owned a ship which in December, 1956, they chartered to the defendants for the carriage of coal from the United States to Europe. The charter was to remain in force for two years' consecutive voyages. The defendants agreed to load and discharge cargoes at specified rates; and, if there was any delay, they were to pay a thousand dollars a day as demurrage. In September, 1957, the plaintiffs claimed that they were entitled to treat the contract as repudiated by the defendants' delays in loading and discharging cargoes. The defendants rejected this contention. In October, 1957, the parties agreed (without prejudice to their dispute) to continue with the contract. The defendants subsequently made eight round voyages. The plaintiffs then claimed all the money which they had lost through the delays. The defendants argued that the claim must be limited to the agreed demurrage for the actual days in question. The plaintiffs replied that the delays were such as to entitle them to treat the contract as repudiated: the demurrage clause therefore did not apply, and they could recover their full loss.

Mr. Justice Mocatta, the Court of Appeal and the House of Lords all held that the plaintiffs must fail. They had elected to affirm the contract, and the demurrage clause applied. But in the House of Lords the plaintiffs argued that the defendants had broken a fundamental obligation of the contract and that this breach prevented the defendants from relying on any " limiting term ". The House of Lords rejected this argument. (1) There was, on the facts, no fundamental breach. (2) The demurrage clause was not a " limiting term ", but a statement of agreed damages in the event of delay. But their Lordships felt that they should examine the issues of general contractual importance which the plaintiffs had raised.]

Lord Wilberforce. The appellants' main argument in law is formulated as follows: First, they say that a breach of contract which goes to the root of the contract or which conflicts with its main purpose is a deviation from, or a repudiation or fundamental breach of, such contract. Secondly, they contend that exceptions clauses do not apply to breaches which are deviations from, or repudiations or fundamental breaches of, the contract. These propositions contain in themselves implicitly or explicitly several distinct lines of argument. It is necessary to separate the strands before attempting to examine them. It is convenient first to segregate the reference to what is sometimes (and conveniently) described as the main purpose rule. This is a rule of construction, a classic statement of which is found in Lord Halsbury's speech in *Glynn* v. *Margetson*[1]: it can be summed up in his words:

> " Looking at the whole of the instrument, and seeing what one must regard
> . . . as its main purpose, one must reject words, indeed whole provisions, if
> they are inconsistent with what one assumes to be the main purpose of the
> contract."

The decision in that case was that printed words in a document intended to be used in a variety of contracts of affreightment between a variety of ports ought to be restricted so as to be consistent with the purpose of the particular charter-party which was for a voyage from Malaga to Liverpool. There is no difficulty as to this, and I shall consider in due course whether it has any application to the relevant clause (i.e., the demurrage clause) in the contract.

Next for consideration is the argument based on " fundamental breach " or, which is presumably the same thing, a breach going " to the root of the contract ". These expressions are used in the cases to denote two quite different things, namely, (i) a performance totally different from that which the contract contemplates, (ii) a breach of contract more serious than one which would entitle the other party merely to damages and which (at least) would entitle him to refuse performance or further performance under the contract. Both of these situations have long been familiar in the English law of contract; and it will have to be considered whether the conception of " fundamental breach " extends beyond them. What is certain is that to use the expression without distinguishing to which of these, or to what other, situations it refers is to invite confusion. The importance of the difference between these meanings lies in this, that they relate to two separate questions which may arise in relation to any contract. These are (as to (i)) whether an " exceptions " clause contained in the contract applies as regards a particular breach and (as to (ii)) whether one party is entitled to elect to refuse further performance.

The appellants, in their submission that exceptions clauses do not apply to " fundamental breaches " or " repudiations ", confuse these two questions. There is in fact no necessary coincidence between the two kinds of (so-called fundamental) breach. For, though it may be true generally, if the contract contains a wide exceptions clause, that a breach sufficiently serious to take the case outside that clause will also give the other party the right to refuse further performance, it is not the case, necessarily, that a breach of the latter character has the former consequence. An act which, apart from the exceptions clause, might be a breach sufficiently serious to justify refusal of further performance, may be reduced in effect, or made not a breach at all, by the terms of the clause. The present case is concerned with the application of what may be said (with what justice will be later considered) to be an exceptions clause to a possible type of " fundamental breach ". I treat the words " exceptions clause " as covering broadly such clauses in a contract as profess to exclude or limit, either quantitatively or as to the time within which action

---

[1] [1893] A.C. 351 at p. 357; [1891–4] All E. R. Rep. at p. 696.

must be taken, the right of the injured party to bring an action for damages. Such a clause must, *ex hypothesi*, reflect the contemplation of the parties that a breach of contract, or what apart from the clause would be a breach of contract, may be committed, otherwise the clause would not be there; but the question remains open in any case whether there is a limit to the type of breach which they have in mind. One may safely say that the parties cannot, in a contract, have contemplated that the clause should have so wide an ambit as in effect to deprive one party's stipulations of all contractual force; to do so would be to reduce the contract to a mere declaration of intent. To this extent it may be correct to say that there is a rule of law against the application of an exceptions clause to a particular type of breach. But short of this it must be a question of contractual intention whether a particular breach is covered or not, and the courts are entitled to insist, as they do, that the more radical the breach the clearer must the language be if it is to be covered. As Lord Parmoor said in *Cunard S.S. Co., Ltd.* v. *Buerger*[1] in relation to exception clauses:

" [they] do not apply when such loss or damage has occurred outside the route or voyage contemplated by the parties . . . unless the intention that such limitations should apply is expressed in clear and unambiguous language."

And in *The Cap Palos*[2] Atkin, L.J., similarly said:

" I am far from saying that a contractor may not make a valid contract that he is not to be liable for any failure to perform his contract, including even wilful default; but he must use very clear words to express that purpose . . ."

In application to more radical breaches of contract, the courts have sometimes stated the principle as being that a " total breach of the contract " disentitles a party to rely on exceptions clauses. This formulation has its use so long as one understands it to mean that the clause cannot be taken to refer to such a breach, but it is not a universal solvent; for it leaves to be decided what is meant by a " total " breach for this purpose—a departure from the contract? but how great a departure? a delivery of something or a performance different from that promised? but how different? No formula will solve this type of question, and one must look individually at the nature of the contract, the character of the breach and its effect on future performance and expectation and make a judicial estimation of the final result.

A few illustrations from three groups of decided cases may explain how the courts have dealt with this problem:

(i) *Supply of a different article.* As long ago as 1838, where the contract provided for the supply of peas, but beans were delivered, Lord Abinger, C.B., explained the difference between this case and a breach of " condition ". " The contract is to sell peas, and if he sends him anything else in their stead, it is a non-performance of it ": *Chanter* v. *Hopkins*[3]. This was followed (after the Sale of Goods Act, 1893) in *Pinnock Bros.* v. *Lewis & Peat, Ltd.*[4] (copra cake), and Pearson, L.J., accepted the principle, while modernising the illustration (chalk for cheese) in *U.G.S. Finance, Ltd.* v. *National Mortgage Bank of Greece and National Bank of Greece, S.A.*[5]. Since the contracting parties could hardly have been supposed to contemplate such a mis-performance, or to have provided against it without destroying the whole

---

[1] [1927] A.C. at p. 13; [1926] All E.R. Rep. at p. 108.
[2] [1921] P. at pp. 471, 472; [1921] All E.R. Rep. at p. 254.
[3] (1838), 4 M. & W. 339 at p. 404. The reference to peas and beans was a hypothesis assumed by Lord Abinger to illustrate his point.   [4] [1923] 1 K.B. 690.
[5] [1964] 1 Lloyd's Rep. 446.

contractual substratum, there is no difficulty here in holding exception clauses to be inapplicable.

(ii) *Hire-purchase cases.* In several recent decisions, the courts have been able to hold wide exception clauses inapplicable by finding that what was delivered was totally different from that promised. Such are *Karsales (Harrow), Ltd.* v. *Wallis*[1] and *Charterhouse Credit Co., Ltd.* v. *Tolly*[2]. These cases, and others, follow the judgment of Devlin, J., in *Smeaton Hanscomb & Co., Ltd.* v. *Sassoon I. Setty, Son & Co. (No. 1)*[3], where he expressed the test as being whether there was a performance totally different from that contemplated by the contract. In some of these cases difficult questions of fact have arisen in deciding whether there is the total difference, or merely a serious breach of contract, as can be seen by comparing the *Karsales* case[1] with *Astley Industrial Trust, Ltd.* v. *Grimley*[4], and some doubt may be felt whether the right result on the facts was reached in *Charterhouse Credit Co., Ltd.* v. *Tolly*[5]; but the principle is well in line with that of the cases mentioned under (i).

(iii) *Marine cases relating to deviation.* There is a long line of authority, the commencement of which is usually taken from the judgment of Tindal, C.J., in *Davis* v. *Garrett*[6], which shows that a shipowner, who deviates from an agreed voyage, steps out of the contract, so that clauses in the contract (such as exceptions or limitation clauses) which are designed to apply to the contracted voyage are held to have no application to the deviating voyage. The basis for the rule was explained in *Stag Line, Ltd.* v. *Foscolo Mango and Co., Ltd.*[7] by Lord Russell of Killowen in these terms:

> " It was well settled before the Act [of 1924] that an unjustifiable deviation deprived a ship of the protection of exceptions. They only applied to the contract voyage."

In *The Cap Palos*[8] Atkin, L.J., had applied this principle to contracts generally, adopting for this purpose the formulation of Scrutton, L.J., in *Gibaud* v. *Great Eastern Rail. Co.*[9]:

> " It is a fairly well-known principle—and *Lilley* v. *Doubleday*[10] is perhaps the best illustration of it—that if you undertake to do a thing in a certain way, or to keep a thing in a certain place with certain conditions protecting it, and you have broken the contract by not doing the thing contracted for in the way contracted for or not keeping the article in the place in which you have contracted to keep it, you cannot rely on the conditions which were only intended to protect you if you carried out the contract in the way in which you had contracted to do it."

The words " intended to protect you " show quite clearly that the rule is based on contractual intention.

The conception, therefore, of " fundamental breach " as one which, through ascertainment of the parties' contractual intention, falls outside an exceptions clause is well recognised and comprehensible. Is there any need, or authority, in relation to exceptions clauses, for extension of it beyond this? In my opinion, there is not. The principle that the contractual intention is to be ascertained—not just grammatically from words used, but

[1] [1956] 2 All E. R.866.   [2] [1963] 2 Q.B. 683; [1963] 2 All E.R. 432.
[3] [1953] 2 All E.R. 1471.   [4] [1963] 2 All E.R. 33.
[5] [1963] 2 Q.B. 683; [1963] 2 All E.R. 432.
[6] (1830), 6 Bing. 716.
[7] [1932] A.C. 328 at p. 347; [1931] All E.R. Rep. 666 at p. 675.
[8] [1921] P. at p. 471; [1921] All E.R. Rep. at p. 254.
[9] [1921] 2 K.B. at p. 435; [1921] All E.R. Rep. at p. 39.
[10] (1881), 7 Q.B.D. 510.

by consideration of those words in relation to commercial purpose (or other purpose according to the type of contract)—is surely flexible enough, and, though it may be the case that adhesion contracts give rise to particular difficulties in ascertaining or attributing a contractual intent, which may require a special solution, those difficulties need not be imported into the general law of contract nor be permitted to deform it.

The only new category of " fundamental breach " which in this context I understand to have been suggested is one of " deliberate " breaches. This most clearly appears in the Privy Council case of *Sze Hai Tong Bank, Ltd.* v. *Rambler Cycle Co., Ltd.*[1]. The decision itself presents no difficulty and seems to have been based on construction; it was that an exceptions clause referring to " discharge " of the goods did not apply to a discharge wholly outside the contract, a case I would have thought well within the principle of the " deviation " cases. But the appellants rely on one passage in the judgment of the Board which seems to suggest that " deliberate " breaches may, of themselves, form a separate category, citing three previous English decisions. Two of them—*Alexander* v. *Railway Executive*[2] and *Karsales (Harrow), Ltd.* v. *Wallis*[3] (on which I have already commented)—are straightforward cases of " total departure " from what is contractually contemplated and present no difficulty. The third, *Bontex Knitting Works, Ltd.* v. *St. John's Garage*[4] does not appear to be based on the deliberate character of the breach. The decision may be justified on the basis that there was a breach of contract equivalent to a deviation, but if it goes beyond this I would regard it as of doubtful validity. The " deliberate " character of a breach cannot, in my opinion, of itself give to a breach of contract a " fundamental " character, in either sense of that word. Some deliberate breaches there may be of a minor character which can appropriately be sanctioned by damages; some may be, on construction, within an exceptions clause (for example, a deliberate delay for one day in loading). This is not to say that " deliberation " may not be a relevant factor; depending on what the party in breach " deliberately " intended to do, it may be possible to say that the parties never contemplated that such a breach would be excused or limited; and a deliberate breach may give rise to a right for the innocent party to refuse further performance because it indicates the other party's attitude towards future performance. All these arguments fit without difficulty into the general principle; to create a special rule for deliberate acts is unnecessary and may lead astray.

I now come to the facts of the present case. First, it is necessary to decide what is the legal nature of the demurrage clause; is it a clause by which damages for breach of the contract are agreed in advance, a liquidated damages clause as such provisions are commonly called, or is it, as the appellants submit, a clause limiting damages?[5] If it is the latter, the appellants are evidently a step nearer the point when they can invoke cases in which clauses of exception, or exemption, do not apply to particular breaches of contract. The appellants' strongest argument here rests on the discrepancy which they assert to exist between the demurrage rate of $1000 per diem and the freight rate for which the charterparty provides. The extent of the discrepancy is said to be shown by the difference between the appellants' claim for lost freight (which is of the order of $900,000 on one calculation and

---

[1] [1959] A.C. 576; [1959] 3 All E.R. 182.
[2] [1951] 2 K.B. 882; [1951] 2 All E.R. 442.   [3] [1956] 2 All E.R. 866.
[4] [1944] 1 All E.R. 381, n.; [1943] 2 All E.R. 690; C.A.
[5] On liquidated damages see *infra*, p. 481.

$600,000 on another) and the amount which they would receive under the demurrage provision, which is approximately $150,000. So, the argument runs, the $1000 per diem cannot be a pre-estimate of damage; it must be a limit in the respondents' favour. I am unable to accept this. Leaving aside that figures quoted for lost freight represent merely the appellants' claim, it must be borne in mind that the $1000 a day figure has to cover a number of possible events. There might have been delay for one day or a few days beyond the laytime, in which case the appellants might, and probably would, lose nothing in the way of freight and only suffer through increased over-heads in port. Even if a case were to arise where freight was lost over a period of two years, circumstances might well change which would affect adversely the appellants' anticipated rate of profit. So I am far from satisfied that any such discrepancy has been shown between the agreed figure and reality as requires the conclusion that the clause is not what on its face it purports to be—particularly when one bears in mind that each side derives an advantage from having the figure fixed and so being assured of payment without the expense and difficulty of proof.

The form of the clause is, of course, not decisive, nor is there any rule of law which requires that demurrage clauses should be construed as clauses of liquidated damages; but it is the fact that the clause is expressed as one agreeing a figure, and not as imposing a limit; and, as a matter of commercial opinion and practice, demurrage clauses are normally regarded as liquidated damage clauses. (This has the authority of Scrutton on Charterparties, 10th and following editions and see *Chandris* v. *Isbrandtsen Moller Co., Inc.*[1], per Devlin, J.)

The clause being, then, one which fixes, by mutual agreement, the amount of damages to be paid to the owners of the vessel if " longer detained " than is permitted by the contract, is there any reason why it should not apply in the present case in either of the assumed alternatives, i.e., either that the aggregated delays add up to a " frustrating " breach of contract, or that the delays were " deliberate " in the special sense? In answering these questions, it is necessary to have in mind what happened. It appears that there was an initial dispute between the appellants and the respondents in which the appellants claimed that they were entitled to treat the respondents as having repudiated the charterparty. This dispute was resolved by an agreement on October 8, 1957, under which the respondents agreed to pay an agreed sum as demurrage, leaving it to arbitration to decide whether the appellants' claim was correct and, if so, what damages they should recover. It was further agreed that the charterparty should be performed for the remainder of the agreed two-year period. The manner in which it was performed is set out in a schedule to the Consultative Case. There were eight voyages in all, the last terminating on March 7, 1959, three days before the termination date. It is as regards these eight voyages that it is claimed that the delays in question occurred. During the whole of the period, although the periods spent in port on either side of the Atlantic (in fact at Rotterdam and, in every case but the first, Newport) must have been known to the appellants, who must also have been in a position to ascertain the availability of cargo and of loading and discharging facilities, the appellants took no steps which would indicate that they regarded the charterparty as repudiated; they did not sail their vessel away but allowed it to continue with further voyages and took demurrage at

---

[1] [1951] 1 K.B. at p. 249; [1950] 1 All E.R. at p. 775.

the agreed rate for the delays. So there is no question here of any termination of the contract having taken place. Is there, then, any basis on which
the appellants can escape from their bargain as regards detention of the vessel?
In my opinion there is not. The arbitrators can (on the assumptions required)
only find that the breach of contract falls within one, or other, or both of the
two stated categories, namely, that they " frustrate the commercial purpose
of the charterparty ", or that the delays were " deliberate " (in the special
sense). In either case, why should not the agreed clause operate? Or what
reason is there for limiting its application to such delays as fall short of such
as " frustrate the commercial purpose " or such as are not " deliberate "? I
can see no such reason for limiting a plain contractual provision, nor is there
here any such conflict between the demurrage clause and the main purpose
of the contract as to bring into play the doctrine of *Glynn* v. *Margetson*[1]. On
a consideration of the nature of this clause, together with the events which
took place, and in particular the fact that the appellants did not during its
currency put an end to the contract, I reach the conclusion that the appellants
are clearly bound by it and can recover no more than the appropriate amount
of demurrage.

I find support for this conclusion in two decisions of the Court of Appeal.
In *Inverkip S.S. Co., Ltd.* v. *Bunge & Co.*[2], there was a detention of the ship
beyond (as was held) a reasonable time for keeping it on demurrage. The
demurrage clause was in a similar form to that in the present case: " If
detained longer than five days ", and was held to be applicable to the whole
period of delay. The Court of Appeal did not decide the question whether
the delay was such as to amount to a " repudiatory breach ", so that the
master could have sailed away, but the implication at least of the judgment of
Warrington, L.J., is that the same result would have followed if this had been
so. Then in *Ethel Radcliffe S.S. Co.* v. *Barnett*[3], there was a deliberate
detention. The arbitrators' actual finding (which it is relevant to compare
with the possible finding here) was that " the respondents neglected and
refused to give such orders until August 29, 1924, and did so deliberately as
it suited their business arrangements to keep the steamer at St. Vincent ".
It was argued that the charterer had repudiated the contract and that the
demurrage clause did not cover wilful detention, but the Court of Appeal
held to the contrary. Counsel for the appellants submitted that these cases
were wrongly decided, but they seem to me to be entirely in accordance with
principle, and I respectfully agree with them.

On the whole case, I would dismiss the appeal.

VISCOUNT DILHORNE, LORD REID, LORD HODSON and LORD UPJOHN
also delivered judgments dismissing the plaintiffs' appeal.

Alexander v. Railway Executive

[1951] 2 All E.R. 442

ACTION for damages for breach of contract. On August 22, 1948, the
plaintiff, in company with one Colmar and others, took some trunks and other
baggage belonging to the plaintiff to Launceston station. Having, with
Colmar's help, repacked some of the trunks, the plaintiff, who had been

---

[1] [1893] A.C. 351; [1891–94] All E.R. Rep. 693. See *supra*, p. 98.
[2] [1917] 2 K.B. 193.   [3] (1926), 24 Lloyd L.R. 277.

engaged locally in a theatrical performance with Colmar, deposited the baggage at the station, and, in return for the due payment of the booking charges, he received cloak-room tickets in respect of it. Most of the trunks and cases were locked or roped. On September 2, 1948, when the parcels clerk, one Wakeford, came on duty, he found Colmar inside the parcels office with one of the trunks opened. Wakeford (who had not originally accepted the deposit) was informed by another member of the station staff that Colmar was one of those who had packed the baggage, and Colmar persuaded Wakeford to let him remove various articles on his signing a list of them. On September 25, 1948, after Colmar had alleged that the plaintiff had sent the tickets to him, Colmar, or to the station, but that they must have been lost in the post, Wakeford again permitted Colmar to remove various articles. Colmar paid the excess charges in respect of the baggage, and signed a form of indemnity. He then re-deposited the baggage and received new tickets in respect of it. On October 19, 1948, Colmar wrote from Liverpool enclosing the tickets and asking that the baggage be sent to Rochdale railway station where he would collect it and pay the charges. The baggage was sent as asked, and Colmar disposed of a large proportion of it. He was later prosecuted and pleaded Guilty to a charge of larceny.

Laski, K.C., and *Lloyd-Davies* for the plaintiff.
Berryman, K.C., and *W. G. Wingate* for the defendants.

DEVLIN, J., stated the facts and continued: The question which I now have to determine is whether there is any liability in the defendants. *Prima facie*, they are bailees of the goods, and, *prima facie*, the liability of a bailee is to restore the goods to the bailor in the same condition as they were deposited, and that the defendants have failed to do. They base their defence on two conditions which they said formed part of the contract of bailment and excused them from liability. These conditions were contained in very small print on the cloak-room tickets and were also contained on a large notice which was exhibited in the waiting room and in the parcels office.

The defendants rely, first, on condition No. 2 (*a*), which provides:

> " The company shall not be liable for loss, misdelivery or detention of, or damage to—Any article or property, which separately or in aggregate exceed the value of £5, unless at the time of deposit the true value and nature thereof shall have been declared by the depositor, and 1*d*. per £ sterling of the declared value paid for each day, or part of a day, in addition to the ordinary cloak-room charges . . . "

It is not disputed that these articles exceeded the value of £5. I find that their true value was never declared and the 1*d*. per £ sterling was not paid. Accordingly, the defendants say that they are not liable for loss, misdelivery or detention, and claim that what happened was a loss or misdelivery. Secondly, the defendants rely on condition No. 3, which provides:

> " The company shall be entitled to withhold the articles or property deposited except on production of the ticket issued in respect thereof. The company may deliver such articles or property to—(*a*) any person producing the ticket, or (*b*) any person, who fails to produce the ticket, upon such evidence of the loss of the ticket, and of ownership or authority to receive the articles or property, as the company's servants may consider satisfactory, in which case the company's form of indemnity must be signed by the person to whom the articles or property are delivered. The delivery of the articles or property shall acquit the company from all further claims in respect thereof."

Under this clause the defendants contend that they delivered the articles to Colmar, as a person who failed to produce the ticket, on evidence of the loss of the ticket and of ownership and authority which was satisfactory to Mr. Wakeford who was concerned with the matter, and, accordingly, the delivery to Colmar acquits the defendants from all further claims in respect thereof.

[His Lordship rejected arguments by the plaintiff that there was a special contract made between himself and the defendants excluding the conditions on which the defendants relied, and that the conditions were not reasonably brought to his notice, and continued:] The next argument which the plaintiff puts forward is that there was a breach of the terms of the bailment on Sept. 2, 1948, which disentitled the defendants from relying thereafter on the exceptions in the contract, and, indeed, put an end to the contract of bailment. In the statement of claim it is alleged that the defendants in breach of the agreement

> " on or about Sept. 1, 1948, allowed one William George Colmar without the knowledge or authority of the plaintiff and without any possible right in the said Colmar so to do to enter the said parcels office, break open the said packages, extract articles therefrom, and finally remove from the said parcels office and take into his possession the said articles and one of the said packages."

That has been made out by the evidence in relation to five of the articles that were taken away on Sept. 2. In answer to the plea of the conditions, it is pleaded:

> " The plaintiff will contend that the defendants can rely upon the said conditions provided that and so long as the defendants themselves are not in breach of the said conditions . . . The defendants are in breach of the said conditions in that they wrongfully and in breach of condition No. 4 allowed the said Colmar to have access in the manner set forth in . . . the statement of claim and the particulars furnished thereunder to the said six packages."

Condition No. 4 provides: " Depositors are not permitted access to any article deposited." The breach of that condition is a breach of the contract, so the plaintiff alleges, and it is a fundamental breach which goes to the root of the matter and determines the bailment. This sort of point has been considered in a number of cases which, themselves on rather different lines, are comprehended within the same principle. The well-known case of *Lilley* v. *Doubleday*[1] deals with bailments and with exceptions applying or not applying when the articles are moved to an unauthorised place. Cases such as *Hain S.S. Co., Ltd.* v. *Tate and Lyle, Ltd.*[2] deal with fundamental breaches of a contract of affreightment when there has been a deviation from the contract voyage and the effect thereof on the exceptions contained in the contract of affreightment. Counsel for the plaintiff relied on the recent case of *North Central Wagon and Finance Co., Ltd.* v. *Graham*[3]. Counsel referred to the following passage in the judgment of Cohen, L. J.[4]:

> " I must further point out that [the hirer], in instructing the defendant to sell, and in selling, the car, committed a breach of the contract which goes to the root of it. In those circumstances, a passage in *Halsbury*, Hailsham ed., vol. 1, p. 736, para. 1211, seems in point. It says: ' The act of the bailee in doing something inconsistent with the terms of the contract terminates the bailment, causing the possessory title to revert to the bailor, and entitling him to maintain an action of trover.' That view is stated in somewhat similar language in *Pollock and Wright on Possession in the Common Law*, p. 132, where it is said: ' Any act or disposition which is wholly repugnant to or as it were an absolute disclaimer of the holding as bailee re-vests the bailor's right to possession, and therefore also his immediate right to maintain trover or detinue even where the bailment is for a term or is otherwise not revocable at will, and so

---

[1] (1881), 7 Q. B. D. 510.
[2] [1936] 2 All E.R. 597.
[3] [1950] 1 All E. R. 780.
[4] *Ibid.*, at 784.

a fortiori in a bailment determinable at will.' The authority cited for both those passages is *Fenn* v. *Bittleston*[1], the relevant passage occurring in the judgment of Parke, B.[2]"

The learned lord justice goes on to say that those passages are a correct statement of the law. Substantially the same thing was stated by Asquith, L.J., earlier where he said[3] in effect, that as a general principle of law it was right to say that a bailee who comports himself in a manner utterly repugnant to the terms of the bailment terminates the bailment and thereupon the right to possession re-vests in the bailor.

These principles are clearly laid down. The difficulty always is to see how they apply to the facts of the case. I must first ask myself whether there was a breach of contract on Sept. 2, 1948; secondly, whether it was a breach of a fundamental term[4]; and, thirdly, what are its consequences in law. That there has been a breach of contract is, I think, hardly denied. There is obviously a duty on a bailee to take care of the goods, and that means to keep them safe from interference by third parties. Accordingly, quite apart from the delivery of the five articles, when the defendants' servants allowed Colmar to enter the parcels room and to open at least one of the trunks and have access to the articles there, they were breaking what was an essential term of the bailment and one that was plainly implied in the contract between these parties. Whether when the five articles were taken away there was a misdelivery which could come within one of the exceptions I do not think I need for this purpose determine, because I think that before the five articles were taken away, when access was allowed, there was a breach of the contract which the defendants are unable to justify, and which they do not, I think, seek to justify, by reference to any one of the conditions and terms in the contract which protected them.

Was that, then, a fundamental breach of contract? I think, on consideration, that it was. There can be no doubt that the duty to take care is an essential part of the duty of a bailee, and the importance that should be attached to the exclusion of unauthorised persons from access to articles which are in a cloak-room can hardly be over-emphasised. The view that the defendants themselves take is shown by the fact that they specifically provide in their contract that not even the depositor himself is to be entitled to have access to the articles, and still more must it, therefore, be that no third person should be entitled to have access thereto. Furthermore, to permit the breaking open of locked articles appears to me to come within the character of a fundamental breach. The evidence is not entirely clear on that point, but I think, on the whole, that I ought to draw the inference that on Sept. 2 the probability is that one of the locked articles was broken into. In *Bontex Knitting Works, Ltd.* v. *St. John's Garage*[5] it was held that the leaving of a delivery van untended by the driver was a fundamental breach of contract which disentitled the bailees of the goods in the van from relying on the exceptions in the contract. If that be so, then it is certainly a much greater breach of contract to allow access by unauthorised persons to articles which are deposited in a cloak-room. On that view, therefore,

---

[1] (1851), 7 Exch. 152.   [2] *Ibid.* at 159.   [3] [1950] 1 All E. R. 780 at p. 782.
[4] DEVLIN, J. seems, both here and on p. 107, to have used the expressions " breach of a fundamental term and " fundamental breach of contract" as synonyms. In view of the judgments in the case of the *Suisse Atlantique* (*supra*, p. 97) the second of these expressions —"fundamental breach of contract "—seems preferable.
[5] [1943] 2 All E. R. 690.

counsel for the plaintiff contends that, in accordance with the passage which I have cited from *North Central Wagon & Finance Co., Ltd.* v. *Graham*[1], the bailment was brought to an end. The result of that would be, of course, that the defendants could not thereafter rely in relation to the other incidents when they parted with the main bulk of the goods, apart from the articles already removed, on the terms and conditions of the contract which were inserted for their protection.

The matter may, perhaps, be put in another way, quite apart from the law of bailment. The ordinary law of contract, as it is discussed in *Hain S.S. Co., Ltd.* v. *Tate and Lyle, Ltd.*[2] in the House of Lords, involves that where there has been a breach of a fundamental term of the contract which gives the other party the right to rescind the contract, then, unless and until with full knowledge of all the facts the other party elects to affirm and not to rescind, the special terms of the contract go and cannot be relied on by the defaulting party. There is no question that the plaintiff ever knew of the circumstances in this case which entitled him to rescind or that he ever elected to affirm the contract.

I think, therefore, that this point succeeds and provides a good answer to the defendants' reliance on the conditions and that this defence fails. I think, however, that I ought also to examine the conditions which have been relied on, partly because I desire to sustain the conclusion which I have already expressed by the further conclusion that, even if the conditions were applicable, they would not, in the circumstances of this case, assist the defendants, and partly because those further conditions involve findings of fact which it is necessary that I should make in case the view which I have expressed is wrong in law.

I will take, first of all, condition No. 3, because it is the one which is obviously designed to deal with this sort of situation. Counsel for the defendants concedes that, although it is not expressly so stated in the condition, there must be reasonable grounds for the satisfaction of the defendants. The condition reads " such evidence . . . as the company's servants may consider satisfactory." Counsel concedes that that must mean " may reasonably consider satisfactory " and that there must be reasonable grounds for the decision of Mr. Wakeford, who was the official responsible in this case. It has been contended on the part of the plaintiff that there were no such reasonable grounds. [His Lordship considered the evidence and continued:] I have come to the conclusion that there were no reasonable grounds and no evidence which should have satisfied Mr. Wakeford, first, that the tickets had been lost, and, secondly, that Colmar had authority to receive the goods.

Counsel for the defendants, however, says that, apart from the question of the applicability of condition No. 3, there was a loss or misdelivery under condition No. 2. I do not think it is contended that there was any loss except in the sense that there was a misdelivery. Therefore, the question which arises is whether in the circumstances of this case a delivery to Colmar can rightly be regarded as a misdelivery within the meaning of that word as it is used in condition No. 2. No doubt, if " misdelivery " means any delivery to the wrong person, even a deliberate delivery to the wrong person, then the case is covered, and it may well be true to say that in many cases that is the right meaning of the word "misdelivery". It appears to be the

---

[1] [1950] 1 All E. R. 780.   [2] [1936] 2 All E. R. 597.

dictionary meaning. There is no authority that directly bears on the point.
Counsel has cited several cases to me, but I do not think it is necessary that
I should review them, because they do not really deal with the sort of point
which I have to consider. The alternative argument is that " misdelivery "
in its natural and ordinary meaning conveys to the ordinary man that there has
been some mistake or inadvertence. If, for example, there are two conflicting
claims between A. and B. and the bailee who holds the goods weighs them
carefully up and decides, on the whole, that he ought to deliver to A., and
decides wrongly, I doubt that in the ordinary sense of the word he would be
said to have misdelivered to A, although he has wrongly delivered. When,
for example, Mr. Wakeford in this case allowed Colmar to abstract the five
articles on Sept. 2, he, Wakeford, knowing quite well that it was in breach
of the regulations, but being moved to do so by the rather pitiful tale which
Colmar told him, was he misdelivering them to A ? If, taking a third
example, he had taken all the articles out of all the trunks and distributed
them to anybody who came to ask for them, could it be said, in the ordinary
use of language, that he was misdelivering ? I am disposed to think that
while in certain contexts the word " misdelivery " may bear the wider meaning, in its more natural and popular meaning it is restricted to a wrong
delivery involving some form of mistake or inadvertence, and that it is
intended to cover the sort of situation where a package is delivered to the
wrong person or address by error or inadvertence, or where the wrong
article is handed out over a counter or in a cloak-room. No principle is
more firmly settled than that when one is construing exceptions to the general
liability of a carrier or a bailee, those exceptions are to be construed strictly,
and, if a word is capable of bearing two meanings, it is the narrower meaning
which ought to be given to it. I think that where " misdelivery " is used
in an exception designed to protect a bailee, it does not cover more, and would
not be regarded by the ordinary man who read such conditions as covering
more, than what I might call accidental misdelivery by mistake or error;
and that, if a bailee in such circumstances wants to protect himself against
every sort of wrongful delivery, however deliberately made, he must use
clear and express terms to that end. Accordingly, I should hold that that
condition, if it applied, would not protect the defendants in this case. For
these reasons, the plaintiff's claim succeeds on liability, and there must be an
inquiry into the amount of the damage which he has sustained.

Judgment for the plaintiff.

IMPLIED TERMS

THE MOORCOCK

GARDNER v. COUTTS & CO.

The Court may supply a term in a contract if to do so is necessary in order
to give " business efficacy " to the contract. Such an implication is based
upon the presumed and common intention of the parties and is designed to
repair their oversight.

But the Court will intervene in this way only if the oversight is obvious
and if an obligation, clearly intended as such, must fail to take effect unless
the term is supplied.   " I do not think that the court will read a term into a
contract unless, considering the matter from the point of view of business
efficacy, it is clear beyond a peradventure that both parties intended a given

term to operate, although they did not include it in so many words" (*per* Jenkins, L.J., in *Sethia* (*K.C.*) (1944), *Ltd.* v. *Partabmull Rameshwar* [1950] 1 All E.R. 51, 59).

The Moorcock

(1889), 14 P.D. 64

APPEAL by the defendants from a judgment of Butt, J.[1], by which they were held liable for the damage sustained by the plaintiff's vessel whilst lying at their jetty.

The facts, which are fully set out in the report in the Court below[1], were shortly as follows :

The appellants were wharfingers possessed of a wharf abutting on, and a jetty extending into, the River Thames. The respondent was the owner of the steamship *Moorcock*.

In November, 1887, it was agreed between the appellants and the respondent that the vessel should be discharged and loaded at the wharf, and for that purpose should be moored alongside the jetty where she would take the ground at low water.

No charge was made in respect of the vessel being moored alongside, or lying at, the jetty, but the shipowner paid for the use of the cranes in discharging the cargo, and rates were payable to the appellants on all goods landed, shipped, or stored.

Whilst the *Moorcock* was lying moored at the extremity of the jetty discharging her cargo, the tide ebbed, and when she ceased to be water-borne, she sustained damage, owing to the centre of the vessel settling on a ridge of hard ground beneath the mud.

Butt, J., came to the conclusion that there was no warranty by the wharfinger that the place was safe for the vessel to lie in, and that the evidence negatived any express representation by him that the place was suitable for the vessel; but the learned judge held that as the use of the wharfingers' premises by the owner of the *Moorcock* required that the vessel should take the ground when moored alongside the jetty, there was an implied representation by the wharfinger that he had taken reasonable care to ascertain that the bottom of the river at the jetty was in such a condition as not to endanger the vessel.

BOWEN, L.J. The question which arises here is whether, when a contract is made to let the use of this jetty to a ship which can only use it, as is known by both parties, by taking the ground, there is any implied warranty on the part of the owners of the jetty, and if so, what is the extent of the warranty. Now, an implied warranty, or, as it is called, a covenant in law, as distinguished from an express contract or express warranty, really is in all cases founded on the presumed intention of the parties, and upon reason. The implication which the law draws from what must obviously have been the intention of the parties, the law draws with the object of giving efficacy to the transaction and preventing such a failure of consideration as cannot have been within the contemplation of either side ; and I believe if one were to take all the cases, and they are many, of implied warranties or covenants in law, it will be found that in all of them the law is raising an implication from the presumed intention of the parties with the object of giving to the transaction such efficacy as both parties must have

---

[1] Reported (1888), 13 P. D. 157.

intended that at all events it should have.   In business transactions such as this, what the law desires to effect by the implication is to give such business efficacy to the transaction as must have been intended at all events by both parties who are business men ; not to impose on one side all the perils of the transaction, or to emancipate one side from all the chances of failure, but to make each party promise in law as much, at all events, as it must have been in the contemplation of both parties that he should be responsible for in respect of those perils or chances.

Now what did each party in a case like this know ? For if we are examining into their presumed intention we must examine into their minds as to what the transaction was.   Both parties knew that this jetty was let out for hire, and knew that it could only be used under the contract by the ship taking the ground.   They must have known that it was by grounding that she used the jetty ; in fact, except so far as the transport to the jetty of the cargo in the ship was concerned, they must have known, both of them, that unless the ground was safe the ship would be simply buying an opportunity of danger, and that all consideration would fail unless some care had been taken to see that the ground was safe.   In fact the business of the jetty could not be carried on except upon such a basis.   The parties also knew that with regard to the safety of the ground outside the jetty the shipowner could know nothing at all, and the jetty owner might with reasonable care know everything.   The owners of the jetty, or their servants, were there at high and low tide, and with little trouble they could satisfy themselves, in case of doubt, as to whether the berth was reasonably safe.   The ship's owner, on the other hand, had not the means of verifying the state of the jetty, because the berth itself opposite the jetty might be occupied by another ship at any moment.

Now the question is how much of the peril of the safety of this berth is it necessary to assume that the shipowner and the jetty owner intended respectively to bear—in order that such a minimum of efficacy should be secured for the transaction, as both parties must have intended it to bear ? Assume that the berth outside had been absolutely under the control of the owners of the jetty, that they could have repaired it and made it fit for the purpose of the unloading and the loading.   If this had been the case, then the case of *The Mersey Docks Trustees* v. *Gibbs*[1] shews that those who owned the jetty, who took money for the use of the jetty, and who had under their control the *locus in quo*, would have been bound to take all reasonable care to prevent danger to those who were using the jetty—either to make the berth outside good, or else not to invite ships to go there—either to make the berth safe, or to advise persons not to go there.   But there is a distinction in the present instance.   The berth outside the jetty was not under the actual control of the jetty owners.   It is in the bed of the river, and it may be said that those who owned the jetty had no duty cast upon them by statute or common law to repair the bed of the river, and that they had no power to interfere with the bed of the river unless under the licence of the Conservators.   Now it does make a difference, it seems to me, where the entire control of the *locus in quo*—be it canal, or be it dock, or be it river berth— is *not* under the control of the persons who are taking toll for accommodation which involves its user; and, to a certain extent, the view must be modified of the necessary implication which the law would make about the duties of

---

[1] (1866), L. R. 1 H. L. 93.

the parties receiving the remuneration. This must be done exactly for the reason laid down by Lord Holt in his judgment in *Coggs* v. *Bernard*[1], where he says, " it would be unreasonable to charge persons with a trust further than the nature of the thing puts it in their power to perform." Applying that modification, which is one of reason, to this case, it may well be said that the law will not imply that the persons who have not the control of the place have taken reasonable care to make it good, but it does not follow that they are relieved from all responsibility. They are on the spot. They must know that the jetty cannot be used unless reasonable care is taken, if not to make it safe, at all events to see whether it is safe. No one can tell whether reasonable safety has been secured except themselves, and I think if they let out their jetty for use they at all events imply that they have taken reasonable care to see whether the berth, which is the essential part of the use of the jetty, is safe; and if it is not safe, and if they have not taken such reasonable care, it is their duty to warn persons with whom they have dealings that they have not done so. This is a business transaction as to which at any moment the parties may make any bargain they please, and either side may by the contract throw upon the other the burden of the unseen and existing danger. The question is what inference is to be drawn where the parties are dealing with each other on the assumption that the negotiations are to have some fruit, and where they say nothing about the burden of this kind of unseen peril, leaving the law to raise such inferences as are reasonable from the very nature of the transaction. So far as I am concerned I do not wish it to be understood that I at all consider this is a case of any duty on the part of the owners of the jetty to see to the access to the jetty being kept clear. The difference between access to the jetty and the actual use of the jetty seems to me, as Mr. Finlay says it is, only a question of degree, but when you are dealing with implications which the law directs, you cannot afford to neglect questions of degree, and it is just that difference of degree which brings one case on the line and prevents the other from approaching it. I confess that on the broad view of the case I think that business could not be carried on unless there was an implication to the extent I have laid down, at all events in the case where a jetty like the present is so to be used, and, although the case is a novel one, and the cases which have been cited do not assist us, I feel no difficulty in drawing the inference that this case comes within the line.

LORD ESHER and FRY, L.J., delivered judgments to the same effect.

Gardner v. Coutts & Co.

[1967] 3 All E.R. 1064

CROSS, J.: At the beginning of July, 1948, a Mr. Francis Walter Jekyll owned two adjoining properties near Godalming. One was called Munstead Wood. That was a largish house, standing in extensive grounds—over $13\frac{1}{2}$ acres in all. The other was Munstead Hut, a smaller house, which with its garden amounted only to a little over half an acre, and had apparently been cut out of the larger property. Mr. Jekyll was living in Munstead Hut and a Mrs. Lawson, who I take it was his tenant, was living in Munstead Wood.

---

[1] (1703), 2 Ld. Raym. 909.

On July 6, 1948, Mr. Jekyll conveyed Munstead Wood to Mrs. Lawson for £10,500. On the next day, July 7, Mr. Jekyll and Mrs. Lawson entered into an agreement, most of which I shall have to read. The parties to that agreement are Mr. Jekyll, who is described as

" of Munstead Hut Godalming in the county of Surrey of the one part and the Hon. Flora Lawson (hereinafter called ' Mrs. Lawson ') which expression shall where the context admits include her successors in title to her freehold property known as Munstead Wood Godalming "

of the other part. The agreement provides:

" In consideration of the sum of 10s. paid by Mrs. Lawson to Mr. Jekyll (the receipt whereof Mr. Jekyll hereby acknowledges) It is agreed as follows: 1 (a) In the event of Mr. Jekyll at any time during his lifetime desiring to sell his freehold property known as Munstead Hut Godalming aforesaid and coloured pink on the plan hereto annexed and in any case on Mr. Jekyll's death (if he is still the owner in fee simple of the said property) Mrs. Lawson shall have the option of purchasing the fee simple of Munstead Hut aforesaid (subject to but with the benefit of any furnished tenancy thereof) at the price of £3000; (b) The said option shall become exercisable during Mr. Jekyll's lifetime on his sending to Mrs. Lawson an offer in writing to sell as aforesaid and such offer shall remain open for acceptance by Mrs. Lawson for a period of one month from the date thereof and if such offer is declined or shall not be accepted within such period of one month Mr. Jekyll may thereafter sell or dispose of the property as he shall think fit. Any acceptance by Mrs. Lawson shall be sent in writing to Mr. Jekyll or his solicitors and Mrs. Lawson shall at the same time pay to him or them the usual deposit of ten per cent. of the purchase money. In the event of Mr. Jekyll still being the owner in fee simple of the said property at his death the above option in favour of Mrs. Lawson shall be exercisable by her by giving notice in writing to Mr. Jekyll's personal representatives or their solicitors within three months of Mr. Jekyll's death and at the same time paying to them or their solicitors the usual ten per cent. deposit, and if such notice is not given within the said period of three months Mr. Jekyll's personal representatives may thereafter sell or dispose of the property as they shall think fit."

Clause 1 (c) deals with the date for completion and cl. 1 (d) deals with title to the property. I need not read either of them. Then cl. 1 of the agreement provides:

" (e) During the subsistence of the said first refusal or option the said property shall be maintained in as good a state of repair as the same is now in and shall not be let to any person except furnished and then only to a person who has been approved by Mrs. Lawson.
" (f) During the subsistence of the said first refusal but so long only as Mrs. Lawson or her devisee or legatee shall be the owner of Munstead Wood aforesaid Mr. Jekyll to have the right to walk through the said property Munstead Wood as hitherto enjoyed."

Paragraph 2 deals with another property nearby called Munstead Orchard, and I need not read it. Paragraph 3 deals with the costs, and again I need not read that.

The contract for the sale of Munstead Wood by Mr. Jekyll to Mrs. Lawson did not contain any provision for the grant of the rights contained in the agreement which I have just read. Nevertheless, it is sufficiently obvious that the conveyance and the agreement, though they were not part and parcel of the same contract, yet were parts of the same transaction.

In 1950 Mrs. Lawson sold Munstead Wood, together with the benefit of the agreement, to a Mrs. Gill, and in 1958 Mrs. Gill conveyed Munstead Wood, together with the benefit of the agreement, to the plaintiff, Robert Oswald Guy Gardner. On January 14, 1963, Mr. Jekyll conveyed Munstead Hut to his sister, Lady Freyberg, by way of gift for no consideration. He had not previously offered the property to the plaintiff, who was then, as I have said, the owner of Munstead Wood and the person entitled to the benefit of the first refusal or option contained in the agreement. Mr. Jekyll died on March 27, 1965, and on June 25, 1965, probate of his will was granted to the defendants, Coutts & Co., the executors named in the will.

The plaintiff contends that by giving Munstead Hut to his sister without first giving the plaintiff the opportunity of buying it for £3000 Mr. Jekyll broke the agreement of July 7, 1948. He does not seek to compel Lady Freyberg to sell the property to him. He is simply claiming damages against Mr. Jekyll's estate.

The defendants deny that the gift to Lady Freyberg was a breach of the agreement. If that contention fails two further problems will arise: first, what is the amount of the damages payable; and secondly, whether, if that amount exceeds the assets remaining in the hands of the defendants as executors, they can, in all the circumstances (including for instance when they had notice of the claim), be made liable beyond the value of the assets in their hands. However, counsel on each side have agreed that I cannot decide those questions now. So if I decide the question of liability in favour of the plaintiff I will have to direct appropriate inquiries on those points.

The agreement does not provide expressly for the event of Mr. Jekyll giving away Munstead Hut in his lifetime. The whole question is whether there ought to be implied in the agreement a provision to the following effect —and I now quote from para. 2 of the statement of claim:

> " . . . that Mr. Jekyll should not during his lifetime make a gift of Munstead Hut without first giving to Mrs. Lawson or her successor in title to Munstead Wood the option of purchasing the fee simple of Munstead Hut in like manner and on the like terms as if Mr. Jekyll had been desirous of selling Munstead Hut."

When one hears the words " implied term " one thinks at once of MacKinnon, L.J., and his officious bystander. It appears, however, that that individual, though not yet so characterised, first made his appearance as long ago as 1918 in a judgment of Scrutton, L.J. I shall read a passage from that judgment and then the well-known passage from the judgment of MacKinnon, L.J., in a later case. In *Reigate* v. *Union Manufacturing Co. (Ramsbottom), Ltd.*[1], Scrutton, L.J., said:

> " The first thing is to see what the parties have expressed in the contract; and then an implied term is not to be added because the court thinks it would have been reasonable to have inserted it in the contract. A term can only be implied if it is necessary in the business sense to give efficacy to the contract; that is, if it is such a term that it can confidently be said that if at the time the contract was being negotiated someone had said to the parties, ' What will happen in such a case ', they would both have replied, ' Of course, so and so will happen; we did not trouble to say that; it is too clear '. Unless the court comes to some such conclusion as that, it ought not to imply a term which the parties themselves have not expressed."

In the case of *Shirlaw* v. *Southern Foundries (1926), Ltd. and Federated Foundries, Ltd.*[2], MacKinnon, L.J., said:

> " I recognise that the right or duty of a court to find the existence of an implied term or implied terms in a written contract is a matter to be exercised with care, and a court is too often invited to do so upon vague and uncertain grounds. Too often, also, such an invitation is backed by the citation of a

---

[1] [1918] 1 K.B. 592 at p. 605; [1918–19] All E.R. Rep. 143 at p. 149.
[2] [1939] 2 K.B. 206 at p. 227; [1939] 2 All E.R. 113 at p. 124.

sentence or two from the judgment of Bowen, L.J., in *The Moorcock*[1]. They are sentences from an extempore judgment as sound and sensible as are all the utterances of that great judge, but I fancy that he would have been rather surprised if he could have foreseen that these general remarks of his would come to be a favourite citation of a supposed principle of law, and I even think that he might sympathise with the occasional impatience of his successors when *The Moorcock*[1] is so often flushed for them in that guise. For my part, I think that there is a test that may be at least as useful as such generalities. If I may quote from an essay which I wrote some years ago, I then said: ' Prima facie that which in any contract is left to be implied and need not be expressed is something so obvious that it goes without saying '. Thus, if, while the parties were making their bargain, an officious bystander were to suggest some express provision for it in their agreement, they would testily suppress him with a common: ' Oh, of course! ' At least it is true, I think, that, if a term were never implied by a judge unless it could pass that test, he could not be held to be wrong.''

I agree wholeheartedly that a judge ought to be very cautious over implying terms in contracts[2]. It is so easy to say to oneself '' That is an eminently reasonable provision. If the parties had thought of it they would certainly have put it in, and so I ought to imply it ''. That sort of approach is, of course, quite wrong. If Mr. Jekyll's reaction to the question '' What if you want to give the property away? '' would have been '' Well, that is a new point; and I do not suppose that in fact I will ever want to give it away, but as you have raised this point I am prepared to agree to offer it to Mrs. Lawson for £3000 if I do want to give it away. So put that in too '', then as I see it the plaintiff must fail. For him to succeed I must be reasonably confident that on the question being raised Mr. Jekyll would have agreed with Mrs. Lawson in saying '' Oh, but of course that event is included too. What goes for a projected sale goes also for a projected gift ''.

With those general considerations in mind I must now consider the submissions made by counsel. Counsel for the defendants first made a general submission based on the fact that the consideration given by Mr. Jekyll for the rights given by him to Mrs. Lawson was only 10s., and the rather tenuous right of walking through Munstead Wood as long as Mrs. Lawson was the owner of it, conferred by cl. 1 (f). He then referred to what Bowen, L.J., said about failure of consideration in *The Moorcock*[3] and argued that I ought to be slower to imply the suggested term here than I might have been if the contract for the sale of Munstead Wood itself provided for the grant of these rights as part of the consideration for the purchase price of £10,500. I do not accept that submission. It does not seem to me that the question whether or not a term should be implied in a contract can depend on the amount of the consideration, and in any case, as I have said, the sale and the agreement, although they were not the subject of one contract, were plainly part and parcel of the same transaction.

Passing to the wording of the agreement, counsel for the defendants placed reliance on the words which appear both in cl. 1 (a) and in cl. 1 (b) '' if he is still the owner in fee simple of the said property ''. That—said counsel—shows that Mr. Jekyll might have parted with the property in his lifetime and yet not have sold it to Mrs. Lawson because she is to have the option at his death, if he is then still the owner of the property. It may well be—he argued—that the parties were contemplating that he might have given

[1] [1886–90] All E.R. Rep. 530; (1889), 14 P.D. 64.
[2] *See Lupton* v. *Potts*, [1969] 3 All E.R. 1083; [1969] 1 W.L.R. 1749.
[3] (1889), 14 P.D. at p. 68; [1886–90] All E.R. Rep. at p. 534.

the property away in his lifetime. To my mind the explanation of these words which counsel for the plaintiff gave is to be preferred. It might well happen that Mrs. Lawson, on the property being offered to her by Mr. Jekyll in his lifetime, would not desire to purchase it and then Mr. Jekyll would be at liberty to deal with it as he liked. He might sell it, or give it away or deal with it as he liked, and if at his death he was not still the owner of it no question of Mrs. Lawson being able to exercise any option over it would arise.

On the other hand, counsel for the plaintiff placed reliance on the words " if such offer is declined or shall not be accepted within such period of one month Mr. Jekyll may thereafter sell *or dispose* of the property as he shall think fit " and the similar provision that his personal representatives, if the option is not exercised within the period of three months after the death of Mr. Jekyll, " may thereafter sell *or dispose* of the property as they shall think fit ". He submitted that the use of the word " dispose " as well as " sell " indicated that it was not contemplated that Mr. Jekyll should be able to dispose of the property in some way other than sale, without first offering it to Mrs. Lawson. To that counsel for the defendants replied that the word " dispose " was directed to the possibility of Mr. Jekyll letting the property. It will be remembered that cl. 1 (e) provided expressly that during the subsistence of the first refusal or option Mr. Jekyll was not to let the property to anybody except on a furnished letting and then only to a person who had been approved by Mrs. Lawson. So counsel says that what was meant was that, if Mrs. Lawson did not accept the offer to purchase, Mr. Jekyll should then be at liberty not only to sell the property but also to let it if he wanted to, whereas previously he could not let it. I agree that the word " dispose " can be explained in this way and does not necessarily negative the idea that Mr. Jekyll could give the property away during his lifetime without having first to offer it to Mrs. Lawson. It seems to me, however, that the scheme of the agreement was that Mrs. Lawson should have the opportunity of buying the property if Mr. Jekyll wished to part with it in his lifetime, and, if he did not wish to part with it in his lifetime, should have the right to get it if she wished on his death from his executors. That general scheme is quite inconsistent to my mind with the idea that Mr. Jekyll could give the property away in his lifetime without giving her a chance of buying it. The right given to Mrs. Lawson, during Mr. Jekyll's lifetime, is strictly speaking a first refusal rather than an option, and is indeed, so described in sub-cl. (e) of cl. 1. During Mr. Jekyll's lifetime she could not set the machinery in motion; she could not compel Mr. Jekyll to do anything. It was only on his death that she could do that. To my mind the notion of a first refusal is inconsistent with the idea that the person who has to give the first refusal should be entitled to give the property away without offering it to the other party. In support of that way of looking at a first refusal counsel for the plaintiff referred me to a passage in *Manchester Ship Canal Co.* v. *Manchester Racecourse Co.*[1], where Vaughan Williams, L.J., in giving the judgment of the Court of Appeal said:

"The contract here to give the canal company the 'first refusal' involves a negative contract not to part with the land to any other company or person without giving that first refusal."

It is fair to say, however, that in all probability the Court of Appeal had not

---

[1] [1901] 2 Ch. 37 at p. 51.

the possibility of a gift of the property in mind at all, and in using the words " not to part with the land " meant no more than not to sell the land.   Nevertheless, viewing this matter apart from authority, I think that it is implicit in a grant of first refusal that the person who has to offer the property to the other party, should not be entitled to give it away without offering it and so to defeat the first refusal.   That being the way that I view the matter, if I apply the test laid down by Scrutton, L.J.[1], and MacKinnon, L.J.[2], I am confident that at the time, whatever views Mr. Jekyll may have formed later, if somebody had said to him " You have not expressly catered for the possibility of your wanting to give away the property ", he would have said, as undoubtedly Mrs. Lawson would have said, " Oh, of course that is implied. What goes for a contemplated sale must go for a contemplated gift ".   In my judgment, therefore, the plaintiff succeeds on the question of liability.

Judgment for the plaintiff.

---

[1] [1918] 1 K.B. at p. 605; [1918–19] All E.R. Rep. at p. 149.
[2] [1939] 2 K.B. at p. 227; [1939] 2 All E.R. at p. 124.

MISTAKE

BELL *v.* LEVER BROTHERS, LTD.

HUDDERSFIELD BANKING CO., LTD. *v.* HENRY LISTER & SON, LTD.

SOLLE *v.* BUTCHER

MAGEE *v.* PENNINE INSURANCE CO. LTD.

COMMON MISTAKE. Discussion by the House of Lords in *Bell* v. *Lever* of the scope and effect of common mistake at common law. Is a contract void if based on a false and fundamental assumption of any character? Or is it void only if the subject-matter is non-existent ?
The latter alternative preferred by Denning, L.J., in *Solle* v. *Butcher*.[1] But a contract, even though not void at common law for common mistake, may be set aside in equity upon such terms as seem fit to the court.

Bell v. Lever Brothers, Ltd.

[1932] A.C. 161

LORD ATKIN.[2]—My Lords, this case involves a question of much importance in the formation and dissolution of contracts. The facts are not very complicated, though in the course of eliciting them the legal proceedings have undergone vicissitudes which have made the task of determining the issues more difficult than need be. In 1923, the Niger Company, Ltd., was controlled by Lever Brothers, Ltd., whom I shall call Levers, who held over 99 per cent. of its shares. The Niger Company dealt in West African produce, including cocoa, and at this time appears to have been making trading losses. To restore the position Levers approached the appellant Bell, who had banking experience, and the appellant Snelling, a chartered accountant, with a view to their taking part in the management of the Niger Company's affairs. In August, 1923, an agreement was made between Levers and Bell, under which Bell entered the service of Levers for a term of five years from November 1, 1923, on the terms of letters of August 8, 1923, which provided that Bell's salary was to be 8,000*l.* a year. Levers were to pay the premiums on an endowment policy maturing at the age of sixty for a sum of 16,200*l.* Levers were to appoint and maintain Bell as chairman of the Niger Company during his service. Bell was only to be responsible to the Committee of Control of Lever Brothers and to the shareholders of the Niger Company. In October an agreement was made between Snelling and Levers whereby Snelling was to be in the service of the company for five years from October 1, 1923, on the terms of a letter of September 12, which provided that Snelling was to serve Levers in regard to its West African interests at a salary of 10,000*l.* per annum to March 31, 1925, and 6,000*l.* for the remainder of the five years. On September 14, both Bell and Snelling were appointed by the Niger Company directors of the company, and Bell was appointed chairman of the Board. In April, 1924, Snelling was appointed a vice-chairman. The result of the appointments was a success. The Niger Company began to prosper and in

---

[1] See also *Harrison and Jones, Ltd.* v. *Bunten and Lancaster, Ltd.*, [1953] 1 Q. B. 646: [1953] 1 All E. R. 903.
[2] It will be observed that in several passages of his speech Lord Atkin uses the expression " mutual mistake." This must have been done *per incuriam*, for it is clear that the facts disclosed a case of common mistake. The epithets " common " and " mutual " are often confused both in and out of the reports. They are thus defined in the O.E.D.: " Common " means " possessed or shared alike by both or all the persons or things in question ". " Mutual " means " possessed or entertained by each of two persons towards or with regard to the other ".

July, 1926, the agreements of both Bell and Snelling with Levers were cancelled and new agreements substituted for a further period of five years from July 1, 1926, at the same salaries but with a commission on the profits of the Niger Company. The Niger Company continued to prosper, and in March, 1929, arrangements were concluded for an amalgamation between the Niger Company and its principal trade competitor, the African and Eastern Trade Corporation. The terms of the amalgamation appear to have left no room for Bell or Snelling. It was necessary, therefore, to dispose of the agreements between them and Levers. Mr. D'Arcy Cooper, the chairman of Levers, saw both gentlemen and arranged terms with them which are recorded in two letters of March 19, 1929. The letter to Bell is as follows :

> Dear Bell,—As promised at our interview to-day, I write to record the agreement then arrived at between us, viz., that on the provisional agreement for amalgamation of the African and Eastern Trading Corporation and the Niger Company becoming effective as from the 1st May next, you will on that date retire from the Boards of the Niger Company and its subsidiaries, including H.C.B. and its subsidiaries, and in consideration of your so doing Lever Brothers, Ltd., will pay you as compensation for the termination of your agreement(s) and the consequent loss of office the sum of £30,000 in full satisfaction and discharge of all claims and demands by you of every nature and kind and howsoever arising against Lever Brothers, Ltd., the Niger Company, the H.C.B., and any company, person or firm associated with them or any of them either directly or indirectly. With regard to the insurance premium payable on the policy on your life with the Yorkshire Insurance Company it was agreed that Lever Brothers will continue to pay such premium until the policy matures. Will you please let me have your reply confirming the above arrangment. I should like to be allowed to say how deeply the Board of Messrs. Lever Brothers appreciate the work that you have done for the Niger Company during the period that you have been in control.
>
> Yours sincerely,
> " F. D'Arcy Cooper."

The letter to Snelling is in similar terms except that the compensation given was 20,000*l.* Both sums were duly paid on May 1, 1929, on which date the two appellants retired from their service with Levers, and from the Boards of the Niger Company and various subsidiary companies to which they had been appointed. Very little attention appears to have been paid at the trial to these subsidiary companies, and there is a scarcity of evidence about them. The position in regard to them may demand further consideration; at present I leave them on one side. The position then is that in March, 1929, the two appellants left the service of Levers with substantial compensation in their pockets and mutual expressions of respect and esteem.

In July, 1929, Levers discovered facts which indicated that their expenditure of 50,000*l.* and their expressions of regard had been misplaced. For the years October to October, 1926-7, 1927-8, and 1928-9, the Niger Company, together with three of its trading competitors, including the African and Eastern Trade Corporation, had been parties to what were called " Pooling Agreements," under which the parties undertook to disclose to one another their dealings in Gold Coast cocoa; not to buy cocoa produced elsewhere without the consent of the Pool Committee; agreed to fix from time to time buying and selling prices and not to sell without consent below the agreed selling price; and made provision for distributing in agreed proportions the proceeds of the pool. It appears to have been considered necessary that the operations of the Niger Company under the pool should be carried out without excessive publicity; and the broker's contracts for the Niger Company were recorded under initials. In November and December, 1927, the two appellants, at a time when the Pool Committee were lowering the pool purchase price of cocoa, on several occasions sold cocoa short, and, closing in a few days at the reduced price, made profits. A few days later they bought for the rise and made a small profit. Altogether the dealings resulted in a profit of 1,360*l*. The transaction was of course conducted without the knowledge of Levers or any responsible official of the Niger Company. It was carried out in secrecy, and payment of the profit was made by the brokers at the appellants' request in a draft for American dollars. No defence can be offered for this piece of misconduct. The appellants were acting in a business in which their employers were concerned ; their interests and their employers' conflicted ; they were taking a secret advantage out of their employment, and committing a grave breach of duty both to Levers and to the Niger Company. The jury have found that had the facts been discovered during the service, Levers could and would have dismissed them, and no objection can be taken to this finding.

Having made this discovery it naturally occurred to Levers that instead of spending 50,000*l*. to cancel the two service agreements they might, if they had known the facts, have got rid of them for nothing. They, therefore, claimed the return of the money from the appellants, as well as the amount of the profits made ; and on August 7, 1929, issued the writ in the present action, claiming damages for fraudulent misrepresentation and concealment, on account of the defendants' dealings in cocoa, and repayment of money paid under a mistake of fact.

The pleadings were in conformity with the endorsement on the writ. The defendants admitted the dealings in cocoa, alleging that they were speculative dealings in differences. They denied that they were wrongful but pleaded tender of the profit of 1,360*l*., which sum by an amended defence they paid into Court. It was not disputed in the Court of Appeal or before this House that the dealings were wrongful ; and no question remains on this issue or as to the remedy ordered in respect of it.

The trial began on March 24, 1930, before Wright, J., and a City of London special jury. On the fourth day on the conclusion of their evidence the plaintiffs sought and obtained permission to amend their pleadings by alleging a series of fraudulent dealings in cocoa by the defendants involving misappropriation of the Niger Company's funds. At the same time for the first time the Niger Company were added as plaintiffs. The defendants were eventually acquitted of all the new charges. On May 5, 1930, the trial commenced anew before the same judge and a new jury. At the conclusion of the evidence there was some discussion as to the questions to be put to the jury. The Court adjourned for a day or two before the summing-up of the judge. There had been some discussion as to the issue raised by the plea of mistake, and when the case was resumed counsel for the plaintiffs suggested an additional question : " Did the plaintiffs in entering into the said agreements for the payment of and in paying the 30,000*l*. and 20,000*l*. respectively, act in ignorance of the defendants' conduct (my Lord, that avoids the word mistake to which your Lordship took objection) and was such ignorance due to non-disclosure by the defendants of such conduct ? " So far this seems to have been the only reference to the matter of mistake in the proposed questions. The learned judge said : " I have been thinking about that matter ; probably yours is better ; but what I thought of asking was this : ' When Levers entered into the agreement of March 19, 1929, did they know of the actions of the defendants or either of them in regard to the dealings C.T.C., R.T.D. and G.S.2? If Levers had known would they have made these agreements or either of them ? At the date of the respective interviews prior to these agreements had the defendants or either of them in mind their actions in respect of these transactions ? ' "

To the last question Mr. Pritt for the defendants objected that there was no evidence that they had. Whereupon the judge said : " The point must really arise ; that issue of fact will have to be dealt with by the jury when they are considering the question of fraudulent misrepresentation or fraudulent concealment. On the other hand the verdict of the jury on this point may have some bearing hereafter on the question of mistake."

The circumstances under which this last question was admitted are relevant to the complaint of the appellants as to the subsequent admission of any issue as to mutual mistake. They say that the only issue raised by the pleadings was as to a unilateral mistake by the plaintiffs ; that the question propounded by the plaintiffs shows this ; and that it cannot be assumed that the judge, while stating that the plaintiffs' questions might be better, but he preferred his own, should have asked a question for the purpose of solving an issue as to mutual mistake which was not upon the pleadings and upon which no witness had been examined or cross-examined and on which no word had been said to the jury by counsel on either side. At present it is unnecessary to say more on the topic.

The questions as finally left to the jury and their answers have been stated to the House and I need not repeat them. The judge heard argument as to how judgment should be entered. At some stage of the proceedings the parties had agreed that rescission of the agreements must be left to the judge, and that on any point left to him he must have leave to draw inferences of fact. Eventually the judge gave judgment for apparently both plaintiffs for 31,224*l.*, against the defendant Bell, and 20,000*l.* against the defendant Snelling, on the ground that " there was a total failure of consideration such as to vitiate the bargain " because " the parties dealt with one another under a mutual mistake as to their respective rights." On appeal this judgment was affirmed. The three Lords Justices accepted the view of Wright, J., that there was a mutual mistake which entitled the plaintiffs to recover. They were also agreed that there was a duty upon the defendants to disclose to the plaintiffs their misconduct as to the cocoa dealings and that the contracts under which the money was paid were in consequence voidable.

Before the Court of Appeal and before this House the appellants contended that no issue as to mutual mistake had been raised by the pleadings, and that it was not open to the learned judge or to the Court of Appeal to determine the case without an amendment of the pleadings and upon an issue of fact which was not submitted to the jury. The Lords Justices appear to have held varying views on this point. Scrutton, L.J., thought that the point was not pleaded, but that it was the practice of the Courts to deal with the legal result of pleaded facts; though the particular legal result is not pleaded except where to ascertain the validity of the legal result would require the investigation of new and disputed facts which had not been investigated at the trial. Here he thought that there were no such disputed facts, and the question could be dealt with without amend-ment. Lawrence, L.J., on the assumption that mutual mistake was not pleaded, thought that all the facts relevant to mutual mistake had been fully investigated and ascertained at the trial : and that the objection was a mere technical objection without merits. Greer, L.J., thought that mutual mistake was sufficiently pleaded.

I think it is sufficient to say for present purposes that it seems to me clear when the pleadings and particulars are examined that the pleading was confined to unilateral mistake. In these circumstances the judge on a trial with a jury has without consent of the parties no jurisdiction to determine issues of fact not raised by the pleadings ; nor, in my opinion, would a general consent to determine issues not decided by the jury include a power, without express further consent after the jury had been discharged, to amend pleadings so as to raise further issues of fact. Similarly, the powers of the Court of Appeal which, under Order LVIII., r. 4, are wider than those of the judge, are limited in the case of trials by jury to determine issues of fact in cases where only one finding by a jury could be allowed to stand. Further, I think that the Court of Appeal cannot without amendment decide a case upon an unpleaded issue of law which depends upon an unpleaded issue of fact. If the issue of fact can be fairly determined upon the existing evidence they may of course amend : but in any such case amendment appears to me to be necessary. In this House in the course of the hearing an amendment was tendered by the plaintiffs which did aver a mutual mistake. In the view that I take of the whole case it becomes unnecessary to deal finally with the appellants' complaint that the points upon which the plaintiffs succeeded were not open to them. I content myself with saying that much may be said for that contention.

Two points present themselves for decision. Was the agreement of March 19, 1929, void by reason of a mutual mistake of Mr. D'Arcy Cooper and Mr. Bell ?

Could the agreement of March 19, 1929, be avoided by reason of the failure of Mr. Bell to disclose his misconduct in regard to the cocoa dealings ?

My Lords, the rules of law dealing with the effect of mistake on contract appear to be established with reasonable clearness. If mistake operates at all it operates so as to negative or in some cases to nullify consent. The parties may be mistaken in the identity of the contracting parties, or in the existence of the subject-matter of the contract at the date of the contract, or in the quality of the subject-matter of the contract. These mistakes may be by one party, or by both, and the legal effect may depend upon the class of mistake above mentioned. Thus a mistaken belief by A. that he is contracting with B., whereas in fact he is contracting with C., will negative consent where it is clear that the intention of A. was to contract only with B. So the agreement of A. and B. to purchase a specific article is void if in fact the article had perished before the date of sale. In this case, though the parties in fact were agreed about the subject-matter, yet a consent to transfer or take delivery of something not existent is deemed useless: consent is nullified. As codified in the Sale of Goods Act the contract is expressed to be void if the seller was in ignorance of the destruction of the specific chattel. I apprehend that if the seller with knowledge that a chattel was destroyed purported to sell it to a purchaser, the latter might sue for damages for non-delivery though the former could not sue for non-acceptance, but I know of no case where a seller has so committed himself. This is a case where mutual mistake certainly, and unilateral mistake by the seller also, will prevent a contract from arising. Corresponding to mistake as to the existence of the subject-matter is mistake as to title in cases where, unknown to the parties, the buyer is already the owner of that which the seller purports to sell to him.   The parties intended to effectuate a transfer of ownership : such a transfer is impossible : the stipulation is *naturali ratione inutilis*. This is the case of *Cooper* v. *Phibbs*[1], where A. agreed to take a lease of a fishery from B., though contrary to the belief of both parties at the time A. was tenant for life of the fishery and B. appears to have had no title at all.   To such a case Lord Westbury applied the principle that if parties contract under a mutual mistake and misapprehension as to their relative and respective rights the result is that the agreement is liable to be set aside as having proceeded upon a common mistake.   Applied to the context the statement is only subject to the criticism that the agreement would appear to be void rather than voidable.   Applied to mistake as to rights generally it would appear to be too wide.   Even where the vendor has no title, though both parties think he has, the correct view would appear to be that there is a contract : but that the vendor has either committed a breach of a stipulation as to title, or is not able to perform his contract.   The contract is unenforceable by him but is not void.

Mistake as to quality of the thing contracted for raises more difficult questions.   In such a case a mistake will not affect assent unless it is the mistake of both parties, and is as to the existence of some quality which makes the thing without the quality essentially different from the thing as it was believed to be.   Of course it may appear that the parties contracted that the article should possess the quality which one or other or both mistakenly believed it to possess.   But in such a case there is a contract and the inquiry is a different one, being whether the contract as to quality amounts to a condition or a warranty, a different branch of the law.   The principles to be applied are to be found in two cases which, as far as my knowledge goes, have always been treated as authoritative expositions of the law.   The first is *Kennedy* v. *Panama Royal Mail Co.*[2]

In that case the plaintiff had applied for shares in the defendant company on the faith of a prospectus which stated falsely but innocently that the company had a binding contract with the Government of New Zealand for the carriage of mails.   On discovering the true facts the plaintiff brought an action for the recovery of the sums he had paid on calls.   The defendants brought a cross action for further calls.   Blackburn, J., in delivering the judgment of the Court (Cockburn, C.J., Blackburn, Mellor and Shee, JJ.), said : " The only remaining question is one of much greater difficulty. It was contended by Mr. Mellish, on behalf of Lord Gilbert Kennedy, that the effect of the prospectus was to warrant to the intended shareholders that there really was such a contract as is there represented, and not merely to represent that the company *bona fide* believed it ; and that the difference in substance between shares in a company with such a contract and shares in a company whose supposed contract was not binding, was a difference in substance in the nature of the thing ; and that the shareholder was entitled to return the shares as soon as he discovered this, quite independently of fraud, on the ground that he had applied for one thing and got another. And, if the invalidity of the contract really made the shares he obtained different things in substance from those which he applied for, this would, we think, be good law.   The case would then resemble *Gompertz* v. *Bartlett*[3] and *Gurney* v. *Womersley*[4], where the person who had honestly sold what

---

[1] (1867), L. R. 2 H. L. 149.   [2] (1867), L. R. 2 Q. B. 580 at p. 586.
[3] (1853), 2 E. & B. 849.   [4] (1854), 4 E. & B. 133.

he thought a bill without recourse to him, was, nevertheless, held bound to return the price on its turning out that the supposed bill was a forgery in the one case, and void under the stamp laws in the other ; in both cases the ground of this decision being that the thing handed over was not the thing paid for. A similar principle was acted on in *Ship's* case[1]. There is, however, a very important difference between cases where a contract may be rescinded on account of fraud, and those in which it may be rescinded on the ground that there is a difference in substance between the thing bargained for and that obtained. It is enough to show that there was a fraudulent representation as to any part of that which induced the party to enter into the contract which he seeks to rescind ; but where there has been an innocent misrepresentation or misapprehension, it does not authorize a rescission unless it is such as to show that there is a complete difference in substance between what was supposed to be and what was taken, so as to constitute a failure of consideration. For example, where a horse is bought under a belief that it is sound, if the purchaser was induced to buy by a fraudulent representation as to the horse's soundness, the contract may be rescinded. If it was induced by an honest misrepresentation as to its soundness, though it may be clear that both vendor and purchaser thought that they were dealing about a sound horse and were in error, yet the purchaser must pay the whole price unless there was a warranty ; and even if there was a warranty, he cannot return the horse and claim back the whole price, unless there was a condition to that effect in the contract : *Street* v. *Blay.*"[2]

The Court came to the conclusion in that case that, though there was a misapprehension as to that which was a material part of the motive inducing the applicant to ask for the shares, it did not prevent the shares from being in substance those he applied for.

The next case is *Smith* v. *Hughes*[3], the well-known case as to new and old oats. The action was in the County Court, and was for the price of oats sold and delivered and damages for not accepting oats bargained and sold. Cockburn, C.J., cites Story on Contracts as follows : " Mr. Justice Story[4] in his work on Contracts (vol. i., section 516), states the law as to concealment as follows : ' The general rule, both of law and equity, in respect to concealment, is that mere silence with regard to a material fact, which there is no legal obligation to divulge, will not avoid a contract, although it operate as an injury to the party from whom it is concealed.' ' Thus,' he goes on to say (section 517), ' although a vendor is bound to employ no artifice or disguise for the purpose of concealing defects in the article sold, since that would amount to a positive fraud on the vendee ; yet, under the general doctrine of *caveat emptor*, he is not, ordinarily, bound to disclose every defect of which he may be cognizant, although his silence may operate virtually to deceive the vendee.' ' But,' he continues (section 518), ' an improper concealment or suppression of a material fact, which the party concealing is legally bound to disclose, and of which the other party has a legal right to insist that he shall be informed, is fraudulent, and will invalidate a contract.' Further, distinguishing between extrinsic circumstances affecting the value of the subject-matter of a sale, and the concealment of intrinsic circumstances appertaining to its nature, character, and condition,

---

[1] (1865), 2 De G. J. & Sm. 544.   [2] (1831), 2 B. & Ad. 456.
[3] (1871), L.R. 6. Q.B. 597, at pp. 604, 606.
[4] [This attribution was mistaken : the author was not the celebrated text-writer and judge but his son, W. W. Story, later in life better known as a sculptor and a writer about Rome, where he resided.—F.P.].

he points out (section 519) that with reference to the latter the rule is, ' that mere silence as to anything which the other party might by proper diligence have discovered, and which is open to his examination, is not fraudulent, unless a special trust or confidence exist between the parties, or be implied from the circumstances of the case.' In the doctrine thus laid down I entirely agree."

In a further passage he says : " It only remains to deal with an argument which was pressed upon us, that the defendant in the present case intended to buy old oats, and the plaintiffs to sell new, so the two minds were not *ad idem* ; and that consequently there was no contract. This argument proceeds on the fallacy of confounding what was merely a motive operating on the buyer to induce him to buy with one of the essential conditions of the contract. Both parties were agreed as to the sale and purchase of this particular parcel of oats. The defendant believed the oats to be old and was thus induced to agree to buy them, but he omitted to make their age a condition of the contract. All that can be said is, that the two minds were not *ad idem* as to the age of the oats ; they certainly were *ad idem* as to the sale and purchase of them. Suppose a person to buy a horse without a warranty, believing him to be sound, and the horse turns out unsound, could it be contended that it would be open to him to say that, as he had intended to buy a sound horse, and the seller to sell an unsound one, the contract was void, because the seller must have known from the price the buyer was willing to give, or from his general habits as a buyer of horses that he thought the horse was sound ? The cases are exactly parallel."

Blackburn, J., said : " In this case I agree that on the sale of a specific article, unless there be a warranty making it part of the bargain that it possesses some particular quality, the purchaser must take the article he has bought though it does not possess that quality. And I agree that even if the vendor was aware that the purchaser thought that the article possessed that quality, and would not have entered into the contract unless he had so thought, still the purchaser is bound, unless the vendor was guilty of some fraud or deceit upon him, and that a mere abstinence from disabusing the purchaser of that impression is not fraud or deceit ; for, whatever may be the case in a court of morals, there is no legal obligation on the vendor to inform the purchaser that he is under a mistake, not induced by the act of the vendor."

The Court ordered a new trial. It is not quite clear whether they considered that if the defendant's contention was correct, the parties were not *ad idem* or there was a contractual condition that the oats sold were old oats. In either case the defendant would succeed in defeating the claim.

In these cases I am inclined to think that the true analysis is that there is a contract, but that the one party is not able to supply the very thing whether goods or services that the other party contracted to take ; and therefore the contract is unenforceable by the one if executory, while, if executed, the other can recover back money paid on the ground of failure of the consideration.

We are now in a position to apply to the facts of this case the law as to mistake so far as it has been stated. It is essential on this part of the discussion to keep in mind the finding of the jury acquitting the defendants of fraudulent misrepresentation or concealment in procuring the agreements in question. Grave injustice may be done to the defendants and confusion introduced into the legal conclusion, unless it is quite clear that in considering mistake in this case no suggestion of fraud is admissible and cannot strictly be regarded by the judge who has to determine the legal issues raised. The agreement which is said to be void is the agreement contained in the letter of March 19, 1929, that Bell would retire from the Board of the Niger Company and its subsidiaries, and that in consideration of his doing so Levers would pay him as compensation for the termination of his agreements and consequent loss of office the sum of 30,000*l*. in full satisfaction and discharge of all claims and demands of any kind against Lever Brothers, the Niger Company or its subsidiaries. The agreement, which as part of the contract was terminated, had been broken so that it could be repudiated. Is an agreement to terminate a broken contract different in kind from an agreement to terminate an unbroken contract, assuming that the breach has given the one party the right to declare the contract at an end ? I feel the weight of the plaintiffs' contention that a contract immediately determinable is a different thing from a contract for an unexpired term, and that the difference in kind can be illustrated by the immense price of release from the longer contract as compared with the shorter. And I agree that an agreement to take an assignment of a lease for five years is not the same thing as to take an assignment of a lease for three years, still less a term for a few months. But, on the whole, I have come to the conclusion that it would be wrong to decide that an agreement to terminate a definite specified contract is void if it turns out that the agreement had already been broken and could have been terminated otherwise. The contract released is the identical contract in both cases, and the party paying for release gets exactly what he bargains for. It seems immaterial that he could have got the same result in another way, or that if he had known the true facts he would not have entered into the bargain. A. buys B.'s horse ; he thinks the horse is sound and he pays the price of a sound horse ; he would certainly not have bought the horse if he had known as the fact is that the horse is unsound. If B. has made no representation as to soundness and has not contracted that the horse is sound, A. is bound and cannot recover back the price. A. buys a picture from B.; both A. and B. believe it to be the work of an old master, and a high price is paid. It turns out to be a modern copy. A. has no remedy in the absence of representation or warranty. A. agrees to take on lease or to buy from B. an unfurnished dwelling-house. The house is in fact uninhabitable. A. would never have entered into the bargain if he had known the fact. A. has no remedy, and the position is the same whether B. knew the facts or not, so long as he made no representation or gave no warranty. A. buys a roadside garage business from B. abutting on a public thoroughfare : unknown to A., but known to B., it has already been decided to construct a byepass road which will divert substantially the whole of the traffic from passing A.'s garage. Again A. has no remedy. All these cases involve hardship on A. and benefit B., as most people would say, unjustly. They can be supported on the ground that it is of paramount importance that contracts should be observed, and that if parties honestly comply with the essentials of the formation of contracts —i.e., agree in the same terms on the same subject-matter—they are bound, and must rely on the stipulations of the contract for protection from the effect of facts unknown to them.

This brings the discussion to the alternative mode of expressing the result of a mutual mistake. It is said that in such a case as the present there is to be implied a stipulation in the contract that a condition of its efficacy is that the facts should be as understood by both parties—namely, that the contract could not be terminated till the end of the current term. The question of the existence of conditions, express or implied, is obviously one that affects not the formation of contract, but the investigation of the terms of the contract when made. A condition derives its efficacy from the consent of the parties, express or implied. They have agreed, but on what terms? One term may be that unless the facts are or are not of a particular nature, or unless an event has or has not happened, the contract is not to take effect. With regard to future facts such a condition is obviously contractual. Till the event occurs the parties are bound. Thus the condition (the exact terms of which need not here be investigated) that is generally accepted as underlying the principle of the frustration cases is contractual, an implied condition. Sir John Simon formulated for the assistance of your Lordships a proposition which should be recorded ; " Whenever it is to be inferred from the terms of a contract or its surrounding circumstances that the consensus has been reached upon the basis of a particular contractual assumption, and that assumption is not true, the contract is avoided ; i.e., it is void *ab initio* if the assumption is of present fact and it ceases to bind if the assumption is of future fact."

I think few would demur to this statement, but its value depends upon the meaning of " a contractual assumption," and also upon the true meaning to be attached to " basis," a metaphor which may mislead. When used expressly in contracts, for instance in policies of insurance, which state that the truth of the statements in the proposal is to be the basis of the contract of insurance, the meaning is clear. The truth of the statements is made a condition of the contract, which failing, the contract is void unless the conditon is waived. The proposition does not amount to more than this that, if the contract expressly or impliedly contains a term that a particular assumption is a condition of the contract, the contract is avoided if the assumption is not true. But we have not advanced far on the inquiry how to ascertain whether the contract does contain such a condition. Various words are to be found to define the state of things which make a condition. " In the contemplation of both parties fundamental to the continued validity of the contract," " a foundation essential to its existence," " a fundamental reason for making it," are phrases found in the important judgment of Scrutton, L.J., in the present case. The first two phrases appear to me to be unexceptionable. They cover the case of a contract to serve in a particular place, the existence of which is fundamental to the service, or to procure the services of a professional vocalist, whose continued health is essential to performance. But " a fundamental reason for making a contract " may, with respect, be misleading. The reason of one party only is presumedly not intended, but in the cases I have suggested above, of the sale of a horse or of a picture, it might be said that the fundamental reason for making the contract was the belief of both parties that the horse was sound or the picture an old master, yet in neither case would the condition as I think exist. Nothing is more dangerous than to allow oneself liberty to construct for the parties contracts which they have not in terms made by importing implications which would appear to make the contract more businesslike or more just. The implications to be made are to be no more than are " necessary " for giving business efficacy to the transaction, and it appears to me that, both as to existing facts and future facts, a condition would not be implied unless the new state of facts makes the contract something different in kind from the contract in the original state of facts. Thus, in *Krell* v. *Henry*[1], Vaughan Williams, L.J., finds that the subject of the contract was " rooms to view the procession " : the postponement, therefore, made the rooms not rooms to view the procession. This also is the test finally chosen by Lord Sumner in *Bank Line* v. *Arthur Capel & Co.*[2] agreeing with Lord Dunedin in *Metropolitan Water Board* v. *Dick Kerr*,[3] where, dealing with the criterion for determining the effect of interruption in " frustrating " a contract, he says : " An interruption may be so long as to destroy the identity of the work or service, when resumed, with the work or service when interrupted." We therefore get a common standard for mutual mistake and implied conditions, whether as to existing or as to future facts. Does the state of the new facts destroy the identity of the subject-matter as it was in the original state of facts ? To apply the principle to the infinite combinations of facts that arise in actual experience will continue to be difficult, but if this case results in establishing order into what has been a somewhat confused and difficult branch of the law it will have served a useful purpose.

I have already stated my reasons for deciding that in the present case the identity of the subject-matter was not destroyed by the mutual mistake, if any, and need not repeat them.

It now becomes necessary to deal with the second point of the plaintiffs —namely, that the contract of March 19, 1929, could be avoided by them in consequence of the non-disclosure by Bell of his misconduct as to the cocoa dealings. Fraudulent concealment has been negatived by the jury ; this claim is based upon the contention that Bell owed a duty to Levers to disclose his misconduct, and that in default of disclosure the contract was voidable. Ordinarily the failure to disclose a material fact which might influence the mind of a prudent contractor does not give the right to avoid the contract. The principle of *caveat emptor* applies outside contracts of sale. There are certain contracts expressed by the law to be contracts of the utmost good faith, where material facts must be disclosed ; if not, the contract is voidable. Apart from special fiduciary relationships, contracts for partnership and contracts of insurance are the leading instances. In such cases the duty does not arise out of contract ; the duty of a person proposing an insurance arises before a contract is made, so too of intending partners. Unless this contract can be brought within this limited category of contracts *uberrimæ fidei* it appears to me that this ground of defence must fail. I see nothing to differentiate this agreement from the ordinary contract of service ; and I am aware of no authority which places contracts of service within the limited category I have mentioned. It seems to me clear that master and man negotiating for an agreement of service are as unfettered as in any other negotiation. Nor can I find anything in the relation of master and servant, when established, that places agreements between them within the protected category. It is said that there is a contractual duty of the servant to disclose his past faults. I agree that the duty in the servant to protect his master's property may involve the duty to report a fellow servant whom he knows to be wrongfully dealing with that property. The servant owes a duty not to steal, but, having stolen, is there superadded a duty to confess that he has stolen ? I am satisfied

---

[1] [1903] 2 K. B. 740, at p. 754.
[2] [1919] A. C. 435.
[3] [1918] A. C. 119, at p. 128.

that to imply such a duty would be a departure from the well established usage of mankind and would be to create obligations entirely outside the normal contemplation of the parties concerned. If a man agrees to raise his butler's wages, must the butler disclose that two years ago he received a secret commission from the wine merchant ; and if the master discovers it, can he, without dismissal or after the servant has left, avoid the agreement for the increase in salary and recover back the extra wages paid ? If he gives his cook a month's wages in lieu of notice can he, on discovering that the cook has been pilfering the tea and sugar, claim the return of the month's wages ? I think not. He takes the risk ; if he wishes to protect himself he can question his servant, and will then be protected by the truth or otherwise of the answers.

I agree with the view expressed by Avory, J., in *Healey* v. *Société Anonyme Française Rubastic*[1] on this point. It will be noticed that Bell was not a director of Levers, and, with respect, I cannot accept the view of Greer, L.J., that if he was in fiduciary relationship to the Niger Company he was in a similar fiduciary relationship to the shareholders, or to the particular shareholders (Levers) who held 99 per cent. of the shares. Nor do I think that it is alleged or proved that in making the agreement of March 19, 1929, Levers were acting as agents for the Niger Company. In the matter of the release of the service contract and the payment of 30,000*l.* they were acting quite plainly for themselves as principals. It follows that on this ground also the claim fails.

The result is that in the present case servants unfaithful in some of their work retain large compensation which some will think they do not deserve. Nevertheless it is of greater importance that well established principles of contract should be maintained than that a particular hardship should be redressed ; and I can see no way of giving relief to the plaintiffs in the present circumstances except by confiding to the Courts loose powers of introducing terms into contracts which would only serve to introduce doubt and confusion where certainty is essential.

I think, therefore, that this appeal should be allowed ; and I agree with the order to be proposed by my noble and learned friend, Lord Blanesburgh.

LORD BLANESBURGH and LORD THANKERTON delivered judgments to the same effect ; VISCOUNT HAILSHAM and LORD WARRINGTON dissented.

Huddersfield Banking Co., Ltd. v. Henry Lister & Son, Ltd.
[1895] 2 Ch. 273

In 1889 Henry Lister had mortgaged his mills and the fixtures therein to the Huddersfield Banking Co. Ltd. In 1890 he converted himself into a limited company—*Henry Lister & Son, Ltd.*—which in 1892 went into liquidation. The bank, as mortgagees, claimed to be entitled, as against the liquidator, to thirty-five power looms in the mills. The question was whether these were fixtures within the terms of the mortgage deed. The agents of the bank and of the liquidator inspected the premises and agreed that the looms were not attached to the mills and were therefore not fixtures. On that assumption the bank concurred in an order made by the court for their sale by the liquidator. It later appeared that the looms were affixed to the mills at the time when the mortgage was made and had subsequently been wrongly separated by some unauthorised person.

---

[1] [1917] 1 K. B. 946.

The bank applied to the court to set aside the order on the ground that it represented an agreement based on a common mistake.

VAUGHAN WILLIAMS, J., gave judgment for the bank, and an appeal by the defendants was dismissed by the Court of Appeal.

LINDLEY, L.J.   Messrs. Lister & Son, Limited, the appellants, contend that there is no jurisdiction to set aside the consent order upon such materials as we have to deal with; and they go so far as to say that a consent order can only be set aside on the ground of fraud.   I dissent from that proposition entirely.   A consent order, I agree, is an order; and so long as it stands it must be treated as such, and so long as it stands I think it is as good an estoppel as any other order.   I have not the slightest doubt on that; nor have I the slightest doubt that a consent order can be impeached, not only on the ground of fraud, but upon any grounds which invalidate the agreement it expresses in a more formal way than usual.

If authority for this be wanted, it will be found in two cases which were referred to in the course of the argument, and which I do not propose to examine at any length—I mean *Davenport* v. *Stafford*[1] and *A.-G.* v. *Tomline*[2].   To my mind, the only question is whether the agreement upon which the consent order was based can be invalidated or not.   Of course, if that agreement cannot be invalidated the consent order is good.   If it can be, the consent order is bad.

Now, on the question of jurisdiction let us see what there is against setting aside the agreement.   How does that stand?   The agreement in this case has been carried out, and under it the receiver has sold certain property and has received the purchase-money.   But I take it that an agreement founded upon a common mistake, which mistake is impliedly treated as a consideration which must exist in order to bring the agreement into operation, can be set aside, formally if necessary, or treated as set aside and as invalid without any process or proceedings to do so.   In point of law, the moment you have got rid of the consent order, it is quite plain that an action would lie at law for money had and received at the instance of the bank against the receiver upon the ground of the mutual mistake; or, rather, as it would be put in law, a total failure of consideration.   If authority for that be wanted, the cases will be found collected in the ordinary books on contract; but in particular *Strickland* v. *Turner*[3] is one of them. That case related to the sale of an annuity by trustees.   The annuitant had died shortly before the sale was effected, but the death was unknown to the purchaser, who paid over his purchase-money.   He afterwards brought an action to recover it back, and his success was a matter of course.

On the same principle, there are cases in equity, of which *Bingham* v. *Bingham*[4] may be referred to as a leading example, in which an agreement to purchase a property was set aside and the money restored, upon the ground that the property really belonged to the man who had professed to buy it.   It was a common mistake, and the transaction was set aside.   I am aware that *Bingham* v. *Bingham*[4] has been occasionally criticised, and in some of the earlier editions of Lord St. Leonard's book on Vendors and Purchasers he seemed to think there was something wrong about it.   In his later editions, however, he changed his opinion; and *Bingham* v. *Bingham*[4] was carefully examined in the House of Lords in *Cooper* v. *Phibbs*[5], and was distinctly affirmed.   The principle of it was assented to and laid down

---

[1] (1845), 8 Beav. 503.   [2] (1877), 7 Ch. D. 388.   [3] (1852), 7 Ex. 208.
[4] (1748), 1 Ves. Sen. 126.   [5] (1867), L. R. 2 H. L. 149.

to be correct; and in a still later case of *Jones* v. *Clifford*[1] Hall, V.-C., again went through the whole of the cases relied on, and came to the conclusion that *Bingham* v. *Bingham*[2] was sound law. As I understand the case, I cannot conceive on what ground there should be any question of its soundness. It appears to me to be in perfect accordance with well-settled principles of law, both of this country and of all civilised countries, as far as I know. In the case now before the Court there is, as far as I can see, no difficulty in getting rid of the consent order or of the agreement under which the receiver received the money. For the agreement was based upon a mistake of fact common to both parties, the mistake being that both parties thought and believed that these thirty-three looms never had been fixed at all, whereas in fact they had.

KAY, L.J.   I will add a few words on my own behalf, because one of the questions raised in this case is of very considerable importance. It was denied in argument that the Court had any jurisdiction whatever to set aside a consent order except in the case of fraud.

Now, what is this consent order? After all, it is only the order of the Court carrying out an agreement between the parties. Supposing the order out of the way and the agreement only to exist, there can be no sort of doubt that the agreement could be set aside, not merely for fraud, but in case it was based upon a mistake of material fact which was common to all the parties to it. Then, if it could be set aside on that ground, why should the Court be unable to set it aside simply because an order has been founded upon it? It seems to me that, both on principle and on authority, when once the Court finds that an agreement has been come to between parties who were under a common mistake of a material fact, the Court may set it aside, and the Court has ample jurisdiction to set aside the order founded upon that agreement. Of course, if the order had been acted upon, and third parties' interests had intervened and so on, difficulties might arise; but nothing of that kind occurs here. Here we have got simply the parties to this agreement and order before us. No one else seems to have obtained any kind of interest under it; and therefore, if it be made out that the order proceeded upon the common mistake of a material fact, there is ample jurisdiction in the Court to set it aside.

Now, the only bodies or persons who were parties to this agreement and this consent order were the original mortgagees and the subsequent debenture-holders. The question was, which of the looms on the mortgaged property were in the nature of fixtures. It was agreed that two were, and it was agreed that thirty-three were not; but as to the thirty-three there does not seem to have been any dispute or contest whether they were fixtures or not. Experts went down and examined what the condition of things was, and found that these thirty-three looms were completely loose. Therefore, they came to the conclusion that they never had been fixed, and these looms were not treated as fixtures at all. That was not the fact. The fact was that they had been fixtures just as much as the two that were treated as fixtures. On the whole, I think the learned judge came correctly to the conclusion that they had been, owing to the manner in which they were fixed to the floor, as much fixtures as the two which it was agreed must be treated as fixtures.

[The Lord Justice then dealt with the contention that, although these

---

[1] (1876), 3 Ch. D. 779.   [2] (1748), 1 Ves. Sen. 126.

looms might have become fixtures, they were never affixed to the mills with
the authority of the mortgagors who were in possession, and, after considering
the evidence upon this point, came to the conclusion that beyond the
possibility of reasonable question they were fastened down by the authority
of the mortgagors.   His Lordship then continued :—]

I therefore think there was a mistake of a material fact which was
common both to the mortgagees and to the debenture-holders between whom
this agreement was made, and on whose behalf this consent order was made.
The mortgagees were induced to consent by ignorance of this material fact,
which also the other side were ignorant of.   That seems to me to give the
Court jurisdiction to set aside the agreement based upon a common mistake
of a material fact, and consequently to set aside the order which was founded
upon it.

LOPES, L.J., gave judgment to the same effect.

Solle v. Butcher
[1950] 1 K.B. 671

APPEAL from Bromley county court.

In 1947, the plaintiff, Godfrey Frank Solle, a surveyor, became a
partner with the defendant, Charles Butcher, in a business of estate agents
styled Godfrey and Charles.   At about that time, the plaintiff introduced
the defendant to the representative of the head lessor of Maywood House,
Beckenham.   This dwelling-house was converted into five flats in 1931, and
in 1938 flat No. 1 was let to one Taylor for three years at an annual rent of
140*l*.   There was a room at the north-west corner of the flat, a part of the
main building, which formed a garage.   Taylor's lease contained no mention
of a garage, but evidence was given by the landlord that Taylor had the right
to use a garage.   In 1947 the flats were unoccupied, a land mine having
exploded near them during the war and done them considerable damage.
In 1947 the defendant took a long lease of the house containing the five
flats with the intention of repairing the war damage and carrying out substantial alterations to the flats.   The defendant was the managing director
of a building company which carried out the works at the flats.   The plaintiff
arranged the finance of the undertakings and negotiated with the rating
authorities as to the new rateable values of the flats, and it was his work to
let the flats.   The plaintiff and the defendant had conversations as to the
rents to be charged for the flats after the works had been completed.   According to the plaintiff, he said, on the question of the standard rent : " Be careful,
because the flats may be within the Rent Acts "; and the defendant said
that he would obtain legal advice on that.   Later the plaintiff presented to the
defendant counsel's opinion which was not produced in court.   It appeared
from the evidence of the defendant that both he and the plaintiff were
satisfied that the rent of 140*l*. in 1938 did not apply as the standard rent.
The defendant said that he relied on the plaintiff on this subject of rents and
that he did not take any action to calculate the permitted additions to the
standard rent in respect of the improvements and structural alterations at
the flats (see s. 7, sub-s. 4 of the Rent and Mortgage Interest (Restrictions)
Act, 1938).   It was stated that because of the works at the flat the permitted
increases might have brought the total permitted rent of flat No. 1 to
about 250*l*.

The defendant spent 6,420*l*. for repair of war damage and about 1,000*l*.

on other alterations and substantial decorations of the five flats. So far as flat No. 1 was concerned, he cut away two broken walls, that at the south end of the main bedroom and that at the north end of the living room, and a transverse brick wall between them where there was a passage and a cupboard. The weight of the structure overhead was taken by steel joists, and some underpinning was done in the cellar below. As a result, space was subtracted from the bedroom and incorporated in the living room so as to form part of a dining recess in the latter. This was a substantial alteration and the work was difficult and expensive. Some wooden partitions were put up in a second bedroom to make a small box-room, and two cupboards were placed in a third bedroom. Three or four electric fires were put in and the hot-water system throughout the building was improved.

Flat No. 1 was let by the defendant to the plaintiff from September 29, 1947, for a term of seven years at a yearly rent of 250*l*. In the lease the garage was expressly included. Once this lease was executed no notice of intention to increase the rent could be given under the Acts of 1920 and 1923 during the contractual tenancy.

Relations between the parties having deteriorated, the plaintiff sued the defendant in the county court, alleging that the standard rent of flat No. 1 was 140*l*. and claiming recovery of the amount of rent which he had overpaid. The defendant by his defence alleged that he granted the lease to the plaintiff on his oral assurance that the rent of 250*l*. was in no way controlled by any letting of the flat before it suffered war damage. He denied that the premises were controlled by virtue of any " pre-war damage " letting. In the alternative, the defendant contended that the plaintiff was estopped by his conduct from asserting that any such control relieved him of his personal obligation to pay the rent of 250*l*. By way of counterclaim, the defendant asserted that the lease was entered into in circumstances amounting to a common mistake of fact, and he asked for rescission of the lease.

The county court judge, Sir Gerald Hurst, K.C., who preferred the evidence of the defendant when it was in conflict with that of the plaintiff, gave judgment for the plaintiff, making a declaration that the standard rent of flat No. 1 was 140*l*. He said: " I find that there was no mistake of fact—possibly a mistake of law—in that both parties for some obscure reason imagined that the Rent Acts did not apply. I do not think they ever addressed their minds to the material issue of identity." He held also that the plea of estoppel was no defence against the provisions of the Rent Restriction Acts. He made an order for the recovery of the amount of rent overpaid, 137*l*. 10*s*. 0*d*. The defendant, the landlord, appealed.

The relevant questions for the court were: (1) whether on the facts of the case the county court judge was right in finding that the standard rent of the premises was 140*l*. a year; if so (2) whether the landlord was right in his contentions that he was entitled to a rescission of the lease on the ground of (*a*) common mistake, or (*b*) innocent material misrepresentation by the plaintiff; and (3) whether the tenant was estopped from claiming the benefit of the Rent Restriction Acts.

DENNING, L.J. The first question is, what is the rent which may lawfully be charged for this flat and garage? The judge has, I think, misdirected himself in several respects, so it is open to this court to review his findings: *British Launderers Research Association* v. *Borough of Hendon Rating Authority*[1]. On this review I think that the structural alterations

---

[1] [1949] 1 K. B. 462.

and improvements were not such as to destroy the identity of the original flat. The landlord was entitled, therefore, to increase the rent by 8 per cent. of their cost, but was not able on this account to charge a new rent unrestricted by the Acts.

The inclusion in the lease of a garage, which had previously not formed part of the demise, gives rise to difficult questions. Even when taken together with the structural alterations, the addition of the garage does not change the identity of the flat. The standard rent, therefore, remains at 140*l.*: *Hemns* v. *Wheeler*[1] and *Langford Property Co., Ltd.* v. *Batten*[2]. It does not follow, however, that the tenant gets the benefit of the garage for nothing. The landlord is probably entitled to increase the rent on account of it. Such an increase is justified by s. 2, sub-s. 3 of the Act of 1920 as interpreted by this court in *Seaford Court Estates, Ltd.* v. *Asher*[3]. Just as the landlord was entitled in that case to increase the rent because the tenant was relieved of the contingent burden of providing himself with hot water, if he wanted it, so here the tenant is relieved of the contingent burden of providing himself with a garage, if he wants one. I do not, however, pursue the point, because it was not argued before us. It is said that, even allowing nothing for the garage, the permitted increases for structural alterations and improvements and increase of rates bring up the rent lawfully payable from 140*l.* to 250*l.* If, therefore, the landlord had served the prospective tenant with a proper notice of increase, the lease at 250*l.* a year would have been valid. But he did not serve any notice at all, because he thought that, owing to the improvements, the new rent was not restricted by the Acts. The tenant says that, there having been no notice, the landlord can only recover 140*l.* a year for the seven years of the lease.

So long as the lease stands the tenant's argument is unanswerable. The Rent Restriction Acts prevent the landlord from recovering any more than the standard rent unless a notice of intention to increase the rent is given either to the sitting tenant or to a prospective tenant; and, although errors or omissions in a notice are not necessarily fatal, nevertheless there must be a notice, however informal. In this case the landlord conceded that no notice was served before the new lease was granted. It follows that the raising of the rent from 140*l.* to 250*l.* was invalid, and the landlord can do nothing now to repair the omission because no fresh notice of increase can be effective so long as the lease continues. The landlord tried to overcome this difficulty by saying that the tenant was estopped from saying that the rent of 250*l.* was invalid; but, just as parties cannot contract out of the Acts, so they cannot defeat them by any estoppel.

In this plight the landlord seeks to set aside the lease. He says, with truth, that it is unfair that the tenant should have the benefit of the lease for the outstanding five years of the term at 140*l.* a year, when the proper rent is 250*l.* a year. If he cannot give a notice of increase now, can he not avoid the lease? The only ground on which he can avoid it is on the ground of mistake. It is quite plain that the parties were under a mistake. They thought that the flat was not tied down to a controlled rent, whereas in fact it was. In order to see whether the lease can be avoided for this mistake it is necessary to remember that mistake is of two kinds: first, mistake which renders the contract void, that is, a nullity from the beginning, which is the kind of mistake which was dealt with by the courts of common law; and,

---

[1] [1948] 2 K. B. 61.　　　　　　　　[2] [1949] 2 All E. R. 422.

[3] [1949] 2 K. B. 481.

secondly, mistake which renders the contract not void, but voidable, that is, liable to be set aside on such terms as the court thinks fit, which is the kind of mistake which was dealt with by the courts of equity. Much of the difficulty which has attended this subject has arisen because, before the fusion of law and equity, the courts of common law, in order to do justice in the case in hand, extended this doctrine of mistake beyond its proper limits and held contracts to be void which were really only voidable, a process which was capable of being attended with much injustice to third persons who had bought goods or otherwise committed themselves on the faith that there was a contract. In the well-known case of *Cundy* v. *Lindsay*[1], Cundy suffered such an injustice. He bought the handkerchiefs from the rogue, Blenkarn, before the Judicature Acts came into operation. Since the fusion of law and equity there is no reason to continue this process, and it will be found that only those contracts are now held void in which the mistake was such as to prevent the formation of any contract at all.

Let me first consider mistakes which render a contract a nullity. All previous decisions on this subject must now be read in the light of *Bell* v. *Lever Brothers, Ltd.*[2] The correct interpretation of that case, to my mind, is that, once a contract has been made, that is to say, once the parties, whatever their inmost states of mind, have to all outward appearances agreed with sufficient certainty in the same terms on the same subject matter, then the contract is good unless and until it is set aside for failure of some condition on which the existence of the contract depends, or for fraud, or on some equitable ground. Neither party can rely on his own mistake to say it was a nullity from the beginning, no matter that it was a mistake which to his mind was fundamental, and no matter that the other party knew that he was under a mistake. *A fortiori*, if the other party did not know of the mistake but shared it. The cases where goods have perished at the time of sale, or belong to the buyer, are really contracts which are not void for mistake but are void by reason of an implied condition precedent, because the contract proceeded on the basic assumption that it was possible of performance. So far as cases later than *Bell* v. *Lever Bros., Ltd.*[2] are concerned, I do not think that *Sowler* v. *Potter*[3] can stand with *King's Norton Metal Co., Ltd.* v. *Edridge*[4] which shows that the doctrine of French law as enunciated by Pothier is no part of English law. Nor do I think that the contract of *Nicholson and Venn* v. *Smith-Marriott*[5] was void from the beginning.

Applying these principles, it is clear that here there was a contract. The parties agreed in the same terms on the same subject-matter. It is true that the landlord was under a mistake which was to him fundamental; he would not for one moment have considered letting the flat for seven years if it meant that he could only charge 140*l.* a year for it. He made the fundamental mistake of believing that the rent he could charge was not tied down to a controlled rent; but, whether it was his own mistake or a mistake common to both him and the tenant, it is not a ground for saying that the lease was from the beginning a nullity. Any other view would lead to remarkable results, for it would mean that, in the many cases where the parties mistakenly think a house is outside the Rent Restriction Acts when it is really within them, the tenancy would be a nullity, and the tenant would have to go; with the result that the tenants would not dare to seek to

[1] (1876), 1 Q. B. D. 348; (1878), 3 App. Cas. 459.
[2] [1932] A.C. 161, at pp. 222, 224, 225-7, 236.
[3] [1940] 1 K. B. 271.   [4] (1897), 14 T. L. R. 98.   [5] (1947), 177 L. T. 189.

have their rents reduced to the permitted amounts lest they should be turned out.

Let me next consider mistakes which render a contract voidable, that is, liable to be set aside on some equitable ground. Whilst presupposing that a contract was good at law, or at any rate not void, the court of equity would often relieve a party from the consequences of his own mistake, so long as it could do so without injustice to third parties. The court, it was said, had power to set aside the contract whenever it was of opinion that it was unconscientious for the other party to avail himself of the legal advantage which he had obtained: *Torrance* v. *Bolton*[1] *per* James, L.J.

The court had, of course, to define what it considered to be unconscientious, but in this respect equity has shown a progressive development. It is now clear that a contract will be set aside if the mistake of the one party has been induced by a material misrepresentation of the other, even though it was not fraudulent or fundamental; or if one party, knowing that the other is mistaken about the terms of an offer, or the identity of the person by whom it is made, lets him remain under his delusion and concludes a contract on the mistaken terms instead of pointing out the mistake. That is, I venture to think, the ground on which the defendant in *Smith* v. *Hughes*[2] would be exempted nowadays, and on which, according to the view by Blackburn, J. of the facts, the contract in *Lindsay* v. *Cundy*[3], was voidable and not void; and on which the lease in *Sowler* v. *Potter*[4], was, in my opinion, voidable and not void.

A contract is also liable in equity to be set aside if the parties were under a common misapprehension either as to facts or as to their relative and respective rights, provided that the misapprehension was fundamental and that the party seeking to set it aside was not himself at fault. That principle was first applied to private rights as long ago as 1730 in *Lansdown* v. *Lansdown*[5]. There were four brothers, and the second and third of them died. The eldest brother entered on the lands of the deceased brothers, but the youngest brother claimed them. So the two rival brothers consulted a friend who was a local schoolmaster. The friend looked up a book which he then had with him called the Clerk's Remembrancer and gave it as his opinion that the lands belonged to the youngest brother. He recommended the two of them to take further advice, which at first they intended to do, but they did not do so; and, acting on the friend's opinion, the elder brother agreed to divide the estate with the younger brother, and executed deeds and bonds giving effect to the agreement. Lord Chancellor King declared that the documents were obtained by a mistake and by a misrepresentation of the law by the friend, and ordered them to be given up to be cancelled. He pointed out that the maxim *ignorantia juris non excusat* only means that ignorance cannot be pleaded in excuse of crimes. Eighteen years later, in the time of Lord Hardwicke, the same principle was applied in *Bingham* v. *Bingham*[6].

If and in so far as those cases were compromises of disputed rights, they have been subjected to justifiable criticism, but, in cases where there is no element of compromise, but only of mistaken rights, the House of Lords in 1867 in the great case of *Cooper* v. *Phibbs*[7], affirmed the doctrine there acted

---

[1] (1872), 8 Ch. App. 118, at p. 124.   [2] (1871), L. R. 6 Q. B. 597.
[3] (1876–8), 1 Q. B. D. 348, at p. 355; (1878), 3 App. Cas. 459.
[4] [1940] 1 K. B. 271.   [5] (1730), Mos. 364; 2 Jac. & W. 205.
[6] (1748), 1 Ves. Sen. 126; Belt's Supp. 79.   [7] (1867), L. R. 2 H. L. 149, at p. 170.

on as correct.   In that case an uncle had told his nephew, not intending to misrepresent anything, but being in fact in error, that he (the uncle) was entitled to a fishery; and the nephew, after the uncle's death, acting in the belief of the truth of what the uncle had told him, entered into an agreement to rent the fishery from the uncle's daughters, whereas it actually belonged to the nephew himself.   The mistake there as to the title to the fishery did not render the tenancy agreement a nullity.   If it had done, the contract would have been void at law from the beginning and equity would have had to follow the law.   There would have been no contract to set aside and no terms to impose.   The House of Lords, however, held that the mistake was only such as to make it voidable, or, in Lord Westbury's words, " liable to be set aside " on such terms as the court thought fit to impose; and it was so set aside.

The principle so established by *Cooper* v. *Phibbs*[1] has been repeatedly acted on: see, for instance, *Earl Beauchamp* v. *Winn*[2], and *Huddersfield Banking Co. Ltd.* v. *Lister*[3].   It is in no way impaired by *Bell* v. *Lever Brothers, Ltd.*[4], which was treated in the House of Lords as a case at law depending on whether the contract was a nullity or not.   If it had been considered on equitable grounds, the result might have been different.   In any case, the principle of *Cooper* v. *Phibbs*[1] has been fully restored by *Norwich Union Fire Insurance Society Ltd.* v. *William H. Price, Ltd.*[5]

Applying that principle to this case, the facts are that the plaintiff, the tenant, was a surveyor who was employed by the defendant, the landlord, not only to arrange finance for the purchase of the building and to negotiate with the rating authorities as to the new rateable values, but also to let the flats.   He was the agent for letting, and he clearly formed the view that the building was not controlled.   He told the valuation officer so.   He advised the defendant what were the rents which could be charged.   He read to the defendant an opinion of counsel relating to the matter, and told him that in his opinion he could charge 250*l*. and that there was no previous control. He said that the flats came outside the Act and that the defendant was " clear ".   The defendant relied on what the plaintiff told him, and authorized the plaintiff to let at the rentals which he had suggested.   The plaintiff not only let the four other flats to other people for a long period of years at the new rentals, but also took one himself for seven years at 250*l*. a year.   Now he turns round and says, quite unashamedly, that he wants to take advantage of the mistake to get the flat at 140*l*. a year for seven years instead of 250*l*. a year, which is not only the rent he agreed to pay but also the fair and economic rent; and it is also the rent permitted by the Acts on compliance with the necessary formalities.   If the rules of equity have become so rigid that they cannot remedy such an injustice, it is time we had a new equity, to make good the omissions of the old.   But, in my view, the established rules are amply sufficient for this case.

On the defendant's evidence, which the judge preferred, I should have thought there was a good deal to be said for the view that the lease was induced by an innocent material misrepresentation by the plaintiff.   It seems to me that the plaintiff was not merely expressing an opinion on the law: he was making an unambiguous statement as to private rights; and a

---

[1] (1867), L.R. 2 H.L. 149, at p. 170.
[2] (1873), L.R. 6 H.L. 223, at p. 234.　　　[3] [1895] 2 Ch. 273, *supra*, p. 128.
[4] [1932] A. C. 161, *supra*, p. 117.　　　[5] [1934] A.C. 455, at pp. 462–3.

misrepresentation as to private rights is equivalent to a misrepresentation of fact for this purpose: *MacKenzie* v. *Royal Bank of Canada*[1]. But it is unnecessary to come to a firm conclusion on this point, because, as Bucknill, L.J., has said, there was clearly a common mistake, or, as I would prefer to describe it, a common misapprehension, which was fundamental and in no way due to any fault of the defendant; and *Cooper* v. *Phibbs*[2] affords ample authority for saying that, by reason of the common misapprehension, this lease can be set aside on such terms as the court thinks fit.

The fact that the lease has been executed is no bar to this relief. No distinction can, in this respect, be taken between rescission for innocent misrepresentation and rescission for common misapprehension, for many of the common misapprehensions are due to innocent misrepresentation; and *Cooper* v. *Phibbs*[2] shows that rescission is available even after an agreement of tenancy has been executed and partly performed. The observations in *Seddon* v. *North Eastern Salt Co., Ltd.*[3], have lost all authority since Scrutton, L.J., threw doubt on them in *Lever Brothers, Ltd.* v. *Bell*[4], and the Privy Council actually set aside an executed agreement in *MacKenzie* v. *Royal Bank of Canada*[5]. If and in so far as *Angel* v. *Jay*[6] decided that an executed lease could not be rescinded for an innocent misrepresentation, it was in my opinion a wrong decision. It would mean that innocent people would be deprived of their right of rescission before they had any opportunity of knowing they had it. I am aware that in *Wilde* v. *Gibson*[7], Lord Campbell said that an executed conveyance could be set aside only on the ground of actual fraud; but this must be taken to be confined to misrepresentations as to defects of title on the conveyance of land.

In the ordinary way, of course, rescission is only granted when the parties can be restored to substantially the same position as that in which they were before the contract was made; but, as Lord Blackburn said in *Erlanger* v. *New Sombrero Phosphate Co.*[8]: " The practice has always been for a court of equity to give this relief whenever, by the exercise of its powers, it can do what is practically just, though it cannot restore the parties precisely to the state they were in before the contract." That indeed was what was done in *Cooper* v. *Phibbs*[1]. Terms were imposed so as to do what was practically just. What terms then, should be imposed here ? If the lease were set aside without any terms being imposed, it would mean that the plaintiff, the tenant, would have to go out and would have to pay a reasonable sum for his use and occupation. That would, however, not be just to the tenant.

The situation is similar to that of a case where a long lease is made at the full permitted rent in the common belief that notices of increase have previously been served, whereas in fact they have not. In that case, as in this, when the lease is set aside, terms must be imposed so as to see that the tenant is not unjustly evicted. When Sir John Romilly, M.R., was faced with a somewhat similar problem, he gave the tenant the option either to agree to pay the proper rent or to go out: see *Garrard* v. *Frankel*[9]; and when Bacon, V.C., had a like problem before him he did the same, saying that " the object of the court is, as far as it can, to put the parties into the position in which they would have been in if the mistake had not happened "; see

---

[1] [1934] A. C. 468.   [2] (1867), L. R. 2 H. L. 149.   [3] [1905] 1 Ch. 326.
[4] [1931] 1 K. B. 557, at p. 588.   [5] [1934] A. C. 468.
[6] [1911] 1 K. B. 666.   [7] (1848), 1 H. L. Cas. 605.
[8] (1878), 3 App. Cas. 1218, at pp. 1278-9.   [9] (1862), 30 Beav. 445.

Paget v. *Marshall*[1]. If the mistake here had not happened, a proper notice of increase would have been given and the lease would have been executed at the full permitted rent. I think that this court should follow these examples and should impose terms which will enable the tenant to choose either to stay on at the proper rent or to go out.

The terms will be complicated by reason of the Rent Restriction Acts, but it is not beyond the wit of man to devise them. Subject to any observations which the parties may desire to make, the terms which I suggest are these: the lease should only be set aside if the defendant is prepared to give an undertaking that he will permit the plaintiff to be a licensee of the premises pending the grant of a new lease. Then, whilst the plaintiff is a licensee, the defendant will in law be in possession of the premises, and will be able to serve on the plaintiff, as prospective tenant, a notice under s. 7, sub-s. (4), of the Act of 1938 increasing the rent to the full permitted amount. The defendant must further be prepared to give an undertaking that he will serve such a notice within three weeks from the drawing up of the order, and that he will, if written request is made by the plaintiff, within one month of the service of the notice, grant him a new lease at the full permitted amount of rent, not, however, exceeding 250*l.* a year, for a term expiring on September 29, 1954, subject in all other respects to the same covenants and conditions as in the rescinded lease. If there is any difference of opinion about the figures stated in the notice, that can, of course, be adjusted during the currency of the lease. If the plaintiff does not choose to accept the licence or the new lease, he must go out. He will not be entitled to the protection of the Rent Restriction Acts because, the lease being set aside, there will be no initial contractual tenancy from which a statutory tenancy can spring.

In my opinion, therefore, the appeal should be allowed. The declaration that the standard rent of the flat is 140*l.* a year should stand. An order should be made on the counter-claim that, on the defendant's giving the undertakings which I have mentioned, the lease be set aside. An account should be had to determine the sum payable for use and occupation. The plaintiff's claim for repayment of rent and for breach of covenant should be dismissed. In respect of his occupation after rescission and during the subsequent licence, the plaintiff will be liable to pay a reasonable sum for use and occupation. That sum should, *prima facie*, be assessed at the full amount permitted by the Acts, not, however, exceeding 250*l.* a year. Mesne profits as against a trespasser are assessed at the full amount permitted by the Acts, even though notices of increase have not been served, because that is the amount lost by the landlord. The same assessment should be made here, because the sums payable for use and occupation are not rent, and the statutory provisions about notices of increase do not apply to them. All necessary credits must, of course, be given in respect of past payments, and so forth.

BUCKNILL, L.J., delivered judgment, agreeing with the terms proposed by DENNING, L.J. JENKINS, L.J., dissented on the ground that the common mistake made by the parties was a mistake not of fact but of law.

---

[1] (1884), 28 Ch. D. 255, at p. 267.

Magee v. Pennine Insurance Co., Ltd.

[1969] 2 All E.R. 891

APPEAL. This was an appeal by the defendants, Pennine Insurance Co., Ltd., from a judgment of His Honour JUDGE LEIGH given on July 1, 1968, whereby he gave judgment for the plaintiff, Thomas Magee, for £385. The facts are set out in the judgment of LORD DENNING, M.R.

G. A. Carman for the defendant insurance company.

K. J. Taylor for the plaintiff.

LORD DENNING, M.R. In 1961 the plaintiff, Mr. Thomas Magee, aged 58, acquired an Austin car. He signed a proposal form for insurance. In it he said that the car belonged to him. He was asked to give details of his driving licence " and of all other persons who to your present knowledge will drive ". These were the details he gave:

" (i) Thomas Magee [that is himself] provisional licence, aged 58. (ii) John Magee [that is his elder son] Police mobile driver, aged 35. [He had an annual licence.] (iii) John Magee [that is the younger son] joiner, aged 18— provisional licence."

The plaintiff signed this declaration:

" I do hereby declare that the Car described is and shall be kept in good condition and that the answers above given are in every respect true and correct and I hereby agree that this Declaration shall be the basis of the Contract of Insurance between the Company and myself."

Those details were not written by the plaintiff. They were written in by Mr. Atkinson at the garage where he got the car. The details unfortunately were completely wrong. The plaintiff had never driven a car himself. He had never had a licence, not even a provisional one. He was getting the car really for his son of 18 to drive. And we all know that a young man of 18 has to pay a much higher insurance than a man of 25 or over. The insurance company said they would not have insured a young man of 18.

The judge found that the plaintiff had not been fraudulent. He did not himself fill in the details. They were filled in by Mr. Atkinson, the man at the garage, and then the plaintiff signed them. It was Mr. Atkinson who made some mistake or other; but there it was. A misrepresentation was made, and on the faith of it being true the insurance company granted an insurance policy to the plaintiff.

Thereafter the policy was renewed each year and the premiums were paid. In 1964 that car was replaced by another. The policy was renewed for the new car without anything further being said about the drivers or the ownership. The insurance company assumed, no doubt, that the same details applied.

On April 25, 1965, there was an accident. The younger son, John Magee, was driving the new car at 4.0 a.m. He ran into a shop window. The plate glass was smashed and the car was a complete wreck. The plaintiff put in a claim form, in which he said that the car was £600 in value. That was clearly wrong because the price new was only £547 the year before. The insurance company thereupon got its engineer to look at it. On May 12, 1965, the broker sent a letter to the plaintiff, in which he wrote:

"... we have today been advised by [the insurance company] that their engineer considers your vehicle is damaged beyond repair. The engineer considers that the pre-accident market value of the vehicle was £410 and they are therefore prepared to offer you this amount, less the £25 accidental damage excess in settlement of your claim. We should be pleased to receive your confirmation that this is acceptable . . .''

There was no written acceptance, but it was accepted by word of mouth. That seemed to be a concluded agreement whereby the insurance company agreed to pay £385.

But within the next few days the insurance company made further enquiries. One of its representatives saw the plaintiff and took a statement from him. Then the truth was discovered. The plaintiff did not drive at all. He had never had a driving licence, not even a provisional one. He said that the car was never his property but was his son's car: and that it was his son, the younger son, who had driven the car and was the only person who had ever driven it. On discovering those facts, the insurance company stated that it was not liable on the insurance policy. They had been induced to grant it, they said, by the misrepresentations in the original proposal form; and also by reason of non-disclosure of material facts, namely, that the son aged 18 was normally to be the driver.

The plaintiff brought an action in the county court in which he claimed the £385. He said it was payable under the insurance policy, or, alternatively, on an agreement of compromise contained in the letter of May 12. The judge rejected the claim on the policy itself, because the insurance was induced by misrepresentation. He found that the insurance company was entitled to repudiate the policy because of the inaccuracy of the plaintiff's answers. That finding was not challenged in this court. Counsel for the plaintiff admitted that he could not claim on the policy.

But the judge upheld the claim on the letter of May 12. He said it was a binding contract of compromise. I am not so sure about this. It might be said to be a mere quantification of the account which should be paid in case the insurance company was liable; and that it did not preclude it from afterwards contesting liability. But, on the whole, I do not think that we should regard it as a mere quantification. The letter contains the important words: '' in settlement of your claim '', which import that it is to be settled without further controversy. In short, it bears the stamp of an agreement of compromise. The consideration for it was the ascertainment of a sum which was previously unascertained.

But then comes the next point. Accepting that the agreement to pay £385 was an agreement of compromise, is it vitiated by mistake? The insurance company was clearly under a mistake. It thought that the policy was good and binding. It did not know, at the time of that letter, that there had been misrepresentations in the proposal form. If the plaintiff knew of its mistake—if he knew that the policy was bad—he certainly could not take advantage of the agreement to pay £385. He would be '' snapping at an offer which he knew was made under a mistake ''; and no man is allowed to get away with that. But I prefer to assume that the plaintiff was innocent. I think we should take it that both parties were under a common mistake. Both parties thought that the policy was good and binding. The letter of May 12, 1965, was written on the assumption that the policy was good whereas it was in truth voidable.

What is the effect of this common mistake? Counsel for the plaintiff said that the agreement to pay £385 was good, despite this common mistake. He relied much on *Bell* v. *Lever Brothers, Ltd*[1] and its similarity to the present

---

[1] [1932] A.C. 161; [1931] All E.R. Rep. 11.

case. He submitted that, inasmuch as the mistake there did not vitiate that contract, the mistake here should not vitiate this one. I do not propose today to go through the speeches in that case. They have given enough trouble to commentators already. I would say simply this: A common mistake, even on a most fundamental matter, does not make a contract void at law; but it makes it voidable in equity. I analysed the cases in *Solle* v. *Butcher*[1], and I would repeat what I said there[2]:

> " A contract is also liable in equity to be set aside if the parties were under a common misapprehension either as to facts or as to their relative and respective rights, provided that the misapprehension was fundamental and that the party seeking to set it aside was not himself at fault."

Applying that principle here, it is clear that, when the insurance company and the plaintiff made this agreement to pay £385, they were both under a common mistake which was fundamental to the whole agreement. Both thought that the plaintiff was entitled to claim under the policy of insurance, whereas he was not so entitled. That common mistake does not make the agreement to pay £385 a nullity, but it makes it liable to be set aside in equity.

This brings me to a question which has caused me much difficulty. Is this a case in which we ought to set the agreement aside in equity? I have hesitated on this point, but I cannot shut my eyes to the fact that the plaintiff had no valid claim on the insurance policy; and, if he had no claim on the policy, it is not equitable that he should have a good claim on the agreement to pay £385, which the insurance company would not have dreamt of making if it had not been under a mistake. I would, therefore, allow the appeal and give judgment for the insurance company.

WINN, L.J. This appeal has given me pleasure because it has been so well argued by both the learned counsel who have appeared in it; and, of course, the problem which it presents is not one the solution of which is going to impose frightful actual loss or consequences on the particular individuals or companies who are involved. It is a neat and teasing problem, the difficulty of which is slightly indicated, though by no means established, by the regrettable circumstance that I find myself respectfully having to dissent from the views of LORD DENNING, M.R., and of FENTON ATKINSON, L.J. I agree with LORD DENNING, M.R., that the letter of May 12, 1965, is of very great importance, though I take the point of counsel for the insurance company that it is not the insurers' letter; it is only what purports to be a report, probably of a telephone conversation, written by the brokers, who were the agents of the plaintiff, of what they were told by some representative of the insurance company. I attach importance to it not because of its terms, which may not be an accurate representation of what the insurers had said, but because it contemplates a complete clearance of the whole matter and a termination of the dispute arising out of the claim, insofar as there was any, by return of various documents, which clearly was regarded as the final, terminal phase of the matter. Whether or not this could be regarded, on a strict construction, as no more than an offer to fix a figure, which, subject to being liable to pay at all, the insurance company was prepared to pay, seems to me to be excluded as a reality by the considerations which I have mentioned. This must have evinced an offer by the insurance company to dispose of the matter by paying £385 in settlement. As I see the matter, it is not

---

[1] [1950] 1 K.B. 671; [1949] 2 All E.R. 1107.
[2] [1950] 1 K.B. 693; [1949] 2 All E.R. 1120.

a question of whether thereby a contract was formed, since it seems to me it is clear that there was a contract formed by that offer from the insurance company and the acceptance of it, again through the brokers, by the plaintiff. The question is whether, as LORD DENNING, M.R., has indicated clearly, that contract is, for one reason or another, invalid and unenforceable by the plaintiff against the insurers.

I do not desire to take long in expressing my opinion that the principles of *Bell* v. *Lever Brothers, Ltd*[1], applied to the circumstances of this case, suggest the contrary conclusion to that which LORD DENNING, M.R., has expressed as correct. It appears to me that the parties were under a misapprehension. If there was any misapprehension shared commonly by both the plaintiff and the insurance company as to the value of any rights that he had against it arising from the insurance policy, that seems to me to have been precisely the subject-matter of the common misapprehension in *Bell* v. *Lever Brothers, Ltd.*[1]. One could pick out and read, and it would be instructive to re-read them many times, several passages from the speech of LORD ATKIN and indeed also from that of LORD THANKERTON; but I content myself with the point made by LORD ATKIN, when he said that[2]:

> " Various words are to be found to define the state of things which make a condition. [i.e., a condition, non-compliance with which, will avoid a contract, and LORD ATKIN instances, quoting them, the phrases]   ' In the contemplation of both parties fundamental to the continued validity of the contract ', ' a foundation essential to its existence ', ' a fundamental reason for making it ', . . . all of which, as LORD ATKIN said, were to be found in the judgment of SCRUTTON, L.J., in the same case[3]. The first two phrases appear to me to be unexceptionable . . . But [by contrast, he said] ' a fundamental reason for making a contract ' may, with respect, be misleading."

And LORD ATKIN goes on to give instances of such misleading assertions or misleading definitions of what is meant by a foundation essential to the contract.

For my part, I think that here there was a misapprehension as to rights, but no misapprehension whatsoever as to the subject-matter of the contract, namely, the settlement of the rights of the plaintiff with regard to the accident that happened. The insurance company was settling his rights, if he had any. He understood it to be settling his rights; but each of them, on the assumption that the learned county court judge's view of the facts was right, thought his rights against the insurance company were very much more valuable than in fact they were, since in reality they were worthless; the insurance company could have repudiated—or avoided, that being the more accurate phrase on the basis of the mis-statements which my Lord has narrated.

LORD THANKERTON also said[4]:

> " The phrase ' underlying assumption by the parties ', as applied to the subject-matter of a contract, may be too widely interpreted so as to include something which one of the parties had not necessarily in his mind at the time of the contract; in my opinion it can only properly relate to something which both must necessarily have accepted in their minds as an essential and integral element of the subject-matter."

I venture respectfully to contrast that sentence with any such sentence as this: " which the parties both must necessarily have accepted in their minds

---

[1] [1932] A.C. 161; [1931] All E.R. Rep. 11.
[2] [1932] A.C. at pp. 225, 226; [1931] All E.R. Rep. at p. 31. See *supra*, p. 126.
[3] [1931] 1 K.B. 557.
[4] [1932] A.C. 235; [1931] All E.R. Rep. 36.

as an essential reason, motive, justification or explanation for the making of the contract ". In my view the mistake must be a mistake as to the nature or at the very least the quality of the subject-matter and not as to the reason why either party desires to deal with the subject-matter as the contract provides that it should be dealt with.

And LORD THANKERTON also said[1]:

"I think that it is true to say that in all the cases—and he is referring to a number of them—it either appeared on the face of the contract that the matter as to which the mistake existed was an essential and integral element of the subject-matter of the contract, or it was an inevitable inference from the nature of the contract that all parties so regarded it."

Since I think there is a most important peripheral implication which might be read into the judgment of this court given today, I want to add only this, that, in my opinion, in a case such as this, there is no rule of law that a warranty, given at the inception of a contract of insurance by the terms of the proposal form and its acceptance by the insured, is to be embodied, or tacitly read, into any contract which is made between such a proposer and the insurers, in settlement of a claim which he makes under the contract. I do not even think, so far as I am aware, that there is any authority for the proposition that a warranty, given in the way I have mentioned, is to be implied indefinitely into renewals of the first contract of insurance which is made of which that warranty is an express term as a condition precedent to liability. In every case it must depend on the length of time elapsed, the probability of changes of circumstances, the practicability of adjusting some ages by the addition of a year or more perhaps, and many other considerations, such, for example, as the improbability that the proposer who has called himself the holder of a provisional licence will continue to be either a holder of a provisional licence or a holder of any licence at all indefinitely. He is likely to have been dealt with by the magistrates in one way or another in the time which has elapsed.

For the reasons which I have endeavoured to state quite briefly—though I think there are many other considerations which are relevant to this interesting problem—I find myself, respectfully and diffidently, unable to agree with the judgment of LORD DENNING, M.R.

FENTON ATKINSON, L.J. Before hearing my Lords' judgments I had been inclined to the view that the letter of May 12, 1965, was not an offer to enter into a contract independent of the policy, but merely an offer of quantification of a claim made under a policy, both parties at that stage believing that there was a valid policy under which the insurers could have no answer to a claim. On reflection, I agree that that is an incorrect approach to the case, and I go on to consider the question of mistake, and on that issue I agree with the judgment of LORD DENNING, M.R. It does seem to me that the basic assumption of both parties at the time of the agreement relied on was that there was a valid enforceable claim under the policy. In fact, counsel for the plaintiff does not seek here to challenge the finding of the learned county court judge that the insurance company was entitled to repudiate any liability under that policy by reason of the untrue and incorrect statements made in the proposed form in 1961; and, applying in this case the proposition which was accepted by all of their Lordships in *Bell* v. *Lever Brothers, Ltd.*[2] set out in para. 207 of CHITTY ON CONTRACTS, vol. 1 (23rd Edn.), in these terms:

---

[1] [1932] A.C. 236; [1931] All E.R. Rep. 37.
[2] [1932] A.C. 161; [1931] All E.R. Rep. 11.

" Whenever it is to be inferred from the terms of a contract or its surrounding circumstances that the *consensus* has been reached upon the basis
of a particular contractual assumption, and that assumption is not true, the
contract is avoided. [And to that has to be added the additional rider] . . . the
assumption must have been fundamental to the continued validity of the contract, or a foundation essential to its existence."

Applying the rule there laid down to the facts of this case, I think it is clear
that when the agreement relied on by the plaintiff was made it was made on
the basis of a particular and essential contractual assumption, namely, that
there was in existence a valid and enforceable policy of insurance, and that
assumption was not true.   In my view it is the right and equitable result of
this case that the insurance company should be entitled to avoid that agreement on the ground of mutual mistake in a fundamental and vital matter.
I agree that this appeal should succeed on that ground.

Appeal allowed.   Leave to appeal to the House of Lords refused.

Joscelyne v. Nissen

[1970] 1 All E.R. 1213

COMMON MISTAKE: RECTIFICATION.   Where it is proved that, owing to
a common mistake, a document does not represent the real intention of the
parties, the court may rectify the incorrect expression of their intention.
It may also, if it thinks fit, decree specific performance of the agreement as
thus rectified.   It is not necessary that the document whose rectification is
sought should itself constitute a finally binding contract.   " It is sufficient
to find a common continuing intention in regard to a particular provision or
aspect of the agreement."[1]

The plaintiff, who shared a house with the defendant, his daughter,
proposed that she should take over his car-hire business. At an early stage in
the ensuing conversations, it was made clear that, if the proposals were
accepted, the daughter should pay all the household expenses, including the
electricity, gas and coal bills due in respect to that part of the house occupied
by her father.   This oral bargain indicated the common intention of the
parties, but it could not be described as a finally binding contract.   The discussions culminated in a written contract which, on its true construction,
placed no liability on the daughter to pay these household expenses. After
honouring the oral bargain for a time, she later refused to pay the electricity,
gas and coal bills, though she continued to take the profits of the business.

The father brought an action in the county court for rectification of the
written agreement so as specifically to include the daughter's liability for
these bills.   The county court judge ordered rectification of the written
agreement.   The daughter appealed against this order, but the appeal was
dismissed by the Court of Appeal.

RUSSELL, L.J. gave the judgment of the Court.   After stating the facts, he
said:[2]

"For the daughter it is argued that the law is that the father cannot get
rectification of the written instrument save to accord with a complete antecedent concluded oral contract with the daughter, and, as was found by the
judge, there was none.   For the father it is argued that, if in the course of negotia-

---

[1] SIMONDS, J. in *Crane* v. *Hegeman-Harris Co. Inc.*, [1939] 1 All E.R. 662, at pp. 664–
665.   *Infra*, p. 145.
[2] [1970] 1 All E.R. 1213, at p. 1216.

tion a firm accord has been expressly reached on a particular term of the proposed contract and both parties continue minded that the contract should contain appropriate language to embrace that term, it matters not that the accord was not part of a complete antecedent concluded oral contract."

RUSSELL, L.J. traced the history of judicial opinion upon the point of law thus involved from the case of *Mackenzie* v. *Coulson* onwards[1]. He cited and stressed a long passage from the judgment of SIMONDS, J. in *Crane* v. *Hegeman—Harris Co. Inc.*[2]

SIMONDS, J. said:

" Before I consider the facts and come to a conclusion whether the defendants are right in their contention, it is necessary to say a few words upon the principles which must guide me in this matter. I am clear that I must follow the decision of CLAUSON, J., as he then was, in *Shipley Urban District Council* v. *Bradford Corpn.*[3], the point of which is that, in order that this court may exercise its jurisdiction to rectify a written instrument, it is not necessary to find a concluded and binding contract between the parties antecedent to the agreement which it is sought to rectify. The judge held, and I respectfully concur with his reasoning and his conclusion, that it is sufficient to find a common continuing intention in regard to a particular provision or aspect of the agreement. If one finds that, in regard to a particular point, the parties were in agreement up to the moment when they executed their formal instrument, and the formal instrument does not conform with that common agreement, then this court has jurisdiction to rectify, although it may be that there was, until the formal instrument was executed, no concluded and binding contract between the parties. That is what the judge decided, and, as I say, with his reasoning I wholly concur, and I can add nothing to his authority in the matter, except that I would say that, if it were not so, it would be a strange thing, for the result would be that two parties binding themselves by a mistake to which each had equally contributed, by an instrument which did not express their real intention, would yet be bound by it. That is a state of affairs which I hold is not the law, and, until a higher court tells me it is the law, I shall continue to exercise the jurisdiction which CLAUSON, J., as I think rightly, held might be entertained by this court. Secondly, I want to say this upon the principle of the jurisdiction. It is a jurisdiction which is to be exercised only upon convincing proof that the concluded instrument does not represent the common intention of the parties. That is particularly the case where one finds prolonged negotiations between the parties eventually assuming the shape of a formal instrument in which they have been advised by their respective skilled legal advisers. The assumption is very strong in such a case that the instrument does represent their real intention, and it must be only upon proof which LORD ELDON, I think, in a somewhat picturesque phrase described as " irrefragable " that the court can act. I would rather, I think, say that the court can only act if it is satisfied beyond all reasonable doubt that the instrument does not represent their common intention, and is further satisfied as to what their common intention was. For let it be clear that it is not sufficient to show that the written instrument does not represent their common intention unless positively also one can show what their common intention was. It is in the light of those principles that I must examine the facts of this somewhat complicated case."

RUSSELL, L.J.: It is we think probable that the eminent counsel concerned in the case did not really dispute that Clauson, J's opinion represented the law on the relevant point; it does not appear from the judgment that they did, and very many more cases would have been cited had they done so. Equally in the Court of Appeal[4], Sir Wilfrid Greene, M.R. said[5]:

" Two arguments on behalf of the present appellant were before SIMONDS, J., and these arguments are before us. They were these. First, that upon the facts of the case no case for rectification had been made out: secondly, that the matter

[1] (1869), L.R. 8 Eq. 368.   [2] [1939] 1 All E.R. 662, at pp. 664–665.
[3] [1936] Ch. 375.   [4] [1939] 4 All E.R. 68.   [5] *Ibid.*, at p. 71.

in question, namely, the issue between the parties as to whether or not the agreement ought to be rectified was a matter which fell within the terms of the arbitration submission, which could have been raised before the arbitrator, and ought to have been raised before him, and could not be raised after he had issued his award and was *functus officio* . . . Simonds, J., in a judgment of conspicuous clarity, rejected the appellant's argument on both points. He found that the facts brought to his mind that high degree of conviction which unquestionably is to be insisted upon in rectification cases."

Sir Wilfrid Greene, M.R. continued[1]:

> " The case is no doubt one of importance to the parties and for that reason I have thought proper to put in my own language my reasons for saying that this appeal should be dismissed, but I might have been content to say that the judgment of SIMONDS, J., both on law and on fact, is one with which I am in entire agreement."

Clauson and Goddard, L.JJ. agreed. In referring particularly to the judge's rejection of the argument on rectification, in our view Sir Wilfrid Greene M.R. was referring in fact to his rejection of argument on the facts, not the law. Accordingly, we have in *Crane* v. *Hegeman-Harris Co. Inc*[2] in both courts an acceptance of the law on rectification as not requiring a complete antecedent concluded contract, in a case in which the decision must have been otherwise if such an antecedent contract was essential to rectification. But it seems to us that the contrary was not really argued, and we leave aside for the moment whether in those circumstances the principles of precedent require us to be bound by this case on the relevant point.

Next we refer to the horsebeans case in this court, *Frederick E. Rose* v. *Wm. H. Pim Junr. & Co. Ltd.*[3]. That was a case in which there was nothing that could be described as an outward expression between the parties of an accord on what was to be involved in a term of a proposed agreement. It turned out that locked separately in the breast of each party was the misapprehension that the word " horsebeans " meant another commodity, but as we understand the case there was no communication between them to the effect that when they should speak of horsebeans that was to be their private label for the other commodity. The decision in our judgment does not assert or reinstate the view that an antecedent complete concluded contract is required for rectification: it only shows that prior accord on a term or the meaning of a phrase to be used must outwardly have been expressed or communicated between the parties. Denning, L.J. said[4]:

> " It is not necessary that all the formalities of the contract should have been executed so as to make it enforceable at law: see *Shipley Urban District Council* v. *Bradford Corpn.*[5], but, formalities apart, there must have been a concluded contract. There is a passage in *Crane* v. *Hegeman-Harris Co. Inc.*[6] which suggests that a continuing common intention alone will suffice, but I am clearly of opinion that a continuing common intention is not sufficient unless it has found expression in outward agreement. There could be no certainty at all in business transactions if a party who had entered into a firm contract could afterwards turn round and claim to have it rectified on the ground that the parties intended something different. He is allowed to prove if he can, that they *agreed something different*: see *Lovell and Christmas* v. *Wall*[7], per LORD COZENS-HARDY, M.R., and per BUCKLEY, L.J.; but not that they *intended* something different."

---

[1] [1939] 4 All E.R. 72.
[2] [1939] 1 All E.R. 662, on appeal [1939] 4 All E.R. 68.
[3] [1953] 2 Q.B. 450; [1953] 2 All E.R. 739.
[4] [1953] 2 All E.R. at pp. 747–748; [1953] 2 Q.B. at pp. 461–462.
[5] [1936] Ch. 375.
[6] [1939] 1 All E.R. 664.
[7] (1911), 104 L.T. 88, at p. 93.

[RUSSELL, L.J., after citing these words of DENNING, L.J., commented upon them.] In so far as this passage might be taken to suggest that an antecedent complete concluded contract is necessary, it would be in conflict with the views of both courts in *Crane* v. *Hegeman-Harris*[1], and is not supported by the other judgments. In so far as it speaks of agreement in the more general sense of an outwardly expressed accord of minds, it does no more than assent to the argument of counsel for the defendants on the true width of the views of SIMONDS, J. . . .

In our judgment the law is as expounded by SIMONDS, J. in *Crane's case*, with the qualification that some outward expression of accord is required. We do not wish to attempt to state in any different phrases that with which we thoroughly agree, except to say that it is in our view better to use only the phrase " convincing proof " without echoing an old-fashioned word such as " irrefragable " and without importing from the criminal law the phrase " beyond all reasonable doubt ". Remembering always the strong burden of proof that lies on the shoulders of those seeking rectification, and that the requisite accord and continuance of accord may be the more difficult to establish if a complete antecedent concluded contract be not shown, it would be a sorry state of affairs if, when that burden is discharged, a party to a written contract could, on discovery that the written language chosen for the document did not on its true construction reflect the accord of the parties on a particular point, take advantage of the fact.

Appeal dismissed

SCOTT *v.* LITTLEDALE

RAFFLES *v.* WICHELHAUS

SCRIVEN BROTHERS & CO. *v.* HINDLEY & CO.

MUTUAL MISTAKE. " There is a distinction between the intention of the parties and the sense of the promise, and it is the sense of the promise rather than the intention of the parties which governs the contract. Of course the sense of the promise may be different to different persons; the promisor may consider that his words bear one sense, the promisee may consider that they bear another, and a stranger may consider that they bear a third. But the judge, who has to decide what legal obligation has resulted from the transaction, determines what the sense is " (Markby, Elements of Law, Para. 622).

If, after an examination of all the evidence, ambiguities remain unresolved and the judge finds himself unable to determine the " sense of the promise," he will conclude that no binding contract has been made.

[These statements are offered as fair inferences from the results of decided cases. The judgments in these cases are singularly unhelpful, and it will be seen from the three which follow and which are usually cited in this context with what wisps of judicial straw the academic bricks have to be made.]

Scott v. Littledale

(1858), 8 E. & B. 815

DECLARATION: that the defendants bargained and sold to the plaintiff, on the usual conditions of private sales, 100 chests of Congou tea, then lying in bond, " *ex* the ship *Star of the East*," at the price of 1s. 3½d. per

---

[1] [1939] 1 All E.R. 662.

pound, the said tea to be delivered on payment, &c. Averments: that the plaintiff had always been ready and willing to do and had done all things necessary on his part which he should be ready and willing to do and should do; of the fulfilment of all conditions precedent; and that all time has elapsed, &c. Breach: the non-delivery of the said tea. Special damage, that the plaintiff, relying, &c., had made a resale of the tea to one Peter Cornthwaite, at advanced prices, and had been obliged to break his contract, and had thereby lost profits, and had become liable to damages.

Plea, being a defence on equitable grounds, that, before the defendants entered into the said contract with the plaintiff, they, the defendants, had in their possession a certain sample of tea, which had been delivered to them as, and which they believed to be, a sample of the said 100 chests of tea *ex* the ship *Star of the East*; and that they, the defendants, before the said contract was made, delivered to one Rae, who was a broker employed by the plaintiff to purchase tea for him, a sample taken from the said sample as and for a sample of the said 100 chests of tea, *ex* the *Star of the East*; and that afterwards the said contract between the plaintiff and the defendants was made through the agency of the said Rae as such broker as aforesaid; and by the said contract the defendants agreed that the tea in the said 100 chests should be equal to the said sample; and that the said sample, which was so in the possession of the defendants before they made the said contract, and of which the defendants so as aforesaid delivered a portion to the said Rae, was not a sample at all of the said 100 chests of tea, *ex* the *Star of the East*, but was a sample of a totally different tea; and that they, the defendants, afterwards, and on the same day when the said contract had been entered into, discovered that there had been a mistake respecting the said sample, and forthwith, and before the plaintiff had in any respect altered his position on account of the said contract having been made, gave notice of the said mistake respecting the said sample to the said Rae, and to the plaintiff, and gave notice to them that the defendants would, on account of the said mistake, treat the said contract as void; and that the said contract was entered into solely through the mistaken belief, on the part of the defendants and the said Rae, that the said sample was a sample of the tea in the said 100 chests, and would not have been entered into but for the said mistake.

There was a replication by the plaintiff to the plea and the defendants then demurred.

Mellish, in support of the demurrer. The plea is good; and the replication is bad. First, as to the plea. It discloses that the contract sued on was founded on a mistake by both contracting parties of a material fact on which it was founded, and that the plaintiff had notice of the mistake before his position was altered. The mistake of fact was: that the sample on which the contract was made was by mistake supposed to be a sample taken from the cargo which was bought and sold, whereas it was not. The consequence was that the defendants could not possibly perform the contract. [LORD CAMPBELL, C.J. Why not? They might have purchased tea equal to the sample and delivered it.] That would not have been a fulfilment of this contract, which was for the purchase and sale of a specific cargo *ex Star*. [CROMPTON, J. The plaintiff by his declaration says that he was always ready and willing to accept the cargo *ex Star*; if he was, were not you bound at least to deliver that cargo? Do you not claim too large a relief?] In the contemplation of a Court of equity there was no contract, because the contract was founded on a mistake of both parties to it. A

Court of equity will relieve against a contract made on a mistake of facts by both parties; *Story's Commentaries on Equity Jurisprudence*, cap. 5, § 134.; though not where compensation cannot be made to the party against whom relief is sought; *M'Alpine* v. *Swift*[1]. [CROMPTON, J. Suppose that the defendants had sought relief against the whole contract in equity, and that the plaintiff had answered that he was ready to accept the cargo *ex Star* without insisting upon any claim for a difference in quality between it and the sample: would the Court have relieved against the whole contract, or would they have enforced the contract and relieved only against the term in it as to sample?] They would have relieved against the whole contract, because it was founded solely on the sample, and that was a mistake. [CROMPTON, J. Is the contract more than an undertaking to deliver tea equal to sample if the vendee insist on it? If he do not insist, will equity decree that the vendor need not deliver any tea? LORD CAMPBELL, C.J. Would equity at the mere option of the vendor simply rescind the contract? That is what you ask us to do.] No doubt it is necessary to show, not only that equity would grant relief, but that it would grant such relief as this Court will alone grant, namely simple, complete, unconditioned relief. It would grant such relief in this case, because the contract was entirely based upon the supposed truth of a fact as to which both parties were mistaken. [CROMPTON, J. We say, not that there is no equity, but that the equity, which would be given elsewhere, is not such an equity as this Court can administer or recognise.]

Hugh Hill, *contra*, was not called on.

LORD CAMPBELL, C.J. We are all of opinion that the plea cannot be supported. It is founded on the assumption that in equity this contract would be void at the option of the vendor. But we are of opinion that the contract would be held to be still subsisting, and that the relief in equity, if any, would be partial or conditional. We have no authority in this Court to settle such equities.

COLERIDGE, WIGHTMAN and CROMPTON, JJ. concurred.

Judgment for plaintiff.

Raffles v. Wichelhaus
(1864), 2 H. & C. 906

DECLARATION.—For that it was agreed between the plaintiff and the defendants, to wit, at Liverpool, that the plaintiff should sell to the defendants, and the defendants buy of the plaintiff, certain goods, to wit, 125 bales of Surat cotton, guaranteed middling fair merchant's Dhollorah, to arrive *ex Peerless* from Bombay; and that the cotton should be taken from the quay, and that the defendants would pay the plaintiff for the same at a certain rate, to wit, at the rate of $17\frac{1}{4}d$. per pound, within a certain time then agreed upon after the arrival of the said goods in England. Averments: that the said goods did arrive by the said ship from Bombay in England, to wit, at Liverpool, and the plaintiff was then and there ready, and willing and offered to deliver the said goods to the defendants, &c. Breach: that the defendants refused to accept the said goods or pay the plaintiff for them.

Plea.—That the said ship mentioned in the said agreement was meant and intended by the defendants to be the ship called the *Peerless*, which

---

[1] (1810), Ball & B. 285.

sailed from Bombay, to wit, in October; and that the plaintiff was not ready and willing and did not offer to deliver to the defendants any bales of cotton which arrived by the last mentioned ship, but instead thereof was only ready and willing and offered to deliver to the defendants 125 bales of Surat cotton which arrived by another and different ship, which was also called the *Peerless*, and which sailed from Bombay, to wit, in December.

Demurrer, and joinder therein.

Milward, in support of the demurrer.—The contract was for the sale of a number of bales of cotton of a particular description, which the plaintiff was ready to deliver. It is immaterial by what ship the cotton was to arrive, so that it was a ship called the *Peerless*. The words " to arrive *ex Peerless*," only mean that if the vessel is lost on the voyage, the contract is to be at an end. [POLLOCK, C.B.—It would be a question for the jury whether both parties meant the same ship called the *Peerless*.] That would be so if the contract was for the sale of a ship called the *Peerless*; but it is for the sale of cotton on board a ship of that name. [POLLOCK, C.B.—The defendant only bought that cotton which was to arrive by a particular ship. It may as well be said, that if there is a contract for the purchase of certain goods in warehouse A, that is satisfied by the delivery of goods of the same description in warehouse B.] In that case there would be goods in both warehouses; here it does not appear that the plaintiff had any goods on board the other *Peerless*. [MARTIN, B.—It is imposing on the defendant a contract different from that which he entered into. POLLOCK, C.B.—It is like a contract for the purchase of wine coming from a particular estate in France or Spain, where there are two estates of that name.] The defendant has no right to contradict by parol evidence a written contract good upon the face of it. He does not impute misrepresentation or fraud, but only says that he fancied the ship was a different one. Intention is of no avail, unless stated at the time of the contract. [POLLOCK, C.B.—One vessel sailed in October and the other in December.] The time of sailing is no part of the contract.

Mellish (*Cohen* with him), in support of the plea.—There is nothing on the face of the contract to shew that any particular ship called the *Peerless* was meant; but the moment it appears that two ships called the *Peerless* were about to sail from Bombay there is a latent ambiguity, and parol evidence may be given for the purpose shewing that the defendant meant one *Peerless* and the plaintiff another. That being so, there was no *consensus ad idem*, and therefore no binding contract.—He was then stopped by the Court.

Per Curiam[1].—There must be judgment for the defendants.

Scriven Brothers & Co. v. Hindley & Co.

[1913] 3 K.B. 564

The action was brought to recover 476*l*. 12*s*. 7*d*., the price of some Russian tow alleged to have been sold at auction on behalf of the plaintiffs to the defendants. The defendants denied that they had agreed to buy the tow, and alleged that they had bid at the auction for Russian hemp, and that the tow had been knocked down to them under a mistake of fact. The facts as stated by the learned judge in his written judgment were as follows:—

---

[1] Pollock, C.B., Martin, B., and Pigott, B.

Mr. Northcott, an auctioneer and broker doing business at the Commercial Sale Rooms, London, was employed by the plaintiffs to sell, *inter alia*, a large quantity of Russian hemp and tow. The goods were lying in the docks, and samples were on view at Cutler Street show-rooms. The catalogue prepared by Northcott contained the shipping mark " S. L.," and the numbers of the bales in two lots, namely, 63 to 67, 47 bales, and 68 to 79, 176 bales. The former were hemp, and the latter were tow; the catalogue did not disclose this difference in the nature of the commodity. At the show-rooms bales from each of these two lots were on view, and on the floor of the room in front of the bales was written in chalk " S. L. 63 to 67 " opposite the samples of hemp, and " S. L. 68 to 79 " opposite the samples of tow. These marks were placed on the floor of the gangway along which persons inspecting samples walked. Macgregor, the defendants' buyer, bid for the 47 bales, and these were ultimately knocked down to him at 24*l.* 0*s.* 6*d.* per ton. The 176 bales were then put up, the defendants' buyer bid 17*l.* per ton (an extravagant price for this tow), and they were at once knocked down to him. The auctioneer said that he announced this lot as " mixed tow," but this was denied. It was ultimately admitted at the trial that the defendants' buyer bid under the belief that the goods were hemp, whereas in fact the lot consisted of very inferior tow, " mere rubbish," as several witnesses said. It was stated by witnesses on both sides that in their experience Russian hemp and Russian tow were never landed from the same ship under the same shipping marks. The defendants' manager, Mr. Gill, who had inspected the samples of " S. L." hemp at Cutler Street, had been shewn two bales of hemp as " samples of the ' S. L.' goods " by Calman, the foreman in charge of the show-rooms. He did not wish to buy tow, and consequently had not inspected the samples of tow, or had his attention in any way called to the fact that the tow was also marked " S. L." He instructed Macgregor to bid for the 47 bales up to a limit of 25*l.*, and for the 176 bales to a limit of 23*l.*, in the belief that both lots were hemp. He had given no instructions for the purchase of tow and had no intention of buying tow. His reduction in price was due, he said, to his requirements and the size of the second lot.

The plaintiffs contended that the mistake was only a mistake as to value and was not one as to the subject-matter of the apparent contract.

The jury in answer to questions found: (1.) That hemp and tow are different commodities in commerce. (2.) That the auctioneer intended to sell 176 bales of tow. (3.) That Macgregor intended to bid for 176 bales of hemp. (4.) That the auctioneer believed that the bid was made under a mistake when he knocked down the lot. (5.) That the auctioneer had reasonable ground for believing that the mistake was merely one as to value. (6.) That the form of the catalogue and the conduct of Calman, or one of them, contributed to cause the mistake that occurred. (7.) That Mr. Gill's " negligence " in not taking his catalogue to Cutler Street and more closely examining and identifying the bales with the lots contributed to cause Macgregor's mistake.

A. T. LAWRENCE, J., read the following judgment:—In this case the plaintiffs brought an action for 476*l.* 12*s.* 7*d.*, the price of 560 cwt. 2 qrs. 27 lb. of Russian tow, as being due for goods bargained and sold. The defendants by their defence denied that they agreed to buy this Russian tow, and alleged that they bid for Russian hemp and that the tow was knocked down to them under a mistake of fact as to the subject-matter of the supposed contract. The circumstances were these. [The learned judge stated the facts and the findings of the jury as set out above, and continued:] Upon these findings both plaintiffs and defendants claimed to be entitled to judgment. A number of cases were cited upon either side. I do not propose to examine them in detail because I think that the findings of the jury determine what my judgment should be in this case.

The jury have found that hemp and tow are different commodities in commerce. I should suppose that no one can doubt the correctness of this finding. The second and third findings of the jury shew that the parties were never *ad idem* as to the subject-matter of the proposed sale; there was therefore in fact no contract of bargain and sale. The plaintiffs can recover from the defendants only if they can shew that the defendants are estopped from relying upon what is now admittedly the truth. Mr. Hume Williams for the plaintiffs argued very ingeniously that the defendants were estopped; for this he relied upon findings 5 and 7, and upon the fact that the defendants had failed to prove the allegation in paragraph 4 of the defence to the effect that Northcott knew at the time he knocked down the lot that Macgregor was bidding for hemp and not for tow.

I must, of course, accept for the purposes of this judgment the findings of the jury, but I do not think they create any estoppel. Question No. 7 was put to the jury as a supplementary question, after they had returned into Court with their answers to the other questions, upon the urgent insistence of the learned junior counsel for the plaintiffs. It begs an essential question by using the word " negligence " and assuming that the purchaser has a duty towards the seller to examine goods that he does not wish to buy, and to correct any latent defect there may be in the sellers' catalogue.

Once it was admitted that Russian hemp was never before known to be consigned or sold with the same shipping marks as Russian tow from the same cargo, it was natural for the person inspecting the " S. L." goods and being shewn hemp to suppose that the " S. L." bales represented the commodity hemp. Inasmuch as it is admitted that someone had perpetrated a swindle upon the bank which made advances in respect of this shipment of goods it was peculiarly the duty of the auctioneer to make it clear to the bidder either upon the face of his catalogue or in some other way which lots were hemp and which lots were tow.

To rely upon a purchaser's discovering chalk marks upon the floor of the show-room seems to me unreasonable as demanding an amount of care upon the part of the buyer which the vendor had no right to exact. A buyer when he examines a sample does so for his own benefit and not in the discharge of any duty to the seller; the use of the word " negligence " in such a connection is entirely misplaced, it should be reserved for cases of want of due care where some duty is owed by one person to another. No evidence was tendered of the existence of any such duty upon the part of buyers of hemp. In so far as there was any evidence upon the point it was given by a buyer called as a witness for the plaintiffs who said he had marked the word " tow " on his catalogue when at the show-rooms " for his own protection." I ought probably to have refused to leave the seventh question to the jury; but neither my complaisance nor their answer can create a duty. In my view it is clear that the finding of the jury upon the sixth question prevents the plaintiffs from being able to insist upon a contract by estoppel. Such a contract cannot arise when the person seeking to enforce it has by his own negligence or by that of those for whom he is responsible caused, or contributed to cause, the mistake.

I am therefore of opinion that judgment should be entered for the defendants.

CUNDY *v.* LINDSAY

PHILLIPS *v.* BROOKS, LTD.

LEWIS *v.* AVERAY

UNILATERAL MISTAKE. A. may allege that he intended to contract with B. and with B. only, but that by mistake he was induced to make an apparent contract with C. The presumption here is that, despite the mistake, a contract has been concluded between A. and C. If A. now seeks to treat this presumed contract as void, the onus lies upon him to prove (1) that he intended to deal with B. and not with anyone else; (2) that C. knew of this intention; (3) that at the time of negotiating the contract he, A., regarded the identity of the other contracting party as a matter of crucial importance; (4) that he took reasonable steps to verify the identity of that party. The application of these requirements has provoked a number of decisions which are not always readily differentiated.

Cundy v. Lindsay

(1878), 3 App. Cas. 459

A fraudulent person named Blenkarn, writing from " 37 Wood St., Cheapside," offered to buy goods from the plaintiffs, and he signed his letter in such a way that his name appeared to be " Blenkiron & Co." The latter were a respectable firm carrying on business at 123 Wood St. Blenkarn occupied a room which he called 37 Wood St., but in fact its entrance was from an adjoining street. The plaintiffs, who were aware of the high reputation of Blenkiron & Co., though they neither knew nor troubled to ascertain the number of the street where they did business, purported to accept the offer and despatched the goods to " Messrs. Blenkiron & Co., 37 Wood St., Cheapside." These were received by the rogue Blenkarn, and he in turn sold them to the defendants, who took them in all good faith. The plaintiffs now sued the defendants for conversion.

At first instance BLACKBURN, J. held that there was a contract between the plaintiff and the rogue, though one that was voidable for fraud. He therefore found for the defendants who, as innocent persons, had acquired a title to the goods before the plaintiff had taken steps to avoid the contract. This decision was reversed in the Court of Appeal, where it was held that the presumed contract was void for mistake. No title had passed to the rogue, and none could pass to the defendants, innocent though they were. The House of Lords affirmed the decision of the Court of Appeal.

THE LORD CHANCELLOR (Lord Cairns):

My Lords, you have in this case to discharge a duty which is always a disagreeable one for any Court, namely to determine as between two parties, both of whom are perfectly innocent, upon which of the two the consequences of a fraud practised upon both of them must fall. My Lords, in discharging that duty your Lordships can do no more than apply, rigorously, the settled and well known rules of law. Now, with regard to the title to personal property, the settled and well known rules of law may, I take it, be thus expressed : by the law of our country the purchaser of a chattel takes the chattel as a general rule subject to what may turn out to be certain infirmities in the title.   If he purchases the chattel in market overt, he obtains a title which is good against all the world ; but if he does not purchase the chattel in market overt, and if it turns out that the chattel has been found by the person who professed to sell it, the purchaser will not obtain a title good as against the real owner.   If it turns out that the chattel has been stolen by the person who has professed to sell it, the purchaser will not obtain a title.   If it turns out that the chattel has come into the hands of the person who professed to sell it, by a *de facto* contract, that is to say, a contract which has purported to pass the property to him from the owner of the property, there the purchaser will obtain a good title, even although afterwards it should appear that there were circumstances connected with that contract, which would enable the original owner of the goods to reduce it, and to set it aside, because these circumstances so enabling the original owner of the goods, or of the chattel, to reduce the contract and to set it aside, will not be allowed to interfere with a title for valuable consideration obtained by some third party during the interval while the contract remained unreduced.

My Lords, the question, therefore, in the present case, as your Lordships will observe, really becomes the very short and simple one which I am about to state.   Was there any contract which, with regard to the goods in question in this case, had passed the property in the goods from the Messrs. Lindsay to Alfred Blenkarn ?   If there was any contract passing that property, even although, as I have said, that contract might afterwards be open to a process of reduction, upon the ground of fraud, still, in the meantime, Blenkarn might have conveyed a good title for valuable consideration to the present appellants.

Now, my Lords, there are two observations bearing upon the solution of that question which I desire to make.   In the first place, if the property in the goods in question passed, it could only pass by way of contract ; there is nothing else which could have passed the property.   The second observation is this : your Lordships are not here embarrassed by any conflict of evidence, or any evidence whatever as to conversations or as to acts done, the whole history of the whole transaction lies upon paper.   The principal parties concerned, the respondents and Blenkarn, never came in contact personally—everything that was done was done by writing.   What has to be judged of, and what the jury in the present case had to judge of, was merely the conclusion to be derived from that writing, as applied to the admitted facts of the case.

Now, my Lords, discharging that duty and answering that inquiry, what the jurors have found is in substance this : it is not necessary to spell out the words, because the substance of it is beyond all doubt.   They have found that by the form of the signatures to the letters which were written by Blenkarn, by the mode in which his letters and his applications to the respondents were made out, and by the way in which he left uncorrected the mode and form in which, in turn, he was addressed by the respondents ; that by all those means he led, and intended to lead, the respondents to believe, and they did believe, that the person with whom they were communicating was not Blenkarn, the dishonest and irresponsible man, but was a well known and solvent house of Blenkiron & Co., doing business in the same street. My Lords, those things are found as matters of fact, and they are placed beyond the range of dispute and controversy in the case.

If that is so, what is the consequence? It is that Blenkarn—the dishonest man, as I call him—was acting here just in the same way as if he had forged the signature of Blenkiron & Co., the respectable firm, to the applications for goods, and as if, when, in return, the goods were forwarded and letters were sent accompanying them, he had intercepted the goods and intercepted the letters, and had taken possession of the goods, and of the letters which were addressed to, and intended for, not himself, but the firm of Blenkiron & Co. Now, my Lords, stating the matter shortly in that way, I ask the question, how is it possible to imagine that in that state of things any contract could have arisen between the respondents and Blenkarn, the dishonest man? Of him they knew nothing, and of him they never thought. With him they never intended to deal. Their minds never, even for an instant of time, rested upon him, and as between him and them there was no *consensus* of mind which could lead to any agreement or any contract whatever. As between him and them there was merely the one side to a contract, where, in order to produce a contract, two sides would be required. With the firm of Blenkiron & Co. of course there was no contract, for as to them the matter was entirely unknown, and therefore the pretence of a contract was a failure.

The result, therefore, my Lords, is this, that your Lordships have not here to deal with one of those cases in which there is *de facto* a contract made which may afterwards be impeached and set aside, on the ground of fraud ; but you have to deal with a case which ranges itself under a completely different chapter of law, the case namely in which the contract never comes into existence. My Lords, that being so, it is idle to talk of the property passing. The property remained, as it originally had been, the property of the respondents, and the title which was attempted to be given to the appellants was a title which could not be given to them.

My Lords, I therefore move your Lordships that this appeal be dismissed with costs, and the judgment of the Court of Appeal affirmed.

Lord Hatherley and Lord Penzance delivered judgment to the same effect ; Lord Gordon concurred.

Phillips v. Brooks, Ltd.

[1919] 2 K.B. 243

Action tried by Horridge, J.

The plaintiff, who was a jeweller, sued the defendants, who were pawnbrokers, for the return of a ring or, alternatively, its value, and damages for its detention.

On April 15, 1918, a man entered the plaintiff's shop and asked to see some pearls and some rings. He selected pearls at the price of 2,550*l.* and a ring at the price of 450*l.* He produced a cheque book and wrote out a cheque for 3,000*l.* In signing it, he said : " You see who I am, I am Sir George Bullough," and he gave an address in St. James's Square. The plaintiff knew that there was such a person as Sir George Bullough, and finding on reference to a directory that Sir George lived at the address mentioned, he said, " Would you like to take the articles with you ? " to which the man replied : " You had better have the cheque cleared first, but I should like to take the ring as it is my wife's birthday to-morrow," whereupon the plaintiff let him have the ring. The cheque was dishonoured, the person who gave it being in fact a fraudulent person named North who was subsequently convicted of obtaining the ring by false pretences. In the meantime, namely on April 16, 1918, North, in the name of Firth, had pledged the ring with the defendants who, *bona fide* and without notice, advanced 350*l*. upon it.

In his evidence the plaintiff said that when he handed over the ring he thought he was contracting with Sir George Bullough, and that if he had known who the man really was he would not have let him have it. In re-examination he said that he had no intention of making a contract with any other person than Sir George Bullough.

HORRIDGE, J., read the following judgment : This is an action brought by the plaintiff, who is a jeweller in Oxford Street, London, for the return of a ring or its value, and for damages for detaining the same. The value of the ring was agreed as being 450*l*., and no evidence was given before me of any damage, apart from the value of the ring which was taken. I have carefully considered the evidence of the plaintiff, and have come to the conclusion that, although he believed the person to whom he was handing the ring was Sir George Bullough, he in fact contracted to sell and deliver it to the person who came into his shop, and who was not Sir George Bullough, but a man of the name of North, who obtained the sale and delivery by means of the false pretence that he was Sir George Bullough. It is quite true the plaintiff in re-examination said he had no intention of making any contract with any other person than Sir George Bullough ; but I think I have myself to decide what is the proper inference to draw where a verbal contract is made and an article delivered to an individual describing himself as somebody else.

After obtaining the ring the man North pledged it in the name of Firth with the defendants, who *bona fide* and without notice advanced 350*l*. upon it. The question, therefore, in this case is whether or not the property had so passed to the swindler as to entitle him to give a good title to any person who gave value and acted *bona fide* without notice. This question seems to have been decided in an American case of *Edmunds* v. *Merchants' Despatch Transportation Co.*[1] The headnote in that case contains two propositions, which I think adequately express my view of the law. They are as follows : (1) " If A., fraudulently assuming the name of a reputable merchant in a certain town, buys, in person, goods of another, the property in the goods passes to A." ; (2) " If A., representing himself to be a brother of a reputable merchant in a certain town, buying for him, buys, in person, goods of another, the property in the goods does not pass to A."

The following expressions used in the judgment of Morton, C.J., seem to me to fit the facts in this case : " The minds of the parties met and agreed upon all the terms of the sale, the thing sold, the price and time of payment, the person selling and the person buying. The fact that the seller was induced to sell by fraud of the buyer made the sale voidable, but not void. He could not have supposed that he was selling to any other person ; his intention was to sell to the person present, and identified by sight and hearing; it does not defeat the sale because the buyer assumed a false name or

---

[1] 135 Mass. 283, at p. 284.

practised any other deceit to induce the vendor to sell." Further on, Morton, C.J., says : " In the cases before us, there was a *de facto* contract, purporting, and by which the plaintiffs intended, to pass the property and possession of the goods to the person buying them ; and we are of opinion that the property did pass to the swindler who bought the goods."

The rule laid down by Lord Cairns, L.C., in *Cundy* v. *Lindsay*[1] is as follows : " If it turns out that the chattel has been stolen by the person who has professed to sell it, the purchaser will not obtain a title. If it turns out that the chattel has come into the hands of the person who professed to sell it, by a *de facto* contract, that is to say, a contract which has purported to pass the property to him from the owner of the property, there the purchaser will obtain a good title, even although afterwards it should appear that there were circumstances connected with that contract which would enable the original owner of the goods to reduce it, and to set it aside, because these circumstances so enabling the original owner of the goods, or of the chattel, to reduce the contract and to set it aside, will not be allowed to interfere with a title for valuable consideration obtained by some third party during the interval while the contract remained unreduced."

The question whether or not the property would pass if a fraudulent person had gone himself to the firm from whom he wished to obtain the goods and had represented that he was someone else was raised in the argument in *Cundy* v. *Lindsay*[1]. In the speech of Lord Penzance, he says[2] : " Hypothetical cases were put to your Lordships in argument in which a vendor was supposed to deal personally with a swindler, believing him to be someone else of credit and stability, and under this belief to have actually delivered goods into his hands. My Lords, I do not think it necessary to express an opinion upon the possible effect of some cases which I can imagine to happen of this character, because none of such cases can I think be parallel with that which your Lordships have now to decide."

Lord Hatherley, in his speech, seems to me to have rather put the case of a man's obtaining goods by representing that he was a member of one of the largest firms in London, which would be a case of representation as to authority to contract, as he says[3] : " Now I am very far, at all events on the present occasion, from seeing my way to this, that the goods being sold to him as representing that firm, he could be treated in any other way than as an agent of that firm."

The illustration given by Lord Hatherley and the facts in the case of *Hardman* v. *Booth*[4] seem to me to be cases which fall within the second proposition in the headnote in *Edmunds* v. *Merchants' Despatch Transportation Co.*[5], namely, representation by a person present that he was an agent for somebody else so as to induce the seller to make a contract with a third person whom the person present had no authority to bind.

It was argued before me that the principle quoted from Pothier (Traité des Obligations, section 19), in *Smith* v. *Wheatcroft*[6], namely, " Whenever the consideration of the person with whom I am willing to contract enters as an element into the contract which I am willing to make, error with regard to the person destroys my consent and consequently annuls the contract " applies. I do not think, however, that that passage governs this case, because

---

[1] (1878), 3 App. Cas. 459, at p. 464.
[2] *Ibid.*, 471.
[3] *Ibid.*, 469.
[4] (1863), 1 H. & C. 803.
[5] 135 Mass. 283. *Supra*, p. 156.
[6] (1878), 9 Ch. D. 223, at p. 230.

I think the seller intended to contract with the person present, and there was no error as to the person with whom he contracted, although the plaintiff would not have made the contract if there had not been a fraudulent misrepresentation. Moreover, the case of *Smith* v. *Wheatcroft* was an action for specific performance and was between the parties to the contract and had no relation to rights acquired by third parties innocently under the contract; and misrepresentation would have been an answer to the enforcement of the contract. In this case, I think, there was a passing of the property and the purchaser had a good title, and there must be judgment for the defendants with costs.

Lewis v. Averay

[1971] 3 All E.R. 907

LORD DENNING, M.R. This is another case where one of two innocent persons has to suffer from the fraud of a third. It will no doubt interest students and find its place in the textbooks.

Mr. Lewis is a young man who is a postgraduate student of chemistry. He lives at Clifton near Bristol. He had an Austin Cooper motor car. He decided to sell it. He put an advertisement in the newspaper offering it for £450. On May 8, 1969, in reply to the advertisement, a man—I will simply call him the " rogue ", for so he was—telephoned and asked if he could come and see the car. He did not give his name. He said he was speaking from Glamorganshire in Wales. Mr. Lewis said that he could come and see it. He came in the evening to Mr. Lewis's flat. Mr. Lewis showed him the car which was parked outside. The rogue drove it and tested it. He said that he liked it. They then went along to the flat of Mr. Lewis's fiancée, Miss Kershaw (they have since married). He told them that he was Richard Green and talked much about the film world. He led both of them to believe that he was the well-known film actor, Richard Green, who played Robin Hood in the " Robin Hood " series. They talked about the car. He asked to see the log book. He was shown it and seemed satisfied. He said he would like to buy the car. They agreed a price of £450. The rogue wrote out a cheque for £450 on the Beckenham branch of the Midland Bank. He signed it " R. A. Green ". He wanted to take the car at once. But Mr. Lewis was not willing for him to have it until the cheque was cleared. To hold him off, Mr. Lewis said that there were one or two small jobs he would like to do on the car before letting him have it, and that would give time for the cheque to be cleared. The rogue said: " Don't worry about those small jobs. I would like to take the car now." Mr. Lewis said: " Have you anything to prove that you are Mr. Richard Green? " The rogue thereupon brought out a special pass of admission to Pinewood Studios, which had an official stamp on it. It bore the name of Richard A. Green and the address, and also a photograph which was plainly the photograph of the man, who was the rogue. On seeing this pass, Mr. Lewis was satisfied. He thought that this man was really like Mr. Richard Green, the film actor. By that time it was 11.00 p.m. Mr. Lewis took the cheque and let the rogue have the car and the log book and the Ministry of Transport test certificate. Each wrote and signed a receipt evidencing the transaction. Mr. Lewis wrote:

" Received from
Richard A Green
59 Marsh Rd,
Beckenham
Kent

the sum of £450 in return for Austin Cooper " S " Reg. No. AHT 484B chassis No. CA257—549597

Signed Keith Lewis."

The rogue wrote:

" Received log-book No. 771835 and M.O.T. for Mini Cooper " S " No. AHT 484B.   R. A. Green."

Next day, May 9, 1969, Mr. Lewis put the cheque into the bank.   A few days later the bank told him it was worthless.   The rogue had stolen a cheque book and written this £450 on a stolen cheque.

Meanwhile, whilst the cheque was going through, the rogue sold the car to an innocent purchaser.   He sold it to a young man called Mr. Averay. He was at the time under 21.   He was a music student in London at the Royal College of Music.   His parents live at Bromley.   He was keen to buy a car. He put an advertisement in the Exchange and Mart, seeking a car for £200. In answer he had a telephone call from the rogue.   He said that he was speaking from South Wales.   He said that he was coming to London to sell a car.   Mr. Averay arranged to meet him on May 11, 1969.   The rogue came with the car.   Young Mr. Averay liked it, but wanted to get the approval of his parents.   They drove it to Bromley.   The parents did approve.   Young Mr. Averay agreed to buy it for £200.   The rogue gave his name as Mr. Lewis. He handed over the car and log book to young Mr. Averay.   The log book showed the owner as Mr. Lewis.   In return Mr. Averay, in entire good faith, gave the rogue a cheque for £200.   The rogue signed this receipt:

" Sale of Cooper S to A. J. Averay.   Received £200 for the Cooper S Registration No. AHT 484B, the said car being my property absolutely, there being no hire-purchase charges outstanding or other impediment to selling the car.

Signed Keith Lewis
May 13th 1969."

A fortnight later, on May 29, 1969, Mr Averay wanted the workshop manual for the car.   So his father on his behalf wrote to the name and address of the seller as given in the log book, that is, to Mr. Lewis.   Then, of course, the whole story came to light.   The rogue had cashed the cheque and disappeared. The police have tried to trace him, but without success.

Now Mr. Lewis, the original owner of the car, sues young Mr. Averay. Mr. Lewis claims that the car is still his.   He claims damages for conversion. The judge found in favour of Mr. Lewis and awarded damages of £330 for conversion.

The real question in the case is whether on May 8, 1969, there was a contract of sale under which the property in the car passed from Mr. Lewis to the rogue.   If there was such a contract, then, even though it was voidable for fraud, nevertheless Mr. Averay would get a good title to the car.   But if there was no contract of sale by Mr. Lewis to the rogue—either because there was, on the face of it, no agreement between the parties, or because any apparent agreement was a nullity and void *ab initio* for mistake, then no property would pass from Mr. Lewis to the rogue.   Mr. Averay would not get a good title because the rogue had no property to pass to him.

There is no doubt that Mr. Lewis was mistaken as to the identity of the person who handed him the cheque.   He thought that he was Richard

Greene, a film actor of standing and worth; whereas in fact he was a rogue whose identity is quite unknown. It was under the influence of that mistake that Mr. Lewis let the rogue have the car. He would not have dreamed of letting him have it otherwise.

What is the effect of this mistake? There are two cases in our books which cannot, to my mind, be reconciled the one with the other. One of them is *Phillips* v. *Brooks*[1], where a jeweller had a ring for sale. The other is *Ingram* v. *Little*[2], where two ladies had a car for sale. In each case the story is very similar to the present. A plausible rogue comes along. The rogue says that he likes the ring, or the car, as the case may be. He asks the price. The seller names it. The rogue says that he is prepared to buy it at that price. He pulls out a cheque book. He writes or prepares to write a cheque for the price. The seller hesitates. He has never met this man before. He does not want to hand over the ring or the car not knowing whether the cheque will be met. The rogue notices the seller's hesitation. He is quick with his next move. He says to the jeweller, in *Phillips* v. *Brooks*[1]: " I am Sir George Bullough of 11, St. James' Square "; or to the ladies in *Ingram* v. *Little*[2]: " I am P. G. M. Hutchinson of Stanstead House, Stanstead Road, Caterham "; or to Mr. Lewis in the present case: " I am Richard Green, the film actor of the Robin Hood series ". Each seller checks up the information. The jeweller looks up the directory and finds there is a Sir George Bullough at 11, St. James's Square. The ladies check up too. They look at the telephone directory and find there is a " P. G. M. Hutchinson of Stanstead House, Stanstead Road, Caterham ". Mr. Lewis checks up too. He examines the official pass of the Pinewood Studios and finds that it is a pass for " Richard A. Green " to the Pinewood Studios with this man's photograph on it. In each case the seller feels that this is sufficient confirmation of the man's identity. So he accepts the cheque signed by the rogue and lets him have the ring, in the one case, and the car and log book in the other two cases. The rogue goes off and sells the goods to a third person who buys them in entire good faith and pays the price to the rogue. The rogue disappears. The original seller presents the cheque. It is dishonoured. Who is entitled to the goods? The original seller or the ultimate buyer? The courts have given different answers. In *Phillips* v. *Brooks Ltd*[1] the ultimate buyer was held to be entitled to the ring. In *Ingram* v. *Little*[2] the original seller was held to be entitled to the car. In the present case the deputy county court judge has held the original seller entitled.

It seems to me that the material facts in each case are quite indistinguishable the one from the other. In each case there was, to all outward appearance, a contract; but there was a mistake by the seller as to the identity of the buyer. This mistake was fundamental. In each case it led to the handing over of the goods. Without it the seller would not have parted with them.

This case therefore raises the question: what is the effect of a mistake by one party as to the identity of the other? It has sometimes been said that, if a party makes a mistake as to the identity of the person with whom he is contracting, there is no contract, or, if there is a contract, it is a nullity and void, so that no property can pass under it. This has been supported by a a reference to the French jurist Pothier[3]; but I have said before, and I repeat

---

[1] [1919] 2 K.B. 243; [1918–19] All E.R. Rep. 246. *Supra*, p. 155.
[2] [1961] 1 Q.B. 31; [1960] 3 All E.R. 332.
[3] Traité des obligations, 1806, s. 19.

now, his statement is no part of English law. I know that it was quoted by Viscount Haldane in *Lake* v. *Simmons*[1] and, as such, misled Tucker, J. in *Sowler* v. *Potter*[2] into holding that a lease was void whereas it was really voidable. But the statement by Pothier has given rise to such refinements that it is time it was dead and buried altogether.

For instance, in *Ingram* v. *Little*[3] the majority of the court suggested that the difference between *Phillips* v. *Brooks*[4] and *Ingram* v. *Little*[3] was that in *Phillips* v. *Brooks*[4] the contract of sale was concluded (so as to pass the property to the rogue) before the rogue made the fraudulent misrepresenta- tion[5], whereas in *Ingram* v. *Little*[3] the rogue made the fraudulent mis- representation before the contract was concluded. My own view is that in each case the property in the goods did not pass until the seller let the rogue have the goods.

Again it has been suggested that a mistake as to the identity of a person is one thing; and a mistake as to his attributes is another. A mistake as to identity, it is said, avoids a contract; whereas a mistake as to attributes does not. But this is a distinction without a difference. A man's very name is one of his attributes. It is also a key to his identity. If then, he gives a false name, is it a mistake as to his identity? or a mistake as to his attributes? These fine distinctions do no good to the law.

As I listened to the argument in this case, I felt it wrong that an innocent purchaser (who knew nothing of what passed between the seller and the rogue) should have his title depend on such refinements. After all, he has acted with complete circumspection and in entire good faith; whereas it was the seller who let the rogue have the goods and thus enabled him to commit the fraud. I do not, therefore, accept the theory that a mistake as to identity renders a contract void.

I think the true principle is that which underlies the decision of this court in *King's Norton Metal Co Ltd* v. *Eldridge, Merrett & Co Ltd*[6] and of Horridge, J. in *Phillips* v. *Brooks Ltd*[4], which has stood for these last 50 years. It is this: when two parties have come to a contract—or rather what appears, on the face of it, to be a contract—the fact that one party is mistaken as to the identity of the other does not mean that there is no con- tract, or that the contract is a nullity and void from the beginning. It only means that the contract is voidable, that is, liable to be set aside at the instance of the mistaken person, so long as he does so before third parties have in good faith acquired rights under it.

Applied to the cases such as the present, this principle is in full accord with the presumption stated by Pearce, L.J. and also by Devlin, L.J. in *Ingram* v. *Little*[7]. When a deal is made between a seller like Mr Lewis and a person who is actually there present before him, then the presumption in law is that there is a contract, even though there is a fraudulent impersona- tion by the buyer representing himself as a different man than he is. There is a contract made with the very person there, who is present in person. It is liable no doubt to be avoided for fraud but it is still a good contract under

---

[1] [1927] A.C. 487 at p. 501, [1927] All E.R. Rep. 49 at p. 53.
[2] [1940] 1 K.B. 271; [1939] 4 All E.R. 478.
[3] [1961] 1 Q.B. 31; [1960] 3 All E.R. 332.
[4] [1919] 2 K.B. 243; [1918–19] All E.R. Rep. 246.
[5] See [1961] 1 Q.B. 51, at p. 60; [1960] 3 All E.R. 337, at p. 343.
[6] (1897) 14 T.L.R. 98.
[7] [1961] 1 Q.B. 61, at p. 66; [1960] 3 All E.R. 344, at p. 347.

which title will pass unless and until it is avoided. In support of that presumption, Devlin, L.J. quoted[1], not only the English case of *Phillips* v. *Brooks*, but other cases in the United States where[2]:

> " The Courts hold that if A appeared in person before B, impersonating C, an innocent purchaser from A gets the property in the goods against B."

That seems to me to be right in principle in this country also.

In this case Mr. Lewis made a contract of sale with the very man, the rogue, who came to the flat. I say that he " made a contract " because in this regard we do not look into his intentions, or into his mind to know what he was thinking, or into the mind of the rogue. We look to the outward appearances. On the face of the dealing, Mr. Lewis made a contract under which he sold the car to the rogue, delivered the car and the log book to him, and took a cheque in return. The contract is evidenced by the receipts which were signed. It was, of course, induced by fraud. The rogue made false representations as to his identity. But it was still a contract, though voidable for fraud. It was a contract under which this property passed to the rogue, and in due course passed from the rogue to Mr. Averay, before the contract was avoided.

Although I very much regret that either of these good and reliable gentlemen should suffer, in my judgment it is Mr. Lewis who should do so. I think the appeal should be allowed and judgment entered for the defendant.

PHILLIMORE L.J. I share the regret expressed by Lord Denning, M.R. I think that the law was conveniently stated by Pearce, L.J. in the course of his judgment in *Ingram* v. *Little*[3], to which reference has already been made. He said this:

> " Each case must be decided on its own facts. The question in such cases is this. Has it been sufficiently shown in the particular circumstances that, contrary to the *prima facie* presumption [and I would emphasise those words] a party was not contracting with the physical person to whom he uttered the offer, but with another individual whom (to the other party's knowledge) he believed to be the physical person present. The answer to that question is a finding of fact."

Now, in that particular case the Court of Appeal, by a majority and in the very special and unusual facts of the case, decided that it had been sufficiently shown in the particular circumstances that, contrary to the *prima facie* presumption, the lady who was selling the motor car was not dealing with the person actually present. But in the present case I am bound to say that I do not think that there was anything which could displace the *prima facie* presumption that Mr. Lewis was dealing with the gentleman present there in the flat—the rogue. It seems to me that when, at the conclusion of the transaction, the car was handed over, the log book was handed over, the cheque was accepted and the receipts were given, it is really impossible to say that a contract had not been made. I think this case really is on all fours with *Phillips* v. *Brooks Ltd*[4], which has been good law for over 50 years. True the contract was induced by fraud, and Mr. Lewis, when he discovered that he had been defrauded, was entitled to avoid it; but in the meanwhile the rogue had parted with the property in this motor car, which he had obtained, to Mr. Averay, who bought it *bona fide* without any notice of the fraud;

[1] [1961] 1 Q.B. at 66; [1960] 3 All E.R. 347.
[2] This quotation is from *Corbin on Contracts*, vol. 3, s. 602.
[3] [1961] 1 Q.B. 31 at p. 61; [1960] 3 All E.R. 332 at p. 344.
[4] [1919] 2 K.B. 243, [1918–19] All E.R. Rep. 246.

and accordingly he thereby, as I think, acquired a good title. This action was in my judgment one which was bound to fail. I think the judge was wrong in the decision to which he came and this appeal must be allowed.

MEGAW, L.J. For myself, with very great respect, I find it difficult to understand the basis, either in logic or in practical considerations, of the test laid down by the majority of the court in *Ingram* v. *Little*[1]. That test is I think accurately recorded in the headnote[2]:

"... where a person physically present and negotiating to buy a chattel fraudulently assumed the identity of an existing third person, the test to determine to whom the offer was addressed was how ought the promisee to have interpreted the promise . . ."

The promisee, be it noted, is the rogue. The question of the existence of a contract and therefore the passing of property, and therefore the right of third parties, if this test is correct, is made to depend on the view which some rogue should have formed, presumably knowing that he is a rogue, as to the state of mind of the opposite party to the negotiation, who does not know that he is dealing with a rogue.

However that may be, and assuming that the test as so stated is indeed valid, in my view this appeal can be decided on a short and simple point. It is the point which was put at the outset of his argument by counsel for the defendant. The well-known textbook on the Law of Contract, Cheshire and Fifoot[3], deals with the question of invalidity of a contract by virtue of unilateral mistake, and in particular unilateral mistake relating to mistaken identity. The learned editors describe what in their submission are certain facts that must be established in order to enable one to avoid a contract on the basis of unilateral mistake by him as to the identity of the opposite party. The first of those facts is that at the time when he made the offer he regarded the identity of the offeree as a matter of vital importance. To translate that into the facts of the present case, it must be established that at the time of offering to sell his car to the rogue, Mr. Lewis regarded the identity of the rogue as a matter of vital importance. In my view, counsel for the defendant is abundantly justified, on the notes of the evidence and on the findings of the learned judge, in his submission that the mistake of Mr. Lewis went no further than a mistake as to the attributes of the rogue. It was simply a mistake as to the creditworthiness of the man who was there present and who described himself as Mr. Green. I should say that I think that the learned judge may possibly have been to some extent misled, because he seems to have assumed that the evidence given by the lady who is now Mrs. Lewis and who was then Mr. Lewis's fiancée was of some assistance. The learned judge refers in many places to " they saw " or " they thought ". That is all very well, if there were evidence that Mr Lewis himself heard or knew the same things as his fiancée heard or knew, or if she, having heard, for example, the name of Mr. Green when he first arrived, had mentioned that fact to Mr. Lewis. But there was no such evidence, and therefore all that the learned judge recites about what Miss Kershaw heard and thought appears to me, with great respect, not to assist in this matter. When one looks at the evidence of Mr. Lewis himself, it is, I think, clear, as counsel for the defendant submits, that there was not here any evidence that would justify the finding that he,

---

[1] (1961) 1 Q.B. 31; [1960] 3 All E.R. 332.
[2] [1961] 1 Q.B. at p. 31.
[3] 7th Edn, 1969, pp. 213, 214.

Mistake

Mr. Lewis, regarded the identity of the man who called himself Mr. Green as a matter of vital importance.

I agree that the appeal should be allowed.

Appeal allowed.

FOSTER *v.* MACKINNON

GALLIE *v.* LEE

DOCUMENTS MISTAKENLY SIGNED.[1] A person may escape liability on a document which he has signed if he can prove that it is of a nature essentially different from what he had supposed it to be. Clear evidence is required to persuade a court that he was the victim of such a mistake.

Two points deserve special mention. (1) In a number of cases a distinction was made between the "character" and the " contents " of a document.[2] This distinction, in itself difficult to draw, has now been virtually abandoned.[3] (2) If the mistake is due to the negligence of the signatory, the latter will be barred from pleading it against an innocent third party who has acted to his loss upon the faith of the document. In the present context the word " negligence " bears no such technical significance as is given to it in the law of torts, and no question arises of a duty of care. The word simply means carelessness. It is, moreover, for the party raising the mistake to prove that he acted with care, and not for the third party to prove the contrary.[4]

Foster v. Mackinnon

(1869), L.R. 4 C.P. 704

ACTION by indorsee against indorser on a bill of exchange for 3,000*l*. drawn on the 6th of November, 1867, by one Cooper upon and accepted by one Callow, payable six months after date, and indorsed successively by Cooper, the defendant, J. P. Parker, T. A. Pooley & Co., and A. G. Pooley, to the plaintiff, who became the holder for value (having taken it in part-payment of a debt due to him from A. G. Pooley) before it became due, and without notice of any fraud.

The pleas traversed the several indorsements, and alleged that the defendant's indorsement was obtained from him by fraud.

The cause was tried before Bovill, C.J., at the last spring assizes at Guildford. The defendant, who was a gentleman far advanced in years, swore that the indorsement was not in his handwriting, and that he had never accepted nor indorsed a bill of exchange; but there was evidence that the signature was his; and Callow, who was called as a witness for the plaintiff, stated that he saw the defendant write the indorsement under the following circumstances:—Callow had been secretary to a company engaged in the formation of a railway at Sandgate, in Kent, in which the defendant

---

[1] The doctrine now under discussion derives from the medieval rule that a blind or illiterate person might prove that a deed on which he was sued was so contrary to his intention and understanding that it could not properly be called his deed at all; *non est factum*. See Fifoot, *History and Sources of the Common Law*, pp. 232–233, 248–249.

[2] e.g. Howatson *v.* Webb, [1908] 1 Ch. 1.

[3] *Infra*, pp. 169 and 172.

[4] *Infra*, pp. 170 and 173–174.

(who had property in the neighbourhood) was interested; and the defendant had some time previously, at Callow's request, signed a guarantee for 3,000*l*., in order to enable the company to obtain an advance of money from their bankers. Callow took the bill in question (which was drawn and indorsed by Cooper) to the defendant, and asked him to put his name on it, telling him it was a guarantee; whereupon the defendant, in the belief that he was signing a guarantee similar to that which he had before given (and out of which no liability had resulted to him), put his signature on the back of the bill immediately after that of Cooper. Callow only showed the defendant the back of the paper: it was, however, in the ordinary shape of a bill of exchange, and bore a stamp, the impress of which was visible through the paper.

The Lord Chief Justice told the jury that, if the indorsement was not the signature of the defendant, or if, being his signature, it was obtained upon a fraudulent representation that it was a guarantee, and the defendant signed it without knowing that it was a bill, and under the belief that it was a guarantee, and if the defendant was not guilty of any negligence in so signing the paper, he was entitled to the verdict.

The jury returned a verdict for the defendant.

The plaintiff obtained a rule nisi for a new trial on the grounds of misdirection and that the verdict was against the evidence.

BYLES, J., delivered the judgment of the Court of Common Pleas.

BYLES, J. This was an action by the plaintiff as indorsee of a bill of exchange for 3,000*l*., against the defendant, as indorser. The defendant by one of his pleas traversed the indorsement, and by another alleged that the defendant's indorsement was obtained from him by fraud. The plaintiff was a holder for value before maturity, and without notice of any fraud.

There was contradictory evidence as to whether the indorsement was the defendant's signature at all; but, according to the evidence of one Callow, the acceptor of the bill, who was called as a witness for the plaintiff, he, Callow, produced the bill to the defendant, a gentleman advanced in life, for him to put his signature on the back, after that of one Cooper, who was payee of the bill and first indorser, Callow not saying that it was a bill, and telling the defendant that the instrument was a guarantee. The defendant did not see the face of the bill at all. But the bill was of the usual shape, and bore a stamp, the impress of which stamp was visible at the back of the bill. The defendant signed his name after Cooper's, he, the defendant, (as the witness stated) believing the document to be a guarantee only.

The Lord Chief Justice told the jury that, if the indorsement was not the defendant's signature, or if, being his signature, it was obtained upon a fraudulent representation that it was a guarantee, and the defendant signed it without knowing that it was a bill, and under the belief that it was a guarantee, and if the defendant was not guilty of any negligence in so signing the paper, the defendant was entitled to the verdict. The jury found for the defendant.

A rule nisi was obtained for a new trial, first, on the ground of misdirection in the latter part of the summing-up, and secondly, on the ground that the verdict was against the evidence.

As to the first branch of the rule, it seems to us that the question arises on the traverse of the indorsement. The case presented by the defendant is, that he never made the contract declared on; that he never saw the face of the bill; that the purport of the contract was fraudulently misdescribed to him; that, when he signed one thing, he was told and believed that he was signing another and an entirely different thing; and that his mind never went with his act.

It seems plain, on principle and on authority, that, if a blind man, or a man who cannot read, or who for some reason (not implying negligence) forbears to read, has a written contract falsely read over to him, the reader misreading to such a degree that the written contract is of a nature altogether different from the contract pretended to be read from the paper which the blind or illiterate man afterwards signs; then, at least if there be no negligence, the signature so obtained is of no force.   And it is invalid not merely on the ground of fraud, where fraud exists, but on the ground that the mind of the signer did not accompany the signature; in other words, that he never intended to sign, and therefore in contemplation of law never did sign, the contract to which his name is appended.

The authorities appear to us to support this view of the law.   In *Thoroughgood's Case*[1] it was held that, if an illiterate man have a deed falsely read over to him, and he then seals and delivers the parchment, that parchment is nevertheless not his deed.   In a note to *Thoroughgood's Case*[1], in Fraser's edition of Coke's Reports, it is suggested that the doctrine is not confined to the condition of an illiterate grantor; and a case in Keilwey's Reports[2] is cited in support of this observation.   On reference to that case, it appears that one of the judges did there observe that it made no difference whether the grantor were lettered or unlettered.   That, however, was a case where the grantee himself was the defrauding party.   But the position that, if a grantor or covenantor be deceived or misled as to the *actual contents* of the deed, the deed does not bind him, is supported by many authorities: see Com. Dig. *Fait* (B. 2); and is recognized by Bayley, B., and the Court of Exchequer, in the case of *Edwards* v. *Brown*[3].   Accordingly, it has recently been decided in the Exchequer Chamber, that, if a deed be delivered, and a blank left therein be afterwards improperly filled up (at least if that be done without the grantor's negligence), it is not the deed of the grantor: *Swan* v. *North British Australasian Land Company*[4].

These cases apply to deeds; but the principle is equally applicable to other written contracts.   Nevertheless, this principle, when applied to negotiable instruments, must be and is limited in its application.   These instruments are not only assignable, but they form part of the currency of the country.   A qualification of the general rule is necessary to protect innocent transferees for value.   If, therefore, a man write his name across the back of a blank bill-stamp, and part with it, and the paper is afterwards improperly filled up, he is liable as indorser.   If he write it across the face of the bill, he is liable as acceptor, when the instrument has once passed into the hands of an innocent indorsee for value before maturity, and liable to the extent of any sum which the stamp will cover.

In these cases, however, the party signing knows what he is doing: the indorser intended to indorse, and the acceptor intended to accept, a bill of exchange to be thereafter filled up, leaving the amount, the date, the maturity, and the other parties to the bill undetermined.

But, in the case now under consideration, the defendant, according to the evidence if believed, and the finding of the jury, never intended to

---

[1] (1584), 2 Co. Rep. 9. b.   [2] Keilw. 70, pl. 6.   [3] (1831), 1 Cr. & J. 307.
[4] (1863), 2 H. & C. 175.

indorse a bill of exchange at all, but intended to sign a contract of an entirely different nature. It was not his design, and, if he were guilty of no negligence, it was not even his fault that the instrument he signed turned out to be a bill of exchange. It was as if he had written his name on a sheet of paper for the purpose of franking a letter, or in a lady's album, or on an order for admission to the Temple Church, or on the fly-leaf of a book, and there had already been, without his knowledge, a bill of exchange or a promissory note payable to order inscribed on the other side of the paper. To make the case clearer, suppose the bill or note on the other side of the paper in each of these cases to be written at a time subsequent to the signature, then the fraudulent misapplication of that genuine signature to a different purpose would have been a counterfeit alteration of a writing with intent to defraud, and would therefore have amounted to a forgery. In that case, the signer would not have been bound by his signature, for two reasons, first, that he never in fact signed the writing declared on, and, secondly, that he never intended to sign any such contract.

In the present case, the first reason does not apply, but the second reason does apply. The defendant never intended to sign that contract, or any such contract. He never intended to put his name to any instrument that then was or thereafter might become negotiable. He was deceived, not merely as to the legal effect, but as to the *actual contents* of the instrument.

We are not aware of any case in which the precise question now before us has arisen on bills of exchange or promissory notes, or been judicially discussed. In the case of *Ingham* v. *Primrose*[2], and the case of *Nance* v. *Lary*[3], both cited by the plaintiff, the facts were very different from those of the case before us, and have but a remote bearing on the question. But in *Putnam* v. *Sullivan*, an American case, reported in 4 Mass. 45, and cited in Parsons on Bills of Exchange, vol. i, p. 111, n., a distinction is taken by Chief Justice Parsons between a case where an indorser intended to indorse such a note as he actually indorsed, being induced by fraud to indorse it, and a case where he intended to indorse a different note and for a different purpose; and the Court intimated an opinion that, even in such a case as that, a distinction might prevail and protect the indorsee.

The distinction in the case now under consideration is a much plainer one; for, on this branch of the rule, we are to assume that the indorser never intended to indorse at all, but to sign a contract of an entirely different nature.

For these reasons we think the direction of the Lord Chief Justice was right.

With respect, however, to the second branch of the rule, we are of opinion that the case should undergo further investigation. We abstain from giving our reasons for this part of our decision only lest they should prejudice either party on a second inquiry.

The rule, therefore, will be made absolute for a new trial.

---

[1] (1859), 7 C.B.(N.S.) 83; 28 L. J. (C.P.) 294.
[2] 5 Alabama, 370, cited 1 Parsons on Bills, 114, n.

Gallie v. Lee

[1970] 3 All E.R. 961[1]

In 1962, the plaintiff, Mrs. Rose Maud Gallie, a widow then aged seventy-eight, executed a deed assigning certain leasehold premises to one William Robert Lee. She did not read the document, but supposed it to be a deed of gift in favour of her nephew, Walter William Parkin. Lee mortgaged the premises to the Anglia Building Society to secure a loan of £2,000.

In 1968 the plaintiff brought an action against Lee and against the building society, claiming that the assignment was void for mistake. STAMP, J. gave judgment for the plaintiff. He made a declaration that the assignment was void and ordered the building society to deliver the title deeds to the plaintiff. In 1969 the Court of Appeal allowed the appeal of the building society against this judgment. In 1970 the House of Lords affirmed the decision of the Court of Appeal. The material facts are set out by LORD HODSON.

LORD HODSON. My Lords, on June 25, 1962, the plaintiff executed an assignment of her leasehold interest in 12, Dunkeld Road, Goodmayes, to one Lee, the first defendant in the action. Her case is that her intention was to give the house to her nephew Walter William Parkin on condition that he was to permit her to reside there for the rest of her life and that she handed the title deeds to Mr. Parkin believing that the house thereupon became his property. She admitted that she signed the deed of assignment to Mr. Lee but said that she believed that this was a deed of gift giving effect to the transaction in favour of Mr. Parkin. She claimed accordingly that the deed was void just as if she had not signed it at all, e.g. as if her signature had been forged. She pleaded *non est factum*.

On the day when the deed was signed by her she was 78 years of age and her pleaded case was that Mr. Lee came to her house with Mr. Parkin and produced a document to her. This he asked her to sign saying words to the effect that he was asking her to sign it as a deed of gift to Wally (Mr. Parkin) and everything was in order. The plaintiff had broken her spectacles so that she could not use them. She could not read without them so she did not read the document. Giving her evidence on commission she said that she thought that Mr. Parkin and Mr. Lee were getting money on the house and that the whole purpose of giving the house to Mr. Parkin was so that he could get money on it. She said—" When they came and spoke to me about the house I said to (Mr. Parkin) ' I don't mind what I do to help you along'." As against Mr. Lee the deed was voidable as having been induced by fraud and the learned judge[2] accordingly held it to be void against him. Mr. Lee has not appealed. The position of the second defendant, the Anglia Building Society, which is the respondent to the appeal, is entirely different. The building society has advanced £2,000 on a deed which on its face is good security for its loan. The learned judge[2], however, held that the plaintiff was entitled to succeed against the building society also. He held that the deed was void, accepting the plea *non est factum* put forward by the plaintiff on the basis

---

[1] This case is reported under the above name in the Law Reports at first instance, in the Court of Appeal and in the House of Lords, [1971] A.C. 1004. In the All England Reports it appears as *Gallie* v. *Lee* both at first instance and in the Court of Appeal; but in the House of Lords it is reported under the name *Saunders* (*executrix of the estate of Rose Maud Gallie, deceased*) v. *Anglia Building Society*.

[2] [1968] 2 All E.R. 322; [1968] 1 W.L.R. 1190.

that she was misled as to the character, not only as to the contents, of the deed. He held that the assignment for consideration to her was of a different character from a deed of gift to Mr. Parkin. Relying on the long-accepted distinction between character and contents he gave judgment against the building society as well as against Mr. Lee. This distinction stems from *Howatson* v. *Webb*[1] (affirmed in the Court of Appeal[2]), a decision of Warrington, J.

The majority of the Court of Appeal[3] in this case, applying the same test as the trial judge, arrived at a different conclusion. Russell, L.J. accepting an argument which had been rejected by the trial judge, said that the essential character of the document which the plaintiff was intending to execute was such as to divest herself of her leasehold property by transferring it to another so that the transferee should be in a position to deal with the property, in particular by borrowing money on the security of the property. Her evidence showed that she understood that Mr. Lee and Mr. Parkin were jointly concerned in raising money on the security of the property. It was her intention that this should be done. This was, as Russell, L.J. said[4], " the object of the exercise ". I agree with him that the identity of the transferee (i.e. Mr. Lee instead of Mr. Parkin) does not make the deed of a totally different character from that which she intended to sign. On this ground the plea of *non est factum* must fail. Salmon, L.J. put the matter somewhat differently, but to the same effect, in concluding from the plaintiff's evidence that she would have executed the assignment to Mr. Lee even if the transaction had been properly explained to her. Lord Denning, M.R. reached the same conclusion but was not prepared to be fettered by the distinction between character and contents.

The distinction is a valid one in that it emphasises that points of detail in the contents of a document are not to be relied on in support of a plea of *non est factum*. Lord Denning, M.R. did, however, demonstrate that using the words as terms of art for test purposes may produce ludicrous results; e.g. a mistake as to the amount of money involved may be described as a mistake as to contents although the difference between two figures may be so great as to produce a document of an entirely different character from the one the signer intended.

It is better to adopt the test which is supported by the authorities prior to *Howatson* v. *Webb*[5] and is sound in principle. This is that the difference to support a plea of *non est factum* must be in a particular which goes to the substance of the whole consideration or to the root of the matter. Where, as in this case, there is an error of personality it may or may not be fundamental; the question cannot be answered in isolation. There is a distinction between a deed and a contract in that the former does not require consensus and the latter does. Hence, in the case of deeds, error of personality is not necessarily so vital as in the case of contracts.

The plea of *non est factum* requires clear and positive evidence before it can be established. As Donovan, L.J. said, delivering the judgment of the Court of Appeal in *Muskham Finance Ltd.* v. *Howard*[6]: " The plea of *non est factum* is a plea which must necessarily be kept within narrow limits."

---

[1] [1907] 1 Ch. 537.
[2] [1908] 1 Ch. 1.
[3] [1969] 2 Ch. 17; [1969] 1 All E.R. 1062.
[4] [1969] 2 Ch. at p. 41; [1969] 1 All E.R. at 1075.
[5] [1907] 1 Ch. 537; on appeal [1908] 1 Ch. 1.
[6] [1963] 1 Q.B. 904 at p. 912; [1963] 1 All E.R. 81 at p. 83.

To take an example, the man who in the course of his business signs a pile of documents without checking them takes the responsibility for them by appending his signature. It would be surprising if he was allowed to repudiate one of those documents on the ground of *non est factum.*

I agree with the robust conclusion reached by Lord Denning, M.R. on the facts of this case that the plaintiff having signed the questioned document, obviously a legal document, on which the building society advanced money on the faith of it being her document, cannot now be allowed to disavow her signature. I should have arrived at this conclusion even if I had thought that the law applicable was that which had previously been accepted, namely that the distinction between character and contents should be maintained.

Want of care on the part of the person who signs a document which he afterwards seeks to disown is relevant. The burden of proving *non est factum* is on the party disowning his signature; this includes proof that he or she took care. There is no burden on the opposite party to prove want of care. The word " negligence " in this connection does not involve the proposition that want of care is irrelevant unless there can be found a specific duty to the opposite party to take care. *Carlisle and Cumberland Banking Co.* v. *Bragg*[1] was on this point, in my opinion, wrongly decided and seems to be due to a confusion of thought by introducing the kind of negligence which founds an action in tort.

A person may be precluded by his own negligence, carelessness or inadvertence from averring his mistake. The word " estoppel " has often been used in this context but, for my part, I agree with Salmon, L.J. that this is not a true estoppel but an illustration of the principle that no man may take advantage of his own wrong. If it were treated as estoppel one would have to face the argument put forward by the plaintiff that if there is no deed there can be no estoppel established by the document itself. If there was no estoppel by deed there was no other foundation for that doctrine to be invoked since there was no conduct by way of representation to the building society that the questioned deed was good.

The plea of *non est factum* was originally available, it seems, only to the blind and the illiterate (*c.f. Thoroughgood's Case, Thoroughgood* v. *Cole*[2]) but by the middle of the last century the modern approach to the matter is illustrated by the leading case of *Foster* v. *Mackinnon*[3], in which the judgment of the court was delivered by Byles, J. I need not cite the whole passage but note that the judgment extends the scope of the doctrine to a person[3]—

> ". . . who, for some reason (not implying negligence) forbears to read, has a written contract falsely read over to him, the reader misreading to such a degree that the written contract is of a nature altogether different from the contract pretended to be read from the paper which the blind or illiterate man afterwards signs; then, at least if there be no negligence, the signature so obtained is of no force. And it is invalid not merely on the ground of fraud, where fraud exists, but on the ground that the mind of the signer did not accompany the signature . . ."

It is, I think, plain that the word " negligence " is not used in this passage in the restricted sense of breach of duty.

The case for the plaintiff stands or falls by her evidence. On no reasonable interpretation of this can she, in my opinion, succeed. I would dismiss the appeal.

---

[1] [1911] I K.B. 489.   [2] (1582), 2 Co. Rep. 9a.   [3] (1869), L.R. 4 CP. 704 at p. 711.

LORD WILBERFORCE. My Lords, the present case is fairly typical of many where a person, having signed and had witnessed his signature to a formal legal document, contends that the fact of signing should not bind him to the effect of it. Such situations, in many legal systems, are regulated by the requirements of execution before a notary who, if he is competent and honest, as he usually is, can do much to ensure that the signer understands and intends what he is doing. In other systems, such as ours, dependence has to be placed on the level of education and prudence of the signer and on the honesty and competence of his professional adviser. But as, inevitably, these controls are sometimes imperfect, the law must provide some measure of relief. In so doing it has two conflicting objectives: relief to a signer whose consent is genuinely lacking (I expand on this later); and protection to innocent third parties who have acted on an apparently regular and properly executed document. Because each of these factors may involve questions of degree or shading, any rule of law must represent a compromise and must allow to the court some flexibility in application.

The plea of *non est factum* has a long history. In mediaeval times, when contracts were made by deeds, and the deed had a kind of life in the law of its own, illiterate people who either could not read, or could not understand, the language in which the deed was written, were allowed this plea (that is what *non est factum* is—a plea); the result of it, if successful, was that the deed was not their deed. I think that three things can be said about the early law. First, that no definition was given of the nature or extent of the difference which must exist between what was intended and what was done—whether such as later appeared as the distinction between " character " and " contents ", or otherwise. (See *Thoroughgood's Case, Thoroughgood* v. *Cole*[1] when the decision was based on the reading of the deed " in other words than in truth it is ", and the sixteenth century case recorded in Keilwey[2]— difference between one acre and two acres. See also the nineteenth century note C to *Whelpdale's Case*[3] referring to the inconsistency of the cases: *Shulter's Case*[4]—of a man aged 115 years.) Secondly, these cases are for the most part as between the original parties to the deed, or if a third party is concerned (e.g. *Thoroughgood's Case*) he is a successor to the estate granted. Thirdly, there is some indication that the plea was not available where the signer had been guilty of a lack of care in signing what he did; there is no great precision in the definition of the disabling conduct. If Fleta is to be relied on, there was an exception of *negligentia* or *imperitia*—see Holdsworth[5].

In the nineteenth century, the emphasis had shifted toward the consensual contract, and the courts, probably unconscious of the fact, had a choice. They could either have discarded the whole doctrine on which *non est factum* was based, as obsolete, or they could try to adapt it to the prevailing structure of contract (" these cases apply to deeds; but the principle is equally applicable to other written contracts "—*Foster* v. *Mackinnon*[6]). They chose the course of adaptation, and, as in many other fields of the law, this process of adaptation has not been logical, or led to a logical result. The modern version still contains some fossilised elements.

We had traced, in arguments at the bar, the emergence of the distinction, which has come to be made between a difference (of intention from result)

---

[1] (1582), 2 Co. Rep. 9a.   [2] Keil 70 p. 6.
[3] (1604), 5 Co. Rep. 119a.   [4] (1611), 12 Co. Rep. 90.
[5] *History of English Law*, Vol. 8, p. 50, note (2).
[6] (1869), L.R. 4 C.P. 704 at p. 712.

of character, which may render a document void, and a difference of contents which at most makes it voidable. As it emerged (see *Edwards* v. *Brown*[1]) it was expressed as being between the actual contents, on the one hand, and its legal effect on the other (see *per* Bayley, B[2]). Here "actual contents " evidently means " character ". In this form it was taken into the leading case of *Foster* v. *Mackinnon*[3]. In the well-known passage from the judgment of the court, Byles, J. used the words[4] " to such a degree that the written contract is of a nature altogether different from the contract pretended to be read ", and later in his conclusion[5]: " He was deceived, not merely as to the legal effect, but as to the *actual contents* of the instrument." The language used may have been imperfect; but I think that the courts were groping for the test of what should enable a man to say that the document was not his document, his consent no consent, the contract no contract. It was really the language used in the second leading case of *Howatson* v. *Webb*[6] which has given rise to difficulty. There, in a judgment of Warrington, J., which has carried much conviction and authority, we find that, although the judgment of Byles, J. in *Foster* v. *Mackinnon*[3] is quoted, the use of the word " contents " is switched to mean what the deed actually (as a matter of detail) contains, and contrasted with what is called its legal character[7], " The misrepresentation was as to the contents of the deed, and not as to the character and class of the deed ".

The distinction, as restated, is terminologically confusing and in substance illogical, as the judgments in the Court of Appeal[8] demonstrate. On the one hand, it cannot be right that a document should be void through a mistake as to the label it bears, however little this mistake may be fundamental to what the signer intends; on the other hand, it is not satisfactory that the document should be valid if the mistake is merely as to what the document contains, however radical this mistake may be and however cataclysmic its result.

The existing test, or at least its terminology, may be criticised, but does it follow that there are no definable circumstances in which a document to which a man has put his signature may be held to be not his document, and so void rather than merely voidable? The judgment of Lord Denning, M.R. seems at first sight to suggest that there are not and that the whole doctrine ought to be discarded; but a closer reading shows that he is really confining his observations to the plainest, and no doubt commonest, cases where a man of full understanding and capacity forbears, or negligently omits, to read what he has signed. That, in the present age, such a person should be denied the *non est factum* plea I would accept; so to hold follows in logical development from the well-known suggested question of Mellish, L.J. in *Hunter* v. *Walters*[9] and from what was said by Farwell, L.J. in *Howatson* v. *Webb*[10]. But there remains a residue of difficult cases. There are still illiterate or senile persons who cannot read, or apprehend, a legal document; there are still persons who may be tricked into putting their signature on a piece of paper which has legal consequences totally different from anything they intended. Certainly the first class may in some cases, even without

[1] (1831), 1 Cr. & J. 307.
[2] (1831), 1 Cr. & J. 312.
[3] (1869), L.R. 4 C.P. 704.
[4] (1869), L.R. 4 C.P. 711.
[5] (1869), L.R. 4 C.P. 713.
[6] [1907] 1 Ch. 537.
[7] [1907] 1 Ch. 549.
[8] [1969] 1 All E.R. 1062, [1969] 2 Ch. 17.
[9] (1871), 7 Ch. App. 75.
[10] [1908] 1 Ch. 4.

Gallie v. Lee 173

the plea, be able to obtain relief, either because no third party has become involved, or, if he has, with the assistance of equitable doctrines, because the third party's interest is equitable only and his conduct such that his rights should be postponed (see *National Provincial Bank of England* v. *Jackson*[1] and of *Hunter* v. *Walters*[2]).   Certainly, too, the second class may in some cases fall under the heading of plain forgery. in which event the plea of *non est factum* is not needed, or indeed available (*c.f. Swan* v. *North British Australasian Co. Ltd.*[3]) and in others be reduced if the signer is denied the benefit of the plea because of his negligence.   But accepting all that has been said by learned judges as to the necessity of confining the plea within narrow limits, to eliminate it altogether would, in my opinion, deprive the courts of what may be, doubtless on sufficiently rare occasions, an instrument of justice.

How, then, ought the principle, on which a plea of *non est factum* is admissible, to be stated?   In my opinion, a document should be held to be void (as opposed to voidable) only when the element of consent to it is totally lacking, i.e. more concretely, when the transaction which the document purports to effect is essentially different in substance or in kind from the transaction intended.   Many other expressions, or adjectives, could be used—" basically " or " radically " or " fundamentally ".   In substance, the test does not differ from that which was applied in the leading cases of *Thoroughgood's Case*[4] and *Foster* v. *Mackinnon*[5], except in moving from the character/ contents distinction to an area better understood in modern practice.

To this general test it is necessary to add certain amplifications.   First, there is the case of fraud.   The law as to this is best stated in the words of the judgment in *Foster* v. *Mackinnon*[6] where it is said that a signature obtained by fraud:

"... is invalid not merely on the ground of fraud, where fraud exists, but on the ground that the mind of the signer did not accompany the signature; in other words, that he never intended to sign, and therefore in contemplation of law never did sign, the contract to which his name is appended."

In other words, it is the lack of consent that matters, not the means by which this result was brought about.   Fraud by itself may do no more than make the contract voidable.

Secondly, a man cannot escape from the consequences, as regards innocent third parties, of signing a document, if, being a man of ordinary education and competence, he chooses to sign it without informing himself of its purport and effect.   This principle is sometimes found expressed in the language that " he is doing something with his estate " (*Hunter* v. *Walters*[7], *Howatson* v. *Webb*[8]) but it really reflects a rule of common sense on the exigency of busy lives.

Thirdly, there is the case where the signer has been careless, in not taking ordinary precautions against being deceived.   This is a difficult area.   Until 1911 the law was reasonably clear; it had been stated plainly in *Foster* v. *Mackinnon*[5] that negligence —i.e. carelessness—might deny the signer the benefit of the plea.   Since *Bragg's* case[9] was decided in 1911 (*Carlisle and Cumberland Banking Co.* v. *Bragg*[9]) the law has been that, except in relation

---

[1] (1886), 33 Ch. D 1.
[2] (1871), 7 Ch. App. at p. 89.
[3] (1863), 2 H. & C. 175.
[4] (1582), 2 Co. Rep. 9a.
[5] (1869), L.R. 4 C.P. 704.
[6] (1869), L.R. 4 C.P. 711.
[7] (1871), 7 Ch. App. 75.
[8] [1907] 1 Ch. 537.
[9] [1911] 1 K.B. 489.

to negotiable instruments, mere carelessness is not disabling; there must be negligence arising from a duty of care to the third person who ultimately relies on the document. It does not need much force to demolish this battered precedent. It is sufficient to point to two major defects in it. First, it confuses the kind of careless conduct which disentitles a man from denying the effect of his signature with such legal negligence as entitles a person injured to bring an action in tort. The two are quite different things in standard and scope. Secondly, the judgment proceeds on a palpable misunderstanding of the judgment in *Foster* v. *Mackinnon*[1]; for Byles, J. so far from confining the relevance of negligence to negotiable instruments (as *Bragg's case*[2] suggests), clearly thought that the signer of a negotiable instrument would be liable, negligence or no negligence, and that negligence was relevant in relation to documents other than negotiable instruments; e.g. (as in the actual case before him) to a guarantee.

In my opinion, the correct rule, and that which in fact prevailed until *Bragg's case*[2], is that, leaving aside negotiable instruments to which special rules may apply, a person who signs a document, and parts with it so that it may come into other hands, has a responsibility, that of the normal man of prudence, to take care what he signs, which, if neglected, prevents him from denying his liability under the document according to its tenor. I would add that the onus of proof in this matter rests on him, i.e. to prove that he acted carefully and not on the third party to prove the contrary. I consider therefore that *Carlisle and Cumberland Banking Co.* v. *Bragg*[2] was wrong, both in the principle it states and in its decision, and that it should no longer be cited as an authority for any purpose.

The preceding paragraphs contemplate persons who are adult and literate: the conclusion as to such persons is that, while there are cases in which they may successfully plead *non est factum*, these cases will, in modern times, be rare. As to persons who are illiterate, or blind, or lacking in understanding, the law is in a dilemma. On the one hand, the law is traditionally, and rightly, ready to relieve them against hardship and imposition. On the other hand, regard has to be paid to the position of innocent third parties who cannot be expected, and often would have no means, to know the condition or status of the signer. I do not think that a defined solution can be provided for all cases. The law ought, in my opinion, to give relief if satisfied that consent was truly lacking but will require of signers even in this class that they act responsibly and carefully according to their circumstances in putting their signature to legal documents.

This brings me to the present case. The plaintiff was a lady of advanced age, but, as her evidence shows, by no means incapable physically or mentally. It certainly cannot be said that she did not receive sympathetic consideration or the benefit of much doubt from the judge as to the circumstances in which the assignment was executed. But accepting all of this, I am satisfied, with Russell, L.J. that she fell short, very far short, of making the clear and satisfactory case which is required of those who seek to have a legal act declared void and of establishing a sufficient discrepancy between her intentions and her act. I am satisfied to adopt, without repetition, the analysis of the facts which appears in the judgment of Russell, L.J. as well as that of my noble and learned friend, Lord Pearson.

I would dismiss the appeal.

---

[1] (1869), L.R. 4 C.P. 704.   [2] [1911] 1 K.B. 489.

MISREPRESENTATION

Bisset v. Wilkinson

[1927] A.C. 177

The expression of an opinion is not *per se* a representation of fact. But (a) an expression of opinion may involve a representation of fact : (b) whether the opinion is in truth held raises a question of fact.

An appeal to the Judicial Committee from a judgment of the Court of Appeal of New Zealand reversing a judgment of the Supreme Court.

LORD MERRIVALE. The appellant in this litigation brought his action in the Supreme Court of New Zealand to recover a sum of money payable to him under an agreement for sale and purchase of land. The defendants by way of defence and counterclaim alleged misrepresentation by the appellant in a material particular as to the character and quality of the land in question and claimed rescission of the agreement with consequential relief or alternatively damages for fraudulent misrepresentation or breach of warranty. Upon the trial of the action judgment was given for the plaintiff on the claim and the counterclaim. The Court of Appeal of New Zealand, by a majority, set aside the judgment of the trial judge and decreed rescission of the contract between the parties with consequential relief as prayed. The appellant claims to have the judgment of the Supreme Court reinstated.

The contract between the parties was an agreement in writing made in May, 1919, whereby the respondents agreed for the purchase by them of two adjoining blocks of land at Avondale, in the Southern Island of New Zealand, called " Homestead " and " Hogan's," containing respectively 2,062 acres and 348 acres or thereabouts, for 13,260*l.* 10*s.* ; 2,000*l.* payable— and it was in fact paid—on the signing of the agreement, and the balance payable in May, 1924, interest to be paid half-yearly in the meantime. The lands in question formed parts of an area of 5,225 acres which the appellant had bought in 1907 and after sundry works of reclamation and improvement had in 1911 subdivided for sale. He sold lots containing 1500 acres and upwards, 964 acres, 350 acres, and Hogan's block of about 348 acres, retaining the Homestead block of 2,400 acres which he used for his business of a sheep-farmer and sheep-dealer until 1919—during the war under some difficulties with regard to labour. Hogan's block was thrown on the appellant's hands by failure of the purchaser to complete, and in September, 1918, on the breakdown of a provisional arrangement which the appellant had made with another intending purchaser, he resumed his occupation of it. During the spring and summer, September, 1918, to April, 1919, the appellant carried out renewal work and stocked part of Hogan's block with young sheep, and in May he made his agreement for sale of the combined areas to the respondents, who had agreed upon a partnership as farmers.

Sheep-farming was the purpose for which the respondents purchased the lands of the plaintiff. One of them had no experience of farming. The other had been before the war in charge of sheep on an extensive sheep-farm carried on by his father, who had accompanied and advised him in his negotiation with the appellant and had carefully inspected the lands at Avondale. In the course of coming to his agreement with the respondents the appellant made statements as to the property which, in their defence and counterclaim, the respondents alleged to be misrepresentations.

At an early period after the respondents went into occupation and commenced their farming operations they found themselves in difficulties. They sought and obtained extensions of time for payment of the interest which fell due to the appellant. Sheep-farming became very unprofitable and they changed their user of the land. One of them withdrew from the partnership. The other made an assignment of the valuable part of his property to his wife, and on being eventually pressed by the appellant for payments under the agreement disclosed this assignment as an answer to the practical enforcement by the appellant of his demands. The appellant brought his action for a half-year's interest on the unpaid purchase money and the respondents set up their case of misrepresentation.

By their defence and counterclaim the respondents alleged that the appellant had " represented and warranted that the land which was the subject of the agreement had a carrying capacity of two thousand sheep if only one team were employed in the agricultural work of the said land." It was common ground at the hearing and in the Court of Appeal that the carrying capacity of a sheep-farm is its capacity the year round. As was said by Reed, J., in the Court of Appeal : " The meaning of the representation as alleged was that the carrying capacity of the farm during the winter, with such special food and new pasture as could be grown by the proper use in ploughing of one team of horses regularly employed throughout the year was two thousand sheep." " It is also common ground," said the same learned judge, " that to bring a farm to its full carrying capacity skilled management is required. It is admitted that the respondents were not experienced farmers."

The appellant made these admissions at the hearing : " I told them that if the place was worked as I was working it, with a good six-horse team, my idea was that it would carry two thousand sheep. That was my idea and still is my idea." Further, he said : " I do not dispute that they bought it believing it would carry the two thousand sheep."

The learned judge who tried the action, Sim, J., based his judgment in favour of the appellant upon conclusions at which he arrived upon his examination of the evidence, first, that the representation made by the plaintiff was a representation only of his opinion of the capacity of the farm, not a representation of what that capacity in fact was ; and secondly, that this representation of opinion was honestly made by the appellant. " It seems to me," the learned judge said, " that the defendants were not justified in regarding anything said by the plaintiff as to the carrying capacity as being anything more than an expression of his opinion on the subject. I am satisfied that what he said was, and still is, his honest opinion on the subject." These conclusions—if warranted by the evidence—were sufficient to dispose of the whole case of misrepresentation, whether as grounding a claim for rescission or a claim for damages. By them the charge of fraud in the pleadings is also specifically negatived. The cause of action founded on alleged warranty which is set up in the defence and counterclaim was, it has been agreed, not asserted at the trial, and the fact is not without bearing on the true effect of the claims which were relied upon.

In the Court of Appeal, as is said in the judgment of Stout, C.J., " the real question in dispute turned out to be whether the appellants were entitled to rescission of the contract. They did not rely upon the breach of warranty, but they asked for rescission of the contract, though their claim for damages for misrepresentation had not been formally withdrawn." The learned judges of the Court of Appeal differed in opinion. Reed, J.—who thought

the appeal failed—dealt with the case upon the contention of the defendants
—the now respondents—that the representation made to them by the
plaintiff was a representation of fact. He found it to be conclusively established by the defendants' own evidence that, given proper management, the
farm was fully capable of carrying at least two thousand sheep. Stout, C.J.,
held that the statement relied upon was made and accepted as a statement
of fact. "It would surely be improbable," the learned Chief Justice said,
"that when a seller is asked to say what the carrying capacity of his farm
is he should not answer the question, but volunteer his opinion or estimate."
As to truth of the representation, the learned Chief Justice said : "The
evidence in my opinion is clear that this place never carried all the year
round two thousand sheep." He added this : "The respondent allowed
the appellants to purchase the farm from him believing that it would carry
two thousand sheep, and, therefore, they were misled." Adams and Ostler,
JJ., alike held that the statement was a representation of fact and was proved
to be untrue.

In an action for rescission, as in an action for specific performance of
an executory contract, when misrepresentation is the alleged ground of relief
of the party who repudiates the contract, it is, of course, essential to ascertain
whether that which is relied upon is a representation of a specific fact, or a
statement of opinion, since an erroneous opinion stated by the party affirming
the contract, though it may have been relied upon and have induced the
contract on the part of the party who seeks rescission, gives no title to relief
unless fraud is established. The application of this rule, however, is not
always easy, as is illustrated in a good many reported cases, as well as in this.
A representation of fact may be inherent in a statement of opinion and, at
any rate, the existence of the opinion in the person stating it is a question
of fact. In *Karberg's* case[1] Lindley, L.J., in course of testing a representation which might have been, as it was said to be by interested parties, one
of opinion or belief, used this inquiry : "Was the statement of expectation
a statement of things not really expected ?" The Court of Appeal applied
this test and rescinded the contract which was in question. In *Smith* v.
Land and House Property Corporation[2] there came in question a vendor's
description of the tenant of the property sold as "a most desirable tenant"—
a statement of his opinion, as was argued on his behalf in an action to enforce
the contract of sale. This description was held by the Court of Appeal to
be a misrepresentation of fact, which, without proof of fraud, disentitled the
vendor to specific performance of the contract of purchase. "It is often
fallaciously assumed," said Bowen, L.J., "that a statement of opinion
cannot involve the statement of fact. In a case where the facts are equally
well known to both parties, what one of them says to the other is frequently
nothing but an expression of opinion. The statement of such opinion is
in a sense a statement of fact about the condition of the man's own mind,
but only of an irrelevant fact, for it is of no consequence what the opinion
is. But if the facts are not equally well known to both sides, then a statement
of opinion by one who knows the facts best involves very often a statement
of a material fact, for he impliedly states that he knows facts which justify
his opinion." The kind of distinction which is in question is illustrated
again in a well known case of *Smith* v. *Chadwick*[3]. There the words under

[1] [1892] 3 Ch. 1, at p. 11. [2] (1884), 28 Ch. D. 7, at p. 15.
[3] (1882), 20 Ch. D. 27; affirmed (1884), 9 App. Cas. 187.

consideration involved the inquiry in relation to the sale of an industrial concern whether a statement of " the present value of the turnover or output " was of necessity a statement of fact that the produce of the works was of the amount mentioned, or might be, and was a statement that the productive power of the works was estimated at so much. The words were held to be capable of the second of these meanings. The decisive inquiries came to be : what meaning was actually conveyed to the party complaining ; was he deceived, and, as the action was based on a charge of fraud, was the statement in question made fraudulently ?

In the present case, as in those cited, the material facts of the transaction, the knowledge of the parties respectively, and their relative positions, the words of representation used, and the actual condition of the subject-matter spoken of, are relevant to the two inquiries necessary to be made : What was the meaning of the representation ? Was it true ?

In ascertaining what meaning was conveyed to the minds of the now respondents by the appellant's statement as to the two thousand sheep, the most material fact to be remembered is that, as both parties were aware, the appellant had not and, so far as appears, no other person had at any time carried on sheep-farming upon the unit of land in question. That land as a distinct holding had never constituted a sheep-farm. The two blocks comprised in it differed substantially in character. Hogan's block was described by one of the respondents' witnesses as " better land." " It might carry," he said, " one sheep or perhaps two or even three sheep to the acre." He estimated the carrying capacity of the land generally as little more than half a sheep to the acre. And Hogan's land had been allowed to deteriorate during several years before the respondents purchased. As was said by Sim, J. : " In ordinary circumstances, any statement made by an owner who has been occupying his own farm as to its carrying capacity would be regarded as a statement of fact. . . . This, however, is not such a case. The defendants knew all about Hogan's block and knew also what sheep the farm was carrying when they inspected it. In these circumstances . . . the defendants were not justified in regarding anything said by the plaintiff as to the carrying capacity as being anything more than an expression of his opinion on the subject." In this view of the matter their Lordships concur.

Whether the appellant honestly and in fact held the opinion which he stated remained to be considered. This involved examination of the history and condition of the property. If a reasonable man with the appellant's knowledge could not have come to the conclusion he stated, the description of that conclusion as an opinion would not necessarily protect him against rescission for misrepresentation. But what was actually the capacity in competent hands of the land the respondents purchased had never been, and never was, practically ascertained. The respondents, after two years' trial of sheep-farming, under difficulties caused in part by their inexperience, found themselves confronted by a fall in the values of sheep and wool which would have left them losers if they could have carried three thousand sheep. As is said in the judgment of Ostler, J. : " Owing to sheep becoming practically valueless, they reduced their flock and went in for cropping and dairy-farming in order to make a living."

The opinions of experts and of their neighbours, on which the respondents relied, were met by the appellant with evidence of experts admitted to be equally competent and upright with those of his opponents, and his own practical experience upon part of the land, as to which his testimony was unhesitatingly accepted by the judge of first instance. It is of dominant importance that Sim, J., negatived the respondents' charge of fraud.

After attending to the close and very careful examination of the evidence which was made by learned counsel for each of the parties their Lordships entirely concur in the view which was expressed by the learned judge who heard the case. The defendants failed to prove that the farm if properly managed was not capable of carrying two thousand sheep.

Their Lordships will humbly advise His Majesty that the appeal should be allowed, and the judgment of Sim, J., restored. The respondents must bear the appellant's costs here and below.

Edgington v. Fitzmaurice

(1884), 29 Ch.D. 459

A misrepresentation of intention may be a misrepresentation of fact.
A misrepresentation is ground for relief if it is one of the causes, though not the sole cause, that induced the plaintiff to make the contract.

This action was brought by the Rev. Charles Nattali Edgington against the Hon. J. T. Fitzmaurice, Colonel Rich, Colonel Snow, General Taylor, and Major Clench, directors of the Army and Navy Provision Market (Limited), and against Mr. Hunt, the secretary, and Mr. Hanley, the manager, asking for the repayment by them of a sum of £1,500 advanced by the plaintiff on debentures of the company, on the ground that he was induced to advance the money by the fraudulent misrepresentations of the defendants.

Early in November, 1880, the plaintiff, who was a shareholder of the company, received a prospectus or circular which had been issued by order of the directors inviting subscriptions for debenture bonds to the amount of £25,000 with interest at 6 per cent., which contained the following statements :—

"The society purchased for their market, at the price of £44,500, the valuable property known as Newman's Yard, comprising more than a quarter of an acre, situate in and with a frontage to Regent Street. This property is held direct from the Crown under a lease from the Commissioners of Woods and Forests for a term of ninety-nine years from the 5th of April, 1824, at a ground rent of £196 11s. 1d., and £15 6s. 9d. yearly, in lieu of land tax, and subject to the half yearly payment of £500 in redemption of a mortgage of which £21,500 is outstanding."

The circular further stated that the company had expended on the property £20,679, and in fittings £2,943. The objects for which the issue of debentures was made were thus stated :—

" 1. To enable the society to complete the present alterations and additions to the buildings and to purchase their own horses and vans whereby a large saving will be effected in the cost of transport.
" 2. To further develop the arrangements at present existing for the direct supply of cheap fish from the coast, which are still in their infancy.
" The changes contemplated in the transport service of the society are the results of past experience, which proves that dealing with contractors is not only expensive but unsatisfactory, for the society being often at their mercy they may almost with impunity horse the vans in such an inefficient manner as to render faulty deliveries unavoidable. With sound horses at the command of the transport department the many evils at present inseparable from employing horses under contract will be prevented.

"The society now consists of upwards of 13,000 members, and since the altered management the numbers have been daily increasing."

The statements in the prospectus were impeached on the following grounds :—

1. That the prospectus was so framed as to lead to the belief that the debentures would be a charge on the property of the company.

2. That the prospectus omitted to refer to a second mortgage for £5,000 to Messrs. Hores & Pattisson which had been made on the 10th of August, 1880.

3. That the prospectus stated that the property was subject to the half-yearly payment of £500 in redemption of the mortgage for £21,500, but omitted to state that on the 5th of April, 1884, the whole balance of the mortgage which would be then due, namely, £18,000, might be at once called in.

4. That the real object of the issue of debentures was to pay off pressing liabilities of the company, and not to complete the buildings or to purchase horses and vans or to develop the business of the company.

On November 8, 1880, the plaintiff, supposing that the debentures would be a charge upon the property mentioned in the prospectus, wrote to Mr. Hunt, the secretary of the company, asking him whether they would be a first charge on the property.

Mr. Hunt replied on November 10, 1880, in a letter in which he said:

"The debentures will be a first charge on this property after providing for the interest payable in respect of the existing mortgage for £21,000, the redemption of which is spread over a period of twenty-one years, and it cannot be called in except at the rate of £1,000 a year."

The plaintiff was also informed verbally by Mr. Hanley, the general manager, that the debenture holders would have the security of the company's property.

The plaintiff accordingly took debenture bonds to the amount of £1,500. The debentures were delivered to him on February 19, 1881, and were in the form of a covenant by the company to pay to the bearer the amount advanced with interest, and contained no charge on the property of the company.

The company was wound up by an order dated July 22, 1881, and the assets were not sufficient to pay the debenture holders more than a small dividend.

The plaintiff claimed repayment of the sum advanced by him with interest, on the ground that it had been obtained from him by the fraudulent misstatements and omissions in the prospectus and the fraudulent misrepresentations of Hunt and Hanley; or, in the alternative, £2,000 damages for non-fulfilment of the agreement to give the plaintiff a charge on the property ; or, in the alternative, repayment of £1,500 advanced by the plaintiff on the promise and representation that it would be secured by debentures specifically charging it on the property of the company, subject only to a mortgage then existing ; whereas the debentures did not specifically charge it on any property, and were made subject to various other charges which were fraudulently concealed from the plaintiff by the defendants.

The defendants appeared separately, but the defences put in by them were substantially the same, namely, that the mortgage for £5,000 was a temporary charge only, and was intended to be paid off before the issue of the debentures, and therefore it was not considered necessary to mention it in the prospectus ; that they were not aware that the mortgage for £21,500 could be called in in 1884 ; that they believed, and had fair grounds for believing, that the money raised by the debentures would be expended on the objects stated in the prospectus, and that some part of it was so expended. They also denied that they had given any authority to Messrs. Hunt and Hanley to represent that the debenture holders would have any charge on the property of the company. Major Clench also relied upon the fact that he resigned his office of director on August 12, 1880, although he was present by special invitation at some of the board meetings at which the prospectus was discussed and assisted in drawing it up.

The plaintiff in his evidence swore that he understood the prospectus as holding out that he would have a charge on the property, and that he would not have taken the debentures unless he had understood that he was to have a charge upon it. He also said that he relied on the fact that the company wanted the money for the objects stated in the prospectus. And he stated that he did not read the bonds when he received them, but only looked at the amounts, and that he did not ascertain their nature till after the company was wound up.

It appeared from the minutes of the board of directors that the company was in financial difficulties at the time when the debentures were issued ; their banking account with Messrs. Ransom, Bouverie & Co. being over-drawn to the extent of £5,000; that the advance by Messrs. Hores & Pattisson had been expended in altering and improving the building in which the company's business was carried on; that a small part of the money raised by the debentures was expended in improving the premises and in the purchase of horses and vans; but the rest was applied in payment of pressing liabilities, including the mortgage debt of £5,000 due to Messrs. Hores & Pattisson. Many facts shewing the company to have been in difficulties are stated in the judgment of Mr. Justice Denman.

The action came on for hearing before Mr. Justice Denman on May 7, 1884.

Denman, J., gave judgment against the five directors, but dismissed the action against Hunt and Hanley. His judgment was affirmed by the Court of Appeal.

BOWEN, L.J. This is an action for deceit, in which the plaintiff complains that he was induced to take certain debentures by the misrepresentations of the defendants, and that he sustained damage thereby. The loss which the plaintiff sustained is not disputed. In order to sustain his action he must first prove that there was a statement as to facts which was false ; and secondly, that it was false to the knowledge of the defendants, or that they made it not caring whether it was true or false. For it is immaterial whether they made the statement knowing it to be untrue, or recklessly, without caring whether it was true or not, because to make a statement recklessly for the purpose of influencing another person is dishonest. It is also clear that it is wholly immaterial with what object the lie is told. That is laid down in Lord Blackburn's judgment in *Smith* v. *Chadwick*[1], but it is material that the defendant should intend that it should be relied on by the person to whom he makes it. But, lastly, when you have proved that the statement was false, you must further shew that the plaintiff has acted upon it and has sustained damage by so doing : you must shew that the statement was either the sole cause of the plaintiff's act, or materially

---

[1] (1884), 9 App. Cas. 187.

contributed to his so acting. So the law is laid down in *Clarke* v. *Dickson*[1],
and that is the law which we have now to apply.

The alleged misrepresentations were three. First, it was said that the
prospectus contained an implied allegation that the mortgage for £21,500
could not be called in at once, but was payable by instalments. I think that
upon a fair construction of the prospectus it does so allege ; and therefore
that the prospectus must be taken to have contained an untrue statement on
that point ; but it does not appear to me clear that the statement was
fraudulently made by the defendants. It is therefore immaterial to consider
whether the plaintiff was induced to act as he did by that statement.

Secondly, it is said that the prospectus contains an implied allegation
that there was no other mortgage affecting the property except the mortgage
stated therein. I think there was such an implied allegation, but I think it
is not brought home to the defendants that it was made dishonestly ;
accordingly, although the plaintiff may have been damnified by the weight
which he gave to the allegation, he cannot rely on it in this action : for in
an action of deceit the plaintiff must prove dishonesty. Therefore if the
case had rested on these two allegations alone, I think it would be too
uncertain to entitle the plaintiff to succeed.

But when we come to the third alleged misstatement I feel that the
plaintiff's case is made out. I mean the statement of the objects for which
the money was to be raised. These were stated to be to complete the
alterations and additions to the buildings, to purchase horses and vans, and
to develope the supply of fish. A mere suggestion of possible purposes to
which a portion of the money might be applied would not have formed a
basis for an action of deceit. There must be a misstatement of an existing
fact : but the state of a man's mind is as much a fact as the state of his
digestion. It is true that it is very difficult to prove what the state of a
man's mind at a particular time is, but if it can be ascertained it is as much
a fact as anything else. A misrepresentation as to the state of a man's mind
is, therefore, a misstatement of fact. Having applied as careful consideration to the evidence as I could, I have reluctantly come to the conclusion
that the true objects of the defendants in raising the money were not those
stated in the circular. I will not go through the evidence, but looking only
to the cross-examination of the defendants, I am satisfied that the objects
for which the loan was wanted were misstated by the defendants, I will not
say knowingly, but so recklessly as to be fraudulent in the eye of the law.

Then the question remains—Did this misstatement contribute to induce
the plaintiff to advance his money? Mr. Davey's argument has not convinced
me that they did not. He contended that the plaintiff admits that he would
not have taken the debentures unless he had thought they would give him
a charge on the property, and therefore he was induced to take them by his
own mistake, and the misstatement in the circular was not material. But
such misstatement was material if it was actively present to his mind when
he decided to advance his money. The real question is, what was the state
of the plaintiff's mind, and if his mind was disturbed by the misstatement
of the defendants, and such disturbance was in part the cause of what he
did, the mere fact of his also making a mistake himself could make no
difference. It resolves itself into a mere question of fact. I have felt some
difficulty about the pleadings, because in the statement of claim this point
is not clearly put forward, and I had some doubt whether this contention as

---

[1] (1859), 6 C. B. N. S. 453.

to the third misstatement was not an afterthought. But the balance of my judgment is weighed down by the probability of the case. What is the first question which a man asks when he advances money ? It is, what is it wanted for ? Therefore I think that the statement is material, and that the plaintiff would be unlike the rest of his race if he was not influenced by the statement of the objects for which the loan was required. The learned Judge in the Court below came to the conclusion that the misstatement did influence him, and I think he came to a right conclusion.

COTTON, L.J. and FRY, L.J., gave judgment to the same effect.

London Assurance v. Mansel

(1879), 11 Ch.D. 363

> All contracts of insurance are *uberrimæ fidei*. The assured is therefore under a duty to disclose all material facts which are known to him. The question in each case is not whether the assured believed any particular circumstance to be material but whether it was in fact material.

This was an action by the plaintiffs, who were duly incorporated by the name of *The London Assurance*, and were empowered to grant assurances on lives, to set aside an agreement to grant a policy of life assurance to the defendant.

On August 16, 1878, the plaintiffs, on the application of the defendant's solicitor, sent him forms of proposal for life assurance, and on August 20, 1878, the defendant left with the plaintiffs at their office a proposal for assurance on his life for £10,000 filled up on one of the plaintiffs' forms of proposal, and signed by the defendant. The questions and answers contained in this proposal, so far as material, were as follows:—

Questions.	Answers.
" Are you now and have you always been of temperate habits ? "	" Yes."
" State if there be any other material circumstance affecting your past or present state of health or habits of life to which the foregoing questions do not extend ? "	" Not to my knowledge."
" Has a proposal ever been made on your life at any other office or offices ? If so, where ? " " Was it accepted at the ordinary premium, or at an increased premium, or declined ? "	" Insured now in two offices for £16,000 at ordinary rates. Policies effected last year ? "

At the foot of the proposal the defendant signed the following declaration. " I declare that the above written particulars are true, and I agree that this proposal and declaration shall be the basis of the contract between me and the *London Assurance*."

On the same day the defendant had an interview with the medical officer of the plaintiffs, and in reply to his inquiries gave substantially the same answers as those in the proposal before stated.

The plaintiffs being, as they alleged, satisfied with and relying upon the said proposal, and with the report of their medical officer, and with the answers they had received from two friends of the defendant to whom he had referred them, sent to the defendant's solicitor a written acceptance of the proposal for an assurance of £10,000 on the defendant's life, and, on August 23, 1878, received from him a cheque for the first year's premium, and on August 24, 1878, the plaintiffs sent him the usual certificate as to the assurance being effected.

The plaintiffs alleged that, shortly after the last-mentioned date, they discovered that, though the defendant's life had been assured for £10,000 in the *Rock Life Assurance Company*, and also for £6,000 in the *Equity and Law Life Assurance Society*, the last-named assurance society had in November, 1877, when the defendant applied for a further assurance of £3,000, decided not to increase the amount at risk on his life; also that the defendant had shortly afterwards made proposals to the *Scottish Equitable Society* and to the *Crown Insurance Society*, who had respectively declined his proposals, to the *North British and Mercantile Insurance Society*, which proposal was withdrawn, and to the *Liverpool, London and Globe Company*, by whom the proposal was not accepted; that in June, 1878, the *English and Scottish Law Life Assurance Association*, after accepting a proposal for an assurance of £5,000 on the life of the defendant, had refused to proceed with it on learning that the *Equity and Law Life Society* had declined the further assurance of the defendant's life; also, that in August, 1878, the defendant had applied for assurances on his life to the *Clerical Medical and General Life Assurance Society*, to the *Scottish Amicable Assurance Society*, and the *Law Life Assurance Society*, but that each of the said offices had declined his proposals.

The plaintiffs alleged that they thereupon determined not to proceed with the assurance, and that their solicitors wrote to the defendant's solicitor to that effect, and sent a cheque for the amount of the premium, which was returned by the defendant.

The plaintiffs then brought their action, setting out in their statement of claim the facts before stated, and alleging that it was the duty of the defendant to have informed them that his life had been refused by the said several offices, that such fact was a very material fact in a contract of life assurance, and that the plaintiffs would not have entertained the defendant's proposal for assurance had he informed them that his life had been refused by other offices, which the defendant had concealed.

The plaintiffs claimed a declaration that the acceptance by the plaintiffs of the defendant's proposal for assurance on his life for £10,000, and the contract by the plaintiffs for the assurance on the life of the defendant, were void.

The defendant, by his statement of defence, admitted the plaintiffs' allegations as to the proposal and as to the two policies that had been effected, also that the *Equity and Law Life Society* had decided not to increase their risk, the reason being that they considered their risk sufficiently large. With regard to the other proposals, the defendant stated as follows:—

" The defendant admits that proposals were made to the *Clerical, Medical, and General Life Assurance Society*, the *Scottish Amicable Life Assurance Society*, and the *Law Life Assurance Society*, for an assurance on his life, and such proposals were declined, without any medical examination."

In paragraph 15 he stated as follows:—" The defendant is not and never has been of intemperate habits of life, and although proposals for assurances on the defendant's life had been made to and declined by the several offices in the statement of claim mentioned, the defendant's life was never rejected by an office, but was passed as a first-class life by every medical officer who examined him." The defendant also stated that the *English and Scottish Law Life Assurance Society* passed his life as a first-class life, but they reserved the right of declining to complete the transaction at any time before the receipt of the premium; but that, having learned that the *Equity and Law Life Assurance Society* had decided not to increase their risk on the defendant's life, and would not take any part of the new risk, exercised their right of declining to complete the transaction."

The defendant submitted that there had been no concealment such as to vitiate the contract.

The case was heard on motion for judgment on admissions in the pleading.

JESSEL, M.R.: The action in this case is to set aside an agreement for assurance for life on the ground of concealment of a material fact in effecting the assurance.

The first question to be decided is, what is the principle on which the Court acts in setting aside contracts of assurance? As regards the general principle I am not prepared to lay down the law as making any difference in substance between one contract of assurance and another. Whether it is life, or fire, or marine assurance, I take it good faith is required in all cases, and, though there may be certain circumstances from the peculiar nature of marine insurance which require to be disclosed, and which do not apply to other contracts of insurance, that is rather, in my opinion, an illustration of the application of the principle than a distinction in principle.

But I think the law has been laid down very often, and I am going to refer to two or three statements of it, which at all events are binding on me.

In the case of *Dalglish* v. *Jarvie*[1], a case which had nothing to do with insurance, but which referred to the principles on which a special injunction ought to be granted *ex parte*, Lord Cranworth, then the Lord Commissioner Rolfe, says this: " Upon one point it seems to me proper to add this much, namely, that the application for a special injunction is very much governed by the same principles which govern insurances, matters which are said to require the utmost degree of good faith, ' *uberrima fides.* ' In cases of insurance a party is required not only to state all matters within his knowledge, which he believes to be material to the question of insurance, but all which in point of fact are so. If he conceals anything that he knows to be material, it is a fraud; but besides that, if he conceals anything that may influence the rate of premium which the underwriter may require, although he does not know that it would have that effect, such concealment entirely vitiates the policy."

Here it is to be observed that he says, " In cases of insurance "; he does not say one kind of insurance or another kind of insurance, but it is the more valuable because he is stating the law as settled as a mere illustration of the similar law which he considers to apply to applications for special injunctions when a man comes for one *ex parte*. If he conceals anything he knows to be material, it is fraud, and if he conceals anything that may influence the rate of premium, although he does not know it, it still vitiates the policy.

In another case, which again is not directly in point, turning on a contract, the case of *Moens* v. *Heyworth*[2], we have a *dictum* of Baron Parke. It was a case of ordinary mercantile contract, not of an insurance contract. Baron Parke says: " The case of a policy of insurance does not appear to me to be analogous to the present; those instruments are made upon an

---

[1] (1850), 2 Mac. & G. 231, at p. 243.   [2] (1842), 10 M. & W. 147, at p. 157.

implied contract between the parties that everything material known to the
assured should be disclosed by them. That is the basis on which the
contract proceeds, and it is material to see that it is not obtained by means of
untrue representation or concealment in any respect "; that means, of course,
concealment in any material respect.

Then in the case, which was an action on a policy of insurance, of
Lindenau v. *Desborough*[1], Lord Tenterden says: " Then it is said that the
party is not bound to do more than answer the questions proposed, unless
he can be charged with some fraudulent concealment. Admitting this not
to fall within any of the specific questions, which is not by any means clear,
still the general question put by the office requires information of every fact
which any reasonable man would think material." That passage shews
that the non-answering of a specific question in Lord Tenterden's opinion
would amount to concealment if the man knew the fact and was able to
answer it.

Mr. Justice Bayley says[2]: " I think that in all cases of insurance "—
then he goes on to add what Lord Cranworth did not add, but which he
meant—" whether on ships, houses or lives, the underwriter should be
informed of every material circumstance within the knowledge of the assured;
and that the proper question is, whether any particular circumstance was
in fact material, and not whether the party believed it to be so. The contrary
doctrine would lead to frequent suppression of information, and it would
often be extremely difficult to shew that the party neglecting to give the
information thought it material. But if it be held that all material facts
must be disclosed, it will be the interest of the assured to make a full and
fair disclosure of all the information within their reach." Then Mr. Justice
Littledale says: " I am of the same opinion. It is the duty of the assured
in all cases to disclose all material facts within their knowledge. In cases
of life insurance certain specific questions are proposed as to points affecting
in general all mankind. But there may be also circumstances affecting
particular individuals which are not likely to be known to the assurers, and
which, had they been known, would no doubt have been made the subject of
specific enquiries." He puts it more strongly, therefore, when it is a specific
inquiry.

Now I come to the facts of the case, which certainly appear to me to
be very plain and clear indeed. The office of the *London Assurance* asks
these questions: " Has a proposal ever been made on your life at any other
office or offices; if so, where? Was it accepted at the ordinary premium,
or declined? " and there is an agreement at the end, " That this proposal
and declaration shall be the basis of the contract between the assured and the
company." Here is the answer: " Insured now in two offices for £16,000
at ordinary rates. Policies effected last year." It is to be observed that
the man proposing the assurance, who knows the facts, does not answer the
question. The question was, " Has a proposal been made at any office or
offices; if so, where? " He does not state, " I proposed to half a dozen
offices," which was the truth, but simply says, " Insured now in two offices,"
which of course must have been intended to represent an answer, and therefore would mislead the persons receiving it, who did not look at it with the
greatest attention, into the belief that he was insured in two offices, and
that they were the only proposals that he had made. " Was it accepted
at the ordinary premiums or an increased premium? " His answer is,

---
[1] (1828), 8 B. & C. 586.   [2] (1828), 8 B. & C. 592.

" At ordinary rates." That is the answer to the second branch of the inquiry, but he has not answered the question, " or declined ? " The inference, therefore, which must have been intended to be produced on the mind of the person reading the answer was that it had not been declined. And in my opinion that is the fair meaning of the answer, and the assured is not to be allowed to say, " I did not answer the question." But if it were so it would make no difference, because if a man purposely avoids answering a question, and thereby does not state a fact which it is his duty to communicate, that is concealment. Concealment properly so called means nondisclosure of a fact which it is a man's duty to disclose, and it was his duty to disclose the fact if it was a material fact.

The question is whether this is a material fact ? I should say, no human being acquainted with the practice of companies or of insurance societies or underwriters could doubt for a moment that it is a fact of great materiality, a fact upon which the offices place great reliance. They always want to know what other offices have done with respect to the lives. But in this case there could be no question as to its materiality. In the first place we have this in the answer: " The defendant admits that proposals were made to the *Clerical, Medical, and General Life Assurance Society*, the *Scottish Amicable Life Assurance Society*, and the *Law Life Assurance Society* for an assurance on his life, and such proposals were declined." There are three proposals, as admitted by the answer, declined in the very words of the question; and then he goes on:—[His Lordship then stated paragraph 15 of the answer, and added:—] We have an admission by the defendant that no less than five insurance offices had declined to accept his life.

Now, to suppose that any one who knows anything about life insurance, that any decent special juryman could for a moment hesitate as to the proper answer to be given to the inquiry, when you go to the insurance office and ask for an insurance on your life, ought you to tell them that your proposals had been declined by five other assurance offices ? is, I say, quite out of the question. There can be but one answer—that a man is bound to say, " My proposals have been declined by five other offices. I will give you the reasons, and shew you that it does not affect my life," as he admits it to be by this answer; but of that the office could judge. There can be no doubt, as a proposition to be decided by a jury, that such a circumstance is material. But in fact I have elements here admitted on the pleadings for deciding that question quite irrespective of the ordinary knowledge of the practice of mankind in respect of these matters which is to be imputed to a good special juryman, because I have here two things admitted, first of all that the proposal which forms the basis of the contract asks a question—Has a proposal been declined ?

Now where it is to form the basis of the contract it is material, because, as was held in a case in the House of Lords of *Anderson* v. *Fitzgerald*[1], where it is part of the contract, the other side cannot say it is not material. So here we have the proposal as the basis of the contract. It is impossible for the assured to say that the question asked is not a material question to be answered, and that the fact which the answer would bring out is not a material fact.

Further, we have this, that within the defendant's own knowledge the *English and Scottish Law Life Assurance Society*, having accepted his life, which had been duly passed by their medical officer as a first-class life after

---

[1] (1853), 4 H. L. Cas. 484.

examination, and merely reserving a right to decline, when they found that one other office, not five, but one, had declined the life, or rather the proposal, at once withdrew from their acceptance and declined his proposal. So that the defendant had the strongest reasons for believing from actual knowledge that the fact of a proposal having been declined was a most material circumstance, and would have the greatest effect on the mind of the proposed assurers.

It seems to me a very plain and clear case, and that the plaintiffs are consequently entitled to judgment.

The order will be—The plaintiffs being willing and hereby offering to return the premium, we declare that the acceptance by the plaintiffs of the defendant's life was void and of no effect, that they were not bound to deliver the policy, and that the contract be delivered up to be cancelled.

Leaf v. International Galleries (A Firm)

[1950] 2 K.B. 86

In principle the categories of term and " mere " representation are mutually exclusive. At common law, if a party to a contract claims damages for a non-fraudulent misrepresentation, he must prove that it constitutes a term in that contract.[1] But he may ask for rescission on the ground that the contract was induced by the representation, provided that he sues within a reasonable time.

Since 1967 the injured party's rights have been enlarged by statute. By s. 1 of the Misrepresentation Act, 1967, he may be able to obtain rescission for a non-fraudulent misrepresentation whether or not it has become a term in the contract and whether or not the contract has been performed. By s. 2 of the Act he may be able to claim damages for a non-fraudulent misrepresentation by which he was induced to make a contract and, as a result, has suffered loss.[2]

APPEAL from Westminster county court.

The plaintiff, Ernest Louis Leaf, on March 8, 1944, purchased from the defendants, International Galleries, a firm, a picture called " Salisbury Cathedral " for 85*l*. At the time of the purchase the defendants represented that the picture was painted by John Constable, but when five years later the plaintiff tried to sell it he was informed that it was not by Constable. Thereupon he returned it to the defendants and asked them to refund the 85*l*. which he had paid for it. The defendants having refused to do so, the plaintiff by this action claimed to rescind the contract and to have repayment of the 85*l*.

When the hearing began in the county court, the judge suggested that the plaintiff's proper remedy was a claim for damages, and asked if he wished to amend his claim. It was then stated that no such amendment was desired. At the end of the hearing, however, the plaintiff applied for leave to amend and add a claim for damages, but this was refused on the ground that the application had been made too late. The county court judge found that the defendants had made an innocent misrepresentation and that the picture had not been painted by Constable. He gave judgment for them, however, holding, on the authority of *Angel* v. *Jay*[3], that the

---

[1] *Supra,* p. 60.
[2] *Infra,* p. 194. It is also possible that he may be able to sue for the tort of negligence under the principle laid down by the House of Lords in *Hedley Byrne & Co. Ltd.* v. *Heller & Partners, Ltd.*, [1964] A.C. 465; [1963] 2 All E.R. 575. But this principle still awaits development by the courts.   [3] [1911] 1 K. B. 666.

equitable remedy of rescission was not available in the case of an executed contract.

The plaintiff appealed.

Weitzman for the plaintiff. The plaintiff is entitled to rescind this contract. He agreed to purchase a picture painted by Constable and it is now established that the picture was not painted by Constable. In *Wilde* v. *Gibson*[1] Lord Campbell said that where there had been an innocent misrepresentation rescission would not be ordered after conveyance. Joyce, J., expressed the same opinion in *Seddon* v. *North Eastern Salt Co., Ltd.*[2], and that principle was applied in *Angel* v. *Jay*[3]. Similar views have been expressed in *Redgrave* v. *Hurd*[4], *Whittington* v. *Seale-Hayne*[5], and *Armstrong* v. *Jackson*[6]. Since those cases were decided, however, many judges have expressed the opinion that rescission could be granted of an executed contract where there had been an innocent misrepresentation: see *per* Lord Atkin in *Bell* v. *Lever Bros., Ltd.*[7], *MacKenzie* v. *Royal Bank of Canada*[8], and the decision of the Court of Appeal in *Solle* v. *Butcher*[9]. The principle that rescission cannot be obtained of an executed contract has been criticized in an article in the Law Quarterly Review, vol. 55, p. 90. It is submitted that the true view is that rescission can be obtained of an executed contract so long as *restitutio in integrum* is possible. Here the parties can be restored to their original position, since the plaintiff can return the picture to the defendants. The plaintiff was under no obligation to have the picture examined when he purchased it. He has only now discovered that he has not got what he purchased.

He is entitled to elect whether he will claim damages under s. 11 of the Sale of Goods Act, 1893, for breach of warranty or whether he will claim rescission. Time did not begin to run against the plaintiff until he discovered that the picture was not in fact painted by Constable.

John Perrett and *K. G. Jupp*, for the defendants, were not called on.

DENNING, L.J. [asked by Evershed, M.R., to deliver the first judgment, stated the facts and continued:] The question is whether the plaintiff is entitled to rescind the contract on the ground that the picture in question was not painted by Constable. I emphasize that it is a claim to rescind only: there is no claim in this action for damages for breach of condition or breach of warranty. The claim is simply one for rescission. At a very late stage before the county court judge counsel did ask for leave to amend by claiming damages for breach of warranty, but it was not allowed. No claim for damages is before us at all. The only question is whether the plaintiff is entitled to rescind.

The way in which the case is put by Mr. Weitzman, on behalf of the plaintiff, is this: he says that this was an innocent misrepresentation and that in equity he is, or should be, entitled to claim rescission even of an executed contract of sale on that account. He points out that the judge has found that it is quite possible to restore the parties to their original position. It can be done by simply handing back the picture to the defendants.

In my opinion, this case is to be decided according to the well known principles applicable to the sale of goods. This was a contract for the sale of goods. There was a mistake about the quality of the subject-matter, because both parties believed the picture to be a Constable; and that

---

[1] (1848), 1 H. L. Cas. 605, at p. 632.   [2] [1905] 1 Ch. 326, at p. 332.
[3] [1911] 1 K. B. 666.   [4] (1881), 20 Ch. D. 1.   [5] (1900), 82 L. T. 49.
[6] [1917] 2 K. B. 822.   [7] [1932] A. C. 161, at p. 224.   [8] [1934] A. C. 468, at p. 475.
[9] [1950] 1 K.B. 671.

mistake was in one sense essential or fundamental. But such a mistake does not avoid the contract: there was no mistake at all about the subject-matter of the sale. It was a specific picture, " Salisbury Cathedral." The parties were agreed in the same terms on the same subject-matter, and that is sufficient to make a contract: see *Solle* v. *Butcher*[1].

There was a term in the contract as to the quality of the subject-matter: namely, as to the person by whom the picture was painted—that it was by Constable. That term of the contract was, according to our terminology, either a condition or a warranty. If it was a condition, the buyer could reject the picture for breach of the condition at any time before he accepted it, or is deemed to have accepted it; whereas, if it was only a warranty, he could not reject it at all but was confined to a claim for damages.

I think it right to assume in the buyer's favour that this term was a condition, and that, if he had come in proper time he could have rejected the picture; but the right to reject for breach of condition has always been limited by the rule that, once the buyer has accepted, or is deemed to have accepted, the goods in performance of the contract, then he cannot thereafter reject, but is relegated to his claim for damages: see s. 11, sub-s. 1 (*c*), of the Sale of Goods Act, 1893, and *Wallis, Son and Wells* v. *Pratt and Haynes*[2].

The circumstances in which a buyer is deemed to have accepted goods in performance of the contract are set out in s. 35 of the Act, which says that the buyer is deemed to have accepted the goods, amongst other things, " when, after the lapse of a reasonable time, he retains the goods without intimating to the seller that he has rejected them." In this case the buyer took the picture into his house and, apparently, hung it there, and five years passed before he intimated any rejection at all. That, I need hardly say, is much more than a reasonable time. It is far too late for him at the end of five years to reject this picture for breach of any condition. His remedy after that length of time is for damages only, a claim which he has not brought before the court.

Is it to be said that the buyer is in any better position by relying on the representation, not as a condition, but as an innocent misrepresentation? I agree that on a contract for the sale of goods an innocent material misrepresentation may, in a proper case, be a ground for rescission even after the contract has been executed. The observations of Joyce, J., in *Seddon* v. *North Eastern Salt Co., Ltd.*[3], are, in my opinion, not good law. Many judges have treated it as plain that an executed contract of sale may be rescinded for innocent misrepresentation: see, for instance, *per* Warrington, L.J., and Scrutton, L.J., in *T. and J. Harrison* v. *Knowles and Foster*[4]; *per* Lord Atkin in *Bell* v. *Lever Brothers, Ltd.*[5]; and *per* Scrutton, L.J., and Maugham, L.J., in *L'Estrange* v. *F. Graucob, Ltd.*[6]

Apart from that, there is now the decision of the majority of this court in *Solle* v. *Butcher*[7], which overrules the first ground of decision in *Angel* v. *Jay*[8]. But it is unnecessary to explore these matters now.

---

[1] [1950] 1 K. B. 671.

[2] [1910] 2 K.B. 1003; on appeal, [1911] A.C. 394. By s. 11, sub-s. 1 (c) of the Sale of Goods Act, 1893, it was enacted that " where a contract of sale is not severable and the buyer has accepted the goods or part thereof, or where the contract is for specific goods, the property in which has passed to the buyer, the breach of any condition to be fulfilled by the seller can only be treated as a breach of warranty, and not as a ground for rejecting the goods and treating the contract as repudiated, unless there be a term of the contract, express or implied, to that effect." See now Misrepresentation Act, 1967, s. 4 (1), *infra*, p. 195.

[3] [1905] 1 Ch. 326.

[4] [1918] 1 K. B. 608, at pp. 609, 610.

[5] [1932] A. C. 161, at p. 224.

[6] [1934] 2 K. B. 394, 400, at p. 405.

[7] [1950] 1 K. B. 671.

[8] [1911] 1 K. B. 666.

Although rescission may in some cases be a proper remedy, it is to be remembered that an innocent misrepresentation is much less potent than a breach of condition; and a claim to rescission for innocent misrepresentation must at any rate be barred when a right to reject for breach of condition is barred. A condition is a term of the contract of a most material character, and if a claim to reject on that account is barred, it seems to me *a fortiori* that a claim to rescission on the ground of innocent misrepresentation is also barred.

So, assuming that a contract for the sale of goods may be rescinded in a proper case for innocent misrepresentation, the claim is barred in this case for the self-same reason as a right to reject is barred. The buyer has accepted the picture. He had ample opportunity for examination in the first few days after he had bought it. Then was the time to see if the condition or representation was fulfilled. Yet he has kept it all this time. Five years have elapsed without any notice of rejection. In my judgment he cannot now claim to rescind. His only claim, if any, as the county court judge said, was one for damages, which he has not made in this action. In my judgment, therefore, the appeal should be dismissed.

JENKINS, L.J. I agree. So far as dealings in land are concerned there is a considerable body of authority to the effect that rescission on the ground of innocent misrepresentation will not be allowed after conveyance. For instance, there are the observations of Lord Campbell to that effect in *Wilde* v. *Gibson*[1]; and the doctrine has also been applied to leases in *Angel* v. *Jay*[2]. In some of the cases, on the strength of the authorities concerning sales of land, the proposition has been stated in general terms to the effect that no executed contract can after completion be rescinded on the ground of innocent misrepresentation. As appears from the recent decision of the majority of this court in *Solle* v. *Butcher*[3], it seems probable that the proposition thus generally stated is unduly wide. In particular, it cannot be assumed that it necessarily holds good with respect to a sale of chattels passing by delivery. For the purposes of this case, however, I find it unnecessary to decide how far it is possible to claim, on the ground of innocent misrepresentation, rescission of a contract for the sale of chattels passing by delivery after the contract has been completed by delivery of those chattels; and I propose to confine myself to considering whether, assuming such a claim to be open, this is a case in which it should properly be allowed.

In my judgment, that question must clearly be answered in the negative on the facts of this case. It is true that the plaintiff bought the picture on the faith of the representation, innocently made, that it was a painting by Constable. It is true that this was a representation of great importance, which went to the root of the contract and induced him to buy. Clearly if, before he had taken delivery of the picture, he had obtained other advice and come to the conclusion that the picture was not a Constable, it would have been open to him to rescind. It may be that if, having taken delivery of the picture on the faith of the representation and having taken it home, he had, within a reasonable time, taken other advice and satisfied himself that it was not a Constable, he might have been able to make good his claim to rescission notwithstanding the delivery. That point I propose to leave open. What in fact happened was that he took delivery of the picture, kept it for some five years, and took no steps to obtain any further evidence

---

[1] (1848), 1 H. L. Cas. 605, 632.   [2] [1911] 1 K. B. 666.   [3] [1950] 1 K. B. 671.

as to its authorship; and that, finally, when he was minded to sell the picture at the end of a matter of five years, the untruth of the representation was brought to light.

In those circumstances, it seems to me to be quite out of the question that a court of equity should grant relief by way of rescission. It is perfectly true that the county court judge held that there had been no laches, and, of course, it may be said that the plaintiff had no occasion to obtain any further evidence as to the authorship of the picture until he wanted to sell; but in my judgment contracts such as this cannot be kept open and subject to the possibility of rescission indefinitely. Assuming that completion is not fatal to his claim, I think that, at all events, it behoves the purchaser either to verify or, as the case may be, to disprove the representation within a reasonable time, or else stand or fall by it. If he is allowed to wait five, ten, or twenty years and then re-open the bargain, there can be no finality at all. I, for my part, do not think that equity will intervene in such a case, more especially as in the present case it cannot be said that, apart from rescission, the plaintiff would have been without remedy. The county court judge was of opinion, and it seems to me that he was clearly right, that the representation that the picture was a Constable amounted to a warranty. If it amounted to a warranty, and that was broken, as on the findings of the county court judge it was, then the plaintiff had a right at law in the shape of damages for breach of warranty. That remedy he did not choose to exercise, and, although he was invited at the hearing to amend his claim so as to include a claim for breach of warranty, he declined that opportunity. That being so, it seems to me that he has no justification at all for now coming to equity five years after the event and claiming rescission. Accordingly, it seems to me that this is not a case in which the equitable remedy of rescission, assuming it to be available in the absence of fraud in respect of a completed sale of chattels, should be allowed to the plaintiff. For these reasons, I agree that the appeal fails and should be dismissed.

EVERSHED, M.R. I also agree that this appeal should be dismissed, for the reasons which have already been given. On the facts of this case it seems to me that the plaintiff ought not now to be allowed to rescind this contract. In the circumstances it is unnecessary, as my Brethren have already observed, to express any conclusion on the more general matter whether the so-called doctrine which finds expression in the headnote to *Seddon* v. *North Eastern Salt Co., Ltd.*[1] ought now to be treated as of full effect and validity. The doubt on that matter is the greater since the observations of the majority of this court in the recent decision in *Solle* v. *Butcher*[2]; but out of respect to the forceful argument of Mr. Weitzman and because the matter is one of interest to lawyers (see, for example, the article in the Law Quarterly Review, vol. 55, p. 90, which has been read to us), I venture to add some observations which may be relevant when the general application of this doctrine has to be further considered.

The plaintiff's case rested fundamentally upon this statement which he made: " I contracted to buy a Constable. I have not had, and never had, a Constable." Though that is, as a matter of language, perfectly intelligible, it nevertheless needs a little expansion if it is to be quite accurate. What he contracted to buy and what he bought was a specific chattel, namely, an oil painting of Salisbury Cathedral; but he bought it on the faith of a representation, innocently made, that it had been painted by John Constable.

---

[1] [1905] 1 Ch. 326.   [2] [1950] 1 K. B. 671.

It turns out, as the evidence now stands and as the county court judge has found, that it was not so painted. Nevertheless it remains true to say that the plaintiff still has the article which he contracted to buy. The difference is no doubt considerable, but it is, as Denning, L.J., has observed, a difference in quality and in value rather than in the substance of the thing itself.

That leads me to suggest this matter for consideration: the attribution of works of art to particular artists is often a matter of great controversy and increasing difficulty as time goes on. If the plaintiff is right in saying that he is entitled, perhaps years after the purchase, to raise the question whether in truth a particular painting was rightly attributed to a particular artist, most costly and difficult litigation may result. There may turn out to be divergent views on the part of artists and critics of great eminence, and the prevailing view at one date may be quite different from that which prevails at a later date.

There is, moreover, a further point: the county court judge has found here that *restitutio in integrum* is possible, meaning thereby, as I understand it, that the picture itself retains the condition and quality that it had on the sale in 1944: it can therefore be returned to the sellers and they can return the 85*l.* paid. But, if the view for which Mr. Weitzman has contended is to prevail and be of general application, many cases may arise in which other controversies of equal difficulty and complexity may have to be determined; for example, whether in the interval there has been a change through wear and tear, or otherwise, in the article which has been sold. A set of chairs attributed to Chippendale might after being used for six years well be said to have suffered damage which, though it does not substantially or greatly alter their value as chairs, may, nevertheless, appreciably diminish their market value. Again, the fashion in these things, and consequently their value, varies from time to time.

It seems to me, therefore, that if Mr. Weitzman's view is to be accepted, there may arise matters for determination of great difficulty and complexity leading to uncertainty and considerable litigation; and, as between one case and another, the alleged rule of equity may work somewhat capriciously. Those are results which, as it seems to me, are in themselves undesirable. If a man elects to buy a work of art or any other chattel on the faith of some representation, innocently made, and delivery of the article is accepted, there is much to be said for the view that on acceptance there is an end of that particular transaction, and that, if it were otherwise, business dealings in these things would become hazardous, difficult and uncertain.

A representation of this kind may either be a warranty or not, or equivalent to a warranty or not. If not, then the matters to which I have already referred seem to me to gain in importance. I need not elaborate the point by example. But if the representation does amount to a warranty, then, as Jenkins, L.J., has pointed out, there is available, when the breach is discovered, a remedy at law which is reasonably certain, and capable of giving adequate compensation to the injured party. And if such a remedy at law is available, then, as it seems to me, there is less ground for invoking a rule of equity to supplement the law.

Finally, I add this: true it is that since the observations of Scrutton, L.J., in *Lever Bros., Ltd.* v. *Bell*[1], and of this court in *Solle* v. *Butcher*[2], much greater doubt may be entertained about the validity of Joyce, J.'s,

---

[1] [1931] 1 K. B. 557.   [2] [1950] 1 K. B. 671.

decision in 1905. Still, it was given forty-five years ago. The article that Mr. Weitzman read to us was written eleven years ago. There has been opportunity for Parliament to alter the law if it was thought to be inadequate. I am not saying that that is a ground on which we should conclude that the so-called doctrine of *Seddon* v. *North Eastern Salt Co., Ltd.*[1] is well stated or is in all respects correct; but the fact that it has stood for such a length of time, even though qualified, is another consideration deserving of some weight, when this matter has further to be debated and to be adjudicated upon.

I have added those remarks out of respect to the argument and because of the importance of the case; but I base my conclusion upon those grounds which have already been stated by my brethren and which it would be mere repetition on my part to state again.

Appeal dismissed.

MISREPRESENTATION ACT

Elizabeth II, 1967, Chapter 7

An Act to amend the law relating to innocent misrepresentations and to amend sections 11 and 35 of the Sale of Goods Act 1893   [22nd March 1967]

Be it enacted by the Queen's most Excellent Majesty, by and with the advice and consent of the Lords Spiritual and Temporal, and Commons, in this present Parliament assembled, and by the authority of the same, as follows:—

Removal of certain bars to rescission for innocent misrepresentation

1. Where a person has entered into a contract after a misrepresentation has been made to him, and—

(*a*) the misrepresentation has become a term of the contract; or

(*b*) the contract has been performed;

or both, then, if otherwise he would be entitled to rescind the contract without alleging fraud, he shall be so entitled, subject to the provisions of this Act, notwithstanding the matters mentioned in paragraphs (*a*) and (*b*) of this section.

Damages for misrepresentation

2.—(1) Where a person has entered into a contract after a misrepresentation has been made to him by another party thereto and as a result thereof he has suffered loss, then, if the person making the misrepresentation would be liable to damages in respect thereof had the misrepresentation been made fraudulently, that person shall be so liable notwithstanding that the misrepresentation was not made fraudulently, unless he proves that he had reasonable ground to believe and did believe up to the time the contract was made that the facts represented were true.

(2) Where a person has entered into a contract after a misrepresentation has been made to him otherwise than fraudulently, and he would be entitled, by reason of the misrepresentation, to rescind the contract, then, if it is claimed, in any proceedings arising out of the contract, that the contract ought to be or has been rescinded, the court or arbitrator may declare the

---

[1] [1905] 1 Ch. 326.

contract subsisting and award damages in lieu of rescission, if of opinion that it would be equitable to do so, having regard to the nature of the misrepresentation and the loss that would be caused by it if the contract were upheld, as well as to the loss that rescission would cause to the other party.

(3) Damages may be awarded against a person under subsection (2) of this section whether or not he is liable to damages under subsection (1) thereof, but where he is so liable any award under the said subsection (2) shall be taken into account in assessing his liability under the said subsection (1).

Avoidance of certain provisions excluding liability for misrepresentation

3. If any agreement (whether made before or after the commencement of this Act) contains a provision which would exclude or restrict—

(a) any liability to which a party to a contract may be subject by reason of any misrepresentation made by him before the contract was made; or

(b) any remedy available to another party to the contract by reason of such a misrepresentation;

that provision shall be of no effect except to the extent (if any) that, in any proceedings arising out of the contract, the court or arbitrator may allow reliance on it as being fair and reasonable in the circumstances of the case.

Amendments of Sale of Goods Act 1893

4.—(1) In paragraph (c) of section 11 (1) of the Sale of Goods Act 1893 (condition to be treated as warranty where the buyer has accepted the goods or where the property in specific goods has passed) the words " or where the contract is for specific goods, the property in which has passed to the buyer " shall be omitted.

(2) In section 35 of that Act (acceptance) before the words " when the goods have been delivered to him, and he does any act in relation to them which is inconsistent with the ownership of the seller " there shall be inserted the words " (except where section 34 of this Act otherwise provides) ".

Saving for past transactions

5. Nothing in this Act shall apply in relation to any misrepresentation or contract of sale which is made before the commencement of this Act.

Short title, commencement and extent

6.—(1) This Act may be cited as the Misrepresentation Act 1967.

(2) This Act shall come into operation at the expiration of the period of one month beginning with the date on which it is passed.

(3) This Act, except section 4 (2), does not extend to Scotland.

(4) This Act does not extend to Northern Ireland.

Low v. Bouverie

[1891] 3 Ch. 82

A person who makes a statement with the intention that it should be acted upon and which is acted upon is estopped from contesting its truth although it was not fraudulently made.

No statement can operate as an estoppel unless it is precise and unambiguous.

In January, 1888, Vice-Admiral *F. W. P. Bouverie*, who under the trusts of his marriage settlement, dated the 1st of September, 1845, was entitled for his life to the income of a sum of £5523 6s. 3d. Metropolitan 3½ per cent. Stock, applied to a firm of solicitors who were in the habit of acting on behalf of the plaintiff, *Robert Low*, in all loan transactions, to make him, Vice-Admiral *Bouverie*, an advance on the security of his life interest, and of certain policies of assurance on his life. The defendant, *Henry Hales Pleydell Bouverie*, a banker, was one of the trustees of the settlement. In consequence of this application the plaintiff's solicitors, on the 22nd of February, 1888, wrote on his behalf the following letter to the defendant :—

" Dear Sir,—We are doing business with Vice-Admiral *Bouverie*, and he says you will give us information as to his means and position. He says he is entitled to a life interest in some funds held in trust, under a settlement dated September 1, 1845, of which you are trustee. Will you kindly tell us what those funds are, and whether Vice-Admiral *Bouverie* is still entitled to the full benefit of his life interest therein. We understand he has not in any way mortgaged or parted with such life interest. Is this so ? Your early reply will oblige."

On the 23rd of February, 1888, the defendant replied as follows :—

" Gentlemen,—In reply to your letter of 22nd inst., I beg to inform you that Vice-Admiral *Bouverie* has a life interest in £5,523 6s. 3d. Metropolitan 3½ Stock, but the same life interest is charged with the payment of the premiums on two life policies, one of which amounts to £35 17s., and the other is extinct. Also it is charged with payment of interest for money already advanced to him to the extent of £34 per annum."

On the 25th of February, 1888, the defendant wrote again to the plaintiff's solicitors as follows :—

" Gentlemen,—In furtherance of my letter to you of a day or two since, I beg to state that I hold a policy of insurance on Admiral *Bouverie's* life in the *Mutual Life Assurance Society* for £300, as security for the money advanced to him, for which the £34 mentioned to you is the annual charge of interest."

On the same day the plaintiff's solicitors had written to the defendant as follows :—

" Dear Sir,—Will you kindly inform us whether you hold any mortgage or know of any incumbrance upon Vice-Admiral *Bouverie's* life interest in the funds mentioned in your letter of the 23rd inst., or on his life interest under his marriage settlement. By so doing you will much oblige."

On the 27th of February, 1888, the defendant replied to the last letter as follows :—

" Sirs,—I don't see how I can explain myself more clearly than I did the other day in my letter to you. I hold no mortgage from Admiral *Bouverie* for the charge of interest on money advanced to him ; but this charge of interest is in the ordinary course of business ; but the two policies of insurance, whose premiums now amount to £35, are mortgaged to his trustees."

The plaintiff thereupon, without any further inquiry, agreed to advance £600 to Vice-Admiral *Bouverie* on the security of a mortgage of his life interest and two policies of assurance on his life. The advance was accordingly made, and a mortgage was executed on the 1st of March, 1888, of which notice was duly given to the defendant.

Towards the close of the year 1888, Vice-Admiral *Bouverie* was in pecuniary difficulties, and at present he was an undischarged bankrupt and residing out of the jurisdiction.

The interest on the plaintiff's mortgage being in arrear, he, through his solicitors, in April, 1889, requested the defendant to pay to him in future the balance of Vice-Admiral *Bouverie's* life income, after satisfying the charges mentioned in the defendant's letters. A correspondence then ensued between the plaintiff's and the defendant's solicitors, from which the plaintiff for the first time became aware that at the date of his mortgage Vice-Admiral *Bouverie's* life interest was already subject to no less than six prior mortgages, including a mortgage to secure the premiums on the policies mentioned in the defendant's letter of the 23rd of February, 1888, two of the mortgages being to the trustees of the settlement of the 1st of September, 1845. It appeared, however, that, at the time he was corresponding with the plaintiff's solicitors as above-mentioned, the defendant had forgotten the existence of these prior mortgages, though he had had notice of them in the sense that they were recited in a deed of the 15th of February, 1885, by which he was appointed trustee of the settlement of the 1st of September, 1845.

The amounts secured by the six prior mortgages exceeded the capital value of the life interest and policies comprised in the plaintiff's mortgage, and the interest payable on those six mortgages more than exhausted the income payable in respect of the life interest. To preserve his security the plaintiff paid the premiums on the policies mortgaged to him.

Under these circumstances, there being due to him, besides the principal mortgage debt of £600, a sum due for interest, premiums, and costs, the plaintiff brought this action, claiming a declaration that the defendant was liable to pay to him the total amount due under his mortgage, and payment accordingly.

NORTH, J., gave judgment for the plaintiff, and the defendant appealed. The Court of Appeal allowed the appeal.

LINDLEY, L.J. (after stating the facts and reading the correspondence, continued) :—

This appeal raises several extremely important questions. First, it is necessary to consider what are the duties of trustees towards persons about to deal with their *cestuis que trust*, and who, before dealing with them, make inquiries of their trustees as to any assignments or incumbrances known to them.

In *Browne* v. *Savage*[1], Vice-Chancellor *Kindersley* said that trustees " must, for their own security, give correct information, when inquiry is made of them, whether they have had notice of any prior assignments affecting their trust property." Mr. *Lewin*, in his well-known work (Lewin on Trusts[2]), refers to that case as an authority for the proposition that trustees are bound to answer such inquiries. But when this opinion is examined it can scarcely be supported, and if such a doctrine were logically carried out it would impose very serious duties upon trustees. The duty of a trustee is properly to preserve the trust fund, to pay the income and the *corpus* to those who are entitled to them respectively, and to give all his *cestuis que trust*, on demand, information with respect to the mode in which the trust fund has been dealt with, and where it is. But it is no part of the duty of a trustee to tell his *cestui que trust* what incumbrances the latter has created, nor which of his incumbrancers have given notice of their respective charges. It is no part of the duty of a trustee to assist his *cestui que trust* in selling or mortgaging his beneficial interest and in squandering or anticipating his fortune ; and it is clear that a person who proposes to buy or lend money on it has no greater rights than the *cestui que trust* himself. There is no trust or other relation between a trustee and a stranger about to deal with a *cestui que trust*, and although probably such a person in making inquiries

---

[1] (1859), 4 Drew. 635, at p. 639.   [2] 8th Ed., p. 704.

may be regarded as authorized by the *cestui que trust* to make them, this view of the stranger's position will not give him a right to information which the *cestui que trust* himself is not entitled to demand. The trustee, therefore, is, in my opinion, under no obligation to answer such an inquiry. He can refer the person making it to the *cestui que trust* himself.

I will next take the case of a trustee who answers the inquiry. What in this case is the extent of his obligation ? Is he bound to find out the facts—bound to make inquiries of his co-trustees, or of the solicitor to the trust ? Or is his obligation limited to giving such information as he himself can give without inquiry or research ? I am not aware of any principle or authority which imposes upon him any obligation to do more than give an honest answer to the inquiry—that is to say, to do more than answer to the best of his actual knowledge and belief. He may, no doubt, undertake a greater responsibility ; he may bind himself by a warranty, or he may so express himself as to be estopped from afterwards denying the truth of what he said ; but unless he does one or the other, I do not know on what principle consistent with *Derry* v. *Peek*[1] he can, if he answer honestly, expose himself to liability. I say, " consistent with *Derry* v. *Peek*," because, until that case was decided, it was generally supposed to be settled in Equity that liability was incurred by a person who carelessly, although honestly, made a false representation to another about to deal in a matter of business upon the faith of such representation : *Burrowes* v. *Lock*[2] ; *Slim* v. *Croucher*[3]. This general proposition is, however, quite inconsistent with *Derry* v. *Peek*. I do not, however, understand *Derry* v. *Peek* to apply where there is a legal obligation on the part of the defendant towards the plaintiff to give him correct information. If such an obligation exists, an action for damages will, I apprehend, lie for its non-performance, even in the absence of fraud : see *per* Lord *Denman* in *Barley* v. *Walford*[4]. It is for this reason that I have examined the obligation of trustees to answer inquiries made by persons about to deal with their *cestuis que trust*. There is no equitable, as distinguished from legal, obligation to answer such inquiries, and if a trustee gives an honest answer he discharges the only obligation which he is under.

Again, *Derry* v. *Peek*[1] does not in any way affect the law relating to warranties, unless it be by negativing the notion that promoters who issue a prospectus impliedly warrant the truth of the statements contained in it. Nor does *Derry* v. *Peek*[1] in any way affect the law relating to estoppel where such law is applicable. But estoppel is not a cause of action—it is a rule of evidence which precludes a person from denying the truth of some statement previously made by himself. Lord *Herschell*, in his judgment in *Derry* v. *Peek*, did not profess to overrule *Burrowes* v. *Lock*[5] and *Slim* v. *Croucher*[6], and it was strenuously contended that those cases were still law, and that they governed the present case. It becomes necessary, therefore, to examine those cases with care.

Burrowes v. *Lock*, as appears from the Registrar's book, was a suit by the assignee of one of several residuary legatees for his share of the residue of a testator's estate. The amount of the residue was not in controversy, and a general administration decree was not sought. The defendants to the suit were the plaintiff's assignor and the trustee of his share of the residue. The trustee had (as appears from the report in *Vesey*) informed the plaintiff

---

[1] (1889), 14 App. Cas. 337.
[2] (1805), 10 Ves. 470.
[3] (1860), 1 De G. F. & J. 518, at p. 525.
[4] (1846), 9 Q. B. 197, at p. 208.
[5] (1805), 10 Ves. 470.
[6] (1860), 1 De G. F. & J. 518.

that this share was unincumbered, whereas, in fact, it was not. The decree was, in effect, that the trustee should pay the full amount of the share to the plaintiff without deducting the incumbrance. The trustee, even if he acted honestly, which is, perhaps, questionable, was clearly estopped from denying that the share was unincumbered. This decision was in 1805, more than thirty years before *Pickard* v. *Sears*[1], and at a time when the doctrine of estoppel was less accurately defined than it has since become. Regarded as a decision on the ground of estoppel, *Burrowes* v. *Lock* appears to me not only to have been quite right, but to remain wholly untouched by *Derry* v. *Peek*. Lord *Blackburn* seems to have thought that the representation in *Burrowes* v. *Lock* was scarcely distinguishable from a warranty : *Brownlie* v. *Campbell*[2] ; and if this be the proper view to take of it, *Burrowes* v. *Lock*[3] can stand on that ground, although I confess my own inability to sustain it on the ground of warranty.

Slim v. *Croucher*[4], in which *Burrowes* v. *Lock*[3] was recognized and extended, cannot, in my opinion, be supported on the ground of estoppel. *Slim* v. *Croucher* was a suit in equity to recover money advanced on a lease granted by the defendant to the borrower, and which the defendant had told the plaintiff would be granted. The lease proved to be invalid. Unless the defendant's statement amounted to a warranty that the lease when granted would be valid, I do not myself see how to avoid the conclusion that *Slim* v. *Croucher* is inconsistent with, and therefore overruled by, *Derry* v. *Peek*[5]. Lord Herschell, in his judgment, did not himself examine these cases, but intimated that the two might stand together upon the grounds explained by Lord *Selborne* in *Brownlie* v. *Campbell*[2]. I am not, however, myself able to reconcile those grounds with the decision in *Derry* v. *Peek*. *Slim* v. *Croucher* evidently proceeded upon the notion, sanctioned by the high authority of Lord *Campbell*, that in that case an action for damages might have been maintained at law upon the defendant's representation, and that in such a case the Court of Chancery had a concurrent jurisdiction with the Courts of Common Law. There would be no such jurisdiction in the case of a warranty. *Slim* v. *Croucher* was not decided, nor did Lord *Selborne* approve it, on any such ground.

The only conclusion I can arrive at is, that whilst *Burrowes* v. *Lock* can be supported and taken as a guide on the ground of estoppel or possibly fraud, *Slim* v. *Croucher* cannot any longer be regarded as having been rightly decided, fraud having been negatived. As pointed out by Lord *Blackburn* in *Brownlie* v. *Campbell* the line between fraud and warranty is often very narrow, and the same observation is true of the line between warranty and estoppel. Narrow, however, as the line often is, the three words denote fundamentally different legal conceptions which must not be confounded.

Reverting now to the grounds of liability on which this action may be supported, it is obvious that, as regards warranty, the plaintiff and the defendant were not contracting parties. There was no intention to contract, nor was there any consideration which is essential for the purpose of treating what the defendant said as a promise or a warranty. As regards estoppel, if the defendant had said that there were no incumbrances on Admiral *Bouverie's* life interest except those mentioned by the defendant in his

---

[1] (1837), 6 Ad. & El. 469. [2] (1880), 5 App. Cas. 925. [3] (1805), 10 Ves. 470.
[4] (1860), 1 De. G. F. & J. 518. [5] (1889), 14 App. Cas. 337.

letters, the case would be clearly one of estoppel; it would be undistinguishable from *Burrowes* v. *Lock*[1]; and the plaintiff would be entitled to relief, not to damages for a misrepresentation, but to an order on the defendant as trustee for the plaintiff to pay to him the Admiral's life interest in the fund in question, subject only to the incumbrances disclosed by the defendant. This is not the relief sought by the plaintiff, nor is it the relief given to him by the Court below, but it is relief to which he would be entitled on the ground of estoppel. But the difficulty of affording the plaintiff relief on this ground arises from the ambiguity of the defendant's letters. They are quite consistent with the view that the incumbrances mentioned by the defendant were all he knew of or remembered. A statement, however, to that effect would not estop him from shewing that there were others which he did not know of or did not remember. But then it is said that he ought to have known of them and remembered them, as notice of them had been given to him; and it is admitted that if he had looked into the deeds and documents relating to the trust, he would have found that there were other incumbrances besides those which he did in fact know of and did accordingly mention. Knowledge and means of knowledge are very different things; and if a person truly says he only knows or remembers so and so, is it right to treat him as saying that he knows more, even if it is his duty to inform himself accurately before he speaks? I do not think that so to hold would be consistent with *Derry* v. *Peek*[2]. To treat him in the case supposed as saying more than he did, would be to resuscitate the doctrine condemned in *Derry* v. *Peek*, and to hold him liable in damages for a negligent misrepresentation.

But then it is said that the defendant's language was such as to be calculated to mislead, and as in fact to mislead, the plaintiff's solicitors, who applied to the defendant for information; and reliance is placed on the judgment of Baron *Parke* in *Freeman* v. *Cooke*[3], and of the present Master of the Rolls in *Carr* v. *London and North-Western Railway Company*[4]. But the answer to this argument is, that the plaintiff too hastily inferred from the defendant's letters that there were no other incumbrances besides those which he mentioned. He never said this in terms; I cannot think he meant to be so understood; and although the plaintiff's solicitors may have so understood him, I do not think they had more reason to be satisfied with his last letter than with his first, which they saw was too loosely expressed to justify them in acting upon it. It must be remembered that in this case the defendant was not the only trustee, and it does not appear that the plaintiff's advisers applied to the other trustee. It is often said that notice to one trustee is notice to all: *Browne* v. *Savage*[5]; but this is one of those misleading generalities against which it is necessary to be on one's guard. An incumbrancer of a trust fund who first gives notice to any of its trustees obtains priority over any prior incumbrancer who has given no notice to any of them; but notice to one does not affect the other trustees so as to make them liable for what they may do in ignorance of the notice to their co-trustee. There is no law which precludes them from saying they do not know what he knows; and notice given to one who dies or retires without communicating it to his co-trustee cannot, I apprehend, render them liable for not giving effect to a notice of which they know absolutely

---

[1] (1805), 10 Ves. 470.   [2] (1889), 14 App. Cas. 337.   [3] (1848), 2 Exch. 654.
[4] (1875), L. R. 10 C. P. 307.   [5] (1859), 4 Drew. 635.

nothing : see on this subject, *Phipps* v. *Lovegrove*.[1]   The doctrine of implied notice cannot create an estoppel in such a case any more than it can create a personal liability.

Fraud, breach of duty, warranty, estoppel, being therefore all negatived in the present case, no ground remains on which this action can be supported.

The appeal, therefore, must be allowed, with costs here and below.

BOWEN and KAY, L.JJ., delivered judgments to the same effect.

---

[1] (1873), L. R. 16 Eq. 80.

UNDUE INFLUENCE

Allcard v. Skinner
(1887), 36 Ch.D. 145

The cases in which a contract may be rescinded for undue influence fall into two groups :
- (i) Those in which the parties come within certain specified relations, such as parent and child, solicitor and client, religious superior and inferior. Here, undue influence is presumed to have been exercised, and the burden of rebutting this presumption lies upon the defendant.[1]
- (ii) Those in which no special relation exists between the parties. Here, the burden lies upon the plaintiff of proving that undue influence has in fact been exercised.

The plaintiff must seek relief within a reasonable time after the removal of the influence under which the contract was made.

LINDLEY, L.J. :—In 1867 the plaintiff was living with her mother in London, and on the recommendation of some clergymen the plaintiff went to the Rev. Mr. Nihill, vicar of St. Michael's, Finsbury, for confession, and she asked him for work in his parish of Shoreditch. By him she was introduced to the defendant Miss Skinner, who was then and is still the lady superior of the sisterhood of St. Mary at the Cross.

Shortly afterwards, that is, in 1868, the plaintiff joined the sisterhood as an associate ; and about this time she promised to devote her property to the service of the poor. She explained to him that she had not much property then but that she would have more, and she said she would bring all into the sisterhood. This promise Mr. Nihill tells us he considered binding upon her in conscience ; and it is plain that the plaintiff herself so considered it. But this promise was purely gratuitous, and it does not appear that the plaintiff ever knew that the promise in question was not binding upon her in point of law ; and her evidence shews that she did not realize its full meaning or the position she would find herself in if she should ever desire to leave the sisterhood. Such an event never occurred to her as one which could ever happen.

In 1870 the plaintiff became a postulant, and later in the same year a novice, and finally in August, 1871, a sister. Each of these steps was accompanied by religious services and bound the plaintiff more and more closely to the sisterhood, and alienated her more and more from the world at large.

When the plaintiff became a postulant she ceased to reside with her mother and resided with the sisterhood, and whilst a postulant the plaintiff made a will by which she left the whole of her property to the sisterhood. This was done at the request of the lady superior. The will when made was laid upon the altar and was regarded as a consecrated document. Why is not explained, and is left to inference. The only reason I can suggest for such a step is that it was intended to impress on the plaintiff that she was doing a very solemn thing, and one which was never to be undone. The will, laid upon the altar and consecrated, would, I imagine, cease to be regarded by the plaintiff and the lady superior as a revocable instrument. The plaintiff was twenty-seven years of age, or thereabouts, when she

---

[1] Whether the presumption applies to persons engaged to be married was discussed by the Court of Appeal in *Zamet* v. *Hyman,* [1961] 3 All E.R. 933.

first joined the sisterhood. She sought Mr. Nihill: he did not seek her. She wished to join the sisterhood, and she was resolved to devote herself and her property to it and to charitable work. This wish and determination were naturally strengthened by the religious services of the sisterhood and by the influence of those around her. There is evidence that, when a novice, and before she became a sister, she wished to leave the sisterhood ; but that she did not feel that she could do so, and that she felt even then bound to the sisterhood. After she became a sister she again wished to leave, but she was told by the lady superior that she could not do so, and that she was bound to the sisterhood for life. On another and later occasion she was not allowed to leave, although she wished to do so.

On becoming a sister the plaintiff took vows of obedience to the lady superior and of poverty and chastity ; and there can be no doubt that the plaintiff regarded these vows as binding on her, not only when she took them but ever afterwards, until she finally left the sisterhood and became a Roman Catholic. On becoming a sister the plaintiff also became subject to the rules of the sisterhood. These rules, although not reduced into their final shape until 1872 or 1873, were practically in force before, and were well known to the plaintiff when she became a sister. The important rules are those which require (1) Implicit obedience to the lady superior ; (2) Poverty. A third rule (No. XXXI) is thus worded : " Let no sister seek advice of any extern without the superior's leave."

The vow of poverty and the rule as to poverty obliged each sister to give away all her property. But the rule did not require her to give it, or any of it, to the sisterhood. She could give it to her relations or to the poor if she wished. But it would be idle to suppose that a sister would not feel that she ought to give some of her property at least to the sisterhood ; and it would be equally idle to suppose that she would not be expected to do so.

The forms of deeds in the Schedules A. and B. to the rules are very significant. The donee is inserted as " —her heirs, executors, administrators, and assigns." The introduction of *her* is very unusual in a legal form, and shews plainly enough who the donee was expected to be. Further, the deeds when filled up are by the rules to be placed on the altar, in order, I suppose, to add to their solemnity, and impress the donor with a sense of their irrevocability. The plaintiff never executed any such deed as was contemplated by the rules ; but they and the schedules shew what was expected to be done. In this particular case, moreover, the plaintiff had expressly promised to give all she had to the sisterhood, and Mr. Nihill tells us that non-performance of this promise would have been regarded as dishonourable.

The vow and rule obliging to implicit obedience to the lady superior, and the exhortation or command to regard her voice as the voice of God, produce very different effects on different minds. There can, however, be no question that the plaintiff felt bound by the vow and by the rule until she emancipated herself from both of them, which she did when she left the sisterhood.

It is important, however, to bear in mind that the fetter thus placed on the plaintiff was the result of her own free choice. There is no evidence that pressure was put upon her to enter upon the mode of life which she adopted. She chose it as the best for herself ; she devoted herself to it, heart and soul ; she was, to use her own expression, infatuated with the life and with the work.   But though infatuated, there is no evidence to shew that she was in such a state of mental imbecility as to justify the inference that she was unable to take care of herself or to manage her own affairs.

The rule against obtaining advice from externs without the consent of the lady superior invites great suspicion.   It is evidently a rule capable of being used in a very tyrannical way, and so as to result in intolerable oppression.   I have carefully examined the evidence to see how this rule practically worked, but I can find nothing on the subject.   I can find nothing to shew one way or the other what would have been the effect, for example, of a request for leave to consult a friend, or to obtain legal or other advice respecting any disposition of property, or respecting leaving the sisterhood. There, however, is the rule, and a very important one it is.   I shall have occasion to refer to it again hereafter.   Such being the nature of the vows and rules which the plaintiff had taken, and to which she had submitted herself, and by which she felt herself bound by the highest religious sanctions, it is necessary to examine what she did with her property, and the circumstances under which she gave it to the sisterhood.

The evidence shews that her brother, who was one of her trustees, kept her fully informed of what her property consisted of, and he remitted to her from time to time cheques and transfers of railway stock and other securities to which she was entitled.   The brother's letters and the cheques and transfers all passed through the hands of the lady superior, it being the rule that she should see all letters to sisters.   The plaintiff gave all the cheques to the lady superior after indorsing them, and also transferred to her all the railway stock and securities as they were received.   The cheques were handed over to Mr. Nihill, who was the treasurer of the sisterhood, and were paid by him into a bank to an account kept in his own name, and on which he alone could draw.   The sisterhood was building an hospital in which the plaintiff took great interest, and most of the plaintiff's money was spent in defraying the expenses of the building.   I have examined the evidence with care in order to see whether any pressure was put upon the plaintiff in order to induce her to give her property to the sisterhood, or whether any deception was practised upon her, or whether any unfair advantage was taken of her, or whether any of her money was applied otherwise than *bona fide* for the objects of the sisterhood, or for any purpose which the plaintiff could disapprove.   The result of the evidence convinces me that no pressure, except the inevitable pressure of the vows and rules, was brought to bear on the plaintiff ; that no deception was practised upon her ; that no unfair advantage was taken of her ; that none of her money was obtained or applied for any purpose other than the legitimate objects of the sisterhood.   Not a farthing of it was either obtained or applied for the private advantage of the lady superior or Mr. Nihill; nor indeed did the plaintiff ever suggest that such had been the case.   The real truth is that the plaintiff gave away her property as a matter of course, and without seriously thinking of the consequences to herself.   She had devoted herself and her fortune to the sisterhood, and it never occurred to her that she should ever wish to leave the sisterhood or desire to have her money back. In giving away her property as she did she was merely acting up to her promise and vow and the rule of the sisterhood, and to the standard of duty which she had erected for herself under the influences and circumstances already stated.

In May, 1879, the plaintiff left the sisterhood, and on the 16th of that month she was received into the Roman Catholic Church, and she then regarded herself as freed from the vows she had taken on joining the sister-hood. Soon after she had left the sisterhood the plaintiff had some conversation with her brother about getting her money back, and he said he did not want the trouble, and she had better leave it alone. She was also advised by a Roman Catholic priest not to trouble about it. In February, 1880, she consulted her present solicitor about making a new will, and she then had some conversation with him about the money she had given to the sisterhood, and he told her it was too large a sum to leave behind without asking for it back, and she said she would not trouble about it. Some time in 1884 the plaintiff heard that another sister, a Miss Merriman, had left the sisterhood, and had asked for her money back, and had had it returned to her, and then the plaintiff made up her mind to try and get her money back. Upon her re-examination by Sir *C. Russell*, the plaintiff said that she had no idea that she could get it back until after she had heard that Miss Merriman had recovered hers. But the evidence already alluded to shews clearly that she had considered the matter, and had come to the conclusion that it was not worth troubling about. As a matter of fact, although she asked the lady superior in 1880 to give her back her will, she never asked for any of her money back until 1884, more than five years after she had left the sisterhood, and the present action was not brought until August 20, 1885.

By her action the plaintiff sought to recover the whole of the money back which she had given to the sisterhood, amounting to nearly £8,500. Mr. Justice Kekewich tried the action, and gave judgment for the defendant. From this judgment the plaintiff has appealed, but she has limited her appeal to two sums of £500 and £1,171, railway stock transferred by her to the lady superior, and still standing in her name.

Two questions are raised by the appeal, namely, 1st, Whether the gifts made by the plaintiff to the sisterhood were revocable or irrevocable when made ? 2nd, Whether, assuming them to have been revocable when made, it was competent for the plaintiff to revoke them when she did ?

The first question is one of great importance and difficulty. Its solution requires a careful consideration of the legal effect of gifts by persons of mature age who feel bound by vows and rules to give away their property, but who have taken the vows and submitted to the rules voluntarily and without pressure, and who are subject to no other coercion or influence than necessarily result from the vows and rules themselves, and from the state of their own mind.

There is no statutory law in this country prohibiting such gifts unless what is given is land or money to be laid out in land. These are provided for by the Mortmain and Charitable Uses Acts. But they have no application to this case. The common law, as distinguished from equity, does not invalidate such gifts as these. There being no duress or fraud, the only ground for impeaching such gifts at law would be want of capacity on the part of the donor ; and although the plaintiff was a religious enthusiast, no one could treat her as in point of law *non compos mentis*. There is no authority whatever for saying that her gifts were invalid at law. It is to the doctrines of equity, then, that recourse must be had to invalidate such gifts, if they are to be invalidated. The doctrine relied upon by the appellant is the doctrine of undue influence expounded and enforced in

Huguenin v. *Baseley*[1] and other cases of that class. These cases may be subdivided into two groups, which, however, often overlap.

First, there are the cases in which there has been some unfair and improper conduct, some coercion from outside, some overreaching, some form of cheating, and generally, though not always, some personal advantage obtained by a donee placed in some close and confidential relation to the donor. *Norton* v. *Relly*[2], *Nottidge* v. *Prince*[3], *Lyon* v. *Home*[4], and *Whyte* v. *Meade*[5], all belong to this group. In *Whyte* v. *Meade* a gift to a convent was set aside, but the gift was the result of coercion, clearly proved. The evidence does not bring this case within this group.

The second group consists of cases in which the position of the donor to the donee has been such that it has been the duty of the donee to advise the donor, or even to manage his property for him. In such cases the Court throws upon the donee the burden of proving that he has not abused his position, and of proving that the gift made to him has not been brought about by any undue influence on his part. In this class of cases it has been considered necessary to shew that the donor had independent advice, and was removed from the influence of the donee when the gift to him was made. *Huguenin* v. *Baseley*[1] was a case of this kind. The defendant had not only acquired considerable spiritual influence over the plaintiff, but was intrusted by her with the management of her property. His duty to her was clear, and it was with reference to persons so situated that Lord Eldon used the language so often quoted and so much relied on in this case. He said[6] : " Take it that she (the plaintiff) intended to give it to him (the defendant) : it is by no means out of the reach of the principle. The question is not whether she knew what she was doing, had done, or proposed to do, but how the intention was produced : whether all that care and providence was placed round her, as against those who advised her, which, from their situation and relation with respect to her, they were bound to exert on her behalf." This principle has been constantly recognized and acted upon in subsequent cases, but in all of them, as in *Huguenin* v. *Baseley*[1] itself, it was the duty of the donee to advise and take care of the donor. Where there is no such duty the language of Lord Eldon ceases to be applicable.

Rhodes v. *Bate*[7] was determined on the same principle as *Huguenin* v. *Baseley*, the Court having come to the conclusion that the relation of the defendant to the plaintiff was really that of a solicitor to his client.

I have not been able to find any case in which a gift has been set aside on the ground of undue influence which does not fall within one or other or both of the groups above mentioned. Nor can I find any authority which actually covers the present case. But it does not follow that it is not reached by the principle on which the Court has proceeded in dealing with the cases which have already called for decision. They illustrate but do not limit the principle applied to them.

The principle must be examined. What then is the principle ? Is it that it is right and expedient to save persons from the consequences of their own folly ? or is it that it is right and expedient to save them from being victimized by other people ? In my opinion the doctrine of undue influence is founded upon the second of these two principles. Courts of

---

[1] (1807), 14 Ves. 273.

[2] (1764), 2 Eden, 286. [3] (1860), 2 Giff. 246. [4] (1868), L. R. 6 Eq. 655.
[5] (1840), 2 I. Eq. R. 420. [6] (1807), 14 Ves. 299. [7] (1866), 1 Ch. App. 252.

Equity have never set aside gifts on the ground of the folly, imprudence, or want of foresight on the part of donors. The Courts have always repudiated any such jurisdiction. *Huguenin* v. *Baseley*[1] is itself a clear authority to this effect. It would obviously be to encourage folly, recklessness, extravagance and vice if persons could get back property which they foolishly made away with, whether by giving it to charitable institutions or by bestowing it on less worthy objects. On the other hand, to protect people from being forced, tricked or misled in any way by others into parting with their property is one of the most legitimate objects of all laws ; and the equitable doctrine of undue influence has grown out of and been developed by the necessity of grappling with insidious forms of spiritual tyranny and with the infinite varieties of fraud.

As no Court has ever attempted to define fraud[2] so no Court has ever attempted to define undue influence, which includes one of its many varieties. The undue influence which Courts of Equity endeavour to defeat is the undue influence of one person over another ; not the influence of enthusiasm on the enthusiast who is carried away by it, unless indeed such enthusiasm is itself the result of external undue influence. But the influence of one mind over another is very subtle, and of all influences religious influence is the most dangerous and the most powerful, and to counteract it Courts of Equity have gone very far. They have not shrunk from setting aside gifts made to persons in a position to exercise undue influence over the donors, although there has been no proof of the actual exercise of such influence ; and the Courts have done this on the avowed ground of the necessity of going this length in order to protect persons from the exercise of such influence under circumstances which render proof of it impossible. The Courts have required proof of its non-exercise, and, failing that proof, have set aside gifts otherwise unimpeachable. In this particular case I cannot find any proof that any gift made by the plaintiff was the result of any actual exercise of power or influence on the part of the lady superior or of Mr. Nihill, apart from the influence necessarily incidental to their position in the sisterhood. Everything that the plaintiff did is in my opinion referable to her own willing submission to the vows she took and to the rules which she approved, and to her own enthusiastic devotion to the life and work of the sisterhood. This enthusiasm and devotion were nourished, strengthened and intensified by the religious services of the sisterhood and by the example and influence of those about her. But she chose the life and work ; such fetters as bound her were voluntarily put upon her by herself ; she could shake them off at any time she thought fit, and had she had the courage so to do ; and no unfair advantage whatever was taken of her. Under these circumstances it is going a long way to hold that she can invoke the doctrine of undue influence to save her from the consequences of her own acts, and to entitle her to avoid the gifts she made when in a state of mind different from that in which she now is. I am by no means insensible of the difficulty of going so far.

Nevertheless, consider the position in which the plaintiff had placed herself. She had vowed poverty and obedience, and she was not at liberty to consult externs without the leave of her superior. She was not a person who treated her vows lightly ; she was deeply religious and felt bound by

---

[1] (1807), 14 Ves. 273.
[2] I.e., as an equitable doctrine: for the common law see *Derry* v. *Peek* (1889), 14 App. Cas. 337.

her promise, by her vows, and by the rules of the sisterhood. She was absolutely in the power of the lady superior and Mr. Nihill. A gift made by her under these circumstances to the lady superior cannot in my opinion be retained by the donee. The equitable title of the donee is imperfect by reason of the influence inevitably resulting from her position, and which influence experience has taught the Courts to regard as undue. Whatever doubt I might have had on this point if there had been no rule against consulting externs, that rule in my judgment turns the scale against the defendant. In the face of that rule the gifts made to the sisterhood cannot be supported in the absence of proof that the plaintiff could have obtained independent advice if she wished for it, and that she knew that she would have been allowed to obtain such advice if she had desired to do so. I doubt whether the gifts could have been supported if such proof had been given, unless there was also proof that she was free to act on the advice which might be given to her. But the rule itself is so oppressive and so easily abused that any person subject to it is in my opinion brought within the class of those whom it is the duty of the Court to protect from possible imposition. The gifts cannot be supported without proof of more freedom in fact than the plaintiff can be supposed to have actually enjoyed.

The case is brought within the principle so forcibly expressed by the late Lord Justice Knight Bruce in *Wright* v. *Vanderplank*[1], in which a gift by a daughter to her father was sought to be set aside. If any independent person had explained to the plaintiff that her promise to give all her property to the sisterhood was not legally binding upon her, and that her vows of poverty and obedience had no legal validity and that if she gave her property away and afterwards left the sisterhood she would be unable to get her property back, it is impossible to say what she might or might not have done. In fact she never had the opportunity of considering this question.

Where a gift is made to a person standing in a confidential relation to the donor, the Court will not set aside the gift if of a small amount simply on the ground that the donor had no independent advice. In such a case, some proof of the exercise of the influence of the donee must be given. The mere existence of such influence is not enough in such a case ; see the observations of Lord Justice Turner in *Rhodes* v. *Bate*[2]. But if the gift is so large as not to be reasonably accounted for on the ground of friendship, relationship, charity, or other ordinary motives on which ordinary men act, the burden is upon the donee to support the gift. So, in a case like this, a distinction might well be made between gifts of capital and gifts of income, and between gifts of moderate amount and gifts of large sums, which a person unfettered by vows and oppressive rules would not be likely to wish to make. In this case the plaintiff gave away practically all she could, although, having a life interest in other property, she did not reduce herself to a state of poverty.

As I have already stated, I believe that in this case there was in fact no unfair or undue influence brought to bear upon the plaintiff other than such as inevitably resulted from the training she had received, the promise she had made, the vows she had taken, and the rules to which she had submitted herself. But her gifts were in fact made under a pressure which, whilst it lasted, the plaintiff could not resist, and were not, in my opinion, past recall when that pressure was removed. When the plaintiff emancipated herself from the spell by which she was bound, she was entitled to invoke

---

[1] (1856), 8 De G. M. & G. 133.   [2] (1866), 1 Ch. App. 252.

the aid of the Court in order to obtain the restitution from the defendant of so much of the plaintiff's property as had not been spent in accordance with the wishes of the plaintiff, but remained in the hands of the defendant. The plaintiff now demands no more.

I proceed to consider the second point which arises in this case, namely, whether it is too late for the plaintiff to invoke the assistance of the Court. More than six years had elapsed between the time when the plaintiff left the sisterhood and the commencement of the present action. The action is not one of those to which the Statute of Limitations in terms applies; nor is that statute pleaded. But this action very closely resembles an action for money had and received where laches and acquiescence are relied upon as a defence: and the question is whether that defence ought to prevail. In my opinion it ought. Taking the statute as a guide, and proceeding on the principles laid down by Lord Camden in *Smith* v. *Clay*[1], and by Lord Redesdale in *Hovenden* v. *Lord Annesley*[2], the lapse of six years becomes a very material element for consideration. It is not, however, necessary to decide whether this delay alone would be a sufficient defence to the action. The case by no means rests on mere lapse of time. There is far more than inactivity and delay on the part of the plaintiff. There is conduct amounting to confirmation of her gift. Gifts liable to be set aside by the Court on the ground of undue influence have always been treated as voidable and not void.

If authority for this proposition be wanted, such authority will be found in *Wright* v. *Vanderplank*[3] and *Mitchell* v. *Homfray*[4]. Moreover, such gifts are voidable on equitable grounds only. A gift intended when made to be absolute and irrevocable, but liable to be set aside by a Court of Justice, not on the ground of a change of mind on the part of the donor, but on grounds of public policy based upon the fact that the donor was not sufficiently free relatively to the donee, such a gift is very different from a loan which the borrower knows he is under an obligation to repay, and is also different from a gift expressly made revocable and never intended to be absolute and unconditional. A gift made in terms absolute and unconditional naturally leads the donee to regard it as his own ; and the longer he is left under this impression the more difficult it is justly to deprive him of what he has naturally so regarded. So long as the relation between the donor and the donee which invalidates the gift lasts, so long is it necessary to hold that lapse of time affords no sufficient ground for refusing relief to the donor. But this necessity ceases when the relation itself comes to an end ; and if the donor desires to have his gift declared invalid and set aside, he ought, in my opinion, to seek relief within a reasonable time after the removal of the influence under which the gift was made. If he does not the inference is strong, and if the lapse of time is long the inference becomes inevitable and conclusive, that the donor is content not to call the gift in question, or, in other words, that he elects not to avoid it, or, what is the same thing in effect, that he ratifies and confirms it. This view is not only conformable to the well-settled rules relating to other voidable transactions (see the judgment in *Clough* v. *London and North Western Railway Company*[5]), but is also warranted by *Wright* v. *Vanderplank*[3] and *Mitchell* v. *Homfray*[4]. It is true that in those cases the donors had died ; but it is clear, I think, that

---

[1] (1767), 3 Bro. C. C. 639, n.   [2] (1806), 2 Sch. & Lef. 607, at p. 630.
[3] (1856), 8 De G. M. & G. 133.   [4] (1881), 8 Q. B. D. 587.
[5] (1871), L. R. 7 Exch. 26.

the decisions proceeded upon the ground that the donors, if alive, could not have obtained relief. A right to have a gift set aside for fraud or undue influence does not cease on the death of the donor but passes to his representatives ; and if in *Mitchell* v. *Homfray* the donor had been entitled when he died to have his gift set aside, his executors would have succeeded to his rights, and would have obtained the relief they sought. In this particular case the plaintiff considered when she left the sisterhood what course she should take, and she determined to do nothing, but to leave matters as they were. She insisted on having back her will, but she never asked for her money until the end of five years or so after she left the sisterhood. In this state of things I can only come to the conclusion that she deliberately chose not to attempt to avoid her gifts but to acquiesce in them, or, if the expression be preferred, to ratify or confirm them. I regard this as a question of fact, and upon the evidence I can come to no other conclusion than that which I have mentioned. Moreover, by demanding her will and not her money, she made her resolution known to the defendant.

It was urged that the plaintiff did not know her rights until shortly before she asked for her money back. But, in the first place, I am not satisfied that the plaintiff did not know that it was at least questionable whether the defendant could retain the plaintiff's money if she insisted on having it back. In the next place, if the plaintiff did not know her rights, her ignorance was simply the result of her own resolution not to inquire into them. She knew all the facts ; she was in communication with her present solicitor in 1880, his remark that " it was too large a sum to leave behind without asking for it back," was a clear intimation to her that she ought to ask for her money back, and was a distinct invitation to her to consider her rights. She declined to do so ; she preferred not to trouble about it. Under these circumstances it would, in my opinion, be wrong and contrary to sound principle to give her relief on the ground that she did not know what her rights were. Ignorance which is the result of deliberate choice is no ground for equitable relief ; nor is it an answer to an equitable defence based on laches and acquiescence. Again, it was urged that the defendant has not been prejudiced by the delay, and that nothing has been done on the faith that the plaintiff would not require her money to be returned to her. But I do not think this material. I treat the money as absolutely given to the sisterhood when the plaintiff determined not to ask for it back, which she did in 1880. But, further, I cannot come to the conclusion that nothing has been done on the faith of the money being the property of the sisterhood. It is contrary to human nature to suppose that the plaintiff's money was not for years regarded as the money of the sisterhood, and that the sisterhood did not act on that assumption and make their arrangements accordingly. Mr. Nihill's evidence satisfies me that they did so, although I do not think he shews that they took any particular step on the faith of having the particular sum now sought to be taken from them. It is not, however, in my opinion, necessary to prove so much as this. Whether the plaintiff's conduct amounts in point of law to acquiescence or laches, or whether it amounts to an election not to avoid a voidable transaction, or whether it amounts to a ratification or a confirmation of her gifts, are questions of mere words which it is needless to discuss. In my judgment, it would not be fair or right to the defendant to compel her now to restore the money sought to be recovered by this appeal. Nor, in my opinion, would such a result be in conformity with sound legal or equitable principles. Upon this ground, therefore, I am of opinion that this appeal ought to be dismissed.

Bowen, L.J., delivered judgment to the same effect. Cotton, L.J., dissented, holding that the plaintiff had not unduly delayed her application for relief.

CONTRACTS RENDERED VOID BY STATUTE:

WAGERING CONTRACTS

Ellesmere (Earl) v. Wallace

[1929] 2 Ch. 1

There cannot be more than two parties, or groups of parties, to a wagering contract.

The essence of a wagering contract is that either party stands to win or lose upon the determination of the event in question.

RUSSELL, L.J.   In this action the Jockey Club sue the defendant to recover payment of the sum of 4*l.* alleged to be due from him, as to 2*l.* as the result of his having entered his horse " Master Michael " for the Peel Handicap to be run at the Newmarket First Spring Meeting last year, and as to the remaining 2*l.* as the result of his having entered the same horse for the Long Course Selling Plate to be run at the same meeting.   The only defence raised and argued was that the contracts made by the defendant in nominating his horse for those races were " contracts by way of gaming or wagering " within section 18 of the Gaming Act, 1845.

Clauson, J., held this to be the case, and dismissed the action.   The plaintiffs appeal.

The first thing to do is to ascertain what in regard to each race was the contract and between whom was it made ; and I will deal in the first place with the Peel Handicap.

I may say at once that I agree with the learned judge that the parties to the contracts are the defendant on the one hand and the Jockey Club on the other.   There is nothing in the Rules of Racing or other documents to suggest or justify the view that the nominators made any contract with each other collectively or individually.   This appeal must in my opinion be decided upon that footing.

The conditions governing the Peel Handicap were advertised in the Racing Calendar of April 12, 1928, and are set out in para. 2 of the statement of claim.   They incorporate the Rules of Racing.   By that advertisement the Jockey Club invites owners to nominate horses for that race upon the stated conditions, one of which is a liability to pay to the Jockey Club the sum of 5*l.* if the horse nominated starts in the race, or the sum of 2*l.* only if the horse does not start.   At this point two views are possible, but it is I think immaterial which is adopted.   Either the advertisement in the Racing Calendar is an offer by the Jockey Club, which becomes a contract by the acceptance of the nominator in making the nomination, or the advertisement is an invitation to the horse owners to make an offer by the nomination which becomes a contract by the acceptance of the nomination.   The phrase " nominations can only be made and accepted on the condition," etc., lends colour perhaps to the latter view.

However that may be, a contract was here established between the defendant and the Jockey Club.   The terms of the contract were in my opinion as follows : the defendant on his part undertook to pay 5*l.* for the right to run " Master Michael " over the Peel Course in the Peel Handicap on May 3, 1928, carrying the weight allotted by the handicapper, the defendant's liability to be reduced to 2*l.* in the event of his not exercising that right.   The Jockey Club on their part undertook : (1) To run the Peel

Handicap on the said date. (2) To allow the defendant to run " Master Michael " over their Peel Course in the Peel Handicap as aforesaid. (3) To pay to the nominator whose horse wins the race (*a*) a sum of 200*l*., and (*b*) the entrance moneys to be paid by the various nominators less a sum of 30*l*. (4) To pay to the nominator whose horse is placed second the said sum of 30*l*. Those appear to me to be the promises on either side in this contract, which however is subject to an overriding provision (which in the present case never operated), that if fewer than 15 entries were obtained the Jockey Club might cancel the race and with it (under rule 169) the defendant's pecuniary liability. This statement of the contract differs from the view of Clauson, J., only in this respect : that I think that the true promise by the Jockey Club is to pay the added money and entrance fees to the nominators of the first and second horses, although no doubt that involves a promise to pay the defendant if he should answer either description.

Now is that a contract by way of wagering ? In making that contract have the Jockey Club and the defendant made a bet between themselves ?

To the unsophisticated racing man (if such there be) I should think that nothing less like a bet can well be imagined. It is payment of entrance money to entitle an owner to compete with other owners for a prize built up in part by entrance fees, the winning of the prize to be determined not by chance but by the skill and merit of horse and jockey combined. Lord Falmouth, the most prominent and successful patron of the turf in the second half of last century, used to pride himself on the fact that (with the exception of a single sixpence wagered with the wife of his trainer) he had never made a bet on a horse race. If the defendant's counsel are correct in their contention here, he was sadly mistaken ; for, according to them, he spent his life in betting with the various racing executives in this country and elsewhere. We must see if they are right, for it may be that the microscope of the law is enabled and bound to detect some betting bacillus lurking within, which converts this apparently innocent bargain into " a contract by way of gaming or wagering," and which turns the 2*l*. which the defendant promised to pay in the event which happened into " a sum of money . . . . alleged to be won upon a wager " for the recovery of which the stewards are forbidden to bring or maintain any suit.

Let us clear our minds of the betting atmosphere which surrounds all horse racing, and affirm a few relevant propositions. There is nothing illegal in horse racing : it is a lawful sport. There is nothing illegal in betting *per se*. There is all the difference in the world between a club sweepstakes on the result of the Derby and a sweepstakes horse race as defined in the Rules of Racing. In each no doubt the winner is ascertained by the result of an uncertain event, but in the case of the former the winner is ascertained by chance, i.e., the luck of the draw not the result of the race (for the result is the same whether the draw is made before or after the race) ; in the case of the latter the winner is ascertained not by chance, but by merit of performance. The former is a lottery ; the latter is not. Finally, but for the presence in the Gaming Act, 1845, of section 18, there can be no doubt that the liability of the defendant to pay his 2*l*. is enforceable here. The defence accordingly depends wholly upon the provisions contained in that section. It runs as follows : " All contracts or agreements whether by parole or in writing, by way of gaming or wagering, shall be null and void ; and no suit shall be brought or maintained in any Court of law or equity for recovering any sum of money or valuable thing alleged to be won upon any wager, or which shall have been deposited in the hands of any person to abide the event on which any wager shall have been made : Provided always, that this enactment shall not be deemed to apply to any subscription or contribution, or agreement to subscribe or contribute, for or towards any plate, prize, or sum of money to be awarded to the winner or winners of any lawful game, sport, pastime, or exercise."

At the outset one is struck by the proviso which (apart from authority) one would have thought qualified the previous part of the section and exempted from its operation a transaction which might otherwise have been subject to it, if the transaction could properly be said to fall within the language of the proviso. Such a view fits in with the usual function of a proviso and with the words which here occur, " shall not be deemed to apply." It is said however that the Court of Appeal has definitely decided to the contrary in *Diggle* v. *Higgs*[1], and has laid it down, as a matter of construction of this section, that if a transaction can be made to fall within the earlier part of the section the proviso has no operation on it at all, and that the proviso only applies to cases which never did or could fall within the earlier words of the section. If this be the true view of *Diggle* v. *Higgs*[1] it binds us, and only the House of Lords can effectively entertain a different opinion ; but *Diggle* v. *Higgs*[1] needs careful scrutiny. The facts were such that the transaction was a bet pure and simple between the two foot racers. Diggle promised to pay Simonite 200*l.* upon one possible issue of an uncertain event ; Simonite promised to pay Diggle 200*l.* upon the other possible issue of the uncertain event. That was quite clearly a contract for a bet. The only matter alleged to bring the transaction within the proviso was that each 200*l.* was deposited with a stakeholder, and so it was said the transaction was merely a subscription of sums to a money prize for the winner. It was held that the contract was clearly a wager, and that the proviso did not take it out of the enactment, because the deposit of the money in the hands of the stakeholder did not turn a bet into an agreement to contribute to a money prize. As I read the case the decision was not (as suggested in argument here) that the proviso only applies to contributions by non-competitors, but that the facts of the particular case (there being only the two competitors) fell clearly within the words of the section and did not fall within the words of the proviso at all.

That is what I think Lord Cairns means when he says[2] that the Legislature never intended to say that if the wager is in the form of a subscription or contribution the winner may recover it. In my opinion there is nothing in the decision in *Diggle* v. *Higgs*[1] which excludes what I believe is the true operation of the proviso—namely, that while it does not enable a man to recover that which is nothing but a wager, though it masquerades as a prize, it does exclude from the operation of the section what are prizes, though composed in part of stakes contributed by competitors. In other words, I should like to decide the present case upon the simple ground that, even if the contributions by competitors do introduce some element of gaming or wagering into the transaction, which would *prima facie* defeat this action under section 18, nevertheless the proviso operates according to its tenor, and the section does not invalidate the contract (whatever it be) or disentitle the plaintiffs to sue. I realize however, more particularly in view of what was said in *Trimble* v. *Hill*[3], that a decision on those lines is

---

[1] (1877), 2 Ex. D. 422.   [2] *Ibid.*, 422, at p. 426.
[3] (1879), 5 App. Cas. 342.

probably open only to the House of Lords. I realize also that the language used in the judgments in *Diggle* v. *Higgs*[1] may justify a wider view of the effect of that decision. I will therefore assume that we must act upon the view that if a transaction once falls within the words " contracts or agreements . . . . by way of gaming or wagering " the proviso can never save it.

Does the defendant's contract in relation to the Peel Handicap fall within those words ? Some subtle distinction was attempted to be drawn before us between " a contract of gaming or wagering " and " a contract by way of gaming or wagering." I am not equal to this. To me the two forms of expression carry the same meaning. To me the first question for solution here is, did the Jockey Club and the defendant by their contract make a bet with each other ?

To define a bet was never an easy task until the job was tackled by Hawkins, J., after careful consideration of the relevant authorities. The result appears in his judgment in *Carlill* v. *Carbolic Smoke Ball Co.*[2] ; every word is thought out and deserves careful attention. The definition has been cited over and over again without so far as I know any judicial criticism. I need not read the passage, because it has already been read.

I draw attention to certain features stated to be essential to the existence of a wagering contract.

There must be two persons (or groups of persons) to the bet. One (the loser) must be bound to pay money (or money's worth) to the other (the winner) if an event happens. The other (the loser) must be bound to pay money (or money's worth) to the one (the winner) if the event does not happen. The bet is decided according as one event does or does not happen. The commonest example is the bookmaker who lays say 5 to 1 in sovereigns to A.B., a member of the public, against a particular horse for a race. In that case A.B. is backing the horse, and is being promised by the bookmaker 5*l.* if the positive event happens of the horse winning ; the bookmaker is backing the field, and A.B. is promising to pay him 1*l.* if the negative event happens of the horse backed by A.B. not winning. I omit the consideration of a case of a dead heat to which special betting rules apply by which each wins and loses a moiety of the bet.

Let me now try and fit these essential features to the defendant's contract in relation to the Peel Handicap. The alleged wager falls to be decided according to the positive event of the defendant's horse winning or the negative event of his horse not winning. If the defendant's horse wins he get the first prize, which consists of (*a*) the added money, and (*b*) the total entrance moneys less 30*l.* In one view he get his 5*l.* back, in that (*a*) plus (*b*) will exceed 5*l.* in value ; but from another point of view part of his entrance money remains behind to make up the 30*l.* But do the Jockey Club, by reason of the event happening that the defendant's horse

---

[1] (1877), 2 Ex. D. 422.

[2] [1892] 2 Q.B. 484, at p. 490. The definition was as follows: " A wagering contract is one by which two persons, professing to hold opposite views touching the issue of a future uncertain event, mutually agree that, dependent on the determination of that event, one shall win from the other, and that other shall pay or hand over to him, a sum of money or other stake ; neither of the contracting parties having any other interest in that contract than the sum or stake he will so win or lose, there being no other real consideration for the making of such contract by either of the parties. It is essential to a wagering contract that each party may under it either win or lose, whether he will win or lose being dependent on the issue of the event, and, therefore, remaining uncertain until that issue is known. If either of the parties may win but cannot lose, or may lose but cannot win, it is not a wagering contract."

wins, lose anything ?   In my opinion they do not, and cannot, under their contract with the defendant, lose anything by reason of that event.   Their contract is to pay away 200*l*. and the entrance fees less 30*l*. to the winner of the race.   Their liability to lose or part with the 200*l*. is absolute whichever way the two events issue, and is in no way contingent upon or affected by the fact of the defendant nominating the winner.

If the defendant's horse does not win the matter stands thus.   The defendant has to pay his 5*l*. or 2*l*. as the case may be.   To that extent he is out of pocket ; but he has not paid or become liable to pay the money because his horse failed to win.   He paid, or became liable to pay it, as the price of that which he in fact obtained—namely, the right to run his horse in the race.

Further, have the Jockey Club won anything ?   So far as I can see, not a sixpence.   By the terms of their contract with the defendant the moneys paid by him are earmarked for the nominators of the first and second horses, and in addition by the same contract they have agreed to provide 200*l*. for the winner.

The essential features of a wagering contract are absent, for although under the terms of the contract it may be said that in one event the defendant wins, in the other event he does not really lose ; and it must be added that whichever way the event issues the Jockey Club can never win.   The result of this is, that the contract between the Jockey Club and the defendant in relation to the Peel Handicap is not a contract by way of wagering within section 18.

But it was suggested, rather than argued, before us, that the true contract was not a bipartite contract between the defendant and the Jockey Club, but a multipartite contract between the defendant and the other nominators, and also (but I am not certain of this) the Jockey Club.   In his judgment Clauson, J., says that he was not sure whether counsel for the defendant disputed that the contract was one between the Jockey Club and the defendant.   I have read the shorthand notes of the proceedings below, and I can find no argument based on the contrary view, nor do I recollect any such argument before us.   But when the suggestion was made of a multipartite wagering contract, I invited counsel to state in terms of wagers the contracts alleged to be made by the nominators *inter se*.   I could get no answer ; nor was I surprised.   The difficulties are obvious.   Let me suppose that the defendant contracts with all the other nominators jointly ; what is the bet made by him with them ?   If the defendant's horse does not win, then I suppose the defendant loses the alleged bet ; but do the other parties to the alleged bet win it ?   Not at all.   One of them only may be said to win, but the other persons who have made the alleged bet with the defendant (who has lost his bet) must rank as losers also.   Let me suppose that the defendant contracts with each of the other nominators separately.   What is the bet made by him with each ?   If the defendant's horse does not win the defendant loses the alleged bet ; but does the other party to the bet win it ?   Only if his horse is the one which wins the race, but not otherwise.   If the horse of one of the other nominators wins the race, the result of the " bet " which I am considering is that nothing is won or lost by either party to the alleged bet.

Let me try to express in words the alleged contract between the defendant and each fellow nominator separately.   It is not easy, but I think it may be done thus if we omit the complication introduced by the existence of the prize of 30*l*. for the owner of the second horse : The defendant promises A.B. that if A.B.'s horse wins the race he, the defendant, will pay to the Jockey Club to the use of A.B. 5*l*. (if the defendant starts a horse in the race) or 2*l*. (if he does not).   A.B. promises the defendant that if the defendant's horse wins the race, he, A.B., will pay to the Jockey Club to the use of the defendant 5*l*. (if A.B. starts a horse in the race) or 2*l*. (if he does not).   These are two contingent promises, each of which may be the consideration for the other—but they do not constitute a bet.   The failure of one contingency does not carry with it the fulfilment of the other, for a third party—namely, C.D.—may be the winner.

Let me try to clothe the defendant's promise under this contract in the language of a bet and test it that way.   The defendant lays A.B. X to Y against A.B.'s horse winning the race.   If X and Y represent money or money's worth, that is a bet.   In this case X must be 5*l*. or 2*l*., according as the defendant does or does not himself run a horse in the race.   But what is Y ?   Y is and can only be nothing.   For no liability arises in A.B. to pay anything to the use of the defendant in the event of A.B. failing to win the race.   A.B.'s only liability arises under the supposed promise by him to pay 5*l*. or 2*l*. to the defendant, which is contingent not on A.B. losing the race, but on the defendant winning it.   If a man lays another 2*l*. to nothing against a horse, there is no bet ; there is only a contingent promise to pay 2*l*., which may or may not be *nudum pactum*.

The truth is that you cannot have more than two parties or two sides to a bet.   You may have a multipartite agreement to contribute to a sweep-stake (which may be illegal as a lottery if the winner is determined by chance, but not if the winner is determined by skill), but you cannot have a multi-partite agreement for a bet unless the numerous parties are divided into two sides, of which one wins or the other wins, according to whether an uncertain event does or does not happen.

Take a simple case of five horse owners each agreeing to contribute 10*l*. for a horse race to be run by their five horses, the owner of the winning horse to take the whole 50*l*.   The only way in which that transaction could, as it seems to me, be twisted into a wager or series of wagers is to say that each one of the five has made a separate bet with each one of the other four in these terms : " I bet you a level 10*l*. that my horse will beat yours, one to win."   The last three words must be added, otherwise the owner of the horse which finished last would find himself saddled with a liability of 40*l*., not 10*l*.   The addition, however, of the last three words makes the wager a contingent wager.   But are the results as to pecuniary liability identical with the results of the promises to subscribe 10*l*. each ?   If one horse wins outright I think they are.   Each of the four losers loses one contingent bet of a level 10*l*., as to his three other bets, the contingency does not materialize.   Suppose, however, that A.'s horse dead heats for first place with B.'s horse and the dead heat is not run off.   How then ?   Have A. and B. both won within the meaning of the bets, so that C., D. and E. each loses his alleged bets of 10*l*. with A. and B. ?   Or does neither A. nor B. win the race within the meaning of the bets, so that no money passes under the bets at all ?   Or do the rules of betting as to halving each bet apply, with the same resulting cancellation of liability all round ?   The answer to each question in fact is " No "—because the stakes are divided. This establishes the objection to twisting a transaction which is not a wager, and was never intended to be a wager, into a wager, and shows how in so doing you may achieve a result never intended by the parties. . . .

In the result I hold that the contract entered into by the defendant in relation to the Peel Handicap was a contract with the Jockey Club, and was not a contract by way of gaming or wagering within section 18 of the Act of 1845. The whole case here depends upon the provisions of that section. In my opinion, the contract sued upon is not within the first portion of the section, and this action is not within the second portion, which prohibits a suit by the winner against the loser or a wager, nor is it within the third portion, which prohibits a suit by a winner of stakes against a stakeholder.

So far, I have only dealt with the Peel Handicap. I will now turn to the Long Course Selling Plate. This appears to be an *a fortiori* case. The prize of 200*l*. is provided by the race fund—i.e., by the executive. The entrance fees are not earmarked in any way for the winner. Under the Rules of Racing they go to the race fund, subject to the provisions of rule 159. The race being a Selling Plate carries with it certain features as to the sale by auction of the winner and other matters which appear irrelevant to the questions with which this appeal is concerned. The only relevant new feature of the contract between the Jockey Club and the defendant in regard to the Long Course Selling Plate (as compared with the Peel Handicap contract) is this : that if the entries exceeded 100 in number the entrance fees received by the Jockey Club would exceed in value the prize of 200*l*. offered by them. But for rule 159 it might in these circumstances be impossible to say that in no event could the Jockey Club win. But rule 159 in my opinion cuts out that argument. It forms part of the contract between the Jockey Club and the defendant, and effectually prevents the Jockey Club from making a gain from the transaction. If the Jockey Club in fact made a gain, they would do so not in pursuance of but in violation of their contract with the defendant.

The result is that I hold that in neither case was there a contract by way of gaming or wagering, and that the sums sued for are recoverable in this action.

I am not sorry to arrive at this conclusion, for I think it would be a travesty of the true facts to say that an owner in entering his horse for a race is gaming or wagering with the racecourse authorities. Neither he nor they intend to do any such thing. He is asked for and intends to pay an entrance fee, and nothing else. I confess I am glad that the law does not compel me to decide otherwise. I think the learned judge erred in coming to the conclusion that the Jockey Club stood to lose the 200*l*. added money and the amount of the Plate in the event of the defendant's horse proving the winner. Those amounts were never at risk at all under the contracts with the defendant : their payment never depended upon the issue of the question did the defendant's horse win or not. Under the contract (which involved holding the race on the advertised terms) those sums had to be paid away by the Jockey Club whether the defendant's horse won or not. Further I think the learned judge erred in holding that the defendant lost money in the event of his horse not winning the race. His liability to pay the 5*l*. or 2*l*. did not depend on his not winning the race It was the price of the right to run his horse in the race.

The appeal should be allowed, the order below discharged, and in lieu thereof an order for payment should be made in the terms indicated by the Master of the Rolls.

LORD HANWORTH, M.R., delivered judgment to the same effect; LAWRENCE, L.J., dissented as to the case of the Peel Handicap.

Hill v. William Hill (Park Lane), Ltd.

[1949] A.C. 530

A new agreement to pay what is in effect the amount of a lost bet is not actionable whether it is made for fresh consideration or not.

APPEAL from the Court of Appeal (Lord Goddard, C.J., Tucker and Evershed, L.JJ.).

The facts, summarized from their Lordships' opinions, were as follows: The appellant (the defendant in the action) Tom Hill, who was a licensed victualler and also an owner of race horses, had betting transactions on horse racing and dog racing with the respondents (the plaintiffs in the action), William Hill (Park Lane), Ltd., a company carrying on business as bookmakers, as the result of which he had by March, 1946, lost to them the sum of 3,835*l.* 12*s.* 6*d.* In April he declared himself unable to pay and, following the common practice, the case was reported to the Committee of Tattersalls by the respondents, who referred the matter of their claim against him to them. They heard evidence and adjudicated on the subject-matter of the complaint on July 22, 1946. They decided that 3,635*l.* 12*s.* 6*d.* was due from the appellant and further that this sum ought to be met by a payment of 635*l.* 12*s.* 6*d.* within fourteen days and the remaining 3,000*l.* by monthly instalments of 100*l.* The discrepancy between the sums of 3,835*l.* 12*s.* 6*d.* and 3,635*l.* 12*s.* 6*d.* was due to the fact that 200*l.* of the former sum had been lost in betting on dog races with which the Committee had no concern. As to the functions and procedure of the Committee, it appeared that it was open to anyone alleging that he had won a bet from another on horse racing and that he had not been paid by the date of settlement, to report the matter to them. The Committee then held an inquiry, at which evidence might be taken, and decided whether a bet had been lost and, if so, of what amount. They might then make a written order for payment on terms and by instalments. If the loser failed to make payment in compliance with their direction, the next step was that the creditor might report the default to them and request them to send the loser a letter described as " the usual ten day letter " calling on him to comply with their order within ten days and stating that, if he failed to comply, they would report him to the Stewards of the Jockey Club. If that were done the automatic result would be that he would be warned off Newmarket Heath and that his name would be posted as a defaulter. He would thereby be precluded from entering a horse for any race in his own name and from attending race meetings on any course controlled by the Stewards of the Jockey Club. In effect he would be unable to place any further bets on race horses, since it would be unlikely that reputable bookmakers would be willing to accept them. He would also incur a serious social stigma. In fact the appellant did not pay the 635*l.* 12*s.* 6*d.* within fourteen days and the following letters then passed between the parties:

> " Ye Olde Chequers Inne,
> Cutnall Green, Nr. Droitwich.

" Wm. Hill Ltd.,
London.

> Telephone—Cutnall Green 228
> August 15th, 1946.

" Dear Sir,

" I am sorry that I have not yet been able to comply with the order made against me by Messrs. Tattersalls but as my financial position at the moment is bad I have not been in a position to do so. The best I can do at the moment is to send you a post-dated cheque for October 10 for 635*l*. 12*s*. 6*d*. and the rest as agreed by Tattersalls. If you cannot see your way clear to accept this offer, then I am afraid there is nothing else I can do.

Yours faithfully,
Tom Hill."

To this letter the respondents replied by a letter of August 17, 1946, in the following terms:

" Tom Hill, Esq.,
 Ye Olde Chequers Inne,
  Cutnall Green,
   Nr. Droitwich.
" Dear Sir,

re Account—3,835l. 12s. 6d.

" We have to acknowledge receipt of your letter of the 15th instant, in which you state that up to the present you have been unable to comply with the order of Tattersalls' Committee of the 22nd ultimo.

We note your suggestion that you are prepared to forward to us a cheque for 635*l*. 12*s*. 6*d*. post-dated to October 10, 1946, the balance of our account of 3,200*l*. to be paid in monthly instalments of 100*l*. as adjudicated by the Committee of Tattersalls.

We agree to your suggestion, and in consideration of your forwarding your cheque for 635*l*. 12*s*. 6*d*. post-dated to October 10, 1946, and of the said cheque being honoured by the bank, and in further consideration of the balance of our account of 3,200*l*. being paid by instalments of 100*l*. commencing November, 1946, and each subsequent month thereafter until our account is clear, we on our part will refrain from enforcing the order made by Tattersalls' Committee on July 22, 1946.

Yours faithfully,
for William Hill (Park Lane) Limited "

The appellant replied in the following letter of August 20, 1946:

" Ye Olde Chequers Inne,
Cutnall Green, Nr. Droitwich.
Telephone—Cutnall Green 228.
20th Aug. 1946

" Wm. Hill Ltd.,
 London.
" Dear Sirs,

" With reference to your letter of the 17th inst. re account 3,835*l*. 12*s*. 6*d*. I am enclosing cheque for 635*l*. 12*s*. 6*d*. post-dated to October 10 as agreed with instalments of 100*l*. per month commencing in Nov. to follow. Thanking you for your helpful consideration in this matter and assuring you that as soon as my financial position improves I shall do all I possibly can to settle this account as soon as possible.

Yours faithfully,
Tom Hill."

The cheque, on due presentation, was not honoured and the appellant failed to pay any instalments. The first payment which was made was an amount of 335*l*. 12*s*. 6*d*. sent by cheque to the respondents on November 19, 1946. This was accepted by them " without prejudice to the legal position " and on the understanding that the terms of the agreement of August 20, 1946, remained unaltered. This cheque was honoured. The appellant made no further payment and on February 21, 1947, the respondents issued a specially endorsed writ. The endorsement was as follows:

" STATEMENT OF CLAIM

The plaintiffs' claim is for the sum of 700*l*. 0*s*. 0*d*. instalments in arrear and payable by the defendant to the plaintiffs under an agreement between the plaintiffs and the defendant on August 20, 1946.

PARTICULARS

1946		£	s.	d.
10 Oct.	To balance of instalment due on this date ..	300	0	0
10 Nov.	To instalment due on this date	100	0	0
Dec.	To instalment due on this date	100	0	0
1947				
Jan.	To instalment due on this date	100	0	0
Feb.	To instalment due on this date	100	0	0
		£700	0	0 "

The appellant was given leave to defend on filing an affidavit stating that the money claimed had been won upon wagers on horse races and setting up s. 18 of the Gaming Act, 1845, as an answer. Hallett, J., gave judgment in favour of the respondents. He said (*inter alia*): " It is quite clear . . . that the decision of the majority of the Court of Appeal in *Hyams* v. *Stuart King*[1] is binding upon me. . . . All I have got to decide is: Does this case fall within the spirit of that decision? I think it quite clearly does. I think this is a plain case where the defendant made a fresh bargain in August in consideration of the plaintiffs refraining from following up the procedure with Tattersalls' Committee which would inevitably have led to the defendant being then and there posted as a defaulter and warned off Newmarket Heath." In the Court of Appeal it was conceded that the case was covered by the former decision and the judgment of Hallett, J., was affirmed. The appellant appealed to the House of Lords.

VISCOUNT SIMON. My Lords, the conclusion to be reached by the House in this appeal will determine the answer to a question which has been the subject of considerable debate among legal text-writers and commentators for forty years past, viz., whether the decision arrived at by the Court of Appeal in *Hyams* v. *Stuart King*[1] is good law. In that case, the promise, at the request of the loser of a bet, by the winner not to present or seek to enforce payment of the loser's cheque for the amount he had lost, together with the winner's promise not to expose his default, was held by the majority of the court (Gorell Barnes, P., and Farwell, L.J.) to be good consideration for a new and enforceable agreement by the loser to pay what was owing. Inasmuch as forbearance to claim prompt payment of an unenforceable debt like a bet cannot constitute good consideration for a legally binding promise to pay the amount later on, the real point of the decision of the majority was that the promise not to expose the loser's default to his detriment constituted effective consideration, in consequence of which the sum owing could be recovered in an action. Fletcher Moulton, L.J., delivered a dissenting judgment, holding that the language of s. 18 of the Gaming Act, 1845 (8 & 9 Vict. cap. 109) prevented the winner from recovering in the action the sum sued for, as in his opinion it was " a sum of money alleged to be won upon a wager," notwithstanding that the fresh promise had been made. The present appellant admits that if the view of the majority in *Hyams* v. *Stuart King*[1] is correct, his appeal must fail, but he contends that the minority view of Fletcher Moulton, L.J., correctly construes the section and that by applying this view to the facts of the case now before us the appeal should succeed.

As a result of betting with the respondents the appellant lost, on balance of account, the sum of 3,835*l*. 12*s*. 6*d*., all but 200*l*. of which was lost in

---

[1] [1908] 2 K. B. 696.

betting on horse racing. In April, 1946, the appellant declared himself unable to pay and the respondents thereupon referred the matter of their claim against the appellant to the Committee of Tattersalls. This Committee concerns itself solely with bets on horse racing and, after hearing evidence, made an order in respect of the 3,635*l*. 12*s*. 6*d*. so lost, directing the appellant to pay to the respondents the sum of 635*l*. 12*s*. 6*d*. forthwith and thereafter to pay the remainder of the gambling debt at the rate of 100*l*. per month. So far, there can be no question that the debt, though a debt of honour, was not a debt payment of which could be enforced by law, for the promise to pay it, by the first words of s. 18, was " null and void." What followed, however, is said by the respondents to constitute a new agreement which is untouched by the section.

The real issue in this case is not whether there was " a fresh bargain," or whether the respondents gave good consideration for the appellant's agreement to pay in the manner defined in the letters of August 17 and August 20, but whether the payments he thus contracted to make were payments of " a sum of money alleged to be won upon a wager " within the meaning of the second limb of s. 18. The contract sued on is identified in the writ as being the agreement made on August 20, and if it was not so identified details of it could have been obtained by demanding particulars. What then is this contract alleged by the respondents upon which the suit is brought ? It is a contract to pay what Tattersalls' Committee ordered the appellant to pay, though the respondents are giving more time for such payment. But there can be no question that what the Committee ordered the appellant to pay was a sum of money won by the respondents from him upon wagers as to the result of horse races. Tattersalls' Committee did not profess to have any jurisdiction to deal with any other subject matter, and indeed the respondents' letter of August 17 correctly interprets the letter of August 15, to which it is a reply, as containing the statement, " that up to the present you have been unable to comply with the order of Tattersalls' Committee." The arrangement, by the very terms of the letter of August 17, is to pay by instalments " the balance of our account " and the account is an account of betting transactions and of nothing else. The first limb of s. 18 does not apply to the case because the contract sued on is not " by way of gaming or wagering " but is a new bargain; but inasmuch as the new bargain was to pay the betting account, an action brought upon it, as it seems to me, is nevertheless brought for recovering sums won by betting.

In opposition to this view of the matter three considerations are urged and I must deal with them in turn. First, it is said that the second limb of the section is mere repetition of the first and thus if the action is not defeated under the first limb it cannot fail under the second. Secondly, this last contention is varied by arguing that the second limb is not entirely tautologous, but is governed by the opening provision which enacts a substantive change in the law, by following this up with the corresponding provision relating to procedure. Thirdly, it is suggested that the word " alleged " in the second limb creates a difficulty which shows that the appellants' construction of the section is wrong.

As regards the first of these objections, it is to be observed that though a Parliamentary enactment (like Parliamentary eloquence) is capable of saying the same thing twice over without adding anything to what has already been said once, this repetition in the case of an Act of Parliament is not to be assumed. When the legislature enacts a particular phrase in a statute the presumption is that it is saying something which has not been said immediately before. The rule that a meaning should, if possible, be given to every word in the statute implies that, unless there is good reason to the contrary, the words add something which would not be there if the words were left out. If the choice is between tautology and retrospective effect (as in *Hough* v. *Windus*[1]) it is natural to prefer a construction which implies the reproach that Parliament has said the same thing twice over in preference to a construction which would have the result of undeclared retrospective interference, but no difficulty of choice of that sort arises here. Indeed, the proper construction of one section can seldom be assisted by reference to a decision on the construction of quite a different section in another statute. The presumption, therefore, is that the second limb of s. 18 is not coincident in effect with the first limb. It is noteworthy that in *Hyams* v. *Stuart King*[2] the report of the argument contains no trace of a submission to this effect and Fletcher Moulton, L.J., observes[3] that " too little attention has been paid to the distinction between the two parts of this enactment, and the second part has been treated as being in effect merely a repetition of the first part." This is the more striking because the actual facts in that case as set out[4] show that the winner of the bet wrote to the loser " You promised faithfully that, if I kept quiet and did not injure your business by telling any of the s.p. men, or take proceedings, you would pay every farthing that was owing " and reproached him for breaking his word, so that the argument would have been a powerful one that it was this debt which the plaintiff was seeking to recover. It appears to me that Fletcher Moulton, L.J., was entirely justified in saying that the statute was so framed as to defeat an action, though not brought upon the original wagering contract, if it was brought upon an alleged new contract to pay a sum won on the wager. Gorell Barnes, P.,[5] refers briefly to this contention that the second limb of s. 18 goes further than the first limb, but dismisses it by saying " . . . when the nature of the contract, as I have stated it, is considered, the contract does not, in my opinion, fall within the language nor the meaning of the statute." What the President meant by " the contract as I have stated it " appears from the previous page where he describes it as one " that in consideration that the plaintiff would give the defendants a reasonable time within which to pay the amount which the defendants ought to have paid him on November 4, and would forbear to declare them defaulters if they paid within that further time, they would pay him on or before the expiration of that time the amount which both parties considered was due to the plaintiff in honour, though not by law." But it seems to me that the amount which was due to the plaintiff in honour was a sum won upon a wager, as Fletcher Moulton, L.J., proceeded to point out. Farwell, L.J.'s, judgment does not appear to contain any implied reference to Fletcher Moulton, L.J.'s, view, and indeed he regards " the gist of the case "[6] as concerned with the question whether threatening to post a defaulter for failure to pay a lost bet would properly be described as blackmail. I should agree that in ordinary circumstances it would not amount to a criminal offence, but that does not touch the point raised in Fletcher Moulton, L.J.'s, dissenting judgment upon which the present appellant relies. What happens in such a case as this is that by a new contract it is sought to transform an obligation of honour into a legal liability and the argument against

---

[1] (1884), 12 Q. B. D. 224.   [2] [1908] 2 K. B. 696.   [3] *Ibid.*, 712–3.
[4] *Ibid.*, 697.   [5] *Ibid.*, 705.   [6] *Ibid.*, 696, 726.

the appellant on this part of the case must be that this transformation turns money which was in the first place won on a wager into something else. But it appears to me that, at any rate on the facts of the present case, it is clear that the sum of money sought to be recovered not only owes its origin to the fact that bets were made but is itself a sum of money so won. When the long history of our legislation to discourage gaming in this country is considered, it is difficult to suppose that the legislature in 1845 did not realize that the object in view would not be attained merely by enacting that bets could not be recovered as such. The Act of 1845 begins with a preamble reciting that previous legislation had not proved completely effective to prevent the mischiefs arising from this cause. I would accept without further comment the passage in Fletcher Moulton, L.J.'s, judgment where he says[1]: " One cannot read the Gaming Act, 1845, without perceiving that it was a very serious attempt on the part of the legislature to put down wagering, and I decline to think that such an obvious and fatal blot was permitted to exist in it, which would well-nigh neutralize its practical effect, when I find language used which is perfectly apt to meet the case and which to my mind can fairly bear no other interpretation than that which would thus render it effective."

As for the second suggested objection, it is enough to say that if all the legislature had wanted to do after providing that contracts by way of wagering should be null and void was to add that, as a matter of procedure, no suit should be brought to enforce them, it would have been quite simple to say so. Instead of this, the second limb of the section is framed in quite different and much wider terms and in my opinion aims at defeating the attempt to recover betting losses by such a device as the present.

Lastly, as to the word " alleged." No difficulty arises in the present case from the use of this word, for the respondents do in terms allege that the sum they seek to recover is claimed under a contract to pay the balance of the betting account and to satisfy an order of Tattersalls' Committee which is concerned with nothing but establishing betting liability. Even if the case was one in which this did not clearly appear from the claim itself, particulars as to the nature of the contract relied on would disclose it. The language of the second limb of the section appears to be apt to cover the case where a plaintiff's declaration was of this nature and would justify the defendant in meeting the declaration by a demurrer. In modern practice, as soon as the nature of the plaintiff's case is found to fall within the second limb, the procedure would be to seek to strike out the statement of claim and to dismiss the action on the ground that such a claim could not possibly succeed. It may be that if a plaintiff managed to launch an action to recover his winnings on betting without either alleging that this was the nature of his claim or being compelled to give particulars to disclose it, the truth of the matter could be established by the defendant, though in that event the language of the section is awkward because the defendant's success would depend not on what he alleged but on what was proved. In any event, I do not see how the suggested difficulty in construing the word " alleged " assists the contention of the present respondents.

The view which I adopt involves the overruling of the decision in *Bubb* v. *Yelverton*[2]. There Lord Romilly, M.R., in the year 1870 held[3] that a bond given by the loser of a bet as security for paying the sum involved

---

[1] [1908] 2 K. B. at pp. 713–4.   [2] (1870), L. R. 9 Eq. 471.   [3] *Ibid.*, 474.

could be enforced on the ground that " it was given, not to pay racing debts, but to avoid the consequences of not having paid them." There were special circumstances in that case which may have induced the Master of the Rolls to reach his conclusion, but I agree with Fletcher Moulton, L.J., that the bond constituted an agreement to pay money won on wagers, notwithstanding the new consideration, and is thus unenforceable under the second limb of s. 18. There is an indication in the report of the argument for the loser that this contention was put forward and it ought to have prevailed. Subsequent cases which essentially depend on following *Bubb* v. *Yelverton*[1] must also be regarded as wrongly decided.

We were referred to dicta to be found in some of the judgments in *Varney* v. *Hickman*[2] and in *Diggle* v. *Higgs*[3]. These two cases arose out of a demand by the plaintiff to recover money which he had deposited with a stakeholder to abide the event in respect of which he had made a bet. In the earlier case the plaintiff had repudiated the wager before the event was ascertained and it was held that he was entitled to recover the amount as money had and received. In the later case the plaintiff succeeded even after the event had been decided and the plaintiff had lost his bet, inasmuch as the money was still in the hands of the stakeholder and had not been paid over to the winner. Neither of these cases, therefore, directly involved the portion of s. 18 of the Act of 1845 which prohibits the maintenance of actions for the recovery of money won upon any wager, and the decisions turned on the proper application of a later limb of the section dealing with the recovery of what has been deposited in the hands of a stakeholder, and lay down that the language of that limb does not deprive a party who deposits money with a stakeholder to abide the event of a wager of what Parke, B., in *Martin* v. *Hewson*[4] (a cock-fighting case) calls a *locus pœnitentiæ*. But Maule, J., in *Varney* v. *Hickman*[2] and Lord Cairns and Bramwell, L.J., in *Diggle* v. *Higgs*[3] expressed a view as to the interpretation of the second limb of the section upon which the present respondents rely. Maule, J., said[5] " Now, the first branch of this section declares the contract to be null and void; the second prevents the winner from bringing an action to recover the amount of the bet from the loser: and the third prevents the winner from suing the stakeholder. It certainly is true that the second branch is involved in the first: that is to say, that, if the section had stopped at the end of the first branch, it would have followed that no action could be brought to enforce a contract so declared to be void. But I apprehend there is nothing unusual in an Act of Parliament stating a legal consequence in this way." Logically, it does not follow that because the second branch was not needed to prevent the success of an action to recover a bet, therefore the ambit of the second branch is limited to the case where the action would fail even apart from what the second branch says, for it would still be a possible view that the second branch also covers some actions which were not rendered void by the first limb. But I think Maule, J., did mean to express the view that the second limb was merely tautologous, and this is certainly the effect of Bramwell, L.J.'s, observation in *Diggle* v. *Higgs*[6] where he roundly declares that the words of the second limb are " unnecessary, and might have been left out of the statute." These dicta, however, were not essential to the correctness of the decisions in which they occur and it

---

[1] (1870), L. R. 9 Eq. 471.
[2] (1847), 5 C. B. 271.
[3] (1877), 2 Ex. D 422.
[4] (1855), 10 Exch. 737, at p. 738.
[5] (1847), 5 C. B. 271, at p. 280.
[6] (1877), 2 Ex. D. 422, at p. 429.

is to be observed that Cockburn, C.J.[1], while concurring in the actual decision in *Diggle* v. *Higgs*[2], entertained a different opinion of the true construction of the section as a whole. Now that the question of the proper range of the second limb of s. 18 comes up as the direct issue for final decision the dicta to which I have referred must give way before the analysis and reasoning which Fletcher Moulton, L.J., first set on foot.

In the course of the argument before us hypothetical illustrations were put in which it was suggested that a " valuable thing " agreed by the loser of a bet to be given to the winner, in consideration of the bet being treated as wiped out and no complaint being made of the failure to pay it promptly in cash, might not be shown to be sued for as " won on a wager." If such a situation were to arise it would be for the judge of fact to decide whether this was or was not the case. But on the evidence in the present appeal it was plainly the sum won on wagering that it was sought to compel the appellant to pay. That, in my opinion, is a claim which under the second limb of s. 18 cannot be enforced by legal proceedings, notwithstanding the new agreement, and consequently in my opinion the appeal should succeed.

LORDS GREENE, NORMAND and MACDERMOTT delivered similar judgments, allowing the appeal: LORDS OAKSEY, JOWITT and RADCLIFFE dissented.

Fitch v. Jones

(1855), 5 E. & B. 238

> A negotiable instrument is normally presumed to have been given for consideration. If it is given in respect of any wager other than on a game this presumption holds good, and it is for the party sued on it to prove the contrary. But if given in respect of a wager on a game, it is deemed to have been given for an illegal consideration, and the party suing on it must prove that subsequent to the illegality value has been given in good faith (Gaming Act, 1835).

Action on a promissory note at two months after date by indorsee against maker. Plea : that the defendant made the note and delivered it to the indorser in payment of a bet on the amount of hop duty ; and that plaintiff took it when overdue and without value. Issue thereon.

On the trial, it was proved that the note was made and given for the bet to the indorser in January, 1855; it bore date 1st January, 1854, but across it, at the time it was delivered by the maker, was written " Due the 4 March, 1855." In fact the date of 1854 was a mistake for 1855, not noticed by any one. It was indorsed to plaintiff in January, 1855. The Judge reserved leave to enter a verdict for the plaintiff if the note was overdue. He left it to the jury to say whether there was value for the indorsement, telling them that the burthen lay on the defendant to prove that there was none.

Held, that the memorandum that the note was due on 4th *March*, 1855, was equivalent to a memorandum correcting the error in the date, and, being made before the note was issued, operated as a correction ; and, consequently, that the note was not overdue.

Held, also, that there was no misdirection ; for that, though proof that a negotiable instrument was affected with fraud or illegality in the hands of a previous holder raises a presumption that he would indorse it

---

[1] (1877), 2 Ex. D. 422.   [2] *Ibid.*, 422, 429.

away to an agent without value, and consequently calls on the plaintiff for proof that he gave value, the presumption does not arise when the previous holder merely held without consideration. And that a bet, though void, and therefore no consideration, was not illegal so as to raise a presumption that the indorsement was without value.

LORD CAMPBELL, C.J. I am of opinion that this rule must be discharged. On the first point, it is quite clear to my mind that, taking the whole of what was written together, the instrument purported on the face of it to be dated in the year 1855. The whole that was on the face of the instrument was written there, whilst the instrument was in the course of inception, before it was issued. It is dated " Jan. 1, 1854 "; and if that was the real date it would, giving effect to the days of grace, be due 4th March, 1854. But on it is written " Due the 4 March, 1855," which would indicate to any one exercising an ordinary understanding that the date must have been intended to be January 1, 1855. It is therefore in effect the case my brother Erle puts, and is exactly as if, contemporaneously and to correct a mistake, there had been written, on the note, " In the date, for four read five."

The other question is one of general importance. It is, whether in such a case as this it lies on the plaintiff to shew that there was consideration for the indorsements, or on the defendant to shew that there was none ; or in other words whether the facts proved raised a presumption that there was no consideration. It is clear that, when there is illegality or fraud shewn in a previous holder, a presumption that there is no consideration for the indorsements does arise ; for the person who is guilty of illegality or fraud, and knows that he cannot sue himself, is likely to hand over the instrument to some other person to sue for him. It is not properly that the burthen of proof as to there being consideration is shifted, but that the defendant, on whom the burthen of proof that there was no consideration lies, has by proving fraud or illegality in the former holder raised a *prima facie* presumption that the plaintiff is agent for that holder, and has therefore, unless that presumption be rebutted, proved that there was no consideration. But no such presumption arises where there was in the former holder a mere want of consideration, without any illegality or fraud. The question therefore comes to be whether this note was given for a consideration merely equivalent to no consideration, or whether the note was given in an illegal transaction. I am of opinion that the note did not take its inception in illegality within the meaning of the rule. The note was given to secure payment of a wagering contract, which, even before stat. 8 & 9 Vict. c. 109, the law would not enforce : but it was not illegal ; there is no penalty attached to such a wager ; it is not in violation of any statute nor of the common law, but is simply void, so that the consideration was not an illegal consideration, but equivalent in law to no consideration at all. Though it is said in *Atherfold* v. *Beard*[1] that a wager as to the amount of hop duty is contrary to public policy, it is not there meant that it was punishable, but merely that it was an idle wager on a matter in which the parties had no concern, and the discussion of which might prejudice others, like the wager on the sex of the Chevalier D'Eon[2], and therefore was a wager not enforceable by law, though not a breach of any law. The note then being given, not on an illegal consideration, but merely on a void consideration, the presumption which the plaintiff would

---

[1] (1788), 2 Term. Rep. 610.   [2] See *Da Costa* v. *Jones* (1778), 2 Cowp. 729.

be called upon to rebut did not arise ; and consequently what my brother Coleridge said to the jury was accurate.

ERLE, J.   Taking the whole writing on the paper together, the instrument is self-contradictory.   In the ordinary place for the date is put " Jan. 1, 1854 " ; but on the face of the written instrument is put a statement that it was " Due the 4 March, 1855," which could not be unless its date was January 1, 1855.   It was for the Judge to construe that instrument; and, taking it altogether, I think he was right in construing it as purporting to be dated on 1st January, 1855.

Then was the Judge right in telling the jury that the burthen of proving that there was no consideration lay upon the defendant ?   It is clear that the general rule of law is that, when a party to a negotiable instrument pleads a plea excusing him from the fulfilment of the duty of paying according to the tenor of the instrument, the burthen of proving the plea lies on him. It is also clear that, when the plea alleges that the instrument had its inception in illegality or fraud, and that the plaintiff took it without value, proof that the instrument had its inception in illegality or fraud raises a presumption that the plaintiff took it without value ; and so far shifts the burthen of proof that, unless the defendant gives satisfactory evidence that there was consideration for the instrument, the allegation in the plea that there was no consideration will be taken to be proved.   The question in the present case is whether this note was brought within the category of notes tainted with illegality within the meaning of the rule.   I am of opinion that it was not.   I think that the defendant might without violating any law make a wager.   If he lost he might without violating any law pay what he had lost, or give a note for the amount.   I am of opinion, therefore, that the proof in this case had the same legal effect as if it had been proved that the defendant made Needham a present of this note.   It is not as if the note had been given for an illegal consideration, or a fraudulent consideration ; but the defendant is in the predicament of a person who voluntarily, as far as law is concerned, gives a negotiable instrument.   That being so, the presumption did not arise; and my brother Coleridge was quite accurate if he did say that the burthen of proving that there was consideration was not cast upon the plaintiff.   On the facts, it appears that, if the burthen had been cast upon the plaintiff, he did prove consideration in a most satisfactory manner : but that is not material.

CONTRACTS PROHIBITED BY STATUTE

ANDERSON, LTD. *v.* DANIEL

ST. JOHN SHIPPING CORPORATION *v.* JOSEPH RANK, LTD.

ARCHBOLDS LTD. *v.* S. SPANGLETT, LTD.

AMAR SINGH *v.* KULUBYA

SPECTOR *v.* AGEDA

A contract which, as made, is expressly or implicitly prohibited by statute, is illegal and void whether there is an intention to break the law or not. The question whether a contract is implicitly forbidden depends upon the construction of the statute.

A contract which, as made, is not prohibited by statute, does not become illegal merely because some collateral act of illegality is committed during the course of performance.

Anderson, Ltd. v. Daniel

[1924] 1 K.B. 138

BANKES, L.J. This appeal raises an important question under the Fertilisers and Feeding Stuffs Act, 1906. The parties are the vendors and purchaser of some stuff which is known to the artificial manure trade in Hull as " salvage," and consists of the sweepings of the holds of vessels that have carried cargoes of nitrate of soda, sulphate of ammonia, potash, superphosphates, or basic slag. These sweepings, whatever they may in fact consist of, are sold under the name of " salvage " for manure. In this case the sale was of ten tons at £7 10s. a ton. The stuff was delivered, and upon the vendors suing in the county court to recover the price the purchaser took the point that the contract was illegal, or at any rate that he was under no obligation to pay for the stuff. Whether he was right in that contention depends upon the construction to be put on two sections of the statute: s. 1, sub-s. 1, and s. 6, sub-s. 1. The former section provides that " Every person who sells for use as a fertiliser of the soil any article . . . . which has been imported from abroad, shall give to the purchaser an invoice stating the name of the article and what are the respective percentages, if any, of nitrogen, soluble phosphates, insoluble phosphates, and potash contained in the article." That section is imperative in its requirement that the statutory invoice shall be given, but it does not specify the time at which it is to be given. That is provided by s. 6, sub-s. 1 (*a*): " If any person who sells any article for use as a fertiliser of the soil . . . . (*a*) fails without reasonable excuse to give, on or before or as soon as possible after the delivery of the article, the invoice required by this Act," he shall be liable to a penalty. The statute does not require the invoice to be given at the time of the sale, for in the majority of cases that would be impossible from a commercial point of view, but only on or before or as soon as possible after delivery. What then is the effect upon the contract of a failure to comply with that condition?

It is said that this is one of those statutes which do not by imposing a penalty render the contract illegal in the event of a breach of the statutory provisions, but mean the enforcement of the penalty to be the only remedy for the breach. Upon that point I should like to refer to what Lord Wrenbury, then Buckley, J., said in one of the moneylender cases: *Victorian Daylesford Syndicate, Ltd.* v. *Dott*[1]: " The next question is whether the Act is so expressed that the contract is prohibited so as to be rendered illegal. There is no question that a contract which is prohibited, whether expressly or by implication, by a statute is illegal and cannot be enforced. I have to see whether the contract is in this case prohibited expressly or by implication. For this purpose statutes may be grouped under two heads, those in which a penalty is imposed against doing an act for the purposes only of the protection of the revenue, and those in which a penalty is imposed upon an act not merely for revenue purposes, but also for the protection of the public. That distinction will be found commented on in numerous cases, including those which have been cited of *Cope* v. *Rowlands*[2] and *Fergusson* v. *Norman*[3]. Parke, B., in the former case says the question to determine is whether the Act is ' meant *merely* to secure a revenue to the city, and for that purpose to render the person acting as a broker liable to a penalty if he does not pay it ? or whether *one* of its objects be the protection of the public, and the prevention of *improper* persons acting as brokers ?' If I arrive at the conclusion that one of the objects is the protection of the public, then the act is impliedly prohibited by the statute and is illegal." In my opinion that language applies directly to this case. Here the penalty is imposed wholly for the protection of the public, and the purchaser is entitled to take the objection that as the vendors have failed to give the required invoice the contract of sale is illegal and they cannot sue for the price.

But it has been contended that a contract cannot be avoided for illegality save where it was illegal ab initio; and although no doubt a contract for the sale of a fertiliser, which expressly stipulated that no invoice of the statutory kind should be given or required, would be illegal ab initio, it is otherwise where, as here, the contract is silent on the subject of the invoice. It was said that in such a case the contract is perfectly legal when made, and cannot be avoided by a subsequent omission to do some act which the statute requires to be done. I do not think it is necessary to show that the contract was illegal ab initio in order to avoid it, it is enough to show that the vendors failed to perform it in the only way in which the statute allows it to be performed. In reference to that matter I will refer to two authorities. One is *Little* v. *Poole*[4], which was very like the present case in that by the section there relied upon as affording a defence to an action for the price of the coals supplied, it was provided that the delivery of the coal should be accompanied by a ticket stating the name of the coal sent and signed by the meter. In that case Bayley, J., said: " The object of the Legislature will be best effected, therefore, by holding that the seller shall not recover the value of his coals where he does not cause to be delivered to the purchaser a ticket signed by the meter, pursuant to the provisions of the Act of Parliament." He there clearly indicates that where a person fails to perform the contract in the only way in which the statute says it may be performed, he is in exactly the same position as if the contract had been illegal and void ab initio.

---

[1] [1905] 2 Ch. 624, at p. 629.   [2] (1836) 2 M. & W. 149.   [3] (1838) 5 Bing. N.C. 76.
[4] 9 B. & C. 192, at pp. 202–3.

And Parke, J., said: " The provision which requires that the meter shall be a party to the vendor's ticket, which is to contain a description of the quality of the coals, is a regulation intended to protect the purchaser; and, that being so, according to *Law* v. *Hodson*[1], the plaintiff cannot recover." The other authority to which I wish to refer is *Bonnard* v. *Dott*[2], where it was held that a moneylender who had not registered himself as such under the Money-lenders Act, 1900, which prohibits unregistered persons from making any money-lending agreement, though compellable to surrender any securities given to him by a borrower, could not recover back the amount that he had advanced. Collins, M.R., said: " Any person who is in fact a money-lender must comply with the terms of the Act as to registration in order to take advantage of any contract." So here I say that a vendor of fertilisers must comply with the provisions as to invoice in order to take advantage of the contract of sale. From that point of view it is unnecessary to consider whether the contract was illegal ab initio.

The last point taken for the respondents, the point on which the county court judge decided the case, was that under the circumstances the vendors had a reasonable excuse for failing to give the invoice, and that consequently there was no offence in their failure to do so. I cannot accept that view. It seems to me quite plain that the prohibitive expense or the physical impossibility of analysis of the fertiliser sold is no excuse for the absence of an invoice. The statute is directed to the sale of articles of which the analysis was impossible, just as much as, or possibly more than, to the sale of those which are difficult of analysis or which are commercially unprofitable to analyse. Here all that was said was that in order to get a fair sample of the bulk of this " salvage " it would be necessary to mix the contents of the different bags so often that it would be commercially unprofitable to go to the expense of analysing it, because it could not, after analysis, be sold at a profit. The particular " salvage " sold may, for all that the purchaser knows, consist wholly of one of the ingredients, or a certain proportion of all five; he has no means of knowing whether it is of any value for the particular purpose for which he wants it. In my opinion there was no evidence upon which the county court judge could properly come to the conclusion that there was any reasonable excuse within s. 6, sub-s. 1 (*a*), for the vendors' failure to deliver an invoice, and under these circumstances they are not entitled to recover the price of the article sold. The appeal must be allowed.

SCRUTTON and ATKIN, L.J.J., delivered judgments to the same effect.

St. John Shipping Corporation v. Joseph Rank, Ltd.

[1957] 1 Q.B. 267

The plaintiffs, St. John Shipping Corporation, were a body incorporated under the laws of Panama and owners of the vessel *St. John*, registered in Panama and a " load line vessel not registered in the United Kingdom " within the meaning of section 57 of the Merchant Shipping (Safety and Load

---

[1] 11 East, 300.   [2] [1906] 1 Ch. 740, at p. 746.

Line Conventions) Act, 1932.[1] The vessel's summer load line corresponded to a mean draft of 27 ft. 8⅞ ins. and her winter load line to a mean draft of 27 ft. 1⅞ ins. The vessel was chartered by a charterparty dated London, October 18, 1955, by the plaintiffs to Gilbert J. McCaul & Co. Ltd., English charterers, to load 9,700 tons of 2,240 lbs. of heavy grain at one safe port, U.S. Gulf, for carriage to London, Avonmouth or Birkenhead, one port only, and deliver the same always afloat agreeable to bills of lading, on being paid freight in cash in British sterling at discharging port.

The defendants, Joseph Rank Ltd., were holders of a bill of lading in respect of 28 parcels of wheat on which the freight due was £18,893 4s. 0d. They paid £16,893 4s. 0d. but withheld the balance of £2,000. The plaintiffs sued for the balance.

The following statement of facts was agreed between the parties.

The goods on which the plaintiffs claimed the balance of freight were loaded on the vessel at Mobile, Alabama, in November, 1955, and were carried by the vessel to Birkenhead pursuant to a bill of lading dated November 2, 1955, whereof the defendants were indorsees to whom the property in the goods passed upon or by reason of such indorsement. The vessel completed loading and sailed from Mobile at 9.30 a.m. on November 2, 1955. On completion of loading the vessel's mean draft, according to a certificate of inspection issued by National Cargo Bureau Inc., dated November 2, 1955, was 27 ft. 8½ ins. The vessel then called at Port Everglades, Florida, for bunkers. She arrived at Port Everglades at 5.30 p.m. on November 5, and sailed at 1.30 a.m. on November 6, having taken on board 600 tons of bunkers. By virtue of the bunkers so taken on board the vessel's mean draft on her departure from Port Everglades was increased to about 28 ft. 7 ins. thereby causing the vessel's summer load line to become submerged by about 10 inches. On November 8 the vessel crossed latitude 36° north and thereby passed into the winter zone, having at all times previously been in the summer zone. The vessel was thereafter throughout in the winter zone and on November 22 she reached the River Mersey. Upon entering the winter zone the vessel's winter load line was submerged by about 16 inches. In the course of the vessel's passage up the River Mersey the master caused the vessel's forepeak tank to be filled for the purpose of trimming the vessel. The capacity of the tank was about 140 tons and the effect of filling the same was to increase the vessel's arrival draft by about 2 ft. 8 ins. On arrival at Birkenhead the vessel's mean draft was

---

[1] Merchant Shipping (Safety and Load Line Conventions) Act, 1932—

S. 44: " (1) A British load line ship registered in the United Kingdom shall not be so loaded as to submerge in salt water, when the ship has no list, the appropriate load line on each side of the ship, that is to say, the load line indicating or purporting to indicate the maximum depth to which the ship is for the time being entitled under the load line rules to be loaded. (2) If any such ship is loaded in contravention of this section, the owner or master of the ship shall for each offence be liable to a fine not exceeding one hundred pounds and to such additional fine, not exceeding the amount hereinafter specified, as the court thinks fit to impose having regard to the extent to which the earning capacity of the ship was, or would have been, increased by reason of the submersion. (3) The said additional fine shall not exceed one hundred pounds for every inch or fraction of an inch by which the appropriate load line on each side of the ship was submerged, or would have been submerged if the ship had been in salt water and had no list ".

S. 57: " The provisions of section 44 of this Act shall apply to load line ships not registered in the United Kingdom, while they are within any port in the United Kingdom, as they apply to British load line ships registered in the United Kingdom. . . . : "

about 28 ft. 1 in. and the vessel was accordingly laden below her winter marks by about 11 inches.

Proceedings were thereafter instituted against the master in a court of summary jurisdiction held at Wallasey wherein the master was charged with an offence under sections 44 and 57 of the Merchant Shipping (Safety and Load Line Conventions) Act, 1932, in respect of the vessel being overloaded at Birkenhead, and on November 28, 1955, the master was fined the sum of £1,200. Evidence was tendered in the proceedings that the vessel's dead-weight scale was out of date. The vessel loaded in fresh water at Mobile and it was accordingly necessary to load by reference to the vessel's dead-weight scale.

In the present action the plaintiffs claimed the amount of freight with-held by the defendants on their parcel. Another receiver also withheld freight to the amount of £295 8s. 10d. The total thus withheld was with-held in consultation with and at the request of the charterers and was the equivalent to freight on about 427 tons of cargo, which tonnage was equiva-lent to the overall additional cargo on board the vessel by reason whereof the vessel was found to be loaded below her winter marks on arrival at Birkenhead.

The Governments of the United States of America and of Panama ratified or acceded to the International Load Line Convention, 1930, in the years 1932 and 1936 respectively, and the United States of America and Panama are " countries to which the Load Line Convention applies " within the meaning of the Act of 1932 by virtue of declarations made by Order in Council pursuant to section 65 of the Act.

It was agreed that (a) in event of the parties agreeing the text of any material legislation of the U.S.A. and/or Panama the court should be free to construe the same and expert evidence as to the effect of such foreign law should be dispensed with; (b) in the event of the parties not having agreed the text of any such material legislation either party should be at liberty to adduce evidence at the trial with regard to the same.

By their defence the defendants alleged that the plaintiffs had per-formed the charter in an illegal manner, by so loading the ship as to sub-merge or allow to be submerged her load line by about 11 inches while in part of the United Kingdom, namely, Birkenhead, contrary to the provisions of the Merchant Shipping (Safety and Load Line Conventions) Act, 1932. They accordingly claimed that the plaintiffs were not entitled to the sum claimed or any part thereof.

The plaintiffs, in reply, contended that the matters relied on by the defendants afforded no ground of defence in point of law to the claim made against them.

Ashton Roskill, Q.C. and *Basil Eckersley* for the plaintiffs. *John Wilmers* for the defendants.

DEVLIN, J., read the following judgment: The continued depreciation of the pound is beginning to take effect on the criminal law. A maximum fine which at the time when Parliament fixed it would have been regarded as a sharp disincentive (if the word was then in use) may now prove to be little or no deterrent. In 1932 Parliament enacted the Merchant Shipping (Safety and Load Line Conventions) Act, 1932, which, *inter alia*, by sections 44 and 57, made it an offence to load a ship so that her load line was submerged. The temptation to overload a freighter and so to submerge her marks is, of course, that the more she carries the more she will earn for the same expenditure on the voyage. So Parliament, when prescribing a fine as the punishment for an offence against section 44, related it to the earning capacity of the ship. The maximum fine was not to exceed the court's estimate of the extent to which the earning capacity of the ship was, or would have been, increased by reason of the submersion; and was also not to exceed £100 for every inch or fraction of an inch by which the load line was submerged. I suppose that in 1932 £100 was considered an outside figure of earning capacity per inch, but freights now are very different from what they were then.

When the master of the plaintiffs' ship *St. John* was prosecuted at Birkenhead under the Act and, on November 28, 1955, found to have overloaded his ship by more than 11 inches, he was fined the maximum of £1,200; but the amount of cargo by which the ship was overloaded was 427 tons and the extra freight earned was £2,295. So the ship came very well out of this situation; and she and other ships will doubtless continue to come very well out of similar situations until the Act of 1932 is amended.

I can see that it is a situation that must cause some concern to cargo owners whose property is at risk. The ship was carrying a cargo of about 10,000 tons of grain from Mobile, Alabama, U.S.A., to Birkenhead. The defendants held a bill of lading for about 3,500 tons of this quantity on which the freight due was nearly £19,000. The defendants, apparently in association with the charterers, decided that some additional punishment should be inflicted on the plaintiffs, and that it should take the form of withholding the £2,295 extra freight. The defendants have withheld £2,000, for which sum they are being sued in this action; and another cargo owner has withheld £295 and is being sued for it in an action that depends on this one.

This is the explanation of how this dispute has arisen. But I, of course, have not got to decide whether the defendants are morally justified in trying to make good deficiencies in the criminal law; nor is any justification of that sort put forward in the case. The defendants' case in law is that since the plaintiffs performed the contract of carriage, evidenced by the bill of lading, in such a way as to infringe the Act of 1932, they committed an illegality which prevents them from enforcing the contract at all; the defendants say they were not obliged to pay any freight, and so cannot be sued for the unpaid balance. If this is right, and if all the consignees had exerted to the full their legal powers, the effective penalty for the plaintiffs' misdeed would have been the loss of the whole freight of more than £50,000.

I do not, of course, regard an offence against the Act of 1932 as a trivial matter, particularly if it is committed deliberately, and if the safety of lives at sea is involved. It is an offence for which the master of a British ship (the plaintiffs' ship was registered in Panama) could be imprisoned. The agreed statement of facts, on which this case is being tried, does not say that the overloading in the U.S.A. was deliberate; for the purposes of the defendants' argument that finding is not required. But there is material in the agreed case which would make such a finding not at all improbable. The vessel was not overloaded when she left her loading port on November 2, 1955; she had then three-eighths of an inch to spare. But it seems plain that she was not then sufficiently bunkered to take her across the Atlantic. On November 5 she called at Port Everglades, Florida, for bunkers, and the 600 tons which she then took on caused her load line to become submerged by about 10 inches. It is hard to believe that that fact was not appreciated at the time. As she went across the Atlantic her load was, of course, lightened by the consumption of bunkers, but, on the other hand, she passed into the winter zone and the net result was that when she arrived in the Mersey her load line, as I have said, was submerged by more than 11 inches.

It is a misfortune for the defendants that the legal weapon which they are wielding is so much more potent than it need be to achieve their purpose. Believing, rightly or wrongly, that the plaintiffs have deliberately committed a serious infraction of the Act and one which has placed their property in jeopardy, the defendants wish to do no more than to take the profit out of the plaintiffs' dealing. But the principle which they invoke for this purpose cares not at all for the element of deliberation or for the gravity of the infraction, and does not adjust the penalty to the profits unjustifiably earned. The defendants cannot succeed unless they claim the right to retain the whole freight and to keep it whether the offence was accidental or deliberate, serious or trivial. The application of this principle to a case such as this is bound to lead to startling results. Mr. Wilmers does not seek to avert his gaze from the wide consequences. A shipowner who accidentally overloads by a fraction of an inch will not be able to recover from any of the shippers or consignees a penny of the freight. There are numerous other illegalities which a ship might commit in the course of the voyage which would have the same effect; Mr. Roskill has referred me by way of example to section 24 of the Merchant Shipping (Safety Conventions) Act, 1949, which makes it an offence to send a ship to sea laden with grain if all necessary and reasonable precautions have not been taken to prevent the grain from shifting. He has referred me also to the detailed regulations for the carriage of timber— similar in character to regulations under the Factories Acts—which must be complied with if an offence is not to be committed under section 61 of the Act of 1932. If Mr. Wilmers is right, the consequences to shipowners of a breach of the Act of 1932 would be as serious as if owners of factories were unable to recover from their customers the cost of any articles manufactured in a factory which did not in all respects comply with the Acts. Carriers by land are in no better position; again Mr. Wilmers does not shrink from saying that the owner of a lorry could not recover against the consignees the cost of goods transported in it if in the course of the journey it was driven a mile an hour over its permitted speed. If this is really the law, it is very unenterprising of cargo owners and consignees to wait until a criminal conviction has been secured before denying their liabilities. A service of trained observers on all our main roads would soon pay for itself. An effective patrol of the high seas would probably prove too expensive, but the maintenance of a corps of vigilantes in all principal ports would be well worth while when one considers that the smallest infringement of the statute or a regulation made thereunder would relieve all the cargo owners on the ship from all liability for freight.

Of course, as Mr. Wilmers says, one must not be deterred from enunciating the correct principle of law because it may have startling or even calamitous results. But I confess I approach the investigation of a legal proposition which has results of this character with a prejudice in favour of the idea that there may be a flaw in the argument somewhere.

Mr. Wilmers puts his case under three main heads. In the first place he submits that, notwithstanding that the contract of carriage between the parties was legal when made, the plaintiffs have performed it in an illegal manner by carrying the goods in a ship which was overloaded in violation of the statute. He submits as a general proposition that a person who performs a legal contract in an illegal manner cannot sue upon it, and he relies upon a line of authorities of which *Anderson, Ltd.* v. *Daniel*[1] is probably the best known. He referred particularly to the formulation of the principle by Atkin, L.J.[2], in the following passage: " The question of illegality in a contract generally arises in connexion with its formation, but it may also arise, as it does here, in connexion with its performance. In the former case, where the parties have agreed to something which is prohibited by Act of Parliament, it is indisputable that the contract is unenforceable by either party. And I think that it is equally unenforceable by the offending party where the illegality arises from the fact that the mode of performance adopted by the party performing it is in violation of some statute, even though the contract as agreed upon between the parties was capable of being performed in a perfectly legal manner."

As an alternative to this general proposition and as a modification of it, Mr. Wilmers submits that a plaintiff cannot recover if, in the course of carrying out a legal contract made with a person of a class which it is the policy of a particular statute to protect, he commits a violation of that statute.

Secondly, he relies upon the well-known principle—most recently considered, I think, in *Marles* v. *Philip Trant & Sons*[3]—that a plaintiff cannot recover money if in order to establish his claim to it, he has to disclose that he committed an illegal act. These plaintiffs, he submits, cannot obtain their freight unless they prove that they carried the goods safely to their destination, and they cannot prove that without disclosing that they carried them illegally in an overloaded ship.

Thirdly, he relies upon the principle that a person cannot enforce rights which result to him from his own crime. He submits that the criminal offence committed in this case secured to the plaintiffs a larger freight than they would have earned if they had kept within the law. A part of the freight claimed in this case is therefore a benefit resulting from the crime and in such circumstances the plaintiff cannot recover any part of it.

I am satisfied that Mr. Wilmers's chief argument is based on a misconception of the principle applied in *Anderson, Ltd.* v. *Daniel*[1], which I have already cited. In order to expose that misconception I must state briefly how that principle fits in with other principles relating to illegal contracts. There are two general principles. The first is that a contract which is entered into with the object of committing an illegal act is unenforceable. The application of this principle depends upon proof of the intent, at the time the contract was made, to break the law; if the intent is mutual the contract is not enforceable at all, and, if unilateral, it is unenforceable at the suit of the party who is proved to have it. This principle is not involved here. Whether or not the overloading was deliberate when it was done, there is no proof that it was contemplated when the contract of carriage was made. The second principle is that the court will not enforce a contract which is expressly or impliedly prohibited by statute. If the contract is of this class it does not matter what the intent of the parties is; if the statute prohibits the contract, it is unenforceable whether the parties meant to break the law or not. A significant distinction between the two classes is this. In the former class you have only to look and see what acts the statute prohibits; it does not matter whether or not it prohibits a contract; if a contract is deliberately made to do a prohibited act, that contract will be unenforceable.

[1] [1924] 1 K. B. 138.   [2] *Ibid.*, 149.
[3] [1954] 1 Q. B. 29; [1953] 1 All E. R. 651.

In the latter class, you have to consider not what acts the statute prohibits, but what contracts it prohibits; but you are not concerned at all with the intent of the parties; if the parties enter into a prohibited contract, that contract is unenforceable.

The principle enunciated by Atkin, L.J.[1], and cited above is an offshoot of the second principle that a prohibited contract will not be enforced. If the prohibited contract is an express one, it falls directly within the principle. It must likewise fall within it if the contract is implied. If, for example, an unlicensed broker sues for work and labour, it does not matter that no express contract is alleged and that the claim is based solely on the performance of the contract, that is to say, the work and labour done; it is as much unenforceable as an express contract made to fit the work done. The same reasoning must be applied to a contract which, though legal in form, is performed unlawfully. Jenkins, L.J., in his illuminating judgment in *B. and B. Viennese Fashions* v. *Losane*[2] has shown how illogical it would be if the law were otherwise. In that case the regulations required that the seller of utility goods should furnish to the buyer an invoice containing certain particulars. The plaintiff made a contract of sale for non-utility goods, to which the regulations did not apply; but he purported to perform it by delivering to the buyer without objection utility garments to which the regulations did apply; and he did not furnish the invoice. If the court enforced his claim for the price of the garments, it would have, in effect, been enforcing a contract for the supply of utility garments without furnishing an invoice, which, had it originally been made in that form, would have been prohibited. But whether it is the terms of the contract or the performance of it that is called in question, the test is just the same: is the contract, as made or as performed, a contract that is prohibited by the statute?

Mr. Wilmers's proposition ignores this test. On a superficial reading of *Anderson, Ltd.* v. *Daniel*[3] and the cases that followed and preceded it, judges may appear to be saying that it does not matter that the contract is itself legal, if something illegal is done under it. But that is an unconsidered interpretation of the cases. When fully considered, it is plain that they do not proceed upon the basis that in the course of performing a legal contract an illegality was committed; but on the narrower basis that the way in which the contract was performed turned it into the sort of contract that was prohibited by the statute.

All the cases which Mr. Wilmers cited in support of his submission show, I think, that this is the true basis. Some of the earlier cases on which he relied—those in which the principle was first being formulated—show this most clearly; and I take as an example of them *Cope* v. *Rowlands*[4]. In that case the plaintiff brought an action for work and labour done by him as a broker and the plea was that he was not duly licensed to act as a stockbroker pursuant to the statute. The statute imposed a penalty on any unlicensed person acting as a broker. Parke, B.[5] (the italics below are those in the report) declared the law to be as follows: " It is perfectly settled that where the contract which the plaintiff seeks to enforce, be it express or implied, is expressly or by implication forbidden by the common or statute law, *no court will lend its assistance to give it effect.* It is equally

---

[1] [1924] 1 K. B. 149.
[3] [1924] 1 K. B. 138.
[2] [1952] 1 All E. R. 909, at p. 913.
[4] (1836), 2 M. & W. 149.
[5] *Ibid.*, 157.

clear that a contract is void if prohibited by a statute, though the statute inflicts a penalty only, because such a penalty implies a prohibition. . . . And it may be safely laid down, notwithstanding some dicta apparently to the contrary, that if *the contract* be rendered illegal, it can make no difference, in point of law, whether the statute which makes it so has in view the protection of the revenue or any other object. The sole question is, whether the statute *means to prohibit the contract* ? " After considering the language of the Act Parke, B., went on to say[1] that the language " shows clearly that the legislature had in view, as *one* object, the benefit and security of the public in those important transactions which are negotiated by brokers. The clause, therefore, which imposes a penalty, must be taken . . . to imply a prohibition of all unadmitted persons to act as brokers, and consequently to prohibit, by necessary inference, all contracts which such persons make for compensation to themselves for so acting; and this is the contract on which this action is . . . brought."

Now this language—and the same sort of language is used in all the cases—shows that the question always is whether the statute meant to prohibit the contract which is sued upon. One of the tests commonly used, and frequently mentioned in the later cases, in order to ascertain the true meaning of the statute is to inquire whether or not the object of the statute was to protect the public or a class of persons, that is, to protect the public from claims for services by unqualified persons or to protect licensed persons from competition. Mr. Wilmers (while saying that, if necessary, he would submit that the Act of 1932 was passed, *inter alia*, to protect those who had property at sea) was unable to explain the relevance of this consideration to his view of the law. If in considering the effect of the statute the only inquiry that you have to make is whether an act is illegal, it cannot matter for whose benefit the statute was passed; the fact that the statute makes the act illegal is of itself enough. But if you are considering whether a contract not expressly prohibited by the Act is impliedly prohibited, such considerations are relevant in order to determine the scope of the statute.

This, then, is the principle which I think is to be derived from the classes of cases which Mr. Wilmers cited. Not unnaturally, he cited those cases in which the result at least was consistent with the proposition for which he was contending. Had he cited those cases in which the claim succeeded because the statute was held not to imply a prohibition of any contract, he would, I think, have seen the fallacy in his argument. For that submits the point to the crucial test. The plaintiff does an illegal act, being one prohibited by the statute, but he does it in performance of a legal contract, since the statute is construed as prohibiting the act merely and not prohibiting the contract under which it is done. If in such a case it had been held that it did not matter whether the contract was legal or not since the mode of performing it was illegal, Mr. Wilmers's argument would be well supported. But in fact the contrary has been held. I take as an example of cases of this type, *Wetherell* v. *Jones*[2]. The plaintiff sued for the price of spirits sold and delivered. A statute of George IV provided that no spirits should be sent out of stock without a permit. The court held that the permit obtained by the plaintiff was irregular because of his own fault and that he was therefore guilty of a violation of the law, but that the statute did not prohibit the contract. Tenterden, C.J., stated the law as follows[3]:

---

[1] 2 M. & W. 159. [2] (1832), 3 B. & Ad. 221.

[3] *Ibid.*, 225.

" Where a contract which a plaintiff seeks to enforce is expressly, or by implication, forbidden by the statute or common law, no court will lend its assistance to give it effect: and there are numerous cases in the books where an action on the contract has failed, because either the consideration for the promise or the act to be done was illegal, as being against the express provisions of the law, or contrary to justice, morality, and sound policy. But where the consideration and the matter to be performed are both legal, we are not aware that a plaintiff has ever been precluded from recovering by an infringement of the law, not contemplated by the contract, in the performance of something to be done on his part."

The last sentence in this judgment is a clear and decisive statement of the law; it is directly contrary to the contention which Mr. Wilmers advances, which I therefore reject both on principle and on authority.

So Mr. Wilmers's wider proposition fails. Mr. Roskill is right in his submission that the determining factor is the true effect and meaning of the statute, and I turn therefore to consider Mr. Wilmers's alternative proposition that the contract evidenced by the bill of lading is one that is made illegal by the Act of 1932. I have already indicated the basis of this argument, namely, that the statute, being one which according to its preamble is passed to give effect to a convention " for promoting the safety of life and property at sea," is therefore passed for the benefit of cargo owners among others. That this is an important consideration is certainly established by the authorities. But I follow the view of Parke, B., in *Cope* v. *Rowlands*[1], which I have already cited, that it is one only of the tests. The fundamental question is whether the statute means to prohibit the contract. The statute is to be construed in the ordinary way; one must have regard to all relevant considerations and no single consideration, however important, is conclusive.

Two questions are involved. The first—and the one which hitherto has usually settled the matter—is: does the statute mean to prohibit contracts at all? But if this be answered in the affirmative, then one must ask: does this contract belong to the class which the statute intends to prohibit? For example, a person is forbidden by statute from using an unlicensed vehicle on the highway. If one asks oneself whether there is in such an enactment an implied prohibition of all contracts for the use of unlicensed vehicles, the answer may well be that there is, and that contracts of hire would be unenforceable. But if one asks oneself whether there is an implied prohibition of contracts for the carriage of goods by unlicensed vehicles or for the repairing of unlicensed vehicles or for the garaging of unlicensed vehicles, the answer may well be different. The answer might be that collateral contracts of this sort are not within the ambit of the statute.

The relevant section of the Act of 1932, section 44, provides that the ship " shall not be so loaded as to submerge " the appropriate load line. It may be that a contract for the loading of the ship which necessarily has this effect would be unenforceable. It might be, for example, that the contract for bunkering at Port Everglades which had the effect of submerging the load line, if governed by English law, would have been unenforceable. But an implied prohibition of contracts of loading does not necessarily extend to contracts for the carriage of goods by improperly loaded vessels. Of course, if the parties knowingly agree to ship goods by an overloaded vessel, such a contract would be illegal; but its illegality does not depend on whether it is impliedly prohibited by the statute, since it

---

[1] (1836), 2 M. & W. 149.

falls within the first of the two general heads of illegality I noted above where there is an intent to break the law. The way to test the question whether a particular class of contract is prohibited by the statute is to test it in relation to a contract made in ignorance of its effect.

In my judgment, contracts for the carriage of goods are not within the ambit of this statute at all. A court should not hold that any contract or class of contracts is prohibited by statute unless there is a clear implication, or " necessary inference," as Parke, B., put it[1], that the statute so intended. If a contract has as its whole object the doing of the very act which the statute prohibits, it can be argued that you can hardly make sense of a statute which forbids an act and yet permits to be made a contract to do it; that is a clear implication. But unless you get a clear implication of that sort, I think that a court ought to be very slow to hold that a statute intends to interfere with the rights and remedies given by the ordinary law of contract. Caution in this respect is, I think, especially necessary in these times when so much of commercial life is governed by regulations of one sort or another, which may easily be broken without wicked intent. Persons who deliberately set out to break the law cannot expect to be aided in a court of justice, but it is a different matter when the law is unwittingly broken. To nullify a bargain in such circumstances frequently means that in a case—perhaps of such triviality that no authority would have felt it worth while to prosecute—a seller, because he cannot enforce his civil rights, may forfeit a sum vastly in excess of any penalty that a criminal court would impose; and the sum forfeited will not go into the public purse but into the pockets of someone who is lucky enough to pick up the windfall or astute enough to have contrived to get it. It is questionable how far this contributes to public morality. In *Vita Food Products Inc.* v. *United Shipping Co., Ltd.*[2] Lord Wright said[3]: " Nor must it be forgotten that the rule by which contracts not expressly forbidden by statute or declared to be void are in proper cases nullified for disobedience to a statute is a rule of public policy only, and public policy understood in a wider sense may at times be better served by refusing to nullify a bargain save on serious and sufficient grounds." It may be questionable also whether public policy is well served by driving from the seat of judgment everyone who has been guilty of a minor transgression. Commercial men who have unwittingly offended against one of a multiplicity of regulations may nevertheless feel that they have not thereby forfeited all right to justice, and may go elsewhere for it if courts of law will not give it to them. In the last resort they will, if necessary, set up their own machinery for dealing with their own disputes in the way that those whom the law puts beyond the pale, such as gamblers, have done. I have said enough, and perhaps more than enough, to show how important it is that the courts should be slow to imply the statutory prohibition of contracts, and should do so only when the implication is quite clear. I have felt justified in saying as much because, to any judge who sits in what is called the Commercial Court, it must be a matter of special concern. This court was instituted more than half a century ago so that it might solve the disputes of commercial men in a way which they understood and appreciated, and it is a particular misfortune for it if it has to deny that service to any except those who are clearly undeserving of it.

I think also that it is proper, in determining the scope of the statute,

---

[1] 2 M. & W. 159.
[2] [1939] A. C. 277; [1939] 1 All E. R. 513.
[3] [1939] A. C. 277, at p. 293.

to have regard to the consequences I have already described and to the inconveniences and injury to maritime business which would follow from upholding the defendants' contention in this case. In the light of all these considerations I should not be prepared to treat this statute as nullifying contracts for the carriage of goods unless I found myself clearly compelled by authority to do so. I can find no such authority in the cases which Mr. Wilmers has cited, nor even any analogous cases in which the law has been stretched as far. Of course, the construction of each Act depends upon its own terms, but I can find no authority in which any Act has been given anything like so wide an effect as Mr. Wilmers wants the Act of 1932 to be given. In the statutes to which the principle has been applied, what was prohibited was a contract which had at its centre—indeed often filling the whole space within its circumference—the prohibited act; contracts for the sale of prohibited goods, contracts for the sale of goods without accompanying documents when the statute specifically said there must be accompanying documents; contracts for work and labour done by persons who were prohibited from doing the whole of the work and labour for which they demanded recompense. It is going a long way further to say that contracts which depend for their performance upon the use of an instrument which has been treated in a forbidden way should also be forbidden. In the only case I have seen where the contention appeared to go as far as that the claim failed. The relevant facts in *Smith* v. *Mawhood*[1] appear sufficiently from the judgment of Alderson, B.,[2] where he also dealt with the contention: " But here the legislature has merely said that where a party carries on the trade or business of a dealer in or seller of tobacco, he shall be liable to a certain penalty, if the house in which he carries on the business shall not have his name, etc., painted on it, in letters publicly visible and legible, and at least an inch long, and so forth. He is liable to the penalty, therefore, by carrying on the trade in a house in which these requisites are not complied with; and there is no addition to his criminality if he makes fifty contracts for the *sale* of tobacco in such a house. It seems to me, therefore, that there is nothing in the Act of Parliament to prohibit every act of sale, but that its only effect is to impose a penalty, for the purpose of the revenue, on the carrying on of the trade without complying with its requisites."

A contract for the sale of tobacco was therefore not to be considered void merely because the premises in which the tobacco was sold did not comply with the law. So it might be said that a contract for carriage of goods is not to be considered void merely because the ship in which they are carried does not comply with the law. But I recognize that each case must be determined by reference to the relevant statute and not by comparison with other cases. I reach my conclusion—in the words of Lord Wright in *Vita Food Products Inc.* v. *United Shipping Co., Ltd.*[3]—on " the true construction of the statute, having regard to its scope and its purpose and to the inconvenience which would follow from any other conclusion."

In view of the importance of this question, I have thought it right to determine it upon general grounds rather than upon the particular wording of section 44. But I must note that Mr. Roskill also particularly relies upon the wording of subsection (2) of that section. This subsection, to which I have already referred, is the one which says that the fine is to be such " as the court thinks fit to impose having regard to the extent to which the

---

[1] (1845), 14 M. & W. 452. [2] *Ibid.*, 464.
[3] [1939] A. C. 277, at p. 295.

earning capacity of the ship was, or would have been, increased by reason of the submersion." Mr. Roskill submits that this shows that the statute contemplated that, notwithstanding the breach of it, there would be an " earning capacity " and, therefore, that contracts for the payment of freight must be intended to remain alive. I note that a similar point was taken in *Forster* v. *Taylor*[1], but it was not necessary for the court to deal with it.

I turn now to Mr. Wilmers's second point. He submitted that the plaintiffs could not succeed in a claim for freight without disclosing that they had committed an illegality in the course of the voyage; or, put another way, that part of the consideration for the payment of freight was the safe carriage of the goods, and therefore they must show that they carried the goods safely. In the passage I have quoted from the judgment in *Wetherell* v. *Jones*[2], Tenderden, C.J.[3], carefully distinguished between an infringement of the law in the performance of the contract and a case where " the consideration and the matter to be performed " were illegal. There is a distinction there—of the sort I have just been considering—between a contract which has as its object the doing of the very act forbidden by the statute, and a contract whose performance involves an illegality only incidentally. It may be, therefore, that the second point is the first point looked at from another angle. However that may be, there is no doubt that if the plaintiffs cannot succeed in their claim for freight without showing that they carried the goods in an overloaded ship, they must fail.

But, in my judgment, the plaintiffs need show no more in order to recover their freight than that they delivered to the defendants the goods they received in the same good order and condition as that in which they received them. Indeed, they are entitled to recover their freight without deduction (but subject to counterclaim) if the goods they delivered were substantially the same as when loaded: see Scrutton on Charterparties, 16th ed., p. 391, art. 144. It may be true that it is a term of the contract of carriage that the goods should be carried safely. Article III of the Hague Rules provides, for example, in rule 2, " that the carrier shall properly and carefully load, handle, stow, carry, keep, care for and discharge the goods carried." But no one has ever heard of a claim for freight being supported by a string of witnesses describing the loading, handling, stowing, keeping, caring for and discharging the goods. The truth is that if the goods have been delivered safely, it must follow that they have been carried safely. If, therefore, they are proved to have been delivered undamaged, the shipowner need prove no more. The law is that they shall be carried safely— not that they should not be exposed to danger on the voyage. If the plaintiffs had to prove that they were not exposed to danger on the voyage, then no doubt they would also have to prove that the ship complied with all the safety regulations affecting her; but in the claim for freight they need only prove safe delivery. This point fails.

On Mr. Wilmers's third point I take the law from the dictum in *Beresford* v. *Royal Insurance Co., Ltd.*[4] that was adopted and applied by Lord Atkin[5]: " no system of jurisprudence can with reason include amongst the rights which it enforces rights directly resulting to the person asserting them from the crime of that person." I observe in the first place that in the

---

[1] (1834), 5 B. & Ad. 887, at p. 889.
[3] *Ibid.*, 225. *Supra*, pp. 238–239.
[4] [1938] A. C. 586; [1938] 2 All E. R. 602.
[5] [1938] A. C. 586, at p. 596.

[2] (1832), 3 B. & Ad. 221.

Court of Appeal in the same case Lord Wright[1] doubted whether this principle applied to all statutory offences. His doubt was referred to by Denning, L.J., in *Marles* v. *Philip Trant & Sons*[2], which I have already cited. The distinction is much to the point here. The Act of 1932 imposes a penalty which is itself designed to deprive the offender of the benefits of his crime. It would be a curious thing if the operation could be performed twice—once by the criminal law and then again by the civil. It would be curious, too, if in a case in which the magistrates had thought fit to impose only a nominal fine, their decision could, in effect, be overridden in a civil action. But the question whether the rule applies to statutory offences is an important one which I do not wish to decide in the present case. The dicta of Lord Wright[3] and Denning, L.J.[4], suggest that there are cases where its application would be morally unjustifiable; but it is not clear that they go as far as saying that the application would not be justified in law. I prefer, therefore, to deal with Mr. Wilmers's submission in another way.

The rights which cannot be enforced must be those " directly resulting " from the crime. That means, I think, that for a right to money or to property to be unenforceable the property or money must be identifiable as something to which, but for the crime, the plaintiff would have had no right or title. That cannot be said in this case. The amount of the profit which the plaintiffs made from the crime, that is to say, the amount of freight which, but for the overloading, they could not have earned on this voyage, was, as I have said, £2,295. The quantity of cargo consigned to the defendants was approximately 35 per cent. of the whole and, therefore, even if it were permissible to treat the benefit as being divisible *pro rata* over the whole of the cargo, the amount embodied in the claim against the defendants would not be more than 35 per cent. of £2,300. That would not justify the withholding of £2,000. The fact is that the defendants and another cargo owner have between them withheld money, not on a basis that is proportionate to the claim against them, but so as to wipe out the improper profit on the whole of the cargo. I do not, however, think that the defendants' position would be any better if they had deducted no more than the sum attributable to their freight on a pro rata basis. There is no warrant under the principle for a *pro rata* division; it would be just as reasonable to say that the excess freight should be deemed to attach entirely to the last 427 tons loaded, leaving the freight claim on all the rest unaffected. But in truth there is no warrant for any particular form of division. The fact is that in this type of case no claim or part of a claim for freight can be clearly identified as being the excess illegally earned.

In *Beresford* v. *Royal Insurance Co., Ltd.*[5] the court dismissed the claim of a personal representative who claimed on policies of life insurance which had matured owing to the assured committing suicide in circumstances that amounted to a crime.[6] Mr. Wilmers submitted that the only benefit which the assured or his estate derived from the claim was the acceleration of the policies and that, notwithstanding that some of the policies had been in force for a considerable time and therefore, I suppose, had a surrender value before the suicide was committed, the plaintiff was not allowed to recover anything. So in the present case, he submits, the commission of the crime

[1] [1937] 2 K. B. 197, at p. 220; [1937] 2 All E. R. 243.
[2] [1954] 1 Q. B. 29, at p. 37.   [3] [1937] 2 K. B. 197, at p. 220.
[4] [1954] 1 Q. B. 29, at p. 37.   [5] [1938] A. C. 586.
[6] See now Suicide Act, 1961, s. 1.

defeats the whole claim to freight notwithstanding that the earning of the greater part of it was irrespective of the crime.

The comparison does not seem to me to be just. In *Beresford* v. *Royal Insurance Co., Ltd.*[1], but for the crime committed by the assured, no part of the policy moneys could have been claimed in that form, that is to say, as money repayable on the happening of the event insured against, or at that time. That does not necessarily mean that, so far as public policy was concerned, the plaintiff could recover nothing. If the plaintiff, for example, had sued for the return of premiums, assuming the contract permitted it, I have not been referred to any observation in the case which would suggest that an action in that form would fail on the grounds of public policy. The claim which the court was considering under the policy depended entirely upon proof of death, and the death was a crime. In the present case the right to claim freight from the defendants was not brought into existence by a crime; the crime affected only the total amount of freight earned by the ship.

The result is that there must be judgment for the plaintiffs for £2,000. But the defendants will not have fought the action altogether in vain if it brings to the attention of the competent authorities the fact that section 44 of the Act of 1932 is out of date and ought to be amended. I have already noted that for a similar offence a British master can be imprisoned and it must be very galling for those concerned to see a foreign master do the same thing without the law providing any effective deterrent.

Archbolds (Freightage), Ltd. v. S. Spanglett, Ltd.

(Randall, Third Party)

[1961] 1 All E.R. 417

PEARCE, L.J.: Judgment was given for the plaintiffs for £3,674 18s. 3d. damages in respect of the loss of a consignment of whisky which was stolen from the defendants owing to their negligence while they were transporting it as carriers for the plaintiffs from Leeds to the London Docks. Various matters raised in the defence were decided in the plaintiffs' favour. The issue on this appeal is whether the judge[2] should have held that the plaintiffs could not recover damages because the contract of carriage was illegal.

The facts material to this issue are these. The defendants are furniture manufacturers in London and own five vans for use in their business. Those vans have " C " licences under the Road and Rail Traffic Act, 1933, which enable them to carry the defendants' own goods but do not allow them to carry for reward the goods of others. The plaintiffs are carriers with offices at London and Leeds and also have a clearing house to assist with sub-contracting contracts of carriage. Their vehicles have " A " licences which enable them to carry the goods of others for reward. When some other carrier is returning home with an empty van having made a delivery, he may ask the plaintiffs if they have a load available for him; and if they have one available, it is obviously an economy for them to sub-contract that load to him instead of sending their own van with the risk of its having to return empty.

---

[1] [1938] A. C. 586   [2] Slade, J.

At the time of the Suez crisis there was a shortage of petrol and the Minister of Transport enlarged the scope of " C " licences to permit licensees to carry the goods of others which would normally be carried under " C " licences. This limited extension was presumably designed to leave the trade of " A " licence-holders unaffected. Although it was not strictly proved, it was assumed that the whisky in question was not whisky that would normally be carried under a " C " licence. Therefore it could not legally be carried for reward on any of the defendants' vans. The plaintiffs' London office as a result of a telephone conversation with some unidentified person who spoke from the defendants' office believed that the defendants' vehicles had " A " licences and were entitled to carry general goods. They therefore employed the defendants to carry for them a part load of goods on the defendants' van which was taking some of the defendants' own furniture from London to the Leeds area. On Mar. 27, 1956, Mr. Randall, the defendants' driver, having delivered those goods, spoke on the telephone to Mr. Field, the traffic manager at the plaintiffs' office in Leeds, in order to see if he could obtain a load for his empty van back from Leeds to London. Mr. Randall said who he was, that he was from the defendants and that he had just carried goods from the plaintiffs' London office to Leeds and " if possible would like a return load." He then said: " Have you anything for a covered van ?" Mr. Field replied that he had three and three-quarter tons. He left the telephone to make certain that the load was suitable for a covered van, returned to the telephone and told Mr. Randall to come to the plaintiffs' Leeds office. Mr. Field made no inquiry about Mr. Randall's licence because, to use his own words, " I knew he had been loaded by our London office." Mr. Randall came to the office, the van was loaded with the three and three-quarter tons, which was in fact two hundred cases of whisky, and set off for the London docks. The whisky was stolen owing to Mr. Randall's negligence.

On the issue of illegality the judge said this:

> " This case is one which falls within the class of case where the contract is not ab initio illegal, or indeed illegal at all vis-a-vis the plaintiffs in this action. In the contract of carriage, no stipulation was made as to what form the carriage should take. It was open to the defendants to carry the goods in any vehicle they liked so far as the plaintiffs were concerned. It is, of course, true that Mr. Field would contemplate that as it was a return load, it would in fact be taken back by Mr. Randall in the vehicle in which he brought the goods to Leeds on the outward journey, but Mr. Field never even saw the vehicle. No one whose knowledge could possibly be imputed to these plaintiffs ever did see the vehicle, and I have already found as a fact that they did not know that the vehicle in which Mr. Randall intended to take the goods to the Royal Albert Docks had in fact only a ' C ' licence. In so far, therefore, as it is a question of fact, I find the fact, and in so far as it is a question of law, I hold as a matter of law, that this contract was not of itself illegal, and that any illegality arose only in the method of its performance by the defendant company. I therefore find that the plea of illegality fails."

Mr. Karmel, in a concise and powerful argument for the defendants, contends that the learned judge should have found as a fact that the plaintiffs knew or that they ought to have known that the defendants' van had only a " C " licence and therefore could not legally carry the whisky. He also argues that even assuming that the plaintiffs were imposed on (as the judge found) and did not know of the " C " licence and were not negligent in failing to find out, yet the plaintiffs must fail because the contract of carriage was in fact unlawful, since it was a contract for carriage in that particular van (Mr. Randall's van) which could not be performed legally. The judge is in error, he contends, in saying: "It was open to the defendants to carry the goods in any vehicle they liked so far as the plaintiffs were concerned." On the question of the plaintiffs' knowledge the matters which were urged before us were urged before the trial judge, but he heard the witnesses and he decided otherwise. He said:

> "What is clear is that the most wilful piece of deception was practised on the plaintiffs by the defendants to persuade them to be allowed to carry this load, and to carry this load as I know now it was carried, on a 'C' licence vehicle. That is material only to the issue of illegality which is raised on the pleadings in this case."

Later the judge said:

> "As to the words ' as the plaintiffs well knew,' I asked counsel for the defendants, and he conceded that there was no evidence at all that the plaintiffs well knew, and I find as a fact that the plaintiffs did not know. I think that the high-water mark of what can be imputed to the plaintiffs or any servants of theirs—and of this there is no evidence—is that during the loading of the cases of whisky at the plaintiffs' Leeds warehouse, somewhere about a mile or some distance away from their offices, there was the vehicle as large as life, stamped all over as what I may call a furniture van, and anyone who had taken the trouble to look would have seen a ' C ' licence on its windscreen. There is no evidence that anyone did look or that the people whose sole task, having been instructed by their foreman, who authorised the loading, was to load the cases on to the lorry, directed their minds for one moment to the question of whether it was a ' C ' licence vehicle or a furniture van or a Carter Paterson van, or anything of the kind. As I say, I find as a fact that the plaintiffs did not know."

Again, he says:

> "No one whose knowledge could possibly be imputed to these plaintiffs ever did see the vehicle, and I have already found as a fact that they did not know that the vehicle in which Mr. Randall intended to take the goods to the Royal Albert Docks had in fact only a ' C ' licence."

He also held that any suggestion that Mr. Field ought to have inquired what licence was held by Mr. Randall's vehicle was completely answered by the fact that Mr. Field knew that Mr. Randall had made the journey to Leeds with a load put on the lorry by the plaintiffs' London office. The judge dealt very fully and carefully with the evidence, he heard the witnesses and he came to conclusions on their credibility. It is in just such a case as this, cases that turn on bona fides and knowledge and half-knowledge, that the trial judge has so great an advantage over a court that relies on the colourless, impersonal and sometimes misleading transcript. There were cogent arguments based on cross-examination of the witnesses that the plaintiffs must have known or suspected the true facts about the licence of Mr. Randall's vehicle, but in spite of them he came to the conclusion that the plaintiffs were imposed on and did not know, and he acquitted them of any bad faith in the matter. I am not prepared to disturb that finding. In so many cases of deception it is hard even for the persons deceived to imagine in retrospect how they could have made such a mistake, yet the fact remains that people are misled into foolish errors. In my judgment we should not be justified in making any finding that the plaintiffs knew or that they should have known that Mr. Randall's van had only a " C " licence.

It having been proved, therefore, that the plaintiffs were imposed on and believed that the goods could be lawfully carried on Mr. Randall's van, are they disentitled to sue ? Counsel for the defendants argues that the goods had to be carried in Mr. Randall's van alone and no other, and that the judge was wrong in holding that this contract of carriage was a general one to be performed by the defendants in any way that they might choose. Counsel for the plaintiffs argues on the other hand that this contract like many others was made with a particular method of performance in mind but was not restricted to that particular method of performance, and that haulage contracts are not so personal to the carrier that they cannot be vicariously performed. The point is not easy. I incline to the view held by the judge, but I do not find it necessary to express a concluded view on it.

Let us assume (although I am far from satisfied on this point) that the learned judge was in error in holding that the haulage contract could have been performed by the defendants in any way they liked (that is to say, lawfully as well as unlawfully). Let us assume first that it was a contract for carriage in Mr. Randall's van only and secondly that it was not by the nature of the contract one which could be performed vicariously. It must then inevitably be carried out unlawfully if (but only if) one adds the fact that Mr. Randall's van had a " C " licence and therefore could not lawfully carry the goods in question; but that fact, though known to the defendants, was unknown to the plaintiffs.

This is not a case where the plaintiffs can assert a cause of action without relying on the contract. Mr. Leonard put forward an ingenious alternative argument for the plaintiffs based on the plaintiffs' rights against the defendants as voluntary bailees of the plaintiffs' property (see *Bowmakers, Ltd.* v. *Barnet Instruments, Ltd.*[1]), so that he might claim in negligence or conversion without having any recourse to the contract or exposing to the court as part of his cause of action its alleged illegality; but I do not think that he can make good that argument. His cause of action comes from the contract, and if the contract is such that the court must refuse its aid, the plaintiffs cannot recover their damages.

If a contract is expressly or by necessary implication forbidden by statute, or if it is ex facie illegal, or if both parties know that though ex facie legal it can only be performed by illegality or is intended to be performed illegally, the law will not help the plaintiffs in any way that is a direct or indirect enforcement of rights under the contract; and for this purpose both parties are presumed to know the law.

The first question, therefore, is whether this contract of carriage was forbidden by statute. The two cases on which the defendants mainly rely are *Re Mahmoud and Ispahani*[2] and *Dennis & Co., Ltd.* v. *Munn*[3]. In both those cases the plaintiffs were unable to enforce their rights under contracts forbidden by statute. In the former case the Seeds, Oils, and Fats Order, 1919, art. 1 (a), provided:

" . . . a person shall not . . . buy or sell . . . [certain] articles . . . except under and in accordance with the terms of a licence . . . "

In the latter case the Defence (General) Regulations, 1939, reg. 56A (1) said:

" Subject to the provisions of this regulation the execution . . . of any operation specified . . . shall be unlawful . . . "

except in so far as authorised. In neither case could the plaintiff bring his contract within the exception that alone would have made its subject-matter lawful, namely, by showing the existence of a licence. Therefore, the core of

---

[1] [1945] K.B. 65; [1944] 2 All E.R. 579.
[2] [1921] 2 K.B. 716; [1921] All E.R. Rep. 217.
[3] [1949] 2 K.B. 327; [1949] 1 All E.R. 616.

both contracts was the mischief expressly forbidden by the statutory order and the statutory regulation respectively. In *Re Mahmoud*[1] the object of the order was to prevent (except under licence) a person buying and a person selling and both parties were liable to penalties. A contract for sale between those persons was therefore expressly forbidden. In *Dennis's* case[2] the object of the regulation was to prevent (except under licence) owners from performing building operations and builders from carrying out the work for them. Both parties were liable to penalties and a contract between these persons for carrying out an unlawful operation would be forbidden by implication.

The case before us is somewhat different. The carriage of the plaintiffs' whisky was not as such prohibited; the statute merely regulated the means by which carriers should carry goods. Therefore this contract was not expressly forbidden by the statute. Was it then forbidden by implication? The Road and Rail Traffic Act, 1933, s. 1 (1), says:

" . . . no person shall use a goods vehicle on a road for the carriage of goods . . . except under a licence,"

and provides that such use shall be an offence. Did the statute thereby intend to forbid by implication all contracts whose performance must on all the facts (whether known or not) result in a contravention of that section? The plaintiffs' part of the contract could not constitute an illegal use of the vehicle by them since they were not " using " the vehicle. If they were aware of the true facts they would, of course, be guilty of aiding and abetting the defendants, but if they acted in good faith they would not be guilty of any offence under the statute (*Davies, Turner & Co., Ltd.* v. *Brodie*[3]; and see *Carter* v. *Mace*[4]). In this case, therefore, the plaintiffs were not committing any offence.

In *St. John Shipping Corpn.* v. *Joseph Rank, Ltd.*[5] Devlin, J., held that the plaintiffs were entitled to recover although there had been an infringement of a statute in the performance of a contract, but in that case the contract was legal when made. Though not directly applicable to the present case, it contains an observation (with which I entirely agree) on the point which arises here. He said[6]:

" For example, a person is forbidden by statute from using an unlicensed vehicle on the highway. If one asks oneself whether there is in such an enactment an implied prohibition of all contracts for the use of unlicensed vehicles, the answer may well be that there is, and that contracts of hire would be unenforceable. But if one asks oneself whether there is an implied prohibition of contracts for the carriage of goods by unlicensed vehicles . . . the answer may well be different. The answer may be that collateral contracts of this sort are not within the ambit of the statute."

In my judgment that distinction is valid.

The object of the Rail and Road Traffic Act, 1933, was not (in this connexion) to interfere with the owner of goods or his facilities for transport, but to control those who provided the transport with a view to promoting its efficiency. Transport of goods was not made illegal but the various licence-holders were prohibited from encroaching on one another's territory, the intention of the Act being to provide an orderly and comprehensive service. Penalties were provided for those licence-holders who went outside the

[1] [1921] 2 K.B. 716; [1921] All E.R. Rep. 217. [2] [1949] 2 K.B. 327; [1949] 1 All E.R. 616.
[3] [1954] 3 All E.R. 283.   [4] [1949] 2 All E.R. 714.
[5] [1957] 1 Q.B. 267; [1956] 3 All E.R. 683.
[6] [1957] 1 Q.B. at p. 287; [1956] 3 All E.R. at p. 690. *Supra*, p. 239.

bounds of their allotted sphere. These penalties apply to those using the vehicle but not to the goods owner. Though the latter could be convicted of aiding and abetting any breach, the restrictions were not aimed at him. Thus a contract of carriage was, in the sense used by Devlin, J.[1] " collateral " and it was not impliedly forbidden by the statute.

This view is supported by common sense and convenience. If the other view were held it would have far-reaching effects. For instance, if a carrier induces me (who am in fact ignorant of any illegality) to entrust goods to him and negligently destroys them, he would only have to show that (though unknown to me) his licence had expired or did not properly cover the transportation or that he was uninsured and I should then be without a remedy against him. Or again, if I ride in a taxicab and the driver leaves me stranded in some deserted spot, he would only have to show that he was (though unknown to me) unlicensed or uninsured, and I should be without remedy. This appears to me an undesirable extension of the implications of a statute.

In *Vita Food Products, Incorporated* v. *United Shipping Co., Ltd.*[2] Lord Wright said:

> " Each case has to be considered on its merits. Nor must it be forgotten that the rule by which contracts, not expressly forbidden by statute or declared to be void, are in proper cases nullified for disobedience to a statute is a rule of public policy only, and public policy understood in a wider sense may at times be better served by refusing to nullify a bargain save on serious and sufficient grounds."

If the court too readily implies that a contract is forbidden by statute, it takes it out of its own power (so far as that contract is concerned) to discriminate between guilt and innocence. If, however, the court makes no such implication, it still leaves itself with the general power, based on public policy, to hold those contracts unenforceable which are ex facie unlawful, and also to refuse its aid to guilty parties in respect of contracts which to the knowledge of both can only be performed by a contravention of the statute (see *Nash* v. *Stevenson Transport, Ltd.*[3]) or which though apparently lawful are intended to be performed illegally or for an illegal purpose (for example, *Pearce* v. *Brooks*[4]). It is for the defendants to show that contracts by the owner for the carriage of goods are within the ambit of the implied prohibition of the Road and Rail Traffic Act, 1933. In my judgment they have not done so.

The next question is whether this contract, though not forbidden by statute, was ex facie illegal. Must any reasonable person on hearing the terms of the contract (with presumed knowledge of the law) realise that it was illegal ? There is nothing illegal in its terms. Further knowledge, namely, knowledge of the fact that Mr. Randall's van was not properly licensed, would show that it could only be performed by contravention of the statute, but that does not make the contract ex facie illegal.

However, if both parties had that knowledge the contract would be unenforceable as being a contract which to their knowledge could not be carried out without a violation of the law (see per Blackburn, J., in *Waugh* v. *Morris*[5]) but where one party is ignorant of the fact that will make the performance illegal, is it established that the innocent party cannot obtain

---

[1] [1957] 1 Q.B. at 287; [1956] 3 All E.R. at 690.
[2] [1939] A.C. at 293; [1939] 1 All E.R. at 523.
[3] [1936] 2 K.B. 128; [1936] 1 All E.R. 906.
[4] (1866), L.R. 1 Exch. 213; *infra*, p. 259.
[5] (1873), L.R. 8 Q.B. at p. 208.

relief against the guilty party ? The case has been argued with skill and care on both sides, and yet no case has been cited to us establishing the proposition that where a contract is on the face of it legal and is not forbidden by statute, but must in fact produce illegality by reason of a circumstance known to one party only, it should be held illegal so as to debar the innocent party from relief. In the absence of such a case I do not feel compelled to so unsatisfactory a conclusion, which would injure the innocent, benefit the guilty, and put a premium on deceit. Such a conclusion (in cases like this where a contract is not forbidden by statute) can only derive from public policy. For the reasons given by Lord Wright, which I have read[1], an extension of the law in this direction would be more harmful than beneficial. No question of moral turpitude arises here. The alleged illegality is, so far as the plaintiffs were concerned, the permitting of their goods to be carried by the wrong carrier, namely, a carrier who, unknown to them, was not allowed by his licence to carry that particular class of goods. The plaintiffs were never in delicto since they did not know the vital fact that would make the performance of the contract illegal.

In my view, therefore, public policy does not constrain us to refuse our aid to the plaintiffs and they are, therefore, entitled to succeed. I would dismiss the appeal.

SELLERS and DEVLIN, L.J.J., delivered judgments to the same effect.

Amar Singh v. Kulubya

[1963] 3 All E.R. 499

Property transferred under a contract, which, as made, is prohibited by statute, can not be recovered unless the plaintiff can establish a cause of action without being compelled to disclose and rely on the illegality. But if the parties are not *in pari delicto* special relief may be given to the less blameworthy party.

A statutory ordinance in Uganda prohibited the sale or lease of " Mailo " land by an African to a non-African, save with the written consent of the Governor. Without obtaining this consent, the plaintiff, an African, agreed to lease such land, of which he was the registered owner, to the defendant, an Indian, for one year and thereafter on a yearly basis. This agreement was therefore illegal and void; and no leasehold interest vested in the defendant. After the defendant had been in possession for several years, the plaintiff (the African) gave him seven weeks' notice to quit, and ultimately sued him to recover the land.

At first instance the plaintiff's action was dismissed. This judgment was reversed by the Court of Appeal for Eastern Africa, and a decree was made in the plaintiff's favour. The defendant (the non-African) appealed to the Judicial Committee of the Privy Council, who affirmed the decision of the Court of Appeal.

LORD MORRIS stated the facts and said:

ON APPEAL by the plaintiff to the Court of Appeal the appeal was allowed and a decree was made, which provided that the defendant should be evicted from the lands and should grant possession to the plaintiff. In the judgments it was pointed out (rightly as their lordships think) that a rejection of the

---

[1] See *supra*, p. 249.

plaintiff's claim would have the result that the defendant, a non-African, would be entitled to remain permanently in possession of African land, to the exclusion of the registered African owner, and without payment of any nature whatsoever.

Although as has been seen, the plaintiff set out in his plaint that he had entered into agreements to lease the plots of land to the defendant his right to claim possession did not depend on those agreements. His claim was in the end based independently of those agreements. Though the plaintiff did in his plaint claim mesne profits and damages he later abandoned those claims and at the trial he made no claim for rent or for mesne profits. He was able to rest his claim on his registered ownership of the property. The defendant did not have and could not show any right to the property. In view of the terms of the legislative provisions he could not assert that he had acquired any leasehold interest. For the same reason the defendant could not assert that he had any right to occupy. As a non-African he had no right without the consent in writing of the Governor to occupy or enter into possession of the land or to make any contract to take the land on lease. Quite irrespective of the circumstance that the plaintiff by giving certain notices to quit had purported to withdraw any permission to occupy, the defendant was not and never had been in lawful occupation. The defendant for his part could not point to or rely on the illegal agreements as justifying any right or claim to remain in possession, and without doing so he could not defeat the plaintiff's claim to possession. In so far as the plaintiff may have thought that in the circumstances it was reasonable to give the defendant notices to quit he could give such notices without their being related to or dependent on the unlawful agreements. Because the agreements were unlawful no leasehold interest vested in the defendant. He had no right to hold over or to hold from year to year. His occupation of the land was contrary to law.

Their lordships consider therefore that the plaintiff's right to possession was in no way based on the purported agreements. It was the defendant who might have needed to rely on them, because, had they been valid and permissible agreements, the defendant would have contended that the tenancies would have needed for their termination longer periods of notice than those contained in the notices to quit that were given. As it was, the contention of the defendant (based on para. 3 of the defence) was that the plaintiff was disabled from suing because he had been a party to illegal agreements. It was quite correct, as set out in that paragraph of the defence, that the plaintiff had been a party to illegal agreements. At the time of the trial, however, he was not basing his claim " on the said agreements ". Indeed he could have presented his claim (if it were limited to a claim for possession) without being under any necessity of setting out the unlawful agreements in his plaint. He required no aid from the illegal transactions in order to establish his case. (Compare *Simpson* v. *Bloss*[1].) It was sufficient for him to show that he was the registered proprietor of the plots of land and that the defendant who was a non-African was in occupation without possessing the consent in writing of the Governor for such occupation and accordingly had no right to occupy. It is true that the plaintiff referred to the purported agreements to which he had been a party and that he repudiated them and acknowledged that they were illegal. It was, however, in spite of and not because of those illegal agreements that he was entitled to possession. Though the plaintiff

---

[1] (1816), 7 Taunt. 246.

had offended by being a party to the illegal and ineffective agreements their lordships do not consider that considerations of public policy demanded the failure of his claim for possession: on the contrary such considerations pointed to the necessity of upholding it in order to eject a non-African who was in unlawful occupation. Their lordships agree with FORBES, V.P.,

> " that it would be contrary to public policy for the courts to refuse to assist an African to eject a non-African in illegal occupation of the former's land, even though the African may have committed an illegal act in permitting the non-African to enter on the land."

This their lordships consider is in line with the decision of the Court of Appeal in *Bowmakers, Ltd.* v. *Barnet Instruments, Ltd*[1], in which case DU PARCQ, L.J., delivering the judgment of the court said[2]:

> " *Prima facie*, a man is entitled to his own property, and it is not a general principle of our law (as was suggested) that when one man's goods have got into another's possession in consequence of some unlawful dealings between them, the true owner can never be allowed to recover those goods by an action. The necessity of such a principle to the interests and advancement of public policy is certainly not obvious. The suggestion that it exists is not, in our opinion, supported by authority."

In his judgment in *Scott* v. *Brown, Doering, McNab & Co., Slaughter and May* v. *Brown, Doering, McNab & Co*[3], LINDLEY, L.J.[4] thus expressed a well-established principle of law:

> " *Ex turpi causa non oritur actio.* This old and well-known legal maxim is founded in good sense, and expresses a clear and well-recognised legal principle, which is not confined to indictable offences. No court ought to enforce an illegal contract or allow itself to be made the instrument of enforcing obligations alleged to arise out of a contract or transaction which is illegal, if the illegality is duly brought to the notice of the court, and if the person invoking the aid of the court is himself implicated in the illegality. It matters not whether the defendant has pleaded the illegality or whether he has not. If the evidence adduced by the plaintiff proves the illegality the court ought not to assist him."

LINDLEY, L.J., added[5]: " Any rights which he may have irrespective of his illegal contract will, of course, be recognised and enforced ". A. L. SMITH, L.J.[6], said:

> " If a plaintiff cannot maintain his cause of action without showing, as part of such cause of action, that he has been guilty of illegality, then the courts will not assist him in his cause of action."

In the earlier case of *Taylor* v. *Chester*[7] it was said[8]:

> " The true test for determining whether or not the plaintiff and the defendant were *in pari delicto*, is by considering whether the plaintiff could make out his case otherwise than through the medium and by the aid of the illegal transaction to which he was himself a party."

In that case it became impossible for the plaintiff to recover except through the medium and by the aid of an illegal transaction to which he was himself a party. He was therefore defeated by the principle which is expressed in the maxim " *in pari delicto potior est conditio possidentis* '. That was a case, therefore, where a plaintiff was forced, in order to support his claim, to

---

[1] [1945] K.B. 65; [1944] 2 All E.R. 579.
[2] [1945] K.B. at p. 70; [1944] 2 All E.R. at p. 582.
[3] [1892] 2 Q.B. 724; [1891–94] All E.R. Rep. 654.
[4] [1892] 2 Q.B. at p. 728; [1891–94] All E.R. Rep. at p. 657.
[5] [1892] 2 Q.B. at p. 729; [1891–94] All E.R. Rep. at p. 657.
[6] [1892] 2 Q.B. at p. 734; [1891–94] All E.R. Rep. at p. 660.
[7] (1869), L.R. 4 Q.B. 309.
[8] (1869), L.R. 4 Q.B. at p. 314.

plead the illegality of a contract. The case was referred to in the judgment of the Court of Appeal, in *Bowmakers, Ltd.* v. *Barnet Instruments, Ltd.*[1], where it was said[2]:

> " In our opinion, a man's right to possess his own chattels will as a general rule be enforced against one who, without any claim of right, is detaining them, or, has converted them to his own use, even though it may appear either from the pleadings, or in the course of the trial, that the chattels in question came into the defendant's possession by reason of an illegal contract between himself and the plaintiff, provided that the plaintiff does not seek, and is not forced, either to found his claim on the illegal contract or to plead its illegality in order to support his claim."

For these reasons their lordships consider that the plaintiff was neither obliged to found his claim on the illegal agreements into which he entered nor, in order to support his claim, to plead or to depend on the agreements. He was not therefore " *in pari delicto* " with the defendant.

This conclusion is reinforced when the scope and purpose of the legislative provisions are considered. Their lordships agree with the view expressed in the Court of Appeal that the legislation was intended to be for the benefit of Africans as a class. In a case in 1957 the Court of Appeal for Eastern Africa recognised that the object of the Land Transfer Ordinance was to protect Africans by regulating any transfer of Mailo land and by controlling (as a matter of public policy) the sale of Mailo land to non-Africans. (See *Motibai Manji* v. *Khursid Begum*[3]). Section 2 of the Land Transfer Ordinance positively prohibits occupation by a non-African unless the consent in writing of the Governor has been given. A non-African who commits a breach of the provisions of the ordinance becomes guilty of an offence. The circumstance that under the Possession of Land Law an owner of " Mailo" land also commits an offence if, without the appoval in writing of the Governor and the Lukiko, he permits " one who is not of the Protectorate " to lease, occupy or use such land does not alter the fact that the purpose of the legislation is to protect Africans and to preserve African land for use by Africans. In this case the plaintiff, in spite of what was set out in his pleadings and in spite of the claims which the pleadings at first contained, did not at the trial in any way rely on or seek to enforce the unlawful agreements, though he had himself made it known that he had entered into them. That however did not make him " *in pari delicto* " with the defendant. He was a member of the protected class.

In his judgment in *Browning* v. *Morris*[4] LORD MANSFIELD said[5]:

> " But, where contracts or transactions are prohibited by positive statutes, for the sake of protecting one set of men from another set of men; the one, from their situation and condition, being liable to be oppressed or imposed upon by the other; there, the parties are not *in pari delicto*; and in furtherance of these statutes, the person injured, after the transaction is finished and completed, may bring his action and defeat the contract,"

So in *Kearley* v. *Thomson*[6] FRY, L.J.[7], referred to the case of oppressor and oppressed,

> " . . . in which case usually the oppressed party may recover the money back from the oppressor. In that class of cases the *delictum* is not *par*, and therefore the maxim does not apply. Again, there are other illegalities which arise

---

[1] [1945] K.B. 65; [1944] 2 All E.R. 579.
[2] [1945] K.B. at p. 71; [1944] 2 All E.R. at p. 582.
[3] [1957] E.A.L.R. 101.   [4] (1778), 2 Cowp. 790.
[5] (1778), 2 Cowp. at p. 792.   [6] (1890), 24 Q.B.D. 742.
[7] (1890), 24 Q.B.D. at p. 745.

where a statute has been intended to protect a class of persons, and the person seeking to recover is a member of the protected class. Instances of that description are familiar in the case of contracts void for usury under the old statutes, and other instances are to be found in the books under other statutes, which are, I believe, now repealed, such as those directed against lottery keepers. In these cases of oppressor and oppressed, or of a class protected by statute, the one may recover from the other, notwithstanding that both have been parties to the illegal contract."

Their lordships agree with the conclusions which were reached in the Court of Appeal and accordingly will humbly advise Her Majesty that the appeal should be dismissed. The defendant must pay the costs of the appeal.

Appeal dismissed.

Spector v. Ageda
[1971] 3 All E.R. 417

A subsequent or collateral contract, which is founded upon or springs from an illegal transaction, is itself illegal and void. This requires little argument when the parties to the original transaction and those to the subsequent or collateral contract are the same persons. If a third person is a party to the subsequent or collateral contract and has full knowledge of the prior illegality, he will, in general, be in no better position than that of the original parties.

A memorandum dated September 8th, 1967, stated that a Mrs. Maxwell, a moneylender, had lent £1,040 to the borrower, to be repaid on November 8, with interest at two per cent. a month. In fact only £1,000 was lent, since interest for two months, amounting to £40, had been added to the principal sum. Such a provision for compound interest is illegal under the Moneylenders Act, 1927, s. 7. The illegal loan was not repaid on November 8; and Mrs. Maxwell sued the borrower in the following February for the recovery of £1,180, the amount then alleged to be due.

At that point the plaintiff entered upon the scene. She was the sister and the solicitor of Mrs. Maxwell, but she was now acting as the solicitor of the borrower. She agreed to advance to the borrower £1,180 with interest at 12 per cent. per annum. She fulfilled this agreement, and the Maxwell loan was repaid. She now sued the borrower for the repayment of £1,180, together with interest at 12 per cent.

MEGARRY, J., stated the facts and said:

The Moneylenders Act 1927, s. 1 (3), provides as follows:

" If any person . . . (b) carries on business as a moneylender without having in force a proper moneylender's excise licence authorising him so to do, or, being licensed as a moneylender, carries on business as such in any name other than his authorised name, or at any other place than his authorised address or addresses, ... he shall be guilty of a contravention of the provisions of this Act and shall for each offence be liable to an excise penalty of one hundred pounds . . ."

Then there is a proviso that I need not read. The loan by Mrs. Maxwell was in breach of this provision. Section 6 (1) provides for a contract for repayment to a moneylender to be unenforceable unless a note or memorandum in writing is made and signed personally by the borrower, and a copy is delivered or sent to him within seven days, and so on. Then s. 6 (2) provides:

" The note or memorandum aforesaid shall contain all the terms of the contract, and in particular shall show the date on which the loan is made, the amount of the principal of the loan, and either the interest charged on the loan expressed in terms of a rate per cent, per annum, or the rate per cent, per annum represented by the interest charged as calculated in accordance with the provisions of the First Schedule to this Act."

The loan by Mrs. Maxwell was also in breach of this provision, in that even in its final form the note or memorandum failed to show the interest as a rate per cent. per annum, the printed words on the blank form which provided for this having been deleted. Section 7 provides:

> " Subject as hereinafter provided, any contract made after the commencement of this Act for the loan of money by a moneylender shall be illegal in so far as it provides directly or indirectly for the payment of compound interest or for the rate or amount of interest being increased by reason of any default in the payment of sums due under the contract . . . ."

There is then a proviso dealing with interest on principal or interest after there has been a default, which neither side has relied on. The memorandum in its final form was a contravention of this provision in that it provided for payment of 2 per cent. per month interest on £1,040, and of that sum £40 was not principal but interest, so that before there had been any default, interest was to be paid on interest. The words " it provides directly or indirectly for the payment of compound interest " are thus satisfied, and to that extent the contract of loan is illegal. I can see no reason why the word " illegal " in s. 7 should not mean " illegal " and not, as counsel for Mrs. Spector contended, merely " void ".

One question that was accordingly debated was whether a loan knowingly made in order to discharge an existing loan that was wholly or partially illegal was itself tainted with illegality. A transaction may simply be void, or it may be unenforceable, and in either case other connected transactions may nevertheless be perfectly valid and enforceable. But illegality is another matter: for it may be contagious. In relation to a transaction that is wholly illegal, Cheshire and Fifoot's Law of Contract[1] in effect answer Yes to the question that I have mentioned. It is there said:

> " If, for example, A and B borrow £500 from C in order to pay a loss that they have suffered in an illegal transaction, C cannot recover the loan if he was aware of the purpose upon which it was to be expended, but presumably he will succeed if he proves his ignorance of that purpose.'

For this proposition, *Cannan* v. *Bryce*[2] is cited. Treitel's Law of Contract[3] is similar:

> ". . . a loan of money is illegal if it is made to enable the borrower to make or to perform an illegal contract, or to pay a debt contracted under an illegal contract."

Again *Cannan* v. *Bryce*[2] is cited as the sole authority for the proposition about paying a debt contracted under an illegal contract.

With respect, I do not think that *Cannan* v. *Bryce*[2] wholly supports the proposition in either book, though that, of course, does not necessarily mean that the proposition is wrong. In *Cannan* v. *Bryce*[2] the statute in question was the Act 7 Geo 2, c. 8, 1734, designed to prevent " the wicked, pernicious and destructive Practice of Stock-jobbing ". Section 5 imposed a penalty of £100 on every person who should " voluntarily compound, make up, pay, satisfy, take or receive " any difference-money or other consideration.

---

[1] 7th Edn., 1969, p. 307.
[2] (1819), 3 B. & Ald. 179, [1814–23] All E.R. Rep. 718.
[3] 3rd Edn, 1970, p. 436.

Abbott, C.J., who delivered the judgment of the court emphasised this, saying that[1]—

> " the act of paying or receiving is prohibited absolutely, and those who pay and those who receive, are both placed *in pari delicto*."

A little later on, he said[1]:

> ". . . as the statute in question has absolutely prohibited the payment of money for compounding differences, it is impossible to say that the making of such payment is not an unlawful act; and if it be unlawful in one man to pay, how can it be lawful for another to furnish him with the means of payment? "

A loan made for the purpose of enabling the borrower to pay or compound differences on a stock-jobbing transaction was thus held itself to be illegal.

On the face of it, this decision does not necessarily cover a case where a loan is made for the purpose of discharging an obligation arising under an illegal contract but there is nothing in the statute to strike the making of any payment under that contract with illegality. If a transaction is illegal, no proceedings can be brought to enforce any payment under it: but it was contended that unless, as in *Cannan* v. *Bryce*[2], statute provides that it shall be illegal to make or receive any payment under the contract, there is nothing to stop one of the parties from voluntarily choosing to make a payment under it, or binding himself to do so. He who wishes may give, or oblige himself to give. If that is so, what is there to affect with illegality any loan made for the purpose of making a voluntary payment of this kind? Thus ran the argument.

Counsel for Miss Ageda sought to meet this by contending that for an unlicensed moneylender to receive payment of a loan was for that moneylender to contravene s. 1 (3) of the Act of 1927 as carrying on business as a moneylender; and then, of course, questions arise as to the lender's knowledge that the moneylender was unlicensed. Without going into that, it seems to me that the answer lies in a case cited on the same page of Cheshire and Fifoot[3] that I have just mentioned as being the leading authority: *Fisher* v. *Bridges*[4]. If one goes back to the decision of the Court of Queen's Bench in that case[5], one can see the court accepting there just the sort of argument that has been put forward in this case. In that case, there was a purchase by way of an illegal lottery, and subsequently the defendant entered into a covenant with the plaintiff to pay him some money remaining due. This was treated as being a mere voluntary agreement to pay a sum of money after the illegal purposes had come to an end, and so was enforceable. The Court of Exchequer Chamber, however, reversed this decision in a judgment delivered by Jervis, C.J. The essence of the decision appears, I think, in this passage[6]:

> " It is clear that the covenant was given for payment of the purchase money. It springs from, and is a creature of, the illegal agreement; and, as the law would not enforce the original illegal contract, so neither will it allow the parties to enforce a security for the purchase money, which by the original bargain was tainted with illegality."

In that case, the subsequent transaction was between the original parties: but a third party who takes part in the subsequent transaction with knowledge of the prior illegality can, in general, be in no better position. Accordingly, it

---

[1] (1819), 3 B. & Ald. at p. 184, [1814–23] All E.R. Rep. at p. 721.
[2] (1819) B. & Ald. 179, [1814–23] All E.R. Rep. 718.   [3] See p. 307.
[4] (1854), 3 E. & B. 642. (See now Cheshire and Fifoot, 8th edn., p. 347.)
[5] (1853), 2 E. & B. 118.
[6] (1854), 3 E. & B. at 649.

seems to me that the propositions stated in the books are in essence correct, even though they need the support of *Fisher* v. *Bridges*[1] in addition to *Cannan* v. *Bryce*[2]. In relation to the case before me, if Mrs. Spector lent money to the borrowers knowing that it was to be used for the discharge of an illegal loan, Mrs. Spector's loan is also tainted with illegality, and she cannot enforce repayment of her loan. I may add that I am, of course, concerned here with the purpose or object type of case, when the attack on the transaction in question is made on the ground of the purpose for which it was entered into. I am not concerned with those cases such as *Simpson* v. *Bloss*[3], where the attack is based on some other form of connection, such as the impossibility of establishing the disputed transaction without also establishing the illegal transaction. I do not, however, think that there is any incompatibility between the two lines of cases.

Now, as I have already held, the illegality in the loan by Mrs. Maxwell falls under the two main heads of her being unlicensed, and the provision for compound interest. As regards the lack of a licence, on the evidence before me I do not think that it has been brought home to Mrs. Spector that she knew that her sister held no moneylender's licence. I think that she ought to have known, but I am far from satisfied that she either had actual knowledge, or that she deliberately shut her eyes to the matter. Accordingly, in my judgment her loan to the borrowers cannot be held to be illegal on this score.

I turn, then, to the illegality in respect of compound interest. Here there is no question but that Mrs. Spector had full knowledge of the facts that constituted the illegality: and, as a solicitor who had admittedly studied the law of moneylending, I think that she knew that these facts constituted an illegality, if, indeed, it is necessary to demonstrate this knowledge. The contract, however, is only made illegal " so far as it provides directly or indirectly for the payment of compound interest ". Quoad the principal sum of £1,000 in truth lent by Mrs. Maxwell to the borrowers, there is no illegality under this head: quoad the £40 untruly represented as being part of the principal sum lent, but in reality constituting interest, the contract is illegal. There has been no satisfactory explanation of the constituent parts of the sum of £1,180 which, when lent by Mrs. Spector, was used to discharge the loan to Mrs. Maxwell. I think that where what is sued on is a loan made with the object of discharging an earlier loan containing an illegality, it is for the party who seeks to rely on that later loan to demonstrate that in some way it has been purged of any connection with the illegal element in the earlier loan. Here Mrs. Spector is relying on a loan that she made with the object of discharging the loan by Mrs. Maxwell which Mrs. Spector knew to be tainted by illegality, and as she has not demonstrated or even suggested that there was any abandonment or exclusion of the illegal segment of Mrs. Maxwell's loan, I cannot hold that there was any such abandonment or exclusion. The loan that Mrs. Spector made to the borrowers was thus manifestly made for the purpose of discharging a contract which was in part illegal. Further, it has not been suggested that the loan that Mrs. Spector made could be apportioned or severed in any way, even though the loan by Mrs. Maxwell was illegal only in part.

---

[1] (1854), 3 E. & B. 642.
[2] (1819) B. & Ald. 179, [1814–23] All E.R. Rep. 718.
[3] (1816), 7 Taunt 246.

No authority has been put before me which states the law applicable to a subsequent transaction which is based on a contract which is illegal only in part, and I do not wish to decide more than is necessary to dispose of this case. It seems to me that where, as here, the subsequent transaction is entered into by a person who not only knows of the partial illegality of the prior contract but also is in a real degree responsible for it and wishes to avoid the consequences of it (as I think that Mrs. Spector probably did), then unless that partial illegality is shown to relate solely to some defined portion of the subsequent transaction, so that only that defined portion is affected, the whole of the subsequent transaction will be affected by the illegality. I cannot see why the court should be astute to limit the effects of the illegality and make some artificial apportionment of the subsequent transaction for this purpose. When the illegality affects only a small part of the prior contract it may seem somewhat Draconian to hold that the whole of the subsequent transaction is affected by the illegality: but illegality is illegality, and it is not for the courts to devise means of preventing those who are implicated from burning their fingers more than to a limited extent.

Of course, the borrowers have had Mrs. Spector's money, and *prima facie* at least they ought to repay it: courts of law do not exist in order to help people to escape from their obligations. But where statute has intervened to strike a transaction with illegality, the courts must give effect not only to the direct provisions of the statute but also to their necessary consequences. Further, in so far as the merits come into the picture, I am not sorry that the result should be in favour of the borrowers. Accordingly, on the ground of illegality Mrs. Spector's claim fails.

[MEGARRY, J., then turned to other questions raised by the action, such as the relationship between solicitor and client.]

CONTRACTS ILLEGAL AT COMMON LAW ON GROUNDS OF PUBLIC POLICY

PEARCE *v.* BROOKS

NAPIER *v.* NATIONAL BUSINESS AGENCY, LTD.

BERG *v.* SADLER AND MOORE

Under the common law doctrine of Public Policy contracts may fall into two classes according to the degree of mischief which they involve. If they violate no basic concept of morality but run counter only to social or economic expediency, they are void. But if, either as formed or as performed, they are so obviously inimical to the interests of the community that they offend basic conceptions of public policy, they are not only void but also illegal.

Pearce v. Brooks

(1866), L.R. 1 Ex. 213

DECLARATION stating an agreement by which the plaintiffs agreed to supply the defendant with a new miniature brougham on hire, till the purchase money should be paid by instalments in a period which was not to exceed twelve months ; the defendant to have the option to purchase as aforesaid, and to pay 50*l.* down ; and in case the brougham should be returned before a second instalment was paid, a forfeiture of fifteen guineas was to be paid in addition to the 50*l.*, and also any damage, except fair wear. Averment, that the defendant returned the brougham before a second instalment was paid, and that it was damaged. Breach, non-payment of fifteen guineas, or the amount of the damage. Money counts.

Plea 3, to the first count, that at the time of making the supposed agreement, the defendant was to the knowledge of the plaintiffs a prostitute, and that the supposed agreement was made for the supply of a brougham to be used by her as such prostitute, and to assist her in carrying on her said immoral vocation, as the plaintiffs when they made the said agreement well knew, and in the expectation by the plaintiffs that the defendant would pay the plaintiffs the moneys to be paid by the said agreement out of her receipts as such prostitute. Issue.

The case was tried before Bramwell, B., at Guildhall, at the sittings after Michaelmas Term, 1865. It then appeared that the plaintiffs were coach-builders in partnership, and evidence was given which satisfied the jury that one of the partners knew that the defendant was a prostitute ; but there was no direct evidence that either of the plaintiffs knew that the brougham was intended to be used for the purpose of enabling the defendant to prosecute her trade of prostitution ; and there was no evidence that the plaintiffs expected to be paid out of the wages of prostitution.

The learned judge ruled that the allegation in the plea as to the mode of payment was immaterial, and he put to the jury the following questions : 1. Did the defendant hire the brougham for the purpose of her prostitution ? 2. If she did, did the plaintiffs know the purpose for which it was hired ? The jury found that the carriage was used by the defendant as part of her display, to attract men ; and that the plaintiffs knew it was supplied to be used for that purpose. They gave nothing for the alleged damage.

On this finding, the learned judge directed a verdict for the defendant, and gave the plaintiffs leave to move to enter a verdict for them for the fifteen guineas penalty.

M. Chambers, Q.C., in Hilary Term, obtained a rule accordingly, on the ground that there was no evidence that the plaintiffs knew the purpose for which the brougham was to be used ; and that if there was, the allegation in the plea that the plaintiffs expected to be paid out of the receipts of defendant's prostitution was a material allegation, and had not been proved : *Bowry* v. *Bennett*[1].

[POLLOCK, C.B., referred to *Cannan* v. *Bryce*[2].]

Digby Seymour, Q.C., and *Beresford*, showed cause. No direct evidence could be given of the plaintiffs' knowledge that the defendant was about to use the carriage for the purpose of prostitution ; but the fact that a person known to be a prostitute hires an ornamental brougham is sufficient ground for the finding of the jury.

[BRAMWELL, B. At the trial I was at first disposed to think that there was no evidence on this point, and I put it to the jury, that, in some sense, everything which was supplied to a prostitute is supplied to her to enable her to carry on her trade, as, for instance, shoes sold to a street walker ; and that the things supplied must be not merely such as would be necessary or useful for ordinary purposes, and might be also applied to an immoral one ; but that they must be such as would under the circumstances not be required, except with that view. The jury, by the mode in which they answered the question, shewed that they appreciated the distinction ; and on reflection I think they were entitled to draw the inference which they did. They were entitled to bring their knowledge of the world to bear upon the facts proved. The inference that a prostitute (who swore that she could not read writing) required an ornamental brougham for the purposes of her calling, was as natural a one as that a medical man would want a brougham for the purpose of visiting his patients ; and the knowledge of the defendant's condition being brought home to the plaintiffs, the jury were entitled to ascribe to them also the knowledge of her purpose.]

Upon the second point, the case of *Bowry* v. *Bennett*[1] falls short of proving that the plaintiff must intend to be paid out of the proceeds of the illegal act. The report states that the evidence of the plaintiffs' knowledge of the defendant's way of life was " very slight " ; and Lord Ellenborough appears to have referred to the intention as to payment not as a legal test, but as a matter of evidence with reference to the particular circumstances of the case. The goods supplied there were clothes ; without other circumstances there would be nothing illegal in selling clothes to a known prostitute ; but if it were shewn that the seller intended to be paid out of her illegal earnings, the otherwise innocent contract would be vitiated. Neither is *Lloyd* v. *Johnson*[3], cited in the note to the last case, an authority for the plaintiffs, for there part of the contract would have been innocent, and all that the Court says is, that it cannot " take into consideration which of the articles were used by the defendant to an improper purpose, and which were not " ; they had no materials for doing so. The present case rather resembles the case of *Crisp* v. *Churchill*, cited in *Lloyd* v. *Johnson*[3], where the plaintiff was not allowed to recover for the use of lodgings let for the purpose of prostitution. *Appleton* v. *Campbell*[4] is to the same effect.

M. Chambers, Q.C., and *J. O. Griffits*, in support of the rule. As to

---

[1] (1808), 1 Camp. 348. [2] (1819), 3 B. & Ald. 179. [3] (1798), 1 Bos. & P. 340.
[4] (1826), 2 C. & P. 347.

the first point, the expressions of Buller, J., in *Lloyd* v. *Johnson*[1], are strongly in the plaintiffs' favour, especially his remarks on the case of the lodgings : " I suppose the lodgings were hired for the express purpose of enabling two persons to meet there." But in this case it is impossible to say that there was any express purpose of prostitution ; the defendant might have used the brougham for any purpose she chose, as to take drives, to go to the theatre, or to shop. Even if there were evidence, the jury have not found the purpose with sufficient distinctness. But secondly, the last allegation in the plea is material, the plaintiffs must intend to be paid out of the proceeds of the immoral act. The words of Lord Ellenborough in *Bowry* v. *Bennett*[2], are very plain, the plaintiff must " expect to be paid from the profits of the defendant's prostitution."

[BRAMWELL, B. At the trial I refused to leave this question to the jury, but it has since occurred to me that the matter was doubtful. The purpose of the seller in selling is, that he may obtain the profit, not that the buyer shall put the thing sold to any particular use ; it is for the buyer to determine how he shall use it. Suppose, however, a person were to buy a pistol, saying to the seller that he means with it to shoot a man and rob him, is the act of the seller illegal, or is it further necessary that he should stipulate to be paid out of the proceeds of the robbery ? If the looking to the proceeds is necessary to make the transaction illegal, is it not also necessary that it should be part of the contract that he *shall* be so paid ?]

Suppose a cab to be called by a prostitute, and the driver directed to take her to some known place of ill-fame, could it be said that he could not claim payment ?

[BRAMWELL, B. If he could, this absurdity would follow, that if a man and a prostitute engaged a cab for that purpose, and if, to meet your argument, the driver reckoned on payment, as to the woman, out of the proceeds of her prostitution, the woman would not be liable, but the man would, although they engaged in the same transaction and for the same purpose.]

If the contract is void for this reason, the plaintiffs were entitled to resume possession, and to bring trover for the carriage ; a test, therefore, of the question will be, whether in such an action, if the jury found the same verdict as they have found here, on the same evidence, the plaintiffs would be entitled to recover.

[MARTIN, B. I think they would ; and that if the carriage had not been returned in this case, the plaintiffs would, on our discharging this rule, be entitled to determine the contract on the ground of want of reciprocity, and to claim the return of the article.]

POLLOCK, C.B. We are all of opinion that this rule must be discharged. I do not think it is necessary to enter into the subject at large after what has fallen from the bench in the course of the argument, further than to say, that since the case of *Cannan* v. *Bryce*[3], cited by Lord Abinger in delivering the judgment of this Court in the case of *M'Kinnell* v. *Robinson*[4], and followed by the case in which it was so cited, I have always considered it as settled law, that any person who contributes to the performance of an illegal act by supplying a thing with the knowledge that it is going to be used for that purpose, cannot recover the price of the thing so supplied. If, to create that incapacity, it was ever considered necessary that the price should be bargained or expected to be paid out of the fruits of the illegal act (which

---

[1] (1798), 1 Bos. & P. at p. 341.
[2] (1808), 1 Camp. 348. [3] (1819), 3 B. & Ald. 179. [4] (1838), 3 M. & W. 434 at p. 441.

I do not stop to examine), that proposition has been overruled by the cases I have referred to, and has now ceased to be law.   Nor can any distinction be made between an illegal and an immoral purpose ; the rule which is applicable to the matter is, *Ex turpi causa non oritur actio*, and whether it is an immoral or an illegal purpose in which the plaintiff has participated, it comes equally within the terms of that maxim, and the effect is the same ; no cause of action can arise out of either the one or the other.   The rule of law was well settled in *Cannan* v. *Bryce*[1] ; that was a case which at the time it was decided, I, in common with many other lawyers in Westminster Hall, was at first disposed to regard with surprise.   But the learned judge (then Sir Charles Abbott) who decided it, though not distinguished as an advocate, nor at first eminent as a judge, was one than whom few have adorned the bench with clearer views, or more accurate minds, or have produced more beneficial results in the law.   The judgment in that case was, I believe, emphatically *his* judgment ; it was assented to by all the members of the Court of King's Bench, and is now the law of the land.   If, therefore, this article was furnished to the defendant for the purpose of enabling her to make a display favourable to her immoral purposes, the plaintiffs can derive no cause of action from the bargain.   I cannot go with Mr. Chambers in thinking that everything must be found by a jury in such a case with that accuracy from which ordinary decency would recoil.   For criminal law it is sometimes necessary that details of a revolting character should be found distinctly and minutely, but for civil purposes this is not necessary.   If evidence is given which is sufficient to satisfy the jury of the fact of the immoral purpose, and of the plaintiffs' knowledge of it, and that the article was required and furnished to facilitate that object, it is sufficient, although the facts are not expressed with such plainness as would offend the sense of decency.   I agree with my brother Bramwell that the verdict was right, and that the rule must be discharged.

BRAMWELL, B.   I am of the same opinion.   There is no doubt that the woman was a prostitute ; no doubt to my mind that the plaintiffs knew it ; there was cogent evidence of the fact, and the jury have so found.   The only fact really in dispute is for what purpose was the brougham hired, and if for an immoral purpose, did the plaintiffs know it ?   At the trial I doubted whether there was evidence of this, but, for the reasons I have already stated, I think the jury were entitled to infer, as they did, that it was hired for the purpose of display, that is, for the purpose of enabling the defendant to pursue her calling, and that the plaintiffs knew it.

That being made out, my difficulty was, whether, though the defendant hired the brougham for that purpose, it could be said that the plaintiffs let it for the same purpose.   In one sense, it was not for the same purpose. If a man were to ask for duelling pistols, and to say : " I think I shall fight a duel to-morrow," might not the seller answer : " I do not want to know your purpose ;   I have nothing to do with it ;   that is your business :   mine is to sell the pistols, and I look only to the profit of trade."   No doubt the act would be immoral, but I have felt a doubt whether it would be illegal; I should still feel it, but that the authority of *Cannan* v. *Bryce*[1] and *M'Kinnell* v. *Robinson*[2] concludes the matter.   In the latter case the plea does not say that the money was lent on the terms that the borrower should game with it ; but only that it was borrowed by the defendant, and lent by the plaintiff " for the purpose of the defendant's illegally playing and gaming therewith."

---

[1] (1819), 3 B. & Ald. 179.   [2] (1838), 3 M. & W. 434.

The case was argued by Mr. Justice Crompton against the plea, and by Mr. Justice Wightman in support of it ; and the considered judgment of the Court was delivered by Lord Abinger, who says (p. 441) : " As the plea states that the money for which the action is brought was lent for the purpose of illegally playing and gaming therewith, at the illegal game of ' Hazard,' this money cannot be recovered back, on the principle, not for the first time laid down, but fully settled in the case of *Cannan* v. *Bryce*. This principle is that the repayment of money, lent for the express purpose of accomplishing an illegal object, cannot be enforced." This Court, then, following *Cannan* v. *Bryce*[1], decided that it need not be part of the bargain that the subject of the contract should be used unlawfully, but that it is enough if it is handed over for the purpose that the borrower shall so apply it. We are, then, concluded by authority on the point ; and, as I have no doubt that the finding of the jury was right, the rule must be discharged.

With respect, however, to the allegation in the plea, which, as I have said, need not be proved, and which I refused to leave to the jury, I desire that it may not be supposed we are overruling anything that Lord Ellenborough has said. It is manifest that he could not have meant to lay down as a rule of law that there would be no illegality in a contract unless payment were to be made out of the proceeds of the illegal act, and that his observation was made with a different view. In the case of the hiring of a cab, which was mentioned in the argument, it would be absurd to suppose that, when both parties were doing the same thing, with the same object and purpose, it would be a lawful act in the one, and unlawful in the other.

BARONS MARTIN and PIGOTT delivered judgments to the same effect.

Napier v. National Business Agency, Ltd.

[1951] 2 All E.R. 264

If it appears from the terms of the contract, or indirectly from other circumstances, that the design of one or of both parties is to defraud the revenue, the contract is contrary to public policy and is illegal at common law. Though part only of the contract may thus be illegal, it may not be severed so as to leave the remainder valid and enforceable. The contract as a whole will be regarded as contaminated.[2]

The defendants engaged the plaintiffs to act as their secretary and accountant at a salary of £13 a week together with £6 a week for expenses. Both parties realised that such expenses would not amount to this sum, and, in fact, they never exceeded £1 a week. Each week the defendants deducted from the salary of £13 a week the amount of income tax appropriate to that sum; and the payment of £6 a week was represented as a re-imbursement of expenses on the returns made to the Inland Revenue Commissioners. The plaintiff was summarily dismissed, and he claimed from the defendants, in lieu of notice, the payment of £13 a week for a certain period.

The case was tried by His Honour JUDGE A. R. THOMAS at the Mayor's and City of London Court. The issue between the parties was confined to the length of notice which the plaintiff should have received. But in the course of the hearing the learned judge formed the view that the contract was intended to evade taxation and was illegal. He therefore held that the plaintiff was unable to enforce any part of it. The Court of Appeal affirmed this decision.

---

[1] (1819), 3 B. & Ald. 179.
[2] Compare the position where a term is void but not illegal: *infra*, pp. 299, 304–5.

SIR RAYMOND EVERSHED, M.R. The agreement sued on was one whereby the plaintiff was engaged by the defendants to act as secretary and accountant. The issue which was disclosed by the pleadings concerned the length of notice to which the plaintiff was entitled under that agreement, for, having served some ten months or so, he was summarily dismissed. In fairness to him it should be said that there is no evidence, and, indeed, no plea on the part of the defendants, that he had committed any disgraceful or wrongful act, and the defendants did not attempt to justify his dismissal without notice. After his dismissal they paid him a certain sum, calculated on the basis that he should have had one month's notice. It was the claim of the plaintiff that he was entitled to six months' notice, or, alternatively, to four months' notice.

Witnesses were called for the purpose of dealing with that aspect of the matter, but when the learned judge began his investigation of the case another and very important question began to emerge. It was no part of the defendants' case that the agreement was tainted in the way in which I use that word, and, therefore, the burden fell on the judge to carry out an investigation into the truth of this matter as best he could without the assistance that he would naturally have had from the other party had this matter been an issue in the action. The terms of the bargain, so far as relevant, were that the plaintiff should be paid for his services in the two capacities which I have mentioned, £13 a week for salary and £6 a week for expenses. The learned judge discerned at an early stage, as the matter developed, the possibility that the figure of £6 a week for expenses was not genuine in the sense that it could be taken as a fair representation on the part of either party of the expenses that the plaintiff would in fact incur.

The plaintiff was paid his salary subject to deduction for income tax by means commonly known as " P.A.Y.E." and the defendants made the appropriate deductions in respect of the £13 a week. They disclosed by indorsement on the appropriate forms that the plaintiff also received £6 a week for expenses. It has been urged forcibly by counsel for the plaintiff that the plaintiff has not attempted any concealment from the revenue authorities. He has been to see them about this matter, and has attempted to obtain a solution of the problem between himself and the revenue as to the amount that could fairly be allowed to him for expenses; but he has conceded that, of the £6 a week, not more than £1 a week could have been treated as fairly representing expenses. The result of the plaintiff's candour *vis-a-vis* the revenue authorities may well be that they will eventually recover from him any tax which ought to have been paid before, but, even assuming that, it is not to be forgotten that in the meantime the defendants will not have accounted, as they ought to have done under the income tax regulations, for the full amount of tax for which they were accountable.

On this aspect of the matter, the learned judge said: " Both parties knew perfectly well that, except on very exceptional occasions, the plaintiff would not incur any expenses," and he then refers to some matters of evidence to support that finding. I venture to make one addition. Before the service began, there was sent in the course of correspondence between the plaintiff and one Hidden, on behalf of the defendant company, a statement of the duties of a secretary plus accountant, and an inspection of that statement discloses that he would not be in the least likely to incur substantial, if, indeed, any, expenses. The case is wholly different from that, say, of a commercial traveller, who has necessarily to be constantly spending money in the way of expenses. The learned judge continued:

" This contract to pay the plaintiff what was undoubtedly, to my mind, part of his salary as expenses I must find was illegal, even if only to the extent that he was receiving money which, or a very large part of which, was liable to tax, and which, or a very large part of which, was not included as salary for the purposes of the returns to the Inland Revenue under the pay-as-you-earn scheme."

Counsel for the plaintiff has observed that the payment by the defendants to the plaintiff of £6 a week expenses was disclosed on the P.A.Y.E. return, but the disclosure, in the form that it took, in itself, as I think, constituted or may be treated fairly as constituting a misrepresentation, for, by stating on the form that £6 a week was paid to the plaintiff for expenses, the defendants were, I should have thought, representing to the revenue that £6 a week or thereabouts was the amount of the expenses which the plaintiff incurred in the course of, and as incidental to, his employment, which was not the fact. The learned judge concludes:

" I cannot help thinking, and I must find as a fact, that when the contract was made the plaintiff intended to allow this to go on, and to avoid paying income tax on it if he possibly could. I think that that was the main attraction of this particular job over the employment he had before he came to the defendant company."

Counsel for the plaintiff has said that the finding is unjust to the plaintiff and is unsupported by evidence, but in all the circumstances I think it impossible for this court to say that the judge was disentitled to find, as he did, that the plaintiff and the defendants together made this bargain knowing well that this was a sham figure which bore no relation to the expenses which, in fact, would be incurred.

If those were the facts, what is the inference? It must surely be that, by making an agreement in that form the parties to it were doing that which they must be taken to know would be liable to defeat the proper claims of the Inland Revenue and to avoid altogether, or at least to postpone, the proper payment of income tax. If that is the right conclusion, it seems to me equally clear (subject to one point which I will mention in a moment) that the agreement must be regarded as contrary to public policy. There is a strong legal obligation placed on all citizens to make true and faithful returns for tax purposes, and, if parties make an agreement which is designed to do the contrary, i.e., to mislead and to delay, it seems to me impossible for this court to enforce that contract at the suit of one party to it.

That being so, the further point arises whether the terms of the agreement relating to the two branches of the plaintiff's reward can be severed, i.e., whether the plaintiff can reject the tainted part of the contract relating to the £6 a week for expenses, and sue only, as he has done, in respect of the £13 a week for remuneration simply so called. I think the answer to that point is in the negative. The contract is, to my mind, not severable. It cannot properly be treated as consisting of two separate and distinct bargains, and, therefore, although it is true that the plaintiff sues only in respect of £13 a week, he is really seeking to enforce a contract which is tainted to the extent I have mentioned. It being so tainted, I think that the court will not enforce it at his suit. I think that this appeal fails and should be dismissed.

DENNING and HODSON, L.JJ., gave judgment to the same effect.

Berg v. Sadler and Moore

[1937] 2 K.B. 158

Money paid under a contract which is illegal in that it involves conduct of a criminal, immoral or otherwise reprehensible character is irrecoverable if the plaintiff cannot substantiate his claim without disclosing such illegality[1].

APPEAL from a decision of Macnaghten, J.

The action was brought by the plaintiff Berg to recover a sum of money paid by him to the defendants Sadler and Moore for certain goods which they refused to deliver and the purchase-money for which they refused to return. The defendants based their refusal on the ground that the plaintiff's scheme was an attempt to obtain the goods by false pretences.

The circumstances which gave rise to the claim were these : There was a body called the Tobacco Trade Association, the members of which were either manufacturers or traders. The object of the Association was to prevent what is called " price-cutting " and to secure price maintenance. The traders agreed, in return for their being supplied by the manufacturers with the particular goods, namely, tobacco, cigarettes and snuff, which came within the category of price-maintained goods, that they would not sell at less than the prices fixed for those goods.

In January, 1934, the plaintiff became a member of the Association; but in April of the same year it was discovered that he was breaking the terms of the agreement, and thereupon he became what was called a " cut-price retailer " and was put on the list of retailers to whom manufacturer members of the Association would not supply goods. He carried on a hairdresser's business, but he apparently did a considerable amount of selling of cigarettes and other classes of tobacco goods.

In or about August, 1935, the plaintiff came into contact with one Reece, who was a member of the Association and in full enjoyment of its privileges. The plaintiff obtained from Reece a large supply of cigarettes which were sold by the defendants, who were also members of the Association, as they thought, to Reece. The transaction, as carried through, involved the plaintiff paying the price of 134*l.* in cash, and the plaintiff's wife and Reece together going with the cash to the defendants and carrying off the cigarettes. The plaintiff paid to Reece a commission or profit of 5*l.*

Towards the end of the same month it was contemplated that the proceedings should be repeated, and Reece gave a written order to the defendants for 39,500 cigarettes at a price of 72*l.* 10*s.* The defendants received the order on the footing that they were supplying Reece, but what really happened was, as Macnaghten, J., found as a fact, that the whole transaction was simply a scheme by which, through the intermediation and under cover of Reece, the plaintiff was to get from the defendants a supply of cigarettes. The defendants would not have supplied the plaintiff with cigarettes had they known that he was the purchaser. It was necessary, therefore, so to arrange the transaction that the defendants would be deceived into supplying the cigarettes and would believe that they were supplying them to Reece, whereas in fact they were supplying them to the plaintiff. The plaintiff therefore sent one Schlisser, one of his assistants in the hairdressing business, accompanied by a representative of Reece, to the defendants with

---

[1] For the similar position when a contract is prohibited by statute, see *supra*, p. 250.

70*l*. to collect the cigarettes. Some little difficulty arose because the price was 72*l*. 19*s*., and the defendants refused to hand over the cigarettes until they were paid the extra 2*l*. 19*s*. Schlisser therefore had to go back to the plaintiff to get another 3*l*., and then, having got it, he paid it and obtained a receipt and the 1*s*. change. The defendant Moore, who was the member of the defendants' firm concerned in the matter, had some doubt or suspicion, and when he handed over the receipt he said he would send the goods to Reece's place of business. Schlisser immediately said that that would not do, and demanded the money back. Moore then said that this was an attempt to get the goods from him by false pretences, and refused to give back the money which had been paid to him; and eventually the writ in this action was issued by the plaintiff claiming a return of the money.

At the trial Macnaghten, J., held that the plaintiff had attempted, although the attempt failed, by deceit to induce a course of action on the part of the defendants which would have been an action to their grave injury. If in fact they had supplied goods to plaintiff, he being on the " stop-list ", the consequences to them might have been of a very serious character in their business. It seemed to him that it was a plain case where there had been an attempt to obtain goods by false pretences, and that it was nothing to the purpose that the fraudulent person who was attempting that crime was in fact willing to pay the full price of the goods. The learned judge then came to the conclusion that the Court would not entertain an action by a man for money dishonestly paid for the purpose of committing an offence against the criminal law and he accordingly dismissed the action.

The plaintiff appealed. The appeal was heard on February 12 and 15, 1937.

LORD WRIGHT, M.R. This case has been very fully put before the Court, but notwithstanding Mr. Cartwright Sharp's argument, I am not able to differ from the conclusion arrived at by the learned judge.

The case in some respects is peculiar, and in some respects involves a novel application of the well known rule which is sometimes expressed in the maxim *ex turpi causa non oritur actio*. This, though veiled in the dignity of learned language, is a statement of a principle of great importance ; but like most maxims it is much too vague and much too general to admit of application without a careful consideration of the circumstances and of the various definite rules which have been laid down by the authorities. Our business here is to apply these rules, either precisely according to the decisions which have been given, or following those decisions very closely and acting on the analogy of those decisions.

The facts here can be very shortly stated. [His Lordship stated the facts substantially as above set out and read the findings of Macnaghten, J. He continued :] This case, as I have said, is in some respects peculiar, and is in some respects to be distinguished from other cases which have been before the Court and in which the Court has refused to entertain the action on the ground of the illegality or immorality which was involved in the proceedings. I need not refer to a common type of case where an action is brought upon a contract and the Court refuses to entertain the action on the ground that, either by express terms or by the understanding of the parties, the contract was intended for the fulfilment of unlawful or immoral purposes. That is the case of *Pearce* v. *Brooks*[1], for instance, and a similar case is *Scott* v. *Brown, Doering, McNab & Co.*[2] This case, I think presents its

---

[1] (1866), L. R. 1 Ex. 213.   [2] [1892] 2 Q. B. 724.

own characteristic features. The plaintiff paid over a sum of money to the defendants, intending the property in that money to pass to them. The defendants took the money intending that the property in it should vest in them, and that it should be paid in pursuance of a contract of sale to Reece. Up to that point the transaction would have been perfectly binding, the money being vested in the defendants. The plaintiff now demands the repayment of that money. He can only do that on the ground that he is entitled to sue for it in an action for money had and received, and that it is contrary to what is *æquum et bonum* for the defendants to retain it. To maintain an action for money had and received he has to prove the exact circumstances in which the money was paid, and the circumstances which he says entitled him on grounds of justice to have an order for repayment. If, however, he proceeds to that proof he can only establish his claim by proving facts which show that he was engaged in a criminal attempt to obtain goods by false pretences. The Court on well-established principles will refuse to give its aid to any claim which can only be established by proving facts of that nature.

For the general proposition which I have just stated I need only refer to two cases. The first is *Simpson* v. *Bloss*[1], which was an action for money had and received. The plaintiff had laid an illegal wager with a third party. The defendant had assumed a part of the bet. The plaintiff won. The third party was the one to pay the debt, but the defendant, as he was going on a journey, asked the plaintiff to advance him his share of the winnings. The third party, however, died insolvent without paying his debt, and the plaintiff sought to recover the amount of his advance from the defendant as money had and received. The Court held that the action must fail. Gibbs, C.J., said[2] : " How can he "—that is the plaintiff—" make out his claim, but by going into proof of the illegal transaction on account of which it is paid ? He says, the payment was on a condition which has failed ; but that condition was, that Brograve, who was concerned with the plaintiff and defendant in this illegal transaction, should make good his part by paying the whole bet to the plaintiff ; and it is impossible to prove the failure of this condition, without going into the illegal contract, in which all the parties were equally concerned." The present case falls, I think, within that general principle, although it is a somewhat different application of it. The illegality here, which necessarily must appear when the plaintiff sets out the facts on which he bases his claim, is his own illegality in attempting to commit a misdemeanour under the criminal law. The principle, I think, is the same.

The principle is very clearly stated by Fry, L.J., in *Kearley* v. *Thomson*[3]. That case involved a further question—namely, whether the contract had or had not been carried into effect. It was held that it had been partially carried into effect, and that was enough to prevent the plaintiff from succeeding. Fry, L.J., in stating the general principle[4] first pointed out that the agreement which was in question was unlawful as interfering with the course of justice, and then said : " As a general rule, where the plaintiff cannot get at the money which he seeks to recover without showing the illegal contract, he cannot succeed. In such a case the usual rule is *potior est conditio possidentis*. There is another general rule which may be thus stated, that where there is

---

[1] (1816), 7 Taunt. 246.   [2] (1816), 7 Taunt., at p. 250.
[3] (1890), 24 Q. B. D. 742.   [4] (1890), 24 Q. B. D., at p. 745.

a voluntary payment of money it cannot be recovered back. It follows in the present case that the plaintiff who paid the 40*l*. cannot recover it back without showing the contract upon which it was paid; and when he shows that, he shows an illegal contract. The general rule applicable to such a case is laid down in the very elaborate judgment in *Collins* v. *Blantern*[1], where the Lord Chief Justice says : ' Whoever is a party to an unlawful contract, if he hath once paid the money stipulated to be paid in pursuance thereof, he shall not have the help of the Court to fetch it back again ; you shall not have a right of action when you come into a court of justice in this unclean manner to recover it back.' " Fry, L.J., went on to distinguish *Taylor* v. *Bowers*[2], where recovery was allowed, as I understand the decision, on the ground that the illegal purpose had been abandoned, and that the plaintiff had so repented that he was not debarred from recovering what he had paid.

Some such argument was put forward in this case, but I should like to add to the expression of opinion of Fry, L.J., on that point the observations which are contained in a judgment of this Court by Romer, L.J., in *Alexander* v. *Rayson*[3] : " Plaintiff's counsel further contended that inasmuch as the plaintiff had failed in his attempted fraud, and could therefore no longer use the documents for an illegal purpose, he was now entitled to sue upon them." (In the case before us the plaintiff had failed to obtain his cigarettes.) " The law, it was said, would allow to the plaintiff a *locus pœnitentiæ*. So, perhaps, it would have done, had the plaintiff repented before attempting to carry his fraud into effect : see *Taylor* v. *Bowers*[4]. But, as it is, the plaintiff's repentance came too late—namely, after he had been found out. Where the illegal purpose has been wholly or partially effected the law allows no *locus pœnitentiæ* ; see Salmond and Winfield's Law of Contract, p. 152. It will not be any the readier to do so when the repentance, as in the present case, is merely due to the frustration by others of the plaintiff's fraudulent purpose." That passage seems to apply very fully to the present case.

Alexander v. *Rayson*[3] also illustrates a further principle which I think is applicable to the facts before this Court. In that case an action was brought on a lease against the defendant, who was the tenant holding under it. It appeared in the proceedings that the lease was at a sum of 450*l*. a year, and that it was accompanied by a further and separate agreement under which the lessee was to pay a further 750*l*. a year ostensibly for the performance of various services in connection with the letting. The Court was of the opinion that the true value of the leasehold interest was 1100*l*. a year, and that that sum was split up into these two figures of 450*l*. and 750*l*. a year in order to deceive the assessment committee. In that action, which was brought by the lessor against the lessee, the lessee being entirely ignorant of and unconcerned in this fraudulent attempt, it was held that the Court would not on the facts as ascertained give effect to the lease, because they held it to have been concocted in the form in which it was in order to effect an unlawful purpose.

Applying that principle to the somewhat different facts of the present case, I think that the 72*l*. 19*s*. here may be regarded as the instrument which the plaintiff was using to carry out his unlawful purpose of obtaining the goods by false pretences. Just as the Court in *Alexander* v. *Rayson*[5] would

---

[1] (1767), 2 Wils. 341, at p. 350 ; 1 Sm. L. C., 13th ed., 406.
[2] (1876), 1 Q. B. D. 291.   [3] [1936] 1 K. B. 169, at p. 190.
[4] (1876), 1 Q. B. D. 291.   [5] [1936] 1 K. B. 169, at p. 190.

not allow the lease to be used as an effective instrument, and would not give any remedy in respect of the lease when once it was established that it was created in order to effect a fraudulent purpose, so I think the Court here should refuse to give any remedy in respect of the 72*l.* 19*s.* when once it is satisfied, as it is satisfied here, that the 72*l.* 19*s.* was used, as it was, in an attempt to effect a fraudulent purpose and was the instrument employed in that attempt. The defendants' position, therefore, is that they are in possession of the money which has passed to them under a contract *prima facie* lawful, but which has turned out to be a contract tainted by fraud, so far as the plaintiff is concerned. The defendants can accordingly rely on the principle *potior est conditio possidentis*, and the Court will refuse to reopen the transaction or order the money to be repaid on the ground of a failure of consideration.

I will only mention one of the other cases to which we have been referred, *Gordon* v. *Chief Commissioner of Metropolitan Police*[1], where the question was quite different. The only objection which was raised against the recovery of the money claimed was that, at some earlier period, and in the course of transactions entirely irrelevant to the matter in question, it had been obtained by unlawful gaming. It was held that that was too remote. Buckley, L.J., said[2] : " It is certainly the law that the Court will refuse to enforce an illegal contract or obligations arising out of an illegal contract, and I agree that the doctrine is not confined to the case of contract. A plaintiff who cannot establish his cause of action without relying upon an illegal transaction must fail : and none the less is this true if the defendant does not rely upon the illegality. If the Court learns of the illegality, it will refuse to lend its aid. The rule is founded not upon any ground that either party can take advantage of the illegality, as, for instance, the defendant, by setting it up as a defence. It is founded on public policy. Lord Mansfield in *Holman* v. *Johnson*[1] said ' *Ex dolo malo non oritur actio*. No Court will lend its aid to a man who founds his cause of action upon an immoral or an illegal act.' " Buckley, L.J., then pointed out that no such consideration arose in that case. It therefore was not one which in any way affects the conclusion at which I have arrived. In my opinion, the appeal should be dismissed, with costs.

ROMER, L.J., and SCOTT, L.J., delivered judgments to the same effect.

---

[1] [1910] 2 K. B. 1080.   [2] *Ibid.*, 1098.

[3] (1775) 1 Cowp. 341, at p. 343.

CONTRACTS VOID AT COMMON LAW ON GROUNDS
OF PUBLIC POLICY

Esso Petroleum Co., Ltd. v. Harper's Garage (Stourport), Ltd.

Attwood v. Lamont

Bennett v. Bennett

Esso Petroleum Co., Ltd. v. Harper's Garage (Stourport), Ltd.

[1967] 1 All E.R. 699

It is a presumption that every contract in restraint of trade is contrary to public policy and therefore *prima facie* void.

Whether a contract is affected by the doctrine of restraint of trade raises two independent questions:—(1) Is the restraint upon the promisor's liberty so manifest that it must be regarded as *prima facie* void? (2) If so, is it nevertheless justifiable and therefore valid as being reasonable in the interests both of the parties and of the community?

It is now established that contracts which restrain competition by an employee against an employer or by the vendor of a business against the purchaser are *prima facie* void. Apart from these two types of contract, the classification of contracts in restraint of trade " must remain fluid, and the categories can never be closed."[1]

This was an appeal by the appellants, Esso Petroleum Co., Ltd., from the judgment of the Court of Appeal (Lord Denning, M.R., Harman and Diplock, L.JJ.), dated Feb. 23, 1966, and reported [1966] 1 All E.R. 725, allowing the appeal of the respondents, Harper's Garage (Stourport), Ltd., from the judgment of Mocatta, J., dated June 15, 1965, and reported [1965] 2 All E. R. 933, given in favour of the appellants in consolidated actions.

The first action, 1964 E. No. 259, described as the " Mustow Green action ", concerned a solus agreement between the appellants and respondents, dated June 27, 1963. The respondents agreed (by cl. 2) to buy from the appellants at the appellants' wholesale schedule price to dealers ruling at the date of delivery the respondents' total requirements of motor fuels for resale at a service station known as Mustow Green garage. The agreement was (by cl. 1) to remain in force for a period of four years and five months from July 1, 1963. By cl. 3 the appellants agreed to allow the respondents a rebate of 1¼d. per gallon on all motor fuels purchased by the respondents under the agreement and to extend to the respondents the advantages of the appellants' Dealer Co-operation Plan. By cl. 4 of this solus agreement the respondents agreed, *inter alia*, (a) to operate the service station in accordance with the plan, which included agreement on the part of the respondents to keep the service station open at all reasonable hours for the sale of the appellants' motor fuel and motor oils; (b) not to resell motor fuels for use in vehicles holding private licences except in accordance with the appellants' retail schedule prices; and (c) before completing any sale or transfer of the service station premises or business to procure the prospective purchaser or transferee to enter into an agreement with the appellants and the respondents

---

[1] *Per* Lord Wilberforce, *infra*, p. 283. The doctrine of restraint of trade has been applied to rules laid down by a professional body for its members: *Dickson* v. *Pharmaceutical Society of Great Britain*, [1967] Ch. 708; [1967] 2 All E.R. 558.

whereby such person would be substituted for the respondents for all future purposes of the agreement.

The second action, 1964 E. No. 1249, which was referred to as the " Corner garage action ", concerned another solus agreement between the appellants and the respondents in the same terms as the Mustow Green agreement save that it related to a service station known as Corner garage, was made on July 5, 1962, and was expressed to remain in force for a period of twenty-one years from July 1, 1962. Under cl. 1 of a charge by way of legal mortgage made between the respondents and the appellants on Oct. 6, 1962, the respondents covenanted to repay the appellants £7,000 with interest by quarterly instalments over a period of twenty-one years from Nov. 6, 1962; it was further provided in the mortgage deed that the respondents should not be entitled to redeem the security otherwise than in accordance with the covenant as to repayment. The respondents charged Corner garage by way of legal mortgage with payment to the appellants of all moneys thereby covenanted to be paid. The respondents further covenanted during the continuance of the mortgage to purchase exclusively from the appellants all motor fuels which the respondents might require for consumption or sale at Corner garage, so long as the appellants should be ready to supply the same at their usual list price, and not to buy, receive or sell or knowingly permit to be bought, received or sold at Corner garage any motor fuels other than such as should be purchased from the appellants.

The two actions were begun by writs issued respectively on Feb. 18 and Aug. 28, 1964, and were consolidated by order dated Mar. 17, 1965. From about the end of the year 1963 and from about August, 1964, the respondents sold at Mustow Green garage and at Corner garage respectively motor fuel that was not supplied by the appellants. On appeal to the Court of Appeal ([1966] 1 All E. R. 725) it was held, briefly stated, that the doctrine of restraint of trade applied to covenants in mortgages as well as to solus agreements; that the restrictions in the solus agreements and in the mortgage were unreasonable and void, and that the proviso in the mortgage prohibiting redemption for twenty-one years, taken with the tie of Corner garage for a like period, rendered the mortgage oppressive, and accordingly the tie was unenforceable.

[The House of Lords (Lord REID, Lord MORRIS, Lord HODSON, Lord PEARCE and Lord WILBERFORCE) reversed the decision of the Court of Appeal as to the Mustow Green garage and affirmed it as to the Corner garage.]

LORD PEARCE: My Lords, on the assumption that the solus agreement relating to the Mustow Green garage comes within the ambit of the doctrine of restraint of trade and that its reasonableness is a matter which the courts must decide, I am of opinion that it is reasonable.

The period of five years has been approved as a reasonable period for agreements of this nature in Canada (*British American Oil Co.* v. *Hey*[1]; *McColl* v. *Avery*[2]; *Great Eastern Oil and Import Co.* v. *Chafe*[3]), and in South Africa (*Shell Co. of South Africa, Ltd.* v. *Gerran's Garages (Pty.), Ltd.*[4]). In the courts of this country there is nothing which suggests that five years is an unreasonable length of time for a tie of this kind in a trade of this kind. In some cases the matter has passed *sub silentio*. Although the point was not relevant in *Regent Oil Co. Ltd.* v. *Strick (Inspector of Taxes)*,[5] the language

---

[1] [1941] 4 D.L.R. 725.
[3] (1956) 4 D.L.R. (2d) 310.
[5] [1966] A.C. 295; [1965] 3 All E.R. 174.

[2] (1928), 34 O.W.N. 275.
[4] [1954] 4 S.A.L.R. 752.

Esso Petroleum Co., Ltd. v. Harper's Garage (Stourport), Ltd. 273

there used (per Lord Reid[1] and Lord Upjohn[2]), seems to suggest that, had the question been raised or relevant, five years would not have been considered unreasonable. So, too, in the cases of *Mobil Oil Australia, Ltd.* v. *Comr. of Taxation of the Commonwealth of Australia*[3] and *B.P. Australia, Ltd.* v. *Comr. of Taxation of the Commonwealth of Australia*[4]. The facts set out in the report of the Monopolies Commission[5] and its conclusions support this view.

Since the war there has been a world-wide re-organisation of the petrol industry. The old haphazard distribution has, in the interests of economy, efficiency and finance, been converted into a distribution by the respective petrol producers through their own individual (and, as a rule, improved and more efficient) outlets. Vast sums have been spent on refineries, the improvement of garages and the like. Hand-to-mouth arrangements are no longer commercially suitable to the industry, and considerable planning (involving, *inter alia*, the geographical spacing of the outlets) is obviously necessary. The garage proprietors were not at any disadvantage in dealing with the various competing producers of petrol. To hold that five-year periods are too long for the ties between the producers and their outlets would, in my opinion, be out of accord with modern commercial needs, would cause an embarrassment to the trade and would not safeguard any public or private interest that needs protection. I would, however, regard twenty-one years as being longer than was reasonable in the circumstances.

It is important that the court, in weighing the question of reasonableness, should give full weight to commercial practices and to the generality of contracts made freely by parties bargaining on equal terms. Undue interference, though imposed on the ground of promoting freedom of trade, may in the result hamper and restrict the honest trader and, on a wider view, injure trade more than it helps it. If a man wishes to tie himself for his own good commercial reasons to a particular supplier or customer, it may be no kindness to him to subject his contract to the arbitrary rule that the court will always reserve to him a right to go back on his bargain if the court thinks fit. For such a reservation prevents the honest man from getting full value for the tie which he intends, in spite of any reservation imposed by the courts, to honour; and it may enable a less honest man to keep the fruits of a bargain from which he afterwards resiles. It may be in this respect similar to imposing on a trader the fetters of infancy; and many an upstanding infant who wishes to trade or buy a house or motorcar has found difficulty and frustration in the rule which the court has imposed for his protection. Where there are no circumstances of oppression, the court should tread warily in substituting its own views for those of current commerce generally and the contracting parties in particular. For that reason, I consider that the courts require on such a matter full guidance from evidence of all the surrounding circumstances and of relevant commercial practice. They must also have regard to the consideration. It is clear that the question of the consideration weighed with Lord Macnaghten in *Nordenfelt* v. *Maxim Nordenfelt Guns and Ammunition Co., Ltd.*[6]. Moreover, although the court may not be able to weigh the details of

---

[1] [1966] A.C. at p. 324; [1965] 3 All E.R. at p. 186, letter D.
[2] [1966] A.C. at p. 345; [1965] 3 All E.R. at p. 199, letter F.
[3] [1966] A.C. 275 at p. 293; [1965] 3 All E.R. 225 at p. 229, letter F.
[4] [1966] A.C. 244 at pp. 265, 267; [1965] 3 All E.R. 209 at p. 218, letter H, p. 220, letter C.
[5] Report on the supply of petrol to retailers in the United Kingdom (chairman, R. F. Levy, Q.C.), H.C. 264.
[6] [1894] A.C. at p. 574; [1891–94] All E.R. Rep. at pp. 22, 23.

the advantages and disadvantages with great nicety, it must appreciate the consideration at least in its more general aspects. Without such guidance they cannot hope to arrive at a sensible and up-to-date conclusion on what is reasonable. That is not to say that, when it is clear that current contracts (containing restraints), however widespread, are in fact a danger and disservice to the public and to traders, the court should hesitate to interfere.

The onus is on the party asserting the contract to show the reasonableness of the restraint. That rule was laid down in the *Nordenfelt* case[1] and in *Herbert Morris, Ltd.* v. *Saxelby*[2]. When the court sees its way clearly, no question of onus arises. In a doubtful case where the court does *not* see its way clearly and the question of onus does arise, there may be a danger in preferring the guidance of a general rule, founded on grounds of public policy many generations ago, to the guidance given by free and competent parties contracting at arms' length in the management of their own affairs. Therefore, when free and competent parties agree and the background provides some commercial justification on both sides for their bargain, and there is no injury to the community, I think that the onus should be easily discharged. Public policy, like other unruly horses, is apt to change its stance; and public policy is the ultimate basis of the courts' reluctance to enforce restraints. Although the decided cases are almost invariably based on unreasonableness between the parties, it is *ultimately* on the ground of public policy that the court will decline to enforce a restraint as being unreasonable between the parties; and a doctrine based on the general commercial good must always bear in mind the changing face of commerce. There is not, as some cases seem to suggest, a separation between what is reasonable on grounds of public policy and what is reasonable as between the parties. There is one broad question: is it in the interests of the community that this restraint should, as between the parties, be held to be reasonable and enforceable?

The rule relating to restraint of trade is bound to be a compromise, as are all rules imposed for freedom's sake. The law fetters traders by a particular inability to limit their freedom of trade, so that it may protect the general freedom of trade and the good of the community; and, since the rule must be a compromise, it is difficult to define its limits on any logical basis.

The court's right to interfere with contracts in restraint of trade (by withholding their enforcement, which is the ultimate sanction of contracts and to which the parties are normally entitled) has been put in very wide words. Those words, though adequate and appropriate to the particular cases in which they were uttered, were not directed towards an exact demarcation of the line where the court will have a right to investigate whether a bargain is reasonable and will decline to enforce it if it is not. The famous passages from the opinion of Lord Macnaghten in the *Nordenfelt* case[1] and the opinion of Lord Parker of Waddington in *A.-G. of Commonwealth of Australia* v. *Adelaide Steamship Co., Ltd.*[3] are not expressly limited in any way. Since any man who sells the whole, or even a substantial part, of his service, his output, his custom or his commercial loyalty to one party is thereby restraining himself from selling them to other persons, it might be argued that the court can investigate the reasonableness of any such contract and allow the contracting party to resile subsequently from any bargain which it considers an unreasonable restraint on his liberty of trade with others. So wide a power

---

[1] [1894] A.C. 535; [1891–94] All E.R. Rep. 1.
[2] [1916] 1 A.C. 688; [1916–17] All E.R. Rep. 305.
[3] [1913] A.C. at p. 793; [1911–13] All E.R. Rep at p. 1122.

of potential investigation, however, would allow to would-be recalcitrants a wide field of chicanery and delaying tactics in the courts. Where, then, should one draw the line?

It seems clear that covenants restraining the use of the land imposed as a condition of any sale or lease to the covenantor (or his successors) should not be unenforceable. It would be intolerable if, when a man chooses of his own free will to buy, or take a tenancy of, land which is made subject to a tie (doing so on terms more favourable to himself owing to the existence of the tie) he can then repudiate the tie while retaining the benefit. I do not accept the argument of counsel for the respondents that such transactions are subject to the doctrine, but will never as a matter of fact be held unreasonable. In my view, they are not subject to the doctrine at all. Certainly public policy gives little justification for their subjection to it. This view would accord with the brewers' cases in which (after an earlier unfavourable protest by Lord Ellenborough, C.J., in *Cooper* v. *Twibill*[1]) the law has, for many years past, been firmly settled in allowing covenants tying the publican (as lessee or purchaser) to a particular brewer (e.g. *Clegg* v. *Hands*[2]). In one case, however, in 1869 (*Catt* v. *Tourle*[3]) a perpetual tie on a sale of land was subjected to scrutiny and was held to be reasonable; but to allow a permanent tie is not very different from holding it exempt from scrutiny.

It may be, however, that when a man fetters with a restraint land which he already owns or occupies, the fetter comes within the scrutiny of the court.

Is one also to place mortgages in the class of cases from which the doctrine is excluded? Counsel for the appellants relies, *inter alia*, on the technical argument that under the mortgage he has in law a demise of three thousand years with cesser on redemption [4]; that this should not be regarded as a mere notional technicality; that he is a lessee for all purposes (see *Regent Oil Co., Ltd.* v. *J. A. Gregory (Hatch End), Ltd.*[5]); that the mortgagor is a lessor in possession; and that, therefore, the covenant should bind him as on a lease. The technicalities of the position where the mortgagor has no subdemise and is only notionally a lessor in possession, however, put it on the wrong side of the line and the mortgagor cannot, therefore, come into the class of lessees to whose covenants the doctrine has no application.

Then, on broader grounds, does the mere fact that a restraint is embodied as an obligation under a mortgage exclude it from critical scrutiny and prevent its being unenforceable if it would have been so apart from the mortgage? I think not. In *Biggs* v. *Hoddinott* [6] the point was not raised and the case is, therefore, of little guidance. The court of equity which declines to enforce the terms of a mortgage, if as a matter of conscience they are harsh and oppressive, cannot be less conscientious with regard to ties which as a matter of public policy the common law courts from earliest times, and thereafter courts of equity, have consistently refused to enforce in contracts. The court has also rightly applied the doctrine against restraint of trade to a tyrannous mortgage of future earnings in *Horwood* v. *Millar's Timber and Trading Co., Ltd.*[7].

Nevertheless, on the question whether a restraint is reasonable, the fact that it is contained as a term in a mortgage may be a determining factor in its

---

[1] (1808), 3 Camp. 286, n. at p. 287.
[2] (1890), 44 Ch.D. 503.
[3] (1869), 4 Ch. App. 654.
[4] See Law of Property Act, 1925, s. 87.
[5] [1966] Ch. 402; [1965] 3 All E.R. 673.
[6] [1898] 2 Ch. 307; [1895–99] All E.R. Rep. 625.
[7] [1917] 1 K.B. 305; [1916–17] All E.R. Rep. 847.

favour. The object of a mortgage is to provide fair security for the lender; and a restraint may be reasonably necessary to protect the security, when it would not have been reasonable without that object. Moreover, it seems usually reasonable for the tie to subsist as long as there is a loan outstanding, which the borrower is unable or unwilling to repay. It may be that even so there must be a limit; but, if so, I would not regard twenty-one years as necessarily excessive since *ex hypothesi* that length of time was commercially necessary for the borrower to have the benefit of the loan for his business. If, therefore, there had been in the mortgage of the Corner garage a right to redeem either when the mortgagor wished or at any time after a reasonable term of years, say five or seven years, and thereby to terminate the tie, I would not have regarded the tie as unreasonable, in view of the amount of the loan; but here there was no such right to redeem. Nor did the tie add anything to the protection of the security. Here, even in the most unlikely event of a shortgage of petrol supplies, the supplier has a discretion not to supply if his own sources of supply fail or go short; and in any other set of circumstances I cannot think that a tied garage would be more valuable than, or even as valuable as, a free garage. Moreover, if the mortgagees entered on their security, they would have to treat it as a free garage and account on that basis. If one regards the mortgage as a whole, the prolonged fetter on the right to redeem seems to have been inserted merely to prolong the tie. In this case, therefore, the existence of the mortgage neither removes the tie from the area to which the doctrine of restraint of trade applies nor, in the particular circumstances, does it assist the appellants on the question whether the tie was reasonable.

Mocatta, J., in his clear and careful judgment[1] held that neither tie was in restraint of trade since it was merely restrictive of the trading use to be made of a particular piece of land, so that the doctrine of restraint of trade had no application. I feel the force of his reasoning, but I do not feel able to accede to it. If the garage proprietor had no obligations to carry on his garage, I might have been persuaded otherwise; but here there was a positive obligation to carry on the business (or to find a transferee who must do likewise) and to purchase from none save the appellants. The practical effect was to create a personal restraint. Although the covenant affected only petrol sold on the particular land it did affect the proprietor with an obligation which he or his agents could not by mere abstention avoid. Both *English Hop Growers, Ltd.* v. *Dering*[2] and *Foley* v. *Classique Coaches, Ltd.*[3], in each of which the restraint was regarded as reasonable, and *McEllistrim* v. *Ballymacelligott Co-operative Agricultural and Dairy Society, Ltd.*[4] where it was not, lend some support to this view.

Finally, there is the important question whether this was a mere agreement for the promotion of trade and not an agreement in restraint of it.

Somewhere there must be a line between those contracts which are in restraint of trade and whose reasonableness can, therefore, be considered by the courts, and those contracts which merely regulate the normal commercial relations between the parties and are, therefore, free from the doctrine. The present case seems near the borderline, as was the case of *Bouchard Servais* v. *Prince's Hall Restaurant*[5], where Sir Richard Henn Collins, M.R., held that

---

[1] [1966] 2 Q.B. at p. 531; [1965] 2 All E.R. at p. 936.
[2] [1928] 2 K.B. 174; [1928] All E.R. Rep. 396.
[3] [1934] 2 K.B. 1; [1934] All E.R. Rep. 88.
[4] [1919] A.C. 548. [5] (1904), 20 T.L.R. 574.

the doctrine did not apply, while the other two lords justices apparently held that it did apply but that the restraint was reasonable.

One of the mischiefs at which the doctrine was aimed originally was the mischief of monopolies; but this was dealt with by legislation and the executive has from time to time taken efficient steps to prevent it. Indeed, in the case of petrol ties there has now been exacted (we are told) from the petrol producers an undertaking which in practice limits these ties to five years.

When Lord Macnaghten said in the *Nordenfelt* case[1] that

> " in the age of Queen Elizabeth all restraints of trade, whatever they were, general or partial, were thought to be contrary to public policy and, therefore, void, "

he was clearly not intending the words " restraints of trade " to cover any contract whose terms, by absorbing a man's services or custom or output, in fact prevented him from trading with others; so, too, the wide remarks of Lord Parker of Waddington in the *Adelaide* case[2]. It was the sterilising of a man's capacity for work and not its absorption that underlay the objection to restraint of trade. This is the rationale of *Young* v. *Timmins*[3], where a brass foundry was during the contract sterilised so that it could work only for a party who might choose not to absorb its output at all but to go to other foundries, with the result that the foundry was completely at the mercy of the other party and might remain idle and unsupported.

The doctrine does not apply to ordinary commercial contracts for the regulation and promotion of trade during the existence of the contract, provided that any prevention of work outside the contract viewed as a whole is directed towards the absorption of the parties' services and not their sterilisation. Sole agencies are a normal and necessary incident of commerce, and those who desire the benefits of a sole agency must deny themselves the opportunities of other agencies. So, too, in the case of a film-star who may tie herself to a company in order to obtain from them the benefits of stardom (*Gaumont-British Picture Corpn., Ltd.* v. *Alexander*[4]; see, too, *Warner Bros. Pictures, Inc.* v. *Nelson*[5]). Moreover, partners habitually fetter themselves to one another.

When a contract ties the parties only during the continuance of the contract, and the negative ties are only those which are incidental and normal to the positive commercial arrangements at which the contract aims, even though those ties exclude all dealings with others, there is no restraint of trade within the meaning of the doctrine and no question of reasonableness arises. If, however, the contract ties the trading activities of either party after its determination, it is a restraint of trade, and the question of reasonableness arises. So, too, if *during* the contract one of the parties is too unilaterally fettered, so that the contract loses its character of a contract for the regulation and promotion of trade and acquires the predominant character of a contract in restraint of trade. In that case the rationale of *Young* v. *Timmins*[6] comes into play and the question whether it is reasonable arises.

The difficult question in this case, as in the case of *Bouchard Servais*[7], is whether a contract regulating commercial dealings between the parties has by

---

[1] [1894] A.C. at p. 564; [1891–94] All E.R. Rep. at p. 17.
[2] [1913] A.C. at p. 794; [1911–13] All E.R. Rep. at p. 1123.
[3] (1831), 1 Cr. & J. 331.
[4] [1936] 2 All E.R. 1686.
[5] [1937] 1 K.B. 209; [1936] 3 All E.R. 160.
[6] (1831), 1 Cr. & J. 331.
[7] (1904), 20 T.L.R. 574.

its restraints exceeded the normal negative ties incidental to a positive commercial transaction and has thus brought itself within the sphere to which the doctrine of restraint applies. If the appellants had assured to the respondents a supply of petrol at a reasonable price, come what may, in return for the respondents selling only the appellants' petrol, it might be that the contract would have come within the normal incidents of a commercial transaction and not within the ambit of restraint of trade; but the appellants did not do this. They hedged their liability around so that they had an absolute discretion in the event, *inter alia*, of a failure in their own sources of supply, whether or not the appellants should have foreseen it, to withhold supplies from the respondents (leaving them the cheerless right in such a situation to seek supplies elsewhere); and then at a later stage it would seem, if and when the appellants were prepared to supply the respondents once more, the appellants could hold the respondents to their tie with the appellants. The price was, also, to be fixed by the appellants; and for the duration of the contract the respondents owed them a contractual obligation to continue to keep the garage open (or find a successor who would do so on like terms). When these contracts are viewed as a whole the balance tilts in favour of regarding them as contracts which are in restraint of trade and which, therefore, can be enforced only if the restraint is reasonable.

I do not here find help in the well-known phrases that a man is not entitled to protect himself against competition *per se*, or that he is only entitled to protect himself if he has an interest to protect. It is clear that a restraint which merely damages a covenantor and confers no benefit on a covenantee is as a rule unreasonable; but here the appellants had a definite interest to protect and secured a definite benefit. They wished to preserve intact their spaced network of outlets in order that they could continue to sell their products as planned over a period of years in competition with the other producers. To prevent them from doing so would be an embarrassment of trade, not a protection of its freedom. If all the other companies owned garages and the appellants were trying for the first time to enter the market, it would stifle trading competition rather than encourage it if the appellants were prevented from being able to enter into a binding solus agreement for a sole outlet in order to compete with the others. Moreover, in a doctrine based on the wide ground of public policy the wider aspects of commerce must always be considered as well as the narrower aspect of the contract as between the parties.

Since the tie for a period of four years and five months was in the circumstances reasonable, I would allow the appeal in respect of the Mustow Green garage. Since the tie for a period of twenty-one years was not in the circumstances reasonable, I would dismiss the appeal in respect of the Corner garage.

LORD WILBERFORCE: My Lords, the main features in the solus agreements entered into by the respondent company, Harper's Garage (Stourport), Ltd., with the appellants, Esso Petroleum Co., Ltd., are that the respondents agreed to purchase from the appellants the whole of their requirements of motor fuel for resale at the relevant service stations, accepted a resale price maintenance clause, agreed to operate the relevant service stations in accordance with the Esso Dealer Co-operation Plan, which included a provision that the service station should be kept open at all reasonable hours for the sale of Esso petrol and oil and, lastly, agreed that, before completing any sale or transfer of the relevant service station, the respondents would notify the appellants and procure the intended successor to assume the respondents' obligations under the agreement.

In the case of the Mustow Green garage, the agreement, dated June 27, 1963, was expressed to operate for four years and five months from July 1, 1963, this being the residue of a longer period which was taken over by the respondents from a previous operator of the station.

In the case of the Corner garage at Stourport-on-Severn the agreement, dated July 5, 1962, was expressed to operate for twenty-one years from July 1, 1962. In addition to this solus agreement, the respondents entered into a mortgage of this station, dated Oct. 6, 1962, by which the station was charged to the appellants to secure a sum not exceeding £7,000 with interest. The principal sum was repayable—and only repayable—by instalments over twenty-one years from Nov. 6, 1962. There were certain special provisions in the mortgage deed which I need not specify at the present stage.

The first main issue is whether these agreements are to be regarded as agreements in restraint of trade so as to be exposed to the tests of reasonableness stated in *Nordenfelt* v. *Maxim Nordenfelt Guns and Ammunition Co., Ltd.*[1]. It is the appellants' contention that they are not, mainly on the ground that they relate to the use of the respondents' land, and that covenants, or contracts, which so relate are by their nature incapable of being regarded as in restraint of trade. This contention has made it necessary to consider how a covenant or contract in restraint of trade is to be defined or identified.

The doctrine of restraint of trade (a convenient, if imprecise, expression which I continue to use) is one which has throughout the history of its subject-matter been expressed with considerable generality, if not ambiguity. The best known general formulations, those of Lord Macnaghten in *Nordenfelt*[2] and of Lord Parker of Waddington in *A.-G. of Commonwealth of Australia* v. *Adelaide Steamship Co., Ltd.*[3], adapted and used by DIPLOCK, L.J., in the Court of Appeal in *Petrofina (Great Britain), Ltd.* v. *Martin*[4], speak generally of all restraints of trade without any attempt at a definition. Often we find the words " restraint of trade " in a single passage used indifferently to denote, on the one hand, in a broad popular sense, any contract which limits the free exercise of trade or business, and, on the other hand, as a term of art covering those contracts which are to be regarded as offending a rule of public policy. Often, in reported cases, we find that instead of segregating two questions (i) whether the contract is in restraint of trade, (ii) whether, if so, it is " reasonable ", the courts have fused the two by asking whether the contract is in " undue restraint of trade ", or by a compound finding that it is not satisfied that this contract is really in restraint of trade at all but, if it is, it is reasonable. A well-known text book describes contracts in restraint of trade as those which " unreasonably restrict " the rights of a person to carry on his trade or profession. There is no need to regret these tendencies: indeed, to do so, when consideration of this subject has passed through such notable minds from Lord Macclesfield onwards, would indicate a failure to understand its nature. The common law has often (if sometimes unconsciously) thrived on ambiguity and it would be mistaken, even if it were possible, to try to crystallise the rules of this, or any, aspect of public policy

---

[1] [1894] A.C. 535; [1891–94] All E.R. Rep. 1.
[2] [1894] A.C. at p. 565; [1891–94] All E.R. Rep. at p. 18.
[3] [1913] A.C. at pp. 793–797; [1911–13] All E.R. Rep. at pp. 1122–1124.
[4] [1966] Ch. at p. 180; [1966] 1 All E.R. at p. 138.

into neat propositions. The doctrine of restraint of trade is one to be applied
to factual situations with a broad and flexible rule of reason.

The use of this expression justifies re-statement of its classic exposition
by White, C.J., in *U.S.* v. *Standard Oil*[1]. Speaking of the statutory words
" every contract in restraint of trade " (Sherman Act, 1890), admittedly
taken from the common law, almost contemporaneous with Lord Macnaghten's formula and just as wide, he said:

> " As the acts which may come under the classes stated in the first section
> and the restraint of trade to which that section applies are not specifically
> enumerated or defined, it is obvious that judgment must in every case be called
> into play in order to determine whether a particular act is embraced within the
> statutory classes, and whether if the act is within such classes its nature or effect
> causes it to be a restraint of trade within the intendment of the Act . . . "

Moreover, he goes on to say that to hold to the contrary would involve either
holding that the statute would be destructive of all right to contract or agree
or combine in any respect whatsoever, or that, the " light of reason " being
excluded, enforcement of the statute was impossible because of its uncertainty.
The right course was to leave it to be determined by the light of reason whether any particular act or contract was within the contemplation of the statute.
One still finds much enlightenment in these words.

This does not mean that the question whether a given agreement is in
restraint of trade, in either sense of these words, is nothing more than a
question of fact to be individually decided in each case. It is not to be supposed, or encouraged, that a bare allegation that a contract limits a trader's
freedom of action exposes a party suing on it to the burden of justification.
There will always be certain general categories of contracts as to which it can
be said, with some degree of certainty, that the " doctrine " does or does not
apply to them. Positively, there are likely to be certain sensitive areas as to
which the law will require in every case the test of reasonableness to be passed:
such an area has long been and still is that of contracts between employer
and employee as regards the period after the employment has ceased. Nega-
tively, and it is this that concerns us here, there will be types of contract as to
which the law should be prepared to say with some confidence that they do
not enter into the field of restraint of trade at all.

How, then, can such contracts be defined or at least identified? No
exhaustive test can be stated—probably no precise, non-exhaustive test. The
development of the law does seem to show, however, that judges have been
able to dispense from the necessity of justification under a public policy test
of reasonableness such contracts or provisions of contracts as, under contemporary conditions, may be found to have passed into the accepted and normal
currency of commercial or contractual or conveyancing relations. The fact
that such contracts have done so may be taken to show at least *prima facie*
that, moulded under the pressures of negotiation, competition and public
opinion, they have assumed a form which satisfies the test of public policy
as understood by the courts at the time, or, regarding the matter from the
point of view of the trade, that the trade in question has assumed such a form
that for its health or expansion it requires a degree of regulation. Absolute
exemption for restriction or regulation is never obtained: circumstances,
social or economic, may have altered, since they obtained acceptance, in such
a way as to call for a fresh examination: there may be some exorbitant or
special feature in the individual contract which takes it out of the accepted

---

[1] (1911), 221 U.S. 1 at p. 63.

category: but the court must be persuaded of this before it calls on the relevant party to justify a contract of this kind.

Some such limitation on the meaning in legal practice of " restraints of trade " must surely have been present to the minds of Lord Macnaghten and Lord Parker of Waddington. They cannot have meant to say that any contract which in whatever way restricts a man's liberty to trade was (either historically under the common law, or at the time of which they were speaking) *prima facie* unenforceable and must be shown to be reasonable. They must have been well aware that areas existed, and always had existed, in which limitations of this liberty were not only defensible, but were not seriously open to the charge of restraining trade. Their language, they would surely have said, must be interpreted in relation to commercial practice and common sense.

Any attempt to trace historically the development of the common law attitude towards " restraints " of different kinds would be out of place here, and generalisations as to it are hazardous; but a few examples of comparatively modern origin show how some such rule of action, however imperfectly I have expressed it in words, has been operated. In some cases the process can be seen whereby a type of contract, initially regarded with suspicion, has later come to be accepted as not, or no longer, calling for justification.

First, there are the brewery cases. Contractual clauses tying a leased public house to the lessor's beers have been known, and commonly current, at least since the early nineteenth century (for an early case see *Hartley* v. *Pehall*[1]). In the form which they then assumed (commonly providing that if the tying covenant was broken there should be an increased rent recoverable by distress) we find them encountering some judicial criticism (*Cooper* v. *Twibill*[2], per Lord Ellenborough, C.J.). But by 1850 they had become current; the attrition of negotiation and competition may be taken to have worn them down to an acceptable shape and in *Catt* v. *Tourle*[3], the Court of Appeal in Chancery not only accepted that such covenants were outside the doctrine of restraint of trade, but were prepared to extend the exclusion to the case where the servient house was sold instead of leased. I quote Selwyn, L.J.'s words[4]:

> " . . . with respect to this particular covenant, it seems to me that the court cannot but take judicial notice of its being extremely common. Every court of justice has had occasion to consider these brewers' covenants, and must be taken to be cognisant of the distinction between what are called free public houses and brewers' public houses which are subject to this very covenant. We should be introducing very great uncertainty into a very large and important trade if we were now to suggest any doubt as to the validity of a covenant so extremely common as this is."

GIFFARD, L.J., added[5] " it does not go beyond the ordinary brewers' covenant ". Neither of the lords justices, it will be seen, puts his decision on the ground (simple and decisive, if he had thought it appropriate) either that the covenant related to the use to be made of land, or that it was imposed on a disposition of land. That it was too late to subject such tying covenants to the test appropriate in restraint of trade was stated in 1889 by Bristowe, V.-C. (*Clegg* v. *Hands*[6]), and the issue was not even debated in the Court of Appeal.

The working of the same principle can be seen even earlier in relation to covenants restricting trade in leases generally. In the normal exploitation

[1] (1792), Peake, 178.
[2] (1803), 3 Camp. 286, n.
[3] (1869), 4 Ch. App. 654.
[4] (1869), 4 Ch. App. at p. 659.
[5] (1869), 4 Ch. App. at p. 662.
[6] (1890), 44 Ch.D. 503.

of property, covenants are entered into, by lessee or lessor, not to trade at all or not to carry on particular trades. In 1613 (*Rogers* v. *Parrey*[1]) the issue, whether a covenant in a lease for twenty-one years not to exercise a particular trade was in restraint of trade, was still susceptible of debate, but Coke, C.J., and the judges of the King's Bench upheld its validity. By 1688 this seems to have become accepted doctrine, for in *Thompson* v. *Harvey*[2] Holt, C.J., was able to say " it was usual to restrain a lessee from such a trade in the house let " giving as the reason " because I will choose whether to let or not ". (Cf. in relation to chattels, *United Shoe Machinery Co. of Canada* v. *Brunet*[3].)

The same has come to be true of dispositions of the freehold: for over one hundred years it has been part of the normal technique of conveyancing to impose and to accept covenants restricting the use of land, including the use for trades or for trade generally, whether of that conveyed or of that retained. A modern example of this is *Newton Abbott Co-operative Society, Ltd.* v. *Williamson and Treadgold, Ltd.*[4].

One may express the exemption of these transactions from the doctrine of restraint of trade in terms of saying that they merely take land out of commerce and do not fetter the liberty to trade of individuals; but I think that one can only truly explain them by saying that they have become part of the accepted machinery of a type of transaction which is generally found acceptable and necessary, so that instead of being regarded as restrictive they are accepted as part of the structure of a trading society. If in any individual case one finds a deviation from accepted standards, some greater restriction of an individual's right to " trade ", or some artificial use of an accepted legal technique, it is right that this should be examined in the light of public policy. An example of this process in a lease (a lessor's covenant as to trading) may be found in *Hinde* v. *Gray*[5], and, in a conveyance, in the Scottish case of *Aberdeen Varieties, Lt.* v. *Donald*[6].

Then there is the well-known type of case where a man sells his business and its goodwill and accepts a limitation on his right to compete. Here, too, we can see the period of scrutiny in the seventeenth century. That, on the sale of the goodwill of a business, a promise might validly be given not to carry on the relevant trade was established, after debate, in *Broad* v. *Jollyfe*[7] —the covenant held void—reversed in the King's Bench[8], where DODDER- IDGE, J., said that it was the usual course of men in their old age to turn over their trade to another; general recognition was given to this type of covenant by LORD MACCLESFIELD in *Mitchel* v. *Reynolds*[9]. So the rule has become accepted that, in the interest of trade itself, restrictions may be imposed on the vendor of goodwill provided that they are fairly and properly ancillary to the sale: if they exceed this limit the " doctrine " may be applied (see *Leather Cloth Co.* v. *Lorsont*[10], where JAMES, V.-C., excepted " natural " covenants from the " doctrine ").

The line of thought that restrictions may in some contexts be imposed, and upheld, where they have become part of the accepted pattern or structure of a trade, as encouraging or strengthening trade, rather than as limiting trade, is I think behind the courts' acceptance of exclusivity contracts and contracts of sole agency. So, in *Bouchard Servais* v. *Prince's Hall Restaurant, Ltd.*[11],

---

[1] (1613), 2 Bulst. 136.
[2] (1688), Comb. 121 at p. 122.
[3] [1909] A.C. 330 at p. 343.
[4] [1952] Ch. 286; [1952] 1 All E.R. 279.
[5] (1840), 1 Man. & G. 195.
[6] 1939 S.C. 788.
[7] (1620), Cro. Jac. 596.
[8] (1620), 2 Roll. Rep. 201.
[9] (1711), 1 P. Wms. at p. 191.
[10] (1869), L.R. 9 Eq. 345.
[11] (1904), 20 T.L.R. 574.

the contract was for exclusive purchase of burgundy for the defendant's restaurant for an indefinite period. The judgments of the lords justices are based on different grounds and it was held, in any event, that the covenant was reasonable; but the judgment of SIR RICHARD HENN COLLINS, M.R., is instructive. He thought that the case did not come within the principle by which restraints of trade were held to be invalid as being contrary to public policy. Contracts of the same class as that now in question, viz., contracts by which persons bound themselves for good consideration to supply their customers with goods obtained from a particular merchant exclusively, were for the benefit of the community. There was need for contracts of this kind and the court must have regard to the fact that contracts for sole agency were matters of every day occurrence (see too *W. T. Lamb & Sons* v. *Goring Brick Co.*[1] where the agreement was not challenged: *British Oxygen Co., Ltd.* v. *Liquid Air, Ltd.*[2]: in the *Adelaide* case[3] an agreement for exclusive purchase of a more comprehensively restrictive character was held to be in restraint of trade).

Lastly (though this is still an uncertain field) certain contracts of employment, with restrictions appropriate to their character, against undertaking other work during their currency may be acceptable (cf. *Warner Brothers Pictures, Inc.* v. *Nelson*[4]; *Gaumont-British Picture Corporation, Ltd.* v. *Alexander*[5]). Here, too, however, if it is found that the restriction is purely limitative or sterilising, it may be subject to examination (see *Gaumont-British Picture Corporation, Ltd.* v. *Alexander*[6], per PORTER, J., and compare the facts in *Young* v. *Timmins*[7]; the decision was mainly based on inadequacy of consideration).

These illustrations are sufficient to show that the courts are not lacking in tools which enable them to select from the whole range of those contracts which in one way or another limit freedom in trading, segments of current and recognisably normal contracts which are not currently liable to be subjected to the necessity of justification by reasonableness. Such contracts may even be listed, provisionally, in categories (see GARE, THE LAW RELATING TO COVENANTS IN RESTRAINT OF TRADE (1935); CHESHIRE & FIFOOT, LAW OF CONTRACT (6th Edn.) (1964) pp. 324, 329 ff.)[8]; but the classification must remain fluid and the categories can never be closed.

I turn now to the agreements. In my opinion, on balance, they enter into the category of agreements in restraint of trade which require justification. They directly bear on, and in some measure restrain, the exercise of the respondents' trade, so the question is whether they are to be treated as falling within some category excluded from the " doctrine " of restraint of trade. The broad test, or rather approach, which I have suggested, is capable of answering this. This is not a mere transaction in property, nor a mere transaction between owners of property: it is essentially a trade agreement between traders. It is not a mere agreement for exclusive purchase of a commodity, though it contains this element: if it were nothing more, there would be a strong case for treating it as a normal commercial agreement of an accepted type. But there are other restrictive elements. There is the tie for a fixed period with no provision for determination by notice: a combination which *McEllistrim* v. *Ballymacelligott Co-operative Agricultural and Dairy Society, Ltd.*[9] shows should be considered together: and there is the fetter

---

[1] [1932] 1 K.B. 710; [1931] All E.R. Rep. 314.   [2] [1925] Ch. 383 at p. 392.
[3] [1913] A.C. at pp. 806–808: *supra*, p. 274.
[4] [1937] 1 K.B. 209; [1963] 3 All E.R. 160.
[5] [1936] 2 All E.R. 1686.   [6] [1936] 2 All E.R. at p. 1692.
[7] (1831). 1 Cr. & J. 331.   [8] See now 8th edn. p. 363.   [9] [1919] A.C. at p. 565.

on the terms on which the station may be sold. Admittedly the respondents could liberate themselves by finding a successor willing to take their place: admittedly, too, being a limited company, they could trade in several places simultaneously, so that even if they remained tied to these sites, and obliged to continue trading there, they could in theory set up business elsewhere. But just as in *McEllistrim's* case[1] the reality of the covenantor's restraint was considered more relevant than his theoretical liberty to depart, so here, in my opinion, addition of all the ingredients takes the case into the category of those which require justification. Finally, the agreement is not of a character which, by the pressure of negotiation and competition, has passed into acceptance or into a balance of interest between the parties or between the parties and their customers; the solus system is both too recent and too variable for this to be said.

The test, suggested by the appellants, seems, by comparison, artificial and unreal. The covenant, they say, is not in restraint of trade because it relates to the use of the respondents' land. Not only does it require an effort of mind to regard the covenant in this way, but also the comment is obvious that an opposite result would be produced by so slight an adjustment as relating the covenant to an area of land instead of to a specific property.

The view which I would take of the agreements, moreover, agrees, as that suggested by the appellants does not, with those reported cases which have been cited as bearing most directly on the present.

In *McEllistrim's* case[1] this House decided that the obligation imposed on a farmer to sell all his milk to the respondent society, a co-operative, was in restraint of trade and unreasonable on the ground that he was thereby prevented from trading both in a wide area in Western Ireland and (effectively) elsewhere and that he had no means open to him to withdraw from the agreement. I find it impossible to extract from the case, even by an argument *ex silentio*, any inference that, had the respondent society's obligations been limited to specified land of theirs, the restrictions would have been exempted from the doctrine. I should be much more inclined to read into it a willingness to accept normal co-operative selling schemes and a rejection of the relevant rule, because it was an unusual and excessive fetter on the farmer's personal liberty. *English Hop Growers, Ltd.* v. *Dering*[2] was another instance of co-operative selling. It is one of those cases to which I have referred in which the decision was a compound one—that the agreement was not in unreasonable restraint of trade. It being apparent that the agreement was both of a normal type (according to ROMER, J., similar agreements were entered into by ninety-five per cent. of the hop growers) and *inter partes* reasonable, it is natural enough that the members of the Court of Appeal based their judgments in different degrees on both these factors. Again one may add that the case lends no support to the appellants' suggestion that the decision was based on the personal character of the agreement or that it would have been any different, or differently expressed, had the agreement related more specifically to the respondent's land. Then there is *Bouchard Servais* v. *Prince's Hall Restaurant, Ltd.*[3]: I have already referred to this case; I need add here only that the decision, upholding the agreements, is not related in any way to the fact that the contract concerned the use to be made of land.

Lastly there is *Foley* v. *Classique Coaches, Ltd.*[4] where on a sale of land

---

[1] [1919] A.C. 548.
[2] [1928] 2 K.B. 174; [1928] All E.R. Rep. 396.
[3] (1904), 20 T.L.R. 574.   [4] [1934] 2 K.B. 1; [1934] All E.R. Rep. 88.

the purchaser agreed to take all the petrol that he needed for his coaching business from the vendor. SCRUTTON, L.J.[1], with whom the other lords justices agreed, described the contract as an ordinary one to purchase petrol from a particular person and held that there was no " undue restraint of trade "; a compound finding, but the ordinary commercial character of the agreement was clearly a strand in it. The fact that the agreement related (as it plainly did) to the use of the defendant's land played no part in the decision.

On this view of the agreements it becomes necessary to subject them to the test of reasonableness. As regards the two solus agreements, having had the benefit of reading the opinions which precede mine, I am content to say that I am in concurrence with them in the view that the Mustow Green agreement does, and that the Corner garage agreement does not (on account of its long duration), satisfy the test of reasonableness in the interests of the parties. I would only add two observations. The first relates to the ground, I think the main ground, on which the Court of Appeal[2] held that even the four years and five months for which the Mustow Green agreement was to last was too long. They were faced with the difficulty (which faces us) that there was very little evidence at the trial, and, because of the course which the trial took, no finding by the judge[3] of facts which would support a tie for any particular period. So the Court of Appeal[2], which had to decide the question of reasonableness for the first time, devised a special and more concrete test of their own. They asked themselves the question, how long it would take the appellants to find an alternative site if the respondents' site were liberated from the tie, and LORD DENNING, M.R., arrived[4] at a period of three years certain and thereafter subject to two years' notice. DIPLOCK, L.J., while not committing himself to any firm period, thought[5] that evidence might have justified a period of two years or so, or an indefinite period subject to two years' notice. I do not feel able to accept this way of dealing with the matter. The parties have contracted in relation to a particular site and no other: who can say what features of it they considered relevant or significant? How can one judge what site, or whether any site, would be an " alternative " or to what lengths the appellants ought to go to find one? What degree of continuity at one place are the appellants entitled to expect, or, conversely, how often may the appellants be expected to move their outlets without losing goodwill or profits? None of these questions can, in my opinion, be answered with certainty, and the question to be answered is a different question. For what the court is endeavouring to ascertain is whether it is unreasonable for the appellants, in relation to the appellants' interest in selling petrol on this location, to bind the respondents to it in the way that the respondents are bound for the period of the tie; or whether, in the public interest of preserving liberty of action to the respondents, they ought not to be held in the fetters which they have accepted. There appears to me to be enough in the evidence to show that, on the appellants' side, to secure a tie for this period was a legitimate commercial objective; and that as regards the respondents, no public policy objection existed against holding them so long bound. On this point it is, I think, legitimate to draw support from a number of decisions in various jurisdictions where restrictions of various kinds, over comparable

---

[1] [1934] 2 K.B. at p. 11; [1934] All E.R. Rep. at p. 91.
[2] [1966] 2 Q.B. at p. 555; [1966] 1 All E.R. 725.
[3] [1966] 2 Q.B. 514; [1965] 2 All E.R. 933.
[4] [1966] 2 Q.B. at p. 564; [1966] 1 All E.R. at p. 729, letter E.
[5] [1966] 2 Q.B. at p. 576; [1966] 1 All E.R. at p. 737, letter A.

periods, have been upheld (see *British American Oil Co.* v. *Hey*[1] (five years); *Peters American Delicacy Co., Ltd.* v. *Patricia's Chocolates and Candies Property, Ltd.*[2] (three years); *Ampol Petroleum, Ltd.* v. *Mutton*[3] (three years); *Shell Co. of South Africa, Ltd.* v. *Gerrans Garage (Pty.), Ltd.*[4] (five years); *Great Eastern Oil and Import Co.* v. *Chafe*[5] (five years)). I should add that I must not be taken either as suggesting that the periods mentioned are maximum periods, or as expressing any opinion as to the validity of ties for periods intermediate between five years and twenty-one years, such as, for example, existed in *Petrofina (Gt. Britain), Ltd.* v. *Martin*[6] (twelve years).

The second observation that I would make is this: the case has been fought exclusively on the first limb of the *Nordenfelt*[7] test of reasonableness (in reference to the interests of the parties), the respondents explicitly disclaiming any reliance on the second limb (in reference to the interests of the public). The first limb itself rests on considerations of public policy: it must do so in order to justify releasing the parties from obligations which they have voluntarily accepted. In relation, however, to many agreements containing restrictions, there may well be wider issues affecting the interests of the public, than those which relate merely to the interests of the parties; these may have been the subject of enquiry, as in this case under statutory powers (Monopolies and Restrictive Practices (Inquiry and Control) Act, 1948[8]), or the subject of a finding by another court (Restrictive Trade Practices Act, 1956[9]) or may be investigated by the court itself. In the present case no separate considerations in this wider field have emerged which are inconsistent with the validity of the Mustow Green solus agreement—on the contrary such as have appeared tend to support it; but I venture to think it important that the vitality of the second limb, or as I would prefer to put it of the wider aspects of a single public policy rule, should continue to be recognized.

Finally it is necessary to deal separately with the mortgage on the respondents' Corner garage, which the appellants contend falls in a separate category, not subject to the " doctrine " of restraint of trade at all. The submission is that, under accepted principles of equity, there is nothing to prevent a mortgage being made irredeemable for a period provided (and this is the only suggested limitation) that the terms of it are not harsh or unconscionable: for this the appellants invoke the well-known judgment of SIR WILFRID GREENE, M.R., in *Knightsbridge Estates Trust, Ltd.* v. *Byrne*[10]. Indeed the appellants' position is even stronger, it is claimed, because the mortgage ranks as a debenture and so may legitimately be made completely irredeemable (Companies Act, 1948, s. 89, s. 455 (1) " debenture "[11]). The steps in this argument are coherent once its foundation is made good—that mortgages as such and restrictions in them fall totally outside the " doctrine " of restraint of trade; but is this foundation sound? I consider first the relevant authorities.

---

[1] [1941] 4 D.L.R. 725.   [2] (1947), 21 A.L.J. 281.
[3] (1952), 53 S.R.N.S.W.1.   [4] [1954] 4 S.A.L.R. 752.
[5] (1956), 4 D.L.R. (2d) 310.
[6] [1966] Ch. 146; [1966] 1 All E.R. 126.
[7] [1894] A.C. 535; [1891–94] All E.R. Rep. 1.
[8] This Act, with Pt. 3 of the Restrictive Trade Practices Act, 1958, which amended it, and the Monopolies and Mergers Act, 1965, constitute the Monopolies and Mergers Acts, 1948 and 1965; see 25 HALSBURY'S STATUTES (2nd Edn.) 751, and 37 HALSBURY'S STATUTES (3rd Edn.) 1972, 177.
[9] See 37 HALSBURY'S STATUTES (3rd Edn.) 77.
[10] [1939] Ch. 441; [1938] 4 All E.R. 618.
[11] See *Knightsbridge Estates Trust, Ltd.* v. *Byrne,* [1940] A.C. 613; [1940] 2 All E.R. 401.

The best known of these is *Biggs* v. *Hoddinott*[1], a brewery mortgage case. The decision is conveniently summarised by LORD DAVEY thus: first, that a stipulation for the continuance of a loan for five years was valid, and secondly, that a covenant to take beer from the mortgagee limited to the continuance of the security did not clog the equity of redemption (see *Bradley* v. *Carritt*[2]). The issue as to restraint of trade was not raised. In *Morgan* v. *Jeffreys*[3] another brewery case, where the contractual right of redemption had passed, a provision against redemption before the expiry of twenty-eight years, coupled with a tie, was held to exceed all reasonable limit, but again no question of restraint of trade was raised. *Biggs* v. *Hoddinott*[1] was recently followed by RUSSELL, J., in *Hill* v. *Regent Oil, Ltd.*[4] where there was a mortgage, coupled with a tie, for twenty years, and it was held that this was not oppressive or unconscionable. The case again was decided purely on the classical principles of equity applicable to mortgages and the judgment makes no reference to restraint of trade. A similar decision was given in Ontario in *Clark* v. *Supertest Petroleum Corporation*[5]. These authorities then establish, and to that extent I have no desire to question them, that as part of a transaction of mortgage, it is permissible, so far as the rules of equity are concerned, both to postpone the date of repayment and, at any rate during the period of the loan, to tie the mortgagor to purchase exclusively the products of the mortgagee. Such an arrangement would fall fairly within the principle which I have earlier suggested, as coming within a recognised and accepted category of transactions, in precisely the same manner as a lease; but just as provisions contained in a lease, affecting the lessees' (or lessors') liberty of trade, which pass beyond what is normally found in and ancillary to this type of transaction and enter on the field of regulation of the parties' trading activities, may fall to be tested as possible restraints of trade, so, in my opinion, may those in a mortgage. The mere designation of a transaction as a mortgage, however true, does not *ipso facto* protect the entire contents of the arrangements from examination however fettering of trade these arrangements may be. If their purpose and nature is found not to be ancillary to the lending of money on security, as, for example, to make the lending more profitable or safer, but some quite independent purpose, they may and should be independently scrutinised. This scrutiny is called for in the present case: for it is clear, on consideration of the mortgage both taken by itself and in its relation to the solus agreement which shortly preceded it, that so far from the tie being ancillary to a predominant transaction of lending money, the mortgage, as was the solus agreement, was entered into as part of a plan, designed by the appellants, to tie the Corner garage to its products for as long as possible. As HARMAN, L.J., put it[6], after a detailed examination of the terms of the mortgage which I forbear from repeating, " the mortgage was intended to bolster up the solus agreement ". It follows, in my opinion, that it must be judged by the test of reasonableness. If this is so, I think that there can be little doubt, once a conclusion adverse to the restrictions is reached as to the solus agreement affecting the Corner garage, that the same must follow as regards the mortgage. I should add that the appellants added to their main argument on this point a subsidiary contention that the stipulations in the mortgage should be

[1] [1898] 2 Ch. 307; [1895–99] All E.R. Rep. 625.
[2] [1903] A.C. 253 at p. 267; [1900–03] All E.R. Rep. 633 at p. 641.
[3] [1910] 1 Ch. 620.
[4] [1962] Estates Gazette Digest 452.
[5] (1958), 14 D.L.R. (2d) 454.
[6] [1966] 2 Q.B. at p. 569; [1966] 1 All E.R. at p. 732, letter H.

regarded in the same legal light as if they had been contained in a lease. For this they referred to s. 85 of the Law of Property Act, 1925, and *Regent Oil Co., Ltd.* v. *J. A. Gregory (Hatch End), Ltd.*[1]. I cannot accept this esoteric argument. For if it be the case that inclusion of the relevant restrictions in a mortgage does not save them from examination, they surely cannot be saved because, for conveyancing purposes, the mortgage also bears the character of a lease. The relationship between the covenant and a lease of the garage site is too technical and notional to bring the case within the recognised exemption which, within limits which I have earlier stated, applies to actual leases of an accepted character.

In my opinion the appeal should be allowed as regards the Mustow Green garage and the judgment and order of MOCATTA, J.[2] so far restored. As regards the Corner garage it should be dismissed.

Attwood v. Lamont

[1920] 3 K.B. 571

A restraint is justifiable on grounds of public policy if, in the light of the circumstances existing at the time when the contract was made, it is no wider than is reasonably necessary to protect the interests of the promisee.

A restraint which prohibits the vendor of a business from competing against the purchaser is justifiable if it is no wider than is reasonably necessary to protect the goodwill in the hands of the purchaser. But a restraint which prohibits an employee from competing against his employer is justifiable only if its sole object is to protect the employer's trade secrets or trade connection.

APPEAL by the defendant from the judgment of a Divisional Court (Bailhache and Sankey, L.JJ.), on appeal from the Kidderminster County Court[3].

The following statement of facts is taken from the judgment of the Master of the Rolls : " In this case the plaintiff is the proprietor of a business which may be called that of a general outfitter. It contained different departments which are enumerated in an agreement referred to later as follows : ' the trade or business of a tailor, dressmaker, general draper, milliner, hatter, haberdasher, gentlemen's, ladies' or children's outfitter.' The defendant was employed as a cutter and head of the tailoring department by the plaintiff and his then partner in 1909. His employment was terminable by a month's notice. He was not concerned with any of the other departments but, no doubt, some of the customers in the tailoring department were also customers in some of the others.

" On entering into the service of the firm he executed the following agreement :

' An agreement made between Harry Attwood and Robert Isaac (hereinafter called " the employers ") of the one part and James Duncan Lamont (hereinafter called " the assistant ") of the other part. Whereas the assistant has requested the employers to employ him as an assistant in their business at Kidderminster at an annual salary commencing at 208*l.*, and two and a half per cent. commission on turnover above 1,000*l.*, in the tailoring department and the employers are only willing to do so upon him entering into the agreement not to trade in opposition with them which is hereinafter expressed. Now this agreement witnesseth that in consideration of the employers employing him in the capacity and at the salary aforesaid the assistant hereby agrees with the employers that

---

[1] [1966] Ch. 402; [1965] 3 All E.R. 673.
[2] [1966] 2 Q.B. 514; [1965] 2 All E.R. 933.   [3] [1920] 2 K. B. 146.

he will not at any time hereafter either on his own account or that of any wife of his or in partnership with or as assistant servant or agent to any other person, persons, or company, carry on or be in any way directly or indirectly concerned in any of the following trades or businesses, that is to say, the trade or business of a tailor, dressmaker, general draper, milliner, hatter, haberdasher, gentlemen's, ladies' or children's outfitter, at any place within a radius of 10 miles of the employers' place of business at Regent House, Kidderminster, aforesaid. And also, that this agreement shall not be affected by any change or changes in the constitution of the employers' firm but that in the event of any change or changes therein the right to enforce this agreement shall continue to the surviving or continuing partner or partners and his or their executors administrators or assigns.'

" In February, 1919, he asked the plaintiff to release him from the agreement or make him a partner, and the plaintiff refused. The defendant then left the plaintiff's service and established himself in business on his own account at Worcester, which is outside the ten-mile radius mentioned in the agreement. There he did business with several of the plaintiff's customers and had personal dealings with them such as taking orders in Kidderminster. The plaintiff then brought an action to restrain him from acting in breach of the agreement and asked for an injunction in the following terms : ' An injunction restraining the defendant from committing any future breach of the said agreement.' The defendant in answer to the claim contended that the agreement was invalid as being in restraint of trade and too wide in its terms to be reasonable.

" It was not seriously contended on behalf of the plaintiff that the agreement could be supported to the full extent of its terms, but it was argued that the restrictions as to the tailoring business could be severed from those relating to the other businesses, and that when so severed it was a reasonable and valid agreement.

" The case was tried in the County Court at Worcester, and the learned County Court judge decided that the contract was not severable and was wider than was reasonably necessary for the protection of the plaintiff's business. He, therefore, gave judgment for the defendant. On appeal to the Divisional Court that Court held that the contract was severable and that when so severed and confined to the tailoring business it was reasonable and valid. Judgment was therefore given for the plaintiff."

The defendant appealed. The appeal was heard on June 18 and 21, 1920.

YOUNGER, L.J. The three questions to which the argument in support of this appeal was directed were : first, whether the stipulations of the restrictive covenant in the agreement of February 15, 1909, were severable, as the Divisional Court thought they were ; secondly, whether if these stipulations were severable they ought in this case to be severed, as the Divisional Court also thought ; and, lastly, whether if they were severed the covenant which would then remain, a covenant confined to the trade or business of a tailor only, was not, contrary to the view of that Court, still void as being in restraint of trade. There was no cross-appeal by the respondent from the finding of the Divisional Court that the covenant unsevered is invalid.

Upon these questions so in debate I have arrived at the conclusion that the stipulations in this covenant are not severable, that the case is not one in which if they were the Court ought to sever them ; and that even if the covenant be severed by deleting what Bailhache, J., called the excess the resulting covenant would still be void as being in restraint of trade.

I regret in expressing these conclusions to find myself at variance with the learned judges of the Divisional Court. But the difference of opinion is really a difference on one matter only. Recent decisions of the House of Lords upon the invalidity of many of these covenants when imposed upon employees in contract of service have, as I read them, effected, in more than one aspect of the subject, a much more fundamental change in hitherto accepted views upon it than has seemed to the learned judges of the Divisional Court to be the case. That is the main difference between us.

Now, we are here dealing with a branch of the law which has at all times been peculiarly susceptible to influence from current views of public policy. Its modern developments have grown up under the shadow of the " laissez faire " school of economics, and, until recently, have, in consequence, been uniformly in the direction of extending the principle of freedom of contract in relation to such bargains, a tendency that has not yet ceased to be operative when the covenant in question is one exacted from a vendor on the sale of the goodwill of his business. But current opinion on the relations between employers and employed has moved rapidly in recent years, and thus it is that the House of Lords, itself bound by comparatively few of the numerous previous decisions on the subject, took the opportunity in 1913, when the validity of a restrictive covenant entered into by an employee came in question before it, to examine the whole problem afresh, with the result that the supreme tribunal, for the guidance of every Court, has now placed upon the permissibility of such covenants a limit which the general interest, including, of course, that of employees themselves, had not previously seemed to require. In consequence it must now, I think, be recognized in all Courts that there is every difference in the matter of its validity between such a covenant as we find here embodied in a contract of service and the same covenant when found in an agreement for the sale of goodwill ; and the dispute between the parties to this action must be decided with due regard to that difference. This declared difference is, as I have said, a matter of recent development, and although it has not been put forward by the House of Lords as a new departure, its effect upon previously accepted views has already been as complete as if it were. Moreover, it may be doubted whether all its incidental consequences have even now become apparent.

A reference to two judgments of long standing and high authority dealing with this subject, one a judgment of the Court of Common Pleas, and the other a judgment of the Court of Chancery, will serve to show that this distinction now so strongly emphasized did not occur at all to the judges of an earlier day. The first of the judgments to which I refer is that of Erle, C.J., in the case of *Mumford* v. *Gething*[1], a case of an employee's restrictive covenant ; and the second, that of James, V.-C., in *Leather Cloth Co.* v. *Lorsont*[2] a case of a vendor's covenant. In each case the necessity in the general interest for upholding such covenants is strongly advocated, but in words so similar as to leave no room for drawing any distinction between the two classes of covenant in any matter of principle.

The passage from the judgment of Erle, C.J., to which I have referred is as follows : " I entirely dissent from the notion thrown out by the defendant's counsel that agreements of this sort are to be discouraged as being contrary to public policy. On the contrary, I think that contracts in partial restraint of trade are beneficial to the public, as well as to the immediate parties ; for, if the law discouraged such agreements as these, employers

---

[1] (1859), 7 C. B. N. S. 305, 319.   [2] (1869), L. R. 9 Eq. 345.

would be extremely scrupulous as to engaging servants in a confidential capacity, seeing that they would incur the risk of their taking advantage of the knowledge they acquired of their customers and their mode of conducting business, and then transferring their services to a rival trader. It appears to me to be highly important that persons like this defendant should be able to enter into contracts of this sort, which will afford some security to their employers that the knowledge acquired in their service will not be used to their prejudice. I think the doctrine laid down by Parke, B., in *Mallan* v. *May*[1] is a correct exposition of the law upon this subject. ' The public,' he says, ' derives an advantage in the unrestrained choice which such a stipulation gives to the employer of able assistants, and the security it affords that the master will not withhold from the servant instruction in the secrets of his trade, and the communication of his own skill and experience, from the fear of his afterwards having a rival in the same business.' And the learned Baron afterwards adds : ' It is justly observed by Lord Wynford, in giving the judgment of the Court in *Homer* v. *Ashford*[2], that it may often happen that individual interest and general convenience render engagements not to carry on trade, or act in a profession, in a particular place, proper ; that engagements of this sort between masters and servants are not injurious restraints of trade, but securities necessary for those who are engaged in it ; and that the effect of such contracts is to encourage rather than cramp the employment of capital in trade, and the promotion of industry.' "

In *Leather Cloth Co.* v. *Lorsont*[3] James, V.-C., dealing with a covenant by the vendor on the sale of goodwill, says :

" The principle is this : Public policy requires that every man shall be at liberty to work for himself, and shall not be at liberty to deprive himself or the State of his labour, skill, or talent, by any contract that he enters into. On the other hand, public policy requires that when a man has by skill or by any other means obtained something which he wants to sell, he should be at liberty to sell it in the most advantageous way in the market ; and in order to enable him to sell it advantageously in the market it is necessary that he should be able to preclude himself from entering into competition with the purchaser. In such a case the same public policy that enables him to do that does not restrain him from alienating that which he wants to alienate, and therefore enables him to enter into any stipulation however restrictive it is, provided that restriction in the judgment of the Court is not unreasonable, having regard to the subject matter of the contract."

Nor again can the existence of the distinction be traced in the historical account given by Lindley, L.J., in the *Nordenfelt* case[4] of the stages in which the law on this subject had, up to that date, gradually been relaxed to suit development of trade and to conform to current ideas and views of public policy and reasonableness : while in his judgment in the same case[5] Bowen, L.J., after an elaborate review of all the cases, states his conclusion to be—a conclusion, be it noted, applicable indifferently to vendors' covenants and to employees' covenants—that by the year 1837 the idea had been fully realized that all partial restraints of trade which satisfied the conditions of the law as to reasonableness and good conduct were not an injury but a benefit to the public ; and that by 1853 the further progress had been made —namely, in *Tallis* v. *Tallis*[6]—that the onus lay upon the person who attacked

---

[1] (1843), 11 M. & W. 653, at p. 666. [2] (1825), 3 Bing. 322, at p. 326 ; 11 Moore, C. P. 91.
[3] (1869), L. R. 9 Eq. 345, at p. 354. [4] [1893] 1 Ch. 630, at p. 647. [5] *Ibid.*, 656.
[6] (1853), 1 E. & B. 391.

a covenant in partial restraint of trade to displace the consideration. The Lord Justice's own view of the law as it then stood he expresses thus[1] : " Partial restraints, or, in other words, restraints which involve only a limit of places at which, or persons with whom, or of modes, in which the trade is to be carried on, are valid when made for a good consideration, and where they do not extend further than is necessary for the reasonable protection of the covenantee." Bowen, L.J.'s view there expressed, a view concurred in by the other judges of the Court of Appeal, and supported by a long line of common law authority, was in other words this—that at that date general or unlimited restraints in trade were, as they had always been, void as being contrary to public policy, but that partial restraints in the sense indicated by him were *prima facie* valid. In the words of Lindley, L.J., every such restraint the Court upheld, unless it was affirmatively shown to be unreasonable as extending further than was required for the protection of the covenantee.

Now it is very important in the present case to bear in mind the confident assertion by the Court of Appeal in the *Nordenfelt* case[2] that these partial restraints were valid. The actual covenant in question in that case was a general restraint, and that covenant—one between vendor and purchaser—was there held valid. And the decision of the Court of Appeal to that effect was upheld by the House of Lords unanimously, while the view of the Court of Appeal as to the *prima facie* validity of partial restraints did not fail to meet with approval in that House, for example, at the hand of Lord Herschell. The Homeric battle which Lord Macnaghten there waged in support of the authorities in equity attacked by Bowen, L.J.—authorities to the effect that all covenants in restraint of trade, partial as well as general, were *prima facie* invalid—had no influence upon the actual decision of the House which was concurred in by all the noble and learned Lords irrespective of their views on that point. Indeed, the decision of the House did not in terms affirm with reference to partial restraints either the one view or the other. Thus it was that until the judgment of the House of Lords in *Mason's* case[3] in 1913, in which Lord Macnaghten's so-called test in the *Nordenfelt* case[2], a test which embodied the equity view, was definitely declared by the House to embody the correct statement of the law, Lord Bowen's opinion particularly, in confining, as it does, all considerations of reasonableness to the position of the covenantee alone, and in treating all partial restraints as *prima facie* good, and not Lord Macnaghten's test indicating the contrary, continued to provide all lower Courts with their working rule. Since *Mason's* case[3], however, Lord Macnaghten's test has become the touchstone of the matter, and the House of Lords has found in it and in the distinction between vendors' covenants and employees' covenants, to which in his speech Lord Macnaghten refers, the foundation for the pronounced views with reference to the limited permissible scope of employees' covenants which the House has then and since developed.

The direct reference to this distinction in Lord Macnaghten's speech is to be found in the following passage from it[4] : " To a certain extent, different considerations must apply in cases of apprenticeship and cases of that sort, on the one hand, and cases of the sale of a business or dissolution of partnership on the other. A man is bound an apprentice because he wishes to learn a trade and to practise it. A man may sell because he is getting too old for the strain and worry of business, or because he wishes

---

[1] [1893] 1 Ch. 662. [2] [1893] 1 Ch. 630. [3] [1913] A. C. 724. [4] [1894] A. C. 535, at p. 566.

for some other reason to retire from business altogether. Then there is obviously more freedom of contract between buyer and seller than between master and servant or between an employer and a person seeking employment." Certainly the distinction is there found in these words, but I cannot find that it had, before *Mason's* case[1], any influence at all upon any intervening decision on employees' covenants. Except in the case of *Leng* v. *Andrews*[2], to which reference will again be made, the views of such covenants enunciated by the common law Courts prior to the *Nordenfelt* case[3] continued to be enforced without any manifest alteration, notwithstanding that the resulting mischief, as he saw it, was more than once alluded to by Neville, J.: see *Leetham* v. *Johnstone-White*[4], where however, the learned Judge felt himself bound to acquiesce in it, so well settled did he conceive the law to be. At length, however, in 1913, as I have said, the House of Lords in *Mason* v. *Provident Clothing and Supply Co.*[1] and in 1916 in the subsequent case of *Morris* v. *Saxelby*[5], defined the limited permissible effect of such a covenant ; and the difference between it and one entered into by a vendor was then at length clearly emphasized. The subject is thus introduced by Lord Haldane in his speech in *Mason's* case[6]: " It is no doubt as a general rule wise to leave adult persons to make their own agreements and take the consequences, but in the present class of case considerations of public policy come in and make it necessary for the Court to scrutinize agreements like the one before your Lordships jealously. The practice of putting into these agreements anything that is favourable to the employer is one which the Courts have to check, and the judges have to see that Lord Macnaghten's test is carefully observed." Lord Shaw in the same case expresses the view that there is much greater room for allowing as between buyer and seller a larger scope for freedom of contract and a correspondingly large restraint in freedom of trade than there is for allowing a restraint of the opportunity for labour in a contract between master and servant or an employer and an applicant for work.

Proceeding upon these lines, the House of Lords has developed this distinction, and the following points may now, I think, be taken to be established.

First, it is the covenantee, the respondent here, who has to show that the restriction sought to be imposed upon the covenantor goes no further than is reasonable for the protection of his business. This obligation was so laid down by Lord Haldane in *Mason's* case[7] and, notwithstanding the judgment of Swinfen-Eady, L.J., in *Eastes* v. *Russ*[8], who pointed out that this view displaced the rule laid down in sundry cases of high authority, it was adhered to by the House in *Morris* v. *Saxelby*[5] : see the speech of Lord Atkinson[9].

Now it is interesting to note how great was the change thereby made. In 1891, that is, before the *Nordenfelt* case[3], Lindley, L.J., in *Mills* v. *Dunham*[10] had said this : " I think that Mr. Levett's contention that you are to treat a restraint of trade as *prima facie* bad, and throw upon the person supporting it the onus of showing that it is reasonable, is introducing a wholly unsound principle into the construction of documents." And in 1899, that is, after the *Nordenfelt* case[3], Romer, L.J., in *Haynes* v. *Doman*[11] expressed himself thus : " Where a man of sufficient age and business

---

[1] [1913] A. C. 724. [2] [1909] 1 Ch. 763. [3] [1894] A. C. 535. [4] [1907] 1 Ch. 189, at p. 194.
[5] [1916] 1 A. C. 688.   [6] [1913] A. C. 724, at p. 734.   [7] [1913] A. C. 724, at p. 734.
[8] [1914] 1 Ch. 468. [9] [1916] 1 A.C. 700. [10] [1891] 1 Ch. 576, at p. 586. [11] [1899] 2 Ch. 13, at p. 30.

capacity knowingly enters into a contract of service which is only in partial restraint of trade, I think the onus lies on him to prove that it goes beyond what was reasonably necessary." That is to say, the Court of Appeal in these decisions after as well as before the *Nordenfelt* case[1] followed the common law rule as therein enunciated by Bowen, L.J., and by Lord Herschell as if it still were the rule of the Court. But when in *Mason's* case[2] Lord Macnaghten's test was definitely accepted as the true one the burden of proof in all these cases necessarily changed, as appears from the following passage in Lord Parker's judgment in *Morris* v. *Saxelby* [3]: " As I read Lord Macnaghten's judgment " in the *Nordenfelt* case[1], Lord Parker says " he was of opinion that all restraints on trade of themselves, if there is nothing more, are contrary to public policy, and therefore void. It is not that such restraints must of themselves necessarily operate to the public injury, but that it is against the policy of the common law to enforce them except in cases where there are special circumstances to justify them. The onus of proving such special circumstances must, of course "—these words " of course " are noticeable—" rest on the party alleging them." Now, when it is remembered that the leading cases on severance were decided at a time when such partial restraints were treated as *prima facie* valid, and when the rule of the Court, dating from *Tallis* v. *Tallis*[4], was that it rested with the covenantor who was bound by and sought to escape from a covenant of partial restriction to establish its invalidity, the importance of this pronouncement on the severance aspect of the present case is obvious.

Secondly—and this is established by the recent cases in the House of Lords—the restraint must be reasonable not only in the interests of the covenantee but in the interests of both the contracting parties. This disposes of the almost passionate protest of Neville, J., in *Leetham* v. *Johnstone-White*[5] that no agreement was invalid, provided the restriction was reasonably necessary for the protection of the employer, however oppressive to the employee and fatal to his chance of obtaining his own living in this country it might be. This is no longer so, although under Bowen, L.J.'s rule the statement was, I think, justified. This modern view of the House of Lords does not, however, involve the restoration of the old principle at one time obtaining that the consideration received by the employee for his covenant must be adequate. It has not. " The Court no longer considers the adequacy of the consideration in any particular case," says Lord Parker in *Morris* v. *Saxelby*[3], but it does involve, per Lord Shaw in the same case[6], and the consideration is of importance in the present case, that as the time of restriction lengthens or the space of its operation grows, the weight of the onus on the covenantee to justify it grows too.

Thirdly, and the most important of all. An employer is not entitled by a covenant taken from his employee to protect himself after the employment has ceased against his former servant's competition *per se*, although a purchaser of goodwill is entitled to protect himself against such competition on the part of his vendor. There are at least two reasons given for this distinction. An employer may not, after his servant has left his employment, prevent that servant from using his own skill and knowledge in his trade or profession, even if acquired when in the employer's service. That skill and knowledge are only placed at the employer's disposal during the employment. They have not been made a subject of sale after that employment has ceased :

---

[1] [1894] A. C. 535.   [2] [1913] A. C. 724, at p. 733.   [3] [1916] 1 A.C. 688.
[4] (1853), 1 E. & B. 391.   [5] [1907] 1 Ch. 189, at p. 194.   [6] [1916] 1 A. C. 715.

see *Leng* v. *Andrews*[1]. Again, when a purchaser takes over the goodwill of a business, if he is to have all its advantages it must in his hands be immune from its former owner exercising his special knowledge and skill to its detriment, and without a covenant on the part of the vendor against competition a purchaser cannot get what he is contracting to buy, nor can the vendor give what he is intending to sell. But, on the other hand, as is pointed out by Lord Parker in *Morris* v. *Saxelby*[2], the case is very different when the employer takes such a covenant from his employee. The employer's goodwill is always necessarily subject to the competition of all persons, including the employee, who choose to engage in a similar trade. " The employer in such a case is not endeavouring to protect what he has, but to gain a special advantage he could not otherwise secure." Accordingly covenants against competition by a former servant are as such not upheld ; and the permissible extent of any covenant imposed upon a servant must be tested in every case with reference to the character of the work done for the employer by the servant while in his service and by the consideration whether in that view the covenant taken from him goes further than is reasonably necessary for the protection of the proprietary rights of the covenantee. " The reason, and the only reason," says Lord Parker in *Morris* v. *Saxelby*[3] " for upholding such a restraint on the part of an employee is that the employer has some proprietary right, whether in the nature of trade connection or in the nature of trade secrets, for the protection of which such a restraint is—having regard to the duties of the employee—reasonably necessary. Such a restraint has, so far as I know, never been upheld, if directed only to the prevention of competition or against the use of the personal skill and knowledge acquired by the employee in his employer's business."

Fourthly, in the opinion at least of two learned Lords, Lord Shaw and Lord Moulton, previously accepted rules as to the doctrine of severance require careful application if not entire reconsideration. To this point I will return[4].

Proceeding now to apply these principles to the facts of the present case, the position appears to be that the respondent is the owner of a considerable business at Kidderminster, described in the agreement in question as a business of drapers, tailors and general outfitters. The business is, I presume for convenience, divided into different departments all under the same roof, customers going from one to another, and many customers dealing in all departments. The agreement into which the appellant entered, a printed form which all managers of departments are required to sign with modifications of salary and detail appropriate to the individual case, is indorsed as " An agreement not to trade in opposition within a radius of 10 miles of Regent House, Kidderminster," and contains a recital " that the assistant," the appellant, " has requested the employers to employ him as an assistant in their business at Kidderminster at an annual salary commencing at 208*l.* and two and a half per cent. commission on turnover above 1,000*l.* in tailoring department; and the employers are only willing to do so upon his entering into the agreement not to trade in opposition to him which is hereinafter expressed " and witnesses " that in consideration of the employers employing him in the capacity and at the salary aforesaid . . . he will not at any time thereafter . . . carry on or be in any way

---

[1] [1909] 1 Ch. 763.   [2] [1916] 1 A. C. 688, at p. 709.   [3] *Ibid.*, 688, at p. 710.
[4] See *infra*, pp. 296–299.

directly or indirectly concerned in any of the following trades or businesses, that is to say, the trade or business of a tailor, dressmaker, general draper, milliner, hatter, haberdasher, gentlemen's, ladies' or children's outfitter at any place, within a radius of 10 miles of the employers' place of business at Regent House, Kidderminster, aforesaid." The agreement is expressed to be and is, in my opinion, nothing more than an agreement not to trade in opposition to the employers in any part of their business. It will be broken if the appellant not only carries on but is directly or indirectly concerned in any of the specified businesses ; and the period of restriction is to cover the whole life of the appellant, although the employment was itself an employment only for a month certain. The appellant, while it is not so stated in the agreement, was manager of the tailoring department and was the principal or only cutter in the respondent's employ. He measured, cut, and fitted on the clothes made in that department, and in doing so, he, of course, became acquainted with the customers. He is said to be an extremely skilful cutter, and the department prospered when under his management. He has now set up in business at Worcester, beyond the ten-mile radius, but he has supplied with clothes former customers of the respondent within that radius, and has also fitted their clothes within it. That is the breach of covenant complained of. The evidence of a Mr. Middleton called to prove one such breach was that he had been measured and fitted by the appellant when he was at the respondents ; that he gave him every satisfaction ; that he met him in Broad Street, Worcester, one day and said : " I hear you have started business in Worcester, I may as well give you an order, send me over some patterns." That evidence confirms me in the conclusion which I should have drawn from the case generally, that it is the appellant's known personal skill as a cutter which attracts to him the customers to whom he attended when with the respondent, and except that they made his acquaintance when he was in the respondent's service, it was not his position there, but it is his own skill which leads them to desire to have the continued benefit of his services, now that he is in business for himself. The question accordingly is whether in these circumstances, and in view of the principles applicable to them enunciated by the House of Lords, this covenant has any validity. In my opinion, as I have already said, it has none. It was apparently strongly urged in the Divisional Court that the covenant was valid as it stands. The learned judges there held that, extending to businesses with which the appellant had had no connection when in the respondent's employment, it was manifestly too wide, and they so held.

But the learned judges held also that they were entitled to sever the covenant by limiting it to the business of a tailor, and this they did.

Now I agree with the Master of the Rolls that this was not a case in which upon any principle this severance was permissible. The learned judges of the Divisional Court, I think, took the view that such severance always was permissible when it could be effectively accomplished by the action of a blue pencil. I do not agree. The doctrine of severance has not, I think, gone further than to make it permissible in a case where the covenant is not really a single covenant but is in effect a combination of several distinct covenants. In that case and where the severance can be carried out without the addition or alteration of a word, it is permissible. But in that case only.

Now, here, I think, there is in truth but one covenant for the protection of the respondent's entire business, and not several covenants for the protection of his several businesses. The respondent is, on the evidence, not carrying on several businesses but one business, and, in my opinion, this covenant must stand or fall in its unaltered form.

But further, I am of opinion that even if this were not so this case is not one in which any severance, even if otherwise technically permissible, ought to be made. In my view the necessary effect of the application of the principle on which *Mason's* case[1] and *Morris* v. *Saxelby*[2] have both been decided has been to render obsolete the cases in which the Courts have severed these restrictive covenants when acting on the view that being *prima facie* valid it was their duty to bind the covenantee to them as far as was permissible. It may well be that these cases are still applicable to covenants between vendor and purchaser, for upon such covenants the effect of Lord Macnaghten's test upon the law as previously understood has been little more than a matter of words, and Lord Moulton's observations, now to be referred to, have no direct application to such covenants. But these authorities do not seem to me to be any longer of assistance in the case of a covenant between employer and employee. To such a covenant I think the statement of Lord Moulton in *Mason's* case[1] necessarily applies. Lord Moulton there says this[3] : " I do not doubt that the Court may, and in some cases will, enforce a part of a covenant in restraint of trade, even though taken as a whole the covenant exceeds what is reasonable. But, in my opinion, that ought only to be done in cases where the part so enforceable is clearly severable, and even so only in cases where the excess is of trivial importance, or merely technical, and not a part of the main purport and substance of the clause. It would in my opinion be *pessimi exempli* if, when an employer had exacted a covenant deliberately framed in unreasonably wide terms, the Courts were to come to his assistance and, by applying their ingenuity and knowledge of the law, carve out of this void covenant the maximum of what he might validly have required. It must be remembered that the real sanction at the back of these covenants is the terror and expense of litigation, in which the servant is usually at a great disadvantage, in view of the longer purse of his master." Then after a passage which does not apply to this case his Lordship goes on : " and the hardship imposed by the exaction of unreasonable covenants by employers would be greatly increased if they could continue the practice with the expectation that, having exposed the servant to the anxiety and expense of litigation, the Court would in the end enable them to obtain everything which they could have obtained by acting reasonably." Lord Shaw expresses the same opinion in his speech where he says[4] : " Courts of law should not be astute to disentangle such contracts and to grant injunctions or restraints which are not justified by their terms." And these opinions are very strongly re-enforced by the following extract from the judgment in *Goldsoll* v. *Goldman*[5] of Neville, J., a learned judge whose words on this subject deserve to have special weight attached to them in that he was a pioneer on the road subsequently taken by the House of Lords. " It seems to me to be in accordance both with principle and justice that if a man seeks to restrain another from exercising his lawful calling to an extent which the law, even as it now stands, deems unreasonable, the contract by which he does so, whether grammatically severable or not, should be held to be void *in toto*.

---

[1] [1913] A. C. 724. [2] [1916] 1 A. C. 688. [3] [1913] A. C. 724, at p. 745.
[4] [1913] A. C. 724, at p. 742. [5] [1914] 2 Ch. 603, at p. 613.

To hold otherwise seems to me to expose the covenantor to the almost inevitable risk of litigation which in nine cases out of ten he is very ill able to afford, should he venture to act upon his own opinion as to how far the restraint upon him would be held by the Court to be reasonable, while it may give the covenantee the full benefit of unreasonable provisions if the covenantor is unable to face litigation."

In my judgment a reference to the very principle which, in the view of the House of Lords, rendered the closest scrutiny of these covenants essential, makes it necessary, if that scrutiny when fruitful is to be operative, that severance where the covenant as a whole is invalid should not in the general case be allowed. I know that this view has not been taken either by Sargant, J., in *Nevanas & Co.* v. *Walker*[1] or by the Court of Appeal in *Goldsoll* v. *Goldman*[2] on the ground generally that the question did not directly arise in *Mason's* case[3] and that the House of Lords could not be supposed in what was there said to have cast doubt on successive decisions of the Court of Appeal which had held that the doctrine of severability applied to such covenants. But it is to be observed that both of these judgments were given before the decision of *Morris* v. *Saxelby*,[4] in which the principles of *Mason's* case[3] were strengthened and re-enforced, and in which it was made plain that the House of Lords had there at least made havoc of strong uniform previous decisions as to the burden of proof, to which I have already referred. Sargant, J., too, held that the covenant in the case before him was invalid even if severed, so that his remarks on severance were by the way, while the covenant in *Goldsoll* v. *Goldman*[5] was one between vendor and purchaser to which the principle of *Mason's* case[3] is not, as I have pointed out, directly applicable[6].

Now, while censure in reference to the covenant with which we have to deal is not fairly attributable to the respondent, for the agreement is dated in 1909 when even the Court of Appeal had, in view of the subsequent decision in *Mason's* case[3], failed fully to appreciate the effect of the *Nordenfelt* case[7]; still, this case is not, I think, one in which the Court, if it need not do so, should be astute to sever its provisions. This system of printed covenants prepared beforehand for signature by every future employee, irrespective of the nature of his employment or his personal qualifications, is to be deprecated in the interests of fair play, and the system is only likely to disappear if it be thoroughly understood by employers that such covenants will not be assisted in cases where in their integrity they are found to be oppressive. I think, therefore, that there ought to be no severance here.

Lastly, I am of opinion that even if the covenant be severable and be severed as the Divisional Court have severed it, it remains invalid.

The severed covenant continues to be a covenant against competition, and in my opinion in the circumstances of this case, a covenant against competition only. The appellant is a dangerous rival of the plaintiff in his own district, not by reason of any knowledge of the plaintiff's connection or customers possessed by the appellant, but by reason of his own skill. The covenant is quite inappropriate to protect the plaintiff against such

---

[1] [1914] 1 Ch. 413.   [2] [1915] 1 Ch. 292.
[3] [1913] A. C. 724.   [4] [1916] 1 A. C. 688.
[5] [1914] 2 Ch. 603.
[6] For the reconciliation of *Goldsoll* v. *Goldman* and *Attwood* v. *Lamont* see *Ronbar Enterprises, Ltd.* v. *Green*, [1954] 2 All E. R. 266.   [7] [1894] A. C. 535.

activities of the appellant as, apart from competition, might be regarded as injurious to his goodwill, and, moreover, being a covenant for life and excluding the appellant for that period from a considerable area with reference to the great bulk of whose residents, in connection with tailoring, the plaintiff has no relation at all, it is, I think, on any view, unreasonably wide. This in my judgment was not a case in which, from the nature of the appellant's employment, the only method by which the respondent could obtain protection for that which he was entitled to protect was by prohibiting competition on the part of the appellant in a defined area. I agree that had that been the case such a restraint, if otherwise reasonable, would not have been illegal by reason of its preventing the appellant from doing within that area acts which the respondent could otherwise not lawfully restrain. But in my opinion this was not such a case. The covenant is essentially inappropriate to the attainment of any legitimate purpose of the respondent, while as it stands it has not been justified by any evidence from him that his connection required so wide a restraint, or, at any rate, a restraint so extended in duration.

I fully share, if I may be allowed to say so, Sankey, J.'s, view that the Court should not lightly absolve parties from the performance of contracts solemnly entered into. Lord Watson's words in the *Nordenfelt* case[1] must also command immediate assent : " that the community has a material interest in maintaining the rules of fair dealing between man and man " ; and that " It suffers far greater injury from the infraction of these rules than from contracts in restraint of trade." Even so, however, there has developed in late years in these employees' covenants a distinct tendency to make them penal rather than protective, and if that mischievous tendency can only be effectively checked by absolving in a few cases from their bargain employees who have no equity to claim release, the result is still not altogether regrettable. It must not, however, be supposed that I take this to be one of these cases. In my judgment the appellant here is deriving no substantial advantage in what he is doing from his previous connection with the respondent's business. Even, however, if he were, the decision in his favour might do this service—it might compel employers to consider the proper limit of restraint which in any particular case they are fairly entitled to insist upon, and having kept the restriction imposed within these limits they will not without success apply to the Courts to exercise their primary function of seeing to it that such bargains like any others fairly entered into are duly observed.

For these reasons I am of opinion that this appeal should be allowed and the judgment of the County Court judge restored with costs here and below.

LORD STERNDALE delivered judgment to the same effect ; ATKIN, L.J., concurred with YOUNGER, L.J.

***

Bennett v. Bennett
[1952] 1 K.B. 249

If a contract contains a number of promises, some void and others valid, the court may allow the contract to stand after eliminating or modifying the void promises; though no severance is possible if any promise is illegal.
Severance may take two forms:—
   (i) The void promise may be eliminated without invalidating the rest of the contract if it forms only a subsidiary part of the contract.

[1] [1894] A. C. 535, at p. 552.

    (ii) The void promise may be reduced in extent if it is so drafted as to be divisible into a number of separate and independent parts.

APPEAL from Devlin, J.[1]

On August 10, 1948, the plaintiff wife presented a petition for dissolution of marriage. She asked for custody of the two sons of the marriage, alimony pending suit, maintenance for the younger son, and maintenance and secured provision for herself. The petition was not defended.

On November 24, 1948, before pronouncement of the decree, the respondent husband entered into a deed whereby he agreed to make financial provision for the petitioner and the younger son, in consideration for which the petitioner covenanted by clause 10 of the deed not to proceed with the prayers for maintenance, to consent to those prayers being dismissed, and not to present any further petition for maintenance.

On the same day, November 24, 1948, the registrar, on being informed of the deed, dismissed the application for maintenance of the petitioner and the younger son contained in the petition. On December 6, 1948, the decree nisi was granted, and in due course was made absolute.

After the execution of the deed the husband made regular payments in accordance with its provisions until financial difficulties rendered him unable to keep up the payments. In those circumstances the wife brought the present action, claiming £262 10s. 0d., being instalments due on December 25, 1950, of the two annuities provided by the deed.

Devlin, J., gave judgment for the husband. He held that the covenant sued upon was void as being contrary to public policy, in that it sought to oust the jurisdiction of the court.

The wife appealed.

SOMERVELL, L.J. . . . The defence to the action is, first, that the consideration, or part of the consideration, moving from the wife was an undertaking not to invoke the jurisdiction of the court in respect of maintenance for herself or for her child, and that this was void as being contrary to public policy: see *Hyman* v. *Hyman*[2]. Therefore, it was said, the whole deed was void. In that case the House of Lords decided that a covenant with regard to a wife not applying to the court was unenforceable. The House did not have before it the question whether the existence of this covenant voided the whole deed, so that the husband could, as he seeks to do here, have repudiated liability on his covenants. They held that the jurisdiction conferred on the court to order maintenance was not only in the interest of the wife but of the public.

Before the judge the main argument appears to have been that no part of the clause in this case was contrary to public policy. The judge held that in so far as the plaintiff had promised not to apply to the court in respect of maintenance for her son, under section 193 of the Supreme Court of Judicature (Consolidation) Act, 1925, this was contrary to public policy. He then proceeded on the basis that if part of the consideration for a promise was contrary to public policy the whole promise was unenforceable, and gave judgment for the defendant.

Before us it was conceded by Mr. Cross, for the plaintiff wife, that so much of the wife's covenant as related to the son was unenforceable. On this basis his argument was, first, that the fact that part of the consideration was unenforceable as contrary to public policy did not in a case of this kind make the whole agreement void. Reliance was placed by way of analogy

---

[1] [1951] 2 K. B. 572.   [2] [1929] A. C. 601.

on the decision in *Czarnikow* v. *Roth, Schmidt & Co.*[1] In that case this court held that part of an arbitration clause which purported to preclude an application to the court for a " consultative case " was void and contrary to public policy as involving an attempt to oust the jurisdiction of the court. It seems, however, clear that the court did not regard that as making void the arbitration clause generally, still less the agreement in which it was contained. Mr. Cross, assuming he established this, further argued that, apart from the promise with regard to the son, the promise with regard to his wife's own maintenance was, having regard to its terms, not contrary to public policy. On that basis, or possibly in any event, he argued that the defendant was not relieved from his obligations; that the agreement should stand, the court striking out only that part of the plaintiff's promises which were objectionable.

Before considering the terms of the deed I will state what seem to me to be the principles to be extracted from the cases. The area is a difficult one in that there are undoubtedly general observations in some cases which, if taken in their generality, appear inconsistent with other decisions. The principle applied by the judge, that if part of the consideration for a promise is " illegal," as being contrary to public policy, the agreement as a whole cannot be enforced, is in accord with statements to be found in more than one reported case. For example, Coltman, J., in *Hopkins* v. *Prescott*[2] and Tindal, C.J., in *Waite* v. *Jones*[3] so stated. In the latter case Tindal, C.J., said: " A party cannot enforce a contract where the consideration is illegal either in the whole or part." It is to be noted that the subject-matter of the promise in the former case was in part the sale of a public office, which was a misdemeanour under 49 George 3, c. 126, and in the latter it was alleged that part of the consideration was for a future separation of spouses. For spouses to separate was not, of course, a criminal offence, but consideration for a future separation was regarded like future cohabitation as *contra bonos mores*.

I have already referred to *Czarnikow* v. *Roth, Schmidt & Co.*[1] where a different principle was applied. In restraint of trade cases there are many decisions under which part only of the restraint has been treated as unenforceable and contrary to public policy. This has not vitiated the rest of the clause. A recent example is *Goldsoll* v. *Goldman*[4]. There was an agreement for the sale of a business which contained a covenant by the vendor not to deal in real or imitation jewellery in the United Kingdom or in various countries abroad. The covenant was restricted by the court to the United Kingdom and dealings in imitation jewellery, the remaining provisions being unenforceable. It was held, in accordance with a long series of authorities, that the covenant could be severed, part being enforceable, and part unenforceable, as contrary to public policy. In these cases, therefore, part is held to be contrary to public policy, the remainder being enforceable. It is to be noted that the severability is one-sided. If in *Goldsoll* v. *Goldman*[4] the purchase price had been split up, so much for the business, so much for the covenant not to trade in the United Kingdom in (*a*) real jewellery, (*b*) imitation jewellery, and so on, there could have been true severability. The court in effect, however, strikes out some of the promises while leaving the consideration on the other side unaffected. This would only be justified if what was struck out was subsidiary to the main purpose. In *Goldsoll's*[4]

---

[1] [1922] 2 K. B. 478.   [2] (1847), 4 C. B. 578, at p. 596.
[3] (1835), 1 Bing. N. C. 656, at p. 662, affirmed *sub. nom. Jones* v. *Waite* (1839), 5 Bing. N. C. 341.   [4] [1915] 1 Ch. 292.

case the purchaser got the business, and what the court held to be reasonable protection against competition. What was struck out was plainly subsidiary to the main purpose. If the purchaser had notionally allocated part of the purchase price to promises held to be contrary to public policy he would have had to abide the consequences. In this class of case the restraint is subsidiary either to a purchaser or to a contract of service. If promises in restraint of trade were the sole subject-matter, and those promises were wholly or in the main contrary to public policy, it seems to me clear that the court would treat the whole contract as void.

The cases to which we were referred seem to me to indicate that if one of the promises is to do an act which is either in itself a criminal offence or *contra bonos mores*, the court will regard the whole contract as void. In restraint of trade cases there is nothing wrong in not trading. What is objectionable is or may be a promise for consideration not to do so. It is not necessary to decide whether this is exhaustive, because I at any rate regard *Czarnikow* v. *Roth, Schmidt & Co.*[1] as an authority binding on this court that in a proper case the doctrine of severability can be applied where the objectionable promise is one purporting to oust the jurisdiction of the court. It seems to me that the court clearly expressed the view that the arbitration clause remained binding, the objectionable words in one clause of it only being in effect struck out.

The first question, therefore, in the present appeal is whether the whole or main consideration moving from the plaintiff wife was a promise or promises purporting to oust the jurisdiction of the court. Under the deed the defendant was to convey to the plaintiff a house to be held by her on trust for herself during her life and on her death for the defendant. The deed acknowledged the gift by the defendant to the plaintiff of the furniture and effects in the house formerly the defendant's property. The defendant covenanted to pay to the plaintiff during her life such a sum as after deduction of income tax would leave £750. The defendant covenanted with the plaintiff and the trustees to pay a secured annuity to the trustees of such sum as after deduction of income tax would leave £300 while her son was alive and under the age of 18 years. There were provisions as to how this should be dealt with during the plaintiff's life, and should she die while the son was under 18. If the proceedings for dissolution of the marriage did not result in a decree absolute the defendant had power to revoke. There are other subsidiary provisions, apart from the plaintiff's covenants, which need not be referred to.

The plaintiff's covenants are contained in clause 10, which reads as follows: " Mrs. Bennett hereby covenants with Mr. Bennett (*a*) to accept the provisions hereby made for her and the younger son in full satisfaction of all rights and claims of Mrs. Bennett and her said two children or any of them against Mr. Bennett in respect of alimony pending suit, maintenance of her two children or either of them, maintenance of herself or secured provision for herself or any like relief whether under section 190 of the Supreme Court of Judicature Act, 1925, or section 10 of the Matrimonial Causes Act, 1937, or otherwise howsoever. (*b*) Not to proceed further with the prayer in her said petition that Mr. Bennett do pay to Mrs. Bennett alimony pending suit, maintenance of the younger son, maintenance and a secured provision and to consent to such prayer being dismissed. (*c*) Not

---

[1] [1922] 2 K. B. 478.

to institute, enter, present or proceed with nor to procure, suggest, assist or encourage directly or indirectly either in her own right or on behalf of her said two children, or either of them, any petition, summons or other proceedings for or in respect of any such alimony pending suit, maintenance of her said two children or either of them, maintenance of herself or secured provision for herself or any like relief. (*d*) Out of her own moneys (including the first annuity and the second annuity) during her life to provide and pay for the maintenance and education of the younger son during his infancy and to keep him at Felstead School until he attains the age of eighteen years. (*e*) At all times to save harmless and keep indemnified Mr. Bennett from and against all actions, proceedings, claims, demands, damages, costs, charges and expenses arising during Mrs. Bennett's life in respect of or in connexion with all or any of the matters or things mentioned or referred to in this clause."

The references to alimony pending suit can for present purposes be disregarded. It is also conceded that the clause is objectionable in so far as it deals with applications for maintenance for the son. What, then, is the effect of the promise not to proceed further with the prayer in her petition for maintenance and secured provision for herself and to consent to such prayer being dismissed ? . . .

I have come to the conclusion, for the reasons I have given, that the promises contained in clause 10 (*a*) to (*c*) of the deed were promises which purported to oust the jurisdiction of the court over the whole field of maintenance. Was it the main consideration ? The indemnity in clause 10 (*e*) is consequential on the undertaking to accept the provisions in full satisfaction and cannot be regarded as any or any appreciable degree of further consideration. Clause 10 (*d*) is, I think, some further consideration. The plaintiff is, as I read it, undertaking that the boy shall remain at Felstead, even though the total cost of his upkeep exceeded the amount of the second annuity. I am, however, clear that the main consideration moving from the wife in accepting this quantification of her rights was her promise not to invoke the jurisdiction of the court. I therefore think the covenants sought to be enforced in the present proceedings are void and unenforceable. I have limited my conclusion in this way because that is the only point before us. If the defendant sought later, as he may not, to reclaim the furniture or the house, there may be an argument that on the terms of the deed these items, particularly the furniture, are unaffected by this judgment. This point, if it be a point, was not argued before us.

I have left to this stage an argument which Mr. Cross, for the plaintiff, based on certain observations in *Hyman* v. *Hyman*[1], because I have, I think, given them full force in the above reasoning. In *Hyman* v. *Hyman*[1], as I have said, the question was whether a covenant by a wife, in a separation deed, not to apply to the court was enforceable when, owing to an alteration of the law, she became entitled to sue for a divorce. The first question was whether the covenant on its terms applied to these altered circumstances. The majority held that it did so and was unenforceable. The House did not have to decide whether this voided the whole deed. The question as to whether it did was, however, referred to by counsel in argument, at any rate in the Court of Appeal. Mr. Cross drew our attention to various passages which proceed, I think, clearly on the basis that the husband remained bound. Both Lord Hailsham[2] and Lord Atkin[3] use words which suggest that the

---

[1] [1929] A. C. 601.   [2] [1929] A. C. 601, at p. 609.   [3] *Ibid.*, 629.

husband would remain bound and that any future application by the wife could only be for an additional sum. The passages referred to above indicate what I have accepted, namely, that in this area the unenforceability or " illegality " is not of the kind which, however small a part of the consideration it may be, necessarily voids the whole agreement. I do not think it would be right to regard these observations as a final authority on a point which was not before the House. The doctrine of severability being applicable might well have prevented the whole agreement from being regarded as void. The main subject of the agreement was the separation. The possibility of divorce was remote and seemed to depend on a change in the law. It might well, in these circumstances, be held to be subsidiary and " severable." In any case separation deeds raise different issues.

Mr. Cross referred to the possible difficulty in which the plaintiff might be in applying for maintenance or secured provision for herself. I hope I shall not be going beyond what is proper in stating what I think the position would be having regard to our decision, if and when she applies. She would, for reasons which I have given, be in the position of having made no application under section 190 of the Act of 1925 or its successor, section 19 in the Matrimonial Causes Act, 1950. The question would, therefore, be whether the application was made in a reasonable time. The court in *Fisher* v. *Fisher*[1] allowed an application by a wife seven years after a decree, the wife having in the interval relied on a continuance of payments of alimony and an undertaking by her former husband to settle certain property on her. Negotiations broke down and it was, as I have said, held that she ought to be given leave to apply. It would seem to me that the plaintiff has, both with regard to time and other circumstances, a stronger case here to have her application entertained. Mr. Sachs for the defendant said, while agreeing that it was a matter for the court, that his client would not resist any application to the court to quantify his liability.

The appeal, therefore, in my opinion, should be dismissed.

DENNING, L.J. In this case the only question to my mind is whether the wife can sue upon the deed by action at law or whether her proper remedy is by application to the Divorce Court. I would not subscribe to a decision which deprived her of all remedy. When husband and wife are separated or divorced, it is often found that they have entered into a deed whereby the husband covenants to pay his wife an annuity and she in turn covenants not to apply to the courts for maintenance. When that happens there is nothing wrong in the husband's covenant to pay the annuity, at any rate where it is taken by itself; but there may be something wrong, or at any rate invalid, in the wife's covenant not to apply to the courts. She has a statutory right to apply to the courts for maintenance; and a covenant, by which she renounces that right, may be unenforceable against her, as being contrary to public policy. A good instance is *Hyman* v. *Hyman*[2]. The question then arises: what is the effect of this on the deed as a whole? and in particular: what is the effect on the husband's covenant to pay the annuity?

In solving this problem a useful analogy may be drawn from covenants in unreasonable restraint of trade. Such covenants offend public policy, just as the covenants of a wife not to apply to the courts may do. They are not " illegal," in the sense that a contract to do a prohibited or immoral act is illegal. They are not " unenforceable," in the sense that a contract

---
[1] [1942] P. 101.   [2] [1929] A. C. 601.

within the Statute of Frauds is unenforceable for want of writing. These covenants lie somewhere in between. They are invalid and unenforceable. The law does not punish them. It simply takes no notice of them. They are void, not illegal. That is how they were described by the full Court of Exchequer Chamber in *Price* v. *Green*[1], and by the Court of Appeal in *Evans & Co.* v. *Heathcote*[2].

The presence of a void covenant of this kind does not render the deed totally ineffective. That has been well shown by Professor Cheshire and Mr. Fifoot in their book on Contract, (8th ed., pp. 381–386). The party who is entitled to the benefit of the void covenant, or rather who would have been entitled to the benefit of it if it had been valid, can sue upon the other covenants of the deed which are in his favour; and he can even sue upon the void covenant, if he can sever the good from the bad (*Goldsoll* v. *Goldman*[3]), even to the extent of getting full liquidated damages for a breach of the good part: *Price* v. *Green*[4]. So also the other party, that is, the party who gave the void covenant and is not bound by its restraints, can himself sue upon the covenants in his favour, save only when his void covenant forms the whole, or substantially the whole, consideration for the deed. If the void covenant goes only to part of the consideration, so that it can be ignored and yet leave the rest of the deed a reasonable arrangement between the parties, then the deed stands and can be enforced in every respect save in regard to the void covenant. That seems to me to be the explanation of *Bishop* v. *Kitchen*[5], *Kearney* v. *Whitehaven Colliery Co.*[6] and *Czarnikow* v. *Roth, Schmidt & Co.*[7]

If the cases on wife's covenants are examined, it will be found that they depend on the same distinction:

1. *Separation agreements.* Once parties are separated, a separation agreement (by which the husband covenants to pay his wife an annuity and she covenants to live separately and apart from him) is perfectly lawful, so long as the agreement is made because of the separation and not with a view to divorce. Sometimes in such a deed there will be found a covenant by the wife not to apply to the court for further maintenance; and that covenant, in some contingencies, is not enforceable against her. For instance, the covenant is not enforceable against her in the event of a subsequent divorce (*Hyman* v. *Hyman*[8]), and it may not be enforceable against her if circumstances so change that the husband can be said to be guilty of " wilful neglect to provide reasonable maintenance " for her, though I would not wish to express a concluded opinion on that point. Nevertheless those contingencies at the time of the deed usually are somewhat remote, and they can be ignored without affecting the reasonableness of the deed as a whole. They do not go to the whole of the consideration for the annuity. The substantial consideration for it is the agreement to live separate and that has been performed. The wife can therefore sue by action at law on the deed, notwithstanding the unenforceability of that particular covenant. That is, I think, implicit in the speeches in the House of Lords in *Hyman* v. *Hyman*[8] particularly in the speech of Lord Atkin[9], where he speaks of statutory maintenance as a " supplement " to the annuity granted by the deed.

2. *Agreements for permanent maintenance on a divorce.* An award of

---

[1] (1847), 16 M. & W. 346, at p. 365.
[3] [1915] 1 Ch. 292.
[5] (1868), 38 L. J. Q. B. 20.
[7] [1922] 2 K. B. 478, at p. 490.
[2] [1918] 1 K. B. 418, at p. 426, 431, 436.
[4] (1847), 16 M. & W. 346.
[6] [1893] 1 Q. B. 700.
[8] [1929] A. C. 601.
[9] *Ibid.*, 629.

permanent maintenance on a divorce is peculiarly a matter for the Divorce Court, and the jurisdiction of that court in regard to it cannot be ousted by the private agreement of the parties. The reason lies in public policy. First, it is in the public interest that the wife and children of a divorced husband should not be left dependent on public assistance, or on charity, when he has the means to support them. They should therefore be able to come to the Divorce Court for maintenance, notwithstanding any agreement to the contrary: *Hyman* v. *Hyman*[1]. Secondly, when maintenance is awarded by the Divorce Court, it is not fixed irrevocably at a named figure. It can be varied thereafter, upwards or downwards, according to the circumstances prevailing at the time. And if the husband is unable to pay, and arrears accumulate, it is in the discretion of the Divorce Court whether to enforce payment of the arrears or not. These beneficent controls would be lost if the parties could, by agreement, without the intervention of the court, fix maintenance permanently at an unalterable figure. Any private agreement of the parties which purports to make maintenance a debt enforceable at law must of necessity impliedly oust the jurisdiction of the Divorce Court to fix it, vary it or discharge it, and it is, by reason of that implication, invalid, for the ouster goes to the whole consideration. There is no consideration moving from the wife except an implied promise to accept the named figure and not to ask for more, and that is invalid, because it impliedly takes away the jurisdiction of the court to give her more. If her promise does not bind her, then his should not bind him: *Gaisberg* v. *Storr*[2]; *Combe* v. *Combe*[3]. Sometimes there may be an implied promise by her to prosecute the divorce proceedings, but that would be worse, for it would be collusion. In the present case, however, the ouster is not merely by implication. It is expressed in clause 10 of the deed. That clause is invalid. It forms the whole, or substantially the whole, consideration for the husband's promise to pay the annuities. His promise is therefore invalid.

   3. *The sanction of the court.* If the parties do not oust the jurisdiction of the Divorce Court, but preserve it by making their agreement subject to the sanction of the court, then, once it is sanctioned, it is valid. The court, however, cannot and will not give its sanction before decree nisi. It has itself no jurisdiction before decree nisi to deal with permanent maintenance. Its jurisdiction only arises " on " the decree. Its sanction should, I think, be obtained in this way: if the parties agree on a figure for maintenance, the court should be asked to make an order for that figure; if they agree on a secured provision, the court should be asked to approve the deed which contains the provision: if they agree on a lump sum in composition of maintenance the court should be asked to dismiss an application for maintenance or to discharge the existing order, as the case may be (*Mills* v. *Mills*[4]); but it would, I think, be entitled to refuse to do so if it did not think it proper to permit the composition.

   In the present case the parties seem to have sought to apply *Mills* v. *Mills*[4], but they made the mistake that they sought to apply it before decree nisi. That was quite wrong, because the court had no jurisdiction before decree nisi to sanction the agreement and did not in fact do so. The agreement was recited in the consent order made by the registrar, and it was no doubt mentioned to the judge who heard the petition. Those circumstances go far to negative any collusion, but they do not validate the deed. They

---

[1] [1929] A. C. 601.   [2] [1950] 1 K. B. 107.   [3] [1951] 2 K. B. 215.
[4] [1940] P. 124, at pp. 134, 136.

do not amount to that sanction by the court which is required to validate it. The proper way of doing it would be to ask the judge to approve the deed as a secured provision for the wife on the ground that it secures to her an assured sum of money by covenant under seal. That was never done. This does not mean that the wife will go destitute. She can still apply to the Divorce Court for maintenance. The consent order dismissing her previous application is no bar, because it was made before the case came on for hearing and there was no adjudication on the merits. At that stage it was no more than an amendment of the petition striking out her claim for maintenance. No adjudication could take place until the decree. Once the consent order is seen to be no obstacle, the case is one in which the Divorce Court would, I think, readily grant her leave to apply for maintenance, notwithstanding that three years have elapsed since the making of the decree. She has a reasonable excuse for not applying earlier because she was relying on an agreement which has turned out to be invalid.

In conclusion I would say this: The avoidance of the wife's covenants in clause 10 makes the covenant to pay the annuities ineffective, but I do not wish to suggest that it vitiates the provisions of the deed relating to the house and furniture. They are severable. When the Divorce Court comes to award maintenance it will no doubt take those benefits into account, and it will also take into account the figures stated in the deed. It may be that the wife will be no worse off. I do not know. At any rate that is her proper remedy, and not this. I agree, therefore, that this appeal should be dismissed.

ROMER, L.J. I agree, and I have nothing I could usefully add.[1]

---

[1] *Note.*—Since 1952, when *Bennett* v. *Bennett* was decided, the common law position has been modified by statute. The Matrimonial Causes Act, 1965, s. 23, enables a wife, who has promised not to apply to the court for maintenance in return for her husband's promise of an allowance, to sue for that allowance; though the husband may not enforce her own promise. But the principles stated in *Bennett* v. *Bennett* still operate in other classes of agreement, such as agreements in restraint of trade; and the case is retained in this book as offering the most helpful judicial pronouncement on the question of severance.

INFANTS[1]

Nash v. Inman

[1908] 2 K.B. 1

" Necessaries " are " goods suitable to the condition of life of [an] infant and to his actual requirements at the time of the sale and delivery ": Sale of Goods Act, 1893, s. 2.

The court must first decide whether the goods are capable of being regarded as necessaries. If it does so decide, it is a question of fact whether they are necessaries in the circumstances of the particular case in issue.

In an action against an infant for necessaries the plaintiff must prove that at the time of sale and delivery the infant did not already possess an adequate supply of goods of the class in question.

The following statement of the facts is taken from the judgment of Buckley, L.J. : The defendant, having been at school at Uppingham, went as a freshman to Trinity College, Cambridge, in October, 1902. The plaintiff, who was a tailor carrying on business in Savile Row, sent a traveller to Cambridge to solicit orders. The traveller has stated in evidence that he was told there was a young man spending money there very freely, so he called upon him. At first he got no order, but he pressed for orders, and subsequently got orders, with the result that between October 29, 1902, and June 16, 1903, the defendant had run up a bill of 145*l.* odd for clothing of an extravagant and ridiculous style having regard to the position of the boy. The tailor now sues the defendant for 145*l.* The defence is infancy. Buckley, L.J., delivered judgment for the defendant.

FLETCHER MOULTON, L.J. I am of the same opinion. I think that the difficulty and at the same time the suggestion of hardship to the plaintiff in such a case as this disappear when one considers what is the true basis of an action against an infant for necessaries. It is usually spoken of as a case of enforcing a contract against the infant, but I agree with the view expressed by the Court in *Re Rhodes, Rhodes* v. *Rhodes*[2], in the parallel case of a claim for necessaries against a lunatic, that this language is somewhat unfortunate. An infant, like a lunatic, is incapable of making a contract of purchase in the strict sense of the words; but if a man satisfies the needs of the infant or lunatic by supplying to him necessaries, the law will imply an obligation to repay him for the services so rendered, and will enforce that obligation against the estate of the infant or lunatic. The consequence is that the basis of the action is hardly contract. Its real foundation is an obligation which the law imposes on the infant to make a fair payment in respect of needs satisfied. In other words the obligation arises *re* and not *consensu*. I do not mean that this nicety of legal phraseology has been adhered to. The common and convenient phrase is that an infant is liable for goods sold and delivered provided that they are necessaries, and there is no objection to that phraseology so long as its true meaning is understood. But the treatment of such actions by the Court of Common Law has been in accordance with that principle I have referred to. That the articles were necessaries had to be alleged and proved by the plaintiff as part of his case, and the sum he recovered was based on a *quantum meruit*. If he claimed anything beyond

---

[1] At common law the age of majority was twenty-one. But by the Family Law Reform Act, 1969, s. 1, a person attains full age at the first moment of the eighteenth anniversary of his birth.

[2] (1890), 44 Ch.D. 94.

this he failed, and it did not help him that he could prove that the prices were agreed prices. All this is very ancient law, and is confirmed by the provisions of section 2 of the Sale of Goods Act, 1893—an Act which was intended to codify the existing law. That section expressly provides that the consequence of necessaries sold and delivered to an infant is that he must pay a reasonable price therefor.

The Sale of Goods Act, 1893, gives a statutory definition of what are necessaries in a legal sense, which entirely removes any doubt, if any doubt previously existed, as to what that word in legal phraseology means. [The Lord Justice read the definition.] Hence, if an action is brought by one who claims to enforce against an infant such an obligation, it is obvious that the plaintiff in order to prove his case must shew that the goods supplied come within this definition. That a plaintiff has to make out his case is, I should have thought, the first lesson that any one studying English law would learn ; and the elaborate argument of Mr. McCardie that if you look at the authorities in the past, going back nearly a hundred years, you will find cases in which particular defendants might have taken a higher stand-point and insisted upon a right which they did not insist on does not appear to me to touch the plain and obvious conclusion that in order to succeed in the action the plaintiff must shew that he has supplied necessaries. That is to say, the plaintiff has to shew, first, that the goods were suitable to the condition in life of the infant ; and, secondly, that they were suitable to his actual requirements at the time—or, in other words, that the infant had not at the time an adequate supply from other sources. There is authority to shew that this was the case even before the Act of 1893. In *Johnstone* v. *Marks*[1] this doctrine is laid down with the greatest clearness, and the *ratio decidendi* of that case applies equally to cases since that Act. Therefore there is no doubt whatever that in order to succeed in an action for goods sold and delivered to an infant the plaintiff must shew that they satisfy both the conditions I have mentioned. Everything which is necessary to bring them within section 2 it is for him to prove.

Passing on from general principles, let me take the facts of the present case. In my opinion they raise no point whatever as to the duty of the judge as contrasted with the duty of the jury arising from the peculiar character of the action. We have only to follow the lines of the law consistently administered by this Court for many more years than I can think of, an example of which as applied to the case of the supply of necessaries to an infant is given by the decision of the Court of Exchequer Chamber in the case of *Ryder* v. *Wombwell*[2]. Questions of law are for the judge ; questions of fact are for the jury ; but, as the Court there laid down, the particular question of fact in issue in such a case, like all other questions of fact, ought not to be left to the jury by the judge unless there is evidence upon which they could reasonably find in the affirmative. The issue in that case was whether certain articles were suitable to the condition in life of the defendant, the infant, and the Court of Exchequer Chamber thought that no jury could reasonably find that those articles were suitable to the condition of that defendant, and therefore they said that the judge—not by reason of any peculiar rule applicable to actions of this kind, but in the discharge of his regular duties in all cases of trial by a jury—ought not to have left the question to the jury because there was no evidence on which

---

[1] (1887), 19 Q. B. D. 509.   [2] (1868), L. R. 4 Exch. 32.

they could reasonably find for the plaintiff. We have before us a similar case, in which the issue is not only whether the articles in question were suitable to the defendant's condition in life, but whether they were suitable to his actual requirements at the time of the sale and delivery ; and how does the evidence stand ? The evidence for the plaintiff shewed that one of his travellers, hearing that a freshman at Trinity College was spending money pretty liberally, called on him to get an order for clothes, and sold him within nine months goods which at cash prices came to over 120*l.*, including an extravagant number of waistcoats and other articles of clothing, and that is all that the plaintiff proved. The defendant's father proved the infancy, and then proved that the defendant had an adequate supply of clothes, and stated what they were. That evidence was uncontradicted. Not only was it not contradicted by any other evidence, but there was no cross-examination tending to shake the credit of the witness, against whose character and means of knowledge nothing could be said. On that uncontradicted evidence the judge came to the conclusion, to use the language of the Court in *Ryder* v. *Wombwell*[1], that there was no evidence on which the jury might properly find that these goods were necessary to the actual requirements of the infant at the time of sale and delivery, and therefore, in accordance with the duty of the judge in all cases of trial by jury, he withdrew the case from the jury and directed judgment to be entered for the defendant. In my opinion he was justified by the practice of the Court in so doing, and this appeal must be dismissed.

Doyle v. White City Stadium, Ltd.

[1935] 1 K.B. 110

A contract of service or of apprenticeship, or a contract closely analogous thereto,[2] is binding upon an infant, provided that in the opinion of the Court it is, when construed as a whole, substantially for his benefit.

APPEAL from a decision of MacKinnon, J., in favour of the plaintiff.

LORD HANWORTH, M.R., delivered judgment allowing the appeal.

SLESSER, L.J.   On March 5, 1932, the plaintiff, who was at all material times an infant, applied for a licence from the British Boxing Board of Control (1929) in order that he might take part in prize fights to be carried on under their licence and control. In that application he agreed to abide by the rules and regulations of the British Boxing Board of Control in the following terms: " I hereby apply for a licence as a boxer and, if this licence is granted me, I declare to adhere strictly to the rules of The British Boxing Board of Control (1929) as printed, and abide by any further rules or alteration to existing rules as may be passed. I agree to pay the fee in accordance with the above." He did so pay the fee, and upon those terms he was granted a licence, and we are told that a year later the licence was renewed. The effect of applying for that licence in those terms and the acceptance of those rules was to make him a member of the British Boxing Board of Control, for by reg. 3 it is provided that: " ' The Members ' of the British Boxing Board of Control (1929) are all the licence holders," and by reg. 15, para. 3, it is provided that any person to whom a licence is issued after payment of the fee " shall be deemed to have read the regulations of the British Board

---

[1] (1868). L. R. 4 Exch. 32.
[2] See *Chaplin* v. *Leslie Frewin* (*Publishers*), *Ltd.*, [1966] Ch. 71; [1965] 3 All E.R. 764.

of Control and shall further be deemed to be a member and to have agreed to accept any decisions under all or any of these regulations, and to submit himself to the constitution and code of the regulations of the British Boxing Board of Control."

In those circumstances, subject to the particular matters which have been argued before us and considered in the Court below and in this Court, it would appear that this plaintiff had agreed, first, by his application, which was accepted, and secondly, by the actual provisions of the rules themselves, to be a member of this society and to be bound by its rules and regulations. It would follow that the rules and regulations would authorize the society dealing with the money which was to be his prize or reward for taking part in this contest in the way in which they have dealt with it. But in substance two arguments have been used in this case to support the view that they are not so entitled to deal with this money and that the plaintiff is entitled himself to have it paid over to him by the promoters. The first of those arguments rests upon the fact that he is an infant. It is said that whatever contract or alleged contract he has entered into under these rules is not binding on him on account of his infancy. If that contention is right, it is an answer to the defendant's claim to keep this money. It is an argument which has not found favour with MacKinnon, J., and it does not find favour with me either. It depends really on two separate considerations—first, whether this agreement is of the order of agreement under which an infant can properly bind himself; and secondly, if it does come within that order, whether this particular agreement can be stated to be so for the benefit of the infant as to be binding upon him. On the first point Serjeant Sullivan has relied very strongly on the argument that for many, many years the types of agreement which are binding upon infants have been narrowly prescribed and defined, and that as this particular agreement is not within that narrow definition and prescription, it is not one which can properly be said to be binding upon the infant.

I would like to associate myself with what has been said by Kay, L.J., in *Clements* v. *London and North Western Rail. Co.*[1] to the effect that it is doubtful whether there is a general principle that if an agreement be for the benefit of the infant it shall bind him. Kay, L.J., there quotes the dictum of Sir George Jessel in *Martin* v. *Gale*[2], where he says: " There must be some mistake in the report of what Buller, J., is stated to have said " in *Maddon & Baker* v. *White*[3]. " No case can be found in which Lord Mansfield or Lord Hardwicke had laid down any such general principle "; and I am not prepared here to say that there is any general principle that all agreements for the benefit of an infant will necessarily bind him. In my view that question does not arise in the present case, because the contract with which we have here to deal is so analogous, so similar in character, to the classes of agreement which have been held to be binding upon infants, if for their benefit, that it can properly be brought within the old category of decisions without having to rely on any more general principle.

The origin so far as we know of the definition of the class of contract binding upon infants on which Serjeant Sullivan relies (and nothing earlier has been suggested) is to be found in Coke upon Littleton, p. 172*a*, where he says: " An infant may bind himself to pay for his necessary meat, drink, apparell, necessary physicke, and such other necessaries, and likewise for his good teaching or instruction, whereby he may profit himselfe after-

---

[1] [1894] 2 Q. B. 482, at p. 493. [2] (1876), 4 Ch. D. 428, at p. 431. [3] (1787), 2 Term Rep. 159.

wards," and to that has been added in the course of years contracts of service which are to his benefit.

The problem which we have here to consider, how far that principle ought to be extended, was considered by this Court in *Clements* v. *London and North Western Rail. Co.*[1] That was a case where, although it was stated by some members of the Court that it might be considered that the contract under consideration was part of the contract of labour, yet at least two members of the Court were at pains to point out that, even if strictly it was not part of the contract of labour, it was so incidental or ancillary to the contract of labour as properly to be one where the infant might bind himself. That case, I think, has dealt with the very problem which Serjeant Sullivan has put before us to-day. Kay, L.J., for example, says[2]: " Suppose, however, as has been argued, that this is not a labour contract, would the same rule apply ? " He says[2], " I will not attempt to say how far the rule extends, but that it does apply to some contracts that are not contracts of labour is clear from many decided cases." He then proceeds to cite a number of cases which, I agree, deal mostly with the marriage settlements of infants, but he is dealing with them for the purpose of showing that an infant's liability under a contract applies in cases other than contracts of labour, and at the end he sums the matter up thus[3]: " Even if this contract were not, as I think it is, a contract concerning the terms of employment of the infant, I think it would come within the rule that I have been discussing, and that the Court might say that the contract was for the benefit of the infant, and elect for him, while he is an infant, to confirm it, treating it as not being a void contract but at most only voidable." A. L. Smith, L.J., as I read his judgment, does not think, or at any rate does not clearly express the view, that the contract there was a part of the contract of service at all. He, as I read it, rather takes the view that it was a contract which was sufficiently akin to a contract of service to be one by which the infant might properly be bound. He says that the contract is binding upon the infant and is a fair contract, because as a result he avoids litigation, and if successful will have a fund out of which he can recover; he avoids the uncertainty of getting a verdict.

If the realities of the present case be looked to and the dicta which are to be found scattered in the authorities that the opportunity of an infant to earn his living is one of the matters which may properly be said to be binding when that opportunity has been given to him by a contract, it becomes clear, I think, that as the licence which this infant obtained was the means whereby he was able to enter into a contract of service or performance, whichever it may be, as a boxer, and thereby to earn his living, it was ancillary and incidental to the contract which he made with the promoter of the fight. As Sir Patrick Hastings pointed out in the course of the case, if Serjeant Sullivan were right, the result would be that no infant could ever obtain a licence from this society, because it would be very unlikely that they would give him one unless he in his turn was bound to some obligation of proper fighting, and he would be debarred for ever from taking part in any boxing contests at all. Whether that would be a good thing in the national interest is not, of course, a matter for me to consider, but that that would be the result it seems difficult to deny.

In all those circumstances I think that without laying down any general

---

[1] [1894] 2 Q. B. 482, at p. 493.　　[2] *Ibid.,* 492.　　[3] *Ibid.,* 494.

principle and looking at the facts of this case, for it is very largely a question of fact, the learned judge was right when he said that he could find in *Clements* v. *London and North Western Rail. Co.*[1] ample authority for saying that this contract was so associated with the class of contract of service which an infant may make so as to be binding upon him that it was binding upon him.

There remains the question, was it for his benefit? Serjeant Sullivan has called our attention to the fact that there are many dicta to the effect that where a contract imposes a penalty or a forfeiture that is not good as against the infant. But I, on the other hand, have been impressed with the consideration which has been pointed out in several of the cases—in *Corn* v. *Matthews*[2] and in the older case of *Wood* v. *Fenwick*[3]—that an infant cannot make a contract of service without having in it some incidents which may not in themselves be directly beneficial to him but may be beneficial to the master. In *Wood* v. *Fenwick*[3] the headnote says: " A contract of hiring and service, for wages, is a contract beneficial to and binding upon an infant, though it contain clauses for referring disputes to arbitration, and for the imposition of forfeitures in case of neglect of duty, to be deducted from the wages." In contracts of apprenticeship, which are admittedly contracts binding upon an infant, the right of the master to proceed not only financially but in the old days corporeally against the infant have not made the contract of apprenticeship invalid as against the infant. Therefore I agree with the learned judge that this contract is for the benefit of the infant and is one binding upon him.

If that be so his position is the same as that of any other member of any association which contains within its rules a power to alter the rules. Here, with respect, I differ from the learned judge in his conclusion that because this particular member did not receive notice of the alteration of the particular rule it is not therefore binding upon him. At one time I thought it was going to be argued that the general meeting which altered the rule was not a valid meeting because this member did not receive notice of it. An omission to send him a notice would not in itself, I think, invalidate the meeting. In reg. 9, para. 4, it is expressly provided that: " The non-receipt of any notice by any member shall not invalidate the proceedings at any general meeting," and I cannot read that as being so limited as merely to mean that when a notice has been sent and not received, the meeting shall not be invalid. I think it is reasonable in the case of a society with a large number of members to hold that the proceedings of the society cannot be set aside merely by pointing to the fact that a particular member has not had a notice sent to him. But as a matter of fact I do not think that argument is open in this Court at all. It apparently was never raised in the Court below, and it formed no part of the judgment of the learned judge.

I come, therefore, to the learned judge's judgment, which is based upon the fact that this particular member is not bound by this alteration of rule because he did not receive a notice. In my opinion that is incorrect. My Lord has referred to the case of *Thellusson* v. *Viscount Valentia*[4], and it is sufficient to quote one passage from the judgment of Lord Cozens-Hardy, M.R., who, after quoting a rule which gives power to alter the rules in a certain way at the annual general meeting, says: " That seems to me to be not a very skilfully drawn rule, I agree, but nevertheless a rule expressly stating that a proposal for adding to or altering the rules of the club is

---

[1] [1894] 2 Q. B. 482.
[3] (1842), 10 M. & W. 195.
[2] [1893] 1 Q. B. 310.
[4] [1907] 2 Ch. 1, 6.

within the competence of the members of the club, and that every member of the club, by joining this club, takes it subject to the contingency that the rules may be altered by this particular majority, at a particular meeting held according to those rules."

Finally I would mention *Burke* v. *Amalgamated Society of Dyers*[1], which dealt with the alteration of the rules of a trade union where the person complaining was insane. It was said, and perhaps said with some force, that in such a case the amended rule was not binding upon him, because he was not mentally in a position to appreciate what had been done. A. T. Lawrence, J., said[2]: " We have had an able argument to the effect that the alteration of rule 39 was ineffective as against the deceased member, because it was made after he had become a lunatic and at a time when it was out of his power to dissent from it. The analogy was suggested of the determination of the authority of an agent "—that was an argument which Mr. Martin O'Connor addressed to us here to-day—" and no doubt the analogy is plausible; but it is not true, for the authority of the majority is not really that of agents. The real ground on which the power of the majority to make an alteration rests is that the original contract entered into between the society and each of its members contained a power of alteration of the rules by the stipulated majority. That power is a fundamental part of the constitution of the society, and no member can claim the benefits while ignoring the existence of the rule." At one time Serjeant Sullivan was inclined to answer Romer, L.J., by saying that the plaintiff could claim the benefits, while disowning the obligations, imposed upon him by the rules. I think that observation is sufficient to dispose of such a contention.

For all these reasons therefore I am of opinion that this appeal should be allowed as stated by my Lord.

ROMER, L.J., delivered judgment to the same effect.

Carter v. Silber, Carter v. Hasluck

[1892] 2 Ch. 278

A contract by which an infant acquires an interest of a permanent nature, or which imposes continuing obligations upon him, is voidable at his option. He must, however, take positive steps to repudiate it at the latest within a reasonable time after attaining his majority.

LINDLEY, L.J. :—This is an appeal from an order made by Mr. Justice Romer, and the question raised by the appeal is a very simple one—namely, whether the defendant, M. A. Silber, was or was not entitled to repudiate his covenant to settle after-acquired property which was contained in the settlement made on his marriage. In order to determine that, it will be convenient to state shortly what the position of affairs was. It appears that by certain settlements made by his father in 1865, 1870, and 1875, certain policies, and also a sum of £40,000 under the last settlement, were settled by the father upon his wife and children ; and by one of those settlements—the settlement of 1870—the son, who is this defendant, was to have a share of the policy monies comprised in that settlement when he attained twenty-one. The father had made a will in 1878 making appointments under these settlements, and he had disposed of the residue to his

---

[1] [1906] 2 K. B. 583.   [2] *Ibid.*, 591.

two sons on attaining twenty-one. The defendant, being under age, in October, 1883, married, and upon that marriage the settlement with which we have to deal was executed. Shortly after that the defendant attained twenty-one. The settlement was carried out in the ordinary course—that is to say, the funds comprised in it and capable of being paid over were paid over to the trustees and applied by them properly. In 1886 the father made a codicil slightly varying his will, but for all practical purposes confirming it ; and in May, 1887, the father died. Then, of course, the policies fell in, and a question arose as to whether the defendant's share of the policy monies comprised in the settlement of 1870 ought to be handed over to the trustees of his marriage settlement or not. That gave rise to a controversy ; and in December, 1887, if not before, his solicitors found out that there was this covenant in the settlement, which they at all events were not aware of before, and the defendant himself says he did not know of it before. The consequence of that was that the money which fell in was paid over to the trustees of the settlement without prejudice to any question. In July, 1888, the defendant repudiated the covenant into which he had entered. The question which has been discussed is, whether it was competent for the defendant then to repudiate that settlement. Now, the settlement in question was made by his father and himself. The father covenanted to pay to the trustees during the life of the wife, and so long as there should be any child or grandchildren of the marriage, £1,500 per annum, and there were provisions in the settlement for reducing that sum if the father put money or capital into the hands of the trustees the income of which would produce it. There was also a settlement by the father of a certain policy. The son took interests both in the £1,500 a year and in the policy ; the exact nature of the limitations I need not refer to. Then there was a covenant by the son to settle any property which he might afterwards acquire under either his father or his mother. That is the short effect of it. He says, and with truth, that when that deed was executed he was a minor : he was a few months under twenty-one.

The first question which we have to consider is the question of law whether that deed so executed by him and his father on the son's marriage was void or voidable. Now, I take it it is quite plain that, applying to this case the principles which were expounded in the well-known case of *Zouch* v. *Parsons*[1] and which have been acted upon ever since, it would be quite impossible to say that this was a void as distinguished from a voidable deed ; and, in fact, none of the counsel who have addressed us have seriously controverted that proposition. It may be for the benefit of the infant. An instrument executed upon the marriage of an infant, settling property on him and by him, must be very strangely framed to justify the conclusion that it could not be for the infant's benefit. Possibly you might conceive such a case ; you might have such a strange settlement that you could say that ; but I do not think anybody in Court ever saw one, and my imagination is not vivid enough to enable me to picture one. I proceed, therefore, upon the assumption that this was a voidable and not a void deed.

Under those circumstances, what is the state of the law with reference to a voidable instrument executed by an infant when that infant attains twenty-one ? Has he to elect to ratify it ? Has he to ratify it, or is it binding upon him until he elects to avoid it ? It appears to me that this

---

[1] (1765), 3 Burr. 1794.

point has been long settled by authority. It is binding upon him until he repudiates it. Further, I take it, the law is perfectly well settled that he must repudiate it, if at all, within a reasonable time after he attains twenty-one —that is, the time from which the reasonable time begins to run. The cases which settle this are those which relate to shares in companies, of which there are a great many in the books. I take it the law is perfectly plain, and there is a very short note of it in a very accurate book, Bullen and Leake on Pleadings[1], which is to this effect :

> " When a person is sued upon obligations arising out of property which he has become possessed of under a contract, as shares in a company, he cannot avoid the obligation by the simple defence that he was an infant at the time of acquiring the property, he must further plead that before coming of age or within a reasonable time in that behalf after coming of age he repudiated the contract on that ground and disclaimed the property."

There are several cases which settle that beyond all controversy, and it is not necessary, therefore, to allude to that further.

Therefore, his legal position was this. Having attained twenty-one, he had a reasonable time to consider what he would do—whether he would repudiate or whether he would not. What is a reasonable time ? That, I agree, depends upon all the circumstances of each particular case. A short time may do in some cases, a longer time may do in others. But what time elapsed before this infant repudiated ? He never repudiated for nearly four years after he attained twenty-one. In the meantime his father had died. It was impossible for his father to rearrange his own affairs, as he very likely would have done if his son had repudiated this deed in his father's lifetime. It is impossible to hold that it was competent for the son to repudiate this settlement when he did. The Court cannot say that three and a half or four years, under the circumstances of this case, is a reasonable time in which to repudiate the settlement. It is not a question of weeks or months. Whether the defendant could have repudiated the deed in five or six or nine months after he came of age I do not care to discuss ; but to ask us to hold that he repudiated within a reasonable time is to ask us to hold that which no reasonable man could think of holding.

That really settles the case so far as this point is concerned.

BOWEN and KAY, L.JJ., delivered judgments to the same effect. The decision of the Court of Appeal was affirmed *sub nom. Edwards* v. *Carter*, [1893] A.C. 360.

Steinberg v. Scala (Leeds), Ltd.

[1923] 2 Ch. 452

> Although an infant may rescind a voidable contract he cannot recover money paid or property delivered under it unless there has been a total failure of consideration.

Appeal from the decision of Roche, J., who gave judgment for the infant plaintiff for the return of 250*l*. paid by her under a contract to purchase shares.

LORD STERNDALE, M.R. I think in this case the appeal must be allowed and judgment must be entered for the defendant company. In saying that I think I am agreeing with what would have been Roche, J.'s own opinion if he had not felt himself bound, as indeed I think he was bound, by the

---

[1] 4th Ed. pt. ii. p. 220.

decision of Stirling, J., in *Hamilton* v. *Vaughan-Sherrin Electrical Engineering Co.*[1] I think I see a possible—I will not say more than that—distinction between this case and that before Stirling, J. If that be not a valid distinction I am afraid I should have to say that I do not agree with that decision, although of course I differ from any judgment of Stirling, J., with great hesitation and trepidation.

The action is brought for two objects : first, for rectification of the register of the defendant company by the removal therefrom of the plaintiff's name, as to which no question now arises because it is not opposed, and, secondly, for judgment for the recovery of money which the plaintiff has paid in order to become a shareholder in the company.

The plaintiff is a young lady still an infant, and when still more an infant some year or two ago she paid 50*l.* as a payment on application for shares in the defendant company and subsequently paid a further sum of 200*l.* for calls after the shares had been allotted to her, so that she paid altogether 250*l.* for shares in the defendant company. There was a question as to certain further calls being made and the plaintiff, who had found the 250*l.* out of money given to her, I think by an uncle, for the purpose of providing her with a dowry, could not find any more money, and then, awaking to the position that she had shares in a company on which there would be calls made and that she had not the money to meet them, she also awoke to the position that she was an infant and could rescind the contract, and she did so. There is no doubt that she was entitled to do so and to have the register rectified by the removal of her name therefrom. But then there came another question. She also wanted the 250*l.* back, and, to a certain extent, I think the argument for the respondent has rather proceeded upon the assumption that the question whether she can rescind and the question whether she can recover her money back are the same. They are two quite different questions, as is pointed out by Turner, L.J., in his judgment in *Re Burrows, Ex parte Taylor*[2]. He there says: " It is clear than an infant cannot be absolutely bound by a contract entered into during his minority. He must have a right upon his attaining his majority to elect whether he will adopt the contract or not." Then he proceeds: " It is, however a different question whether, if an infant pays money on the footing of a contract, he can afterwards recover it back. If an infant buys an article which is not a necessary, he cannot be compelled to pay for it, but if he does pay for it during his minority he cannot on attaining his majority recover the money back." That seems to be only stating in other words the principle which is laid down in a number of other cases that, although the contract may be rescinded, the money paid cannot be recovered back unless there has been an entire failure of the consideration for which the money has been paid. Therefore it seems to me that the question to which we have to address ourselves is : Has there here been a total failure of the consideration for which the money was paid ?

Now the plaintiff has had the shares ; I do not mean to say that she had the certificates ; she could have had them at any time if she had applied for them ; she has had the shares allotted to her and there is evidence that they were of some value, that they had been dealt in at from 9*s.* to 10*s.* a share. Of course her shares were only half paid up and, therefore, if she had attempted to sell them she would only have obtained half of that amount, but that is quite a tangible and substantial sum.

---

[1] [1894] 3 Ch. 589.   [2] (1856), 8 De G. M. & G. 254, at pp. 257, 258.

In those circumstances is it possible to say that there was a total failure
of consideration ?   If the plaintiff were a person of full age suing to recover
the money back on the ground, and the sole ground, that there had been a
failure of consideration it seems to me it would have been impossible for
her to succeed, because she would have got the very thing for which the
money was paid and would have got a thing of tangible value.

The argument for the respondent is I think to this effect : That it is
necessary, in order to show that the consideration has not entirely failed,
to prove that the plaintiff has not only had something which was worth
value in the market and for which she could have obtained value, but that
she has in fact received that value.   It was admitted that if she had in this
case sold the shares and received the 125*l.* which would have been receivable
according to one of the prices mentioned in evidence, she could not have
recovered the money back; but it is said that as she did not in fact do that
and had only an opportunity of receiving that benefit, there has been a total
failure of consideration.   I cannot see that.   If she has obtained something
which has money's worth then she has received some consideration, that is,
she has received the very thing for which she paid her money, and the fact
that, although it has money's worth, she has not turned that money's worth
into money, does not seem to me to prevent it being some valuable consideration for the money which she has paid.   I cannot see any difference, when
you come to consider whether there has been consideration or not, between
the position of a person of full age and an infant.   The question whether
there has been consideration or not must, I think, be the same in the two
cases.   That is, on the face of it, an opinion opposed to the decision of
Stirling, J., in *Hamilton* v. *Vaughan-Sherrin Electrical Engineering Co.*[1],
unless this is a distinction, that in that case there was no evidence at all
that the shares had any marketable value.   I do not mean to say they had
none, but there is no evidence one way or the other, and the learned judge
does not seem to have addressed himself to the question whether that would
make any difference.   He seems, as far as I can make out, rather to have
put as a test, whether the company was a prosperous one out of which money
could be made or whether it was not.   I cannot think that that is the true
test and I am not quite sure that he applied it, but it looks to me rather as
if he did.   If the fact that these shares had a marketable value, whereas
there was no such evidence in the case before Stirling, J., is a valid distinction
between the two cases, then that is not an authority.   If that be not a valid
distinction then, although I say it with great trepidation, I am afraid I do
not agree with the decision of Stirling, J., in *Hamilton* v. *Vaughan-Sherrin
Electrical Engineering Co.*[1]

There is only one other thing I wish to say.   It was argued for the
respondent that my decision is contrary to the judgment of the Court of
Common Pleas in *Corpe* v. *Overton*[2].   I do not think it is so.   The 100*l.*
that was sought to be recovered in that case was in quite a different position
from the money which the plaintiff sues to recover in this case.   In that case
there was an agreement that the infant and another person should enter into
partnership, and there was also beyond that—the consideration for that
agreement being, as it seems to me, the mutual promises of the parties—a
further agreement that to secure the proper fulfilment of the contract when it
was made, because it was for a future contract, the infant should deposit

---

[1] [1894] 3 Ch. 589.   [2] (1833), 10 Bing. 252.

100*l*. as a sort of security for the performance by him of the contract. That 100*l*. seems to me to be in a totally different position from the money which was paid in this case. It is quite true that in that case, in addition to the fact of it being a deposit in the way I have mentioned, the Court did say that it was recoverable as on a total failure of consideration. I think that is quite right. The promise of the partnership was not obtained by the payment of the 100*l*. The 100*l*. was paid down as a deposit for the due performance of the contract by the plaintiff, and when that contract was once rescinded of course there was no consideration for that 100*l*. having been paid and it had to be paid back.

I do not think that my judgment in any way conflicts with *Corpe* v. *Overton*[1]. It does or may conflict with *Hamilton* v. *Vaughan-Sherrin Electrical Engineering Co.*[2] If it does, I regret to say that I do not agree with that case, and I think, for the reasons I have stated, that this appeal should be allowed and judgment should be entered for the defendant company with costs here and below.

YOUNGER and WARRINGTON, L.JJ., delivered judgments to the same effect.

Pearce v. Brain

[1929] 2 K.B. 310

A contract for the exchange of chattels, other than necessaries, entered into by an infant is a contract " for goods supplied " within the meaning of the Infants Relief Act, 1874, s. 1, and is therefore " absolutely void."

The infant, however, cannot recover the chattels unless there has been a complete failure of consideration.

APPEAL from Clerkenwell County Court.

The plaintiff, an infant suing by his next friend, brought this action in the County Court for the recovery of a motor-cycle and side-car or in the alternative for their value on the ground that the contract under which he delivered the motor-cycle to the defendant was void under the Infants Relief Act, 1874, or in the alternative was voidable and had been avoided by him.

The contract in question was made on February 10, 1928, when the plaintiff exchanged his motor-cycle and side-car for a second-hand motor-car belonging to the defendant. For the purpose of the transaction it was agreed that each vehicle was of the value of 30*l*.

The plaintiff took possession of the car and drove it away, handing over his motor-cycle to the defendant.

On February 14, 1928, after being driven by the plaintiff for about 70 miles in all, the car broke down owing to a defect in the back axle. On February 16, 1928, the plaintiff wrote repudiating the contract on the ground that he was an infant when he entered into the contract.

He claimed the return of the motor-cycle and offered to return the damaged car to the defendant. The defendant refused, and the plaintiff then brought this action in the County Court, which was tried at Clerkenwell by a judge and jury. The jury found that the car was not a " necessary "

---

[1] (1833), 10 Bing. 252. [2] [1894] 3 Ch. 589.

for the plaintiff, that the defendant gave no warranty as to the car and that it was worth 15*l*. only, but that the motor-cycle and side-car was worth 30*l*. It was admitted by the plaintiff that the defendant had acted in good faith.

The County Court judge held that the contract was one of exchange and not, as the plaintiff alleged, a sale of the motor-cycle for 30*l*. with a sale of the car by the defendant for 30*l*. ; that it was void under the Infants Relief Act, 1874, section 1, but that as the plaintiff had enjoyed the benefit of the contract he was not entitled to recover the consideration which he had given : *Valentini* v. *Canali*[1].

The plaintiff appealed from this decision.

SWIFT, J. [after stating the facts continued :] The only point left is the contention of the plaintiff that, as he was an infant at the time the contract was entered into, the contract was rendered void by section 1 of the Infants Relief Act, 1874. It was said that the property in the motor bicycle never passed from the plaintiff to the defendant and that the plaintiff was entitled to have it back by virtue of section 1 of the Act, which provided : " All contracts, whether by specialty or by simple contract, henceforth entered into by infants for the repayment of money lent or to be lent, or for goods supplied or to be supplied (other than contracts for necessaries), and all accounts stated with infants, shall be absolutely void : Provided always, that this enactment shall not invalidate any contract into which an infant may, by any existing or future statute, or by the rules of common law or equity, enter, except such as now by law are voidable."

In his able argument counsel for the plaintiff contended that the transaction was one which was void under that section, and that therefore the plaintiff had never ceased to be the owner of the motor bicycle and was entitled to have it back. I am quite clear that the transaction was, as the County Court judge has found, a contract of exchange of goods. But it comes within the words " goods supplied or to be supplied," which are as much applicable to exchange as to sale.

If I were at liberty to decide this case without authority, I should be inclined to accept the argument for the plaintiff and decide that the contract being by way of exchange it was void under the Act and that no property passed. But I cannot see any difference in principle between the recovery of a chattel given in exchange and the recovery of money paid as the purchase price of goods. If the contract were void by statute I should have thought, apart from authority, that money paid could have been recovered as money had and received to the use of an infant plaintiff. Money paid under a merely voidable contract is in a very different position. But there is direct authority that money paid under a void contract cannot be recovered unless there is a total failure of consideration. In *Valentini* v. *Canali*[1], which was decided by Lord Coleridge, C.J., and Bowen, L.J., sitting as a Divisional Court, Lord Coleridge said : " The construction which has been contended for on behalf of the plaintiff would involve a violation of natural justice. When an infant has paid for something and has consumed or used it, it is contrary to natural justice that he should recover back the money which he has paid. Here the infant plaintiff who claimed to recover back the money which he had paid to the defendant had had the use of a quantity of furniture for some months. He could not give back this benefit or replace the defendant in the position in which he was before the contract. The object of the statute would seem to have been to

---

[1] (1889), 24 Q. B. D. 166.

restore the law for the protection of infants upon which judicial decisions were considered to have imposed qualifications. The legislature never intended in making provisions for this purpose to sanction a cruel injustice."

That case the County Court judge treated as binding on him and adopted as the basis of his decision. He came to the conclusion that the plaintiff had had the benefit of the contract and that, although he had not had everything which he expected to get, there was not a total failure of consideration.

In view of *Valentini* v. *Canali*[1] I think his decision was right. I cannot distinguish between the recovery of a specific chattel under a void contract and the recovery of money. If the latter cannot be recovered, neither can the former. In order to succeed here it was incumbent on the plaintiff to show a complete failure of consideration ; this he has failed to do, and in my view the decision of the County Court judge was right and the appeal must be dismissed.

Leslie (R.), Ltd. v. Sheill

[1914] 3 K.B. 607

An infant will be compelled in equity to restore specific property which he has obtained by fraud and which is still in his possession, but he will not be compelled to repay money or to pay the value of specific property that he has parted with.

LORD SUMNER. At the time of the transaction in question the appellant was an infant. He succeeded in deceiving some money-lenders by telling them a lie about his age, and so got them to lend him 400*l.* on the faith of his being adult. Perhaps they were simpler than money-lenders usually are ; perhaps the infant looked unusually mature. At any rate when they awoke to the fact that they could not enforce their bargain and sought to recover the 400*l.* paid, charging him with fraud, the jury found that the appellant had been guilty of fraud, and he does not now complain of the verdict. On further consideration Horridge, J., gave judgment against him for the full amount that he received.

It is not a pretty story to begin life with, and one might have expected that the appellant's chief anxiety would have been to live it down, but money is money, and I suppose 400*l.* is more than he cares to pay, or rather repay, if he can manage to avoid it. Accordingly he appeals, alleging that there is no process of law by which the money-lenders can get their money back from him, and, if this is so, he must succeed on this appeal.

The claim first pleaded is for the amount of principal and interest, as damages sustained because by his fraud the plaintiffs have been induced to make and act upon an unenforceable contract. So long ago as *Johnson* v. *Pye*[2] it was decided that, although an infant may be liable in tort generally, he is not answerable for a tort directly connected with a contract which, as an infant, he would be entitled to avoid. " One cannot make an infant liable for the breach of a contract by changing the form of action to one *ex delicto* " : *per* Byles, J., in *Burnard* v. *Haggis*[3]. " A married woman," says Pollock, C.B., in *Liverpool Adelphi Loan Association* v. *Fairhurst*[4], speaking

---

[1] (1889), 24 Q. B. D. 166, at p. 167.
[2] (1665), 1 Sid. 258.　　　　　　　　[3] (1863), 32 L. J. C. P. 189.
[4] (1854), 9 Exch. 422 ; 23 L. J. Ex. 163.

before the common law had been altered by Married Women's Property Acts, " is liable for frauds committed by her on any person as for any other personal wrong. But when the fraud is directly connected with the contract with the wife and is the means of effecting it and parcel of the same trans- action, the wife cannot be responsible or the husband be sued for it together with the wife. If this were allowed, it is obvious that the wife would lose the protection which the law gives her against contracts made by her during coverture, for there is not a contract of any kind, which a feme covert could make whilst she knew her husband to be alive, that could not be treated as a fraud, for every such contract would involve in itself a fraudulent repre- sentation of her capacity to contract. . . . In the case of an infant it was held for a similar reason that he could not be made liable for a fraudulent representation that he was of full age, whereby the plaintiff was induced to contract with him. . . . If the action should be maintainable ' all the pleas of infancy would be taken away, for such affirmations are in every contract.' " The Chief Baron's quotation is from *Johnson* v. *Pye*[1]. As Lord Kenyon says in *Jennings* v. *Rundall*[2], alluding to *Zouch* v. *Parsons*[3], " this protection was to be used as a shield and not as a sword; therefore if an infant commit an assault or utter slander God forbid that he should not be answerable for it in a Court of Justice. But where an infant has made an improvident contract with a person who has been wicked enough to contract with him, such person cannot resort to a Court of law to enforce such contract." It is perhaps a pity that no exception was made where, as here, the infant's wickedness was at least equal to that of the person who innocently contracted with him, but so it is. It was thought necessary to safeguard the weakness of infants at large, even though here and there a juvenile knave slipped through. The rule is well settled. No action of deceit lay against the present appellant and this claim was abandoned, but for the purposes of this case it is important to observe the principles on which an infant's immunity is established in this regard.

Nor does the other cause of action pleaded fare any better. To the claim for return of the principal moneys paid to the infant under the contract that failed, as money had and received to the plaintiff's use, there are at least two answers; the infancy itself was an answer before 1874 at common law, and the Infants' Relief Act, 1874, is an answer now. An action for money had and received against an infant has been sustained, where in substance the cause of action was *ex delicto*: *Bristow* v. *Eastman*[4], approved before 1874 in *In re Seager*[5], and cited without disapproval in *Cowern* v. *Nield*[6]. Even this has been doubted, but where the substance of the cause of action is contractual, it is certainly otherwise. To money had and received and other *indebitatus* counts infancy was a defence just as to any other action in contract: *Alton* v. *Midland Rail. Co.*, *per* Willes, J.[7]; *In re Jones*, *per* Jessel, M.R.[8]; Dicey on Parties, p. 284; Bullen and Leake's Precedents of Pleadings, 3rd ed., p. 605. Further, under the statute the principle, which at common law relieved an infant from liability for a tort directly connected with a voidable contract, namely, that it was impossible to enforce in a roundabout way an unenforceable contract, equally forbids Courts of law to allow, under the name of an implied contract or in the form of an action *quasi ex contractu*, a proceeding to enforce part of a contract,

---

[1] (1665), 1 Sid. 258.   [2] (1799), 8 Term Rep. 335, at p. 337.   [3] (1765), 3 Burr. 1804.
[4] (1794), 1 Esp. 172.   [5] (1889), 60 L. T. 665.   [6] [1912] 2 K. B. 419.
[7] (1865), 34 L. J. C. P. at pp. 292, 297, 298.   [8] (1881), 18 Ch. D. 109, 118.

which the statute declares to be wholly void. This has been recently illustrated in the closely analogous case of a claim on the footing of money had and received for moneys paid but irrecoverable under what in law was a lending and borrowing *ultra vires: Sinclair* v. *Brougham*[1].

The ground on which Horridge, J., held the appellant liable was that by reason of his fraud he was compellable in equity to repay the money, actually received and professedly borrowed, and compellable too by a judgment *in personam* for the amount, not by any mere proprietary remedy. The rule in equity has been so stated at times by text-writers, both remote and recent (Fonblanque's Equity, 1820, 5th ed., i. 77; Roscoe's Nisi Prius, 16th ed., 642; Wace on Bankruptcy, ed. 1904, p. 6), but of authority for it there is very little. *Esron* v. *Nicholas*[2], a decision of Lord King's, was much relied upon. He is reported to have said " infants have no privilege to cheat men," a wholesome truth indeed, but I should hardly call it a principle. The case was examined by Knight Bruce, V.-C., in *Stikeman* v. *Dawson*[3], who concluded that the facts as reported do not support the decree as made. He procured the note in the registrar's book and found it impracticable to appreciate the decision without knowing the evidence and the pleadings in full, and these unfortunately are not forthcoming. It is a case in which an infant stood by (apparently without actual fraud) while his guardian, or a person purporting to be his guardian, granted a lease. He received or took the benefit of the fine, but when he came of age he repudiated the lease. In a suit to compel him either to grant the plaintiff a new lease or refund the fine, the decree was that, if he did not grant the lease, he should pay back the fine. This seems to be the converse of a line of decisions, both at law and in equity, the gist of which is that a person who takes and keeps property cannot rely on infancy to release him from its burdens, especially if sued when of age, as in some instances was the case : see Year Book, 2 Hen. 6, 318 ; *Kirton* v. *Eliott*[4] ; *Earl of Buckinghamshire* v. *Drury*[5]; *Evelyn* v. *Chichester*[6]; *Lemprière* v. *Lange*[7]; whatever may be thought of some of these decisions, they do not touch the present case. There is a long gap in the cases relied on after *Esron* v. *Nicholas*[8].

For a very long time and in many forms equity has interfered to give relief against frauds committed by infants, or has refused it to infants guilty of fraud ; but the practice and even the principles applicable to such cases were long ill-defined. " An infant," says Knight Bruce, V.-C., in *Stikeman* v. *Dawson*[9], " however generally for his own sake protected by an incapacity to bind himself by contracts, may be *doli capax* in a civil sense and for civil purposes in the view of a Court of Equity, though perhaps only when *pubertati proximus* or older . . . and may therefore commit a fraud for which or the consequences of which he may after his majority be made civilly liable in equity . . . I agree . . . that in what cases in particular a Court of Equity will thus exert itself it is not easy to determine." Though many cases have been decided on this subject, none has been cited to us till one in last year in which the decision has directly been that the defendant must pay back under a judgment purely *in personam* a sum equal to that which he obtained during infancy under a purported contract of lending

---

[1] [1914] A. C. 398. [2] (1733), 2 Eq. Cas. Abr. 488.
[3] (1847), 1 De G. & Sm. 90. [4] (1613), 2 Bulst. 69. [5] (1761), 2 Eden, 60.
[6] (1765), 3 Burr. 1717. [7] (1879), 12 Ch. D. 675. [8] (1733), 2 Eq. Cas. Abr. 488.
[9] (1847), 1 De G. & Sm. 90.

and borrowing, which was entered into by the lender on the faith of the borrower's fraudulent assertion that he was of full age.

There are, however, some dicta of importance and some decisions which are alleged to bear indirectly on the point. In *Nelson* v. *Stocker*[1] Turner, L.J., says : " if the case had depended simply upon the point of the defendant having represented himself to be of age, when he was not of age, I should have felt no doubt about it. . . . Infants are no more entitled than adults are to gain benefit to themselves by fraud, and had the case therefore depended upon this point alone I should have agreed most fully with the decision of the Vice-Chancellor," which was that the defendant should be decreed to pay 1,000*l.* under his covenant, made when an infant, to place that sum in the hands of trustees, contained in a marriage settlement executed by him and by other parties after he had fraudulently represented himself to be of full age. As, however, the party to the settlement who was most concerned, namely the infant's wife, knew the truth, the Lords Justices allowed the appeal. It will be seen that the actual decision in *Nelson* v. *Stocker*[2] does not touch the present case, nor does the dictum, if its principle be estoppel after majority against denying the truth of a statement made when under age, as explained by Sir Ford North in *Mohori Bibee* v. *Dharmodas Ghose*[3] ; and see *Wright* v. *Snowe*[4]. The observations of the Court of Appeal in *Levene* v. *Brougham*[5] that there could be no such estoppel were made apparently without citation of any of these cases, but in such a case the Infants' Relief Act would be an answer to estoppel now.

Much reliance was placed on *In re King, Ex parte Unity Joint Stock Mutual Banking Association*[6], with which should be read the comments on it by Bacon, V.-C., in *Re Jones, Ex parte Jones*[7] (which are in point though his actual decision was overruled) and by Baggallay, L.J., at p. 123. In that case the debtor King, while under age, had obtained advances from the association by a fraudulent misrepresentation that he was of full age. He was adjudicated bankrupt after he came of age and the association was admitted to prove in the bankruptcy for the amount advanced. The Lords Justices arrived at this conclusion somewhat reluctantly on the authority of uncited decisions of Lord Cowper, Lord Hardwicke, and Lord Thurlow. Lord Cowper's case is probably *Watts* v. *Creswell*[8], in which he says that if an infant was old enough and cunning enough to carry on a fraud he ought in a Court of Equity to make satisfaction for it. Lord Hardwicke's opinion may be that in *Earl of Buckinghamshire* v. *Drury*[9]—" minors are not allowed to take advantage of infancy to support a fraud," against which should be set Lord Mansfield's more particular statement in the same case at p. 72, that if the infant took an estate and was to pay rent for it, he should not hold the estate and defend himself against payment of the rent by pretence of infancy. The allusion to Lord Thurlow probably is to the case of *Beckett* v. *Cordley*[10], where he said, " if there was fraud of which the infant was cognizant, she would be bound as much as an adult." If these be the authorities relied on in *Re King, Ex parte Unity Joint Stock Mutual Banking Association*[11], and I can find none nearer, they hardly touch the decision in that case, nor do they, or the decision itself in *Re King*[11], affect the case now before us.

---

[1] (1859), 4 De G. & J. 458, at p. 464.
[2] (1859), 4 De G. & J. 458. [3] (1902), L. R. 30 Ind. App. 114, at p. 122.
[4] (1848), 2 De G. & Sm. 321. [5] (1909), 25 T. L. R. 265.
[6] (1858), 3 De G. & J. 63. [7] (1881), 18 Ch. D. at 115.
[8] (1714), 9 Vin. Abr. tit. Enfant. N., pl. 24, p. 415.
[9] (1761), 2 Eden 60, 71. [10] (1784), 1 Bro. C. C. 353. [11] (1858), 3 De G. & J. 63.

There, the bankruptcy standing unchallenged and the question being how the assets should be administered among competing creditors or claimants, it was held that persons who had been defrauded by the bankrupt when under age and thereby induced to lend him money had a claim on his assets, not against him personally, which was available in competition with creditors in the full sense of the word. It is clear that Jessel, M.R., thought the decision anomalous and one not to be extended: see *Re Jones, Ex parte Jones*[1]. Since then it has been decided in *R.* v. *Wilson*[2] that an infant cannot be convicted, under section 12 of the Debtors Act, 1869, of quitting the country fraudulently with property that ought to be divided among his creditors, since in law he has none. Whatever may be said of *In re King*[3] now, it does not govern the present case, but it must be admitted that the language of the Lords Justices is hardly consistent with any other view than that the bankrupt was in equity personally liable to pay the debt in question. There is further language of a similar kind in *Maclean* v. *Dummett*[4], where the Privy Council speaks of an infant as " contracting debts " in his trade by fraudulently asserting himself to be of full age, but this again was not necessary to the decision. These seem to be all the material dicta.

As to the cases, *Clarke* v. *Cobley*[5] is one in which the Court restored the *status quo* affected by an infant's fraud by ordering him to return promissory notes, the surrender of which he had procured by falsely stating that he was of age, and by putting him under terms not to plead the Statute of Limitations if sued upon them; but a decree against him to pay the amount of the notes, though he was now of age, was expressly refused. In *Cory* v. *Gertcken*[6], where Sir T. Plumer says " though in general a payment to an infant may be bad, yet if the infant practises a fraud he is liable for the consequences," he only decided that a person could not make his trustee pay over again a sum that he had got from him by fraudulently representing himself, while still an infant, to be already of full age, and in *Chubb* v. *Griffiths*[7] Lord Romilly, M.R., when saddling an infant defendant with costs who had been passing off his safes as Chubb's safes, says that he does so " on the principle laid down in *Cory* v. *Gertcken*."[6] What he conceived this principle to be I can hardly tell, but at any rate it is not a general liability in equity for fraud. Jessel, M.R., in *In re Jones*[8] regards *Cory* v. *Gertcken*[6] as a pure action of tort. The grounds of an infant defendant's liability for costs were again discussed in *Woolf* v. *Woolf*[9], another case of similar dishonesty, and the liability was rested on the above principle and authority, also without any hint of a wider one that in equity an infant is generally liable for fraud. I think that the whole current of decisions down to 1913, apart from dicta which are inconclusive, went to shew that, when an infant obtained an advantage by falsely stating himself to be of full age, equity required him to restore his ill-gotten gains, or to release the party deceived from obligations or acts in law induced by the fraud, but scrupulously stopped short of enforcing against him a contractual obligation, entered into while he was an infant, even by means of a fraud. This applies even to *Re King, Ex parte Unity Joint Stock Mutual Banking Association*[10]. Restitution stopped where repayment began; as Kindersley, V.-C., puts it in

---

[1] (1881), 18 Ch. D. at pp. 120–1.
[2] (1879), 5 Q. B. D. 28.
[3] (1858), 3 De G. & J. 63.
[4] (1869), 22 L. T. at p. 711.
[5] (1789), 2 Cox, Eq. Cas. 173.
[6] (1816), 2 Madd. 40.
[7] (1865), 35 Beav. 127.
[8] (1881), 18 Ch. D. at p. 118.
[9] [1899] 1 Ch. 343.
[10] (1858), 3 De G. & J. 63.

Vaughan v. *Vanderstegen*[1], an analogous case, " you take the property to pay the debt."

Last year, in *Stocks* v. *Wilson*[2], an infant, who had obtained furniture from the plaintiff by falsely stating that he was of age and had sold part of it for 30*l.*, was personally adjudged by Lush, J., to pay this 30*l.* as part of the relief granted to the plaintiff. This is the case which more than any other influenced Horridge, J., in the Court below. I think it is plain that Lush, J., conceived himself to be merely applying the equitable principle of restitution. The form of the claim was that, by way of equitable relief, the infant should be ordered to pay the reasonable value of the goods, which he could not restore because he had sold them. The argument was that equity would not allow him to keep the goods and not pay for them, and that if he kept the property he must discharge the burthen, and that he could not better his position by having put it out of his power to give up the property. Lush, J., expressly says[3] " it is a jurisdiction to compel the infant to make satisfaction," and, at p. 246, " the remedy is not on the contract." At pp. 242-243 he says " what the Court of Equity has done in cases of the kind is to prevent the infant from retaining the benefit of what he has obtained by reason of his fraud. It has done no more than this, and this is a very different thing from making him liable to pay damages and compensation for the loss of the other party's bargain. If the infant has obtained property by fraud he can be compelled to restore it " ; but now comes the proposition, which applies to the present case and is open to challenge, " if he has obtained money he can be compelled to refund it." The learned judge thought that the fundamental principle in *Re King, Ex parte Unity Joint Stock Mutual Banking Association*[4] was a liability to account for the money obtained by the fraudulent representation, and that in the case before him there must be a similar liability to account for the proceeds of the sale of the goods obtained by this fraud. If this be his *ratio decidendi* though I have difficulty in seeing what liability to account there can be (and certainly none is named in *Re King, Ex parte Unity Joint Stock Mutual Banking Association*[4]), the decision in *Stocks* v. *Wilson*[2] is distinguishable from the present case and is independent of the above dictum, and I need express no opinion about it. In the present case there is clearly no accounting. There is no fiduciary relation : the money was paid over in order to be used as the defendant's own and he has so used it, and, I suppose, spent it. There is no question of tracing it, no possibility of restoring the very thing got by the fraud, nothing but compulsion through a personal judgment to pay an equivalent sum out of his present or future resources, in a word nothing but a judgment in debt to repay the loan. I think this would be nothing but enforcing a void contract. So far as I can find, the Court of Chancery would never have enforced any liability under circumstances like the present, any more than a Court of law would have done so, and I think that no ground can be found for the present judgment, which would be an answer to the Infants' Relief Act.

Accordingly the appeal succeeds ; the judgment must be set aside and entered for the defendant. He will have the costs here, where he succeeds and of the further consideration below, where he ought to have succeeded. Further than this there should be no costs given him. He cannot be made

---

[1] (1854), 2 Drew. 363.
[3] [1913] 2 K. B. at p. 247.
[2] [1913] 2 K. B. 235.
[4] (1858), 3 De G. & J. 63.

to pay the costs of the action, in which he was entitled to judgment, but I think that, as he was charged with fraud and found guilty of it, he must pay the costs of that issue, to be set off against such costs as he gets, and as to any other general costs of the action, which must be small, I think there is good ground for saying that there be no order for payment on either side.

KENNEDY, L.J., and A. T. LAWRENCE, L.J., delivered judgments to the same effect.

PRIVITY OF CONTRACT

1. THE SCOPE OF THE ORIGINAL CONTRACT

TWEDDLE v. ATKINSON

DUNLOP v. SELFRIDGE

MIDLAND SILICONES, LTD. v. SCRUTTONS, LTD.

A person who is not a party to a contract or who has not furnished consideration may not sue upon it at common law even if he is intended to be the beneficiary. Nor may he rely upon any excluding or limiting term in that contract.

Tweddle v. Atkinson

(1861), 1 B. & S. 393

The declaration stated that the plaintiff was the son of John Tweddle, deceased, and, before the making of the agreement hereafter mentioned, married the daughter of William Guy, deceased; and before the said marriage of the plaintiff the said William Guy, in consideration of the then intended marriage, promised the plaintiff to give to his said daughter a marriage portion, but the said promise was verbal, and at the time of the making of the said agreement had not been performed ; and before the said marriage the said John Tweddle, in consideration of the said intended marriage, also verbally promised to give the plaintiff a marriage portion, which promise at the time of the making of the said agreement had not been performed. It then alleged that after the marriage and in the lifetime of the said William Guy, and of the said John Tweddle, they, the said William Guy and John Tweddle, made and entered into an agreement in writing in the words following, that is to say:

> "*High Coniscliffe, July* 11, 1855.
> "Memorandum of an agreement made this day between William Guy, of etc., of the one part, and John Tweddle, of etc., of the other part. Whereas it is mutually agreed that the said William Guy shall and will pay the sum of 200*l*. to William Tweddle, his son-in-law ; and the said John Tweddle, father to the aforesaid William Tweddle, shall and will pay the sum of 100*l*. to the said William Tweddle, each and severally the said sums on or before the 21st day of August, 1855. And it is hereby further agreed by the aforesaid William Guy and the said John Tweddle that the said William Tweddle has full power to sue the said parties in any Court of law or equity for the aforesaid sums hereby promised and specified."

And the plaintiff says that afterwards and before this suit, he and his said wife, who is still living, ratified and assented to the said agreement, and that he is the William Tweddle therein mentioned. And the plaintiff says that the said 21st day of August, A.D. 1855, elapsed, and all things have been done and happened necessary to entitle the plaintiff to have the said sum of 200*l*. paid by the said William Guy or his executor: yet neither the said William Guy nor his executor has paid the same, and the same is in arrear and unpaid, contrary to the said agreement.

Demurrer and joinder therein.

Edward James, for the defendant.—The plaintiff is a stranger to the agreement and to the consideration as stated in the declaration and therefore cannot sue upon the contract. It is now settled that an action for breach of contract must be brought by the person from whom the consideration moved ; *Price* v. *Easton*[1]. (He was then stopped.)

Mellish, for the plaintiff.—Admitting the general rule as stated by the other side, there is an exception in the case of contracts made by parents for the purpose of providing for their children. In *Dutton and Wife* v. *Poole*[2], affirmed in the Exchequer Chamber, a tenant in fee simple being about to cut down timber to raise a portion for his daughter, the defendant his heir-at-law, in consideration of his forbearing to fell it, promised the father to pay a sum of money to the daughter, and an action of *assumpsit* by the daughter and her husband was held to be well brought. [WIGHTMAN, J. In that case the promise was made before marriage. In this case the promise is post nuptial, and the whole consideration on both sides is between the two fathers.] The natural relationship between the father and the son constituted the father an agent for the son, in whose behalf and for whose benefit the contract was made, and therefore the latter may maintain an action upon it. [CROMPTON, J. Is the son so far a party to the contract that he may be sued as well as sue upon it ? Where a consideration is required there must be mutuality. WIGHTMAN, J. This contract, so far as the son is concerned, is one sided.] In *Bourne* v. *Mason*[3] two cases are cited which support this action. In *Sprat* v. *Agar*, in the King's Bench in 1658, one promised the father that, in consideration that he would give his daughter in marriage with his son, he would settle so much land; after the marriage the son brought an action, and it was held maintainable. The other was the case of a promise to a physician that if he did such a cure he would give such a sum of money to himself and another to his daughter, and it was resolved the daughter might bring *assumpsit*, " Which cases," says the report, " the Court agreed; " and the reason assigned as to the latter is, " the nearness of the relation gives the daughter the benefit of the consideration performed by her father." There is no modern case in which this question has been raised upon a contract between two fathers for the benefit of their children.

WIGHTMAN, J. Some of the old decisions appear to support the proposition that a stranger to the consideration of a contract may maintain an action upon it, if he stands in such a near relationship to the party from whom the consideration proceeds, that he may be considered a party to the consideration. The strongest of those cases is that cited in *Bourne* v. *Mason*[4], in which it was held that the daughter of a physician might maintain *assumpsit* upon a promise to her father to give her a sum of money if he performed a certain cure. But there is no modern case in which the proposition has been supported. On the contrary, it is now established that no stranger to the consideration can take advantage of a contract, although made for his benefit.

CROMPTON, J. It is admitted that the plaintiff cannot succeed unless this case is an exception to the modern and well established doctrine of the action of *assumpsit*. At the time when the cases which have been cited were decided the action of *assumpsit* was treated as an action of trespass upon the case, and therefore in the nature of a tort ; and the law was not settled, as it now is, that natural love and affection is not a sufficient consideration

---

[1] (1833), 4 B. & Ad. 433.
[2] (1677), 2 Lev. 210 ; 1 Vent. 318.   Affirmed on error in the Exch. Ch., T. Raym. 302.
[3] (1669), 1 Vent. 6.   [4] (1669), 1 Vent. 6.

for a promise upon which an action may be maintained ; nor was it settled that the promisee cannot bring an action unless the consideration for the promise moved from him.   The modern cases have, in effect, overruled the old decisions ; they shew that the consideration must move from the party entitled to sue upon the contract.   It would be a monstrous proposition to say that a person was a party to the contract for the purpose of suing upon it for his own advantage, and not a party to it for the purpose of being sued. It is said that the father in the present case was agent for the son in making the contract, but that argument ought also to make the son liable upon it. I am prepared to overrule the old decisions, and to hold that, by reason of the principles which now govern the action of *assumpsit*, the present action is not maintainable.

BLACKBURN, J.   The earlier part of the declaration shews a contract which might be sued on, except for the enactment in section 4 of the Statute of Frauds, 29 Car. 2 c. 3.   The declaration then sets out a new contract, and the only point is whether, that contract being for the benefit of the children, they can sue upon it.   Mr. *Mellish* admits that in general no action can be maintained upon a promise, unless the consideration moves from the party to whom it is made.   But he says that there is an exception ; namely, that when the consideration moves from a father, and the contract is for the benefit of his son, the natural love and affection between the father and son gives the son the right to sue as if the consideration had proceeded from himself.   And *Dutton and Wife* v. *Poole*[1] was cited for this.   We cannot overrule a decision of the Exchequer Chamber ; but there is a distinct ground on which that case cannot be supported.   The cases upon stat. 27 El. c. 4, which have decided that, by section 2, voluntary gifts by settlement after marriage are void against subsequent purchasers for value, and are not saved by section 4, shew that natural love and affection are not a sufficient consideration whereon an action of *assumpsit* may be founded.

Judgment for the defendant.

Dunlop Pneumatic Tyre Co. Ltd. v. Selfridge & Co. Ltd.

[1915] A.C. 847

The plaintiffs sold a number of their tyres to Dew & Co., described as " motor accessory factors ", on the terms that Dew & Co. would not re-sell them below certain scheduled prices and that, in the event of a sale to trade customers, they would extract from the latter a similar undertaking.   Dew & Co. sold the tyres to Selfridge, who, by their contract with Dew, undertook to observe the restriction and to pay to Messrs. Dunlop the sum of £5 for each tyre sold in breach of this agreement.   Selfridge in fact supplied tyres to two of their own customers below the listed price.   As between Dew and Selfridge this act was clearly a breach of contract for which damages could have been recovered.   But the action was brought, not by Dew, but by Messrs. Dunlop, who sued to recover two sums of £5 each as liquidated damages[2], and asked for an injunction to restrain further breaches of agreement.   They were met by the objection that they were not parties to the relevant contract and had furnished no consideration for the defendants' promise.

---

[1] (1677), 2 Lev. 210 ; 1 Vent. 318.   Affirmed on error in the Exch. Ch. T. Raym. 302.
[2] See *infra*, p. 481.

Phillimore, J., gave judgment for the appellants for 10*l.*, the liquidated damages in respect of the two breaches above mentioned, and granted an injunction restraining the respondents from selling Dunlop motor tyres, covers, or tubes below the appellants' current list prices.

The Court of Appeal (Vaughan Williams, Kennedy, and Swinfen Eady, L.JJ.) reversed this decision and gave judgment for the respondents. They held that the contract of January 2 was not a contract between the appellants and the respondents at all, but was a contract between Messrs. A. J. Dew & Co. and the respondents only, and that Messrs. A. J. Dew & Co. were not legally competent at one and the same time to make a contract with the respondents by themselves as principals and as agents of the appellants. They therefore held that the action was not sustainable.

The House of Lords affirmed the decision of the Court of Appeal.

VISCOUNT HALDANE, L.C.   My Lords, in my opinion this appeal ought to fail.

Prior to January 2, 1912, Messrs. Dew had entered into a contract with the appellants to purchase a quantity of tyres and other goods from them at the prices in their list, in consideration of receiving certain discounts. As part of their contract Messrs. Dew undertook, among other things, not to sell to certain classes of customer at prices below the current list prices of the appellants. They were, however, to be at liberty to sell to a class of customer that included the respondents at a discount which was substantially less than the discount they were themselves to receive from the appellants, but in the case of any such sale they undertook, as the appellants' agents in this behalf, to obtain from the customer a written undertaking that he similarly would observe the terms so undertaken to be observed by themselves. This contract was embodied in a letter dated October 12, 1911.

On January 2 the respondents contracted with Messrs. Dew, in terms of a letter of that date addressed to them, that, in consideration of the latter allowing them discounts on goods of the appellants' manufacture which the respondents might purchase from Messrs. Dew, less, in point of fact, than the discount received by the latter from the appellants, the respondents, among other things, would not sell the appellants' goods to private customers at prices below those in the appellants' current list, and that they would pay to the appellants a penalty for every article sold in breach of this stipulation.

The learned judge who tried the case has held that the respondents sold goods of the appellants' manufacture supplied through Messrs. Dew at less than the stipulated prices, and the question is whether, assuming his finding to be correct, the appellants, who were not in terms parties to the contract contained in the letter of January 2, can sue them.

My Lords, in the law of England certain principles are fundamental. One is that only a person who is a party to a contract can sue on it. Our law knows nothing of a *jus quæsitum tertio* arising by way of contract. Such a right may be conferred by way of property, as, for example, under a trust, but it cannot be conferred on a stranger to a contract as a right to enforce the contract *in personam*. A second principle is that if a person with whom a contract not under seal has been made is to be able to enforce it consideration must have been given by him to the promisor or to some other person at the promisor's request. These two principles are not recognized in the same fashion by the jurisprudence of certain Continental countries or of Scotland, but here they are well established. A third proposition is that a principal not named in the contract may sue upon it if the promisee really contracted as his agent. But again, in order to entitle him so to sue, he must have given consideration either personally or through the promisee, acting as his agent in giving it.

My Lords, in the case before us, I am of opinion that the consideration, the allowance of what was in reality part of the discount to which Messrs. Dew, the promisees, were entitled as between themselves and the appellants, was to be given by Messrs. Dew on their account, and was not in substance, any more than in form, an allowance made by the appellants. The case for the appellants is that they permitted and enabled Messrs. Dew, with the knowledge and by the desire of the respondents, to sell to the latter on the terms of the contract of January 2, 1912. But it appears to me that even if this is so the answer is conclusive. Messrs. Dew sold to the respondents goods which they had a title to obtain from the appellants independently of this contract. The consideration by way of discount under the contract of January 2 was to come wholly out of Messrs. Dew's pocket, and neither directly nor indirectly out of that of the appellants. If the appellants enabled them to sell to the respondents on the terms they did, this was not done as any part of the terms of the contract sued on.

No doubt it was provided as part of these terms that the appellants should acquire certain rights, but these rights appear on the face of the contract as *jura quæsita tertio*, which the appellants could not enforce. Moreover, even if this difficulty can be got over by regarding the appellants as the principals of Messrs. Dew in stipulating for the rights in question, the only consideration disclosed by the contract is one given by Messrs. Dew, not as their agents, but as principals acting on their own account.

The conclusion to which I have come on the point as to consideration renders it unnecessary to decide the further question as to whether the appellants can claim that a bargain was made in this contract by Messrs. Dew as their agents ; a bargain which, apart from the point as to consideration, they could therefore enforce. If it were necessary to express an opinion on this further question, a difficulty as to the position of Messrs. Dew would have to be considered. Two contracts—one by a man on his own account as principal, and another by the same man as agent—may be validly comprised in the same piece of paper. But they must be two contracts, and not one as here. I do not think that a man can treat one and the same contract as made by him in two capacities. He cannot be regarded as contracting for himself and for another *uno flatu*.

My Lords, the form of the contract which we have to interpret leaves the appellants in this dilemma, that, if they say that Messrs. Dew contracted on their behalf, they gave no consideration, and if they say they gave consideration in the shape of a permission to the respondents to buy, they must set up further stipulations, which are neither to be found in the contract sued upon nor are germane to it, but are really inconsistent with its structure. That contract has been reduced to writing, and it is in the writing that we must look for the whole of the terms made between the parties. These terms cannot, in my opinion, consistently with the settled principles of English law, be construed as giving to the appellants any enforceable rights as against the respondents.

I think that the judgment of the Court of Appeal was right, and I move that the appeal be dismissed with costs.

LORDS DUNEDIN, ATKINSON, PARKER, SUMNER and PARMOOR delivered judgments to the same effect.[1]

Midland Silicones Ltd. v. Scruttons, Ltd.

[1962] 1 All E.R. 1

The plaintiffs, Midland Silicones, Ltd., had bought a drum of chemicals which was shipped by consignors in New York on a vessel owned by the United States Lines. The bill of lading contained a clause limiting the liability of the shipowners, as carriers, to 500 dollars (£179). The defendants, Scruttons, Ltd., were stevedores who had contracted with the United States Lines to act for them in London on the terms that the defendants were to have the benefit of the limiting clause in the bill of lading. To this bill the defendants were not parties. The plaintiffs knew nothing of the contract between the defendants and the United States Lines. Owing to the defendants' negligence the drum of chemicals was damaged to the extent of £593. The plaintiffs sued the defendants in negligence, and the defendants pleaded the limiting clause in the bill of lading.

DIPLOCK, J. found for the plaintiffs, and his judgment was upheld both by the Court of Appeal and by the House of Lords.

VISCOUNT SIMONDS: My Lords, the facts in this case are not in dispute. They are fully and accurately stated in the judgment of the learned trial judge, DIPLOCK, J.[2], and I do not think it necessary to restate them. I come at once to the question of law which arises on them.

The question is whether the appellants, a well-known firm of stevedores, who admittedly by their negligence caused damage to certain cargo consigned to the respondents under a bill of lading of March 26, 1957, can take advantage of a provision for limitation of liability contained in that document. In judgments, with which I entirely agree and to which, but for the importance of the case, I should think it necessary to add nothing, the learned judge[2] and the Court of Appeal[3] have unanimously answered the question in the negative.

The appellants' claim to immunity (for so I will call it for short) was put in a number of different ways, but I think that I am not unjust to the able argument of their counsel if I say that he rested in the main on the well-known case of *Elder, Dempster & Co.* v. *Paterson, Zochonis & Co.*[4], contending that that is an authority binding this House to decide in his favour.

Let me then get rid shortly of some of the other arguments advanced on behalf of the appellants. In the first place I see no reason for saying that the word "carrier" either in the bill of lading or in the United States Carriage of Goods by Sea Act, 1936 (which the bill of lading incorporated) means or includes a stevedore. This is a proposition which does not admit of any expansion. A stevedore is not a carrier according to the ordinary use of language and, so far from the context supplying an extended meaning to the

---

[1] *Note.*—By s. 1(1) of the Resale Prices Act, 1964, " any term or condition of a contract for the sale of goods by a supplier to a dealer, or of any agreement between a supplier and a dealer relating to such a sale, shall be void in so far as it purports to establish, or provide for the establishment of, minimum prices to be charged on the resale of the goods in the United Kingdom." See also s. 5 (2) of this Act.
[2] [1959] 2 All E.R. 289; [1959] 2 Q.B. 171.
[3] [1960] 2 All E.R. 737; [1961] 1 Q.B. 106.
[4] [1924] A.C. 522; [1924] All E.R. Rep. 135.

latter word, the contrary is indicated, as HODSON, L.J.[1] points out, by cl. 17 of the bill of lading which authorises the carrier or master to appoint stevedores.

Then, to avert the consequences which would appear to follow from the fact that the stevedores were not a party to the contract conferring immunity on the carriers, it was argued that the carrier contracted as agent for the stevedores. They did not expressly do so; if then there was agency, it was a case of an agent acting for an undisclosed principal. I am met at once by the difficulty that there is no ground whatever for saying that the carriers were contracting as agent either for this firm of stevedores or any other stevedores whom they might employ. The relation of the stevedores in this case to the carriers was that of independent contractors. Why should it be assumed that the carriers entered into a contract of affreightment or into any part of it as agents for them?

Next it was urged that there was an implied contract between the cargo owners, the respondents, and the stevedores that the latter should have the benefit of the immunity clause in the bill of lading. This argument presents, if possible, greater difficulties. When A and B have entered into a contract, it is not uncommon to imply a term in order to give what is called " business efficacy " to it—a process, I may say, against the abuse of which the courts must keep constant guard. But it is a very different matter to infer a contractual relation between parties who have never entered into a contract at all. In the present case the cargo owners had a contract with the carrier which provided amongst other things for the unloading of their cargo. They knew nothing of the relations between the carrier and the stevedores. It was no business of theirs. They were concerned only to have the job done which the carriers had contracted to do. There is no conceivable reason why an implication should be made that they had entered into any contractual relation with the stevedores.

But, my Lords, all these contentions were but a prelude to one which, had your Lordships accepted it, would have been the foundation of a dramatic decision of this House. It was argued, if I understood the argument, that if A contracts with B to do something for the benefit of C, then C, though not a party to the contract, can sue A to enforce it. This is independent of whether C is A's undisclosed principal or a beneficiary under a trust of which A is trustee. It is sufficient that C is an " interested person ". My Lords, if this is the law of England, then, subject always to the question of consideration, no doubt, if the carrier purports to contract for the benefit of the stevedore, the latter can enforce the contract. Whether that premise is satisfied in this case is another matter, but since the argument is advanced it is right that I should deal with it.

Learned counsel for the respondents met it, as they had successfully done in the courts below, by asserting a principle which is, I suppose, as well established as any in our law, a " fundamental " principle, as VISCOUNT HALDANE, L.C., called it in *Dunlop Pneumatic Tyre Co., Ltd.* v. *Selfridge & Co., Ltd.*[2] an " elementary " principle, as it has been called times without number, that only a person who is a party to a contract can sue on it. " Our law ", said LORD HALDANE[2], " knows nothing of a *jus quaesitum tertio* arising by way of contract ". Learned counsel for the respondents claimed that this

---

[1] [1961] 1 Q.B. at p. 119; [1960] 2 All E.R. at p. 739.
[2] [1915] A.C. at p. 853.

was the orthodox view and asked your Lordships to reject any proposition that impinged on it. To that invitation I readily respond. For to me heterodoxy, or, as some might say, heresy, is not the more attractive because it is digni-fied by the name of reform. Nor will I easily be led by an undiscerning zeal for some abstract kind of justice to ignore our first duty, which is to ad-minister justice according to law, the law which is established for us by Act of Parliament or the binding authority of precedent. The law is developed by the application of old principles to new circumstances. Therein lies its genius. Its reform by the abrogation of those principles is the task not of the courts of law but of Parliament. Therefore I reject the argument for the appellants under this head and invite your Lordships to say that certain state-ments which appear to support it in recent cases such as *Smith* v. *River Douglas Catchment Board*[1] and *White* v. *John Warrick & Co., Ltd*[2] must be rejected. If the principle of *jus quaesitum tertio* is to be introduced into our law, it must be done by Parliament after a due consideration of its merits and demerits. I should not be prepared to give it my support without a greater knowledge than I at present possess of its operation in other systems of law.

I come finally to the case which is said to require us to decide in favour of the appellants. The *Elder, Dempster case*[3] has been the subject of so much analytical criticism and so many different conclusions that one may well despair of finding out what was decided by which of the five noble and learned Lords who took part in it. In the course of the discussion before your Lord-ships my mind turned to what was said by VISCOUNT DUNEDIN (who was himself a party to the *Elder, Dempster* decision[3]) some four years later in *Great Western Rail Co.* v. *Mostyn (Owners), The Mostyn*[4]. He said:

> ". . . if from the opinions delivered it is clear—as is the case in most in-
> stances—as to what was the *ratio decidendi* which led to the judgment, then
> that *ratio decidendi* is also binding. But if it is not clear, then I do not think
> it is part of the tribunal's duty to spell out with great difficulty a *ratio decidendi*
> in order to be bound by it. That is what the Court of Appeal has done here.
> With great hesitation they have added the opinion of LORD HATHERLEY to that
> of Lord CAIRNS and then, with still greater difficulty, that of LORD BLACKBURN,
> and so have secured what they think was a majority in favour of LORD CAIRNS'
> very clear view. I do not think that the respect which they hold and have ex-
> pressed for the judgments of your Lordships' House compelled them to go
> through this difficult and most unsatisfactory performance."

My LORDS, Lord DUNEDIN'S was a dissenting speech and at a later date this House was able to ascertain the principle which was decided by that case and the case that he was discussing, *River Wear Comrs.* v. *Adamson*[5] (see *Workington Harbour and Dock Board* v. *Towerfield S.S. (Owners)*[6]). But that does not, I think, detract from the value and importance of his observa-tions on the ascertainment of the *ratio decidendi* of a decision which is said to bind this House. I would cast no doubt on the doctrine of *stare decisis*, with-out which law is at hazard. But I do reserve the right at least to say of any decision of this House that it does not depart from a long-established prin-ciple, and particularly does not do so without even mentioning it, unless that is made abundantly clear by the majority of the noble Lords who take part in it. When, therefore, it is urged that the *Elder, Dempster case*[3] decided

[1] [1949] 2 K.B. 500; [1949] 2 All E.R. 179.
[2] [1953] 2 All E.R. 1021.
[3] [1924] A.C. 522; [1924] All E.R. Rep. 135.
[4] [1928] A.C. at p. 73; [1927] All E.R. Rep. at p. 121.
[5] (1877), 2 App. Cas. 743.
[6] [1951] A.C. at p. 157; [1950] 2 All E.R. at p. 441.

that, even if there is no general exception to what I have called the fundamental rule that a person not a party to a contract cannot sue to enforce it,
there is at least a special exception in the case of a contract for carriage of
goods by sea, an exception which is to be available to every person, servant or
agent of the contracting party or independent contractor, then I demand that
that particular exception should be plainly deducible from the speeches that
were delivered. Nor should I forget the warning given by the EARL OF
HALSBURY, L.C., in *Quinn* v. *Leathem*[1] in a passage quoted by DIPLOCK, J.,
in this case[2], which I need not repeat, for it is undeniable that the facts in
Elder, Dempster[3] which enabled the House to hold that both shipowners and
charterers could take advantage of a provision in a bill of lading are remote
from the facts of the present case. The question then is whether there is to
be extracted from *Elder, Dempster*[3] a decision that there is in a contract for
carriage of goods by sea a particular exception to the fundamental rule in
favour of all persons including stevedores and presumably other independent
contractors. This question must clearly, in my opinion, be answered in the
negative.

In the course of this opinion I have already borrowed freely, without
acknowledgment, from the judgment of the late FULLAGAR, J., in *Wilson* v.
Darling Island Stevedoring and Lighterage Co., Ltd.[4] and I shall say something
more about that judgment presently. In the meantime I will quote a passage
from it which expresses my own view of *Elder, Dempster*[3]. After referring to
a passage in CARVER (9th Edn.) at p. 294, that learned judge said[5]:

> " In my opinion, what the *Elder, Dempster* case[3] decided, and all that it
> decided, is that in such a case, the master having signed the bill of lading, the
> proper inference is that the shipowner, when he receives the goods into his
> possession, receives them on the terms of the bill of lading. The same inference
> might perhaps be drawn in some cases even if the charterer himself signed the
> bill of lading, but it is unnecessary to consider any such question."

This appears to me to be the only possible generalisation, or, if your Lordships think " rationalisation " an appropriate word, the only possible rationalisation of *Elder, Dempster*[3], and it is a far cry from the circumstances to which
it is sought to apply that decision in the present case.

I shall not further discuss *Elder, Dempster*[3] except to say two things. The
first is that in so far as the case turned on a question of bailment (which I
think it largely did) it has no relevance to the present case. For I agree with
DIPLOCK, J.[6], in thinking that the appellants were not bailees " whether sub,
bald, or simple ". Secondly, I must say a few words on a passage much
relied on by the appellants in the judgment of SCRUTTON, L.J., in *Mersey
Shipping and Transport Co., Ltd.* v. *Rea, Ltd.*[7] where he pronounced that the
effects of the *Elder, Dempster* decision were as follows:

> ". . . where there is a contract which contains an exception clause, the
> servants or agents who act under that contract have the benefit of the exemption
> clause. They cannot be sued in tort as independent people, but they can claim
> the protection of the contract made with their employers on whose behalf they
> are acting."

---

[1] [1901] A.C. at p. 506.
[2] [1959] 2 Q.B. at p. 187; [1959] 2 All E.R. at p. 295.
[3] [1924] A.C. 522; [1924] All E.R. Rep. 135.
[4] [1956] 1 Lloyd's Rep. 346.
[5] [1956] 1 Lloyd's Rep. at p. 364.
[6] [1959] 2 Q.B. at p. 189; [1959] 2 All E.R. at p. 296.
[7] (1925), 21 Lloyd's Rep. at p. 378.

This observation was admittedly *obiter* and BANKES, L.J., who sat with SCRUTTON, L.J., clearly did not agree with it. Nor do I agree with it: that follows from what I have already said. And with all deference to a very learned judge I do not think that the use of the word " independent " is felicitous. If the cargo-owner sues a stevedore for negligence, he sues him not as a dependent or independent tortfeasor but just as a tortfeasor. It may be that, if he is a " dependent " tortfeasor in the sense that he is the servant or agent of a master or principal, the latter may be made vicariously liable, but that does not touch his personal liability. From that he can only escape if there is a contractual relation between him and the cargo-owner which provides him with immunity for his tort or a principle of law which entitles him to rely on a contract made by another. The first line of escape depends on the facts of the particular case: the second is denied by the fundamental rule which was reasserted in the *Dunlop* case[1]. I will only add that in the passage that I have cited[2] the Lord Justice uses the word "agents", and, whatever else may be attributed to him, I should hesitate to say that he intended to include independent contractors in that word.

It follows from what I have said that the case of *Cosgrove* v. *Horsfall*[3] on which doubt was cast by counsel for the appellants was rightly decided and that DEVLIN, J.'s decision in *Pyrene Co., Ltd.* v. *Scindia Steam Navigation Co., Ltd.*[4] can be supported only on the facts of the case which may well have justified the implication of a contract between the parties.

In the consideration of this case I have not yet mentioned a matter of real importance. It is not surprising that the questions in issue in this case should have arisen in other jurisdictions where the common law is administered and where the Hague Rules have been embodied in the municipal law. It is (to put it no higher) very desirable that the same conclusions should be reached in whatever jurisdiction the question arises. It would be deplorable if the nations should after protracted negotiations reach agreement as in the matter of the Hague Rules and that their several courts should then disagree as to the meaning of what they appeared to agree on: see *Riverstone Meat Co., Pty., Ltd.* v. *Lancashire Shipping Co., Ltd.*[5] and cases there cited. It is therefore gratifying to find that the Supreme Court of the United States in the recent case of *Krawill Machinery Corpn.* v. *Robert C. Herd & Co., Inc.*[6] not only unanimously adopted the meaning of the word " carrier " in the relevant Act, which I invite your Lordships to adopt, but also expressed the view that the *Elder, Dempster* decision[7] did not decide what is claimed for it by the appellants.

Finally, I must refer again to the case of *Wilson* v. *Darling Island Stevedoring and Lighterage Co., Ltd.*[8] which is fortunately reported also in [1956] 1 Lloyd's Rep. 346—fortunately, since the Commonwealth Law Reports are too seldom to be found in counsel's chambers. In that case, in which the facts are not in any material respect different from those in the present case, the late FULLAGAR, J., delivered a judgment with which the Chief Justice, SIR OWEN DIXON, said that he entirely agreed. So do I—with every line and every word of it, and, having read and re-read it with growing admiration. I cannot forbear from expressing my sense of the loss which not only his

---

[1] [1915] A.C. at p. 853.
[2] (1925), 21 Lloyd's Rep. at p. 378.
[3] (1945), 175 L.T. 334.
[4] [1954] 2 Q.B. 402; [1954] 2 All E.R. 158.
[5] [1961] A.C. 807; [1961] 1 All E.R. 495.
[6] [1959] 1 Lloyd's Rep. 307
[7] [1924] A.C. 522; [1924] All E.R. Rep. 135.
[8] (1956), 95 C.L.R. 43.

colleagues in the High Court of Australia but all who anywhere are concerned with the administration of the common law have suffered by his premature death. I have already cited one passage from his judgment. Perhaps I may refer also with respectful approbation to those passages[1] in which he asserts the view that the exceptions to the rule in *Tweddle* v. *Atkinson*[2] are apparent rather than real and explains the so-called on-carrier cases, and in which he protests against a tendency by some artifice to save negligent people from the normal consequence of their fault.

I would dismiss this appeal with costs.

LORDS REID, KEITH and MORRIS delivered judgments to the same effect. LORD DENNING dissented.

RE FLAVELL, MURRAY *v.* FLAVELL
RE SCHEBSMAN

A party to a contract may constitute himself a trustee for a third party of a right under the contract and thus confer an equitable right upon such third party. An action to enforce this right should be in the name of the trustee; but if he refuses to sue, the beneficiary may himself sue, joining the trustee as a defendant.

But the existence of such a trust depends upon the intention of the parties and the circumstances of each case, and an unequivocal intention to constitute the trust must be proved.

Re Flavell, Murray v. Flavell
(1883), 25 Ch.D. 89

This was a creditor's action for the administration of the real and personal estate of T. W. Flavell, who died without issue on January 7, 1883. The defendant was his widow, and she was his sole executrix. On May 24, 1883, an administration judgment was pronounced, and a receiver was appointed of the rents and profits of the testator's real and leasehold estate, and to get in his outstanding personal estate.

The testator was a solicitor, and he carried on business in partnership with J. F. Bowman, under the provisions of articles of partnership dated July 6, 1875. The partnership was to be for the term of ten years from May 1, 1875, if both the partners should so long live.

Clause 3 of the articles provided for the determination of the partnership by notice.

Clause 35 provided that " From the determination of the partnership the retiring partner, his executors or administrators, or the executors or administrators of the deceased partner, shall be entitled, in addition to the moneys payable under the last preceding article, to receive out of the net profits of the partnership business such yearly sums as hereinafter provided during such periods as hereinafter mentioned (that is to say) . . . and during so much (if any) of the term of five years from May 1, 1880, as shall remain after the determination of the partnership, if the retiring or deceased partner shall be the said J. W. Flavell, the sum of £350, and if the retiring or deceased partner shall be the said J. F. Bowman the sum of £250, and during so much (if any) of the term of five years from May 1, 1885, as either the retiring partner or a widow of the retiring or deceased partner shall be living, if such partner shall be the said J. W. Flavell, the sum of £250, and if such partner shall be the said J. F. Bowman the sum of £150 . . . any yearly sum which may under this present article for the time being become

---

[1] [1956] 1 Lloyd's Rep. at pp. 357, 359.   [2] (1861), 1 B. & S. 393.

payable to the executors or administrators of a deceased partner to be applied in such manner as such partner shall by deed or will direct for the benefit of his widow and children or child (if any) or any of them, and in default of such direction to be paid to such widow, if living, for her own benefit, or, if not living, then to the guardian or guardians for the time being of such children or child for the benefit of such children or child."

By clause 36 " the yearly sum payable under the last preceding article shall, so far as legally may be, be constituted a charge upon the net profits of the partnership business."

By his will, dated September 26, 1845, Flavell devised and bequeathed all his real and personal estate to his wife, her heirs, executors, administrators, and assigns, for ever, subject to the payment of his debts and funeral and testamentary expenses. He did not in any way by deed or will direct how the annuity payable to his executors or administrators under the above provisions of the partnership articles was to be applied, unless the will was to be construed as giving such a direction. After his death the question arose whether the annuity thus payable to his executrix formed part of his assets, or whether she was beneficially entitled to it. This summons was taken out by the widow, asking that the receiver might be at liberty to pay the annuity to her for her own use and benefit so long as the same should remain payable or until further order.

The summons came on for hearing before Mr. Justice North on August 6, 1883.

NORTH, J. (after referring to the provisions of the partnership articles and stating the other facts), continued:—

The testator's estate is insufficient for the payment of his debts, but there is no suggestion that the articles were in any way intended to defeat or delay his creditors. The widow claims the annuity which is now payable under the articles. The testator's will contains no express direction as to its payment. The testator's creditors resist this claim, and allege that the annuity forms part of the testator's estate. It seems to me that, if the widow is entitled to the annuity at all, she is entitled to it in priority to the creditors. If the creditors are entitled to it in priority to her this can only be, I think, on the basis that she would not be entitled to it at all, however solvent the testator's estate might be. Of the cases which have been cited the one most like the present case is *Page* v. *Cox*[1]. There a trader bequeathed his residuary estate, including his stock-in-trade, to trustees, on certain trusts for the benefit of his wife, her sister, and another person. After the date of the will he entered into partnership, and the articles of partnership contained a proviso that, if the testator should die during the partnership, leaving a widow surviving him, such widow might, if she should think fit, continue to carry on the business with the surviving partner, and should be entitled to the testator's share of the profits, and of the property of the partnership. The testator died, leaving his widow surviving him, and it was held that the effect of the articles was to take the testator's share of the business entirely out of the provisions of the will, and that the widow was entitled to that share. Vice-Chancellor Turner said[2], " The effect of the clause " (in the articles) " cannot, I think, be stated lower than that it was an agreement by both parties, that, upon the death of either of them, his share should be dealt with according to the provisions which the clause contains. We have

---

[1] (1852), 10 Hare, 163.   [2] *Ibid.*, 168.

to consider then what is the effect of such an agreement. Is it not to create an obligation in equity upon the surviving partner, in whom the legal interest would be, and was contemplated as being, vested; and in what respect does such an obligation differ from a trust? I see no difference between them; and I am of opinion, therefore, that, in the event which happened, these articles created a trust in favour of the widow; and I have less difficulty in so holding, as I consider it to be now settled, in *Kekewich* v. *Manning*[1], that, in cases of this nature, the Court is to regard the substance and effect and not the mere form of the instrument; and that a trust may well be created, although there may be an absence of any expression in terms importing confidence. It was argued that this was a mere case of contract between two persons for the benefit of a third party, and that the third party could not enforce such a contract, and *Colyear* v. *Countess of Mulgrave*[2] was cited upon that point. But it seems to have been considered in *Kekewich* v. *Manning*[1] that that case was not free from doubt; and, at all events, I think it is distinguishable from the present case. . . . A trust certainly cannot be the less capable of being enforced because it is founded on contract." The difference between that case and the present is this, that there the testator's share of the partnership business and assets was to go to his widow, while here there is an agreement by the surviving partner to pay the widow an annuity which is to be a charge on the partnership assets. It is said that *Ponton* v. *Dunn*[3] is at variance with *Page* v. *Cox*[4]. In *Ponton* v. *Dunn* there was a stipulation in a partnership deed that the testator's interest should after his death and during the term of partnership go to such persons as he should by will name or appoint, and in default of appointment to his wife; if she should be dead, to his surviving children, in equal shares, and in case of the death of all his children, to his executors or administrators. By his will he, without alluding to the partnership deed, gave all his estate and effects to one of his children, and it was held that his interest in the partnership passed by the bequest. Sir John Leach, M.R., said[5], " It is true the words ' name and appoint ' are used in the deed; but, considering the relation of the parties, I cannot understand them to be used with a view to create a power of appointment in its technical sense, and to limit the testator's power of disposition by will over this part of his property. Without this stipulation, those who claimed through him would have had no title to share in the partnership profits after his death; and it is a mere bargain with his partner that he should have a power of disposition by will, and, if he died without a will, that the property should devolve to his family in the manner stated. This property will, therefore, pass under the description in his will of ' all other his estate and effects of whatsoever nature or description.' " When that case is closely looked at it is clear that all that was decided was this, that, although the words " nominate and appoint " were used in the deed, the use of those words was not essential to the validity of an exercise of the power of disposition given, and that the power was well exercised though the will contained no reference to the power or to the subject of it. It is clear that the Master of the Rolls recognised the provisions of the deed in favour of the testator's family as good, and held they were rendered nugatory only because the power of appointment was carried into effect by the terms of the will. The decision in *Page* v. *Cox*[4] is rather put on the ground that

---

[1] (1851), 1 De G. M. & G. 176.   [2] (1836), 2 Keen, 81.   [3] (1830), 1 Russ. & M. 402.
[4] (1852), 10 Hare, 163.   [5] 1 Russ. & M. 406.

there was a trust for the benefit of the widow, and that view of it is taken by Lord Justice Lindley in his book on Partnership[1]. I have already noticed the distinction between *Page* v. *Cox* and the present case, and the question is whether that distinction really makes any difference. The first case referred to on that point is in *Re Empress Engineering Co.*[2] There A. and B. had agreed with C. on behalf of an intended company that A. and B. should sell, and the company should buy a certain business, and it was a term of the agreement that sixty guineas should be paid to Jones & Pride, solicitors, for their expenses and charges in registering the company. The memorandum of association of the company which was subsequently formed adopted this agreement, and the directors afterwards ratified it. In the winding-up of the company it was held that the agreement had never been made binding on the company, and that, even if it had, Jones & Pride, not having been parties to the contract between A. and B. and the company, could not proceed against the company for the sixty guineas. During the argument Jessel, M.R., said[3], " If you can make out that Jones & Pride are *cestuis que trust*, that alters the case. It appears to me that they are not. The promoters were liable to Jones & Pride, who are simply their creditors. A. being liable to B., C. agrees with A. to pay B. That does not make B. a *cestui que trust*." The case of *Gregory* v. *Williams*[4] was relied on there in support of the claim, and Jessel, M.R.,[5] said that the agreement there was that the defendant would, " out of the produce " of certain property pay what was due by Parker to Gregory on a promissory note, and apply the residue, as far as it would extend, in satisfaction of the defendant's own demand, and pay the surplus (if any) to Parker. " It was a parol agreement part performed, and it created a trust of property," and in his judgment Jessel, M.R., said[6], " It is then contended that a mere contract between two parties that one of them shall pay a certain sum to a third person not a party to the contract will make that third person a *cestui que trust*. As a general rule that will not be so. A mere agreement between A. and B. that B. shall pay C. (an agreement to which C. is not a party either directly or indirectly), will not prevent A. and B. from coming to a new agreement the next day releasing the old one. If C. were a *cestui que trust* it would have that effect. I am far from saying that there may not be agreements which may make C. a *cestui que trust*. There may be an agreement like that in *Gregory* v. *Williams*[7], where the agreement was to pay out of property, and one of the parties to the agreement may constitute himself a trustee of the property for the benefit of the third party." And Lord Justice James said[6], " I think it is perhaps as well that we should say that *Gregory* v. *Williams* seems to be misunderstood. When that case is considered with the careful criticism with which the Master of the Rolls has examined it, it appears quite clear that there was there a transfer of property with a declaration of trust in favour of a third person, which was a totally different thing from a mere covenant to pay money to that person." This shews how near a mere agreement may come to a declaration of trust. The Lord Justice afterwards said[8], " I may add, as the Master of the Rolls pointed out to me in the course of the argument, that in *Gregory* v. *Williams* the man with whom the contract was made was one of the plaintiffs, and the only defence there

---

[1] 4th Ed. vol. ii, pp. 851, 852.
[3] (1880), 16 Ch. D. 127. [4] (1817), 3 Mer. 582.
[6] (1880), 16 Ch. D. 129. [7] (1817), 3 Mer. 582.

[2] (1880), 16 Ch. D. 125.
[5] (1880), 16 Ch. D. 128.
[8] (1880), 16 Ch. D. 130.

would have been misjoinder of plaintiffs, and that is a defence which the Court was not likely to view with much favour." The same subject was again very fully considered in *Lloyd's* v. *Harper*[1], in which a father, on the occasion of his son being admitted as an underwriting member of the association known as Lloyd's, gave a guarantee to the managing committee of the association by which he held himself responsible for all his son's engagements in that capacity. The association, in whom the rights of the committee had become vested by statute, sixteen years after the date of contract sought to enforce the guarantee for the benefit of the persons, whether members of Lloyd's or not, with whom the son had contracted engagements as an underwriting member, he having become a bankrupt, and it was held that the plaintiffs were entitled so to do. It is clear that the association were not nominees on behalf of the persons who were to benefit by the guarantee, and moreover they entered into the contract for the benefit of persons who were not in existence at the date of the contract. The point was taken that, assuming that Lloyd's were entitled to sue on the guarantee at all, the utmost which they could recover was nominal damages, because the association had not sustained any loss, the loss having been sustained by the persons who had entered into the contracts with the son. Lord Justice James said[2], " The defendants say, ' You, Lloyd's, have sustained no loss, and can only recover nominal damages, because you can only recover for your own loss, and not for the losses sustained by other persons.' That might be true if Lloyd's were not trustees, but I am of opinion that Mr. Justice Fry was well warranted in the conclusion at which he arrived, that the engagement was made with the committee as trustees for and on behalf of persons beneficially interested. That brings the case within the authorities, of which there are more than one, viz., *Gregory* v. *Williams*[3], *Lamb* v. *Vice*[4], and many other cases which proceed on the obvious principle that, if A. is trustee for B., A. can sue on behalf of B." Lord Justice Cotton, in giving judgment to the same effect, referred also[5] to *Tomlinson* v. *Gill*[6], and said that the principle there laid down by Lord Hardwicke " is, I think, a good and sound one, and one upon which we can properly act, and are bound to act in the present case, treating the plaintiffs, Lloyd's, as trustees for those for whose benefit this contract was entered into." And Lord Justice Lush said[7], " I consider it to be an established rule of law that where a contract is made with A. for the benefit of B., A. can sue on the contract for the benefit of B., and recover all that B. could have recovered if the contract had been made with B. himself." There is one further observation to be made on that case, viz., that *West* v. *Houghton*[8] was cited in the argument. In that case the lessee of sporting rights over an estate covenanted with the lessor to keep down the rabbits on the estate, so that no appreciable damage might be done to the crops, and it was held that the lessor, being under no obligation to compensate the farming occupier for damages to the crops, and not being a trustee for him, could not recover more than nominal damages for the breach of the covenant. My reason for referring to that case is this, that both Lord Justice James and Lord Justice Cotton[9] intimated an opinion that that decision could not be supported. If then *West* v. *Houghton* ought to have been decided the other way, it would shew that the person who

---

[1] (1880), 16 Ch. D. 290. [2] (1880), 16 Ch. D. 315. [3] (1817), 3 Mer. 582.

[4] (1840), 6 M. & W. 467. [5] (1880), 16 Ch. D. 317. [6] (1756), Amb. 330.

[7] (1880), 16 Ch. D. 321. [8] (1879), 4 C. P. D. 197. [9] (1880), 16 Ch. D. 311.

had really sustained damage by the game might sue the lessee through the landlord as his trustee. This case of *Lloyd's* v. *Harper*[1] appears to me to go far enough to shew that in the present case the widow, the person for whose benefit the covenant to pay the money was really entered into, is entitled to sue the defendant upon it.

NORTH, J., concluded by declaring that the widow was entitled to the charge which she claimed, and his decision was affirmed by the Court of Appeal.

Re Schebsman, *ex parte* The Official Receiver.
The Trustee v. Cargo Superintendents (London), Ltd. and Others
[1943] 2 All E.R. 768

S. was for many years employed by a Swiss company and its subsidiary, an English company. His employment came to an end on Mar. 31, 1940, and by an agreement dated Sept. 20, 1940, made between S. and the two companies, it was agreed that, in consideration of his loss of employment, the English company would pay to S. the sum of £2,000 immediately and a further sum of £5,500 by instalments over a period of 6 years and that, if he should die within that period, certain sums would be paid to his widow over a number of years, and, if she should die during that time, payments would be made to his daughter. S. was adjudicated bankrupt on Mar. 5, 1942, and died on May 12, 1942. His trustee in bankruptcy claimed that the sums payable under the agreement to the widow or possibly the daughter formed part of the deceased bankrupt's estate. The contention was based on the ground that S. always had the right to intercept the sums in question and this right was now vested in the trustee in bankruptcy.

Uthwatt, J., held (1) that in respect of the payments to the widow and daughter S. was not a trustee for them, (2) that it was impossible to imply in the contract a term whereby S. or his successors in title could have a right to intercept the payments and that the trustee in bankruptcy had thus no right to intercept them.

The Court of Appeal upheld the judgment of Uthwatt, J.

DU PARCQ, L.J.: It is, in my opinion, convenient to approach the problems raised in this appeal by first considering the position of the parties at common law. It is clear that Mrs. Schebsman, who was not a party to the agreement of Sept. 20, 1940, acquired no rights under it and has never been in a position to maintain an action upon it. It is common ground, also, that the personal representatives of Schebsman (whom I will call the debtor) could not have recovered any sums which had been paid to Mrs. Schebsman under the agreement as money had and received or by any process known to the common law. It is not disputed that the English company, which under the agreement was liable to make the payments, properly performed that agreement by paying into the hands of Mrs. Schebsman those sums which it had bound itself to pay to Mrs. Schebsman, and, at common law, could not be called upon to pay them to the personal representatives of the debtor. Nor, I think, is it disputed, and it may be said to be self-evident, that the English company's agreement to pay these moneys into the hands of Mrs. Schebsman was a valid agreement, a breach of which would be regarded by the courts as an " unlawful act " and a " legal wrong." I borrow these expressions from a well-known passage in the speech of Lord Lindley in *South Wales Miners' Federation* v. *Glamorgan Coal Co.*[2] The rules

---

[1] (1880), 16 Ch. D. 290.   [2] [1905] A.C. 239.

according to which damages for breach of contract are assessed sometimes allow a person guilty of the legal wrong constituted by the breach to escape very lightly, but that fact does not affect the illegality of his act.

So far there is general agreement. I may now express my own agreement with a proposition submitted by counsel for the appellant. He said that the duty to pay into the hands of a nominated person is discharged when the money has been paid to that person, and that the party bound to make a payment has no control over its destination. As a general proposition, that is true and can hardly be questioned. In the case before us Mrs. Schebsman, being no party to the contract, is clearly under no obligation to the English company to apply the money in any particular way, nor is the English company concerned with any agreement which she may choose to make with third parties binding herself to apply it in a particular manner. But the proposition, accurate as it is, may be misleading unless it is considered together with another proposition which I take to be equally unexceptionable and which I will now state.

It is open to parties to agree that, for a consideration supplied by one of them, the other will make payments to a third person for the use and benefit of that third person, and not for the use and benefit of the contracting party who provides the consideration. Whether or not such an agreement has been made in a given case is clearly a question of construction, but assuming that the parties have manifested their intention so to agree, it cannot, I think, be doubted that the common law would regard such an agreement as valid and as enforceable (in the sense of giving a cause of action for damages for its breach to the other party to the contract), and would regard the breach of it as an unlawful act. If the party from whom the consideration moved somehow succeeded in intercepting a payment intended for the named payee, he would be guilty of a tort, and, in certain circumstances, of a crime, and he would also be breaking his contract, since it would be implicit in his agreement with the other party that he would do nothing to prevent the money paid from reaching the payee. If he sought to argue that, because he had himself provided the consideration, he alone was interested in the destination of the money, the answer would be that the other contracting party had not agreed (and perhaps might never have thought of agreeing) to make a payment either to him or for his benefit. If he can persuade the payee to hand the money over to him by lawful means, he is, of course, at liberty to do so, and there may be circumstances *dehors* the contract which would give him rights against the payee. Subject to that qualification, he can never, in the case of such a contract as I have supposed, lawfully claim payment of the money for himself while the contract remains unaltered. That the common law allows it to be varied nobody doubts. At any time the parties may agree that payment shall in future be made not to the payee named in the contract, but to the party from whom the consideration moved, or, for that matter, to any other person. But in the case of such a contract there cannot be a variation at the will of one of the parties, any more than a condition introduced into a contract for the benefit of both parties can be waived by only one of them.

I have said that the question whether a contract imposes a liability on one of the parties to confer a benefit on a third party, not privy to the contract, is always one of construction. From the point of view of the common law, with which alone I am now dealing, I have no doubt that the general rule of construction laid down by Blackburn, J., in *Burges* v. *Wickham*[1] must be applied. According to the general law of England, the written record of a contract must not be varied or added to by verbal evidence of what was the intention of the parties.

I now turn to the agreement in the present case, in order to seek in the document itself the answer to the question whether the parties intended that, after the debtor's death, the company should be under an obligation to make payments to Mrs. Schebsman for her own benefit, and the debtor's personal representatives under a corresponding obligation to accept payment to Mrs. Schebsman for her own benefit as a fulfilment of the contract. It seems to me to be plain upon the face of the contract that this was the intention of the parties. In this connection the most striking feature of the agreement, in my opinion, is that, after the deaths of Mrs. and Miss Schebsman (assuming that the debtor were to predecease them, as in fact he did), all payments were to cease, even though a large part of the amount payable by the company might remain unpaid. This provision points clearly, as it seems to me, to the conclusion that both parties were concerned with benefiting Mrs. Schebsman and the daughter, and that the company did not intend to bind itself to pay a penny for the benefit of the debtor's estate after the death of these ladies. It is impossible, in my judgment, to regard this as in effect an aleatory contract, under which the amount of payments intended to accrue for the benefit of the debtor's estate was to be dependent on events so uncertain as the duration of the two lives. Further, it is, I think, proper to have regard to the fact that, in the circumstances disclosed by the agreement itself, both parties might be expected to wish to confer a benefit on the debtor's dependents. Lastly, I attach some importance to the language of cl. 6 which speaks of payments " due to " Mrs. and Miss Schebsman.

I may now summarise the position at common law as follows: (i) It is the right, as well as the duty, of the company to make the prescribed payments to Mrs. Schebsman and to no other person. (ii) Mrs. Schebsman may dispose of the sums so received as she pleases, and is not accountable for them to the personal representatives of the debtor, or to anyone claiming to stand in the shoes of the debtor. (iii) If anyone standing in the shoes of the debtor were to intercept the sums payable to Mrs. Schebsman and refuse to account to her for them, he would be guilty of a breach of the debtor's contract with the company. (iv) The obligation undertaken by the company cannot be varied at the will of the other party to the contract, but may be varied consensually at any time although the debtor is no longer living, as it could have been in his life-time.

It now remains to consider the question whether, and if so to what extent, the principles of equity affect the position of the parties.

It was argued by counsel for the appellant that one effect of the agreement of Sept. 20, 1940, was that a trust was thereby created, and that the debtor constituted himself trustee for Mrs. Schebsman of the benefit of the covenant under which payments were to be made to her. Uthwatt, J., rejected this contention, and the argument has not satisfied me that he was wrong. It is true that, by the use possibly of unguarded language, a person may create a trust, as Monsieur Jourdain talked prose, without knowing it, but unless an intention to create a trust is clearly to be collected from the language used and the circumstances of the case, I think that the court ought not to be astute to discover indications of such an intention. I have little doubt that,

---

[1] (1863), 3 B. & S. 669.

in the present case, both parties (and certainly the debtor) intended to keep alive their common law right to vary consensually the terms of the obligation undertaken by the company, and, if circumstances had changed in the debtor's life-time, injustice might have been done by holding that a trust had been created and that those terms were accordingly unalterable. On this point, therefore, I agree with Uthwatt, J.[1]

It was contended by counsel for the appellant in an attractive and (to me) instructive argument, that, although the company might be bound to make payments to Mrs. Schebsman, she must necessarily be held liable in a court of equity to hand over the money she received to the debtor's representatives on the ground that the debtor had provided all the consideration for the payments so that there was a resulting trust in his favour. If I am right in the views which I have expressed as to the position of the parties at common law, it seems to me plain that this contention cannot prevail. Counsel for the appellant submitted that, on facts identical with the present, notice having been given to the company that the debtor's representative required payment to be made, not to Mrs. Schebsman, but to himself, a court of equity before the Judicature Acts (i) would have been prepared to restrain the company from making a payment to Mrs. Schebsman, or (ii) supposing that, notwithstanding the notice, the company had made the payment, would have treated Mrs. Schebsman as a bare trustee and compelled her to pay the money which she had received to the debtor's estate. Now it follows from what I have already said that, by taking the first course, the court of equity would have prevented the company from doing what the contract permitted and required it to do. By taking the second course, the court of equity would have permitted and assisted the debtor's representative to break the contract which he was bound to perform. There is, I believe, no instance in which equity compels a man to pay money to someone other than the person to whom alone, and for whose sole benefit, he has bound himself to pay it. Counsel for the appellant sought to find an analogy in the case of an equitable assignment, but what a court of equity did in such a case was not to compel the debtor to pay the assignee, but to compel the assignor to allow the assigneee to sue in the assignor's name. There is certainly no case in which a court of equity has given its protection to a suitor asking to be relieved from the due performance of a contract which was neither unlawful nor unconscionable. To put the matter bluntly and, if my view of the common law is right, fairly, equity, which mends no man's contracts, will not assist any man to commit a breach of contract and so to do an "illegal act." In such a case as that now before us, there cannot be a resulting trust since the party who provided the consideration is bound by the terms of his bargain to permit the payee to retain the money, and would be acting unconscionably if he diverted it to himself against the will of the payee, save with the consent of the other contracting party.

Even if I am wrong in thinking that the present contract is, on the face of it, to be construed as imposing on the company an obligation to confer a benefit on Mrs. Schebsman, and on the debtor an implied obligation to do nothing to deprive her of that benefit, the same result follows when it is

---

[1] In the court below Uthwatt, J. had said: " The cases no doubt are hard to reconcile, but to my mind the explanation of them is that different minds may reach different conclusions on the question whether the circumstances sufficiently show an intention to create a trust; and inferences as to intent may vary. . . . I do not think that any such inference can properly be drawn from these facts ": *Re Schebsman*, [1943] 2 All E.R., at p. 390.

conceded (as it was rightly conceded at the Bar in this case) that at common law no action could be maintained against Mrs. Schebsman for money had and received, or, in other words, that according to the common law she is entitled to retain the money paid to her as against the debtor's estate. When an attempt is made to recover such payments on equitable principles, I am of opinion that the strict rule of evidence, to which I have referred as prevailing when the sole issue is the construction of the contract, is no longer to be applied, and that the court may, and often should, look beyond the four corners of the document. In the words of Sir W. M. James, L.J., in *Fowkes* v. *Pascoe*[1]:

> " Where the Court of Chancery is asked, on an equitable assumption or presumption, to take away from a man that which by the common law of the land he is entitled to, he surely has a right to say: ' Listen to my story as to how I came to have it, and judge that story with reference to all the surrounding facts and circumstances.' "

On this principle Uthwatt, J., in the present case, and Simonds, J., in *Re Stapleton-Bretherton*[2], were right to admit evidence as to the surrounding facts. When that evidence is considered, it seems to me impossible to escape from the conclusion that, as matters now stand, anyone standing in the shoes of the debtor would be guilty of a breach of faith if he contrived to intercept the payments due to Mrs. Schebsman. I need hardly add that there is no equitable doctrine on which, in such circumstances, he could be permitted to rely. On the contrary, there is one known to every student which would disqualify him from access to equity.

It now remains to consider whether the trustee in bankruptcy is entitled to the advantage which he seeks to obtain from the Bankruptcy Act, 1914, s. 42. In my opinion, he is not. On the view which I take of the transaction, the debtor never acquired a right to the sums which were to be paid to Mrs. Schebsman. All he acquired was a right to insist on those payments being made, not to himself, but to her. If it is said that he named her as the person to whom he wished the payments to be made, it may equally well be said that the company named her as a person, and, in certain events, the only person, to whom, and for whose benefit, they would promise to make the payments. The fact is that she was the person whom both parties agreed to make the beneficiary of the contract. The money payable to her was never the " property " of the bankrupt, and it was never in his power to " transfer " it to her.

For these reasons, I agree with the conclusion at which Uthwatt, J., arrived. My reasons do not, I think, differ much in substance from his, though I fear that I have expressed them at greater length. I have done so partly in deference to the very able argument of counsel for the appellant, who put forward the criticism that Uthwatt, J., had not considered or sufficiently dealt with the question whether, after receiving the money, as she lawfully might, Mrs. Schebsman was entitled in equity to retain it. I have endeavoured to deal fully with that aspect of the case. I have only to add, with reference to one of the arguments of counsel for the appellant, that no suggestion was made in this case against the good faith of the parties to the contract. A debtor with an eye to a future bankruptcy might, of course, find a complacent friend who would assist him by entering into a colourable agreement, under which the debtor's earnings were to be put out of his creditor's reach. Fraud commonly simulates honesty. That is no

---

[1] (1875), 10 Ch. App. 343, at 349.　　　　[2] [1941] Ch. 482.

reason for refusing to give full effect to an honest agreement. The law has ample power to deal with cases of fraud. I agree that the appeal should be dismissed.

LORD GREENE, M.R., and LUXMOORE, L.J. delivered judgments to the same effect, dismissing the appeal.

Beswick v. Beswick

[1967] 2 All E.R. 1197

" A person may take an immediate or other interest in land or other property, or the benefit of any condition, right of entry, covenant or agreement over or respecting land or other property, although he may not be named as a party to the conveyance or other instrument " (Law of Property Act, 1925, s. 56(1)).

" In this Act, unless the context otherwise requires ... ' Property ' includes any thing in action and any interest in real or personal property " (Law of Property Act, 1925, s. 205 (1) (xx)).

Despite the above wording, s. 56 (1) is not to be interpreted so as to enable third parties to sue upon a contract.

Peter Beswick was a coal merchant. In March 1962 he contracted to sell the business to his nephew John in consideration (1) that for the rest of Peter's life John should pay him £6 10s. a week, (2) that if Peter's wife survived him John should pay her an annuity of £5 weekly. John took over the business and paid Peter the agreed sum until Peter died in November 1963. He then paid Peter's widow £5 for one week and refused to pay any more. The widow brought an action against John in which she claimed £175 as arrears of the annuity and asked for specific performance of the contract. She sued (a) as administratrix of Peter's estate, (b) in her personal capacity. In the Chancery Court of the County Palatine of Lancaster her action was dismissed. The Court of Appeal reversed this decision.[1] They held that the plaintiff was entitled as her husband's administratrix to enforce the contract by way of an order for specific performance and that the order should enforce the provision in the contract in her own personal favour. Lord Denning and Danckwerts, L.J., held that, by virtue of s. 56 (1) and of s. 205 (1) (xx), the plaintiff was also entitled to enforce the contract in her own personal capacity, although she was not a party to it: upon this latter point Salmon, L.J., preferred to express no opinion. All the members of the Court thought that, especially in view of *Re Schebsman*,[2] it was not possible on the facts to infer the existence of a trust.

The defendant appealed to the House of Lords. Their Lordships (Lord Reid, Lord Hodson, Lord Guest, Lord Pearce and Lord Upjohn) dismissed the appeal. They held that the widow was entitled as administratrix to an order for specific performance and affirmed, on this point, the decision of the Court of Appeal. They also considered s. 56 (1) and s. 205 (1) (xx) of the Law of Property Act 1965, and were of opinion that the effect of these subsections was not to confer upon a third party any right to sue upon a contract.

LORD HODSON. My Lords, the question is whether the respondent, who is the personal representative of her late husband, is entitled in that capacity or personally to enforce payment of an annuity of £5 a week which on Mar. 14, 1962, the appellant agreed to pay to her. This arose from an agreement by the husband to sell his coal merchant's business to the appellant for a consideration. Part of the consideration was to pay the annuity

---

[1] [1966] 3 All E.R. 1.　　　　　　　　[2] [1943] 2 All E.R. 768; *supra*, p. 343.

to the respondent. The respondent, as administratrix and therefore a party by representation to the agreement, has a cause of action to sue on the agreement as, indeed, is admitted in the defence. The only question is, " What is the appropriate remedy? ". It would be strange if the only remedy were nominal damages recoverable at common law or a series of actions at law to enforce the performance of a continuing obligation. Although the point was discussed during the course of the case, it is not now contended that at common law (apart from statute), since the contract by its express terms purports to confer a benefit on a third party, the third party can be entitled to enforce the provision in his own name. Similarly, it is not now argued that the claim can be enforced as a trust. The respondent is no longer making any claim in her personal capacity, save under a statute.

The surviving issues in the case are two: first, whether the Court of Appeal were justified in making an order for specific performance by directing that the appellant do pay to the respondent during the remainder of her life from July 15, 1964 (the date of the issue of the writ) an annuity at the rate of £5 per week in accordance with the agreement; second, whether or not the common law rule, that a contract such as this one which purports to confer a benefit on a stranger to the contract cannot be enforced by the stranger, has been to all intents and purposes (with few exceptions) destroyed by the operation of s. 56 (1) of the Law of Property Act, 1925. I will deal with this section first. It provides:

" A person may take an immediate or other interest in land or other property, or the benefit of any condition, right of entry, covenant or agreement over or respecting land or other property, although he may not be named as a party to the conveyance or other instrument."

The definition s. 205, provides:

" (1) In this Act, unless the context otherwise requires, the following expressions have the meanings hereby assigned to them respectively, that is to say . . . (xx) ' Property ' includes any thing in action, and any interest in real or personal property."

Section 56 replaced s. 5 of the Real Property Act, 1845, which provided:

" That, under an indenture, executed after Oct. 1, 1845, an immediate estate or interest, in any tenements or hereditaments, and the benefit of a condition or covenant, respecting any tenements or hereditaments, may be taken, although the taker thereof be not named a party to the said indenture . . . "

One effect of s. 56 was to make clear that which may not have been plain in the authorities, that those matters dealt with were not confined to covenants, etc., running with the land.

The Law of Property Act, 1925, was a consolidating Act and came into force on Jan. 1, 1926, at the same time as two other Acts, namely, the Law of Property Act, 1922, and the Law of Property (Amendment) Act, 1924. These last two Acts were to be construed as one Act cited together as the Property Acts, 1922 and 1924. Neither of them touched the question raised by the language of s. 56 of the Act of 1925.

One cannot deny that the view of Lord DENNING, M.R., expressed so forcibly, not for the first time, in his judgment in this case[1] reinforced by the opinion of DANCKWERTS, L.J., in this case [2], is of great weight notwithstanding that it runs counter to the opinion of all the other judges who have been faced by the task of interpreting this remarkable section, viz., s. 56 of the Act of 1925. Contained, as it is, in a consolidation Act, an Act moreover dealing

---

[1] [1966] Ch. at p. 549; [1966] 3 All E.R. at p. 4.
[2] [1966] Ch. at p. 558; [1966] 3 All E.R. at p. 9

with real property, is it to be believed that by a side wind, as it were, Parliament has slipped in a provision which has revolutionised the law of contract? Although the presumption is against such an Act altering the law, the presumption must yield to plain words to the contrary.

Apart from the definition section (s. 205) I doubt whether many would have been disposed to the view that the general law which declares who can sue on a contract had received the mortal blow which s. 56 is said to have inflicted on it. The use of the word " agreement " is inapt to describe a unilateral promise. However, the definition section, if it is to be applied expressly, refers to property as including " any interest in real or personal property ". But for the saving words " unless the context otherwise requires" I should have felt grave difficulty in resisting the argument that Parliament, even if it acted *per incuriam*, had somehow allowed to be slipped into consolidating legislation, which had nothing to do with the general law of contract, an extraordinary provision which had such a drastic effect.

The section has been discussed in a number of cases which were cited by WYNN-PARRY, J., in the case of *Re Miller's Agreement, Uniacke* v. *A.G.*[1]. A useful summary of the opinions contained in the cases is in the judgment of WYNN-PARRY, J.[1], where he cited[2] a passage from *Re Foster, Hudson* v. *Foster*[3], which appears in the opinion of my noble and learned friend, LORD PEARCE. Like CROSSMAN, J., I am unable to believe that such an enormous change in the law has been made by s. 56, as to establish that an agreement by A with B to pay money to C gives C a right to sue on the contract.

Section 56 has been discussed in recent common law cases, e.g., *Green* v. *Russell (McCarthy, Third Parties)*[4], where the argument was rejected by the Court of Appeal. In *Midland Silicones, Ltd.* v. *Scruttons, Ltd.*[5] to the best of my recollection the argument based on s. 56 was not pressed. The case came before your lordships[6]. If the section was mentioned, it is not easy to see from the report that it played a great part in the case. VISCOUNT SIMONDS who at first instance had given consideration to the section (see *White* v. *Bijou Mansions, Ltd.*[7]) can scarcely have been unconscious of the section when he said in *Scruttons, Ltd.* v. *Midland Silicones, Ltd.*[8]:

> " If the principle of *jus quaesitum tertio* is to be introduced into our law, it must be by Parliament after a due consideration of its merits and demerits. I should not be prepared to give it my support without a greater knowledge than I at present possess of its operation in other systems of law."

Section 56 had as long ago as 1937 received consideration by the Law Revision Committee presided over by LORD WRIGHT, then Master of the Rolls, and containing a number of illustrious lawyers. The committee was called on to report specially on consideration including the attitude of the common law towards the *jus quaesitum tertio*. It had available to it and considered the decision of LUXMOORE, J., in *Re Ecclesiastical Comrs. for England's Conveyance*[9] which gave the orthodox view of the section. By its

---

[1] [1947] Ch. at pp. 620–622; [1947] 2 All E.R. at pp. 80–82.
[2] [1947] Ch. at p. 621; [1947] 2 All E.R. at p. 81.
[3] [1938] 3 All E.R. 357 at p. 365.
[4] [1959] 2 Q.B. 226; [1959] 2 All E.R. 529.
[5] [1961] 1 Q.B. 106; [1960] 2 All E.R. 737.
[6] [1962] A.C. 446; [1962] 1 All E.R. 1.
[7] [1937] Ch. at p. 625; [1937] 3 All E.R. at p. 277.
[8] [1962] A.C. at p. 468; [1962] 1 All E.R. at p. 7. *Supra*, p. 335.
[9] [1936] 1 Ch. 430 at p. 438; [1934] All E.R. Rep. 118 at p. 122.

report (Cmd. 5449) it impliedly rejected the revolutionary view, for it recommended that—

> " Where a contract by its express terms purports to confer a benefit directly on a third party, it shall be enforceable by the third party in his own name."

Like my noble and learned friend, LORD REID, whose opinion I have had the opportunity of reading, I am of opinion that s. 56, one of twenty-five sections in the Act of 1925 appearing under the cross heading " Conveyances and other instruments ", does not have the revolutionary effect claimed for it, appearing as it does in a consolidation Act. I think, as he does, that the context does otherwise require a limited meaning to be given to the word " property " in the section.

Although, therefore, the appellant would succeed if the respondent relied only on s. 56 of the Act of 1925, I see no answer to the respondent's claim for specific performance and no possible objection to the order made by the Court of Appeal[1] on the facts of this case.

Indeed, on this aspect of the case it seems that most of the appellant's defences were down before the case reached your lordships' House. For example, it was argued at one time that the equitable remedy of specific performance of a contract to make a money payment was not available. This untenable contention was not proceeded with. Further, it was argued that specific performance would not be granted where the remedy at law was adequate and so should not be ordered. The remedy at law is plainly inadequate, as was pointed out by the Court of Appeal[2], as (i) only nominal damages can be recovered, and (ii) in order to enforce a continuing obligation it may be necessary to bring a series of actions whereas specific performance avoids multiplicity of action. Again, it was said[3] that the courts will not make an order which cannot be enforced. This argument also fell by the wayside, for plainly the order can be enforced by the ordinary methods of execution (see R.S.C., Ord. 45, r. 1 and Ord. 45, r. 9).

The peculiar feature of this case is that the respondent is not only the personal representative of the deceased but also his widow and the person beneficially entitled to the money claimed. Although the widow cannot claim specific performance in her personal capacity there is no objection to her doing so in her capacity as administratrix, and when the moneys are recovered they will be in this instance held for the benefit of herself as the person for whom they are intended. The authorities where the remedy of specific performance has been applied in such circumstances as these are numerous. Examples are mentioned in the judgments of the Court of Appeal[4] which have dealt fully with this matter and there is no need to elaborate the topic. *Keenan* v. *Handley*[5] is a very striking example which appears to be exactly in point. It is to be noticed that the learned counsel engaged in this and other cases never took the point now relied on, that the personal representative of the contracting party could not enforce a contract such as this. As I understood the argument for the appellant it was contended that the personal representative could not obtain specific performance as the estate had nothing to gain, having suffered no loss. There is no authority which supports this proposition and I do not think that it has any validity. In *Hohler* v. *Aston*[6] a decision of

---

[1] [1966] Ch. at p. 567; [1966] 3 All E.R. at p. 15.
[2] [1966] Ch. at p. 565; [1966] 3 All E.R. at p. 14.
[3] [1966] Ch. at p. 566; [1966] 3 All E.R. at p. 15.
[4] [1966] Ch. 538; [1966] 3 All E.R. 1.
[5] (1864), 12 W.R. 930.   [6] [1920] 2 Ch. 420.

SARGANT, J., is good authority to the contrary. A Mrs. Aston agreed with her nephew Mr. Hohler to make provision for her niece and her husband, Mr. and Mrs. Rollo. Mrs. Aston died before doing so. Mr. Hohler and Mr. and Mrs. Rollo sued the executors of Mrs. Aston for specific performance and succeeded. SARGANT, J., said[1]:

> " The third parties, of course, cannot themselves enforce a contract made for their benefit, but the person with whom the contract is made is entitled to enforce the contract."

Mr. Hohler, like the respondent in her capacity as administratrix, took no benefit under the contract but was rightly allowed to recover. It is no part of the law that in order to sue on a contract one must establish that it is in one's interest to do so. Absurd results would follow if a defendant were entitled to lead evidence to show that it would pay the plaintiff better not to sue for specific performance of, say, the sale of a house because the plaintiff could sell it for a higher price to someone else. It is true that specific performance would not be ordered so as to disregard the fiduciary position which the appellant occupies as administratrix. Situations might arise in the administration of an estate when there might be conflicting claims between creditors and persons entitled beneficially otherwise, but this is not such a case. There was in the agreement reference to creditors[2] but there was no evidence directed to this matter and no reason to assume the existence of conflicting claims at the present day.

In such a case as this, there having been an unconscionable breach of faith, the equitable remedy sought is apt. The appellant has had the full benefit of the contract and the court will be ready to see that he performs his part (see the judgment of KAY, J., in *Hart* v. *Hart*[3]).

I would dismiss the appeal.

McGruther v. Pitcher
[1904] 2 Ch. 306

> A restrictive condition as to price may not be imposed upon goods at the time of their sale so as to bind subsequent purchasers either at common law or in equity, even if they take with notice of the condition.

APPEAL from a decision of Farwell, J.

The plaintiffs were rubber manufacturers at Preston ; the defendant was a boot and shoe retailer at Brixton.

By their statement of claim the plaintiffs alleged that they were the sole manufacturers of the " Palatine Revolving Rubber Heel Pad " under a licence from a Mr. Roberts, who was the owner of the Wood-Milne Patent for the article, and they alleged that their revolving heel pads were well known in the trade and had a very extensive sale.

The statement of claim contained the following paragraphs :

> " (4) The plaintiffs sell and dispose of their said revolving heel pads on the following conditions of sale, viz. :—
> " ' These revolving heel pads, whether bought directly from us or from any dealer, are sold on the express agreement that the same shall not be retailed at less than the following prices, viz :—
> " ' Ladies' 10*d.* per pair.
> " ' Gent's 1*s.* per pair.
> And shall not be resold except subject to these conditions as a term of sale.
> " ' The acceptance of the goods by any purchaser will be deemed to be an

---

[1] [1920] 2 Ch. at p. 425.
[2] See para. 6 of the agreement which is printed at [1966] 3 All E.R. 4.
[3] (1881), 18 Ch. D. 670 at p. 678.

acknowledgment that they are sold to him on these conditions and on these conditions only, and that he agrees with the vendors (as our agents in this respect) to be bound by the same.

" ' These revolving heel pads are supplied to a dealer on the above express agreement, and also on the additional terms that these conditions shall remain attached to every package sold wholesale, and shall form part of the terms upon which every such dealer resells every such package.'

" (5) The plaintiffs' course of business in the sale and disposal of their said revolving heel pads has always been and is still to pack them in boxes, and on the inside of the lid of each box are printed in large type the said conditions of sale upon which the said revolving heel pads are sold.

" (6) The plaintiffs dispose of considerable quantities of these said revolving heel pads to factors in London and elsewhere for resale by them. All of such revolving heel pads are packed in boxes with the said conditions of sale printed as aforesaid."

The plaintiffs alleged that the defendant had purchased from Charles Howes, one of their factors, some of their revolving heel pads, and that when he made the purchase he was orally informed by Howes of the conditions upon which the pads were sold to him and accepted by him.

Notwithstanding this the defendant had sold the pads at prices less than those mentioned in the conditions, and he threatened and intended to continue so doing.

The plaintiffs claimed an injunction to restrain the defendant from selling rubber heel pads manufactured by the plaintiffs, and purchased by him either directly or indirectly, at less prices than those mentioned in the conditions.

The defendant did not deny that he had sold a few of the plaintiffs' pads at prices lower than those mentioned in the conditions, but he said that when he made the purchase he was not informed by Howes of the conditions and had no notice of them. He did not admit that the conditions were binding on him or that he ever entered into any contract with the plaintiffs regulating the price at which he might sell the pads. And " the defendant will also contend that the said alleged conditions are illegal and void as being in restraint of trade."

At the trial of the action Farwell, J., granted an injunction as claimed by the plaintiffs, but limited its duration to the period of the continuance of the patent.

The defendant appealed.

The Court of Appeal allowed the appeal.

VAUGHAN WILLIAMS, L.J. In my judgment this is both in substance and in form an action for breach of contract. So treating it, I suppose no one will deny the authority of *Price* v. *Easton*[1], in which it was decided that " an action for breach of contract must be brought by the person from whom the consideration moved " ; and that is confirmed by *Tweddle* v. *Atkinson*[2].

Now Mr. McCall very properly and frankly admitted that if an action were brought for the price of these heel pads it could only be brought by Howes. But he said that the plaintiffs, who are licensees from Roberts, the owner of the patent, are entitled to sue for the breach of contract. I cannot assent to that proposition. It is said that the defendant may be sued for breach of the condition as to the prices at which the pads are to be sold. Why ? Because it is said the defendant bought with notice of that condition. Even if the defendant did buy with notice of the condition, I entirely deny that this would give any rights to a person who was not a

---

[1] (1833), 4 B. & Ad. 433.　　　　　　　[2] (1861), 1 B. & S. 393.

party to the bargain. An attempt of this sort was made in *Taddy & Co.* v. *Sterious & Co.*[1] The head-note of that case is as follows :

" T. & Co., manufacturers of tobacco, sold packet tobaccos subject to printed terms and conditions fixing a minimum price below which they were not to be sold, and containing the following proviso : ' Acceptance of the goods will be deemed a contract between the purchaser and T. & Co., that he will observe the stipulations.' " (A much stronger case, be it observed, than the present.) " ' In the case of a purchase by a retail dealer through a wholesale dealer, the latter shall be deemed to be the agent of T. & Co.' T. & Co. sold to N., who resold for his own profit to S. & Co. S. & Co. had notice of the conditions, but sold to the public at a price below the stipulated minimum : *Held*, that there was no contract between T. & Co. and S. & Co. which T. & Co. could enforce, and that conditions cannot be attached to goods so as to bind all purchasers with notice." One need only look at paragraph 5 of the statement of claim in the present case to see that the pleader meant to affirm just the contrary to the decision of Swinfen Eady, J., in *Taddy & Co.* v. *Sterious & Co.*[1] That paragraph contains really the gist of this action. [His Lordship read paragraph 5, and continued :]

The plaintiffs say that because the defendant had notice of these conditions, although he entered into no contract whatsoever directly or indirectly with the plaintiffs, they can sue him for the breach of the conditions. I do not agree, and I think that the decision of Swinfen Eady, J., was perfectly right. He said[2] : " Secondly, they contended that the goods were sold subject to certain conditions, and that, even if Netten or any one else had purported to sell them free from the conditions, Sterious & Co., having notice of the conditions, could not sell goods except according to the conditions, and the plaintiffs were entitled to restrain them from doing so. With regard to this last contention, there is a short answer. Conditions of this kind do not run with the goods, and cannot be imposed upon them. Subsequent purchasers, therefore, do not take subject to any conditions which the Court can enforce. If there was a breach of contract, the plaintiffs could no doubt sue. The question remains, therefore, whether there was any contract. There was no direct contract between Sterious & Co. and Taddy & Co., and the question does not arise as to the effect of a sale by Taddy & Co. direct to a retail trader subject to these terms as to minimum retail price." In my opinion that is perfectly sound, and I think the present plaintiffs have no cause of action. I desire to add that the case does not appear to have been presented to Farwell, J., in the way in which it has been presented to us. Farwell, J., seems to have dealt with the action as if it were brought to enforce the rights of the patentee through his licensees. I say nothing as to those rights, because in my judgment this is simply an action for breach of contract, and the plaintiffs were not parties to the contract.

ROMER, L.J. I have arrived at the same conclusion.

I have tried in vain to see on what ground this case could be successfully based by the plaintiffs, and I am bound to say that I cannot find any secure ground.

In the first place, this case is not one in which the plaintiffs can be fairly regarded as seeking to enforce some patent rights which are vested in them. I can find no trace of such a case. The plaintiffs certainly say

---

[1] [1904] I Ch. 354.   [2] [1904] Ch. at 358.

that the article is patented, but they state that they are mere licensees to manufacture it, and, as I gather also, to sell it. They do not say that as licensees they cannot do that ; and if they could, so far as I can see, the person who would have a right to complain would be the patentee. The plaintiffs do not say that any of the rights of the patentee are vested in them beyond what they have as licensees. At any rate I cannot find any case established which would justify the Court in giving the plaintiffs relief on the footing of patent rights. That being so, they must succeed if at all on some other ground.

Can the plaintiffs succeed on the ground that they are selling goods, and that they purported to attach a condition to the resale of the goods, and that the defendant was informed of this condition when he purchased the goods ? Clearly, to my mind, they cannot. A vendor cannot in that way enforce a condition on the sale of his goods out and out, and, by printing the so-called condition upon some part of the goods or on the case containing them, say that every subsequent purchaser of the goods is bound to comply with the condition, so that if he does not comply with the condition he can be sued by the original vendor. That is clearly wrong. You cannot in that way make conditions run with goods.

The only other possible ground for the action is contract. Have the plaintiffs succeeded in shewing that they have entered into a contract with the defendant ? The evidence utterly fails to prove any such contract. On the contrary, so far as I can see, the defendant has throughout said that he always intended to sell the pads without regard to the conditions, and I certainly cannot find any evidence that he agreed with his vendor to comply with the conditions. And even if the defendant had so contracted with his vendor, I should have a difficulty in holding that that would constitute a contract between the defendant and the plaintiffs. Even if the intermediate vendor was the agent of the plaintiffs, I doubt very much whether the plaintiffs could maintain the action ; but I need not consider that case. In fact, I cannot find any intermediate contract between the defendant and his vendor.

That being so, the ground of contract fails, and, as I have already said, I can find no sure ground on which to rest the plaintiffs' case. In my opinion the action fails, and the appeal must be allowed.

Cozens-Hardy, L.J., delivered judgment to the same effect.[1]

LORD STRATHCONA STEAMSHIP CO. *v.* DOMINION COAL CO.
PORT LINE LTD. *v.* BEN LINE STEAMERS, LTD.

Quaere, whether a contractual interest in a chattel granted by A to B may be enforced in equity by B against a subsequent purchaser of the chattel who, at the time of his purchase, has notice of B's interest.

Lord Strathcona Steamship Co. v. Dominion Coal Co.
[1926] A.C. 108

The judgment of their Lordships was delivered by

LORD SHAW. This is an appeal from a judgment and order of the Supreme Court of Appeal of Nova Scotia (*en banc*), dated March 1, 1924, which affirmed a judgment and order of Mellish, J., in the Supreme Court of Nova Scotia, dated May 18, 1922.

---

[1] *Note.*—See now s. 1 (1) of the Resale Prices Act, 1964, as set out *supra*, p. 333, note.

The questions involved in the case depend upon a consideration of the charter-party about to be mentioned and of the conduct of parties under and in reference to that contract.

The charter-party was dated April 20, 1914, corrected to July 24, 1914. It was made between the Lord Curzon Steamship Company, Ltd., as the owners of the steamship *Lord Strathcona*, and the respondents as charterers thereof. The charter-party was a long term charter-party—namely, for ten consecutive St. Lawrence seasons, commencing with the year 1915, with the option to the respondents of continuing the charter-party for a further period of five more seasons and a still further option of three more seasons thereafter. Should these options be exercised by the respondents as charterers the period of the contract thus extended to eighteen years. The St. Lawrence season referred to was to commence, except as to the first season 1915, five days prior to the opening of navigation to Montreal and not later than May 15 in each year. The re-delivery to the owners of the steamship was to be between November 15 and December 15 in each year.

The ship went into the service of the respondents in 1916. She was delivered, or commenced service on July 10, and she continued during the St. Lawrence season—namely, until December 14, 1916, being used by the respondents for their trade purposes under the charter-party. The British Government, which had previously intimated that the vessel would be required for the purposes of war in 1915, when she was ready for the year, abandoned this position and allowed the use of the vessel under the charter for the season 1916 as stated.

They made, however, an effective requisition of the vessel at the close of the 1916 season, and the vessel remained under requisition for 1917 and 1918 by the British Government. She came on service again by the withdrawal of the Government requisition on July 2, 1919, and remained on service till the end of the season—namely, December, 1919. Shortly put, the vessel was thus under requisition for some two and a half years—namely, from the end of the 1916 season until early in July, 1919. During the course of these years various changes, to be afterwards referred to, were made in the ownership of the vessel.

There are three questions which arise in the appeal—these are, first, whether the contract under the charter-party was frustrated by the action of the Government, as just described. Second, whether any rights of the Dominion Coal Company, as charterers of the vessel, existed as against the appellants, the Lord Strathcona Steamship Company, as owners thereof, there having been no direct privity of contract between those parties. The third question has reference to an order upon the appellants to repay a portion of the hire of the *Lord Strathcona* under an agreement made without prejudice.

The questions will be dealt with in their order.

1. On the question of frustration their Lordships are clearly of opinion that this doctrine, which has been much developed and commented upon in recent years, cannot be applied to the facts of the present case. Put shortly, frustration can only be pleaded when the events and facts on which it is founded have destroyed the subject matter of the contract, or have, by an interruption of performance thereunder so critical or protracted as to bring to an end in a full and fair sense the contract as a whole, or so superseded it that it can be truly affirmed that no resumption is reasonably possible.

It is a mistake to say that the doctrine of frustration is a hard and fast doctrine which can be applied as a general principle in a definite measure to all cases alike. The facts and circumstances of each particular contract as well as the nature and duration of the interruption to performance must all be taken into account. Shipping cases afford easy illustrations of the variety of circumstances alluded to. A voyage is arranged to be made during fixed dates. The substantial interruption of such a voyage almost necessarily concludes the question of frustration in the affirmative. Or, again, a charter is for a short term and into that term such an interruption is projected as to preclude business arrangements being readjusted so as to suit limited and disjointed periods of time ; then, again, it becomes well-nigh clear that frustration has resulted.

In the present case there is a seasonal charter extending over a long period of possibly eighteen years. The interruption has been concluded and the vessel has been restored in good sailing order after a period of use by the Government of, say, three seasons. Upon these facts then in truth the question has really settled itself in the sense that a long balance of time and season remains during which, after resumption, the contract can be effectively carried on. It happens in the present case that, after the Government interruption had ceased, the parties did resume the practice of running the vessel as owners and charterers. The range of business has not been lost, the suitability of the vessel for performance has not been impaired. In these circumstances their Lordships are clear that the judgments of the Courts below upon this topic are right and that frustration of the contract contained in the charter-party did not occur. Had the question accordingly arisen between the original charterers of the vessel the Lord Curzon Steamship Company, as owners, and the respondents as charterers, the case would have been at an end.

2. Upon the point of privity of contract and the nature of the right or remedy still open to the charterers of the vessel the following facts and dates have to be kept in view. The writ was issued by the respondents on July 31, 1920. It was directed against the appellants as present owners and against the Lord Curzon Steamship Company as parties to the charter-party, and it certainly claimed a declaration and made demands which are of a wide character, and have been exposed to considerable criticism. Generally speaking their Lordships look upon the writ as an attempt to substitute the appellants in the entirety of the obligations resting upon the Lord Curzon Steamship Company as the original owners. A declaration was claimed by the respondents under the charter-party, under which the appellants could be called upon as in an action of specific performance to perform the obligations under the charter in the same sense and degree as the original owners, the Lord Curzon Steamship Company. It will be necessary to see whether, under the principles of English jurisprudence, this demand can be justified as stated, or whether, under the other claims made in the writ, English equity is able to afford to the charterers against the present owners, the appellants, any remedy for the wrong arising to them by the threatened loss of their rights under the charter-party.

The charter-party is dated April 20, 1914, corrected to July 24, 1914. The ship had been built in England for the Lord Curzon Steamship Company under plans provided by the Dominion Coal Company, and it was agreed that, when complete, she should be chartered to the respondents, and this was done by the charter-party mentioned. Then occurred a series of transmissions of title to the ship. The dates are : December 14, 1917; Bill of Sale ; Lord Curzon Company to The Century Shipping Company. February 25, 1919 ; Bill of Sale ; Century Shipping Company to Lord Lathom Company. December 18, 1919 ; Bill of Sale ; Lord Lathom Company to Lord Strathcona Company (No. 1). June 22, 1920 ; Bill of Sale ; Lord Strathcona Company (No. 1) to Lord Strathcona Company (incorporated in 1920).

So far as the knowledge of the existence of the charter-party was concerned their Lordships are clearly of opinion that all these successive owners were well aware of it, and this knowledge was, by notice, passed very clearly and properly on from each owner to the successor. It was only very late in the day when any flaw on this point was attempted to be taken.

An important document in the case is that of September 1, 1919— namely, a memorandum of agreement by which the Lathom Company agreed with the Strathcona Company about to be formed, which contained the following clause :

> "The steamer is chartered to the Dominion Coal Company as per charter-party dated New York, April 20, 1914, corrected to July 24, 1914, which charter the buyers undertake to perform and accept all responsibilities thereunder as from date of delivery in consideration of which the buyers shall receive from date of delivery all benefits arising from the said charter. All liabilities up to date of delivery to buyers to be for account of sellers."

In the opinion of the Board the appellants thoroughly understood that the charter-party and its responsibilities and obligations thereunder were to be respected. This is not a mere case of notice of the existence of a covenant affecting the use of the property sold, but it is the case of the acceptance of their property expressly *sub conditione*.

The position of the case accordingly is that the appellants are possessed of a ship with regard to which a long running charter-party is current, the existence of which was fully disclosed, together, indeed, with an obligation which the appellants appear to have accepted to respect and carry out that charter-party. The proposal of the appellants and the argument submitted by them is to the effect that they are not bound to respect and carry forward this charter-party either in law or in equity, but that, upon the contrary, they can, in defiance of its terms, of which they had knowledge, use the vessel at their will in any other way. It is accordingly, when the true facts are shown, a very simple case raising the question of whether an obligation affecting the user of the subject of sale, namely, a ship, can be ignored by the purchaser so as to enable that purchaser, who has bought a ship notified to be not a free ship but under charter, to wipe out the condition of purchase and use the ship as a free ship. It was not bought or paid for as a free ship, but it is maintained that the buyer can thus extinguish the charterer's rights in the vessel, of which he had notice, and that the charterer has no means, legal or equitable, of preventing this in law.

In the opinion of the Board the case is ruled by *De Mattos* v. *Gibson*[1], also a shipping case, the case of the user of a piece of property by a third person (e.g., the respondent company in this case) of " the property for a particular purpose in a specified manner." Their Lordships think that the judgment of Knight Bruce, L.J.[2] plainly applies to the present case : " Reason and justice seem to prescribe that, at least as a general rule, where a man, by gift or purchase, acquires property from another, with knowledge

---

[1] (1858), 4 De G. & J. 276.   [2] *Ibid.*, 282.

of a previous contract, lawfully and for valuable consideration made by him with a third person, to use and employ the property for a particular purpose in a specified manner, the acquirer shall not to the material damage of the third person, in opposition to the contract and inconsistently with it, use and employ the property in a manner not allowable to the giver or seller." A principle, not without analogy, had previously been laid down in reference to the user of land.

In the opinion of their Lordships the case of *De Mattos* v. *Gibson*[1] still remains, notwithstanding many observations and much criticism of it in subsequent cases, of outstanding authority.

The general character of the principle on which a Court of equity acts was explained in *Tulk* v. *Moxhay*[2]. The plaintiff there was owner in fee of Leicester Square, and several houses forming the Square. He sold the property to one Elms in fee, and the deed of conveyance contained a covenant obliging Elms, his heirs and assigns, to " keep and maintain the said piece of ground and Square Garden . . . in its then form . . . in an open state, uncovered with any buildings." Elms sold to others, and the property came into the hands of the defendant, who admitted that he had purchased with notice of the covenant. The defendant, " having manifested an intention to alter the character of the Square Garden, and asserted a right, if he thought fit, to build upon it," the plaintiff, who still remained owner of several houses in the Square, filed a bill for an injunction. All this is familiar knowledge, but it appears to have been sometimes forgotten what was the nature of the argument for the defendant. He contended that the covenant did not run with the land so as to be binding upon him as a purchaser, and Sir Roundell Palmer, on his behalf, relied on the dictum of Brougham, L.C., in *Keppell* v. *Bailey*[3] to the effect that " notice of such a covenant did not give a Court of equity jurisdiction to enforce it by injunction against such purchaser, inasmuch as ' the knowledge by an assignee of an estate, that his assignor had assumed to bind others than the law authorized him to affect by his contract, had attempted to create a burden upon property which was inconsistent with the nature of that property and unknown to the principles of the law and could not bind such assignee by affecting his conscience.' " No reply was called for to this argument, and the Lord Chancellor said that Lord Brougham never could have meant to lay down the doctrine " that this Court would not enforce an equity attached to land by the owner, unless under such circumstances as would maintain an action at law." " If that be the result of his observations," added the Lord Chancellor, " I can only say that I cannot coincide with it."

It has sometimes been considered that *Tulk* v. *Moxhay*[4] and *De Mattos* v. *Gibson*[1] carried forward to and laid upon the shoulders of an alienee with notice the obligations of the alienor, and, therefore, that the former is liable to the covenantee in specific performance as by the law of contract, and under a species of implied privity. This is not so ; the remedy is a remedy in equity by way of injunction against acts inconsistent with the covenant, with notice of which the land was acquired. The former was the view of Kay, J., in *London and South Western Ry. Co.* v. *Gomm*[5] ; but it was corrected by the Court of Appeal substantially in the sense above stated. So confined, that is, to a remedy in equity by injunction against

---

[1] (1858), 4 De G. & J. 276.   [2] (1848), 2 Ph. 774, at pp. 776, 779.
[3] (1834), 2 My. & K. 517, at p. 547.   [4] (1848), 2 Ph. 774, at p. 777.
                    [5] (1881), 20 Ch. D. 562.

the violation of restrictive covenants, the application of the principle of
Tulk v. *Moxhay*[1] was affirmed. The same result had been reached in
Haywood v. *Brunswick Permanent Benefit Building Society*[2], and other
decisions have followed in a like sense.

The cases on this branch of the law are legion. But following the
leading authorities just cited there may be specially mentioned that of
Catt v. *Tourle*[3], in which Selwyn, L.J., affirms, with precision, the principles
of *Tulk* v. *Moxhay*[1] and *De Mattos* v. *Gibson*[4].

But *Tulk* v. *Moxhay*[1] is important for a further and vital consideration
—namely, that it analyses the true situation of a purchaser who, having
bought upon the terms of the restriction upon free contract existing, thereafter, when vested in the lands, attempts to divest himself of the condition
under which he had bought : " it is said that the covenant being one which
does not run with the land, this Court cannot enforce it ; but the question
is, not whether the covenant runs with the land, but whether a party shall
be permitted to use the land in a manner inconsistent with the contract
entered into by his vendor, and with notice of which he purchased. Of
course, the price would be affected by the covenant, and nothing could be
more inequitable than that the original purchaser should be able to sell
the property the next day for a greater price, in consideration of the assignee
being allowed to escape from the liability which he had himself undertaken."

In the opinion of the Board these views, much expressive of the justice
and good faith of the situation, are still part of English equity jurisprudence,
and an injunction can still be granted thereunder to compel, as in a Court
of conscience, one who obtains a conveyance or grant *sub conditione* from
violating the condition of his purchase to the prejudice of the original
contractor. Honesty forbids this ; and a Court of equity will grant an
injunction against it.

It may be mentioned that essentially the same principle has been applied
by the House of Lords in the Scotch case of the *Earl of Zetland* v. *Hislop*[5],
in which the superior of land (according to law holding the *dominium
directum* thereof and, therefore, of course, having a continuing patrimonial
interest therein) granted contracts of feu to various vassals holding the
dominium utile of the land under that permanent tenure. By these contracts
the vassal, his heirs and assignees and their tenants were prohibited from
using the property for carrying on the trade of a publican. Various transactions of sale and transfer of the property had occurred : four of the
purchasers asserted their right to carry on a publican's business, and the
Earl of Zetland asked interdict (or injunction) against such a violation of
the restrictions contained in the feu charter. In the House of Lords, as
stated, the patrimonial interest of the superior was affirmed and also his
right to interdict unless (which was alleged and which was made the subject
of a remit for probation) he was precluded from this remedy by acquiescence
and waiver.

It has been said—it was strongly urged for the appellant in this case
—that a remedy by way of injunction against the owners not disposing of
their ship in any other way than under the charter-party could not be granted
because there was no such negative covenant to enforce by injunction.

Lord Selborne, in *Wolverhampton and Walsall Rail. Co.* v. *London and*

---

[1] (1848), 2 Ph. 774, at p. 777.   [2] (1881), 8 Q. B. D. 403.   [3] (1869), L. R. 4 Ch. App. 654.
[4] (1858), 4 De G. & J. 276.   [5] (1882), 7 App. Cas. 427.

North Western Rail. Co.[1], disposed of such an argument thus, in language which still remains unimpaired in force : " The technical distinction being made, that if you find the word ' not ' in an agreement—' I will not do a thing '—as well as the words ' I will,' even although the negative term might have been implied from the positive, yet the Court, refusing to act on an implication of the negative, will act on the expression of it. I can only say that I should think it was the safer and the better rule, if it should eventually be adopted by this Court, to look in all such cases to the substance and not to the form. If the substance of the agreement is such that it would be violated by doing the thing sought to be prevented, then the question will arise, whether this is the Court to come to for a remedy. If it is, I cannot think that ought to depend on the use of a negative rather than an affirmative form of expression."

A perusal of the numerous decisions on this branch of the law shows that much difficulty has been caused by the attempt to extend these principles to cases to which they could not, by the nature of the case, have been meant to apply. It has been forgotten that—to put the point very simply—the person seeking to enforce such a restriction must, of course, have, and continue to have, an interest in the subject matter of the contract. For instance, in the case of land he must continue to hold the land in whose favour the restrictive covenant was meant to apply. That was clearly the state of matters in the case of *Tulk* v. *Moxhay*[2] applicable to the possession of real estate in Leicester Square. It was also clearly the case in *De Mattos* v. *Gibson*[3], in which the person seeking to enforce the injunction had an interest in the user of the ship. In short, in regard to the user of land or of any chattel, an interest must remain in the subject matter of the covenant before a right can be conceded to an injunction against the violation by another of the covenant in question. This proposition seems so elementary as not to require to be stated. And it is only mentioned because in numerous decisions, as is clearly brought out in the judgment of Lord Wrenbury, then Buckley, L.J., in *London County Council* v. *Allen*[4], it was necessary to shear away this misapplication or improper extension of the equitable principle. As Romer, L.J., said in *Formby* v. *Barker*[5] : " If restrictive covenants are entered into with a covenantee, not in respect of or concerning any ascertainable property belonging to him, or in which he is interested, then the covenant must be regarded, so far as he is concerned, as a personal covenant—that is, as one obtained by him for some personal purpose or object."

Applying that to the case of land and referring to numerous cases upon the subject, Lord Wrenbury says in *London County Council* v. *Allen*[4] : " Inasmuch as at the date when the covenant was taken the covenantee had no land to which the benefit of the covenant could be attached, it was held that the benefit of the restrictive covenant could not enure against a derivative owner even where he took with notice."

The Board notes the observations made by Scrutton, L.J., in the case of *London County Council* v. *Allen*[6], in which, alluding to various decisions, the learned judge puts this point as to the possible inconvenience, not only private but public, which may result from a strict adhesion to the principle that the enforcement of a restrictive covenant must be confined to those

---

[1] (1873), L. R. 16 Eq. 433, at p. 440.   [2] (1848), 2 Ph. 774.   [3] (1858), 4 De G. & J. 276.
[4] [1914] 3 K. B. 642, at p. 656 to 658.   [5] [1903] 2 Ch. 539, at p. 554.
[6] [1914] 3 K. B. 642, at p. 673.

having patrimonial interests in the subject matter. His Lordship takes the not unfamiliar case of restrictive covenants imposed by an owner of a large block of land in the terms of conveyance of the various fractions in which it may be split up for private use, and he observes : " I regard it as very regrettable that a public body should be prevented from enforcing a restriction on the use of property imposed for the public benefit against persons who bought the property knowing of the restriction, by the apparently immaterial circumstance that the public body does not own any land in the immediate neighbourhood. But, after a careful consideration of the authorities, I am forced to the view that the later decisions of this Court compel me so to hold."

The question here alluded to may subsequently arise, and their Lordships are unwilling, because it is unnecessary in the present case, to make any pronouncement upon it ; for the present is, as has been seen, a case as to the user of a ship, with regard to the subject matter of which, namely, the vessel, the respondent has, and will have during the continuance of the period covered by the charter-party, a plain interest so long as she is fit to go to sea. Again, to adopt the language of Knight Bruce, L.J., in the *De Mattos* v. *Gibson*[1] case : " Why should it (the Court) not prevent the commission or continuance of a breach of such a contract, when, its subject being valuable, as for instance, a trading ship or some costly machine, the original owner and possessor, or a person claiming under him, with notice and standing in his right, having the physical control of the chattel, is diverting it from the agreed object, that object being of importance to the other ? A system of laws in which such a power does not exist must surely be very defective. I repeat that, in my opinion, the power does exist here."

In considering the character of the doctrines of equity in a case like the present it is essential to remember that these doctrines are of several kinds and fall partly, though not exclusively, under different heads. If this is not borne in mind uncertainty and confusion are apt to arise. Dicta of eminent judges which apply under one principle get to be regarded as though they illustrated a principle which is in reality different.

Equity has, in addition to the concurrent jurisdiction, auxiliary and exclusive jurisdiction. The enforcement of trusts is in the main an illustration of the exclusive jurisdiction. The scope of the trusts recognized in equity is unlimited. There can be a trust of a chattel or of a chose in action, or of a right or obligation under an ordinary legal contract, just as much as a trust of land. A shipowner might declare himself a trustee of his obligations under a charter-party, and if there were such a trust an assignee, although he could not enforce specific performance of the obligation, would fail to do so only on the broad ground that the Court of equity had no machinery by means of which to enforce the contract. Subject to this an assignee of the charterer could enforce his title to the chose in action in equity, even though he could not have done so at law.

There are cases of a different type in which equity is proceeding, not on the footing of trust, but of following, by the exercise of concurrent and auxiliary jurisdiction, the analogy of the common law. Such are the cases of so-called equitable easements. This was explained by the Court of Appeal in *London County Council* v. *Allen*[2]. There it was held that an owner of land, deriving title under a person who had entered into a restrictive covenant concerning the land, which covenant did not run with the land

---

[1] (1858), 4 De G. & J. 276, at p. 283.   [2] [1914] 3 K. B. 642.

at law, was not bound by the covenant although he took the land with notice of it, if the covenantee were not in possession of or interested in land for the benefit of which the covenant was entered into. In the judgments it was pointed out that such a covenant did not run with the land at law, and that there was a series of authorities which showed that in the case of land mere purchase with notice was not sufficient. The reason was that under this head of its jurisdiction equity had followed law except to the extent of recognizing a negative covenant as capable of operating for the benefit of a dominant tenement. The principle proceeded on the analogy of a covenant running with the land or of an easement, as explained by Jessel, M.R., in *London and South Western Rail. Co.* v. *Gomm*[1]. This restriction of the principle on the analogy of easements at law rendered mere notice insufficient, and cut down the jurisdiction from the wider principle stated by Knight Bruce, L.J., in *De Mattos* v. *Gibson*[2] to the narrower head established in order to accord with the legal analogy in the case of land.

But in no other regard does this or any other decision of commanding importance seem to affect the general principle which Knight Bruce, L.J., laid down. If a man acquires from another rights in a ship which is already under charter, with notice of rights which required the ship to be used for a particular purpose and not inconsistently with it, then he appears to be plainly in the position of a constructive trustee with obligations which a Court of equity will not permit him to violate. It does not matter that this Court cannot enforce specific performance. It can proceed, if there is expressed or clearly implied a negative stipulation. The judgment of Lord St. Leonards, L.C., in *Lumley* v. *Wagner*[3] appears to be conclusive of the principle : " Wherever," says that very eminent judge, " this Court has not proper jurisdiction to enforce specific performance, it operates to bind men's consciences, as far as they can be bound, to a true and literal performance of their agreements ; and it will not suffer them to depart from their contracts at their pleasure, leaving the party with whom they have contracted to the mere chance of any damages which a jury may give."

For the reasons already fully set forth the Board is of opinion that the injunction granted by Mellish, J., in cl. 7 of his order of June 20, 1922, was correct, and was properly affirmed by the Supreme Court for the reasons set forth by Chisholm, J. The fundamental point indicated is thus determined.

(His Lordship then considered briefly a point subsidiary to the main issue.)

Port Line, Ltd. v. Ben Line Steamers, Ltd.

[1958] 2 Q.B. 146

The plaintiffs, Port Line Ltd., chartered a vessel from the then owners, Silver Line Ltd., on a gross time charter for a period of about 30 months, and they took delivery on March 9, 1955. In February, 1956, Silver Line sold the vessel to the defendants, Ben Line Steamers Ltd., and provision was made to cover the unexpired term of the plaintiffs' time charter with Silver Line by the defendants chartering the vessel by demise to Silver Line for the unexpired term of the plaintiffs' charter. The bareboat charter between Silver Line and the defendants contained a clause providing: " If the ship be requisitioned this charter shall thereupon cease." There was no comparable provision in the plaintiffs' gross time charter. On August 22,

---

[1] (1881), 20 Ch. D. 562.   [2] (1858), 4 De G. & J. 276.   [3] (1852), 1 De G. M. & G. 604, at p. 619.

1956, due to the Suez crisis, the Ministry of Transport informed the defendants that the vessel was requisitioned and it was put at the Crown's disposition on August 29. On September 10, the defendants entered into an agreement with the Ministry providing for the rates of hire during the period of requisition. Requisition continued until November 28, 1956, when the vessel was released to the defendants. It was agreed by the parties that when notice of requisition was given on August 22, a reasonable estimate of the duration of the requisition was from three to four months. During the period of requisition the plaintiffs continued to pay the charter hire to Silver Line despite the latter's contention that the plaintiffs' time charter with them was frustrated.

The plaintiffs claimed to recover the whole or part of the compensation received by the defendants from the Crown in respect of the requisition period on the grounds, *inter alia*, that as there was a subsisting contract between the plaintiffs and Silver Line at the material time, the plaintiffs were entitled as against the defendants on the principle laid down in *Lord Strathcona Steamship Co. Ltd.* v. *Dominion Coal Co. Ltd.*[1] to have the vessel used for the carriage of their goods; that they were entitled to recover from the defendants under the Compensation (Defence) Act, 1939, if it applied, the bareboat element of the compensation under section 4 (3)[2]; alternatively, if the Act did not apply, they were entitled to a portion of the compensation in accordance with the principles laid down in *F. A. Tamplin Steamship Co. Ltd.* v. *Anglo-Mexican Petroleum Products Co. Ltd.*[3]

The defendants alleged that the plaintiffs' contract with Silver Line was frustrated by the requisitioning; that the *Strathcona* case[4] was wrongly decided; that, even if rightly decided, it only applied where the subsequent purchaser had express notice of the terms of a subsisting charterparty, and that, in any event, it laid down no principle which entitled the plaintiffs to have the vessel used for the carriage of their goods, and imposed no obligation on the defendants to account as constructive trustees; that the Compensation (Defence) Act, 1939, applied, but gave no rights to the plaintiffs; and that the *Tamplin* case[5] apportionment was excluded by the Act of 1939, and in any event did not apply.

DIPLOCK, J.   The only issue which I have to determine is as to the respective rights of the plaintiffs and the defendants to the compensation or requisition hire which the defendants have received from the Crown in respect of the use of the vessel from August 29 to November 28, 1956.

The plaintiffs contend: (1) that throughout the relevant period they had a valid and subsisting contract with Silver Line Ltd.; (2) that by virtue of that contract they were entitled, as against the defendants, on the principle laid down in *Lord Strathcona Steamship Co. Ltd.* v. *Dominion Coal Co. Ltd.*,[6] to have the vessel used for the carriage of their goods; (3) that they are entitled to recover from the defendants (a) under the Compensation (Defence) Act, 1939, if it applies, the whole compensation, or alternatively, the bareboat

---

[1] [1926] A. C. 108.
[2] Compensation (Defence) Act, 1939, s. 4 (3):
   " Where, on the day on which any compensation accrues due by virtue of paragraph (a) of subsection (1) of this section, a person other than the owner of the vessel . . . is, by virtue of a subsisting charter or contract of hiring, the person who would be entitled to possession of, or to use, the vessel . . . but for the requisition, the person to whom the compensation is paid shall be deemed to receive it as a trustee for the first mentioned person ".
[3] [1916] 2 A. C. 397.   [4] [1926] A. C. 108.   [5] [1916] 2 A. C. 397.
[6] [1926]A. C. 108.

element of the compensation, received by the defendants in respect of the requisition, or (b) if the Compensation (Defence) Act, 1939, does not apply, a portion of the compensation, such portion being ascertained in accordance with the principles laid down by Lord Parker in *F. A. Tamplin Steamship Co., Ltd.* v. *Anglo-Mexican Petroleum Products Co., Ltd.*[1] and applied in *Chinese Mining and Engineering Co., Ltd.* v. *Sale & Co.*[2] and other cases; or (c), as an alternative to (a) and (b), the profits made by the defendants out of the requisition of the vessel.

The defendants challenge these contentions to the polls and to the array. The plaintiffs' contract with Silver Line Ltd., they say, was frustrated by the requisition; the *Strathcona* case[3] was wrongly decided; even if rightly decided it applies only where the subsequent purchaser has express notice of the terms of a subsisting charterparty; in any event it lays down no principle which entitles the plaintiffs to have the vessel used for the carriage of their goods, and it imposes no obligation on the defendants to account as constructive trustees; the Compensation (Defence) Act, 1939, applies, but gives no rights to the plaintiffs. The *Tamplin* case[4] apportionment is excluded by the Compensation (Defence) Act, 1939, and in any event does not apply. It is conceded that if the defendants are right as to the plaintiffs' gross time charter being frustrated by the requisition, their claim must fail.

The requisition in this case took place not under any statutory powers but under the prerogative power of the Crown, a fact which is not without some relevance on the question of frustration, since the Crown's power to retain possession of ships under the prerogative extends only for such period as possession is needed for the defence of the realm, although of this the Crown is no doubt, in the absence of *male fides*, the sole judge. A requisition under the prerogative power is, therefore, necessarily a temporary taking of possession, although the period of possession may be lengthy. It is, however, agreed in this case that on August 22 it would have been reasonably expected that the requisition would last three to four calendar months, as in fact it did. No proclamation or Order in Council is required to entitle the Crown to exercise its prerogative power of requisition, and none had been published by August 22 when notice of requisition of the vessel was given to the defendants. In fact, however, an Order in Council, the Requisition of Ships Order, 1956, regulating the requisition of ships had been made on August 3, but was not published until August 28 when it appeared in the " London Gazette." I shall have to look at its terms later to see what provision it makes for compensation.

Those being the circumstances, the question poses itself neatly: is a time charter for 30 months of which a little over 17 months have expired and a little under 13 months remain to be fulfilled frustrated by a requisition which would be expected to and does in fact last three to four months, and accordingly leaves about 10 months at the end of the requisition when the vessel will be available for use in performing services under the charter? It would appear to be the fate of frustration cases when they reach the highest tribunals that either there should be agreement as to the principle but differences as to its application, or differences as to the principle but agreement as to its application. I do not propose to add to what, according to Lord Radcliffe in *Davis Contractors, Ltd.* v. *Fareham Urban District*

---

[1] [1916] 2 A. C. 397.
[3] [1926] A. C. 108.

[2] [1917] 2 K. B. 599.
[4] [1916] 2 A. C. 397.

Council[1], had already become by 1919 an anthology of phrases, by venturing on any restatement of the principle myself. Lest it be thought, however, that I do not remain an unrepentant adherent of the " implied term " theory of frustration, I would add that I have carefully considered the terms of the plaintiffs' charter, including in particular the " off-hire clause," and have borne in mind that at the time the charter was entered into the Compensation (Defence) Act, 1939—at which I shall have to look later—was in force, and provided in effect for the apportionment between the owner and time charterer of compensation payable by the Crown in respect of requisition.

I think, however, that, whichever of the many suggested tests are applied, the result in this case is the same. Whether one applies the practical test favoured by Lord Loreburn in *Tamplin's* case[2] that in the case of a time charter, if the requisition is likely to last for substantially less than the remaining period of the charterparty, the contract is not frustrated, or whether one asks oneself with Lord Dunedin in *Metropolitan Water Board* v. *Dick, Kerr & Co., Ltd.*[3]: Was the interruption one which was likely to be so long as to destroy the identity of the work or service, when resumed, with the work or service interrupted ?—which was Lord Sumner's favourite of his anthology in *Bank Line, Ltd.* v. *Arthur Capel & Co.*[4], the answer in this case must, I think, be that this charterparty was not frustrated. It is also the answer which MacKinnon, L.J.'s " officious bystander " (see *Shirlaw* v. *Southern Foundries* (1926) *Ltd.*[5]) would I think have received at the time the contract was made had he posed the question to Silver Line and Port Line, or to two disembodied and unincorporated reasonable shipowners (see *per* Lord Radcliffe in *Davis's* case[6]) entering into a contract in similar terms.

Finally, if however reluctantly I had to ask myself the metaphorical question: " Was the basis of the contract overthrown " by the requisition (see *per* Lord Reid in *Davis's* case[7]), or less metaphorically, is the contract not wide enough to apply to the new situation[8], my answer still would be no, and the law accordingly did not step in to terminate the contract when the vessel was requisitioned, or at any time during the requisition.

In the result I hold that at all material times there was a valid and subsisting contract between Silver Line and the plaintiffs for breach of which (if there was any breach during the period of requisition) the plaintiffs could recover damages from Silver Line. But that is a claim with which I am not concerned. What is said, however, is that by virtue of that contract the plaintiffs were entitled as against the defendants, Ben Line, to have the vessel used for the carriage of their goods.

The plaintiffs' charterparty with Silver Line was a gross time charter, not one by demise. It gave the plaintiffs no right of property in or to possession of the vessel. It was one by which Silver Line agreed with the plaintiffs that for 30 months from March 9, 1955, they would render services by their servants and crew to carry the goods which were put on the vessel by the plaintiffs: see *per* MacKinnon, L.J., in *Sea and Land Securities, Ltd.* v. *William Dickinson & Co., Ltd.*[9]. By parting with their property in the vessel on February 8, 1956, and retaining a right to possession and use which terminated on its requisition, Silver Line put it out of their power to con-

---

[1] [1956] A. C. 696, at p. 727; [1956] 2 All E. R. 145, *infra*, p. 415.
[2] [1916] 2 A. C. 397.   [3] [1918] A. C. 119.
[4] [1919] A. C. 435.
[5] [1939] 2 K. B. 206, at p. 227; [1939] 2 All E. R. 113.
[6] [1956] A. C. 696, at p. 728.   [7] *Ibid.*, 719.   [8] *Ibid.*, 721.
[9] [1942] 2 K. B. 65, at p. 69; [1942] 1 All E. R. 503.

tinue to perform their contractual services after the vessel was requisitioned. It is true that during the period of requisition (which is the only period with which I am concerned) Silver Line could not have performed their contractual services to the plaintiffs anyway, but the plaintiffs would have been entitled under section 4 (3) of the Compensation (Defence) Act, 1939, to the bareboat element of any compensation received by Silver Line from the Crown, and would have had to pay to Silver Line a rather larger sum by way of hire under the charterparty. It would seem, therefore, that so far as the period of requisition itself is concerned, the plaintiffs would have gained rather than lost by any breach of the contract by Silver Line which relieved the plaintiffs from paying to Silver Line the chartered hire. This, however, is a matter between Silver Line and the plaintiffs with which I am not called upon to deal except in so far (if at all) as it may be relevant to the determination of the plaintiffs' rights against the defendants. There was no privity of contract between the plaintiffs and the defendants. On what ground, therefore, can they assert against the defendants all or any of the contractual rights they had against Silver Line, or any statutory rights which they would have had against Silver Line by virtue of the existence of such contractual rights ?

It is contended that the plaintiffs' rights against the defendants stem from the principle laid down by Knight Bruce, L.J., in *De Mattos* v. *Gibson*[1] in 1858 as approved by the Privy Council in the *Lord Strathcona* case.[2] The principle laid down by Knight Bruce, L.J., in *De Mattos* v. *Gibson*[1] in granting on appeal an interlocutory injunction to restrain a mortgagee of a ship who had acquired his mortgage with knowledge of the plaintiffs' subsisting charterparty from interfering with the performance of a subsisting voyage charter was in the following oft-quoted terms[3].

" Reason and justice seem to prescribe that, at least as a general rule, where a man, by gift or purchase, acquires property from another, with knowledge of a previous contract, lawfully and for valuable consideration made by him with a third person, to use and employ the property for a particular purpose in a specified manner, the acquirer shall not, to the material damage of the third person, in opposition to the contract and inconsistently with it, use and employ the property in a manner not allowable to the giver or seller."

In 1858 this was new law. In *Tulk* v. *Moxhay*[4] decided 10 years before, on which Knight Bruce, L.J.'s statement has been assumed to be based, Lord Cottenham, L.C.'s *ratio decidendi* was based on the retention, by the covenantee, of land the value of which would be diminished by breach of the covenant. Turner, L.J., who sat with Knight Bruce, L.J., in the interlocutory appeal in *De Mattos* v. *Gibson*[5], gave a separate judgment which was subsequently treated as correctly propounding the questions to be determined at the trial, and expressed no concurrence with Knight Bruce, L.J.'s reasons. When the action came for trial before the Lord Chancellor[6], Lord Chelmsford, L.C., did not grant an injunction. It would appear on analysis of his judgment that he treated the right to an injunction as depending on the same principle as the right to damages in *Lumley* v. *Gye*[7], decided five years before, namely, that it is a tort knowingly to procure a breach of contract by another person.

De Mattos v. *Gibson*[5] was followed five years later with expressed reluc-

---

[1] (1858) 4 De G. & J. 276.
[3] 4 De G. & J. 282.   [4] (1848), 2 Ph. 774.
[6] (1859) 4 De G. & J. 284, at p. 288 *et seq.*

[2] [1926] A. C. 108.
[5] (1858), 4 De G. & J. 276.
[7] (1853), 2 E. & B. 216.

tance by Wood, V.-C., in *Messageries Imperiales Co.* v. *Baines*[1], but I am inclined to think on the principle laid down by Lord Chelmsford, L.C., rather than that laid down by Knight Bruce, L.J. The broad principle as laid down by Knight Bruce, L.J., applies to all species of property—real property, chattels and choses in action alike. It was applied (or at any rate treated as correct) in a number of cases relating to each of those species up to the turn of the century, but as a doctrine dependent upon notice alone was finally discredited in *London County Council* v. *Allen*[2]. Scrutton, L.J., there shed a tear over its demise as respects real property, but five years later in *Barker* v. *Stickney*[3] he regarded the period of mourning as over, and his judgment conveniently lists (and so saves me from citing) the cases which he considered had buried it as respects each class of property. In 1926, however, it rose from the grave in the *Strathcona* case[4] which, being a decision of the Privy Council, is not binding upon me, but being one of a Board which included Lords Haldane, Wrenbury and Blanesburgh, in addition to Lord Shaw, is (so far as it deals with questions of equity) entitled to respect which in a common law lawyer borders upon awe.

It may be relevant to note that in the *Strathcona* case[4] the buyers of the vessel subject to the time charter in favour of the plaintiffs had express notice of the terms of the charter, and had covenanted with the sellers to perform and accept all responsibilities under it. It was, as the Board said[5], not a mere case of notice of the existence of a covenant affecting the use of the property sold, but a case of acceptance of the property expressly *sub conditione*. The initial emphasis on this, and the reference at a later stage to the possibility that a shipowner might declare himself a trustee of his obligations under a charterparty so as to bind his assignee, might suggest as a possible *ratio decidendi* that the *Strathcona* case[4] was one where either the purchaser used expressions which amounted to a declaration of trust in favour of the charterers, or the vendor himself accepted the benefit of the covenant as trustee for the charterers. But an examination of the Board's opinion as a whole seems to indicate that they accepted the full doctrine of Knight Bruce, L.J., as respects chattels, namely, that mere notice does give rise to the equity, the only qualification that the Board imposed being that[6] " an interest must remain " (sc. in the person seeking the remedy) " in the subject matter of the covenant before a right can be conceded to an injunction against the violation by another of the covenant in question." The only remedy which the Board in terms recognized is a remedy by injunction against the use of the ship by the purchaser inconsistent with the charterparty, but they said[7], in a passage on which Mr. Roskill for the plaintiffs strongly relies, that the purchaser " appears to be plainly in the position of a constructive trustee with obligations which a court of equity will not permit him to violate."

These passages pose several problems: (1) If, as the Board states[8], the ship is the " subject-matter " of the covenant of which the violation by another is to be restrained, it is difficult to see in what sense a charterer under a gross time charter has an interest in that subject-matter except in the broad sense that it is to his commercial advantage that his covenantor should continue to use the ship to perform the services which he has covenanted to perform. But the time charter is a contract for services. The time charterer has no proprietary or possessory rights in the ship, and if the

---

[1] (1863), 7 L. T. 763. [2] [1914] 3 K. B. 642. [3] [1919] 1 K. B. 121. [4] [1926] A. C. 108.
[5] *Ibid.*, 116. [6] *Ibid.*, 122. [7] *Ibid.*, 125. [8] *Ibid.* 123.

covenantee's commercial advantage in the observance of the covenant is sufficient to constitute an " interest " in the chattel to which the covenant relates, it is difficult to see why the principle does not apply to price fixing cases such as *Dunlop Pneumatic Tyre Co., Ltd.* v. *Selfridge & Co., Ltd.*[1] The Board[2] explain cases like *Dunlop's case*[3], which had been cited to them, as cases where the plaintiff had no interest in the subject-matter of the contract. They say[4] that the charterer has and will have during the continuance of the charterparty " a plain interest " (in the ship) " so long as she is fit to go to sea." Plain though it may be, if the expression " interest " is used colloquially, the Board nowhere explain what the legal nature of that interest is.

(2) Whether the reference to the subsequent purchaser with notice as being, also " plainly," in the position of a constructive trustee imports that equity provides other remedies against him by his *cestui que trust*, such as the right to an account, the making of a vesting order or the appointment of a new trustee, is nowhere discussed in the *Strathcona* case; but the whole trend of the opinion, the actual order made and the observation of the Board[4]: " It is incredible that the owners will lay up the vessel rather than permit its use under the contract," all strongly suggest that the only remedy in the view of the Board that the charterer acquired against the subsequent purchaser was the purely negative remedy, namely, to restrain a user of the vessel inconsistent with the terms of his charter with the former owner, and the obligation of the purchaser which a court of equity will not allow him to violate is the negative obligation not to make such inconsistent user of the vessel. As a " constructive trustee " the subsequent purchaser seems to be one *sui generis*, and I should hesitate as a common law lawyer to seek to devise other remedies against him which did not apparently occur to the Board.

(3) The Board in the *Strathcona* case[5], beyond saying that that case was not one of " mere notice," did not discuss what kind of notice to the purchaser of the charterer's rights gives rise to the equity, namely, whether at the time of his acquisition of his interest in the vessel he must have actual knowledge of the charterer's rights against the seller, the violation of which it is sought to restrain, or whether " constructive notice " will suffice. " Reason and justice "—the sole though weighty grounds on which Knight Bruce, L.J., based the equity—do not seem to me to prescribe the introduction into commercial matters such as the sale of a ship of the doctrine of constructive notice. I respectfully agree with Lindley, L.J.'s observations in *Manchester Trust* v. *Furness*[6]. Furthermore, as between vendor and purchaser of real property, where the doctrine has been developed, constructive notice—like estoppel in less esoteric matters—is a shield not a weapon of offence. It protects an already existing equitable interest from being defeated by a purchaser for value without notice. It is not itself the source of an equitable interest.

The *Strathcona* case[5], although decided over 30 years ago, has never been followed in the English courts, and has never come up for direct consideration. In *Clore* v. *Theatrical Properties, Ltd.*[7] Lord Wright, M.R., suggested in passing that it might be peculiar to ships, but no such suggestion is to be found in the *Strathcona* case[8] itself. In *Greenhalgh* v. *Mallard*[9]

[1] [1915] A. C. 847.   [2] [1926] A. C. 108, at p. 121.
[3] [1915] A. C. 847.   [4] [1926] A. C. 108, at p. 123.
[5] [1926] A. C. 108. [6] [1895] 2 Q. B. 539, at p. 545. [7] [1936] 3 All E. R. 483, at p. 490.
[8] [1926] A. C. 108.   [9] [1943] 2 All E. R. 234.

Lord Greene, M.R., in a judgment concurred in by Luxmoore, L.J., and Goddard, L.J., was clearly of opinion that it was wrongly decided, although it is only fair to add that as recently as 1952, Denning, L.J., gave it a not unfriendly passing glance in *Bendall* v. *McWhirter*[1].

It seems, therefore, that it is in this case for the first time after more than 30 years that an English court has to grapple with the problem of what principle was really laid down in the *Strathcona* case[2], and whether that case was rightly decided. The difficulty I have found in ascertaining its *ratio decidendi*, the impossibility which I find of reconciling the actual decision with well-established principles of law, the unsolved and, to me, insoluble problems which that decision raises combine to satisfy me that it was wrongly decided. I do not propose to follow it. I naturally express this opinion with great diffidence, but having reached a clear conclusion it is my duty to express it.

If I am wrong in my view that the case was wrongly decided, I am certainly averse from extending it one iota beyond that which, as I understand it, it purported to decide. In particular, I do not think that it purported to decide (1) that anything short of actual knowledge by the subsequent purchaser at the time of the purchase of the charterer's rights, the violation of which it is sought to restrain, is sufficient to give rise to the equity; (2) that the charterer has any remedy against the subsequent purchaser with notice except a right to restrain the use of the vessel by such purchaser in a manner inconsistent with the terms of the charter; (3) that the charterer has any positive right against the subsequent purchaser to have the vessel used in accordance with the terms of his charter. The third proposition follows from the second; *ubi jus, ibi remedium*. For failure by the subsequent purchaser to use the vessel in accordance with the terms of the charter entered into by his seller there is no remedy by specific performance as was held in the *Strathcona* case[2] itself. There is equally no remedy in damages, a consideration which distinguishes the *Strathcona*[2] case from such cases as *Lumley* v. *Wagner*[3] and *Lumley* v. *Gye*[4]. The charterer's only right is coterminous with his remedy, namely, not to have the ship used by the purchaser in violation of his charter.

[DIPLOCK, J., then considered and rejected the plaintiffs' contention that they were entitled to succeed under the Compensation (Defence) Act, 1939. He concluded:]

As is obvious from what I have already said, in my view this claim fails: (1) Because the *Strathcona* case[2] was wrongly decided; (2) because, even if it was rightly decided, the defendants do not come within its principles as they had no actual knowledge at the time of their purchase of the plaintiffs' rights under their charter; (3) because, even if it was rightly decided, and the defendants come within its principles (a) they were in breach of no duty to the plaintiffs since it was by no act of theirs that the vessel during the period of requisition was used inconsistently with the terms of the plaintiffs' charter—it was by act of the Crown by title paramount—and (b) the plaintiffs are not entitled to any remedy against the defendants except a right to restrain the defendants from using the vessel in a manner inconsistent with the terms of the charter. This interesting action—in which I have been very much indebted to counsel for their clear and learned arguments—therefore fails at least so far as this court is concerned.

---

[1] [1952] 2 Q. B. 466; [1952] 1 All E. R. 1307. [2] [1926] A. C. 108.
[3] (1852), 1 De G. M. & G. 604. [4] (1853), 2 E. & B. 216.

PRIVITY OF CONTRACT

2. AGENCY

Jolly v. Rees

(1864), 15 C.B. N.S. 628

As in other cases of agency, a wife cannot bind her husband contractually unless she has his express or implied authority to contract on his behalf. There is, however, a presumption that a wife who lives with her husband has his authority to purchase necessaries suitable to his style of living.

This presumption is rebutted, *inter alia*, if the husband expressly forbids his wife to pledge his credit.

This was an action for goods sold and delivered. Plea, never indebted.

The cause was tried before Byles, J., at the Bristol Spring Assizes, 1863. The facts which appeared in evidence were as follows :—

The plaintiffs, Messrs. Jolly, were hosiers and linendrapers at Bath. The defendant was a gentleman of small fortune residing at Killymanellugh House, about two miles and a half from the railway station at Llanelly, in Carmarthenshire. His family consisted of four sons and two daughters. He was a magistrate for the county ; and his establishment was moderate. The goods in respect of which the action was brought were supplied by the plaintiffs upon the orders of Mrs. Rees during the years 1860 and 1861. They consisted of drapery and millinery goods suitable for persons in the position of Mrs. Rees and her daughters. The prices were fair and reasonable. The orders were conveyed by letter ; and the goods were directed to " Llanelly,"—none being sent directly to the defendant's house.

The defence set up was, that the wife had a sufficient allowance to enable her to obtain articles of the description of those in question without pledging her husband's credit for them : and that he had expressly prohibited her doing so. This defence rested mainly upon the defendant's own evidence, which was in substance as follows :—

" Before 1851, I had reason to be dissatisfied with the expenditure of my wife. In that year I had communication with her as to her future course. She had an income of 65*l.* of her own settled to her separate use, which I never interfered with. On that occasion I distinctly told her not to pledge my credit, and that, if she wanted anything necessary, if she would come to me, I would either give her the money, or give her an order on a tradesman whom I would select. After that, I gave orders to the Llanelly tradesmen for goods required for the house. I afterwards furnished my wife with money for the purpose of supplying what was wanting for the children. In 1861, I gave her a cheque for 50*l.* entirely for drapery for the children. I supplied her with money for what I considered necessary and proper, to the extent to which my income enabled me, and more. I entirely supplied my sons. I supplied my wife with money at the rate of 50*l.* a year since 1851. I had no knowledge of the claim of Messrs. Jolly till I received a letter from them in 1862. I had not known of the goods being supplied by them. The goods were not sent to Llanelly with my knowledge : parcels directed to me are always directed to my house. I never had a bill of particulars at all. I never saw invoices before my wife's death [which took place in January, 1863]. I never exercised any control over her private income."

The defendant was cross-examined at some length as to the extent of his establishment, and as to the payments he had made to his wife for the purpose of clothing herself and daughters during the years 1860, 1861 and 1862 ; but nothing very material was elicited.

A Mr. Jones, an attorney at Llanelly, proved that he received 65*l.* a year for Mrs. Rees, and paid it into her own hands, or to her order.

It was conceded that the plaintiffs had received no notice of the defendant's prohibition to his wife to pledge his credit.

In answer to questions put to them by the learned judge, the jury found : 1. That the articles supplied were necessaries in the sense of suitable to the estate and degree of the defendant's wife and daughters.   2. That the wife's authority was revoked by her husband in 1851.   3. That, if the sum of 115*l.* a year had been regularly paid to the wife, and applied by her to the clothing of herself and daughters, it would have been sufficient.   4. But that 50*l.* a year, or 65*l.* (her private income) would not have been sufficient. 5. That the sum of 115*l.* a year was not regularly paid, and that so much of it as was paid was insufficient.

Upon these findings, the learned judge directed a verdict to be entered for the plaintiffs for 21*l.* 8*s.* 4*d.* ; but with leave to the defendant to move to enter a verdict for him, if the Court should see fit, the Court to draw any inferences of fact not inconsistent with the findings of the jury.   And it was agreed that the parties should abide the judgment of this Court.

ERLE, C.J., now delivered the judgment of himself, WILLIAMS, J., and WILLES, J.[1] :—

This was a rule for setting aside the verdict for the plaintiffs, and entering it for the defendant.

The action was for goods sold.   Upon the trial the plaintiffs raised a presumption of the defendant's liability by shewing that the goods were ordered by his (the defendant's wife), while living with him, for the use of herself and children.   The defendant rebutted this presumption by shewing that he had forbidden his wife to take up goods on his credit, and had told her that if she wanted money to buy goods she was to apply to him for it : and there was no evidence that she had so applied and been refused.   The plaintiffs proved, in reply, that the goods were necessaries suitable to the estate and degree of the defendant ; that the wife had 65*l.* per annum to her separate use ; and that the defendant had promised to allow her 50*l.* per annum in addition, but had not paid it regularly, and had not supplied her with such necessaries or with money sufficient for the purchase thereof. The plaintiffs also shewed that they had received no notice of the defendant's prohibition to his wife against taking up goods on his credit.

These facts are in effect found by the jury : and the question is raised whether the wife had authority to make a contract binding on the husband for necessaries suitable to his estate and degree, against his will and contrary to his order to her, although without notice of such order to the tradesman.

Our answer is in the negative.   We consider that the wife cannot make a contract binding on her husband, unless he gives her authority as his agent so to do.   We lay down this as the general rule, premising that the facts do not raise the question what might have been the rights of the wife, either if she was living separate without any default on her part towards her husband, or if she had been left destitute by him.

---

[1] BYLES, J., dissented.

The whole law upon this subject is well collected in the note to *Manby* v. *Scott* ((1663), 1 Siderfin, 109), 2 Smith's Leading Cases, 385 *et seq.* It is there shewn that the general rule is as above stated ; and that, where a plaintiff seeks to charge a husband on a contract made by his wife, the question is, whether the wife had his authority, express or implied, to make the contract ; and that, if there be express authority, there is no room for doubt, and, if the authority is to be implied, the presumptions which may be advanced on one side may be rebutted on the other ; and, although there is a presumption that a woman living with a man, and represented by him to be his wife, has his authority to bind him by her contract for articles suitable to that station which he permits her to assume, still this presumption is always open to be rebutted. So was the decision of the majority of the judges in *Manby* v. *Scott* ; and to that effect are the words of Lord Holt in *Etherington* v. *Parrot*, (1703), 2 Ld. Raym. 1006, 1 Salk. 118 : and this doctrine has been sanctioned in the cases which have followed. In supporting this conclusion, our decision does not militate against the rule that the husband, as well as every principal, is concluded from denying that the agent had such authority as he was held out by his principal to have, in such a manner as to raise a belief in such authority, acted on in making the contract sought to be enforced. Such liability is not founded on any rights peculiar to the conjugal relation, but on a much wider ground.

The plaintiffs contend that the wife has the power above described ; and they rely on observations made by judges both in *Manby* v. *Scott* and in some later cases : but the answer in point of authority is, that the adjudications have not supported the observations on which they rely. In *Manby* v. *Scott*, those judges were in the minority ; and the observations referred to in later cases have not been the ground of any decision. The weight of authority seems to us to be against the plaintiffs.

Then, if we resort to considerations of principle, they lead to the same conclusion.

It is not our province here to enquire whether it is advisable to give to the wife greater rights. But, taking the law to be, that the power of the wife to charge her husband is in the capacity of his agent, it is a solecism in reasoning to say that she derives her authority from his will, and at the same time to say that the relation of wife creates the authority against his will, by a *presumptio juris et de jure* from marriage : and, if it be expedient that the wife should have greater rights, it is certainly inexpedient that she should have to exercise them by a process tending to disunion at home and pecuniary distress from without. The husband sustains the liability for all debts : he should therefore have the power to regulate the expenditure for which he is to be responsible, by his own discretion, and according to his own means. But, if the wife taking up goods from a tradesman can make her husband's liability depend on the estimate by a jury of his estate and degree, the law would practically compel him to regulate his expenses by a standard to be set up by that jury—a standard depending on appearances, perhaps assumed for a temporary purpose, with intention of change.

Moreover, if the law was clear that the husband was protected from the debts incurred by the wife without his authority, not only in the ranks where wealth abounds would speculations upon the imprudence of a thoughtless wife be less frequent because less profitable, but also in the ranks where the support of the household is from the labour of the man; and where the home must be habitually left in the care of the wife during his absence at his work, more painful evils from debt which the husband never intended to contract would be checked.

As we collect from the report of the learned judge that the verdict is for necessaries suitable to the estate and degree of the husband, obtained from the plaintiffs by the wife of the defendant without his authority and contrary to his order, according to our view of the law this verdict cannot be supported. It follows that the rule for setting it aside and entering a nonsuit should be made absolute.

Keighley, Maxsted & Co. v. Durant

[1901] A.C. 240

A person may ratify a contract made on his behalf by an unauthorized agent, and if he does so he is in the same position as if he had been a party to the contract *ab initio*.

But no contract is capable of ratification unless at the time of the contract the agent professed to be acting on behalf of another.

Roberts, a corn merchant at Wakefield, was authorized by Keighley, Maxsted & Co., the appellants, to buy wheat on a joint account for himself and them at a certain price. Roberts, having failed to buy at the authorized price, on May 11, 1898, without authority from the appellants, made a contract by telegram with the respondent Durant, a corn merchant in London, to buy from him wheat at a higher price. Roberts made the contract in his own name but, as he afterwards said at the trial, intending it to be on a joint account for the appellants, Keighley, Maxsted & Co., and himself. That intention was not disclosed by Roberts to Durant. The next day the appellants, by their manager Wright, agreed with Roberts to take the wheat on joint account with him. Roberts and the appellants having failed to take delivery of the wheat, Durant resold it at a loss and sued them for the amount in an action tried before Day, J., and a special jury. At the close of the plaintiff's case, the jury having been discharged, Day, J., dismissed the action against the appellants on the ground that there was no ratification in law of the contract, and gave judgment against Roberts for the amount claimed. The Court of Appeal (Collins and Romer, L.JJ., A. L. Smith, M.R., then L.J., dissenting) reversed the decision as regards the appellants, and ordered a new trial on the ground that there was evidence for the jury that Roberts contracted on behalf of himself and the appellants.

LORD MACNAGHTEN. I dissent very respectfully from the judgments of the majority of the Court of Appeal, and I agree entirely with the Master of the Rolls.

It is said that there is no decision one way or the other. It is quite true that there is no reported case in which the precise question discussed in the judgments under review has been raised and determined, and it may be that Collins, L.J., is right in thinking that there is no dictum in which that question has been dealt with pointedly and advisedly. But there is a stream of authority all tending in one direction, which it is impossible, I think, to gainsay or resist, and which has been treated as conclusive by text-writers of acknowledged eminence both in this country and in America. And when your Lordships are told that there is no actual decision, nor even any carefully considered expression of opinion in favour of the view which the Master of the Rolls took to be settled law, I cannot help recalling the observation of a great judge : " The clearer a thing is," said James, L.J., " the more difficult it is to find any express authority or any dictum exactly to the point."[1]

My Lords, I will not trouble you by going through the roll of cases bearing upon the question. It would be impossible, I think, with advantage to add anything to the very able and exhaustive review of the Master of the Rolls. I will only say a few words in reference to the two grounds on which his conclusion is challenged by Collins, L.J. Having satisfied himself that the case was not governed by authority, the learned Lord Justice ends his judgment by declaring that he was bound to decide in accordance with what he regarded to be " principle and common sense."

In appealing to common sense, I do not for a moment suppose that Collins, L.J., meant to intimate that the conclusion at which he had arrived, believing himself to be untrammelled by authority, was a self-evident proposition which ought to command the assent of all sensible persons. Admittedly, Lord Cairns and Lord Esher, both sensible persons I should say, took the other view. I rather suppose that the learned Lord Justice meant to appeal to considerations of convenience. But it is difficult to understand how this new departure, if it be a new departure, can be required by any consideration of that sort, seeing that in all these years the question has never before presented itself for decision but once, and then the case was decided on other grounds.

With all deference, I much doubt whether the decision under appeal is in accordance with good sense, whatever that expression means. Still less do I think it is in accordance with principle.

As a general rule, only persons who are parties to a contract, acting either by themselves or by an authorized agent, can sue or be sued on the contract. A stranger cannot enforce the contract, nor can it be enforced against a stranger. That is the rule ; but there are exceptions. The most remarkable exception, I think, results from the doctrine of ratification as established in English law. That doctrine is thus stated by Tindal, C.J., in *Wilson* v. *Tumman*[2] : " That an act done, *for another*, by a person, not assuming to act for himself, but for such other person, though without any precedent authority whatever, becomes the act of the principal, if subsequently ratified by him, is the known and well-established rule of law. In that case the principal is bound by the act, whether it be for his detriment or his advantage, and whether it be founded on a tort or on a contract, to the same effect as by, and with all the consequences which follow from, the same act done by his *previous* authority." And so by a wholesome and convenient fiction, a person ratifying the act of another, who, without authority, has made a contract openly and avowedly on his behalf, is deemed to be, though in fact he was not, a party to the contract. Does the fiction cover the case of a person who makes no avowal at all, but assumes to act for himself and for no one else ? If Tindal, C.J.'s statement of the law is accurate, it would seem to exclude the case of a person who may intend to act for another, but at the same time keeps his intention locked up in his own breast ; for it cannot be said that a person who so conducts himself does assume to act for anybody but himself. But ought the doctrine of

---

[1] *Panama and South Pacific Telegraph Co.* v. *India Rubber Gutta Percha and Telegraph Works Co.* (1875), 10 Ch. App. 515.
[2] (1843), 6 Man. & G. at p. 242.

ratification to be extended to such a case ? On principle I should say
certainly not. It is, I think, a well-established principle in English law
that civil obligations are not to be created by, or founded upon, undisclosed
intentions. That is a very old principle. Lord Blackburn, enforcing it in
the case of *Brogden* v. *Metropolitan Rail. Co.*[1], traces it back to the year-books
of Edward IV. (17 Edw. 4, 2, pl. 2) and to a quaint judgment of Brian, C.J. :
' It is common learning," said that Chief Justice, who was a great authority
in those days, " that the thought of a man is not triable, for the Devil has
not knowledge of man's thoughts."[2] Sir E. Fry quotes the same observation
in his work on Specific Performance, section 295, p. 133, 3rd ed. It is, I
think, a sound maxim—at least, in its legal aspect : and in my opinion it
is not to be put aside or disregarded merely because it may be that, in a
case like the present, no injustice might be done to the actual parties to the
contract by giving effect to the undisclosed intentions of a would-be
agent. . . .

I think the appeal must be allowed.

LORD LINDLEY. My Lords, I do not propose to trouble the House by
stating the facts or by examining in detail the numerous authorities cited in
the course of the argument. I propose to confine my observations to what
appear to me to be the real difficulties in the case, and to the legal doctrines
involved in it.

So much turns on the position of undisclosed principals that I will
first say a few words about them.

The explanation of the doctrine that an undisclosed principal can sue
and be sued on a contract made in the name of another person with his
authority is, that the contract is in truth, although not in form, that of the
undisclosed principal himself. Both the principal and the authority exist
when the contract is made ; and the person who makes it for him is only
the instrument by which the principal acts. In allowing him to sue and
be sued upon it, effect is given, so far as he is concerned, to what is true in
fact, although that truth may not have been known to the other contracting
party.

At the same time, as a contract is constituted by the concurrence of
two or more persons and by their agreement to the same terms, there is
an anomaly in holding one person bound to another of whom he knows
nothing and with whom he did not, in fact, intend to contract. But middle-
men, through whom contracts are made, are common and useful in business
transactions, and in the great mass of contracts it is a matter of indifference
to either party whether there is an undisclosed principal or not. If he
exists it is, to say the least, extremely convenient that he should be able to
sue and be sued as a principal, and he is only allowed to do so upon terms
which exclude injustice.

The reasons upon which a real principal not disclosed can sue or be
sued on a contract made on his behalf by an agent acting with his authority
have no application to contracts made by one person for another, but without
any authority from him. Some other reason must be found to permit a
person to sue or be sued upon a contract not entered into by him through
an agent or otherwise.

The principle relied on, and the only principle which by our law can

---

[1] (1877), 2 App. Cas. at p. 692.

[2] In the original thus : " comen erudition est q̃ l'entent d'un home ne serr trie, car
e Diable n'ad consuance de l'entent de home."

be invoked with any chance of success, is that known as ratification, by which an approval of what has been done is sometimes treated as equivalent to a previous authority to do it. The mere statement of the general nature of what is meant by ratification shews that it rests on a fiction. Where a man acts with an authority conferred upon him, no fiction is introduced ; but where a man acts without authority and an authority is imputed to him a fiction is introduced, and care must be taken not to treat this fiction as fact.

It is not necessary to write a treatise on the doctrine of ratification in order to dispose of this case. Historically that doctrine is no doubt derived from the Roman law ; but it has been extended and developed in this country conformably to our own legal principles and to meet our own commercial necessities ; and it is to our own decisions rather than to the Digest and commentaries upon it that English Courts must look for guidance. It is well known that in matters of contract we pay far less attention judicially to unexpressed intentions than is paid to them in other countries which have followed the Roman law more closely than we have : see *Byrne* v. *Van Tienhoven*[1].

Roberts' evidence, on which the case turns, may be summed up by saying that it amounts to one or other of the two following statements, namely : (1) that he intended to buy, and did buy, as a principal, hoping and expecting that Keighley, Maxsted & Co., would afterwards join him in his speculation ; or (2) that he intended to buy, and did buy, on the joint account of himself and Keighley, Maxsted & Co., as principals, hoping and expecting that they would, when informed of what he had done, ratify the transaction.

The first of these views of his evidence will not avail the plaintiffs ; for in this view Roberts' contract, not having been made for Keighley, Maxsted & Co., as possible principals, will not admit of ratification by them. The plaintiffs' counsel did not contend that it would, and they did not press the first view in argument.

The second view is not open to this objection, and ought to be left to a jury if there is any evidence that Roberts not only intended to buy, but did buy, on the joint account of himself and Keighley, Maxsted & Co. He swears that he did ; so far as his intention is concerned, I will give him credit for what he says, but I am unable to discover any evidence of anything more.

Had Keighley, Maxsted & Co. authorized Roberts to buy for them there would have been a contract in fact, although Durant & Co. did not know of them and did not intend to sell to them. This is, no doubt, an anomaly, as already pointed out ; but there is a reality behind it. To apply the same sort of reasoning to a different state of facts from which the reality is absent is to go further than any existing authority, and to extend a fiction further than is required by those necessities or conveniences of trade which led to its introduction.

The doctrine of ratification as hitherto applied in this country to contracts has always, I believe, in fact given effect in substance to the real intentions of both contracting parties at the time of the contract, as shewn by their language or conduct. It has never yet been extended to other cases. The decision appealed from extends it very materially, and I can find no warrant or necessity for the extension. . . .

That ratification when it exists is equivalent to a previous authority

---

[1] (1880), 5 C. P. D. 344.

is true enough (subject to some exceptions which need not be referred to). But, before the one expression can be substituted for the other, care must be taken that ratification is established.

It was strongly contended that there was no reason why the doctrine of ratification should not apply to undisclosed principals in general, and that no one could be injured by it if it were so applied. I am not convinced of this. But in this case there is no evidence in existence that, at the time when Roberts made his contract, he was in fact acting, as distinguished from intending to act, for the defendants as possible principals, and the decision appealed from, if affirmed, would introduce a very dangerous doctrine. It would enable one person to make a contract between two others by creating a principal and saying what his own undisclosed intentions were, and these could not be tested.

To return to the question whether there was any evidence proper to be left to the jury which would justify a verdict in favour of the plaintiffs against Keighley, Maxsted & Co., I am of opinion that there was none. There was no evidence of any purchase by Roberts for Keighley, Maxsted & Co., as expected principals, except (1) what he says of his own intention ; (2) what he says about the telegram he afterwards sent to Keighley, Maxsted & Co. ; and (3) his own entry in his own book. Assuming all this to be admissible for any purpose, what Roberts intended was never disclosed to Durant & Co., and cannot be inferred from the nature of the transaction itself. His intention, therefore, cannot be allowed to affect the rights of the parties. What he afterwards did, unknown to Durant & Co., cannot in any way affect their position. The appeal, therefore, in my opinion, ought to be allowed with costs here and below.

Judgments to the same effect were delivered by LORD HALSBURY, L.C., LORD SHAND, LORD JAMES OF HEREFORD, LORD DAVEY, LORD BRAMPTON and LORD ROBERTSON.

Clarkson, Booker, Ltd. v. Andjel

[1964], 3 All E.R. 260

If an agent, having authority to contract on behalf of another, makes the contract in his own name and conceals the fact that he is a mere representative, the doctrine of the undisclosed principal comes into play. By this doctrine either the agent or the principal may sue the other party to the contract. As a corollary either the agent or the principal, when disclosed, may be sued. But the other party to the contract must elect which of the two he wishes to sue; and when he has made an unequivocal election he must abide by it and cannot change his mind. Whether an unequivocal choice has been made must be decided by the court in the light of all the relevant circumstances. Thus, if the other party to the contract starts proceedings against either agent or principal, this is strong evidence of a final election. But it is not conclusive. Further evidence may show that he has not in fact abandoned his alternative right of action.

WILLMER, L.J. In this difficult case we have had the greatest possible assistance from counsel on both sides, and for my part I should like to acknowledge my indebtedness to them both for the excellent arguments which they have presented. The appeal is from a judgment of His Honour JUDGE BLOCK given in the Mayor's and City of London Court on January 14, 1964, whereby he found for the plaintiffs for the sum of £728 7s. 6d., being the cost of booking flights for some twelve people from Athens to London in October, 1961. There is no dispute that the plaintiffs (who are travel agents) booked these flights at the request of the defendant. The defendant's case was that in booking the flights he was acting as agent for a company called Peters & Milner, Ltd., who traded as Antigone Travel Services. It was his case at the trial that he disclosed to the plaintiffs that he was acting only as agent for Antigone Travel Services; but the defendant's evidence on this point was not accepted by the judge, who found that the defendant contracted as if he were a principal. There has been no appeal against this finding of the judge.

The defendant also offered some evidence to show that he was in fact acting as an agent, but this evidence was ruled by the judge to be inadmissible. To save the necessity for an adjournment in order to enable the defendant to obtain further evidence as to the fact of his agency, the case proceeded by agreement on the basis, accepted by counsel for the plaintiffs for the purpose of argument, that the defendant was acting as agent for an undisclosed principal. In this court we intimated that we were not prepared to deal with the case on a basis that might prove to be only hypothetical. Counsel for the plaintiffs thereon conceded on instructions that the defendant, in booking the flights in question, did in fact act as agent for undisclosed principals, viz., Peters & Milner, Ltd.

It was proved by evidence which the judge accepted that in supplying the tickets at the request of the defendant the plaintiffs were giving him credit, having previously done business with him on credit terms. The defendant, however, sought to escape liability on the basis that the plaintiffs, on discovering the identity of the undisclosed principals (viz., Peters & Milner, Ltd.) elected to pursue their remedy against the principals. What happened was that on July 26, 1962 (nine months after the issue of the tickets), not having received payment, the plaintiffs through their solicitors wrote both to the defendant and to Peters & Milner, Ltd., holding both of them liable. It is not necessary to quote both of these letters in full, but I think it right to refer to one sentence in the letter addressed to Peters & Milner, Ltd., which was as follows:

> " In our clients' contention this money may well be payable either by you or [the defendant], though not of course by both, and we would inform you that unless we receive payment of the said sum of £784 7s. 6d. by first post on Tuesday, Aug. 7, proceedings against you for the recovery of the same may be commenced without further notice."

A similar threat of proceedings without further notice was contained in the letter addressed to the defendant.

It is abundantly clear that up to this point the plaintiffs had certainly made no election. Eight days later, however, after a further exchange of letters, the plaintiffs wrote to Peters & Milner, Ltd., on Aug. 3, a letter in the following terms:

> " Further to our letter of Aug. 1, our clients have instructed us to proceed to obtain judgment against you in order to safeguard their interests. However, when this has been obtained, they may be prepared to consider terms for payment."

This letter produced no response, and accordingly on September 4, 1962, the plaintiffs issued a writ against Peters & Milner, Ltd., which was duly served. The plaintiffs, however, did not in fact proceed with this action. After an interval the solicitors acting for Peters & Milner, Ltd., wrote to the plaintiffs' solicitors on November 15, 1962, informing them that the company was insolvent, having virtually no assets and substantial liabilities, and

that it had been decided to put the company into voluntary liquidation. The
plaintiffs accordingly took no further action against Peters & Milner, Ltd.
Instead they wrote again, through their solicitors, to the solicitors for the
defendant, again holding the defendant liable, and in due course, on December 13, 1962, issued the writ in the present action.

It is in these circumstances that the point is taken for the defendant that
the plaintiffs, having elected to start proceedings against Peters & Milner,
Ltd., are now debarred from asserting their claim against the defendant. The
contention on behalf of the defendant is that this is a case of true election in
that, with full knowledge of the facts, the plaintiffs deliberately and unequivocally chose to pursue their right against the principals, which was a right
inconsistent with their right against the defendant as agent. Reliance is
placed on a statement contained in POWELL ON AGENCY (2nd Edn.) at p. 270,
where the following is put forward as proposition (v):

> " T. [a third party] starts proceedings against P. [the principal] or A.
> [the agent]. The initiation of proceedings against P. or A. is strong evidence
> of election, though not necessarily conclusive. That is so whether T. issues a
> writ or files proof of his debt in bankruptcy proceedings."

This proposition is not accepted by the plaintiffs as a correct statement of the
law. It has been submitted on their behalf that a plaintiff is barred only if he
has sued one or other (i.e., principal or agent) to judgment. It is conceded that
he cannot then proceed against the other; but that, it is said, is not a true case
of election, for the remedy is barred because the cause of action has merged in
the judgment. It is contended that nothing short of judgment against the
principal is sufficient to bar the plaintiff's remedy against the agent. In the
present case it is said that there has been nothing amounting either in law or
in fact to an election, so as to preclude the present action against the defendant.

The judge, in dealing with this aspect of the case, quoted at some length
from the speech of LORD BLACKBURN in *Scarf* v. *Jardine*[1]. I need not quote
again the passage from LORD BLACKBURN. Suffice it to say that he expressed
the view that there could be no more unequivocal act than instituting proceedings against one of two possible debtors; this, he thought, amounted to a
final election to treat that debtor as liable so as to preclude the plaintiff thereafter from suing the other debtor. The judge, having quoted the passage
from LORD BLACKBURN, described the events which happened in the present
case and then proceeded as follows:

> " The plaintiffs then hear of the pending bankruptcy or voluntary liquida-
> tion of the then defendant company, the travel agency, and in those circum-
> stances they abandon that action and choose to pursue the present defendant.
> It seems to me that this falls far below the determination of election in *Scarf* v.
> *Jardine*[2]. It seems also clear from the authorities that this is a question of fact
> for the determination of the court, and in all the circumstances I am unable to
> see that any election has been made by the plaintiffs which precludes them from
> succeeding against the defendant."

The judge was thus treating the question as one of fact, and he concluded on
the facts that the plaintiffs had not made any final election so as to preclude
them from suing the defendant.

The authorities cited on behalf of the plaintiffs were mostly cases where
one or other of the parties had been sued to judgment. Thus in *Priestly* v.

---

[1] (1882), 7 App. Cas. 345 at p. 360; [1881–85] All E.R. Rep. 651 at p. 658.
[2] (1882), 7 App. Cas. 345; [1881–85] All E.R. Rep. 651.

Fernie[1] the plaintiff, who had sued the master of a ship to judgment and execution in respect of a claim arising out of a bill of lading, was held to be debarred from subsequently suing the shipowner in respect of the same claim, even though the judgment against the master remained unsatisfied. Some reliance, however, was placed on a passage in the judgment of BRAMWELL, B., which appears to indicate that in his view no final election is made until judgment has been taken. What BRAMWELL, B., said was[2]:

" The very expression that where a contract is so made the contractee has an election to sue agent or principal, supposes he can only sue one of them, that is to say, sue to judgment. For it may be that an action against one might be discontinued and fresh proceedings be well taken against the other."

Kendall v. *Hamilton*[3] was another case of one of two debtors being sued to judgment. It was decided by the House of Lords that a fresh action against the other debtor was not maintainable. I think that the ratio of the decision appears from what was said by EARL CAIRNS, L.C., as follows[4]:

" When the appellants sued Wilson and McLay, and obtained judgment against them, . . . they exhausted their right of action, not necessarily by reason of any election between two courses open to them, which would imply that, for an election the fact of both courses being open must be known, but because the right of action which they pursued could not, after judgment obtained, co-exist with a right of action on the same facts against another person."

LORD BLACKBURN also[5] made it clear that his decision did not proceed on the ground of election, the facts not having been fully known at the time of the institution of the first suit. Some reliance is placed on a passage in the speech of LORD CAIRNS[6], in which he appears to contemplate the possibility that at any time up to judgment the plaintiffs might have discontinued against Wilson and McLay and brought a fresh action against the defendant. It is evident that in LORD CAIRNS' view the mere institution of proceedings against one debtor would not amount to such an election as would necessarily preclude a subsequent remedy against the other debtor.

We were also referred to *Morel Brothers & Co., Ltd.* v. *Earl of Westmorland*[7] and *Moore* v. *Flanagan*[8], in both of which judgment against a wife was held to bar any subsequent remedy against the husband. The ratio of these cases is of no help in the present case, but there is a dictum of ATKIN, L.J., in the later case which is of no little relevance. He said[9]:

" Having recovered judgment against the agent he cannot sue the principal. This depends, not on election, but on the construction of the contract. By the language of the contract the plaintiff is prevented, owing to something she has done, from recovering judgment against the husband. Election is a separate principle which may bar the remedy which a person may otherwise have against the principal."

I should also refer to a passage in the speech of LORD ATKIN in *United Australia, Ltd.* v. *Barclays Bank, Ltd.*[10] where he said:

" On the other hand, if a man is entitled to one of two inconsistent rights, it is fitting that, when, with full knowledge, he has done an unequivocal act showing that he has chosen the one, he cannot afterwards pursue the other, which, after the first choice, is by reason of the inconsistency, no longer his to

[1] (1865), 3 H. & C. 977.
[2] (1865), 3 H. & C. at pp. 983, 984.
[3] (1879), 4 App. Cas. 504.
[4] (1879), 4 App. Cas. at p. 515.
[5] (1879), 4 App. Cas. at p. 542.
[6] (1879), 4 App. Cas. at p. 514.
[7] [1904] A.C. 11; [1900–03] All E.R. Rep. 397.
[8] [1920] 1 K.B. 919; [1920] All E.R. Rep. 254.
[9] [1920] 1 K.B. at p. 928; [1920] All E.R. Rep. at p. 258.
[10] [1941] A.C. 1 at p. 29; [1940] 4 All E.R. 20 at p. 37.

choose. Instances are the right of a principal dealing with an agent for an undisclosed principal to choose the liability of the agent or the principal, the right of a landlord, whose forfeiture of a lease has been committed to exact the forfeiture or to treat the former tenant as still tenant, and the like. To those cases the statement of Lord Blackburn in *Scarf* v. *Jardine*[1] applies ' where a man has an option to choose one or other of two inconsistent things, when once he has made his election it cannot be retracted '."

I have ventured to quote these dicta of Lord Atkin because in them he seems clearly to recognise that the mere institution of proceedings against one or other of principal and agent may amount to a case of true election, i.e., the unequivocal choice between one of two inconsistent rights, so as to bar the subsequent assertion of the other, inconsistent right. What Lord Atkin said in these passages seems to me to afford a good deal of support for Professor Powell's proposition (v) to which I have already referred [see p. 380, *ante*].

The leading case on election, and the decision which represents the high water mark in favour of the defendant's submission, is that of *Scarf* v. *Jardine*[2]. That case, it is true, was not a case of election as between principal and agent. The question was whether the institution of proceedings against the partners in a reconstituted partnership amounted to an election which would bar any right to bring subsequent proceedings against the original partners. It seems to me, however, that the same principle must apply, for in either case the choice is between inconsistent rights. This at least seems to have been the view of Lord Atkin, as appears from the passage which I have quoted from his speech in the *United Australia, Ltd.'s* case[3].

Perhaps the case nearest on its facts to the present case is that of *MacClure* v. *Schemeil*[4]. In that case the plaintiffs, who were suing for the price of goods sold, were held not entitled to recover from the principal on two grounds, the second of which was that[5]

"by demanding payment from R., and taking proceedings in bankruptcy against him after they knew him to be only an agent, they had made a final and irrevocable election to treat him as their debtor instead of the defendants."

I cannot, of course, do other than attach the greatest possible weight to the decision of the House of Lords in *Scarf* v. *Jardine*[1], particularly the reasoning of Lord Blackburn. I do not understand him, however, to mean that where proceedings have once been commenced against one of two possible debtors, a plaintiff is necessarily precluded as a matter of law from subsequently taking proceedings against the other. Indeed counsel for the defendant freely conceded that there must at least be some cases where the mere issue of a writ could not be held to amount to a binding election—for instance, where it is done for the purpose of preventing the limitation time from running out. Similarly, it has been held that an abortive writ issued against a company not yet incorporated at the time when the order for the plaintiffs' services was given did not amount to a binding election so as to preclude a subsequent action against the agents through whom the order was given; see *Longman* v. *Lord Hill*[6]. Even allowing for such exceptional cases,

---

[1] (1882), 7 App. Cas. at p. 360; [1881–85] All E.R. Rep. at p. 658.
[2] (1882), 7 App. Cas. 345; [1881–85] All E.R. Rep. 651.
[3] [1941] A.C. at p. 29; [1940] 4 All. E.R. at p. 37.
[4] (1871), 20 W.R. 168.
[5] (1871), 20 W.R. at p. 169.
[6] (1891), 7 T.L.R. 639.

however, it is clear that the institution of proceedings against agent or principal is at least strong evidence of an election such as, if not rebutted, will preclude subsequent proceedings against the other. In other words, it raises a *prima facie* case of election.

That this is the true view appears, I think, from an analysis of *Curtis* v. *Williamson*[1]. In that case the plaintiff had filed an affidavit in proof of his debt in the bankruptcy of the agent. He did not proceed any further on that, but subsequently sued the principal for the same debt and obtained the verdict of the jury in his favour. A rule was sought to discharge the jury's verdict on the ground that the prior proceedings against the agent constituted in law a conclusive bar to the subsequent proceedings against the principal; but it was held that the question was one of fact, and that the verdict of the jury must stand. There is no separate report of the argument in that case, but I think the substance of what was argued sufficiently appears from the judgment delivered by QUAIN, J. He said[2]:

> " The question is, what is sufficient to constitute a binding election in point of law? In general the question of election can only be properly dealt with as a question of fact for the jury, subject to the direction of the presiding judge, as was done in the case of *Calder* v. *Dobell*[3]; but there may no doubt be cases in which the act of the contractee in regard to his dealings with or proceeding against the agent, with full knowledge of the facts and freedom of choice, may be such as to preclude him in point of law from afterwards resorting to the principal. Whether in regard to proceedings taken against the agent by action at law anything short of judgment and satisfaction would be sufficient to exclude resort to the principal was the point raised in the case of *Priestly* v. *Fernie*[4]."

The judge then referred to the facts of *Priestly* v. *Fernie*[4] and continued[5]:

> " But it is clear from the language used by BRAMWELL, B., . . . that whilst it was considered that judgment against the agent, even without satisfaction, would constitute a conclusive election, yet that no legal proceedings short of judgment would have that effect, for he distinctly points out that by the word ' sue ' he means ' sue to judgment '."

QUAIN, J., expressed his conclusion on the case before him in the following terms[6]:

> " We think it would be going too far to hold that this was in point of law a binding election to deal with the agent as alone liable, and abandon all right to take proceedings against his principals. It might possibly, in an appropriate case, constitute with other facts some evidence of election to be submitted to a jury, but we cannot regard it as a legal bar to proceedings against the defendants."

Having regard to these authorities I think that the judge in the present case was plainly right in regarding the question before him as one of fact; but it has been argued that on the evidence he came to a wrong conclusion on the facts. Since the relevant evidence is all contained in the correspondence, we have been invited to review the judge's findings and to draw our own inferences from the correspondence. In a case such as the present we are clearly entitled to take this course, for we are in as good a position as was the judge to draw inferences.

In the light of the authorities to which I have referred, I approach the question to be decided on the basis that the institution of the proceedings against Peters & Milner, Ltd., affords at least *prima facie* evidence of an election on the part of the plaintiffs to look only to them for payment of their

---

[1] (1874), L.R. 10 Q.B. 57.
[3] (1871), L.R. 6 C.P. 486.
[5] (1874), L.R. 10 Q.B. at p. 60.

[2] (1874), L.R. 10 Q.B. at p. 59.
[4] (1865), 3 H. & C. 977.
[6] (1874), L.R. 10 Q.B. at p. 61.

debt. The question is whether there is any sufficient evidence to rebut the
prima facie inference that arises from the institution of those proceedings.

In order to constitute an election which will bar the present proceedings
against the defendant the decision to sue Peters & Milner, Ltd., must, in the
first place, be shown to have been taken with full knowledge of all the relevant
facts. In the circumstances of this case I feel no difficulty on that point, for
it cannot be suggested that when the plaintiffs made their decision to sue
Peters & Milner, Ltd. they were in any way ignorant of their rights against the
defendant. Secondly, it must be shown that the decision to institute proceedings against Peters & Milner, Ltd., was a truly unequivocal act, if it is to
preclude the plaintiffs from subsequently suing the defendant. This, I
think, involves looking closely at the context in which the decision was taken,
for any conclusion must be based on a review of all the relevant circumstances. One highly relevant circumstance is the fact that it was the defendant to whom the plaintiffs gave credit, as they had done over previous transactions. The correspondence shows that down to the letters of July 26,
1962, the plaintiffs throughout were looking to the defendant for payment of
their debt, i.e., to the person to whom they had given credit, although they
also adumbrated a possible claim against Peters & Milner, Ltd. On July
26, as I have already stated, they caused letters to be written to both the
defendant and Peters & Milner, Ltd., threatening proceedings against both.
Clearly up to that time there was no election to proceed only against the latter.

The whole case for the defendant rests on the fact that on Aug. 3, having
taken instructions, the plaintiffs' solicitors wrote to Peters & Milner, Ltd.,
announcing their intention " to obtain judgment " against them. It is true
that they did not at that time write any similar letter to the defendant, but
they did not then or at any other time ever withdraw their threat to take proceedings against him. There is not (and could not be) any suggestion that the
defendant was in any way prejudiced by the course which the plaintiffs took,
or that he was in any sense lulled into a false sense of security. Had the
plaintiffs carried out their threat to obtain judgment against Peters & Milner,
Ltd., they would, of course, have been precluded from subsequently taking
proceedings against the defendants, for their cause of action would then have
been merged in the judgment obtained against Peters & Milner, Ltd.; but
in fact the plaintiffs took no step against Peters & Milner, Ltd., beyond the
issue and service of the writ. On being informed of the proposal to put the
company into liquidation they took no further action whatsoever against that
company. They did not, for instance (as in *Scarf* v. *Jardine*[1] and other cases
cited) seek to prove in the liquidation; instead they proceeded to give effect
forthwith to their already announced, and never withdrawn, threat to sue the
defendant.

On the whole, though I regard the case as being very near the borderline,
I find myself unable to disagree with the conclusion arrived at by the judge. I
do not think that the plaintiffs, by the mere institution of proceedings against
Peters & Milner, Ltd., made such an unequivocal election as to debar them
from taking the present proceedings against the defendant. I would accordingly dismiss the appeal.

DAVIS, L. J., concurred in this judgment; and RUSSELL, L. J., gave
judgment to the same effect.

---

[1] (1882), 7 App. Cas. 345; [1881–85] All E.R. Rep. 651.

Irvine v. Watson
(1880), 5 Q.B.D. 414

A principal who becomes indebted to a third person upon a contract made by his agent remains liable for the debt, notwithstanding that he has already paid the amount to the agent, unless before making such payment he has been led by the third person to believe that the agent has discharged the obligation.

This was an appeal from a judgment of BOWEN, J. in favour of the plaintiffs.

BRAMWELL, L.J. I am of opinion that the judgment must be affirmed.

The facts of the case are shortly these: The plaintiffs sold certain casks of oil, and on the face of the contract of sale Conning appeared as the purchaser. But the plaintiffs knew that he was only an agent buying for principals, for he told them so at the time of the sale. Therefore they knew that they had a right against somebody besides Conning. On the other hand the defendants knew that somebody or other had a remedy against them, for they had authorised Conning, who was an ordinary broker, to pledge their credit; and the invoice specified the goods to have been bought "*per* John Conning". Then, that being so, the defendants paid the broker; and the question is whether such payment discharged them from their liability to the plaintiffs. I think it is impossible to say that it discharged them, unless they were misled by some conduct of the plaintiffs into the belief that the broker had already settled with the plaintiffs, and made such payment in consequence of such belief. But it is contended that the plaintiffs here did mislead the defendants into such belief, by parting with the possession of the oil to Conning without getting the money. The terms of the contract were "cash on or before delivery," and it is said that the defendants had a right to suppose that the sellers would not deliver unless they received payment of the price at the time of delivery. I do not think, however, that that is a correct view of the case. The plaintiffs had a perfect right to part with the oil to the broker without insisting strictly upon their right to prepayment, and there is, in my opinion, nothing in the facts of the case to justify the defendants in believing that they would so insist. No doubt if there was an invariable custom in the trade to insist on prepayment where the terms of the contract entitled the seller to it, that might alter the matter ; and in such cases non-insistence on prepayment might discharge the buyer if he paid the broker on the faith of the seller already having been paid. But that is not the case here ; the evidence before Bowen, J., shews that there is no invariable custom to that effect.

Apart from all authorities, then, I am of opinion that the defendants' contention is wrong, and upon looking at the authorities, I do not think that any of them are in direct conflict with that opinion. It is true that in *Thomson* v. *Davenport*[1] both Lord Tenterden and Bayley, J., suggest in the widest terms that a seller is not entitled to sue the undisclosed principal on discovering him, if in the meantime the state of account between the principal and the agent has been altered to the prejudice of the principal. But it is impossible to construe the dicta of those learned judges in that case literally ; it would operate most unjustly to the vendor if we did. I think the judges who uttered them did not intend a strictly literal interpretation to be put on their words. But whether they did or not, the opinion of Parke, B., in *Heald* v. *Kenworthy*[2] seems to me preferable ; it is this, that " If the conduct

---

[1] (1829), 9 B. & C. 78.   [2] (1855), 10 Exch. 739 ; 24 L. J. Ex. 76.

of the seller would make it unjust for him to call upon the buyer for the money, as for example, where the principal is induced by the conduct of the seller to pay his agent the money on the faith that the agent and seller have come to a settlement on the matter, or if any representation to that effect is made by the seller, either by words or conduct, the seller cannot afterwards throw off the mask and sue the principal." That is in my judgment a much more accurate statement of the law. But then the defendants rely on the case of *Armstrong* v. *Stokes*[1]. Now that is a very remarkable case ; it seems to have turned in some measure upon the peculiar character filled by Messrs. Ryder as commission merchants. The Court seemed to have thought it would be unreasonable to hold that Messrs. Ryder had not authority to receive the money. I think upon the facts of that case that the agents would have been entitled to maintain an action for the money against the defendant, for as commission merchants they were not mere agents of the buyer. Moreover the present is a case, which Blackburn, J., there expressly declines to decide. He expressly draws a distinction between a case in which, as in *Armstrong* v. *Stokes*[1], the seller at the time of the sale supposes the agent to be himself a principal, and gives credit to him alone, and one in which, as here, he knows that the person with whom he is dealing has a principal behind, though he does not know who that principal is.

It is to my mind certainly difficult to understand that distinction, or to see how the mere fact of the vendor knowing or not knowing that the agent has a principal behind can affect the liability of that principal. I should certainly have thought that his liability would depend upon what he himself knew, that is to say whether he knew that the vendor had a claim against him and would look to him for payment in the agent's default. But it is sufficient here that the defendants did know that the sellers had a claim against them, unless the broker had already paid for the goods.

In this view of the case it is unnecessary to consider the further question raised by Mr. Kennedy, as to whether a payment on a general running account, as distinguished from a payment specifically appropriated to the particular purchase, would be sufficient to bring the case within Lord Tenterden's qualification of the general rule.

BRETT, L.J. The material facts of this case are these. There is a contract for the sale of goods made between the plaintiffs and the defendants through the agency of one Conning, a broker. But in making this contract Conning acted solely as agent of the defendants, not as agent of the plaintiffs at all. The contract was for " cash on or before delivery ; " and the goods having been delivered, the defendants pay Conning, who, as I have said before, was their agent and no one else's. Now, apart from authority, I should certainly say that a payment to such an agent could not be a good payment to the plaintiffs. But then it is said that it is a good payment within the dicta of *Thomson* v. *Davenport*[2] ; but there the question for the decision of the Court was, not whether a payment by the principal to the agent precluded the seller from suing the principal, but, whether the seller could sue the principal at all. The main proposition laid down by Lord Tenterden was this, " that if a person sells goods, supposing that at the time of the contract he is dealing with the principal, but afterwards discovers that the person with whom he has been dealing is not the principal, but agent for a third person, though he may in the meantime have debited the

---

[1] (1872), L. R. 7 Q. B. 598.   [2] (1829), 9 B. & C. 78.

agent with it, he may afterwards recover the amount from the real principal."
He then introduces a qualification, " subject, however, to this qualification,
that the state of the account between the principal and the agent is not
altered to the prejudice of the principal." Now the terms of that qualification are certainly very wide, and Bayley, J., in qualifying the above general
rule uses equally wide language : " If the principal has paid the agent,
or if the state of accounts between the agent and the principal would make
it unjust that the seller should call on the principal, the fact of payment or
such a state of accounts would be an answer to the action brought by the
seller where he had looked to the responsibility of the agent."

And Maule, J., in the case of *Smyth* v. *Anderson*[1], expresses himself
in the same general terms. But there again the point did not directly call
for decision. Now, I think it is not fair to put a strictly literal interpretation
on the language used by judges when merely glancing at by matters, with
their minds mainly directed to another question, and, tying them down to
the very words they used, to assume that those words contained in their
opinion an absolutely accurate statement of the law. I do not think those
dicta were so intended to be read. In *Heald* v. *Kenworthy*[2], however, the
question directly arose. And Parke, B., after citing the dictum of Bayley,
J., to the effect that the seller cannot sue the principal if the state of accounts
between the principal and the agent would make it inequitable that he
should do so, proceeds to ask what equity there can be, unless it is something
arising out of the conduct of the seller, something to induce the defendant
to believe that a settlement has already been made with the agent.

If the authorities stood there, I should have no doubt that the limitation
put by Parke, B., on the earlier wide qualification was correct. But it is
suggested that that limitation was overruled in *Armstrong* v. *Stokes*[3]. I
think, however, that the Court there did not intend to overrule it, but to
treat the case before them as one to which the limitation did not apply. I
think they noticed the peculiar character of Manchester commission
merchants. Probably their decision means this, that, when the seller deals
with the agent as sole principal, and the nature of the agent's business is
such that the buyer ought to believe that the seller has so dealt, in such a
case it would be unjust to allow the seller to recover from the principal after
he paid the agent. Or it may perhaps be that Blackburn, J., finding the
wider qualification in the very case which lays down the general rule, felt
himself bound by the terms of that qualification, and applied them to the
case before him.

If the case of *Armstrong* v. *Stokes*[3] arises again, we reserve to ourselves
sitting here the right of reconsidering it.

The only other question is whether the present case falls within the
qualification as limited by Parke, B., whether there was any misleading
conduct on the part of the plaintiffs. But the only thing relied on by the
defendants on that point was the non-insistance on prepayment by the
plaintiffs. And I do not think that that amounted to laches, or was such
an act as would justify the defendants in supposing that Conning had already
paid the plaintiffs.

BAGGALLAY, L.J., delivered judgment to the same effect.

---

[1] (1849), 7 C. B. 21 ; 18 L. J. C. P. 109.
[2] (1855), 10 Exch. 739 ; 24 L. J. Ex. 76.   [3] (1872), L. R. 7 Q.B. 598.

Privity of Contract

Yonge v. Toynbee

[1910] 1 K.B. 215

A person who assumes to act as agent implicitly warrants that he possesses the authority of his principal, and he is liable in damages if the authority does not in fact exist.[1]

He is equally liable if his authority, which did in fact exist, is determined without his knowledge by the death or lunacy of his principal.

APPEAL from refusal by Sutton, J., at chambers to order that solicitors, who had assumed to act for the defendant in an action for libel and slander, should personally pay the plaintiff's costs in the action.

The defendant Toynbee in August, 1908, retained Messrs. Wontner & Sons, the respondents in the appeal, to act as his solicitors in the conduct of his defence to an action which he then expected to be brought against him by the plaintiff, and, on several occasions in September, instructions in the matter were given by him to the respondents. On October 8, 1908, the defendant was certified, and a detention order was made against him, as being a person of unsound mind not so found by inquisition. It appeared that the respondents had at that time been informed that the defendant was suffering from a nervous breakdown, and was in a home and unable to attend to any business, but it was not until April, 1909, that they became aware that he was of unsound mind and that he had been certified as such. On October 26, 1908, the plaintiff brought an action against one Morshead and the defendant for libel and slander. On October 30 the respondents undertook to appear in that action for the defendant, and did, in pursuance of that undertaking, on November 6 enter an appearance for the defendant. The plaintiff, being subsequently advised that the defendant and Morshead were improperly joined as defendants in that action, discontinued that action as against the defendant, and on December 19 commenced a fresh action against him for libel and slander. The respondents on December 21, 1908, undertook to appear for the defendant in this action, and on December 30 entered an appearance accordingly. On February 22, 1909, they delivered a statement of defence in the action, pleading privilege and denying the alleged libel and slander. On February 26, 1909, an order was made in lunacy appointing the defendant's wife receiver of his estate with certain powers of a committee thereof. The plaintiff put in a reply to the defence of the defendant, and other interlocutory proceedings in the action took place. Afterwards, on April 5, 1909, the action not having then come to trial, the respondents, having, as before mentioned, become aware that the defendant had been certified as a person of unsound mind, forthwith communicated that fact to the plaintiff's solicitors. Correspondence ensued between the plaintiff's solicitors and the respondents with regard to the appointment of a guardian *ad litem* for the defendant, but ultimately none was appointed. Application was subsequently made on behalf of the plaintiff to a Master at chambers for an order that the appearance in the action, and all proceedings subsequent thereto, should be struck out, and that the respondents should personally pay to the plaintiff her costs of the action, on the ground that they had acted for the defendant without authority. The Master made an order that the appearance and subsequent proceedings in the action should be struck out, but refused to make an order that the

---

[1] He has in truth made a " collateral contract " which he has broken: see *supra*, p. 21.

respondents should personally pay the plaintiff's costs of the action. On appeal to Sutton, J., at chambers against that refusal, he affirmed the decision of the Master. The plaintiff appealed to the Court of Appeal.

BUCKLEY, L.J. Vaughan Williams, L.J., has asked me to deliver my judgment first.

The interesting and important question in this case is as to the extent to which the principle of *Smout* v. *Ilbery*[1] remains good law after the decision in *Collen* v. *Wright*[2]. In *Smout* v. *Ilbery*[1] Alderson, B., in giving the judgment of the Court, dealt with the authorities under three heads : First, the case where the agent made a fraudulent misrepresentation as to his authority with an intention to deceive. In such case the agent is, of course, personally responsible. Secondly, the case where the agent without fraud, but untruly in fact, represented that he had authority when he had none, instancing under this head *Polhill* v. *Walter*[3]. In that case A., having no authority from B. to accept a bill on his behalf, did accept it as by his procuration, *bona fide* believing that B. would retrospectively approve that which he was doing. In such case again the agent is personally liable, for he induced the other party to enter into a contract on a misrepresentation of a fact within his own knowledge. The third class is where the agent *bona fide* believes that he has, but in fact has not, authority[4]. This third class the learned Baron seems to subdivide into two heads—the first where the agent never had authority, but believes that he had (e.g., when he acted on a forged warrant of attorney which he thought to be genuine), and the second where the agent had in fact full authority originally, but that authority had come to an end without any knowledge, or means of knowledge, on the part of the agent that such was the fact. The latter was the state of facts in *Smout* v. *Ilbery*[5]. I understand *Smout* v. *Ilbery*[5] not to dispute that in the former of these last two cases (that is, where the agent never had authority) he is liable, but to hold that in the latter (namely, where he originally had authority, but that authority has ceased without his having knowledge, or means of knowledge, that it has ceased) he is not liable. The principle is stated in the following words : " If, then, the true principle derivable from the cases is, that there must be some wrong or omission of right on the part of the agent, in order to make him personally liable on a contract made in the name of his principal, it will follow that the agent is not responsible in such a case as the present. And to this conclusion we have come." It seems to me that, if that principle be the true principle, then the former of the last two mentioned cases ought to have been resolved in the same way as the latter. I can see no distinction in principle between the case where the agent never had authority and the case where the agent originally had authority, but that authority has ceased without his knowledge or means of knowledge. In the latter case as much as in the former the proposition, I think, is true that without any *mala fides* he has at the moment of acting represented that he had an authority which in fact he had not. In my opinion he is then liable on an implied contract that he had authority, whether there was fraud or not. That this is the true principle is, I think, shewn by passages which I will quote from three judgments which I have selected out of the numerous cases upon this subject. In *Collen* v.

---

[1] (1842), 10 M. & W. 1.   [2] (1857), 8 E. & B. 647.   [3] (1832), 3 B. & Ad. 114.
[4] This triple classification is a little misleading. There is in law no distinction between the first and the second category. In the latter the learned judge appears to be emphasizing a point of morals rather than of law.   [5] (1842), 10 M. & W. 1.

Wright[1] Willes, J., in giving the judgment of the Court uses the following language : " I am of opinion that a person who induces another to contract with him, as the agent of a third party, by an unqualified assertion of his being authorized to act as such agent, is answerable to the person who so contracts for any damages which he may sustain by reason of the assertion of authority being untrue. . . . The fact that the professed agent honestly thinks that he has authority affects the moral character of his act ; but his moral innocence, so far as the person whom he has induced to contract is concerned, in no way aids such person or alleviates the inconvenience and damage which he sustains. The obligation arising in such a case is well expressed by saying that a person professing to contract as an agent for another, impliedly, if not expressly, undertakes to or promises the person who enters into such contract, upon the faith of the professed agent being duly authorized, that the authority which he professes to have does in point of fact exist." This language is equally applicable to each of the two classes of cases to which I have referred. The language is not, in my opinion, consistent with maintaining that which *Smout* v. *Ilbery*[2] had laid down as the true principle, that there must be some wrong or omission of right on the part of the agent in order to make him liable. The question is not as to his honesty or *bona fides*. His liability arises from an implied undertaking or promise made by him that the authority which he professes to have does in point of fact exist. I can see no difference of principle between the case in which the authority never existed at all and the case in which the authority once existed and has ceased to exist. In *Firbank's Executors* v. *Humphreys*[3] the rule is thus stated by Lord Esher : " The rule to be deduced is that, where a person by asserting that he has the authority of the principal induces another person to enter into any transaction which he would not have entered into but for that assertion, and the assertion turns out to be untrue, to the injury of the person to whom it is made, it must be taken that the person making it undertook that it was true, and he is liable personally for the damage that has occurred."

Lastly, Lord Davey in *Starkey* v. *Bank of England*[4], after stating that the rule extends to every transaction of business into which a third party is induced to enter by a representation that the person with whom he is doing business has the authority of some other person, rejects the argument that the rule in *Collen* v. *Wright*[1] does not extend to cases where the supposed agent did not know that he had no authority, and had not the means of finding out ; cites Lord Campbell's language in *Lewis* v. *Nicholson*[5], that the agent " is liable, if there was any fraud, in an action for deceit, and, in my opinion, as at present advised, on an implied contract that he had authority, whether there was fraud or not " ; and concludes by saying that in his opinion " it is utterly immaterial for the purpose of the application of this branch of the law whether the supposed agent knew of the defect of his authority or not."

The result of these judgments, in my opinion, is that the liability of the person who professes to act as agent arises (*a*) if he has been fraudulent, (*b*) if he has without fraud untruly represented that he had authority when he had not, and (*c*) also where he innocently misrepresents that he has authority where the fact is either (1) that he never had authority or (2) that his original authority has ceased by reason of facts of which he has not know-

---

[1] (1857), 8 E. & B. 647.   [2] (1842), 10 M. & W. 1.   [3] (1886), 18 Q. B. D. 54, at p. 60.
[4] [1903] A. C. 114, at p. 119.   [5] (1852), 18 Q. B. 503.

ledge or means of knowledge. Such last-mentioned liability arises from the fact that by professing to act as agent he impliedly contracts that he has authority, and it is immaterial whether he knew of the defect of his authority or not.

This implied contract may, of course, be excluded by the facts of the particular case. If, for instance, the agent proved that at the relevant time he told the party with whom he was contracting that he did not know whether the warrant of attorney under which he was acting was genuine or not, and would not warrant its validity, or that his principal was abroad and he did not know whether he was still living, there will have been no representation upon which the implied contract will arise. This may have been the *ratio decidendi* in *Smout* v. *Ilbery*[1] as expressed in the passage " The continuance of the life of the principal was, under these circumstances, a fact equally within the knowledge of both contracting parties " ; and this seems to be the ground upon which Story on Agency, section 265a, approves the decision. The husband had left England for China in May, 1839, a time in the history of the world when communication was not what it is now, and the Court seems to have decided upon the ground that the butcher who supplied the goods knew that the facts were such that the wife did not, because she could not, take upon herself to affirm that he was alive. If so, there was no implied contract. The principle, as stated in the words I have quoted, may have been meant to be, but is not in words, rested upon that ground, and, if it is to be understood as it seems to have been understood in *Salton* v. *New Beeston Cycle Co.*[2], it is not, I think, consistent with *Collen* v. *Wright*[3]. The true principle as deduced from the authorities I have mentioned rests, I think, not upon wrong or omission of right on the part of the agent, but upon implied contract.

The facts here are that the solicitors originally had authority to act for Mr. Toynbee ; that that authority ceased by reason of his unsoundness of mind ; that, subsequently, they on October 30, 1908, undertook to appear, and on November 6 appeared, in the first action, and, after that was discontinued, did on December 21 undertake to appear, and did on December 30 enter an appearance, in the second action ; and that they subsequently, on February 22, 1909, delivered a defence pleading privilege, and denying the slander, and did not until April 5 inform the plaintiff that, as the fact was, their client had become of unsound mind. During all this time they were putting the plaintiff to costs, and these costs were incurred upon the faith of their representation that they had authority to act for the defendant. They proved no facts addressed to shew that implied contract was excluded.

It has been pressed upon us that a solicitor is an agent of a special kind with an obligation towards his client to continue to take on his behalf all proper steps in the action. The particular nature of his agency is not, I think, very material. On the other hand it must be borne in mind that after August 21, when the defendant Toynbee wrote to the plaintiff's solicitors, referring them to Messrs. Wontner & Sons, the plaintiff could not consistently with professional etiquette communicate personally with the defendant. During the period from August, 1908, to April, 1909, the solicitors had the means of knowing and did not in fact ascertain that the defendant had become of unsound mind. In the interval they did acts which amounted to representations on their part that they were continuing

---

[1] (1842), 10 M. & W. 1.

[2] [1900] 1 Ch. 43.

[3] (1857), 8 E. & B. 647.

to stand in a position in which they were competent to bind the defendant. This was not the case. They are liable, in my judgment, upon an implied warranty or contract that they had an authority which they had not.

For these reasons I think that the appellant is entitled to succeed and to have an order against the solicitors for damages, and the measure of damage is, no doubt, the amount of the plaintiff's costs thrown away in the action. The appeal, therefore, should be allowed with costs here and below.

SWINFEN EADY, J., delivered judgment to the same effect ; VAUGHAN WILLIAMS, L.J., concurred.

Luxor (Eastbourne), Ltd. v. Cooper

[1941] A.C. 108

A promise not to revoke the agent's authority without just cause is binding on the principal.
Whether such a promise is to be implied in a contract depends upon the facts of each case, but is not easy to establish.
Position illustrated from the case of an estate agent.

VISCOUNT SIMON, L.C. My Lords, in this case the respondent, who was plaintiff in the action, issued his writ in April, 1937, claiming from each of the two appellant companies a sum of 5,000*l.* as commission alleged to be due under an oral agreement made in September, 1935. Alternatively, he claims the same amount as damages for breach of this agreement. The trial judge, Branson, J., decided in favour of the appellants, but the Court of Appeal reversed this decision and gave judgment in favour of the respondent for a total sum of 8,000*l.* as damages for breach of a term alleged to be implied in the commission agreement to the effect that the appellants would not without just cause so act as to prevent the respondent from earning his commission.

The appellants are private companies and were the freeholders of the Luxor Cinema at Eastbourne and of the Regal Cinema at Hastings respectively. The board of directors of each of the appellant companies was composed of the same individuals and a Mr. Garton was solicitor to each company; their auditor was one Ewbank. Prior to his death on September 11, 1935, one Walter Bentley, who was managing director of both companies, held the majority of the issued ordinary shares in Regal (Hastings), Ltd., and also a large block of issued ordinary shares in Luxor (Eastbourne), Ltd. On Mr. Walter Bentley's death, his son, Mr. Harry Bentley, became a director in his place. Mr. Harry Bentley and his mother were administrators of the estate of Mr. Walter Bentley. In the summer of 1935, Mr. Walter Bentley had asked Mr. Ewbank to get an offer for the purchase of the Luxor and Regal Cinemas, and Mr. Ewbank said he would approach his " client," meaning the respondent. Mr. Ewbank gave evidence that Mr. Bentley had said that he would see to it that Mr. Ewbank was paid a commission, but matters had not developed further before Mr. Walter Bentley's death. On September 16 Mr. Ewbank told Mr. Griffiths (who was one of the directors of the two companies) of his conversations with the late Mr. Bentley and two days later, after a directors' meeting of one of the appellant companies (as to which, however, no minute was produced) Mr. Griffiths told Mr. Ewbank that the directors had decided to sell, and that Mr. Ewbank's client should make his offer through Mr. Garton, who had the authority of the directors to deal with the matter. The next day Mr. Ewbank told the respondent of this and the latter shortly afterwards introduced to Mr. Ewbank, Colonel Burton, who was a director of the London and Southern Super Cinemas, Ltd., as willing to negotiate for the properties on behalf of that company. Mr. Ewbank took the respondent and Colonel Burton to meet Mr. Garton. Shortly before the meeting, Mr. Ewbank and the respondent had a preliminary meeting with Mr. Garton, when the respondent told Mr. Garton he wanted 10,000*l.* as commission " to cover both himself and Ewbank."

It appears that the Regal (Hastings) company was in a position to obtain leases of two more cinema theatres at Hastings called the Elite and the De Luxe without cost to themselves, and on September 26, 1935, a company called Hastings Amalgamated Cinemas, Ltd., was formed by Regal (Hastings), Ltd., to acquire these leases, the intention being that they should be included in the proposed sale to Colonel Burton's company. Instead, however, of the shares in Hastings Amalgamated Cinemas, Ltd., being all taken up by Regal (Hastings), Ltd., the directors and Mr. Garton between them hit upon a plan by which they should themselves apply for 3,000 out of the 5,000 shares to be issued at par, so that Regal (Hastings), Ltd., could only be allotted 2,000 shares. As it was intended that out of the total purchase price of the four cinemas 15,000*l.* was to be allotted for the purchase of the two leasehold cinemas (for which Hastings Amalgamated Cinemas, Ltd., had paid nothing), the result of this scheme would have been that the directors and Mr. Garton would have obtained for themselves a profit amounting to 6,000*l.*, which would otherwise have accrued to Regal (Hastings), Ltd., and its shareholders.

The discussions between Mr. Ewbank, Mr. Garton and Colonel Burton continued and at an interview, the date of which is not precisely fixed, but which was some day after September 19, Mr. Garton told Colonel Burton that he wanted a net purchase price for the four cinemas of 175,000*l.*, to which 10,000*l.* would have to be added for commission, making a total of 185,000*l.* Colonel Burton agreed " subject to contract," and gave evidence at the trial that his company, the London and Southern Super Cinemas, Ltd., remained throughout, as the appellants knew, able and willing to buy the properties for this figure.

On October 2 Mr. Ewbank wrote to Mr. Garton, enclosing a letter of the same date written by Colonel Burton on behalf of his company offering 185,000*l.* for the various properties, subject to contract, and Mr. Ewbank's letter went on to say that " These offers are subject to your clients confirming to Mr. Norman Cooper . . . the agreed procuration fees, namely, 5,000*l.* to be paid by each of the vendor companies, making a total of 10,000*l.* The payments to be made on the completion of the purchases."

On October 11, Mr. Garton's firm replied to Mr. Ewbank: " We are instructed by our clients to confirm that, on completion of the sale of the two leasehold cinemas at Hastings, and the freehold cinemas at Hastings and Eastbourne, respectively, to the London and Southern Super Cinemas, Ltd., a procuration fee of 10,000*l.* is to be paid to Mr. Norman Cooper, being 5,000*l.* in respect of each of the freehold cinemas at Hastings and Eastbourne."

There was a board meeting of the directors of Regal (Hastings), Ltd., on October 2, at which Mr. Garton reported the offer which he had received and stated the commission demanded. The majority of the directors present were in favour of accepting the offer, but Mr. Harry Bentley opposed the

motion and this was followed up next day by a letter from Mr. Bentley's
solicitors, writing in the interests of the late Mr. Walter Bentley's estate,
objecting to the size of the commission and also criticizing the way in which
the shares in Hastings Amalgamated Cinemas, Ltd., were being taken up.
The letter asked for an assurance that the proposals put before the board
on the previous day would not be carried out, and added that if this assurance
was not given, it would be necessary to consider the necessity of making an
immediate application to the Court.   There are no directors' minutes produced to show how this letter was dealt with, and it may seem somewhat
surprising that Mr. Garton's firm should none the less have written on
October 8 accepting Colonel Burton's offer and, as already stated, should
have sent a confirmation on October 11 to Mr. Ewbank of the proposed
arrangements about commission to be paid to Mr. Cooper.

Neither Mr. Garton nor any of the directors were called as witnesses
at the trial and these matters were not cleared up.   What, however, is more
important is that, in the light of Mr. Bentley's protest, the sale to Colonel
Burton's company was not proceeded with; indeed, no draft contract was
ever submitted; and the disposal of the cinemas ultimately took place by
way of a sale of shares in the appellant companies to another party.

The question to be now decided is whether the appellant companies
are liable to the respondent in damages for not carrying through the sale to
Colonel Burton's company, in which case the respondent would have earned
his commission.

In the present case no commission note addressed to the respondent is
produced, and the express contract is not contained in any document.
The proof of it mainly depends on evidence given by the respondent at
the trial in February, 1939, of the interview which he had with the appellants'
solicitor, Mr. Garton, apparently in late September, 1935.   There has been
much argument whether it was proved that Mr. Garton had authority to
act for the appellant companies in selling the properties and arranging the
commission.   Direct evidence of authority there is none, but I think (as
did the trial judge and the Court of Appeal) that the minutes of the board
meetings of the two companies, fragmentary as they are, are sufficient to
provide ratification of Mr. Garton's agency.   The respondent's oral account
of the terms of the commission contract may be filled in by the letter from
Garton and Company to Mr. Ewbank (who was to get forty per cent. of the
commission for himself) dated October 11, 1935, confirming that a " procuration fee " of 10,000*l*. was payable on the sale to the London and Southern
Super Cinemas, Ltd., and that the commission was to be provided in equal
shares by the two appellant companies—two points not mentioned in the oral
evidence.

Such being the materials out of which the express contract has to be
pieced together, what is the result ?   It seems to me that the express bargain
was simply this: if a party introduced by the respondent should buy the
cinemas for at least 185,000*l*., each of the two appellants would pay to the
respondent 5,000*l*. on the completion of the sale.   No such sale, however,
took place.   Accordingly, there can be nothing due to the respondent on the
terms of the express bargain.   But it is said that since the proposed purchasers introduced by the respondent were and remained willing and able
to buy the properties for the minimum price, while the appellants did not
close with the offer, the appellants are liable in damages to the respondent for
breach of an implied term of the commission contract.   In the statement of

claim the implied term is said to be that the appellants would " do nothing to prevent the satisfactory completion of the transaction so as to deprive the respondent of the agreed commission." The breach pleaded is the failure to complete the contract of sale with the respondent's client and the disposal of the subject matter in another quarter.

The implied term thus alleged is in any case too widely expressed, for the authorities relied on in support of the view that the express contract involves an implied term of this sort, concede that the alleged obligation on the vendor to complete the transaction if the commission agent's nominee remains able and willing to buy does not extend to cases where the vendor has " reasonable cause " for refusing to complete (*per* Greer, L.J., in *Trollope & Sons* v. *Martyn Brothers*[1]) or as Maugham, L.J., expressed it[2], " where there is no default on the part of the vendor."

But what amounts to " reasonable cause " in this connection ? If in the course of negotiating the contract of sale the parties come to loggerheads, how is the allocation of " default " determined ? In the present case, Branson, J., thought that " reasonable cause " existed, while the Court of Appeal considered that it did not. In his dissenting judgment in *Trollope & Sons* v. *Martyn Brothers*[3] Scrutton, L.J., said that he could not agree with the view that it is " ' necessary ' to imply a term that the employer shall not ' without just cause ' prevent the agent from earning his commission, and as a corollary, that if he ' arbitrarily ' " (i.e., " without alleging any just ' excuse ' ") " refuses to sell, he is " (*vis-à-vis* the agent) " in default, though in an agreement subject to contract he breaks no contract with the purchaser by refusing to complete without giving any reason." " This view," the Lord Justice went on to say, " seems to make the subsidiary matter, the remuneration of the agent who is to obtain a contract of sale, as of more importance than the sale itself, which without breach of any contract with the purchaser has not been completed or materialised. It does not seem to me that a vendor taking an attitude towards the purchaser which by his contract he is entitled to adopt, if he gives no reason why he so acts except that it is in the bond, is acting arbitrarily and therefore in some unspecified default. Every man who receives and refuses without giving a reason an offer which he is not bound to accept, may be said to act arbitrarily, but I cannot understand why he is in default."

The implied term upon which the respondent relies, following *Trollope & Sons* v. *Martyn Brothers*[4], amounts to saying that when once he has introduced his duly qualified nominee the appellants must look in no other direction for a purchaser, but are bound, in the absence of " just excuse," to do their best to sell to that nominee. It appears to me that this proposition leads to great difficulties in its application, and to great uncertainty as to what might amount to a just excuse. In the present case, the respondent was not appointed sole agent, and there might have been half-a-dozen competitors for the proffered commission. If the respondent's introduction of his nominee had been immediately followed by a better offer through another agent, would the appellants have been bound to refuse the latter, or to accept it only with the consequence of paying two commissions ? If, after receiving the respondent's " name," and before becoming bound by contract of sale, the appellants sold the property to another purchaser without the intervention of any agent at all, would this expose the appellants

---

[1] [1934] 2 K. B. 436.   [2] *Ibid.*, 458.   [3] *Ibid.*, 436, at p. 444.
[4] [1934] 2 K. B. 436.

to a claim by the respondent for damages ?　The contrary has been held, I think correctly, by McCardie, J., in *Bentall, Horsley and Baldry* v. *Vicary*[1]. Again, what would be the rights of the agent if he were employed on precisely corresponding terms to find a tenant for a house at a rent named ?　Can it be that the owner would be bound to accept the first tenant so offered to him who was willing to pay the rent ?　How would matters stand in such a case where the house is to be let furnished and the selection of a suitable tenant is therefore of particular concern to the landlord ?

　　I find it impossible to formulate with adequate precision the tests which should determine whether or not a " just excuse " exists for disregarding the alleged implied term, and this leads me to consider whether there really is any such implied term at all.

　　The matter may be tested in this way.　If such an implied term must be assumed, then this amounts to saying that when the owner gives the agent the opportunity of earning commission on the express terms thus stated, the agent might have added, " From the moment that I produce a duly qualified offeror, you must give up all freedom of choice and carry through the bargain, if you reasonably can, with my nominee," and the vendor must reply, " of course; that necessarily follows."[2]　But I am by no means satisfied that the vendor would acquiesce in regarding the matter in this light.　I doubt whether the agent is bound, generally speaking, to exercise any standard of diligence in looking for a possible purchaser.　He is commonly described as " employed ": but he is not " employed " in the sense in which a man is employed to paint a picture or to build a house, with the liability to pay damages for delay or want of skill.　The owner is offering to the agent a reward if the agent's activity helps to bring about an actual sale, but that is no reason why the owner should not remain free to sell his property through other channels.　The agent necessarily incurs certain risks, *e.g.*, the risk that his nominee cannot find the purchase price or will not consent to terms reasonably proposed to be inserted in the contract of sale.　I think, upon the true construction of the express contract in this case, that the agent also takes the risk of the owner not being willing to conclude the bargain with the agent's nominee.　This last risk is ordinarily a slight one, for the owner's reason for approaching the agent is that he wants to sell.

　　If it really were the common intention of owner and agent that the owner should be bound in the manner suggested, there would be no difficulty in so providing by an express term of the contract.　But in the absence of such an express term, I am unable to regard the suggested implied term as " necessary."　The well known line of authorities, of which *Mackay* v. *Dick*[3], is a leading example, do not, in my opinion, lead to the conclusion drawn from them by the majority of the Court of Appeal in *Trollope & Sons* v. *Martyn Brothers*[4].　If A. employs B. for reward to do a piece of work for him which requires outlay and effort on B.'s part and which depends on the continued existence of a given subject-matter which is under A.'s control (as in *Inchbald* v. *Western Neilgherry Coffee Co.*[5]) there may be an implied term that A. will not prevent B. doing the work by destroying the subject-matter.　And, generally speaking, where B. is employed by A. to do a piece of work which requires A.'s co-operation (e.g., to paint A.'s portrait), it is

---

[1] [1931] 1 K. B. 253.　　　　　　　　　　[2] See *supra*, p. 108.
[3] (1881) 6 App. Cas. 251.　　　　　　　　[4] [1934] 2 K. B. 436.
　　　　　　　　　　[5] (1864), 17 C. B. N. S. 733.

implied that the necessary co-operation will be forthcoming (e.g., A. will give sittings to the artist). But the work which the respondent was invited to do was to produce an offer for the property—a piece of work which does not require the appellants' co-operation at all (except in giving a prospective purchaser reasonable opportunity to inspect the property which no doubt would be an implied term)—and I am unable to deduce from the fact that the respondent was invited to produce an offer the implication that the appellants promised the respondent that they would accept it unless " just excuse " for refusal existed.

In my view, therefore, the respondent's claim fails because the implied term suggested is not proved to exist, and it is unnecessary to consider whether the objections taken on behalf of Mr. Harry Bentley in the letter of October 3, and the risk of controversy or litigation arising if the original scheme had been carried through, constituted " just cause " for failing to accept Colonel Burton's offer. I am unwilling unnecessarily to comment on the action of Mr. Garton and the directors in proposing themselves to subscribe for the majority of the shares in Hastings Amalgamated Cinemas, Ltd., since they were not parties to the present litigation and the decision whether they should be called as witnesses or not presumably did not rest with them. Their explanation, whether good or bad, has not been heard in this action.

The present Master of the Rolls, in concluding his judgment in *Trollope & Sons* v. *Caplan*[1], expressed the view that the case law as to the rights and obligations of house agents and their clients with regard to the sort of questions then under discussion was not in a very satisfactory condition, and that it was desirable that the whole position should be reviewed, if opportunity offered, in the House of Lords. du Parcq, L.J., in the present case, expressed his agreement with this view. I have had the advantage of reading the opinion prepared by my noble and learned friend Lord Wright, in which he examines a number of the cases, on which I do not myself comment in this opinion, and I am glad to adopt his conclusions concerning them.

There is, I think, considerable difficulty, and no little danger, in trying to formulate general propositions on such a subject, for contracts with commission agents do not follow a single pattern and the primary necessity in each instance is to ascertain with precision what are the express terms of the particular contract under discussion, and then to consider whether these express terms necessitate the addition, by implication, of other terms. There are some classes of contract in which an implied term is introduced by the requirements of a statute (for example, under the Sale of Goods Act or the Marine Insurance Act); there are other contracts where an implied term is introduced by the force of established custom (for example, the necessity of a month's notice in the case of hiring a domestic servant); but in contracts made with commission agents there is no justification for introducing an implied term unless it is necessary to do so for the purpose of giving to the contract the business effect which both parties to it intended it should have.

It may be useful to point out that contracts under which an agent may be occupied in endeavouring to dispose of the property of a principal fall into several obvious classes. There is the class in which the agent is promised a commission by his principal if he succeeds in introducing to his principal a person who makes an adequate offer, usually an offer of not less than the stipulated amount. If that is all that is needed in order to earn his

---

[1] [1936] 2 K.B. 382, *per* Lord Greene at p. 401.

reward, it is obvious that he is entitled to be paid when this has been done, whether his principal accepts the offer and carries through the bargain or not. No implied term is needed to secure this result. There is another class of case in which the property is put into the hands of the agent to dispose of for the owner, and the agent accepts the employment and, it may be, expends money and time in endeavouring to carry it out. Such a form of contract may well imply the term that the principal will not withdraw the authority he has given after the agent has incurred substantial outlay, or, at any rate, after he has succeeded in finding a possible purchaser. Each case turns on its own facts and the phrase " finding a purchaser " is itself not without ambiguity. *Inchbald's* case[1] might, I think, be regarded as falling within this second class. But there is a third class of case (to which the present instance belongs) where, by the express language of the contract, the agent is promised his commission only upon completion of the transaction which he is endeavouring to bring about between the offeror and his principal. As I have already said, there seems to me to be no room for the suggested implied term in such a case. The agent is promised a reward in return for an event, and the event has not happened. He runs the risk of disappointment, but if he is not willing to run the risk he should introduce into the express terms of the contract the clause which protects him.

The oft-quoted case of *Prickett* v. *Badger*[2] must, I think, be regarded as turning on its special facts, which were very unusual. There the defendant invited the plaintiff to concern himself, for reward, in the sale of a piece of freehold land, although the defendant had no interest in the land whatsoever. I can well understand that in such circumstances the plaintiff, after incurring outlay and exerting himself to produce the would-be purchaser, could make good a claim for a *quantum meruit*. The report attributes to Pollock, C.B., who tried the case at Assizes, the assertion that if a man places in the hands of several house-agents a house which he is desirous of letting or selling, " though the successful agent alone would be entitled to claim commission, the others would clearly be entitled to something for their trouble." If the Chief Baron really made this observation, it certainly is not in accordance with the usual result of arrangements made with house agents, and it should be noted that Williams, J.[3], speaks of " the implied understanding that the agent is only to receive a commission if he succeeds in effecting a sale, but, if not, then he is to get nothing."

Trollope & Sons v. *Martyn Brothers*[4] was also a case with unusual special facts, for, though the offer produced by the plaintiffs was " subject to contract," matters had proceeded so far that the draft terms of contract proposed by the defendant had been accepted and signed by the would-be purchaser, and there was nothing whatsoever to explain why the contract did not go through other than the unwillingness of the defendant to proceed. The judgment of my noble and learned friend, Lord Maugham (then Maugham, L.J.), in favour of the plaintiffs largely turned on these special facts, and for that reason I venture to doubt whether he would necessarily have approved of the later decision in *Trollope & Sons* v. *Caplan*[5], where the Court of Appeal was endeavouring to apply the earlier case. However that may be, for the reasons which I have stated, I prefer the minority view of Scrutton, L.J., in *Trollope & Sons* v. *Martyn Brothers*[4], and am of opinion

---

[1] (1864), 17 C. B. N. S. 733.   [2] (1856), 1 C. B. N. S. 296.
[3] (1856), 1 C.B. N.S., at p. 305.   [4] [1934] 2 K. B. 436.   [5] [1936] 2 K. B. 382.

that that case and the following case of *Trollope & Sons* v. *Caplan*[1] were wrongly decided.

I move that this appeal be allowed. *Appeal allowed.*

PRIVITY OF CONTRACT

3. THE ASSIGNMENT OF CHOSES IN ACTION

Durham Brothers v. Robertson

[1898] 1 Q.B. 765

> No particular form of words is required to constitute a valid equitable assignment.
> An assignment which does not satisfy the requirements of the Judicature Act, 1873, s. 25 (6) (now the Law of Property Act, 1925, s. 136), may be a valid equitable assignment, but the assignor must be a party to any proceedings brought against the debtor.

CHITTY, L.J., read the following judgment :—This is an appeal by the defendant Robertson against a judgment whereby the plaintiffs Durham Brothers recovered judgment for a sum of 1,080*l.* The action was tried by Wills, J., without a jury. The plaintiffs' claim was that under a building contract dated April 1, 1895, made between the defendant, the building owner, and Smith & Co., the contractors, the sum of 1,080*l.* became payable, in the events which had happened, on August 18, 1896, as a premium or purchase-money for an improved or additional ground-rent of 60*l.* ; that this sum before it became payable had been duly assigned by Smith & Co., to the plaintiffs by writing within the meaning of the Judicature Act, 1873, section 25, sub-section 6, and that due notice of the assignment had been given to the defendant. There was no question about the notice. The defences relied upon on the appeal were in substance, first, a denial that the sum of 1,080*l.* ever became payable under the building contract ; and, secondly, that there was no valid assignment of that sum within the Act. Smith & Co. were not parties to the action, nor was George Tapley Smith, to whom a lease, at the improved ground-rent, was in fact granted on August 18, 1896. Wills, J., decided both points in favour of the plaintiffs.

Both points were raised on the appeal. The second point as to the assignment was first argued. Mr. Jelf, for the respondents, admitted (and rightly) that if the decision on this point was adverse to his clients the appeal must succeed. But, on consideration, it appeared to us that a decision on this point alone would be unsatisfactory, because it would leave the other point still open to controversy in some further litigation between the parties. Consequently, the argument on the other point was resumed and concluded ; and we now proceed to give judgment on both the questions.

I will follow the course of the argument, and deal first with the point as to the assignment ; and I shall assume throughout this part of the judgment that the sum of 1,080*l.* did become payable under the building contract of April 1, 1895.

The document, relied on by the plaintiffs as an assignment within

[4] [1936], 2 K. B. 382.

the Act, is a letter dated August 19, 1895, written by Smith & Co. to the plaintiffs. It runs thus :

> "*Re* Building Contract of Middle Class Dwellings, situate on the west side South Lambeth Road, S.W.—In consideration of money advanced from time to time we hereby charge the sum of 1,080*l*., being the agreed price for the sale of 60*l*. per annum ground-rent which will become due to us from John Robertson, Esq., of No. 73, Rosendale Road, West Dulwich, on the completion of the above buildings as security for the advances, and we hereby assign our interest in the above-mentioned sum until the money with added interest be repaid to you."

Now the document divides itself into two parts. First, there is a charge upon 1,080*l*. for the advances ; and, secondly, there is an assignment of the interest of Smith & Co. in the 1,080*l*. in terms not absolute, but until the happening of an event, namely, the repayment of the advances with interest. On repayment of the advances and interest the assignment, according to the import of the document, comes to an end.

Dealing with the case apart from the Judicature Act, there is here unquestionably a valid equitable assignment. To operate as an equitable assignment no particular form of words is required in the document : an engagement or direction to pay, out of a debt or fund, a sum of money constitutes an equitable assignment, though it does not operate as an assignment of the whole fund or debt. A mere charge on a fund or debt operates as a partial equitable assignment. As is well-known, an ordinary debt or chose in action before the Judicature Act was not assignable so as to pass the right of action at law, but it was assignable so as to pass the right to sue in equity. In his suit in equity the assignee of a debt, even where the assignment was absolute on the face of it, had to make his assignor, the original creditor, party in order primarily to bind him and prevent his suing at law, and also to allow him to dispute the assignment if he thought fit. This was *a fortiori* the case where the assignment was by way of security, or by way of charge only, because the assignor had a right to redeem. Further, the assignee could not give a valid discharge for the debt to the original debtor unless expressly empowered so to do. The original debtor, whether he admitted the debt or not, was not concerned with the state of the accounts between the assignor and the assignee where the debt was assigned by way of security ; and the rule was that where he did not dispute the debt he should have his costs of suit out of the debt : he was regarded in the light of a stakeholder. It is unnecessary to cite authorities in support of any of the above propositions.

Now it was in order to afford some remedy for this state of the law that sub-section 6 was passed. It is plain on reading it that it does not apply to every case of equitable assignment of a debt or chose in action.

Two matters, as is apparent on the face of it, had to be regarded : first, the simplifying the remedy in favour of the assignee : and secondly, the protection of the original debtor.

With these preliminary observations, which I have made for the purpose of explaining the language of the sub-section, which at first sight seems peculiar if not awkward, I proceed to examine the sub-section itself : " Any absolute assignment, by writing under the hand of the assignor (not purporting to be by way of charge only), of any debt or other legal chose in action, of which express notice in writing shall have been given to the debtor, trustee, or other person from whom the assignor would have been entitled to receive or claim such debt or chose in action, shall be, and be deemed to have been effectual in law (subject to all equities which would have been entitled to priority over the right of the assignee if this Act had not passed), to pass and transfer the legal right to such debt or chose in action from the date of such notice, and all legal and other remedies for the same, and the power to give a good discharge for the same, without the concurrence of the assignor." This is followed by a proviso that if the debtor (I omit the other words) shall have had notice that such assignment is disputed by the assignor or any one claiming under him, or of any other opposing claims to such debt or chose in action, he shall be entitled, if he think fit, to call upon the claimants to interplead, or he may pay the debt into Court under the Trustee Relief Act.

No argument was addressed to us founded on this proviso. It appeared, from the evidence put in at the trial, that under an agreement in August, 1896, connected with the original building contract, George Tapley Smith (not a member of the contractors' firm) had or might have a claim to the 1,080*l.* in question in this action, or to a sum of like amount ; and we were informed by counsel during the argument on the appeal, that he had issued a writ against the defendant Robertson to recover that sum. But the defendant has taken no step in this action calling on the parties to interplead, supposing that he had a right so to do, which he had not, as he disputed the debt. In these circumstances no question arises on the proviso, and it may be left out of consideration.

To bring a case within the sub-section transferring the legal right to sue for the debt and empowering the assignee to give a good discharge for the debt, there must be (in the language of the sub-section) an absolute assignment not purporting to be by way of charge only. It is requisite that the assignment should be, or at all events purport to be, absolute, but it will not suffice if the assignment purport to be by way of charge only. It is plain that every equitable assignment in the wide sense of the term as used in equity is not within the enactment. As the enactment requires that the assignment should be absolute, the question arose whether a mortgage, in the proper sense of the term, and as now generally understood, was within the enactment. In *Tancred* v. *Delagoa Bay and East Africa Railway*[1] there was an assignment of the debt to secure advances with a proviso for redemption and reassignment upon repayment. It was there held by the Divisional Court (disapproving of a decision in *National Provincial Bank* v. *Harle*[2]), that such a mortgage fell within the enactment. It appears to me that the decision of the Divisional Court was quite right. The assignment of the debt was absolute : it purported to pass the entire interest of the assignor in the debt to the mortgagee, and it was not an assignment purporting to be by way of charge only. The mortgagor-assignor had a right to redeem, and on repayment of the advances a right to have the assigned debt reassigned to him. Notice of the reassignment pursuant to the sub-section would be given to the original debtor, and he would thus know with certainty in whom the legal right to sue him was vested. I think that the principle of the decision ought not to be confined to the case where there is an express provision for reassignment. Where there is an absolute assignment of the debt, but by way of security, equity would imply a right to a reassignment on redemption, and the sub-section would apply to the case of such an absolute assignment. In a well-known judgment of the Exchequer Chamber in *Halliday* v. *Holgate*[3], the late Willes, J., in

---

[1] (1889), 23 Q. B. D. 239. [2] (1881), 6 Q. B. D. 626. [3] (1868), L. R. 3 Exch. 299.

delivering the judgment of the Court, distinguished between lien, pledge, and mortgage, and spoke of a mortgage as passing the property out and out. A mortgage is not mentioned in the enactment ; but where there is an absolute assignment of the debt, the limiting words as to a charge only are not sufficient to exclude mortgage. The respondent's counsel cited a passage from Fisher on Mortgages and from Wharton's Dictionary to the effect that a mortgage was a conditional conveyance. In bygone days mortgages were made by a conveyance subject to a condition making it void if the money was repaid within six months ; but mortgages in this form had become obsolete long before the Judicature Act, 1873, was passed. The form was abandoned because of the difficulty in ascertaining in whom the legal estate was vested, the title being made to depend on the fact whether the money was or was not paid within the time limited by the condition.

The assignment before us complies with all the terms of the enactment save one, which is essential : it is not an absolute but a conditional assignment. The commonest and most familiar instance of a conditional assurance is an assurance until J. S. shall return from Rome. The repayment of the money advanced is an uncertain event, and makes the assignment conditional. Where the Act applies it does not leave the original debtor in uncertainty as to the person to whom the legal right is transferred ; it does not involve him in any question as to the state of the accounts between the mortgagor and the mortgagee. The legal right is transferred, and is vested in the assignee. There is no machinery provided by the Act for the reverter of the legal right to the assignor dependent on the performance of a condition ; the only method within the provisions of the Act for revesting in the assignor the legal right is by a retransfer to the assignor followed by a notice in writing to the debtor, as in the case of the first transfer of the right. The question is not one of mere technicality or of form : it is one of substance, relating to the protection of the original debtor and placing him in an assured position.

It is necessary to refer to *Brice* v. *Bannister*.[1] In that case there was an assignment of 100*l.* out of money due or to become due to the assignor under a contract to build a ship, with an express power to give a good discharge to the debtor. Lord Coleridge, C.J., held that the assignment was within the 25th section. The Court of Appeal decided the case quite apart from the Act. Cotton, L.J., expressly decided the case on the ground of equitable assignment. That is shewn by the opening sentence of his judgment, where he says that the letter was a good equitable assignment. Bramwell, L.J., reluctantly assented to this view. Brett, L.J., dissented, but on general principles. So soon as it was ascertained that there was a good equitable assignment, with power to give a discharge, it became unnecessary to consider whether it fell within the Act or not. In *Re Jones*, *Ex parte Nichols*[2] the present Master of the Rolls, referring to this decision, treated the assignment as an equitable assignment. He said that the decision was founded on the principle that the right of an equitable assignment of a debt cannot be defeated by a voluntary payment by the debtor to the assignor. The decision of Lord Coleridge, C.J., in *Brice* v. *Bannister*[1], that the case fell within the 25th section, appears to me to be open to question. The assignment purported to be by way of charge only. It was a direction to pay the 100*l.* out of money due or to become due. No doubt it purported

---

[1] (1878), 3 Q. B. D. 569.   [2] (1883), 22 Ch. D. 782, at p. 787.

to be a charge of an unredeemable sum of 100*l*. ; but still it was a charge. The section speaks of an absolute assignment of any debt or other chose in action. It does not say " or any part of a debt or chose in action." It appears to me as at present advised to be questionable whether an assignment of part of an entire debt is within the enactment[1]. If it be, it would seem to leave it in the power of the original creditor to split up the single legal cause of action for the debt into as many separate legal causes of action as he might think fit. However, it is not necessary to decide the point in the present case, and I leave it open for future consideration.

The result then, thus far, is this : the plaintiffs' assignment is not within the Act, and they had no legal right to sue for it. The assignment, however, is a valid equitable assignment, but by way of security only, and without power to give a valid discharge to the debtor. No relief can be given to the plaintiffs in this action as it is constituted. It is admitted as between the parties to this action that considerably less than 1,080*l*. is due to the plaintiffs in respect of their advances. In the absence of Smith & Co., the amount due from them to the plaintiffs cannot be ascertained. An account taken in this action of the advances would not bind Smith & Co. Nor could the matters in question, on the footing that the plaintiffs have a mere equitable assignment, be finally determined in the absence of George Tapley Smith, who has or seems to have had an adverse claim to the 1,080*l*. under the documents of August 18, 1896. Mr. Jelf was unquestionably right when he admitted that the plaintiffs' case failed unless it came within the 25th section. The trial has taken place, and it is not possible now to make any amendment by adding parties or otherwise.

[The Lord Justice then dealt with the question whether the 1,080*l*. had become payable, and confirmed the view taken by the learned judge at the trial, and continued :—]

The result is that the plaintiffs fail in the action. The appeal must be allowed, and judgment entered for the defendant.

A. L. SMITH, L.J., delivered judgment to the same effect. COLLINS, L.J., concurred.

Ellis v. Torrington

[1920] 1 K.B. 399

A bare right of action is not assignable. To be assignable, a right of action must be incidental to a proprietary right that is also transferred to the assignee.

APPEAL from the judgment of Sargant, J., sitting in the King's Bench Division.

The action was for damages for breach of a covenant to keep and leave a certain house and premises in repair. The plaintiff claimed as assignee of the benefit of the covenant.

The statement of claim contained the following allegations :—

1. By a deed dated October 24, 1898, made between Earle Tudor Johnson of the one part and Franz Voelklein of the other part the house and premises in question which were situate in the parish of Cookham in the county of Berks,

---

[1] It has since been decided that the assignment of part of a debt is not within the enactment, *Williams* v. *Atlantic Assurance Co.*, [1933] 1 K. B. 81.

and were then known as Felix Cottage, but now as Hazeldene, were let by
E. T. Johnson to F. Voelklein from September 29, 1898, for a term of nineteen
years and one quarter of another year except the last ten days thereof.

By the said deed F. Voelklein covenanted with E. T. Johnson that he would
during the term well and substantially repair and keep in good and substantial
repair in a workmanlike manner and with good materials the house and premises,
damage by fire excepted, and also would save as aforesaid at his own cost in
the second year and in every subsequent third year and in the last year of the
term paint all the outside woodwork ironwork and other work belonging to the
house and premises and all the inside woodwork in the fourth year and once in
every subsequent seven years and in the last year and would colour whitewash
and paper as therein provided and also would at the expiration of the term peace-
ably yield up the house and premises in good and substantial repair and condition
in accordance with the covenants thereinbefore contained, damage by fire
excepted.

2. The term subsequently became vested in the defendant.

3. E. T. Johnson died on March 29,1917, and the reversion upon the term
became vested in his executors.

4. While the defendant was assignee of the term the house and premises
were out of such repair as was required by the covenants above mentioned,
and at the end of the term they were yielded up by the defendant out of such
repair.

5. By a deed dated September 17, 1918, the executors of E. T. Johnson,
in consideration of the covenant hereinafter mentioned, assigned to the plaintiff
the full benefit of the covenants on the part of the lessee contained in the deed
of October 24, 1898 together with the full right to recover receive and retain
for his benefit all damages costs and other sums of money and all other relief
for or in respect of any breach or breaches committed of the said covenants or
any of them and also the right to bring, prosecute, compound, or release any
action or proceeding in respect thereof and all other rights and powers whatsoever
in connection therewith. And the plaintiff covenanted with the executors that
he would at all times keep the executors and the estate of E. T. Johnson effectually
indemnified against all actions and proceedings costs damages claims and demands
in respect of any liability whatsoever on the part of E. T. Johnson or his estate
or effects under the indenture of lease dated March 30, 1868, made between
Albert Ricardo and E. T. Johnson, and referred to below.

Express notice of this assignment was given in writing to the defendant
on September 18, 1918. The plaintiff claimed 334*l*.

The defendant submitted that the statement of claim disclosed no
cause of action.

The following statement of facts is taken from the judgment of Sargant, J.

By an indenture of lease dated February 12, 1868, hereinafter referred
to as lease No. 1, the house and premises were demised by Cooper and
others to Albert Ricardo from Christmas, 1867, for fifty years—i.e., to
Christmas, 1917—at a rent of 96*l*. per annum, and there were covenants
by the lessee to repair, to keep in repair, to do certain specified painting,
and to yield up in good repair.

On March 30, 1868, a lease (lease No. 2) was executed by which Albert
Ricardo, as lessee under lease No. 1, leased the premises to E. T. Johnson
from Christmas, 1867, for fifty years less seven days—i.e., to December 18,
1917—at a rent of 45*l*. per annum. There were covenants by the lessee
to repair and keep in repair, to do certain specified painting, and also to
yield up in good repair. The language of those covenants was substantially
identical with the language of the covenants in lease No. 1.

Some thirty years afterwards, on October 24, 1898, E. T. Johnson by
a lease No. 3, demised the same property to F. Volklein from Michaelmas,
1898, for 19¼ years less ten days for a term expiring on December 15, 1917.
This is the lease referred to in para. 1 of the statement of claim. It contained

the covenant set out therein which was more or less, but not quite, the same, as the covenants contained in leases Nos. 1 and 2. There was an exception of damage by fire in the covenant to yield up. By September 29, 1909, lease No. 3 had got into the hands of one Leon as assignee, who in the same year assigned lease No. 3 to the defendant, Lady Torrington, by a deed of assignment containing the ordinary covenant by the assignee to indemnify the assignor against subsequent breaches of covenant in the lease.

On May 30, 1914, by a lease, No. 4, the defendant leased the premises to the plaintiff from June 24, 1914, for a term of $3\frac{1}{2}$ years less twenty days, that is, to December 5, 1917. The covenants to repair in this lease were different from those in the other leases. They were covenants by which the lessee's liability for fair wear and tear were excepted. The plaintiff was in actual possession when lease No. 4 came to an end.

During the twenty days or so from December 5 to December 25, 1917, all the four leases expired.

On December 18, 1917, the plaintiff contracted with the successors in title of Cooper and others, the lessors under lease No. 1, to purchase the freehold of the premises, and it was part of the terms of the purchase that the plaintiff should have assigned to him the benefit of the covenants by the lessee contained in lease No. 1. The purchase was actually completed on May 1, 1918. On that day two indentures were executed; by one of which the freeholders conveyed the fee simple of the premises to the plaintiff, and by the other of which the freeholders conveyed to the plaintiff the full benefit of the lessee's covenants in lease No. 1, together with the right to sue in respect thereof. Thus the plaintiff was entitled to sue Ricardo or his representatives for breaches by the lessee of the covenants in lease No. 1. Ricardo or his representatives if sued by the plaintiff could, and probably would, sue the executors of E. T. Johnson, who had died on March 29, 1917, for breaches of the almost identical covenants in lease No. 2, and Johnson's executors in their turn could sue the defendant on the covenants in lease No. 3. The defendant was already seeking to recover from the plaintiff under his covenants in lease No. 4.

In these circumstances the representatives of E. T. Johnson executed the assignment mentioned in para. 5 of the statement of claim as set out above.

The question was whether that assignment was valid.

Sargant, J., gave judgment for the plaintiff.

The defendant appealed.

SCRUTTON, L.J. On a careful consideration of the authorities which have been cited to us I find no principle of law to countenance the objection taken to this assignment. The objection is this: The appellant's lessor has assigned to the present owner of the property the right to sue on the appellant's covenant to keep the premises in repair or pay damages; it is said that this assignment is impossible because it contravenes the law of champerty and maintenance. It is elementary knowledge that for a long time Courts of common law and Courts of equity differed as to how far choses in action, and particularly causes of action, could be assigned. The common law treated debts as personal obligations and assignments of debts merely as assignments of the right to bring an action at law against the debtor and, except in a strictly limited number of cases, did not recognize any such assignments. Courts of equity always took a different view. They treated debts as property, and the necessity of an action at law to reduce the property into possession they regarded merely as an incident which followed on the assignment of the property. I am stating the effect of the judgment of Cozens-Hardy, L.J., in *Fitzroy* v. *Cave*[1]. But there came a point on which both Courts would have agreed; to assign a bare right of action, a bare power to bring an action, was not permitted in either Court; and the reason was as pointed out by Warrington, L.J., that both Courts treated such an assignment as offending against the law of maintenance or champerty or both. But early in the development of the law the Courts of equity, and perhaps the Courts of common law also, took the view that where the right of action was not a bare right, but was incident or subsidiary to a right in property, an assignment of the right of action was permissible, and did not savour of champerty or maintenance. In *Glegg* v. *Bromley*[2] Parker, J., defined the exception in this way: " The question was whether the subject matter of the assignment was, in the view of the Court, property with an incidental remedy for its recovery, or was a bare right to bring an action either at law or in equity." Stirling, L.J., in *Dawson's* Case[3] defined it in these words: " We think that great weight must be given to the circumstance that this assignment is incidental and subsidiary to that conveyance and is part of a *bona fide* transaction, the object of which was to transfer to the plaintiff the property of Blake with all the incidents which attached to it in his hands." I will cite one case more, *Dickinson* v. *Burrell*[4], which has been approved in later cases. There Dickinson, having conveyed property by a deed which was voidable in equity, made a second conveyance of the same property by a valid deed. It was held that the second deed carried with it the right to set aside the voidable deed. Lord Romilly, M.R., said, " The distinction is this: if James Dickinson sold or conveyed the right to sue to set aside the indenture of December, 1860, without conveying the property, or his interest in the property, which is the subject of that indenture, that would not have enabled the grantee, A. B., to maintain this bill; but if A. B. had bought the whole of the interest of James Dickinson in the property, then it would. The right of suit is a right incidental to the property conveyed." Those three cases state in various ways the exception which the Courts have recognized to the rule that a bare right of action cannot be conveyed because it savours of champerty and maintenance. The exception and the limits defining it are easily apprehended when the nature of champerty and maintenance is considered. Many acts used to be regarded as acts of maintenance which are not so regarded now. Hawkins in his Pleas of the Crown gives many instances which no one now would think of calling maintenance. Lord Haldane in *Neville* v. *London " Express " Newspaper, Ltd.*[5] said: " It is unlawful for a stranger to render officious assistance by money or otherwise to another person in a suit in which that third person has himself no legal interest, for its prosecution or defence." Champerty is only a particular form of maintenance, namely, where the person who maintains takes as a reward a share in the property recovered. When the person who assists is himself interested in the subject matter of the suit before its commencement there is neither champerty nor maintenance. Three owners of property may assist one of them in suing to protect the property and may share in what is recovered. This is neither maintenance nor champerty, because none of the three has a bare right of action. Each has a right of

---

[1] [1905] 2 K. B. 364.
[3] [1905] 1 K. B. 260, at p. 271.
[5] [1919], A. C. 368, at p. 390.
[2] [1912] 3 K. B. 474, at p. 490.
[4] (1866), L. R. 1 Eq. 337, at p. 342.

action relating to his interest in the property. So in this case when the respondent, who had bought the freehold, took also an assignment of the right to recover damages for dilapidations against the first lessee, he was not buying in order merely to get a cause of action; he was buying property and a cause of action as incidental thereto. That assignment seems clearly to be protected by the principle of *Williams* v. *Protheroe*[1]. The next step is this: if, starting with a valid assignment of the lease, he had sued the first lessee, who had sued the second lessee, who had sued the third lessee, there would have been three actions the last of which would have established the liability of the appellant. Instead of that the respondent by taking an assignment of the action against the third lessee reaches the same result by one action instead of the complicated formalities of three. For these reasons I think the objection taken to this assignment is without foundation.

I wish to add this: There are two much-quoted cases which must in future be accepted with caution. The dictum in *Prosser* v. *Edmonds*[2] would be much modified if that case were decided now for the first time. Secondly, it is not of much use to cite *May* v. *Lane*[3] at the present day without citing the cases in which it has been explained. The judgment of Rigby, L.J., is generally cited without reference to the facts of the case. It ought to be taken with the qualification placed upon it in *Torkington* v. *Magee*[4]. I agree that the appeal should be dismissed.

BANKES and WARRINGTON, L.JJ., delivered judgments to the same effect.

The British Waggon Co. and the Parkgate Waggon Co. v. Lea & Co.

(1880) 5 Q.B.D. 149

1. Contractual obligations cannot be assigned.
2. In certain cases, however, the obligation to perform a contract may be delegated, but such delegation does not affect the rights and liabilities of the contracting parties.
3. Whether delegation is possible or not depends upon the construction of the contract in the light of the surrounding circumstances.

COCKBURN, C.J. This was an action brought by the plaintiffs to recover rent for the hire of certain railway waggons, alleged to be payable by the defendants to the plaintiffs, or one of them, under the following circumstances:—

By an agreement in writing of the 10th of February, 1874, the Parkgate Waggon Company let to the defendants, who are coal merchants, fifty railway waggons for a term of seven years, at a yearly rent of 600*l.* a year, payable by equal quarterly payments. By a second agreement of the 13th of June, 1874, the company in like manner let to the defendants fifty other waggons, at a yearly rent of 625*l.*, payable quarterly like the former.

Each of these agreements contained the following clause: " The owners, their executors, or administrators, will at all times during the said term, except as herein provided, keep the said waggons in good and substantial repair and working order, and, on receiving notice from the tenant of any want of repairs, and the number or numbers of the waggons requiring to be repaired, and the place or places where it or they then is or are, will,

---

[1] (1829), 2 M. & P. 779. [2] (1835), 1 Y. & C. Ex. 481.
[3] (1894), 64 L. J. Q. B. 236. [4] [1902] 2 K. B. 427.

with all reasonable despatch, cause the same to be repaired and put into good working order."

On the 24th of October, 1874, the Parkgate Company passed a resolution, under the 129th section of the Companies Act, 1862, for the voluntary winding-up of the company. Liquidators were appointed, and by an order of the Chancery Division of the High Court of Justice, it was ordered that the winding-up of the company should be continued under the supervision of the Court.

By an indenture of the 1st of April, 1878, the Parkgate Company assigned and transferred, and the liquidators confirmed, to the British Company and their assigns, among other things, all sums of money, whether payable by way of rent, hire, interest, penalty, or damage, then due, or thereafter to become due, to the Parkgate Company, by virtue of the two contracts with the defendants, together with the benefit of the two contracts, and all the interest of the Parkgate Company and the said liquidators therein; the British Company, on the other hand, covenanting with the Parkgate Company " to observe and perform such of the stipulations, conditions, provisions, and agreements contained in the said contracts as, according to the terms thereof were stipulated to be observed and performed by the Parkgate Company." On the execution of this assignment the British Company took over from the Parkgate Company the repairing stations, which had previously been used by the Parkgate Company for the repair of the waggons let to the defendants, and also the staff of workmen employed by the latter company in executing such repairs. It is expressly found that the British Company have ever since been ready and willing to execute, and have, with all due diligence, executed all necessary repairs to the said waggons. This, however, they have done under a special agreement come to between the parties since the present dispute has arisen, without prejudice to their respective rights.

In this state of things the defendants asserted their right to treat the contract as at an end, on the ground that the Parkgate Company had incapacitated themselves from performing the contract, first, by going into voluntary liquidation, secondly, by assigning the contracts, and giving up the repairing stations to the British Company, between whom and the defendants there was no privity of contract, and whose services, in substitution for those to be performed by the Parkgate Company under the contract, they, the defendants, were not bound to accept. The Parkgate Company not acquiescing in this view, it was agreed that the facts should be stated in a special case for the opinion of this Court, the use of the waggons by the defendants being in the meanwhile continued at a rate agreed on between the parties, without prejudice to either, with reference to their respective rights.

The first ground taken by the defendants is in our opinion altogether untenable in the present state of things, whatever it may be when the affairs of the company shall have been wound up, and the company itself shall have been dissolved under the 111th section of the Act. Pending the winding-up, the company is by the effect of ss. 95 and 131 kept alive, the liquidator having power to carry on the business, " so far as may be necessary for the beneficial winding-up of the company," which the continued letting of these waggons, and the receipt of the rent payable in respect of them, would, we presume, be.

What would be the position of the parties on the dissolution of the company it is unnecessary for the present purpose to consider.

The main contention on the part of the defendants, however, was that, as the Parkgate Company had, by assigning the contracts, and by making over their repairing stations to the British Company, incapacitated themselves to fulfil their obligation to keep the waggons in repair, that company had no right, as between themselves and the defendants, to substitute a third party to do the work they had engaged to perform, nor were the defendants bound to accept the party so substituted as the one to whom they were to look for performance of the contract; the contract was therefore at an end.

The authority principally relied on in support of this contention was the case of *Robson* v. *Drummond*[1], approved of by this Court in *Humble* v. *Hunter*[2]. In *Robson* v. *Drummond*[1] a carriage having been hired by the defendant of one Sharp, a coachmaker, for five years, at a yearly rent, payable in advance each year, the carriage to be kept in repair and painted once a year by the maker—Robson being then a partner in the business, but unknown to the defendant—on Sharp retiring from the business after three years had expired, and making over all interest in the business and property in the goods to Robson, it was held that the defendant could not be sued on the contract—by Lord Tenterden on the ground that " the defendant might have been induced to enter into the contract by reason of the personal confidence which he reposed in Sharp, and therefore might have agreed to pay money in advance, for which reason the defendant had a right to object to its being performed by any other person; " and by Littledale and Parke, JJ., on the additional ground that the defendant had a right to the personal services of Sharp, and to the benefit of his judgment and taste, to the end of the contract.

In like manner, where goods are ordered of a particular manufacturer, another, who has succeeded to his business, cannot execute the order, so as to bind the customer, who has not been made aware of the transfer of the business, to accept the goods. The latter is entitled to refuse to deal with any other than the manufacturer whose goods he intended to buy. For this *Boulton* v. *Jones*[3] is a sufficient authority. The case of *Robson* v. *Drummond*[4] comes nearer to the present case, but is, we think, distinguishable from it. We entirely concur in the principle on which the decision in *Robson* v. *Drummond*[4] rests, namely, that where a person contracts with another to do work or perform service, and it can be inferred that the person employed has been selected with reference to his individual skill, competency, or other personal qualification, the inability or unwillingness of the party so employed to execute the work or perform the service is a sufficient answer to any demand by a stranger to the original contract of the performance of it by the other party, and entitles the latter to treat the contract as at an end, notwithstanding that the person tendered to take the place of the contracting party may be equally well qualified to do the service. Personal performance is in such a case of the essence of the contract, which, consequently, cannot in its absence be enforced against an unwilling party. But this principle appears to us inapplicable in the present instance, inasmuch as we cannot suppose that in stipulating for the repair of these waggons by the company— a rough description of work which ordinary workmen conversant with the business would be perfectly able to execute—the defendants attached any importance to whether the repairs were done by the company, or by any one with whom the company might enter into a subsidiary contract to do the work. All that the hirers, the defendants, cared for in this stipulation was that the waggons should be kept in repair; it was indifferent to them by whom the

---

[1] (1831), 2 B. & Ad. 303.
[3] (1857), 2 H. & N. 564.

[2] (1848), 12 Q. B. 310.
[4] (1831), 2 B. & Ad. 303.

repairs should be done. Thus if, without going into liquidation, or assigning these contracts, the company had entered into a contract with any competent party to do the repairs, and so had procured them to be done, we cannot think that this would have been a departure from the terms of the contract to keep the waggons in repair. While fully acquiescing in the general principle just referred to, we must take care not to push it beyond reasonable limits. And we cannot but think that, in applying the principle, the Court of Queen's Bench in *Robson* v. *Drummond*[1] went to the utmost length to which it can be carried, as it is difficult to see how in repairing a carriage when necessary, or painting it once a year, preference would be given to one coachmaker over another. Much work is contracted for, which it is known can only be executed by means of subcontracts; much is contracted for as to which it is indifferent to the party for whom it is to be done, whether it is done by the immediate party to the contract, or by someone on his behalf. In all these cases the maxim *Qui facit per alium facit per se* applies.

In the view we take of the case, therefore, the repair of the waggons, undertaken and done by the British Company under their contract with the Parkgate Company, is a sufficient performance by the latter of their engagement to repair under their contract with the defendants. Consequently, so long as the Parkgate Company continues to exist, and, through the British Company, continues to fulfil its obligation to keep the waggons in repair, the defendants cannot, in our opinion, be heard to say that the former company is not entitled to the performance of the contract by them, on the ground that the company have incapacitated themselves from performing their obligations under it, or that, by transferring the performance thereof to others, they have absolved the defendants from further performance on their part.

That a debt accruing due under a contract can, since the passing of the Judicature Acts, be assigned at law as well as equity, cannot since the decision in *Brice* v. *Bannister*[2] be disputed.

We are therefore of opinion that our judgment must be for the plaintiffs for the amount claimed.

---

[1] (1831), 2 B. & Ad. 303.   [2] (1878), 3 Q. B. D. 569.

DISCHARGE OF CONTRACTS

1. BY PERFORMANCE

SUMPTER *v.* HEDGES

HOENIG *v.* ISAACS

Sumpter v. Hedges

[1898] 1 Q.B. 673

A party to an entire contract who has abandoned it after partly performing his obligations can recover nothing for what he has done, unless a new contract entitling him to payment can be inferred from the circumstances.

A. L. SMITH, L.J.   In this case the plaintiff, a builder, entered into a contract to build two houses and stables on the defendant's land for a lump sum.   When the buildings were still in an unfinished state the plaintiff informed the defendant that he had no money, and was not going on with the work any more.   The learned judge has found as a fact that he abandoned the contract.   Under such circumstances, what is a building owner to do ? He cannot keep the buildings on his land in an unfinished state for ever. The law is that, where there is a contract to do work for a lump sum, until the work is completed the price of it cannot be recovered.   Therefore the plaintiff could not recover on the original contract.   It is suggested however that the plaintiff was entitled to recover for the work he did on a *quantum meruit*.[1]   But, in order that that may be so, there must be evidence of a fresh contract to pay for the work already done.   With regard to that, the case of *Munro* v. *Butt*[2] appears to be exactly in point.   That case decides that, unless the building owner does something from which a new contract can be inferred to pay for the work already done, the plaintiff in such a case as this cannot recover on a *quantum meruit*.   In the case of *Lysaght* v. *Pearson*[3], to which we have been referred, the case of *Munro* v. *Butt*[2] does not appear to have been referred to.   There the plaintiff had contracted to erect on the defendant's land two corrugated iron roofs.   When he had completed one of them, he does not seem to have said that he abandoned the contract, but merely that he would not go on unless the defendant paid him for what he had already done.   The defendant thereupon proceeded to erect for himself the second roof.   The Court of Appeal held that there was in that case something from which a new contract might be inferred to pay for the work done by the plaintiff.   That is not this case.   In the case of *Whitaker* v. *Dunn*[4] there was a contract to erect a laundry on defendant's land, and the laundry erected was not in accordance with the contract, but the official referee held that the plaintiff could recover on a *quantum meruit*.   The case came before a Divisional Court, consisting of Lord Coleridge, C.J., and myself, and we said that the decision in *Munro* v. *Butt*[2] applied, and there being no circumstances to justify an inference of a fresh contract the plaintiff must fail.   My brother Collins thinks that that case went to the Court of Appeal, and that he argued it there, and the Court affirmed the decision of the Queen's Bench Division.   I think the appeal must be dismissed.

---

[1] See *infra*, p. 509.
[2] (1858), 8 E. & B. 738.
[3] Not reported, except in Times Newspaper of March 3, 1879.
[4] (1887), 3 T. L. R. 602.

CHITTY, L.J. I am of the same opinion. The plaintiff had contracted to erect certain buildings for a lump sum. When the work was only partly done, the plaintiff said that he could not go on with it, and the judge has found that he abandoned the contract. The position therefore was that the defendant found his land with unfinished buildings upon it, and he thereupon completed the work. That is no evidence from which the inference can be drawn that he entered into a fresh contract to pay for the work done by the plaintiff. If we held that the plaintiff could recover, we should in my opinion be overruling *Cutter* v. *Powell*[1] and a long series of cases in which it has been decided that there must in such a case be some evidence of a new contract to enable the plaintiff to recover on a *quantum meruit*. There was nothing new in the decision in *Pattinson* v. *Luckley*[2], but Bramwell, B., there pointed out with his usual clearness that in the case of a building erected upon land the mere fact that the defendant remains in possession of his land is no evidence upon which an inference of a new contract can be founded. He says : " In the case of goods sold and delivered, it is easy to shew a contract from the retention of the goods ; but that is not so where work is done on real property." I think the learned judge was quite right in holding that in this case there was no evidence from which a fresh contract to pay for the work done could be inferred.

COLLINS, L.J. I agree. I think the case is really concluded by the finding of the learned judge to the effect that the plaintiff had abandoned the contract. If the plaintiff had merely broken his contract in some way so as not to give the defendant the right to treat him as having abandoned the contract, and the defendant had then proceeded to finish the work himself, the plaintiff might perhaps have been entitled to sue on a *quantum meruit* on the ground that the defendant had taken the benefit of the work done. But that is not the present case. There are cases in which, though the plaintiff has abandoned the performance of a contract, it is possible for him to raise the inference of a new contract to pay for the work done on a *quantum meruit* from the defendant's having taken the benefit of that work, but, in order that that may be done, the circumstances must be such as to give an option to the defendant to take or not to take the benefit of the work done. It is only where the circumstances are such as to give that option that there is any evidence on which to ground the inference of a new contract. Where, as in the case of work done on land, the circumstances are such as to give the defendant no option whether he will take the benefit of the work or not, then one must look to other facts than the mere taking the benefit of the work in order to ground the inference of a new contract. In this case I see no other facts on which such an inference can be founded. The mere fact that a defendant is in possession of what he cannot help keeping, or even has done work upon it, affords no ground for such an inference. He is not bound to keep unfinished a building which in an incomplete state would be a nuisance on his land. I am therefore of opinion that the plaintiff was not entitled to recover for the work which he had done. I feel clear that the case of *Whitaker* v. *Dunn*[3], to which reference has been made, was the case which as counsel I argued in the Court of Appeal, and in which the Court dismissed the appeal on the ground that the case was concluded by *Munro* v. *Butt*[4].

---

[1] (1795), 6 Term Rep. 320.
[2] (1875), L. R. 10 Exch. 330.
[3] (1887), 3 T. L. R. 602.
[4] (1858), 8 E. & B. 738.

Hoenig v. Isaacs

[1952] 2 All E.R. 176

If a contract has been substantially performed by one of the parties, the other party cannot treat himself as discharged from his obligations and refuse payment merely because the performance is not in exact accordance with the contract.

APPEAL by the defendant from an order of His Honour Sir Lionel Leach, Official Referee, dated July 20, 1951, on a claim by the plaintiff for the balance of money alleged to be due to him from the defendant for work and labour and materials supplied.

The plaintiff was an interior decorator and furniture designer. The defendant, the owner of a one room flat, employed the plaintiff to decorate it and provide it with furniture, including bedstead and wardrobe and bookcase fitments, for a sum of £750, the terms of payment being " net cash, as the work proceeds; and balance on completion." On April 12, 1950, the defendant paid £150, and on April 19 he paid a further £150. On August 28, the plaintiff said that he had carried out the work in compliance with the contract and requested payment of the balance of £450. The defendant replied complaining of faulty design and bad workmanship, but he sent the plaintiff a further £100, entered into occupation of the flat, and used the furniture. On a claim by the plaintiff for the balance of £350, the defendant alleged that the plaintiff had failed to perform his contract, and, alternatively, that the work was done negligently, unskilfully, and in an unworkmanlike manner. The official referee held that the door of a wardrobe required replacing, and that a bookshelf, which was too short, would have to be re-made, which would require alterations being made to a bookcase. The defendant contended that this was an entire contract which had not been performed, and, therefore, the plaintiff could not recover. The official referee held that there had been a substantial compliance with the contract and that the defendant was liable for £750 less the cost of remedying the defects which he assessed at £55 18s. 2d., and he gave judgment for £294 1s. 10d.

DENNING, L.J.: This case raises the familiar question: Was entire performance a condition precedent to payment? That depends on the true construction of the contract. In this case the contract was made over a period of time and was partly oral and partly in writing, but I agree with the official referee that the essential terms were set down in the letter of April 25, 1950. It describes the work which was to be done and concludes with these words:

" The foregoing, complete, for the sum of £750 net. Terms of payment are net cash, as the work proceeds; and balance on completion."

The question of law that was debated before us was whether the plaintiff was entitled in this action to sue for the £350 balance of the contract price as he had done. The defendant said that he was only entitled to sue on a *quantum meruit*. The defendant was anxious to insist on a *quantum meruit*, because he said that the contract price was unreasonably high. He wished, therefore, to reject that price altogether and simply to pay a reasonable price for all the work that was done. This would obviously mean an inquiry into the value of every item, including all the many items which were in compliance with the contract as well as the three which fell short of it. That is what the defendant wanted. The plaintiff resisted this course and refused to claim on a *quantum meruit*. He said that he was entitled to the balance of £350 less a deduction for the defects.

In determining this issue the first question is whether, on the true construction of the contract, entire performance was a condition precedent to payment. It was a lump sum contract, but that does not mean that entire performance was a condition precedent to payment. When a contract provides for a specific sum to be paid on completion of specified work, the courts lean against a construction of the contract which would deprive the contractor of any payment at all simply because there are some defects or omissions. The promise to complete the work is, therefore, construed as a term of the contract, but not as a condition. It is not every breach of that term which absolves the employer from his promise to pay the price, but only a breach which goes to the root of the contract, such as an abandonment of the work when it is only half done. Unless the breach does go to the root of the matter, the employer cannot resist payment of the price. He must pay it and bring a cross-claim for the defects and omissions, or, alternatively, set them up in diminution of the price. The measure is the amount which the work is worth less by reason of the defects and omissions, and is usually calculated by the cost of making them good: see *Mondel* v. *Steel*[1]; *H. Dakin & Co., Ltd.* v. *Lee*[2], and the notes to *Cutter* v. *Powell*[3] in Smith's Leading Cases, 13th ed., vol. 2, pp. 19–21. It is, of course, always open to the parties by express words to make entire performance a condition precedent. A familiar instance is when the contract provides for progress payments to be made as the work proceeds, but for retention money to be held until completion. Then entire performance is usually a condition precedent to payment of the retention money, but not, of course, to the progress payments. The contractor is entitled to payment *pro rata* as the work proceeds, less a deduction for retention money. But he is not entitled to the retention money until the work is entirely finished, without defects or omissions. In the present case the contract provided for " net cash, as the work proceeds; and balance on completion." If the balance could be regarded as retention money, then it might well be that the contractor ought to have done all the work correctly, without defects or omissions, in order to be entitled to the balance. But I do not think the balance should be regarded as retention money. Retention money is usually only ten per cent., or fifteen per cent., whereas this balance was more than fifty per cent. I think this contract should be regarded as an ordinary lump sum contract. It was substantially performed. The contractor is entitled, therefore, to the contract price, less a deduction for the defects.

Even if entire performance was a condition precedent, nevertheless the result would be the same, because I think the condition was waived. It is always open to a party to waive a condition which is inserted for his benefit. What amounts to a waiver depends on the circumstances. If this was an entire contract, then, when the plaintiff tendered the work to the defendant as being a fulfilment of the contract, the defendant could have refused to accept it until the defects were made good, in which case he would not have been liable for the balance of the price until they were made good. But he did not refuse to accept the work. On the contrary, he entered into possession of the flat and used the furniture as his own,

---

[1] (1841), 8 M. & W. 858.   [2] [1916] 1 K. B. 566.   [3] (1795), 6 Term. Rep. 320.

including the defective items. That was a clear waiver of the condition precedent. Just as in a sale of goods the buyer who accepts the goods can no longer treat a breach of condition as giving a right to reject but only a right to damages, so also in a contract for work and labour an employer who takes the benefit of the work can no longer treat entire performance as a condition precedent, but only as a term giving rise to damages. The case becomes then an ordinary lump sum contract governed by the principles laid down in *Mondel* v. *Steel*[1] and *H. Dakin & Co., Ltd.* v. *Lee*[2]. The employer must, therefore, pay the contract price subject to a deduction for defects or omissions.

I would point out that in these cases the question of *quantum meruit* only arises when there is a breach or failure of performance which goes to the very root of the matter. On any lump sum contract, if the work is not substantially performed and there has been a failure of performance which goes to the root of it, as, for instance, when the work has only been half done, or is entirely different in kind from that contracted for, then no action will lie for the lump sum. The contractor can then only succeed in getting paid for what he has done if it was the employer's fault that the work was incomplete, or there is something to justify the conclusion that the parties have entered into a fresh contract, or the failure of performance is due to impossibility or frustration: see *Appleby* v. *Myers*[3]; *Sumpter* v. *Hedges*[4]; and s. 1 (3) of the Law Reform (Frustrated Contracts) Act, 1943[5]. In such cases the contractor can recover in an action for restitution such sum as he deserves, or in the words of the Act, " such sum . . . as the court considers just." Those cases do not, however, apply in the present case, because in this case the work has been substantially performed. In my opinion, the official referee was right and this appeal should be dismissed.

SOMERVELL and ROMER, L.JJ., delivered judgments to the same effect.

---

2. BY FRUSTRATION

DAVIS CONTRACTORS, LTD. v. FAREHAM URBAN DISTRICT COUNCIL

TSAKIROGLOU & CO. v. NOBLEE & THORL

JOSEPH CONSTANTINE STEAMSHIP LINE, LTD. v. IMPERIAL SMELTING CORPORATION, LTD.

" Frustration occurs whenever the law recognizes that without default of either party a contractual obligation has become incapable of being performed because the circumstances in which performance is called for would render it a thing radically different from that which was undertaken by the contract ": *per* Lord Radcliffe, *infra*, p. 423.

Davis Contractors, Ltd. v. Fareham Urban District Council

[1956] A.C. 696

Early in 1946 the respondents, in contemplation of a building scheme, drew up bills of quantities and a form of tender which indicated the nature of their requirements, and invited inspection of their drawings, specifications

---

[1] (1841), 8 M. & W. 858.
[3] (1867), L. R. 2 C. P. 651.
[5] *Infra*, p. 442.

[2] [1916] 1 K. B. 566.
[4] [1898] 1 Q. B. 673.

and conditions of contract. Contractors wishing to tender for all or part of the projected work were to deliver their tenders on the form prescribed by March 19, 1946.

On March 18 the appellants sent in a signed tender on the appropriate form undertaking the erection of (*inter alia*) 78 houses at Gudgeheath Lane, Fareham, in the county of Southampton, at a price of £92,425 and within the time limits specified. With it went a covering letter of the same date:

DAVIS CONTRACTORS LIMITED
325, Kilburn High Road,
London, N.W.6
18th March, 1946.

RL/JEM
Clerk of the Council,
Fareham Urban District Council,
Westbury Manor,
Fareham,
Hants.

DEAR SIR,

Re Gudgeheath Lane, Fareham.

We have pleasure in enclosing herewith our tender prepared in accordance with your bills of quantities and specifications submitted by your engineer and surveyor for one hundred and fifty two houses on four sites.

Our tender is subject to adequate supplies of material and labour being available as and when required to carry out the work within the time specified.

It is also based on the present published market prices of materials delivered to site and existing established rates of wages in the various trades for the district.

Purchase tax has not been allowed for in our tender and payment of such will form a nett addition to the contract's sum. Also any variation in price of labour or materials will form nett additions or omissions to or from the contract's sum, as may be determined by calculation.

We have based our price for facings on a p.c. amount of 20s. on the present quoted price for Fletton bricks delivered Fareham station. This has been necessary as we have been unable to get firm quotations for facings delivered to site.

Thank you for this opportunity of serving you, and we assure you always of our best attention.

Yours faithfully,
For and on behalf of
DAVIS CONTRACTORS LTD.
(sd.) W. B. W. C. Curd.
Director.
CONTRACTS MANAGER.

The form of tender which the respondents prescribed had appendix I attached to it, bearing the heading:

" Materials and goods to be purchased directly by the contractor in respect of which variation of the contract sum is desired in accordance with clause 68B of the conditions of contract."

There was then a blank space left under two column headings " *Materials or Goods* " and " *Basic Price*." In this blank space the appellants had written the words,

" As terms of letter attached dated March 18, 1946, reference RL/JEM."

There was nothing else in the appendix except a clause limiting to some extent the contractor's right to vary the contract sum in respect of price variations of materials and goods. Negotiations followed and between March 18 and the date when the formal agreement was entered into the appellants in fact supplied the respondents with a detailed schedule of prices, which was intended to constitute the list of materials and goods called for by appendix I, and was accepted. No further reference was apparently made to the letter of March 18.

The building contract was contained in a short agreement under seal dated July 9, 1946, and its main purpose was to identify several documents which had come into existence during or for the purpose of the preceding negotiations. It recited that

"the employer" (the respondents) ". . . has accepted a tender by the contractors" (the appellants) "for the sum of £92,425 8s. 4d. or such other sum as may become due under the contract also having regard to the intended issue to the contractors of variation orders the effect of which it has been estimated by the employer's engineer and surveyor will reduce the actual expenditure based on the rates submitted by the contractor to a sum not exceeding £85,836 0s. 8d. for the construction, completion and maintenance of such works."

By clause 2:

"The following documents shall be deemed to form and be read and construed as part of this agreement, viz. (*a*) the said tender, (*b*) the drawings, (*c*) the general conditions of contract, (*d*) the specification, (*e*) the bill of quantities, (*f*) the schedule of rates and prices (if any)."

By the general conditions the appellants agreed to build 78 houses at Gudgeheath Lane within a period of eight months, completing 40 houses in six months and 70 houses in seven months. There was a penalty clause of £5 a week for every house uncompleted after the contract period.

The work started on June 20, 1946. For various reasons, the chief of them the lack of skilled labour, the work took, not eight but 22 months. The appellants were in due course paid the contract price which, together with stipulated increases and adjustments, amounted to £94,424. They contended, however, that owing to the long delay the contract price had ceased to be applicable, and that they were entitled to a payment on a *quantum meruit* basis.

[The matter went to arbitration.]
The arbitrator set out the contentions of the appellants as follows:

"(1) That the letter of March 18, 1946, became a term and condition of the contract. (2) That in any event the contract was entered into on the basis that adequate supplies of labour and materials would be available at the times required. (3) That because adequate supplies of labour and materials were not available the footing of the contract was removed and the claimants were entitled to be paid on the basis of a *quantum meruit*."

The arbitrator stated the questions of law which he was requested to state for the decision of the court:

"(*a*) Whether the stipulation as to availability of labour and materials made in the claimants' letter of March 18, 1946, became a term of the contract. (*b*) Whether the claimants are entitled to be paid any sum in excess of £94,424 17s. 9d. already paid them."

Upon the matter coming before the court, Lord Goddard, C.J., was of the opinion that the letter of March 18, 1946, was incorporated in the contract, and upon that basis was further of opinion that there was an implied promise by the respondents to pay a further reasonable sum if the conditions of the letter were not satisfied. [On appeal, the Court of Appeal referred the case back to the arbitrator for further findings of fact.]

The arbitrator in his supplemental award dated October 22, 1954, stated the contentions of the appellants, which repeated their previous contentions. The contentions of the respondents included the following:

" (4) That in any event the footing on which the contract was agreed was not so changed that the contract could be declared or treated as void or the claimants be entitled to payment on a *quantum meruit*. (5) That any claim on a *quantum meruit* basis was precluded by reason of the conduct of the parties after a claim for additional payment was first intimated by the claimants. That the respondents so far from allowing the claimants to continue to work on a different basis consistently maintained that the contract was still applicable."

The arbitrator then stated the questions of law for the opinion of the court:

" (1) Whether the stipulation as to the availability of labour and materials made in the claimants' letter of March 18, 1946, became a term of the contract. (2) Whether the claimants are entitled to be paid any sum in excess of the £94,424 17s. 9d. already paid to them, namely, on a *quantum meruit*, by reason of (a) the footing upon which the contract was made having been so changed in the course of its execution that its provisions no longer applied, or (b) an implied term in the contract that it ceases to bind in the circumstances as found. (3) Whether, if the claimants became entitled to be paid any sum in excess of that already paid to them by the respondents, such a claim was barred by the conduct of the parties. . . ."

The arbitrator found that both parties entered into the contract on the basis that adequate supplies of labour and material would be available at the times required, that such supplies were not so available, and that, as the duration of the work was unavoidably extended from a period of eight months to one of 22 months, the footing of the contract was removed.

The Court of Appeal held that the letter of March 18, 1946 was not incorporated in the contract and that the contract was not frustrated. Davis Contractors Ltd. appealed to the House of Lords. The appeal was dismissed.

LORD REID: In order to determine how far the arbitrator's findings are findings of law and therefore subject to review, I think it is necessary to consider what is the true basis of the law of frustration. Generally this has not been necessary: for example, Lord Porter said in *Denny, Mott & Dickson Ltd.* v. *James B. Fraser & Co. Ltd.*[1]: " Whether this result follows from a true construction of the contract or whether it is necessary to imply a term or whether again it is more accurate to say that the result follows because the basis of the contract is overthrown, it is not necessary to decide." These are the three grounds of frustration which have been suggested from time to time, and I think that it may make a difference in two respects which is chosen. Construction of a contract and the implication of a term are questions of law, whereas the question whether the basis of a contract is overthrown, if not dependent on the construction of the contract, might seem to be largely a matter for the judgment of a skilled man comparing what was contemplated with what has happened. And if the question is truly one of construction I find it difficult to see why we should not apply the ordinary rules regarding the admissibility of extrinsic evidence whereas, if it is only a matter of comparing the contemplated with the actual position, evidence might be admissible on a wider basis.

Further, I am not satisfied that the result is necessarily the same whether frustration is regarded as depending on the addition to the contract of an implied term or as depending on the construction of the contract as it stands. Frustration has often been said to depend on adding a term to the contract by implication: for example, Lord Loreburn in *F. A. Tamplin Steamship Co. Ltd.* v. *Anglo-Mexican Petroleum Products Co. Ltd.*[2], after quoting language of Lord Blackburn, said:

---

[1] [1944] A. C. 265, at p. 281; [1944] 1 All E. R. 678.
[2] [1916] 2 A. C. 397, at p. 404.

" That seems to me another way of saying that from the nature of the contract it cannot be supposed the parties, as reasonable men, intended it to be binding on them under such altered conditions. Were the altered conditions such that, had they thought of them, they would have taken their chance of them, or such that as sensible men they would have said ' if that happens, of course, it is all over between us ' ? What, in fact, was the true meaning of the contract ? Since the parties have not provided for the contingency, ought a court to say it is obvious they would have treated the thing as at an end ? "

I find great difficulty in accepting this as the correct approach because it seems to me hard to account for certain decisions of this House in this way. I cannot think that a reasonable man in the position of the seaman in *Horlock* v. *Beal*[1] would readily have agreed that the wages payable to his wife should stop if his ship was caught in Germany at the outbreak of war, and I doubt whether the charterers in the *Bank Line* case[2] could have been said to be unreasonable if they had refused to agree to a term that the contract was to come to an end in the circumstances which occurred. These are not the only cases where I think it would be difficult to say that a reasonable man in the position of the party who opposes unsuccessfully a finding of frustration would certainly have agreed to an implied term bringing it about.

I may be allowed to note an example of the artificiality of the theory of an implied term given by Lord Sands in *James Scott & Sons, Ltd.* v. *Del Sel*[3]: " A tiger has escaped from a travelling menagerie. The milkgirl fails to deliver the milk. Possibly the milkman may be exonerated from any breach of contract; but, even so, it would seem hardly reasonable to base that exoneration on the ground that ' tiger days excepted ' must be held as if written into the milk contract."

I think that there is much force in Lord Wright's criticism in *Denny, Mott and Dickson, Ltd.* v. *James B. Fraser & Co., Ltd.*[4]: " The parties did not anticipate fully and completely, if at all, or provide for what actually happened. It is not possible, to my mind, to say that, if they had thought of it, they would have said : ' Well, if that happens, all is over between us.' On the contrary, they would almost certainly on the one side or the other have sought to introduce reservations or qualifications or compensations."

It appears to me that frustration depends, at least in most cases, not on adding any implied term, but on the true construction of the terms which are in the contract read in light of the nature of the contract and of the relevant surrounding circumstances when the contract was made. There is much authority for this view. In *British Movietonews, Ltd.* v. *London and District Cinemas, Ltd*[5]. Viscount Simon said: " If, on the other hand, a consideration of the terms of the contract, in the light of the circumstances existing when it was made, shows that they never agreed to be bound in a fundamentally different situation which has now unexpectedly emerged, the contract ceases to bind at that point—not because the court in its discretion thinks it just and reasonable to qualify the terms of the contract, but because on its true construction it does not apply in that situation." In *Sir Lindsay Parkinson & Co., Ltd.* v. *Commissioners of Works*[6] Asquith, L.J., said: " In each case a delay or interruption was fundamental enough to transmute the job the contractor had undertaken into a job of a different kind, which the contract did not contemplate and to which it could not apply, although there was nothing in the express language of either contract to limit its operation

---

[1] [1916] 1 A. C. 486.
[2] [1919] A. C. 435.
[3] 1922 S. C. 592, at p. 597.
[4] [1944] A. C. 265, at p. 275.
[5] [1952] A. C. 166, at p. 185.
[6] [1949] 2 K. B. 632, at p. 667; [1950] 1 All E. R. 208.

in this way." I need not multiply citations, but I might note a reference by Lord Cairns so long ago as 1876 to " additional or varied work, so peculiar, so unexpected, and so different from what any person reckoned or calculated upon "[1]. On this view there is no need to consider what the parties thought or how they or reasonable men in their shoes would have dealt with the new situation if they had foreseen it. The question is whether the contract which they did make is, on its true construction, wide enough to apply to the new situation: if it is not, then it is at an end.

In my view, the proper approach to this case is to take from the arbitrator's award all facts which throw light on the nature of the contract, or which can properly be held to be extrinsic evidence relevant to assist in its construction and then, as a matter of law, to construe the contract and to determine whether the ultimate situation, as disclosed by the award, is or is not within the scope of the contract so construed.

The appellants on March 18, 1946, sent to the respondents with their tender a covering letter. I agree with your Lordships that this letter was not incorporated in the contract of July 9, 1946, and I do not think that it can be used in construing this contract. It was simply part of the preliminary negotiations and we do not know and cannot inquire why it was not incorporated in the contract.

The arbitrator has found that both parties " anticipated that there would be available in the building industry a sufficient labour force and a sufficient supply of materials to enable the work specified in the agreement to be carried out substantially within the time stipulated in the agreement." The nature of the contract is such that they must have expected this. The contract required the appellants to complete the work within eight months, and provided for payment of liquidated damages if the appellants failed to do so, subject to the surveyor being required in certain events to allow such additional time as he might deem fair and reasonable: and it was clearly of great importance to the appellants that there should be no substantial delay because any such delay was bound to add considerably to their costs. It appears from the arbitrator's findings that the parties did not make their expectations known to each other, and I do not think that a finding that the parties in fact expected that there would be no substantial delay adds anything material or alters the legal position.

The arbitrator then found that the conditions in which the work had to be carried out were different from those anticipated, in that at all times there was a serious shortage of labour and difficulty in obtaining adequate supplies of bricks and other material. He found that as a result of this shortage, and the consequent delay in completing the work, the actual cost to the appellants of carrying out the contract was £115,233, whereas the sum paid to them under the contract was £94,424. The arbitrator has not awarded the whole of the difference between these sums. He held that to some extent the appellants were themselves to blame, and awarded £17,651 as the additional cost and expense properly and unavoidably incurred by them.

If the contract continued to apply, then the appellants are not entitled to more than they have already received; but if it was brought to an end, then the respondents admit that the appellants are entitled to the sum awarded subject to a very small adjustment.

The arbitrator found that " the respondents accepted the position and allowed the work to continue until finally completed on May 14, 1948,

[1] *Thorn* v. *London Corporation* (1876), 1 App. Cas. 120, at p. 127.

without serious objections by the respondents." I do not think that that means, or was intended by the arbitrator to mean, that at some time while the work was in progress the parties agreed or must be held to have agreed that their contract should no longer apply and that the work should proceed on some other basis. There is no finding as to when any such agreement must be held to have been made, or what were its terms, and there are no facts found from which such an agreement could be inferred. The respondents no doubt recognized that the delays were not due to the fault of the appellants: they made no claim for liquidated damages, and they made no attempt to take the work out of the hands of the appellants, as they could have done if the appellants had been at fault. But that is no ground for inferring an agreement to terminate the contract and proceed on some different basis.

The appellant's case must rest on frustration, the termination of the contract by operation of law on the emergence of a fundamentally different situation. Using the language of Asquith, L.J. (as he then was), which I have already quoted[1], the question is whether the causes of delay or the delays were " fundamental enough to transmute the job the contractor had undertaken into a job of a different kind, which the contract did not contemplate and to which it could not apply." In most cases the time when the new situation emerges is clear; there has been some particular event which makes all the difference. It may be that frustration can occur as a result of gradual change, but, if so, the first question I would be inclined to ask would be when the frustration occurred and when the contract came to an end. It has been assumed in this case that it does not matter at what point during the progress of the work the contract came to an end, and that, whatever the time may have been, if the contract came to an end at some time the whole of the work must be paid for on a *quantum meruit* basis. I do not pursue this matter because the respondents have admitted that if there was frustration at any time the appellants are entitled to the sum awarded. But, even so, I think one must see whether there was any time at which the appellants could have said to the respondents that the contract was at an end, and that if the work was to proceed there must be a new contract, and I cannot find any time from first to last at which they would have been entitled to say that the job had become a job of a different kind which the contract did not contemplate. There is a difficulty about a party being entitled to go on and finish the work without raising the question that a new agreement is necessary, and then maintain that frustration occurred at some time while the work was in progress, but again I do not pursue that matter because it does not arise in view of the course this case has taken.

In a contract of this kind the contractor undertakes to do the work for a definite sum and he takes the risk of the cost being greater or less than he expected. If delays occur through no one's fault that may be in the contemplation of the contract, and there may be provision for extra time being given: to that extent the other party takes the risk of delay. But he does not take the risk of the cost being increased by such delay. It may be that delay could be of a character so different from anything contemplated that the contract was at an end, but in this case, in my opinion, the most that could be said is that the delay was greater in degree than was to be expected. It was not caused by any new and unforeseeable factor or event: the job proved to be more onerous but it never became a job of a different kind from that contemplated in the contract.

---

[1] [1949] 2 K. B. 632, at p. 667. *Supra*, p. 419.

LORD RADCLIFFE: My Lords, I agree that this appeal fails. Of the two main grounds upon which the appellants rely the shorter is that which concerns the question whether their building contract was made subject to a condition as to the availability of adequate supplies of labour and material by incorporating in its terms the relevant part of a letter from the appellants to the respondents dated March 18, 1946. I will deal with that point first. [LORD RADCLIFFE reviewed the evidence and held that the letter in question was not incorporated into the contract. He then turned to the second argument offered by the appellants, based on the doctrine of frustration.]

Before I refer to the facts I must say briefly what I understand to be the legal principle of frustration. It is not always expressed in the same way, but I think that the points which are relevant to the decision of this case are really beyond dispute. The theory of frustration belongs to the law of contract and it is represented by a rule which the courts will apply in certain limited circumstances for the purpose of deciding that contractual obligations, *ex facie* binding, are no longer enforceable against the parties. The description of the circumstances that justify the application of the rule and, consequently, the decision whether in a particular case those circumstances exist are, I think, necessarily questions of law.

It has often been pointed out that the descriptions vary from one case of high authority to another. Even as long ago as 1918 Lord Sumner was able to offer an anthology of different tests directed to the factor of delay alone, and delay, though itself a frequent cause of the principle of frustration being invoked, is only one instance of the kind of circumstance to which the law attends (see *Bank Line, Ltd.* v. *Arthur Capel & Co.*[1]). A full current anthology would need to be longer yet. But the variety of description is not of any importance so long as it is recognized that each is only a description and that all are intended to express the same general idea. I do not think that there has been a better expression of that general idea than the one offered by Lord Loreburn in *F. A. Tamplin Steamship Co., Ltd.* v. *Anglo-Mexican Petroleum Products Co., Ltd.*[2] It is shorter to quote than to try to paraphrase it: " . . . a court can and ought to examine the contract and the circumstances in which it was made, not of course to vary, but only to explain it, in order to see whether or not from the nature of it the parties must have made their bargain on the footing that a particular thing or state of things would continue to exist. And if they must have done so, then a term to that effect will be implied, though it be not expressed in the contract . . . No court has an absolving power, but it can infer from the nature of the contract and the surrounding circumstances that a condition which is not expressed was a foundation on which the parties contracted." So expressed, the principle of frustration, the origin of which seems to lie in the development of commercial law, is seen to be a branch of a wider principle which forms part of the English law of contract as a whole. But, in my opinion, full weight ought to be given to the requirement that the parties " must have made " their bargain on the particular footing. Frustration is not to be lightly invoked as the dissolvent of a contract.

Lord Loreburn ascribes the dissolution to an implied term of the contract that was actually made. This approach is in line with the tendency of English courts to refer all the consequences of a contract to the will of those who made it. But there is something of a logical difficulty in seeing how the parties could even impliedly have provided for something which

---

[1] [1919] A. C. 435, at pp. 457–460.   [2] [1916] 2 A. C. 397, at p. 403.

ex hypothesi they neither expected nor foresaw; and the ascription of frustration to an implied term of the contract has been criticized as obscuring the true action of the court which consists in applying an objective rule of the law of contract to the contractual obligations that the parties have imposed upon themselves. So long as each theory produces the same result as the other, as normally it does, it matters little which theory is avowed (see *British Movietonews, Ltd.* v. *London and District Cinemas, Ltd.*[1], *per* Viscount Simon). But it may still be of some importance to recall that, if the matter is to be approached by way of implied term, the solution of any particular case is not to be found by inquiring what the parties themselves would have agreed on had they been, as they were not, forewarned. It is not merely that no one can answer that hypothetical question: it is also that the decision must be given " irrespective of the individuals concerned, their temperaments and failings, their interest and circumstances[2]." The legal effect of frustration " does not depend on their intention or their opinions, or even knowledge, as to the event[3]." On the contrary, it seems that when the event occurs " the meaning of the contract must be taken to be, not what the parties did intend (for they had neither thought nor intention regarding it), but that which the parties, as fair and reasonable men, would presumably have agreed upon if, having such possibility in view, they had made express provision as to their several rights and liabilities in the event of its occurrence.[4]"

By this time it might seem that the parties themselves have become so far disembodied spirits that their actual persons should be allowed to rest in peace. In their place there rises the figure of the fair and reasonable man. And the spokesman of the fair and reasonable man, who represents after all no more than the anthropomorphic conception of justice, is and must be the court itself. So perhaps it would be simpler to say at the outset that frustration occurs whenever the law recognizes that without default of either party a contractual obligation has become incapable of being performed because the circumstances in which performance is called for would render it a thing radically different from that which was undertaken by the contract. *Non haec in foedera veni.* It was not this that I promised to do.

There is, however, no uncertainty as to the materials upon which the court must proceed. " The data for decision are, on the one hand, the terms and construction of the contract, read in the light of the then existing circumstances, and on the other hand the events which have occurred[5]." In the nature of things there is often no room for any elaborate inquiry. The court must act upon a general impression of what its rule requires. It is for that reason that special importance is necessarily attached to the occurrence of any unexpected event that, as it were, changes the face of things. But, even so, it is not hardship or inconvenience or material loss itself which calls the principle of frustration into play. There must be as well such a change in the significance of the obligation that the thing undertaken would, if performed, be a different thing from that contracted for.

I am bound to say that, if this is the law, the appellants' case seems to me a long way from a case of frustration. Here is a building contract entered

---

[1] [1952] A. C. 166, at p. 184.
[2] *Hirji Mulji* v. *Cheong Yue Steamship Co., Ltd.*, [1926] A. C. 497, at p. 510.
[3] *Ibid.*, at p. 509.
[4] *Dahl* v. *Nelson* (1881), 6 App. Cas. 38, *per* Lord Watson.
[5] *Denny, Mott and Dickson, Ltd.* v. *James B. Fraser & Co., Ltd.*, [1944] A. C. 265, at pp. 274–275, *per* Lord Wright.

into by a housing authority and a big firm of contractors in all the uncertainties of the post-war world. Work was begun shortly before the formal contract was executed and continued, with impediments and minor stoppages but without actual interruption, until the 78 houses contracted for had all been built. After the work had been in progress for a time the appellants raised the claim, which they repeated more than once, that they ought to be paid a larger sum for their work than the contract allowed; but the respondents refused to admit the claim and, so far as appears, no conclusive action was taken by either side which would make the conduct of one or the other a determining element in the case.

That is not in any obvious sense a frustrated contract. But the appellants' argument, which certainly found favour with the arbitrator, is that at some stage before completion the original contract was dissolved because it became incapable of being performed according to its true significance and its place was taken by a new arrangement under which they were entitled to be paid, not the contract sum, but a fair price on *quantum meruit* for the work that they carried out during the 22 months that elapsed between commencement and completion. The contract, it is said, was an eight months' contract, as indeed it was. Through no fault of the parties it turned out that it took 22 months to do the work contracted for. The main reason for this was that, whereas both parties had expected that adequate supplies of labour and material would be available to allow for completion in eight months, the supplies that were in fact available were much less than adequate for the purpose. Hence, it is said, the basis or the footing of the contract was removed before the work was completed; or, slightly altering the metaphor, the footing of the contract was so changed by the circumstance that the expected supplies were not available that the contract built upon that footing became void. These are the findings which the arbitrator has recorded in his supplemental award.

In my view, these are in substance conclusions of law, and I do not think that they are good law. All that anyone, arbitrator or court, can do is to study the contract in the light of the circumstances that prevailed at the time when it was made and, having done so, to relate it to the circumstances that are said to have brought about its frustration. It may be a finding of fact that at the time of making the contract both parties anticipated that adequate supplies of labour and material would be available to enable the contract to be completed in the stipulated time. I doubt whether it is, but, even if it is, it is no more than to say that when one party stipulated for completion in eight months, and the other party undertook it, each assumed that what was promised could be satisfactorily performed. That is a statement of the obvious that could be made with regard to most contracts. I think that a good deal more than that is needed to form a " basis " for the principle of frustration.

The justice of the arbitrator's conclusion depends upon the weight to be given to the fact that this was a contract for specified work to be completed in a fixed time at a price determined by those conditions. I think that his view was that, if without default on either side the contract period was substantially extended, that circumstance itself rendered the fixed price so unfair to the contractor that he ought not to be held to his original price. I have much sympathy with the contractor, but, in my opinion, if that sort of consideration were to be sufficient to establish a case of frustration, there would be an untold range of contractual obligations rendered uncertain and, possibly, unenforceable.

Two things seem to me to prevent the application of the principle of frustration to this case. One is that the cause of the delay was not any new state of things which the parties could not reasonably be thought to have foreseen. On the contrary, the possibility of enough labour and materials not being available was before their eyes and could have been the subject of special contractual stipulation. It was not made so. The other thing is that, though timely completion was no doubt important to both sides, it is not right to treat the possibility of delay as having the same significance for each. The owner draws up his conditions in detail, specifies the time within which he requires completion, protects himself both by a penalty clause for time exceeded and by calling for the deposit of a guarantee bond and offers a certain measure of security to a contractor by his escalator clause with regard to wages and prices. In the light of these conditions the contractor makes his tender, and the tender must necessarily take into account the margin of profit that he hopes to obtain upon his adventure and also any appropriate allowance for the obvious risks of delay. To my mind, it is useless to pretend that the contractor is not at risk if delay does occur, even serious delay. And I think it a misuse of legal terms to call in frustration to get him out of his unfortunate predicament.

VISCOUNT SIMONDS, LORD MORTON OF HENRYTON and LORD SOMERVELL OF HARROW also delivered judgments dismissing the appeal.

Tsakiroglou & Co., Ltd. v. Noblee and Thorl G.m.b.H.

[1961] 2 All E.R. 179

APPEAL by sellers of groundnuts, Tsakiroglou & Co., Ltd., from an order of the Court of Appeal (Sellers, Ormerod and Harman, L.JJ.), dated Mar. 28, 1960, and reported [1960] 2 All E.R. 160, affirming (on different grounds) an order of Diplock, J., dated Dec. 9, 1958, and reported [1959] 1 All E.R. 45, on an award in the form of a Special Case stated pursuant to s. 21 (1) (b) of the Arbitration Act, 1950, by the Board of Appeal of the Incorporated Oil Seed Association.

LORD REID: My Lords, the appellants agreed to sell to the respondents three hundred tons of Sudan groundnuts at £50 per ton c.i.f. Hamburg. Admittedly the groundnuts had to be shipped from Port Sudan. The usual and normal route at the date of the contract was via Suez Canal. Shipment was to be November/December, 1956, but, on Nov. 2, 1956, the canal was closed to traffic and it was not reopened until the following April. It is stated in the Special Case that " the [appellants] could have transported the goods from Port Sudan to Hamburg via the Cape during November or December, 1956." The freight via Suez would have been about £7 10s. per ton. The freight via the Cape was increased by stages. It was £15 per ton after Dec. 13. I shall assume in favour of the appellants that the proper comparison is between £7 10s. and £15 per ton. The appellants refused to ship the goods via the Cape and, on Feb. 9, the respondents gave notice of their intention to buy in against the appellants. The question now is whether, by reason of the closing of the Suez route, the contract had been ended by frustration.

The appellants' first argument was that it was an implied term of the contract that shipment should be via Suez. It is found in the Case that both parties contemplated that shipment would be by that route, but I find nothing in the contract or in the Case to indicate that they intended to make this a term of the contract, or that any such term should be implied; they left the matter to the ordinary rules of law. Admittedly, the ordinary rule is that a shipper must ship by the usual and customary route, or, if there is no such route, then by a practicable and reasonable route. But the appellants' next contention was that this means the usual and customary route at the date of the contract, while the respondents maintain that the rule refers to the time of performance. There appears to be no decided case about this and, perhaps, that is not surprising because the point cannot often arise. Apart from the opinion of MacNair, J., in *Carapanayoti & Co., Ltd.* v. *E. T. Green, Ltd.*[1] and of the Court of Appeal in this case, which are against the appellants, there are a few expressions of opinion on this matter, but I shall not examine them as the precise point may not have been in the minds of their authors, and I am doing no injustice to the appellants because, on the whole, these opinions favour the respondents' contention. Regarding the question as an open one, I would ask which is the more reasonable interpretation of the rule.

If the appellants are right, the question whether the contract is ended does not depend on the extent to which the parties or their rights and obligations are affected by the substitution of the new route for the old. If the new route, made necessary by the closing of the old, is substantially different, the contract would be at an end, however slight the effect of the change might be on the parties. That appears to me to be quite unreasonable; in effect, it means writing the old route into the contract, although the parties have chosen not to say anything about the matter. On the other hand, if the rule is to ascertain the route at the time of performance, then the question whether the seller is still bound to ship the goods by the new route does depend on the circumstances as they affect him and the buyer; whether or not they are such as to infer frustration of the contract. That appears to me much more just and reasonable and, in my opinion, that should be held to be the proper interpretation of the rule.

I turn, then, to consider the position after the canal was closed, and to compare the rights and obligations of the parties thereafter, if the contract still bound them, with what their rights and obligations would have been if the canal had remained open. As regards the sellers, the appellants, the only difference to which I find reference in the Case—and, indeed, the only difference suggested in argument—was that they would have had to pay £15 per ton freight instead of £7 10s. They had no concern with the nature of the voyage. In other circumstances that might have affected the buyers; and it is necessary to consider the position of both parties because frustration operates without being invoked by either party and, if the market price of groundnuts had fallen instead of rising, it might have been the buyers who alleged frustration. There might be cases where damage to the goods was a likely result of the longer voyage which twice crossed the Equator, or, perhaps, the buyer could be prejudiced by the fact that the normal duration of the voyage via Suez was about three weeks, whereas the normal duration via the Cape was about seven weeks. But there is no suggestion in the Case that the longer voyage could damage the groundnuts or that the

---

[1] [1959] 1 Q. B. 131; [1958] 3 All E. R. 115.

delay could have caused loss to these buyers of which they could complain. Counsel for the appellants rightly did not argue that this increase in the freight payable by the appellants was sufficient to frustrate the contract, and I need not, therefore, consider what the result might be if the increase had reached an astronomical figure. The route by the Cape was certainly practicable. There could be, on the findings in the Case, no objection to it by the buyers, and the only objection to it from the point of view of the sellers was that it cost them more; and it was not excluded by the contract. Where, then, is there any basis for frustration? It appears to me that the only possible way of reaching a conclusion that this contract was frustrated would be to concentrate on the altered nature of the voyage. I have no means of judging whether, looking at the matter from the point of view of a ship whose route from Port Sudan was altered from via Suez to via the Cape, the difference would be so radical as to involve frustration, and I express no opinion about that. As I understood the argument, it was based on the assumption that the voyage was the manner of performing the sellers' obligations and that, therefore, its nature was material. I do not think so. What the sellers had to do was simply to find a ship proceeding by what was a practicable and now a reasonable route—if, perhaps, not yet a usual route— to pay the freight and obtain a proper bill of lading, and to furnish the necessary documents to the buyer. That was their manner of performing their obligations, and, for the reasons which I have given, I think that such changes in these matters as were made necessary fell far short of justifying a finding of frustration. I agree that the appellants cannot rely on the provisions of cl. 6 of the contract regarding prevention of shipment. I, therefore, agree that this appeal should be dismissed.

I should, perhaps, add a few words about the finding in the Case that performance by shipping via the Cape of Good Hope was " not commercially or fundamentally different " from performance by shipping via Suez. This cannot be intended to mean that it was neither different commercially nor different fundamentally. Plainly, there is a commercial difference between paying £7 10s. and paying £15 per ton freight. It must mean that performance was not fundamentally different in a commercial sense. But all commercial contracts ought to be interpreted in light of commercial considerations. I cannot imagine a commercial case where it would be proper to hold that performance is fundamentally different in a legal, though not in a commercial, sense. Whichever way one takes it, the ultimate question is whether the new method of performance is fundamentally different, and that is a question of law. The commercial importance of the various differences involved in the change of route—delay, risk to the goods, cost, etc.—is fact on which specific findings by arbitrators are entirely appropriate. But the inference to be drawn on a consideration of all the relevant factors must, in my view, be a matter of law—was there or was there not frustration?

LORD RADCLIFFE: My Lords, I think that the outcome of this appeal depends on a short point. The real issue, as I see it, is to determine how to define the obligation of the appellants, the vendors, under the sale contract of Oct. 4, 1956, so far as it related to shipment of the goods sold and the provision of shipping documents. Once it is settled what that definition should be, there is not much difficulty in seeing what are the legal consequences that should follow, having regard to the facts found for us by the Special Case.

This is a sale of goods on c.i.f. terms. Such a sale involves a variety of obligations, both those written out in the contract itself and those supplied by implication of law for the business efficacy of the transaction. The only sector of these obligations that is relevant for the purpose of this case is the vendor's duty " to procure a contract of affreightment, under which the goods will be delivered at the destination contemplated by the contract " (see *Biddell Brothers* v. *E. Clemens Horst Co.*[1], per Hamilton, J.). Even within this sector, however, there are gaps which the law has to fill in; for instance, what form of contract of affreightment will meet the needs of the transaction, and what route or routes are permissible for the carrying vessel selected ? In the present case, nothing turns on the form of the bill of lading, which is not in evidence; everything turns on the question of route. The written contract makes no condition about this, its only stipulation being that shipment is to be from an East African port, by which we are asked to assume that the parties in fact meant Port Sudan. So the voyage was to begin at Port Sudan and to end at Hamburg. The primary duty under this part of the contract was to despatch the groundnuts by sea from one port to the destination of the other. At the date when the contract was entered into, the usual and normal route for the shipment of Sudanese groundnuts from Port Sudan to Hamburg was via the Suez Canal. It would be unusual and rare for any substantial parcel of Sudanese groundnuts from Port Sudan to Europe to be shipped via the Cape at any time when the Suez Canal was open. The Suez Canal was blocked on Nov. 2, 1956, and remained blocked until April, 1957. Nevertheless, during the months of November/December, 1956, the period in which the vendors had to ship under the contract, it was feasible for them to transport the goods via the Cape of Good Hope. It would have involved a voyage of some 11,137 miles as against 4,386 miles by way of Suez, and it would have meant a rise in freight rate of twenty-five per cent. (and, in the last two weeks of December, one hundred per cent.) above that ruling when the sale contract was made. These differences did not, however, in the opinion of the Board of Appeal of the Incorporated Oil Seed Association who state the Case, render transport by the Cape route commercially or fundamentally different from transport by way of the Suez Canal.

Now, in these circumstances, were the appellants under obligation to procure a bill of lading for the transport of the goods by the Cape route, the Suez Canal not being available ? That depends on how their obligation is defined. It is said on their behalf that the duty of shipment is a duty to ship by the " customary or usual route," a route which can be ascertained as that followed by settled and established practice (see *Kennedy on C.I.F. Contracts* (2nd Edn.), p. 39). Failing express provision on the point by the terms of the contract, that is, in my opinion, a correct general statement of what the law would imply; but I do not accept the further proposition which the appellants' argument requires, namely that, given the existence of such a route at the date of the contract, the whole of the vendor's obligation with regard to shipment is contained in this phrase, " the customary or usual route." Putting aside exceptional cases in which there never has become established any customary route at all from one port to the other, we have to consider the case in which, while there has been a customary route at or before the date of the sale, that route is not available at the time when the vendor is ready to ship. The appellants say that, since the whole

[1] [1911] 1 K. B., at p. 220.

obligation consists in shipping by the customary or usual route, the contract would, in that event, become unenforceable, either because its terms had become impossible of performance or because it was avoided by frustration. In this context, the two alternatives would amount to the same thing. I think, however, that the vendor's obligation has to be determined in the light of matters as they stand at the date of shipment, and it may be proper for him to take a course in these circumstances which it would not have been proper for him to take at the date of the contract.

In my opinion, there is no magic in the introduction of the formula " customary or usual route " to describe the term implied by law. It is only appropriate because it is in ordinary circumstances the test of what it is reasonable to impose on the vendor in order to round out the imperfect form of the contract into something which, as mercantile men, the parties may be presumed to have intended. The corpus of commercial law has been built up largely by this process of supplying from the common usage of the trade what is the unexpressed intention of the parties. It is necessary first to ascertain what is the commercial nature or purpose of the adventure that is the subject of the contract; that ascertained, it has next to be asked what, within this scope, are the essential terms which, so far as not expressed, must be implied in order to make the contract efficacious as a business instrument. The natural way to answer this question is to find out what is the usual thing in the same line of business. Various adjectives or phrases are employed to describe the point of reference. I can quote the following from judicial decisions:—recognised, current, customary, accustomed, usual, ordinary, proper, common, in accordance with custom or practice or usage, a matter of commercial notoriety; and, of course, reasonable. I put " reasonable " last, because I think that the other phrases are at bottom merely instances of what it is reasonable to imply having regard to the nature and purpose of the contract. The basic proposition is, therefore, that laid down by Brett, M.R., in *Sanders* v. *Maclean*[1]: " The stipulations which are inferred in mercantile contracts are always that the party will do what is mercantilely reasonable." Applying that proposition to the present case, I do not think that it is enough for the appellants to point out that the usual, and customary route for the transport of groundnuts from Port Sudan to Hamburg was via the Suez Canal and that, at the date of the sale contract, both parties contemplated that shipment would be by that route. This contract was a sale of goods which involved despatching the goods from Port Sudan to Hamburg; but, of course, the transport was not the whole but only one of the incidents of the contract, in which particular incident neither vendors nor buyers were directly implicated. There was nothing to prevent the vendors from despatching the goods as contracted, unless they were impliedly bound as a term of the contract to use no other route than that of the Suez Canal. I do not see why that term should be implied; and, if it is not implied, the true question seems to me to be, since shipment was due to be made by some route during November/December, whether it was a reasonable action for a mercantile man to perform his contract by putting the goods on board a ship going round the Cape of Good Hope and obtaining a bill of lading on this basis. A man may habitually leave his house by the front door to keep his appointments; but, if the front door is stuck, he would hardly be excused for not leaving by the back. The question,

---

[1] (1883), 11 Q. B. D., at p. 337; 5 Asp. M. L. C., at p. 163.

therefore, is what is the reasonable mercantile method of performing the contract at a time when the Suez Canal is closed, not at a time when it is open. To such a question the test of " the usual and customary route " is ex hypothesi inapplicable.

On the facts found by the Special Case, I think that the answer is inevitable. The voyage would be a much longer one in terms of miles; but length reflects itself in such matters as time of arrival, condition of goods, increase of freight rates. A change of route may, moreover, augment the sheer hazard of the transport. There is nothing in the circumstances of the commercial adventure represented by the appellants' contract which suggests that these changes would have been material. Time was plainly elastic. Not only did the vendors have the option of choosing any date within a two-month period for shipment, but also there was a wide margin within which there might be variations of the speed capacity of the carrying vessel or vessels selected. There was no stipulated date for arrival at Hamburg. Nothing appears to suggest that the Cape voyage would be prejudicial to the condition of the goods or would involve special packing or stowing, nor does there seem to have been any seasonal market to be considered. With all these facts before them, as well as the measure of freight surcharge that would fall to the vendors' account, the Board of Appeal made their finding that performance by shipping on the Cape route was not " commercially or fundamentally different " from shipping via the Suez Canal. We have no material which would make it possible for us to differ from that conclusion.

It has been a matter of debate whether this finding ought to be treated as a finding of fact, by which a court would be bound, or as a holding of law, which, as such, would be open to review. It was treated as the first by the learned trial judge; it was treated more as the second by the Court of Appeal whose view of it was, I think, that, while of the utmost relevance for the determination of the final issue of the case, it did not bind the court so as to dictate what it should decide. So far as the distinction can be made between law and fact, I agree with the Court of Appeal. I regard it as a mixed question of fact and law whether transport via the Cape of Good Hope was so materially different from transport via the Suez Canal that it was not within the range of the c.i.f. contract or, alternatively, was so radically different that it left that contract frustrated. The ultimate conclusion is a conclusion of law, but, in a case of this sort, that conclusion is almost completely determined by what is ascertained as to mercantile usage and the understanding of mercantile men.

I do not believe that in this, as in many other branches of commercial law, it is possible to analyse very precisely where law begins and fact ends. That is because in this field legal obligations and legal rights are largely founded on usage and practice, which, themselves, are established as matters of fact. Many things which are now regarded as settled principles of law originated in nothing more than common mercantile practice, and the existence and terms of this practice have been vouched sometimes by questions put to and answered by special juries, sometimes by the findings and views of commercial arbitrators and sometimes by the bare statements of the judges, founded on their experience at the Bar or on the Bench. It would be difficult, for instance, to separate the judgments on commercial law delivered by three such masters as Lord Esher, Scrutton, L.J., and Lord Sumner from their personal acquaintance with mercantile usages and their translation of the one into the terms of the other. I do not think, therefore, that it is right to be very analytical in distinguishing between questions of law and questions of fact in matters of this kind. Since Lord Mansfield's day, commercial law has been ascertained by a co-operative exchange between judge and jury, and, now that arbitrators have taken the place of juries, I do not think that we can start all over again with an absolute distinction between the respective spheres of judge and arbitrator. Generally speaking, I do not think that a finding in the form which we have here can ever be conclusive on the legal issue. When all necessary facts have been found, it remains a question of law for the court what, on the true construction of the contract, are the obligations imposed or whether, having regard to the terms of the contract and the surrounding circumstances, any particular term is to be implied. But, when the implication of terms depends essentially on what is customary or usual or accepted practice, it is inevitable that the findings of fact, whatever they may be, go virtually the whole way towards determining the legal result.

The finding in this case is, perhaps, unusual in that it does not speak for any usage or practice of trade—ex hypothesi, there was no established usage once the Suez Canal was blocked—but rather for the view of mercantile men as to the significance of adopting the alternative route. It is a summary way of stating that a voyage by that route would not involve any elements of difference that would be regarded as material by persons familiar with the trade. It would be contrary to common sense that a court, which cannot uninstructed assess the commercial significance of, say, a surcharge of £7 10s. per ton for freight in a c.i.f. contract of this kind, should not pay careful attention to such a view from such a source; just as it would be, I think, contrary to principle that a court should regard a view so expressed as finally conclusive of the legal issue. I must add that I do not think that such a finding is altogether satisfactory for the purposes of a Special Case. It is, in essence, a summary of the commercial significance of several separate aspects of the Cape route as contrasted with the Suez Canal route, and it is embarrassing for a court which has to answer the question raised by the Case to have before it only the summary and not the arbitrators' findings on the individual aspects which make up the conclusion. I can see that, if this form came into general use, a court might feel obliged to send back the Case containing it for further and more explicit findings. It would have been better if the Special Case had identified the several aspects of difference, length, time, cost, risk, etc., which, as it is, the court is left to infer, and had made with regard to them, both separately and together, the finding that was clearly intended that they were not significant from the mercantile point of view.

I agree with the opinion already expressed by my noble and learned friends who have preceded me that the exception clause, cl. 6 of the contract, does not apply. I would dismiss the appeal.

VISCOUNT SIMONDS, LORD HODSON and LORD GUEST delivered judgments to the same effect.

Joseph Constantine Steamship Line, Ltd. v. Imperial Smelting Corporation, Ltd.

[1941] 2 All E.R. 165

An essential feature of frustration is that it should not have been caused by the act of either of the contracting parties. If it is so caused the doctrine will not apply, and the party to whose fault or choice the frustrating act is

due is not discharged from the contract. But the burden of proving such
" self-induced frustration " lies on the party who seeks to enforce the contract: he makes the allegation and he must prove it.

APPEAL by the shipowners from a judgment of the Court of Appeal (Sir
Wilfrid Greene, M.R., Scott and Goddard, L.JJ,), dated June 18, 1940, and
reported [1940] 3 All E.R. 211, reversing a decision of Atkinson, J., dated
March 1, 1940, and reported [1940] 2 All E.R. 46.

LORD WRIGHT: My Lords, this appeal has to deal with an award of an
arbitrator in which he states for the decision of the court the question
whether, on the facts as found, and on the true construction of the charter-
party, the respondents in this appeal are entitled to damages from the
appellants for non-performance of the charterparty. The dispute arose
out of an explosion which occurred in the auxiliary boiler of the appellants'
steamship *Kingswood* while she was anchored in the roads of Port Pirie.
She had arrived there in pursuance of a charterparty dated Aug. 5, 1936,
made between the appellants as owners and the respondents as charterers.
Under it, she was to be ready to load a full ore cargo at Port Pirie at any
customary wharf or wharves as ordered for carriage to a port or ports in
England or Europe. She was expected to arrive at Port Pirie about the end
of Dec., 1936, or early Jan., 1937. On Dec. 26, 1936, she anchored in the
roads of Port Pirie, having sailed in ballast from Lorenzo Marques. It was
agreed between the parties that the *Kingswood* should remain at her anchorage until Jan. 4, 1937, and then proceed to her loading berth, on arrival at
which time should count. While she still lay at the anchorage, and before
she became an arrived ship, the explosion occurred in the auxiliary boiler.
It was of unprecedented character, in the words of the arbitrator, and took
place within the boiler. The arbitrator found that it was due to the fact
that there was a sudden opening of communication between the water and
steam space and one or both of the combustion chambers. The energy
released was such that the main boilers situated aft of the auxiliary boiler
were set aft by the concussion of the explosion 4 ft. and 5 ft. 6 ins. respectively,
at which points their movement was arrested, whereas the auxiliary boiler
itself was projected forward through two watertight bulkheads, finally
piercing the collision bulkhead and breaking the shell plates at the starboard
bow. The damage to the steamer was so serious that the appellants gave
notice that they could not perform the charterparty. The respondents then
claimed damages in the arbitration.

It was admitted in the arbitration that the delay caused by the damage
to the steamer was such as to frustrate the commercial object of the adventure.
The appellants resisted the claim on the ground that the frustration released
them from liability for further performance. The respondents contested
this defence on the ground that such a defence was only maintainable if the
frustration took place without fault on the part of the appellants, and that it
was for the appellants to show absence of fault. There had in fact been a
Board of Trade inquiry, but the arbitrator observed that neither those who
were responsible for conducting the Board of Trade inquiry nor any of the
witnesses who gave evidence before him claimed to be able to state with any
certainty the causes of the disaster or the sequence of events which led up to
it, and that no sequence of events which was other than improbable was
suggested as capable of having given rise to it. The arbitrator stated three
principal theories of the disaster which had been put forward, but the most
he could say was that, though each theory might be possibly correct, he was

not satisfied by it.   He summed up the final result in the words: " I am not satisfied that the true cause of the disaster has as yet been suggested." Subject to the case stated, he awarded in favour of the respondents.

Thus, the question has come before the court whether, in the case of an admitted frustration of the adventure, without default of either party being proved, the promisors—in this case, the appellants—are liable in damages as for breach of contract.   Atkinson, J., before whom the special case came in the King's Bench Division, decided in favour of the appellants, on the ground that no default was established, but the casualty was unexplained, and accordingly he set aside the arbitrator's award.   His decision was overruled by the Court of Appeal and the arbitrator's award was restored. In the Court of Appeal, Scott, L.J., in giving the leading judgment, said, at p. 213:

> " A party *prima facie* guilty of a failure to perform his contract cannot escape under the plea of frustration unless he proves that the frustration occurred without his default.   There is no frustration in the legal sense *unless he proves affirmatively* that the cause was not brought into operation by his default."

The gist of the whole judgment, which is very brief, is contained in the words which I have italicised.   No authority is cited.

The statement of the principle by Scott, L.J., is manifestly different from the statement by Blackburn, J., in *Taylor* v. *Caldwell*[1]:

> " The principle seems to us to be that, in contracts in which the performance depends on the continued existence of a given person or thing, a condition is implied that the impossibility of performance arising from the perishing of the person or thing, shall excuse the performance."

He justified his conclusion on the ground that, by the nature of the contract, it was apparent that the parties contracted on the basis of the continued existence of the music hall, that being essential to the performance, because it was in that building that the preformance was to take place.   From this the condition releasing the parties was to be implied by law.   Blackburn, J., elsewhere in his judgment added as a sort of warning at p. 840, " without fault of either party."   Clearly a party to a contract who by his fault has caused the impossibility cannot take advantage of his own wrong.   In such a case, he has prevented performance in the substantial sense, as in the illustration given by Willes, J., in *Inchbald* v. *Western Neilgherry Coffee, Tea, and Cinchona Plantation Co., Ltd.*[2], of " the case in *Bulstrode* where the defendant contracted to deliver to the plaintiff a horse, but poisoned him before delivery," and was held liable in damages because he had prevented the contemplated performance.

However, Blackburn, J., though he qualified the rule he stated by excepting the fault or default of the contractor, or of either party, did not add that the defendant relying on impossibility of performance must prove affirmatively that the impossibility was not due to his own default.   The Court of Appeal, in so stating the rule, have made a vital change in the rule. I must consider what justification there is for that change.   In order to do so, I must briefly explain my conception of what is meant in this context by impossibility of performance, which is the phrase used by Blackburn, J. In more recent days, the phrase more commonly used is " frustration of the contract," or, more shortly, " frustration."   " Frustration of the contract," however, is an elliptical expression.   The fuller and more accurate phrase is " frustration of the adventure or of the commercial or practical purpose of

---

[1] (1863), 3 B. & S. 826, at p. 839.   [2] (1864), 17 C. B. N. S. 733, at p. 741.

the contract." This change in language corresponds to a wider conception of impossibility, which has extended the rule beyond contracts which depend on the existence, at the relevant time, of a specific object, as in the instances given by Blackburn, J., to cases where the essential object does indeed exist, but its condition has by some casualty been so changed as to be not available for purposes of the contract, either at the contract date or, if no date is fixed, within any time consistent with the commercial or practical adventure. For the purposes of the contract the object is as good as lost. Another case, often described as frustration, is where by state interference or similar over-riding intervention the performance of the contract has been interrupted for so long a time as to make it unreasonable for the parties to be required to go on with it. Yet another illustration is where the actual object still exists and is available, but the object of the contract as contemplated by both parties was its employment for a particular purpose, which has become impossible, as in the Coronation cases. In these and similar cases, where there is not, in the strict sense, impossibility by some casual happening, there has been so vital a change in the circumstances as to defeat the contract. What Willes, J., in *Inchbald's* case[1] described as substantial performance is no longer possible. The common object of the parties is frustrated. The contract has perished *quoad* any rights or liabilities subsequent to the change. The same is true where there has been a vital change of the law, either statutory or common law, operating on the circumstances, as, for instance, where the outbreak of war destroys a contract legally made before the war, but which, when war breaks out, cannot be performed without trading with the enemy. I have given this bare catalogue to illustrate the application in practice of the doctrine of frustration, in order to show how wide and various is the range of circumstances to which it may extend, and how manifold are the complications involved in the rule laid down by the Court of Appeal that there is an affirmative onus of disproving fault on the party claiming to rely on frustration.

The suggested rule seems to me to be both anomalous and unreasonable. The doctrine of frustration is intended to achieve a just and reasonable result. Blackburn, J., in *Taylor* v. *Caldwell*[2] starts his judgment by referring to what he regards as the general rule of English law that a party who positively contracts to do a thing must perform it or pay damages even though, by unforeseen accidents, performance has become impossible, and a *dictum*, unnecessary to the decision, of the Court of King's Bench in *Paradine* v. *Jane*[3], is often quoted:

> " . . . when the party by his own contract creates a duty or charge upon himself, he is bound to make it good, if he may, notwithstanding any accident by inevitable necessity, because he might have provided against it by his contract."

I am not clear what " if he may " means. It may mean " legally may," but the reference to inevitable accident seems inconsistent with reading " if he may " as reserving impossibility. However, the results of holding a man to the absolute terms of a contract would often be so unjust that from early times as the examples of Blackburn, J., in *Taylor* v. *Caldwell* show, the courts set themselves to avoid these results wherever justice seemed to require it. The doctrine of frustration is thus, in the words of Lord Sumner in *Hirji Mulji* v. *Cheong Yue S.S. Co.*[4], at p. 510:

---

[1] (1864), 17 C. B. N. S. 733.
[3] (1647), Aleyn, 26, at p. 27.
[2] (1863), 3 B. & S. 826.
[4] [1926] A. C. 497, at p. 510.

" . . . a device by which rules as to absolute contracts are reconciled with a special exception which justice demands."

It is true that a contract absolute in terms may be absolute also in effect. The contractor, if he cannot perform, must pay damages. *Prima facie*, the actual language governs. However, a contract absolute in terms is not necessarily absolute in effect. It is in all cases a question of construction, as Lord Cranworth, L.C., pointed out in *Couturier* v. *Hastie*[1], at p. 681, a case where, under a contract for the sale of goods, the goods had perished at the date of the contract, both parties being then ignorant of the fact. Lord Cranworth, L.C., said that, looking at the contract alone, what the parties contemplated, those who bought and those who sold, was that there was an existing something to be bought and sold at the time of the contract. The buyer could not be held liable for the price, or the seller for failure to deliver. The court having thus construed the contract, both parties were held, in the event, to be discharged in law. This rule admits of clear and simple statement. This is done in the Sale of Goods Act, 1893, s. 6. Sect. 7 deals with the analogous case of an agreement to sell specific goods. If they perish, without any fault on the part of the seller or buyer, before the risk passes to the buyer, the agreement is thereby avoided. In the same way, the general law as to impossibility or frustration might be stated in positive terms. It is a question of the construction of the particular contract whether the obligation is absolute or whether it is qualified. It is thus seen that the court is not claiming to exercise a dispensing power, or to modify or alter contracts. The parties did not express the qualification because they did not think of the possibility of the occurrence, but, as Lord Watson said in *Dahl* v. *Nelson, Donkin & Co.*[2]:

" . . . when one or other of these possibilities becomes a fact, the meaning of the contract must be taken to be not what the parties did intend (for they had neither thought nor intention regarding it) but that which the parties, as fair and reasonable men, would presumably have agreed upon if, having such possibility in view, they had made express provision as to their several rights and liabilities in the event of its occurrence."

In short, in ascertaining the meaning of the contract and its application to the actual occurrences, the court has to decide, not what the parties actually intended, but what, as reasonable men, they should have intended. The court personifies for this purpose the reasonable man. In the words of Lord Sumner in *Hirji Mulji* v. *Cheong Yue S.S. Co.*[3]:

" An event occurs, not contemplated by the parties and therefore not expressly dealt with in their contract, which, when it happens, frustrates their object. Evidently it is their common object that has to be frustrated, not merely the individual advantage which one party or the other might have gained from the contract. If so, what the law provides must be a common relief from this common disappointment and an immediate termination of the obligations as regards future performance. This is necessary because otherwise the parties would be bound to a contract, which is one which they did not really make. If it were not so, a doctrine designed to avert unintended burdens, would operate to enable one party to profit by the event and to hold the other, if he so chose, to a new obligation."

Then Lord Sumner added, at p. 510, that rights and wrongs which have already come into existence remain, and the contract remains to give effect to them. I have quoted these statements of law to emphasise that the court is exercising its powers, when it decides that a contract is frustrated, in order

---

[1] (1856), 5 H. L. Cas. 673, at p. 681.   [2] (1881), 6 App. Cas. 38, at p. 59.
[3] [1926] A. C. 497, at p. 507.

to achieve a result which is just and reasonable. It would indeed be strange if it clogged its decision with the qualification which the Court of Appeal would impose, but which seems to me, as I shall seek to explain, inconvenient and unreasonable . . . [LORD WRIGHT then explained why he felt it unnecessary in the instant case to discuss the rationale of frustration[1], and continued] . . .

There is another aspect of the doctrine of frustration which I find it difficult to reconcile with the decision of the Court of Appeal. Frustration operates automatically. It does not depend on the choice or election of the parties to the contract. If the court holds that the meaning of the contract is such that its life is dependent on the existence, or continuance in existence, of a thing or state of things and then finds in fact that the frustrating circumstance has come to pass because the thing or state of things has not existed at the date of the contract, or has ceased to exist at some later material date, it follows by operation of law that the contract was either void to begin with or has become avoided, to use the language of the Sale of Goods Act, 1893, ss. 6, 7. This position must accordingly be distinguished from a somewhat analogous, but really quite different, position, which arises when a contract is terminated by the injured party, who rescinds it on the ground of a fundamental breach by the other party, and who further claims damages for the breach while treating it as no longer binding for the future. Such a procedure involves a choice or option by the party who rescinds. In the case of frustration, however, the contract is ended and dead simply by the frustrating event. If the parties choose to go on with it, that is in truth entering into a new contract. This is clearly stated by Lord Sumner in the passage I have quoted above from *Hirji Mulji* v. *Cheong Yue S.S. Co.*[2]. The position of the parties ought to be determined at once, and an indefinite suspense avoided. This result, however, is just what the decision of the Court of Appeal would prevent, because, according to the decision, it cannot be known whether there has been frustration in a legal sense unless and until it is proved affirmatively by one party or the other that the frustration was not brought into operation by his default.

In the Court of Appeal, Scott, L.J., begins his judgment by referring to the fact that there were no exceptions in the charterparty relevant to the facts. That is true enough. The charter was wholly executory, and the exception did not operate until the vessel was placed at the charterers' disposal, which never took place. However, that is not directly material on the question of frustration if the court is satisfied that the contract, though absolute in terms, is not absolute in fact. If, in virtue of the doctrine of frustration, the court holds that the contract is dissolved, the contract as to future performance is at an end and the exceptions go with it. Frustration, if it occurs, is an overriding event. Exceptions can only be relevant at an earlier stage in the controversy, because they may be inconsistent with the idea that the contract admitted of the doctrine of frustration being applied. This aspect was discussed by Lord Finlay, Viscount Haldane and Lord Sumner in *Bank Line, Ltd.* v. *Arthur Capel & Co.*[3]. Exceptions, however, may be important at a late stage as excluding fault if the frustrating event was induced by what, apart from the exceptions, would be an actionable breach of contract. I need not further discuss that aspect here. There

---

[1] See the discussion by Lord Reid and Lord Radcliffe in *Davis Contractors, Ltd.* v. *Fareham Urban District Council, supra*, pp. 418–423.

[2] [1926] A. C. 497. [3] [1919] A. C. 435.

are no exceptions to be considered. Scott, L.J., seems, however, to be leading up to the proposition that frustration is the only possible defence and then excluding it, not on the ground that the appellants cannot rely on their own fault if that had been proved, but on the ground that, though no fault was proved, they had not affirmatively proved absence of fault. I think that Scott, L.J., is basing his decision on the view that affirmative proof of absence of fault is an essential part of the case of the party relying on frustration, so that, if he fails to establish it, there is no case to go to the jury, even though in all other aspects impossibility or frustration is established, as, in the present case, it is indeed admitted.

I have tried to find authority for the rule enunciated by the Court of Appeal, but have found none either in English or in American cases or in the writings of eminent legal authors. Cases in which the courts have refused to give relief on the ground of frustration because the frustration was due to the fault of the promisor or of either party, or have considered the question, are very rare in the English reports. In the vast majority of cases, questions of responsibility do not arise. There is the observation of Lord Sumner in *Bank Line, Ltd.* v. *Arthur Capel & Co.*[1], where the facts did not raise the question:

> " I think it is now well settled that the principle of frustration of an adventure assumes that the frustration arises without blame or fault on either side. Reliance cannot be placed on a self-induced frustration; indeed, such conduct might give the other party the option to treat the contract as repudiated."

In *Mertens* v. *Home Freeholds Co.*[2], a builder was sued for damages for failing to complete a building which he had agreed to erect. He pleaded by way of defence that he was discharged from further performance by a refusal of the Minister of Munitions to give a licence to proceed under the Defence of the Realm Regulations existing in 1916. The defendant had applied for a licence, but it was refused because he had intentionally (as it was found), in order to get out of a losing contract, delayed in the work. It was held by the Court of Appeal, reversing the decision of the Divisional Court, that the defence failed. Lord Sterndale, M.R., without any precise examination of the doctrine of frustration, proceeded on the broad common-sense view that a man could not take advantage, by way of defence to an action for breach of contract, of circumstances as excusing him from further performance of the contract if he had brought those circumstances about himself. Lord Sterndale, M.R., observed that, in *Taylor* v. *Caldwell*[3], if the defendant had burned down the music hall himself, he would not have been entitled to say that the subject-matter was gone and the contract frustrated.   It might be added, however, that no one until now had gone so far as to decide or suggest that the defendant could not have relied on the destruction of the music hall unless he had affirmatively proved that he was not responsible for it and was not in fault. The conclusion of Lord Sterndale, M.R., followed from the facts proved, which showed actual fault on the part of the defendant.

In *Maritime National Fish, Ltd.* v. *Ocean Trawlers, Ltd.*[4], a similar conclusion was reached. The case was somewhat peculiar. The defendants chartered the plaintiffs' trawler, but, it was held, on the basis that it could be used for trawling with the use of otter or similar trawling gear. That could not be done without a licence. A licence was refused, because the defendants

---

[1] [1919] A. C. 435, at p. 452.   [2] [1921] 2 K. B. 526.
[3] (1863), 3 B. & S. 826.   [4] [1935] A. C. 524.

were not permitted to obtain licences for more than three trawlers, and had applied for and obtained licences for three trawlers of their own, thus making it impossible to obtain a licence for the plaintiffs' trawler. The Privy Council held that the defendants were liable. The result is shortly stated at p. 531:

" . . . it was the appellants' own default which frustrated the adventure: the appellants cannot rely on their own default to excuse them from liability under the contract."

That was all that was necessary for the decision of the case. No question of onus of proof was raised, because all the facts were before the court. Earlier in the judgment, the Privy Council had said at p. 530:

" The essence of ' frustration ' is that it should not be due to the act or election of the party."

They had gone on to observe that Lord Sumner in *Hirji Mulji* v. *Cheong Yue S.S. Co.*[1] had quoted from *Dahl* v. *Nelson, Donkin & Co.*[2] the reference of Lord Blackburn to frustration as a matter " caused by something for which neither party was responsible," and again had quoted the words of Brett, J., which postulate that one of the conditions of frustration is that it should be " without any default of either party." But for such expressions of opinion, it would be tempting to say that the more logical view might be that there are two elements to be considered—namely, (i) impossibility or frustration under the contract and the facts, and (ii) the causation of that impossibility or frustration, whether or not it is imputable to the fault of either party. The question has generally been approached from the point of view of a party relying on frustration as an excuse for failure to perform his contract, and, obviously, if frustration means not only that performance has become impossible, but that neither party is responsible, there can be no frustration in that sense unless both conditions are fulfilled. It is that definition which English law seems to have accepted, and I think the Court of Appeal must have proceeded upon it. However, I can conceive a case in which the injured party, instead of electing to rescind on the ground of the other party's breach and claiming damages for a repudiation, might wish to rely on frustration as involving automatically the destruction of the contract and at the same time claim damages for the breach of contract which has frustrated and destroyed the contract, except so far as it remains alive to enforce rights accrued under it. So far as I know, such a case has never arisen, but, logically, it might be open, if the authorities have not excluded it. This way of looking at the matter might explain the reference to the fault of either party, instead of the fault of the party relying upon the doctrine, though " either party " may simply mean " one party or the other, if either is responsible." This view of the matter would obviously be fatal to the conclusion of the Court of Appeal, because there would then be two separate issues to be separately proved by the parties, who severally raised the one or the other. However, I do not desire to decide the question in this appeal on that debatable or untenable ground. The appeal can, I think, be decided, according to the generally accepted view that frustration involves as one of its elements absence of fault, by applying the ordinary rules as to onus of proof. If frustration is viewed, as I think it can be, as analogous to an exception, since it is generally relied upon as a defence to a claim for failure to perform a contract, the same rule will properly be applied to it as

[1] [1926] A. C. 497. [2] (1881), 6 App. Cas. 38.

to the ordinary type of exceptions. The defence may be rebutted by proof of fault, but the onus of proving fault will rest on the plaintiff. This is merely to apply the familiar rule which is applied, for instance, where a carrier by sea relies on the exception of perils of the seas. If the goods owner then desires to rebut that *prima facie* defence on the ground of negligence or other fault on the part of the shipowner, it rests on the goods owner to establish the negligence or fault. Thus, on the view most favourable to the conclusion at the Court of Appeal, I still reject it. In addition, the ordinary rule is that a man is not held guilty of fault unless fault is established and found by the court. This rule, which is sometimes described as the presumption of innocence, is no doubt peculiarly important in criminal cases or matters, but it is also true in civil disputes. Thus, it was said in *Thomas* v. *Thomas*[1], by Wood, V.-C.:

"...possession is never considered adverse if it can be referred to a legal title."

I need not multiply citations for a principle familiar to lawyers. There is, for example, no presumption of fraud. It must be alleged and proved. So also of other wrongful acts or breaches of contract. If it is necessary, in order to defend a claim, to prove that it was a case of *felo de se*, and not merely innocent suicide while of unsound mind, the full fact must be affirmatively proved. An illustration perhaps more germane is afforded by the rules as to the onus of proof in cases of unseaworthiness. If at the end of the case it is not ascertainable on the evidence that the real cause of the loss was unseaworthiness, the defence must fail. The maxim *respice finem* applies, though there may be provisional presumptions, shifting the onus of proof from time to time during the progress of the case. This is well illustrated in *Ajum Goolam Hossen & Co.* v. *Union Marine Insurance Co.*[2], an action on a marine insurance policy for the loss of a ship which had sunk through causes not explained. The defence was that the ship was unseaworthy. The underwriters showed facts which raised a presumption in favour of unseaworthiness, and shifted at that stage the onus of proof, but at the end the court held that the real cause of the loss was unknown, that unseaworthiness was not proved, and that the defence failed. In the same way, if negligence is alleged to override the defence of excepted perils, it must be alleged and proved affirmatively. If the matter is left in doubt when all the evidence has been heard, the party who takes upon himself to affirm fault must fail. If what Scott, L.J., meant was that the failure to tender the *Kingswood* to the charterers in time for the agreed adventure was such a fundamental breach that it could only be excused by affirmative proof of absence of fault, I cannot agree with him.

It is clear that the rule which the Court of Appeal laid down would in many cases work serious injustice and nullify the beneficial operation of the doctrine of frustration which has been somewhat empirically evolved with the object of doing what is reasonable and fair, as I have already explained. That the rule adopted by the Court of Appeal is inconvenient seems to me to be obvious. It is true that in many cases of frustration there is little or no room for human activity. As instances, I might mention earthquakes and unusual floods. In other cases, there is little room for intervention by the parties, such as in case of governmental requisition, or the refusal of a licence. It cannot be, however, that in any of these cases the party claiming that the contract is frustrated has to prove affirmatively

---

[1] (1855), 2 K. & J. 79, at p. 83.   [2] [1901] A. C. 362.

that he has not caused or induced the frustration, and, where natural forces have operated, there may still be room for inquiry. If a ship, however, is lost with all hands in a cyclone, must the shipowners establish affirmatively that the master did not receive or ignored warnings of the danger area? There may be many maritime losses in which evidence as to how they happened is impossible. If a ship is torpedoed with all hands, must the shipowner prove affirmatively absence of fault, such as that a light was not shown on the ship, or that the ship obeyed the convoy regulations? In any case of unexplained sinking, it may be impossible to exclude the possibility of fault on the part of the owner, as in *Ajum Goolam Hossen & Co.* v. *Union Marine Insurance Co.*[1], but indeed the present is a sufficiently good illustration of an unprecedented and unexplained casualty where the real cause cannot be ascertained even after prolonged and exhaustive inquiry.

On the ruling of the Court of Appeal, the shipowner has placed upon him the unusual task of proving a negative. It is sought to say that the rule is not anomalous because of some other cases in which a party is required to prove a negative, but what are cited as parallels are so different and are so few in number as to emphasise the general rule. Thus the law as to the liability of a bailee depends on the special obligation which the law has imposed on him from ancient times. It has recently been discussed by the Court of Appeal in *Brook's Wharf and Bull Wharf, Ltd.* v. *Goodman Brothers.*[2] If the bailee fails duly to redeliver the goods, he must, in the absence of exceptions, show that he has taken reasonable care in keeping them. Similarly the liability of a common carrier depends, according to the old law, on the custom of the realm, like that of the innkeeper. Under this special rule, a carrier is an insurer who is absolutely liable for the safe carriage of the goods unless he can explain the loss as due to an act of God, the King's enemies, or inherent vice. In modern times, the practice of having special contracts has been superimposed on the custom of the realm. These contracts contain exceptions. If the carrier pleads an exception, the goods owner may counter by pleading the fault of the carrier, but the onus of proving that, as also of proving an allegation of unseaworthiness, is, as I have already explained, on the goods owner who makes it. The provisions of the Merchant Shipping Act, 1894, particularly sects. 502 and 503, which concede to a shipowner the right by appropriate proceedings to limit the damages for which he is otherwise responsible under the contract to goods owners or passengers, require as a condition of this privilege that he should show that the casualty happened without his actual fault or privity. All these and similar cases are obviously different and depend on special contracts or statutes. They do not give any support for the rule adopted by the Court of Appeal.

The Court of Appeal do not define what in this context is the meaning of fault or default. In the Sale of Goods Act, 1893, the word " fault " as used in sects. 6 and 7 is defined as meaning " wrongful act or default." That is not perhaps very helpful, but in *Blairmore Sailing Ship Co.* v. *Macredie*[3] Lord Watson observed, at p. 607:

" The rule of law applicable to contracts is that neither of the parties can by his own act or default defeat the obligations which he has undertaken to fulfil."

In the passages cited above from *Inchbald's case*[4], Willes, J., gave as an instance

---

[1] [1901] A. C. 362.
[2] [1937] 1 K. B. 534.
[3] [1898] A. C. 593.
[4] (1864), 17 C. B. N. S. 733, at p. 741.

of a party preventing performance the case of a man poisoning before delivery a horse which he had promised to deliver. Lord Sumner, in speaking of a self-induced frustration, has clearly in mind positive acts against the faith of the contract which amount to a repudiation and would justify rescission. This test would apply to *Mertens* v. *Home Freeholds Co.*[1] and to *Maritime National Fish, Ltd.* v. *Ocean Trawlers, Ltd.*[2] On the other hand, mere negligence seems never to have been suggested as sufficient to constitute fault in this connection. In *Taylor* v. *Caldwell*[3], where the fire was described as accidental, no one suggested an inquiry whether any servant of the defendant had negligently caused the fire, and in the cases of personal incapacity defeating a contract for personal service, like *Poussard* v. *Spiers and Pond*[4], no investigation seems ever to have been suggested whether the party claiming to be excused was careful of his or her health. Even there, however, a case of gross delinquency might perhaps be construed as amounting to a repudiation of the obligations of the contract. I do not here think it necessary to attempt the definition. This difficulty or absence of definition makes the rule enunciated by the Court of Appeal even more open to objection. In my opinion, this is a case in which it is found that there has been an unexplained casualty frustrating the contract. The real cause cannot be ascertained. No fault is shown against the appellants. I think that they are entitled to rely on the frustration as a defence to the claim. The judgment of the Court of Appeal should, in my opinion be set aside and that of Atkinson, J. restored.

VISCOUNTS SIMON and MAUGHAM, LORD RUSSELL of KILLOWEN and LORD PORTER delivered similar judgments.

LAW REFORM (FRUSTRATED CONTRACTS) ACT, 1943

(6 and 7 Geo. 6, c. 40)

[5th August, 1943]

An Act to amend the law relating to the frustration of contracts.

1. *Adjustment of rights and liabilities of parties to frustrated contracts:*

(1) Where a contract governed by English law has become impossible of performance or been otherwise frustrated, and the parties thereto have for that reason been discharged from the further performance of the contract, the following provisions of this section shall, subject to the provisions of section two of this Act, have effect in relation thereto.

(2) All sums paid or payable to any party in pursuance of the contract before the time when the parties were so discharged (in this Act referred to as " the time of discharge ") shall, in the case of sums so paid, be recoverable from him as money received by him for the use of the party by whom the sums were paid, and, in the case of sums so payable, cease to be so payable:

Provided that if the party to whom the sums were so paid or payable incurred expenses before the time of discharge in, or for the purpose of, the performance of the contract, the court may, if it considers it just

---

[1] [1921] 2 K. B. 526.
[3] (1863), 3 B. & S. 826.
[2] [1935] A. C. 524.
[4] (1876), 1 Q. B. D. 410.

to do so having regard to all the circumstances of the case, allow him to retain or, as the case may be, recover the whole or any part of the sums so paid or payable, not being an amount in excess of the expenses so incurred.

(3) Where any party to the contract has, by reason of anything done by any other party thereto in, or for the purpose of, the performance of the contract, obtained a valuable benefit (other than a payment of money to which the last foregoing subsection applies) before the time of discharge, there shall be recoverable from him by the said other party such sum (if any), not exceeding the value of the said benefit to the party obtaining it, as the court considers just, having regard to all the circumstances of the case and, in particular,

(a) the amount of any expenses incurred before the time of discharge by the benefited party in, or for the purpose of, the performance of the contract, including any sums paid or payable by him to any other party in pursuance of the contract and retained or recoverable by that party under the last foregoing sub-section, and

(b) the effect, in relation to the said benefit, of the circumstances giving rise to the frustration of the contract.

(4) In estimating, for the purposes of the foregoing provisions of this section, the amount of any expenses incurred by any party to the contract, the court may, without prejudice to the generality of the said provisions, include such sums as appear to be reasonable in respect of overhead expenses and in respect of any work or services performed personally by the said party.

(5) In considering whether any sum ought to be recovered or retained under the foregoing provisions of this section by any party to the contract, the court shall not take into account any sums which have, by reason of the circumstances giving rise to the frustration of the contract, become payable to that party under any contract of insurance unless there was an obligation to insure imposed by an express term of the frustrated contract or by or under any enactment.

(6) Where any person has assumed obligations under the contract in consideration of the conferring of a benefit by any other party to the contract upon any other person, whether a party to the contract or not, the court may, if in all the circumstances of the case it considers it just to do so, treat for the purposes of sub-section (3) of this section any benefit so conferred as a benefit obtained by the person who has assumed the obligations as aforesaid.

2. *Provision as to application of this Act:*

(1) This Act shall apply to contracts, whether made before or after the commencement of this Act, as respects which the time of discharge is on or after the first day of July, nineteen hundred and forty-three, but not to contracts as respects which the time of discharge is before the said date.

(2) This Act shall apply to contracts to which the Crown is a party in like manner as to contracts between subjects.

(3) Where any contract to which this Act applies contains any provision

which, upon the true construction of the contract, is intended to have effect in the event of circumstances arising which operate, or would but for the said provision operate, to frustrate the contract, or is intended to have effect whether such circumstances arise or not, the court shall give effect to the said provision and shall only give effect to the foregoing section of this Act to such extent, if any, as appears to the court to be consistent with the said provision.

(4) Where it appears to the court that a part of any contract to which this Act applies can properly be severed from the remainder of the contract, being a part wholly performed before the time of discharge, or so performed except for the payment in respect of that part of the contract of sums which are or can be ascertained under the contract, the court shall treat that part of the contract as if it were a separate contract and had not been frustrated and shall treat the foregoing section of this Act as only applicable to the remainder of that contract.

(5) This Act shall not apply:

    (a) to any charterparty, except a time charterparty or a charterparty by way of demise; or to any contract (other than a charterparty) for the carriage of goods by sea; or

    (b) to any contract of insurance, save as is provided by subsection (5) of the foregoing section; or

    (c) to any contract to which section seven of the Sale of Goods Act, 1893 (which avoids contracts for the sale of specific goods which perish before the risk has passed to the buyer) applies, or to any other contract for the sale, or for the sale and delivery, of specific goods, where the contract is frustrated by reason of the fact that the goods have perished.

3. *Short title and interpretation:*

(1) This Act may be cited as the Law Reform (Frustrated Contracts) Act, 1943.

(2) In this Act the expression " court " means, in relation to any matter, the court or arbitrator by or before whom the matter falls to be determined.

---

3. BY BREACH

Mersey Steel and Iron Co. *v.* Naylor, Benzon & Co.

Decro-Wall International S.A. *v.* Practitioners in Marketing, Ltd.

    An option is given to one party to treat a contract as discharged if
    (1) the other acts in such a way as to show an intention to repudiate his obligations, or
    (2) the other breaks a term that is of major importance, as opposed to one that is only of subsidiary importance.
    In neither of these cases does the breach operate as an automatic discharge, but the injured party has it in his election to treat the contract as discharged or to maintain it in operation. It is not easy to determine whether the term broken is of major or of minor importance. A variety of phrases has been used to describe the nature of the task thus thrown upon the courts. Perhaps the approach most favoured is to ask if the term in question " goes to the root of the contract? "[1]

---

[1] See *infra*, p. 450.

Mersey Steel and Iron Co. v. Naylor, Benzon & Co.

(1884), 9 App. Cas. 434

On December 22, 1880, an agreement was entered into by which the appellants agreed to sell and the respondents to purchase 5,000 tons of steel blooms to be delivered on board at Liverpool by instalments of 1,000 tons monthly, commencing with January, 1881, payment to be made within three days after receipt of shipping documents.

On January 31, 1881, the appellants, who had earlier in the month delivered 120 tons, delivered 211 tons, price 1,161*l.* 12*s.*, which became payable on February 5, 1881. At the beginning of February, 1881, they delivered 260 tons 11 cwt., price 1,433*l.* 1*s.*, which became due on February 8, 1881, making a total amount of 2,594*l.* 13*s.* In both January and February, therefore, they had failed to complete their monthly instalments.

On February 2, 1881, a petition was presented in the Court of the County Palatine of Lancaster to wind up the appellant company.

The respondents were mistakenly advised by their solicitors that, pending the petition, they could not safely pay any of the price already due without the leave of the Court, and they so informed the appellant company on February 9. On February 10, the appellants told the respondents that they should treat this refusal to pay as a breach of contract which released them from any further obligations. On February 15, the Court made an order to wind up the appellant company and appointed a liquidator. The respondents informed the liquidator that they were still prepared to accept deliveries under the contract but claimed damages for the failure to deliver the first instalments.

The liquidator made no more deliveries, but sued in the name of the appellant company for the price of the steel actually delivered. The respondents counter-claimed for damages for breach of contract in failing to deliver the proper quantities in accordance with its terms.

LORD COLERIDGE, C.J., held that the respondents, by refusing to pay, had been guilty of such a breach of contract as entitled the appellants to treat it as at an end. He therefore gave judgment for the appellants. The Court of Appeal reversed his decision, and the appellants appealed to the House of Lords.

Cohen, Q.C., and *French* for the appellants:—

As to the first point, the rights of the parties upon the contract, the Court of Appeal did not apply the true principle for the determination of a case like the present. A contract of the kind now sued on is made on the assumption that the parcel already delivered will be paid for punctually and in time to put the manufacturer in funds to provide for the manufacture and delivery of the next parcel. If either party to such a contract breaks it in a material part the other is absolved from performing his part: *Hoare* v. *Rennie*[1]; *Honck* v. *Muller*[2]. Payment for one parcel is a condition precedent to the delivery of the next. If the purchaser is solvent he ought to pay: if insolvent it is unjust that he should have delivery; and the seller is justified in refusing to deliver: *Turnbull* v. *McLean*[3]. The question which must be decided here was left open by Patteson, J., in *Withers* v. *Reynolds*[4]. The Court of Appeal proceeded on the ground that in order to set free the vendor

---

[1] (1859), 5 H. & N. 19.
[2] (1881), 7 Q. B. D. 92.
[3] (1874), 1 R. Ct of Sess. 730.
[4] (1831), 2 B. & Ad. 882, at p.885.

the purchaser must evince an intention not to perform the rest of the contract. That cannot be; it is enough if one party refuses to perform any material part: in other words if the contract originally made is substantially different from the contract which the purchaser seeks to enforce upon the vendor. The law gives no damages or remedy for the breach of a contract to pay money: not even interest unless stipulated or recoverable under the statute: therefore the Courts should be slow to compel the vendor to deliver without payment. Up to the 15th of February the respondents declined to pay, under a mistaken notion that the appellants could not give a discharge: after that date they refused to pay because they claimed to deduct unliquidated damages: they had no right thus to take the law into their own hands. Though not so expressed, payment is implied as a condition precedent; see notes to *Pordage* v. *Cole*[1]; *Graves* v. *Legg*[2]; *Coddington* v. *Paleologo*[3]; *Bradford* v. *Williams*[4], *per* Martin, B. The rule in equity that time is not of the essence of the contract does not apply in mercantile contracts: *Reuter* v. *Sala*[5], *per* Cotton, L.J. *Freeth* v. *Burr*[6] was wrongly decided; but if right is distinguishable.

LORD BLACKBURN. . . . I myself have no doubt that *Withers* v. *Reynolds*[7] correctly lays down the law to this extent, that where there is a contract which is to be performed in future, if one of the parties has said to the other in effect, " If you go on and perform your side of the contract I will not perform mine " (in *Withers* v. *Reynolds*[7] it was, " You may bring your straw, but I will not pay you upon delivery as under the contract I ought to do. I will always keep one bundle of straw in hand so as to have a check upon you "), that in effect amounts to saying, " I will not perform the contract." In that case the other party may say, " You have given me distinct notice that you will not perform the contract. I will not wait until you have broken it, but I will treat you as having put an end to the contract, and if necessary I will sue you for damages, but at all events I will not go on with the contract." That was settled in *Hochster* v. *De La Tour*[8] in the Queen's Bench and has never been doubted since ; because there is a breach of the contract although the time indicated in the contract has not arrived.

That is the law as laid down in *Withers* v. *Reynolds*[7]. That is, I will not say the only ground of defence, but a sufficient ground of defence. In *Freeth* v. *Burr*[6] it was also so laid down ; and Lord Coleridge here thinks the facts were such as to bring the case within that principle. I will not at this time of the day go through them, but when the facts are looked at it is to me clear that that is not so. So far from the respondents saying that when the iron was brought in future they would not pay for it, they were always anxious to get it, and for a very good reason, that the price had risen high above the contract price. There was a statement that for reasons which they thought sufficient they were not willing to pay for the iron at present ; and if that statement had been an absolute refusal to pay, saying, " Because we have power to do wrong we will refuse to pay the money that we ought to pay," I will not say that it might not have been evidence to go to the jury for them to say whether it would not amount to a refusal to go on with the contract in future, for a man might reasonably

---

[1] (1669), 1 Wms. Saund. 319.
[2] (1854), 9 Ex. 709.
[3] (1867), L. R. 2 Exch. 193.
[4] (1872), L. R. 7 Exch. 259.
[5] (1879), 4 C. P. D. 239, at p. 249.
[6] (1874), L. R. 9 C. P. 208.
[7] (1831), 2 B. & Ad. 882.
[8] (1853), 2 E. & B. 678.

so consider it. But there is nothing of that kind here ; it was a *bona fide* statement, and a very plausible statement. I will not say more. I refrain from weighing its value at this moment, but, as I said before, it prevents the case from coming within the authority of *Withers* v. *Reynolds*[1] and *Freeth* v. *Burr*[2], and consequently, as I understand it, Lord Coleridge made a mistake in the ground on which he went. The rule of law, as I always understood it, is that where there is a contract in which there are two parties, each side having to do something (it is so laid down in the notes to *Pordage* v. *Cole*[3]) if you see that the failure to perform one part of it goes to the root of the contract, goes to the foundation of the whole, it is a good defence to say, " I am not going on to perform my part of it when that which is the root of the whole and the substantial consideration for my performance is defeated by your misconduct." But Mr. Cohen contended that whenever there was a breach of contract at all (I think he hardly continued to contend that after a little while, but he said whenever there was a breach of a material part of the contract) it necessarily went to the root of the matter. I cannot agree with that at all. I quite agree that when there were a certain number of tons of the article delivered, it was a material part of the contract that the man was to pay, but it was not a part of the contract that went to the root of the consideration in the matter. There was a delay in fulfilling the obligation to pay the money, it may have been with or without good reason (if that would have made any difference), but it did not go to the root or essence of the contract, nor do I think that there is any sound principle upon which it could do so. I repeatedly asked Mr. Cohen whether or not he could find any authority which justified him in saying that every breach of a contract, or even a breach which involved in it the non-payment of money which there was an obligation to pay, must be considered to go to the root of the contract, and he produced no such authority. There are many cases in which the breach may do so ; it depends upon the construction of the contract. With regard to the case of *Hoare* v. *Rennie*[4] it has been said that the Chief Baron there went so far as to say that it was the essence and substance of the contract that the whole of the 166 tons of iron, and no less, should be delivered. If it was so, it would follow that when in the present case the January shipment had not been made, and the company could only deliver part of the quantity, it went to the essence of the contract. The question depends upon whether the whole and no less is the essence of it. And again in *Honck* v. *Muller*[5], which has been referred to, it is expressly and pointedly shewn that that was the ground taken, and the noble and learned Lord opposite (Lord Bramwell) stated that in his opinion the contract of the one party was to deliver and of the other to take 2,000 tons of iron, and that inasmuch as it was to be by three instalments and the first was gone and there never could be more than two-thirds of the quantity, the thing bargained for being the whole quantity of iron and no less, the defendant was not bound to deliver two-thirds when the plaintiff required the two-thirds only. Supposing that that was the true construction of the contract, I think that that would be the right conclusion. The present Master of the Rolls seems, if I understand him rightly, to have thought that that was not the true construction of the contract—whether it was or not I do not express any opinion, except

[1] (1831) 2 B. & Ad. 882.
[2] (1874), L. R. 9 C. P. 208.
[3] (1669) 1 Wms. Saund. 319.
[4] (1859), 5 H. & N. 19.
[5] (1881), 7 Q. B. D. 92.

to point out that whatever be the construction of other contracts, there is
not in my mind the slightest pretext for saying that such is the construction
of this contract ; and that being so, these cases have really no bearing
upon the matter.

The circumstances being as I have said, the contract not being such
as to make this payment a condition precedent, nor to make punctual payment
for one lot of iron which has been delivered a matter causing the contract
to deliver other iron afterwards to be a dependent contract, being of opinion
that that is not the meaning of the contract, I think that the decision of the
Court of Appeal was right.

The EARL OF SELBORNE, L.C., LORD WATSON and LORD BRAMWELL
delivered judgments to the same effect. The decision of the Court of
Appeal in favour of the respondents was therefore affirmed.

Decro-Wall International S.A. v. Practitioners in Marketing, Ltd.

[1971] 2 All E.R. 216

By an oral agreement made in March, 1967, the plaintiffs, a French
manufacturing company, undertook (i) not to sell their goods in the United
Kingdom to anyone other than the defendants, (ii) to ship goods with reasonable despatch on receipt of the defendants' orders and (iii) to supply the
defendants on demand with certain advertising material; the defendants
undertook (i) not to sell goods competing with the plaintiffs' goods, (ii) to
pay for the goods which they bought by bills of exchange due 90 days from
the date of the invoice, and (iii) to use their best endeavours to create a market
for the plaintiffs' goods in the United Kingdom and to develop it to its maximum potentiality. The agreement was terminable by reasonable notice
on either side. The defendants incurred heavy expenses in promoting the
plantiffs' products in the United Kingdom, but as a result of their efforts the
sales of those products increased very substantially each year and by April,
1970, accounted for 83 per cent. of the defendants' business. The defendants
were however consistently late in meeting the bills of exchange. They were,
as the plaintiffs knew before entering into the contract, short of working
capital and they had to rely on money received from customers to meet the
bills. The delays in payment varied from two to 20 days. The plaintiffs
never doubted that the bills would be paid albeit late. On occasions the time
for payment had been extended with their consent. The financial detriment
to the plaintiffs of the delay in payment was in the area of £20 on each
bill (being the interest on loans from their bank). This loss could have been
but was not debited to the defendants. At the beginning of April, 1970, without a word to the defendants, the plaintiffs arranged for another company to
be appointed their sole concessionaires in the United Kingdom. On April 9,
the plaintiffs wrote to the defendants in effect alleging that the defendants
had wrongfully repudiated the agreement by failing to pay the bills on time
and purporting to accept the repudiation and bring the agreement to an end.
In an action by the plaintiffs claiming the amount of the bills accepted and
unpaid, sums for goods sold and delivered and a declaration that the defendants had ceased to be from April 10, 1970, their sole concessionaires in the
U.K., the trial judge gave judgment for the plaintiffs in respect of the dishonoured bills and the goods sold and delivered, and for the defendants on their

counterclaim for a declaration that they remained the plaintiffs' sole concessionaires in the United Kingdom. He further held that the agreement was only terminable by 12 months' notice by either party and ordered the plaintiffs to pay the defendants damages for their own breach of contract. The plaintiffs undertook (a) to continue supplying the defendants with their products until the expiry of 12 months' notice to terminate the agreement, (b) not to appoint any other persons as concessionaires for their products in the United Kingdom until that date and (c) not themselves to sell or distribute such products in the United Kingdom until that date.

APPEAL

The plaintiffs, Decro-Wall International S.A., appealed against the judgment of Nield, J. given on July 13, 1970, adjudging: (1) that the distribution agreement between the plaintiffs and the defendants, Practitioners in Marketing Ltd, entered into in March, 1967, was still in existence and was only terminable on 12 months' notice; (2) that judgment be entered for the defendants on the counterclaim for a declaration that the defendants were the sole concessionaires for the plaintiffs' products including Magic Mosaic (formerly known as Mosaic Adhesif) and Magic Decor (formerly known as Decrowall, Decrotile and Town and Country) in the United Kingdom of Great Britain and Northern Ireland, and (3) that judgment be entered for the defendants on their counterclaim for an amount to be ascertained by an official referee of the Supreme Court for damages for breach of the distribution agreement.

SACHS, L.J. The key factor to be considered when seeking to resolve the questions raised by this appeal is the nature and scope of the business relationship between the plaintiffs and the defendants which resulted from the original contract of March, 1967, and which subsisted for the three years before the plaintiffs on April 9, 1970, purported to treat the contract as at an end. In essence the defendants became the sole concessionaires for marketing in this country certain products manufactured by the plaintiffs, a French company, in France, but not previously sold in England. The products were mainly self-adhesive wall panels about 12 inches square made of vinyl to have the appearance of ceramic tiles. Each panel when affixed to a wall looked like four tiles. They were marketed in boxes marked " Patents pending " containing some half dozen or so of these panels to be retailed to the public for " do-it-yourself " wall decoration. The mutual objective of the parties was to build up through the efforts of the defendants a market which would grow year by year in the hope that it would eventually reach proportions comparable to that attained in France, where the sales appear to have reached a very high level. Both parties appear from the correspondence to have had in mind promotion efforts over a period of years.

For the successful marketing of this product on such a scale it was essential to provide a large number of " outlets ", i.e. selling points such as Selfridges and John Lewis, at which these tiles could be obtained by members of the public. Later in this judgment further reference will be made to what was entailed in the way of personnel, stocking facilities, and advertising to enable the project to go forward. At this stage it is sufficient to mention that by July, 1969, supplies were being ordered by the defendants on the scale of a " container " carrying 10,000 boxes each fortnight and to quote an illuminating passage in the memorandum of Mr. Josef of April 4, 1969, when the plaintiffs had under consideration the formation in conjunction with the defendants of a new English company to take over the marketing here of the product. In it he stated:

> " It is imperative that there is no break, whatever the form which our relations with [the defendants] must take, in the supplying of 780 points of sale of Decro-Wall now existing in England.'

In this court, though not at first instance, it was rightly conceded on behalf of the plaintiffs that this contract was one which could only be determined by reasonable notice (a point to which it will be necessary to return) and that during its subsistence the plaintiffs were under an obligation to supply, so far as practicable, such goods as might be ordered by the defendants to enable the outlets to meet the demands of the public. The defendants on their side were under an obligation to use their best endeavours to promote sales of the products. The way in which the above terms and certain others fell to be implemented in the changing commercial circumstances of the ensuing three years have already been mentioned by Salmon, L.J., and to some of these matters it will be necessary to refer further. For the present it is sufficient to state that, whilst this arrangement necessarily involved a continuing number of individual transactions for the sale and delivery of goods by the plaintiffs to the defendants it would be wrong to regard the contract between the parties as being merely one of sale of goods. It has a far wider ambit, in that it involved a long-term project for building up to the mutual benefit of both parties a large scale market in a specialised product.

That being the nature and scope of the business relationship, I now turn to the issues which are the subject of this appeal, it being in this court common ground that, if the defendants had not repudiated the contract before the plaintiffs sent their letter of April 9, then the letter constituted a repudiation by the latter: (1) Had the defendants by their conduct before April 9, 1970, repudiated their contract with the plaintiffs, so that the latter were entitled by their letter of that date to end the relationship by accepting the repudiation? (2) If not, were the defendants after that letter entitled to treat the contract as still subsisting, or were they bound to accept that the contract was at an end? (3) Was the length of notice needed to terminate the contract 12 months or three months? (4) Did the plaintiffs' letter of April 9, operate in law as a notice to bring the contract to an end after whatever period constituted reasonable notice? (5) Ought the defendants to have been granted any and if so what injunction?

(1) *Had the defendants by 9th April 1970 repudiated the contract?*

By the terms of the contract payment for the goods was to be by bills of exchange payable 90 days after the date of invoice. All these bills were paid but in almost every case before April 9, 1970, they were not met on the due date, but between two and 20 days after that date: the average delay was eight days. Counsel for the defendants conceded in this court that bills which became due after April 9, were likely only to be met after similar delays and that this had become obvious to the plaintiffs. This situation stemmed from the fact that, as the defendants were, as the plaintiffs well knew before entering into contract, short of working capital, they had to rely on money received from their customers to meet the bills; and as the market expanded their stock had to be increased, and they encountered more delays in getting in payments from their own customers with which to meet the bills. In addition certain further difficulties beyond their control arose. There was, however, never any question of the defendants failing to pay—it was always only a matter of the delays averaging eight days.

The question is whether these past failures to pay on the due date, coupled with the likelihood of further similar failures, constituted a repudiation of the contract. There has been much discussion in this court as to what today is the test by which to judge whether the conduct of a party to a contract constitutes repudiation, where the contract itself does not specifically state what terms are of its essence. It is well said in Cheshire and Fifoot on Contract[1]:

"... it is surely convenient to have some generally recognised language to distinguish terms whose breach entitles the injured party to treat the contract as discharged from those whose breach entitles him only to damages ..."

This statement related to contracts for the sale of goods but it applies equally to contracts generally. For my part I prefer—perhaps at the risk of being dubbed old-fashioned—to adhere to the long standing phraseology used by Lord Ellenborough, C.J. in *Davidson* v. *Gwynne*[2] much cited over the next 150 years by eminent judges (including in 1884 Lord Blackburn in *Mersey Steel and Iron Co., Ltd.* v. *Naylor, Benzon & Co*[3] and adopted again recently by Upjohn, L.J. in the *Hong Kong Fir Shipping Co., Ltd.* v. *Kawasaki Kisen Kaisha, Ltd*[4])—that to constitute repudiation a breach of contract must go to the root of that contract. (Since preparing this judgment our attention has been directed to the use of the same phrase by Lord Denning, M.R. in *The Mihalis Angelos*[5].) That leaves the question whether a breach does thus go to the root as a matter of degree for the court to decide on the facts of the particular case in the same way as it has to decide which terms are warranties and which are conditions. This constitutes the test even when there are recurring breaches —producing differing results according to the degree of non-compliance (*c.f. Maple Flock Co., Ltd.* v. *Universal Furniture Products (Wembley) Ltd*[6]). Notice that a breach is likely to occur or to recur cannot, of course, be treated as being a repudiation unless it would have that effect when it did occur or recur.

Applying that test in the present case involves assessing the defaults of the defendants and their effect in relation to the nature and scope of the business transactions between the parties as a whole. The financial detriment to the plaintiffs of the defendants delaying payment seems in the case of an average bill to have been *at most* in the area of £20. (No evidence was adduced showing what precisely that detriment was in any individual instance, and it may well in practice have been less—and on occasions nil.) The plaintiffs could have charged such losses against the defendants, but on no occasion did they seek so to do—perhaps because the sums concerned were relatively so small. Such defaults even if repeated could not, to my mind, go to the root of this contract.

Moreover, precise time of payment was never made of the essence of the contract. On the contrary, looking at the correspondence as a whole, at the changes in fact made from time to time in the terms of payment, and at the other changes which came under discussion, it seems plain that terms as to payment were at all times negotiable. The plaintiffs incidentally never gave notice that if the defaults continued they would terminate the contract. The

---

[1] 7th Edn., p. 132. See 8th edn., at p. 567.
[2] (1810), 12 East 381, at p. 389; [1803–13] All E.R. Rep. 331, at p. 335.
[3] (1884), 9 App. Cas. 434, at p. 442; [1881–85] All E.R. Rep. 365, at p. 370.
[4] [1962] 2 Q.B. 26, at p. 64; [1962] 1 All E.R. 474, at p. 484.
[5] [1970] 3 All E.R. 125, at p. 128; [1970] 3 W.L.R. 601, at pp. 609, 610.
[6] [1934] 1 K.B. 148, at p. 157; [1933] All E.R. Rep. 15, at pp. 18, 19.

plaintiffs have thus failed to establish that in all the circumstances the defaults and the likelihood of their recurrence were such as to amount to repudiation; so their letter of April 9, stating that no further deliveries would be made constituted a repudiation on their part.

(2) *Were the defendants bound to accept the plaintiffs' repudiation of 9th April 1970?*

The general law as to the effect of repudiation has long been settled. The *locus classicus* for reference purposes is the statement in plain and simple terms in the speech of Viscount Simon, L.C. in *Heyman* v. *Darwins Ltd*[1]:

> ". . . repudiation by one party standing alone does not terminate the contract. It takes two to end it, by repudiation, on the one side, and acceptance of the repudiation, on the other."

Whether the other party accepts is a matter for his option; if he does not, the contract remains alive, as was recently emphasised in *White and Carter (Councils), Ltd.* v. *McGregor*.[2]

Counsel for the plaintiffs pressed on this court as his primary submission that whenever it was necessary for the completion of the contract for the repudiating party to co-operate by doing or refraining from doing some act—affording the other side some facility or at least not barring him from access to work—then the innocent party was bound to accept the repudiation save in exceptional circumstances such as when the remedy of specific performance was available. He argued alternatively that, if this proposition was too wide, nonetheless contracts for personal service were an exception to the general rule that the innocent party has an option and that, the instant contract being analogous to a contract for personal service, the defendants here were bound to accept the plaintiffs' repudiation. In aid of the wider submission he relied on certain passages in the speech of Lord Reid in the *White and Carter* case[2], a case where there was no need for any co-operation by the repudiating party. He referred for instance to a passage where it was said[3]:

> " Of course, if it had been necessary for the defender to do or accept anything before the contract could be completed by the pursuers, the pursuers could not and the court would not have compelled the defender to act, the contract would not have been completed, and the pursuers' only remedy would have been damages."

This echoed what was said earlier[4]:

> " In most cases by refusing co-operation the party in breach can compel the innocent party to restrict his claim to damages."

To my mind, however, neither these nor any other passages in Lord Reid's speech conflict with that of Lord Hodson (with which Lord Tucker agreed) who restated the law regarding an unaccepted repudiation in plain terms, which can be summarised by quoting one sentence[5]:

> " The true position is that the contract survives and does so not only where specific implement is available."

That sentence unequivocally disposes of the primary submission.

The truth of the matter is that there are a great many cases in which it is of no benefit to the innocent party to keep the contract alive for the simple reason that, in the long run, unless the repudiating party can be persuaded or

---

[1] [1942] A.C. 356, at p. 361; [1942] 1 All E.R. 337, at p. 341.
[2] [1962] A.C. 413; [1961] 3 All E.R. 1178.
[3] [1962] A.C., at p. 429; [1961] 3 All E.R., at p. 1182.
[4] [1962] A.C., at p. 428; [1961] 3 All E.R., at p. 1181.
[5] [1962] A.C., at p. 445; [1961] 3 All E.R., at p. 1193.

impelled to change his mind and withdraw his repudiation, the only remedy available to the innocent party will lie in damages. So there are vast numbers of cases where the innocent party can in one sense be said to be forced to adopt the only practicable course because any other would be valueless. In such cases it is the range of remedies that is limited, not the right to elect.

That does not alter the position that the innocent party can if he so chooses elect not to accept the repudiation and may thus in suitable cases keep open, maybe at certain risks, the chances either that the other party may yet take a different course or that it may be one of those special cases where the court will in its discretion grant some form of declaration or injunction on the basis that the contract has not yet been discharged.

The primary submission being ill-founded, it is next necessary to turn to the alternative argument. To dispose of it, it suffices to say that in my view the contract under consideration is not analogous, in the sense propounded by counsel for the plaintiffs, to one for personal services. It is true that the plaintiffs, on a brief acquaintance, thought highly of Mr. Clothier when they first entered into the contract with the defendants, and that in practice it was his efforts that played a great part in the success of the enterprise—but that did not make the contract a personal one which would for instance have determined automatically had Mr. Clothier met with a fatal accident. The contract was in every sense a commercial transaction between two companies.

As the alternative submission fails, for the reason just given, it is unnecessary for me to determine whether on a true analysis contracts of personal service do *in strict law* form an exception to the rule that an innocent party has an option when faced with a repudiation—or whether they form a prime example of the type of case in which in the overwhelming majority of instances the innocent party must *in practice* accept the repudiation because there is no room for a change of mind by the other side nor, if he is the employee, can he either sue for services he does not render or seek any other remedy except damages. As at present advised I favour the latter view, despite the fact that on research phrases may be found which *prima facie* tend the opposite way, in cases (e.g. *Vine* v. *National Dock Labour Board*[1], and *Cranleigh Precision Engineering, Ltd.* v. *Bryant*[2]) where the court was dealing with the practical result of repudiation in a generality of cases rather than the law applicable to exceptional ones.

(3) *Length of notice*

At first instance it was contended on behalf of the plaintiffs that the arrangement between them and the defendants could be determined without giving any notice. In support of that contention reliance was placed on the now somewhat remote decision in *Motion* v. *Michaud*[3], a case usually cited in conjunction with *Joynson* v. *Hunt & Son*[4], each of which concerned contracts in which those asserting that reasonable notice should be given were held to be under no legal obligation to do any specific work but were entitled to commission if sales were effected. Whether there is an implied term in a contract that reasonable notice for its termination must be given and what in that event the length of such notice should be must always depend on the particular facts of the case; moreover the commercial practice current at the date of the

---

[1] [1956] 1 Q.B. 658, at p. 674; [1956] 1 All E.R. 1, at p. 8.
[2] [1965] 1 W.L.R. 1293, at p. 1304.
[3] (1892), 8 T.L.R. 253.
[4] (1905), 93 L.T. 470.

contract may be a relevant factor. Cases such as *Motion* v. *Michaud*[1] are thus nowadays of but little assistance.

In this court it was, as has already been mentioned, rightly conceded that the trial judge came to a correct conclusion in holding that reasonable notice was necessary. His finding that 12 months' notice was required is, however, challenged by the plaintiffs, who put forward three months as the correct period. It has in this court been also rightly conceded on behalf of the plaintiffs that when determining the appropriate length of notice the court must look at the overall state of affairs in March, 1970 (as opposed to the position in March, 1967, when the contract was originally entered into), taking into account what led up to the position at that time. By then, the defendants, by strenuous efforts and by expenditure of large sums on promotion, having started from scratch, had built up a trade that required supplies on the scale to which reference has already been made. The plaintiffs were, incidentally, well satisfied with the progress that had occurred.

To this end the defendants had themselves expended some £30,000 in promoting the product, largely on advertising. For 1970 their plans, with which they kept the plaintiffs in touch (see e.g. their letter of January 6, 1970) included a nation-wide advertising campaign to commence on March 15. They had greatly increased their accommodation for stock. As appears from their letter of November 20, 1969, they were planning greatly to increase—indeed to double by March, 1970, to a total of 14—their sales staff on a regional basis in anticipation of the advertising campaign. The same letter shows they were aiming at a turnover of 1,000,000 boxes a year in 1971. In other words, they were in the middle of developing, with the knowledge and assent of the plaintiffs, the market in the plaintiffs' goods on a really large scale—something which could only be done on a sole-concessionaire basis. Net profits, having regard to heavy promotion expenditure, may well be small in the earlier stages of such operations, the real reward coming in the future. They were also selling products of other firms, but in the first quarter of 1970 83 per cent. of their main business—which was in hardware—was constituted by sales of the plaintiffs' products. In those circumstances any sudden stoppages of supplies by the plaintiffs would, of course, produce disastrous results.

Looking at it from the point of view of two reasonable business men deciding as between themselves what would be the appropriate length of notice required for determining a relationship of the nature already described and involving the work and expenditure just mentioned, it seems to me that no concessionaire would proceed unless he knew the concession could not be terminated by notice of less than 12 months; he might reasonably have stipulated for even longer notice. Similarly no reasonable producer of the product would have expected his concessionaire to carry on the business in this way except on the safeguard that he would not receive notice of less than 12 months. Accordingly the plaintiffs' appeal fails also on this issue.

(4) *Did the 9th April letter operate as a notice?*

On behalf of the defendants it was submitted that in the circumstances of this case the 12 months should run from the date on which a notice was actually given after the trial, i.e. July 17. The plaintiff's case on the other hand, is that the letter of April 9 operated as a notice to determine the relationship and that the 12 months should run from that date. This is an issue which

---

[1] (1892), 8 T.L.R. 253.

I have not found it easy to resolve. In favour of the plaintiffs' submissions is first a reluctance to introduce into commercial transactions any of those complications which attend the giving of notice in landlord and tenant cases, and next some of the reasoning in *Dorling* v. *Honnor Marine, Ltd.*[1]. As against that can be balanced first the practical and undesirable difficulties that could arise if business men were entitled by giving a wrongfully short notice to determine a contractual relationship—or indeed by determining it without notice—and so place the opposite party in a position of great uncertainty and yet retain the same benefits as if they had given a correct notice; it may well be better that they should feel impelled to give a longer notice rather than be entitled to cause such confusion. To that can be added the legal difficulties in the instant case of deeming something which is an unlawful repudiation of the contract to be a lawful notice given under the contract. (A parallel point arises when short notice amounts to an anticipatory breach.)

In the end I have come to the conclusion that in principle a repudiation of a contract cannot operate as a notice given under it—and *a fortiori* a letter wrongly purporting to accept a repudiation that has not occurred cannot so operate. Accordingly the defendants' contentions must succeed unless anything in *Minister of Health* v. *Bellotti*[2] precludes the above conclusion. *Bellotti's* case[2] was concerned with a revocable licence to occupy requisitioned premises—a class of case very much *sui generis*. The essence of the position in such cases was stated by MacKinnon, L.J.[3]:

> " I think the rule of law is that the licensor can revoke his licence at any time, but the licensee has thereafter a reasonable time, having regard to all the circumstances, to comply with the revocation."

Cross, J. put it aptly in *Dorling* v. *Honnor Marine, Ltd*[4]:

> ". . . if a licensor purports to revoke a revocable licence but gives insufficient notice of revocation, the licensee cannot ignore the revocation and treat the licence as still subsisting. On the other hand, he cannot be treated as a wrong-doer for continuing to do what the licence permitted him to do until the expiry of the period which would have constituted reasonable notice."

Dorling's case[1] concerned a personal licence to use a design for sailing boats and involved consideration of the Copyright Act, 1956. Cross, J. dealt with the relevant issues on the footing that the decision in *Bellotti's* case[2] applied to the type of licence before him. To my mind *Bellotti's* case[2] is of limited application and has no real bearing on a case such as the present, which is concerned with a not unusual type of commercial contract. Whether it was correct to apply it to the rather different type of licence in *Dorling's* case[1], where the parties appear to have embarked on a joint venture, it is unnecessary to consider. Suffice it to say that I find nothing in the former case to preclude a finding in this court for the defendants on this issue. I consider that the contract remains in being for 12 months from July 17.

(5) *The injunction*

Having regard to the nature and scope of the transaction and the facts referred to when deciding the length of notice required, it was well within the

---

[1] [1964] Ch. 560; [1963] 2 All E.R. 495.
[2] [1944] K.B. 298; [1944] 1 All E.R. 238.
[3] [1944] K.B., at p. 308; [1944] 1 All E.R., at p. 245.
[4] [1964] Ch., at p. 567; [1963] 2 All E.R., at p. 502.

discretion of the trial judge to grant a negative injunction against the plaintiffs' selling their products in the United Kingdom or appointing someone else to represent them here. It would indeed have been wrong for the courts to allow the plaintiffs freedom in breach of their obligations to inflict on the defendants a ruinous blow—one which would incidentally break up their business in a way for which damages can never provide full compensation. I would accordingly not disturb either of the undertakings (b) and (c) given by the plaintiffs in order to avoid having an injunction granted against them. As regards undertaking (a), however, it seems to me that this should be discharged, for the reasons given by Salmon, L.J. I would accordingly dismiss this appeal.[1]

---

[1] See per SALMON, L.J. [1971] 2 All E.R., at p. 221. It may also be remarked that the first undertaking was couched in positive terms while the other two undertakings were negative: per BUCKLEY, L.J. [1971] 2 All E.R., at p. 235. See also *infra*, p. 491.

REMEDIES

VICTORIA LAUNDRY (WINDSOR), LTD. *v.* NEWMAN INDUSTRIES, LTD.

THE HERON II.

The party who commits a breach of contract is liable for the loss thereby caused to the plaintiff, provided that, in the light of the knowledge, actual or constructive, possessed by him at the time of the contract, he ought reasonably to have contemplated that the loss was " liable to result " or was " likely to occur " or was " a serious possibility ".[1]

Victoria Laundry (Windsor), Ltd. v. Newman Industries, Ltd.

[1949] 2 K.B. 528

APPEAL from Streatfeild, J.

The plaintiffs, a limited company, carrying on a business as launderers and dyers at Windsor, were in January, 1946, minded to expand their business, and to that end required a boiler of much greater capacity than the one they then possessed, which was of a capacity of 1,500-1,600 lbs. evaporation per hour. Seeing an advertisement by the defendants on January 17, 1946, of two " vertical Cochran boilers of 8,000 lb. per hour capacity heavy steaming," the plaintiffs negotiated for the purchase of one of them, and by April 26 had concluded a contract for its purchase at a price of 2,150*l.*, loaded free on transport at Harpenden, where it was installed in the premises of the defendants. The defendants knew that the plaintiffs were launderers and dyers, and wanted the boiler for use in their business. Also, during the negotiations the plaintiffs by letter expressed their intention to " put it into use in the shortest possible space of time." Arrangements were made by the plaintiffs with the defendants to take delivery at Harpenden on June 5, and the plaintiffs on that date sent a lorry to Harpenden to take delivery, but it was then ascertained that four days earlier the third parties, who had been employed by the defendants to dismantle the boiler, had allowed it to fall on its side and sustain damage. The plaintiffs refused to take delivery unless the damage was made good and ultimately the defendants agreed to arrange for the necessary repairs. The plaintiffs did not receive delivery of the boiler until November 8, 1946, and in the present action they claimed damages for breach of contract and sought to include in the damages loss of business profits during the period from June 5 to November 8, 1946.

Streatfeild, J., gave judgment for the plaintiffs against the defendants for 110*l.* damages under certain minor heads, but held that they were not entitled to include in their measure of damages loss of business profits during the period of delay. The boiler, he said, was not a whole plant capable of being used by itself as a profit-making machine. Only the entire plant, including the vats, was a profit-making machine. The defendants were supplying the plaintiffs with only a part, the function of which they did not know, of that plant. The case fell, in his opinion, within the second rule in

---

[1] These and other phrases appear in the judgments of the House of Lords in *The Heron II*; and their lordships indicated their individual preferences or aversions. Lord Morris, indeed, doubted the need to express " any definite preference as between the phrases that were submitted for consideration. . . . Each one of these phrases may be of help, but so may many others "; [1969] 1 A.C. 350, at p. 399; [1967] 3 All E.R. 686, at p. 699.

Hadley v. *Baxendale*[1] and the defendants were not liable for the loss of profits because the special object for which the plaintiffs were acquiring the boiler had not been drawn to the defendants' attention.

The plaintiffs appealed.

ASQUITH, L.J., delivered the judgment of the court[2]: This is an appeal by the plaintiffs against a judgment of Streatfeild, J., in so far as that judgment limited the damages to 110*l*. in respect of an alleged breach of contract by the defendants, which is now uncontested. The breach of contract consisted in the delivery of a boiler sold by the defendants to the plaintiffs some twenty odd weeks after the time fixed by the contract for delivery. The short point is whether, in addition to the 110*l*. awarded, the plaintiffs were entitled to claim in respect of loss of profits which they say they would have made if the boiler had been delivered punctually. Seeing that the issue is as to the measure of recoverable damage and the application of the rules in *Hadley* v. *Baxendale*[1], it is important to inquire what information the defendants possessed at the time when the contract was made, as to such matters as the time at which, and the purpose for which, the plaintiffs required the boiler. The defendants knew before, and at the time of the contract, that the plaintiffs were laundrymen and dyers, and required the boiler for purposes of their business as such. They also knew that the plaintiffs wanted the boiler for immediate use. On the latter point the correspondence is important. The contract was concluded by, and is contained in, a series of letters. In the earliest phases of the correspondence—that is, in letters of January 31 and February 1, 1946 (which letters, as appears from their terms, followed a telephone call on the earlier date)—the defendants undertook to make the earliest possible arrangements for the dismantling and removal of the boiler. The natural inference from this is that in the telephone conversation referred to the plaintiffs had conveyed to the defendants that they required the boiler urgently. Again, on February 7 the plaintiffs wrote to the defendants: " We should appreciate your letting us know how quickly your people can dismantle it "; and finally, on April 26, in the concluding letter of the series by which the contract was made: " We are most anxious that this " (that is, the boiler) " should be put into use in the shortest possible space of time." Hence, up to and at the very moment when a concluded contract emerged, the plaintiffs were pressing upon the defendants the need for expedition; and the last letter was a plain intimation that the boiler was wanted for immediate use. This is none the less so because when, later, the plaintiffs encountered delays in getting the necessary permits and licences, the exhortations to speed came from the other side, who wanted their money, which in fact they were paid in advance of delivery. The defendants knew the plaintiffs needed the boiler as soon as the delays should be overcome, and they knew by the beginning of June that such delays had by then in fact been overcome. The defendants did not know at the material time the precise role for which the boiler was cast in the plaintiffs' economy, e.g., whether (as the fact was) it was to function in substitution for an existing boiler of inferior capacity, or in replacement of an existing boiler of equal capacity, or as an extra unit to be operated side by side with and in addition to any existing boiler. It has indeed been argued strenuously that, for all they knew, it might have been wanted as a " spare " or " stand-by," provided in advance to replace an existing boiler when, perhaps some time hence, the latter should wear out; but such an intention to reserve it for future use

---

[1] (1854), 9 Exch. 341.   [2] TUCKER, ASQUITH and SINGLETON, L.JJ.

seems quite inconsistent with the intention expressed in the letter of April 26, to " put it into use in the shortest possible space of time."

In this connexion, certain admissions made in the course of the hearing are of vital importance. The defendants formally admitted what in their defence they had originally traversed, namely, the facts alleged in para. 2 of the statement of claim. That paragraph reads as follows: " At the date of the contract hereinafter mentioned the defendants well knew as the fact was that the plaintiffs were launderers and dyers carrying on business at Windsor and required the said boiler for use in their said business and the said contract was made upon the basis that the said boiler was required for the said purpose."

On June 5 the plaintiffs, having heard that the boiler was ready, sent a lorry to Harpenden to take delivery. Mr. Lennard, a director of the plaintiff company, preceded the lorry in a car. He discovered on arrival that four days earlier the contractors employed by the defendants to dismantle the boiler had allowed it to fall on its side, sustaining injuries. Mr. Lennard declined to take delivery of the damaged boiler in its existing condition and insisted that the damage must be made good. He was, we think, justified in this attitude, since no similar article could be bought in the market. After a long wrangle, the defendants agreed to perform the necessary repairs and, after further delay through the difficulty of finding a contractor who was free and able to perform them, completed the repairs by October 28. Delivery was taken by the plaintiffs on November 8 and the boiler was erected and working by early December. The plaintiffs claim, as part— the disputed part—of the damages, loss of the profits they would have earned if the machine had been delivered in early June instead of November. Evidence was led for the plaintiffs with the object of establishing that if the boiler had been punctually delivered, then, during the twenty odd weeks between then and the time of actual delivery (1.) they could have taken on a very large number of new customers in the course of their laundry business, the demand for laundry services at that time being insatiable—they did in fact take on extra staff in the expectation of its delivery—and (2.) that they could and would have accepted a number of highly lucrative dyeing contracts for the Ministry of Supply. In the statement of claim, para. 10, the loss of profits under the first of these heads was quantified at 16*l.* a week and under the second at 262*l.* a week.

The evidence, however, which promised to be voluminous, had not gone very far when Mr. Paull, for the defendants, submitted that in law no loss of profits was recoverable at all, and that to continue to hear evidence as to its *quantum* was merely waste of time. He suggested that the question of remoteness of damage under this head should be decided on the existing materials, including the admissions to which we have referred. The learned judge accepted Mr. Paull's submission, and on that basis awarded 110*l.* damages under certain minor heads, but nothing in respect of loss of profits, which he held to be too remote. It is from that decision that the plaintiffs now appeal. It was a necessary consequence of the course which the case took that no evidence was given on behalf of the defendants, and only part of the evidence available to the plaintiffs. It should be observed parenthetically that the defendants had added as third parties the contractors who, by dropping the boiler and causing the injuries to it, prevented its delivery in early June and caused the defendants to break their contract. Those third-party proceedings have been adjourned pending the hearing of the present appeal as between the plaintiffs and the defendants. The third parties, nevertheless, were served with notice of appeal by the defendants and argument was heard for them at the hearing of the appeal.

The ground of the learned judge's decision, which we consider more fully later, may be summarized as follows: He took the view that the loss of profit claimed was due to special circumstances and therefore recoverable, if at all, only under the second rule in *Hadley* v. *Baxendale* and not recoverable in this case because such special circumstances were not at the time of the contract communicated to the defendants. He also attached much significance to the fact that the object supplied was not a self-sufficient profit-making article, but part of a larger profit-making whole, and cited in this connexion the cases of *Portman* v. *Middleton*[1] and *British Columbia Sawmills* v. *Nettleship*[2]. Before commenting on the learned judge's reasoning, we must refer to some of the authorities.

The authorities on recovery of loss of profits as a head of damage are not easy to reconcile. At one end of the scale stand cases where there has been non-delivery or delayed delivery of what is on the face of it obviously a profit-earning chattel; for instance, a merchant or passenger ship: see *Fletcher* v. *Tayleur*[3]; *Re Trent and Humber Co., Ex parte Cambrian Steam Packet Co.*[4]; or some essential part of such a ship; for instance, a propeller, in *Wilson* v. *General Ironscrew Co.*[5], or engines, *Saint Line* v. *Richardson*[6]. In such cases loss of profit has rarely been refused. A second and intermediate class of case in which loss of profit has often been awarded is where ordinary mercantile goods have been sold to a merchant with knowledge by the vendor that the purchaser wanted them for resale; at all events, where there was no market in which the purchaser could buy similar goods against the contract on the seller's default, see, for instance, *Borries* v. *Hutchinson*[7]. At the other end of the scale are cases where the defendant is not a vendor of the goods, but a carrier, see, for instance, *Hadley* v. *Baxendale*[8] and *Gee* v. *Lancashire and Yorkshire Railway*[9]. In such cases the courts have been slow to allow loss of profit as an item of damage. This was not, it would seem, because a different principle applies in such cases, but because the application of the same principle leads to different results. A carrier commonly knows less than a seller about the purposes for which the buyer or consignee needs the goods, or about other " special circumstances " which may cause exceptional loss if due delivery is withheld.

Three of the authorities call for more detailed examination. First comes *Hadley* v. *Baxendale*[8] itself. Familiar though it is, we should first recall the memorable sentence in which the main principles laid down in this case are enshrined: " Where two parties have made a contract which one of them has broken, the damages which the other party ought to receive in respect of such breach of contract should be such as may fairly and reasonably be considered as either arising naturally, i.e., according to the usual course of things, from such breach of contract itself, or such as may reasonably be supposed to have been in the contemplation of both parties, at the time they made the contract, as the probable result of the breach of it." The limb of this sentence prefaced by " either " embodies the so-called " first " rule; that prefaced by " or " the " second." In considering

---

[1] (1858), 4 C. B. N. S. 322. [2] (1868), L. R. 3 C. P. 499.
[3] (1855), 17 C. B. 21. [4] (1868), L. R. 6 Eq. 396.
[5] (1877), 47 L. J. Q. B. 239. [6] [1940] 2 K. B. 99.
[7] (1865), 18 C. B. N. S. 445. [8] (1854), 9 Exch. 341.
[9] (1860), 6 H. & N. 211.

the meaning and application of these rules, it is essential to bear clearly in mind the facts on which *Hadley* v. *Baxendale*[1] proceeded. The head-note is definitely misleading in so far as it says that the defendant's clerk, who attended at the office, was told that the mill was stopped and that the shaft must be delivered immediately. The same allegation figures in the statement of facts which are said on page 344 to have " appeared " at the trial before Crompton, J. If the Court of Exchequer had accepted these facts as established, the court must, one would suppose, have decided the case the other way round; must, that is, have held the damage claimed was recoverable under the second rule. But it is reasonably plain from Alderson, B.'s, judgment that the court rejected this evidence, for on page 355 he says: " We find that the only circumstances here communicated by the plaintiffs to the defendants at the time when the contract was made were that the article to be carried was the broken shaft of a mill and that the plaintiffs were the millers of that mill," and it is on this basis of fact that he proceeds to ask, " How do these circumstances show reasonably that the profits of the mill must be stopped by an unreasonable delay in the delivery of the broken shaft by the carrier to the third person ? "

British Columbia Sawmills v. *Nettleship*[2] annexes to the principle laid down in *Hadley* v. *Baxendale*[1] a rider to the effect that where knowledge of special circumstances is relied on as enhancing the damage recoverable that knowledge must have been brought home to the defendant at the time of the contract and in such circumstances that the defendant impliedly undertook to bear any special loss referable to a breach in those special circumstances. The knowledge which was lacking in that case on the part of the defendant was knowledge that the particular box of machinery negligently lost by the defendants was one without which the rest of the machinery could not be put together and would therefore be useless.

Cory v. *Thames Ironworks Co.*[3]—a case strongly relied on by the plaintiffs—presented the peculiarity that the parties contemplated respectively different profit-making uses of the chattel sold by the defendant to the plaintiff. It was the hull of a boom derrick, and was delivered late. The plaintiffs were coal merchants, and the obvious use, and that to which the defendants believed it was to be put, was that of a coal store. The plaintiffs, on the other hand, the buyers, in fact intended to use it for transhipping coals from colliers to barges, a quite unprecedented use for a chattel of this kind, one quite unsuspected by the sellers and one calculated to yield much higher profits. The case accordingly decides, *inter alia*, what is the measure of damage recoverable when the parties are not *ad idem* in their contemplation of the use for which the article is needed. It was decided that in such a case no loss was recoverable beyond what would have resulted if the intended use had been that reasonably within the contemplation of the defendants, which in that case was the " obvious " use. This special complicating factor, the divergence between the knowledge and contemplation of the parties respectively, has somewhat obscured the general importance of the decision, which is in effect that the facts of the case brought it within the first rule of *Hadley* v. *Baxendale*[1] and enabled the plaintiff to recover loss of such profits as would have arisen from the normal and obvious use of the article. The " natural consequence ", said Blackburn, J., of not delivering the derrick was that 420*l.* representing those normal profits was lost. Cockburn, C.J., interposing during the argument, made the significant observa-

---

[1] (1854), 9 Exch. 341.   [2] (1868), L. R. 3 C. P. 499.   [3] (1868), L. R. 3 Q. B. 181, at p. 187.

tion: " No doubt in order to recover damage arising from a special purpose the buyer must have communicated the special purpose to the seller; but there is one thing which must always be in the knowledge of both parties, which is that the thing is bought for the purpose of being in some way or other profitably applied." This observation is apposite to the present case. These three cases have on many occasions been approved by the House of Lords without any material qualification.

What propositions applicable to the present case emerge from the authorities as a whole, including those analysed above? We think they include the following:—

(1.) It is well settled that the governing purpose of damages is to put the party whose rights have been violated in the same position, so far as money can do so, as if his rights had been observed (*Sally Wertheim* v. *Chicoutimi Pulp Co.*[1]). This purpose, if relentlessly pursued, would provide him with a complete indemnity for all loss *de facto* resulting from a particular breach, however improbable, however unpredictable. This, in contract at least, is recognized as too harsh a rule. Hence,

(2.) In cases of breach of contract the aggrieved party is only entitled to recover such part of the loss actually resulting as was at the time of the contract reasonably foreseeable as liable to result from the breach.

(3.) What was at that time reasonably so foreseeable depends on the knowledge, then possessed by the parties or, at all events, by the party who later commits the breach[2].

(4.) For this purpose, knowledge " possessed " is of two kinds; one imputed, the other actual. Everyone, as a reasonable person, is taken to know the " ordinary course of things " and consequently what loss is liable to result from a breach of contract in that ordinary course. This is the subject matter of the " first rule " in *Hadley* v. *Baxendale*[3]. But to this knowledge, which a contract-breaker is assumed to possess whether he actually possesses it or not, there may have to be added in a particular case knowledge, which he actually possesses, of special circumstances outside the " ordinary course of things," of such a kind that a breach in those special circumstances would be liable to cause more loss. Such a case attracts the operation of the " second rule " so as to make additional loss also recoverable.

(5.) In order to make the contract-breaker liable under either rule it is not necessary that he should actually have asked himself what loss is liable to result from a breach. As has often been pointed out, parties at the time of contracting contemplate not the breach of the contract, but its performance. It suffices that, if he had considered the question, he would as a reasonable man have concluded that the loss in question was liable to result (see certain observations of Lord du Parcq in the recent case of *Monarch Steamship Co., Limited* v. *A/B Karlshamns Oljefabriker*[4].

(6.) Nor, finally, to make a particular loss recoverable, need it be proved that upon a given state of knowledge the defendant could, as a reasonable man, foresee that a breach must necessarily result in that loss. It is enough if he could foresee it as likely so to result. It is indeed enough, to borrow from the language of Lord du Parcq in the same case, at page 233, if the loss (or some factor without which it would not have occurred) is a

---

[1] [1911] A. C. 301.
[2] The House of Lords in *The Heron II, infra,* p. 456, preferred " contemplate " to " foresee". See especially Lord Upjohn, [1969] 1 A.C. 350, at p. 425, [1967] 3 All E.R., at p. 716.   [3] (1854), 9 Exch. 341.   [4] [1949] A. C. 196.

" serious possibility " or a " real danger." For short, we have used the word " liable " to result. Possibly the colloquialism " on the cards " indicates the shade of meaning with some approach to accuracy.

If these, indeed, are the principles applicable, what is the effect of their application to the facts of this case ? We have, at the beginning of this judgment, summarized the main relevant facts. The defendants were an engineering company supplying a boiler to a laundry. We reject the submission for the defendants that an engineering company knows no more than the plain man about boilers or the purposes to which they are commonly put by different classes of purchasers, including laundries. The defendant company were not, it is true, manufacturers of this boiler or dealers in boilers, but they gave a highly technical and comprehensive description of this boiler to the plaintiffs by letter of January 19, 1946, and offered both to dismantle the boiler at Harpenden and to re-erect it on the plaintiffs' premises. Of the uses or purposes to which boilers are put, they would clearly know more than the uninstructed layman. Again, they knew they were supplying the boiler to a company carrying on the business of laundry-men and dyers, for use in that business. The obvious use of a boiler, in such a business, is surely to boil water for the purpose of washing or dyeing. A laundry might conceivably buy a boiler for some other purpose; for instance, to work radiators or warm bath water for the comfort of its employees or directors, or to use for research, or to exhibit in a museum. All these purposes are possible, but the first is the obvious purpose which, in the case of a laundry, leaps to the average eye. If the purpose then be to wash or dye, why does the company want to wash or dye, unless for purposes of business advantage, in which term we, for the purposes of the rest of this judgment, include maintenance or increase of profit, or reduction of loss ? (We shall speak henceforward not of loss of profit, but of " loss of business.") No commercial concern commonly purchases for the purposes of its business a very large and expensive structure like this—a boiler 19 feet high and costing over 2,000*l.*—with any other motive, and no supplier, let alone an engineering company, which has promised delivery of such an article by a particular date, with knowledge that it was to be put into use immediately on delivery, can reasonably contend that it could not foresee that loss of business (in the sense indicated above) would be liable to result to the purchaser from a long delay in the delivery thereof. The suggestion that, for all the supplier knew, the boiler might have been needed simply as a " stand-by," to be used in a possibly distant future, is gratuitous and was plainly negatived by the terms of the letter of April 26, 1946.

Since we are differing from a carefully reasoned judgment, we think it due to the learned judge to indicate the grounds of our dissent. In that judgment, after stressing the fact that the defendants were not manufacturers of this boiler or of any boilers (a fact which is indisputable), nor (what is disputable) people possessing any special knowledge not common to the general public of boilers or laundries as possible users thereof, he goes on to say: " That is the general principle and I think that the principle running through the cases is this—and to this extent I agree with Mr. Beney— that if there is nothing unusual, if it is a normal user of the plant, then it may well be that the parties must be taken to contemplate that the loss of profits may result from non-delivery, or the delay in delivery, of the particular article. On the other hand, if there are, as I think there are here, special circumstances, I do not think that the defendants are liable for loss of profits unless these special circumstances were drawn to their notice. In looking at the cases, I think there is a distinction, as Mr. Paull has pointed out and insists upon, between the supply of a part of the profit-making machine, as against the profit-making machine itself." Then, after referring to *Portman* v. *Middleton*[1], he continues: " It is to be observed that not only must the circumstances be known to the supplier, but they must be such that the object must be taken to have been within the contemplation of both parties.   I do not think that on the facts of the case as I have heard them, and upon the admissions, it can be said that it was within the contemplation of the supplier, namely, the defendants, that any delay in the delivery of this boiler was going to lead necessarily to loss of profits.   There was nothing that I know of in the evidence to indicate how it was to be used or whether delivery of it by a particular day would necessarily be vital to the earning of these profits.   I agree with the propositions of Mr. Paull that it was no part of the contract, and it cannot be taken to have been the basis of the contract, that the laundry would be unable to work if there was a delay in the delivery of the boiler, or that the laundry was extending its business, or that it had any special contracts which they could fulfil only by getting delivery of this boiler.   In my view, therefore, this case falls within the second rule of *Hadley* v. *Baxendale*[2] under which they are not liable for the payment of damages for loss of profits unless there is evidence before the court—which there is not—that the special object of this boiler was drawn to their attention and that they contracted upon the basis that delay in the delivery of the boiler would make them liable to payment of loss of profits."

The answer to this reasoning has largely been anticipated in what has been said above, but we would wish to add: First, that the learned judge appears to infer that because certain " special circumstances " were, in his view, not " drawn to the notice of " the defendants and therefore, in his view, the operation of the " second rule " was excluded, *ergo* nothing in respect of loss of business can be recovered under the " first rule."   This inference is, in our view, no more justified in the present case than it was in the case of *Cory* v. *Thames Ironworks Co.*[3]   Secondly, that while it is not wholly clear what were the " special circumstances " on the non-communication of which the learned judge relied, it would seem that they were, or included, the following:—(a) the " circumstance " that delay in delivering the boiler was going to lead " necessarily " to loss of profits.   But the true criterion is surely not what was bound " necessarily " to result, but what was likely or liable to do so, and we think that it was amply conveyed to the defendants by what was communicated to them (plus what was patent without express communication) that delay in delivery was likely to lead to " loss of business "; (b) the " circumstance " that the plaintiffs needed the boiler " to extend their business."   It was surely not necessary for the defendants to be specifically informed of this, as a pre-condition of being liable for loss of business. Reasonable persons in the shoes of the defendants must be taken to foresee without any express intimation that a laundry which, at a time when there was a famine of laundry facilities, was paying 2,000*l.* odd for plant and intended at such a time to put such plant " into use " immediately, would be likely to suffer in pocket from five months' delay in delivery of the plant in question, whether they intended by means of it to extend their business, or merely to maintain it, or to reduce a loss; (c) the " circumstance " that

[1] (1858), 4 C. B. N. S. 322.   [2] (1854), 9 Exch. 341.   [3] (1868), L. R. 3 Q. B. 181.

the plaintiffs had the assured expectation of special contracts, which they could only fulfil by securing punctual delivery of the boiler. Here, no doubt, the learned judge had in mind the particularly lucrative dyeing contracts to which the plaintiffs looked forward and which they mention in para. 10 of the statement of claim. We agree that in order that the plaintiffs should recover specifically and as such the profits expected on these contracts, the defendants would have had to know, at the time of their agreement with the plaintiffs, of the prospect and terms of such contracts. We also agree that they did not in fact know these things. It does not, however, follow that the plaintiffs are precluded from recovering some general (and perhaps conjectural) sum for loss of business in respect of dyeing contracts to be reasonably expected, any more than in respect of laundering contracts to be reasonably expected.

Thirdly, the other point on which Streatfeild, J., largely based his judgment was that there is a critical difference between the measure of damages applicable when the defendant defaults in supplying a self-contained profit-earning whole and when he defaults in supplying a part of that whole. In our view, there is no intrinsic magic, in this connexion, in the whole as against a part. The fact that a part only is involved is only significant in so far as it bears on the capacity of the supplier to foresee the consequences of non-delivery. If it is clear from the nature of the part (or the supplier of it is informed) that its non-delivery will have the same effect as non-delivery of the whole, his liability will be the same as if he had defaulted in delivering the whole. The cases of *Hadley* v. *Baxendale*[1], *British Columbia Sawmills* v. *Nettleship*[2] and *Portman* v. *Middleton*[3], which were so strongly relied on for the defence and by the learned judge, were all cases in which, through want of a part, catastrophic results ensued, in that a whole concern was paralysed or sterilized; a mill stopped, a complex of machinery unable to be assembled, a threshing machine unable to be delivered in time for the harvest and therefore useless. In all three cases the defendants were absolved from liability to compensate the plaintiffs for the resulting loss of business, not because what they had failed to deliver was a part, but because there had been nothing to convey to them that want of that part would stultify the whole business of the person for whose benefit the part was contracted for. There is no resemblance between these cases and the present, in which, while there was no question of a total stoppage resulting from non-delivery, yet there was ample means of knowledge on the part of the defendants that business loss of some sort would be likely to result to the plaintiffs from the defendants' default in performing their contract.

We are therefore of opinion that the appeal should be allowed and the issue referred to an official referee as to what damage, if any, is recoverable in addition to the 110*l.* awarded by the learned trial judge. The official referee would assess those damages in consonance with the findings in this judgment as to what the defendants knew or must be taken to have known at the material time, either party to be at liberty to call evidence as to the *quantum* of the damage in dispute.

---

[1] (1854), 9 Exch. 341. [2] (1868), L. R. 3 C. P. 499.
[3] (1858), 4 C. B. N. S. 322.

The Heron II

[1967] 3 All E.R. 686

This was an appeal from an order of the Court of Appeal (DIPLOCK and SALMON, L.JJ., SELLERS, L.J., dissenting), dated Apr. 5, 1966 and reported [1966] 2 All E.R. 593, allowing an appeal by the respondents, C. Czarnikow, Ltd., the charterers of the Heron II, from an order of McNAIR, J., dated Dec. 2, 1965, on a Special Case stated by the umpire on a claim by the respondents against the appellant Nicolas Demetrius Koufos, the owner of the ship, for damages for breach of the charterparty causing late arrival of the ship at Basrah, the port of destination. The umpire had awarded the charterers £4,183 16s. 8d. the amount by which the market value of the cargo at Basrah had fallen between the date the ship should have arrived and the date when she did arrive, but McNair, J., held that the charterers were only entitled to interest on the value of the cargo for the period between those dates. The Court of Appeal reversed the order of McNair, J., and restored the award of the umpire.

The House of Lords (LORD REID, LORD MORRIS, LORD HODSON, LORD PEARCE and LORD UPJOHN) unanimously dismissed the appeal and affirmed the decision of the Court of Appeal.

The following statement of facts is taken from the judgment of LORD REID:

By charterparty of Oct. 15, 1960, the respondents chartered the appellant's vessel, Heron II, to proceed to Constanza, there to load a cargo of three thousand tons of sugar; and to carry it to Basrah, or, in the charterers' option, to Jeddah. The vessel left Constanza on Nov. 1. The option was not exercised and the vessel arrived at Basrah on Dec. 2. The umpire has found that "a reasonably accurate prediction of the length of the voyage was twenty days". But the vessel had in breach of contract made deviations which caused a delay of nine days.

It was the intention of the respondent charterers to sell the sugar "promptly after arrival at Basrah and after inspection by merchants". The appellant shipowner did not know this, but he was aware of the fact that there was a market for sugar at Basrah. The sugar was in fact sold at Basrah in lots between Dec. 12 and 22, but shortly before that time the market price had fallen partly by reason of the arrival of another cargo of sugar. It was found by the umpire that if there had not been this delay of nine days the sugar would have fetched £32 10s. per ton. The actual price realised was only £31 2s. 9d. per ton. The charterers claim that they are entitled to recover the difference as damages for breach of contract. The shipowner admits that he is liable to pay interest for nine days on the value of the sugar and certain minor expenses but denies that fall in market value can be taken into account in assessing damages in this case.

McNair, J., following the decision in *The Parana*[1], decided this question in favour of the appellant. He said:

"In those circumstances it seems to me almost impossible to say that the shipowner must have known that the delay in prosecuting the voyage would probably result, or be likely to result, in this kind of loss."

---

[1] (1877), 2 P.D. 118.

The Court of Appeal[1] by a majority (DIPLOCK and SALMON, L.JJ., SELLERS, L.J., dissenting) reversed the decision of the trial judge. The majority held that *The Parana*[2] laid down no general rule, and, applying the rule (or rules) in *Hadley* v. *Baxendale*[3], as explained in *Victoria Laundry* (*Windsor*), *Ltd.* v. *Newman Industries, Ltd.*[4], they held that the loss due to fall in market price was not too remote to be recoverable as damages.

It may be well first to set out the knowledge and intention of the parties at the time of making the contract so far as relevant or argued to be relevant. The charterers intended to sell the sugar in the market at Basrah on arrival of the vessel. They could have changed their mind and exercised their option to have the sugar delivered at Jeddah, but they did not do so. There is no finding that they had in mind any particular date as the likely date of arrival at Basrah or that they had any knowledge or expectation that in late November or December there would be a rising or a falling market. The shipowner was given no information about these matters by the charterers. He did not know what the charterers intended to do with the sugar. But he knew there was a market in sugar at Basrah, and it appears to me that, if he had thought about the matter, he must have realised that at least it was not unlikely that the sugar would be sold in the market at market price on arrival. He must also be held to have known that in any ordinary market prices are apt to fluctuate from day to day: but he had no reason to suppose it more probable that during the relevant period such fluctuation would be downwards rather than upwards—it was an even chance that the fluctuation would be downwards. . . .

LORD HODSON: My Lords, the broad question which arises on the appeal is what is the correct measure of damages for wrongful delay by a shipowner in the performance of a contract for the carriage of goods by sea.

The respondent charterers contend that the ordinary measure of damages for delay in delivery of goods for which there is a market is the difference between the market value of the goods at their destination on the date when they arrive, and the value at the date when they should have arrived if there had been no breach of contract. The loss so measured is one which arises naturally according to the usual course of things. This right to recover does not depend on any special knowledge of the party in breach. It applies to contracts of carriage by sea and by land in all ordinary cases.

The appellant shipowner contends, on the other hand, that except in special circumstances, which are not to be found in this case, the measure of damages is limited to the interest on the value of the goods during the period of delay.

In these circumstances the shipowner admitted liability for £172 consisting of £12 10s. (cable expenses) and £159 9s. 6d. (interest at six per cent. per annum on the full value of the cargo during the period of the delay) on the facts found and stated in the special case. The umpire awarded the charterers, in addition to the above sum of £172, £4,010 16s. 8d. in respect of the fall in value of the goods during the delay. McNair, J., on questions of law being submitted for the decision of the court as to (*inter alia*) the correct measure of damages held that the umpire was wrong in law and that the charterers were entitled only to the admitted sum of £172, made up in the

---

[1] [1966] 2 Q.B. 695; [1966] 2 All E.R. 593.
[2] (1877), 2 P.D. 118.
[3] (1854), 9 Exch. 341; [1843–60] All E.R. Rep. 461.
[4] [1949] 2 K.B. 528; [1949] 1 All E.R. 997.

main of interest charges. The Court of Appeal[1], Diplock and Salmon, L.JJ. (Sellers, L.J., dissenting) restored the umpire's award.

The ultimate question for decision is whether, as a matter of law, contracts for the carriage of goods by sea are in a special class, having regard to the intrinsic differences there are between such contracts and contracts for the carriage of goods by land. For example, in the former class, it is pointed out that goods may be sold before shipment or during the voyage or intended for the purposes of stocking or consumption at the port of destination and that the contemplation of the parties that the goods may be resold by the charterer at the port of destination is not necessarily to be inferred. In addition it is urged that ocean voyages are liable to be affected by weather, by congestion at loading and discharging ports, and similar factors, which account for a different treatment being given to cases of carriage of goods by sea. There is on the face of it no reason why the charterer should not be entitled to the value of that of which he has been deprived by the breach of contract independently of his intention to sell again, and sale during the voyage or before the shipment is in any case irrelevant since the purchaser would stand in the charterer's shoes. There is nothing speculative about the claim, and what the charterer does with the goods should not make any difference. This should apply to contracts of carriage by land or sea.

Consideration of sea and weather conditions has been thought to be the basis of the decision in *The Parana*[2]. This appears from the judgment of SIR RICHARD HENN COLLINS, M.R., in *Dunn v. Bucknall Brothers*[3]. The uncertainties of the Parana's voyage were so great, he said in *Dunn v. Bucknall*[3], that the parties could not be said to have contracted on the footing that the goods would arrive at any particular moment. The headnote to *Dunn v. Bucknall*[4], however, concisely states as a summary of the judgment that there is no rule of law that damages cannot be recovered for loss of market on a contract of carriage by sea. This, I think, was really accepted by the appellant shipowner and also in the main by McNair, J., although Sellers, L.J., went so far as to say[5] that it was desirable, in establishing a basis for damages, to avoid fortuitous elements, unless the parties had already contracted that the chance change of market price should fall on the shipowner if it happened to be less and not equal to or more than the price which could have been obtained without a breach of contract.

That was in substance the position taken up by the shipowner before your lordships. He accepted the established authority of the judgment in *Hadley v. Baxendale*[6]. The case concerned a broken crank shaft delivered to common carriers to be sent to engineers for repair. There was a delay of five days in delivery and the issue was as to the measure of damages for breach of contract. In the judgment of the court, which consisted of PARKE, MARTIN and ALDERSON, BB.[7], it was said:

" We think the proper rule in such a case as the present is this. Where two parties have made a contract which one of them has broken, the damages which the other party ought to receive in respect of such breach of contract should be such as may fairly and reasonably be considered either arising naturally, i.e., according to the usual course of things, from such breach of contract itself,

---

[1] [1966] 2 Q.B. 695; [1966] 2 All E.R. 593.
[2] (1877), 2 P.D. 118.
[3] [1902] 2 K.B. at p. 622; [1900–03] All E.R. Rep. at p. 134.
[4] [1902] 2 K.B. at p. 614.
[5] [1966] 2 Q.B. at p. 723; [1966] 2 All E.R. at p. 600, letter D.
[6] (1854), 9 Exch. 341; [1843–60] All E.R. Rep. 461.
[7] (1854), 9 Exch. at p. 354; [1843–60] All E.R. Rep. at p. 465, letter E.

or such as may reasonably be supposed to have been in the contemplation of both parties, at the time they made the contract, as the probable result of the breach of it."

The phrases beginning " either " and " or " are commonly said to divide the rule laid down by the court into two parts, the one arising " according to the usual course of things " and the other relating to special circumstances in which the contract was made.

The shipowner argued that the fluctuations of market due to unforeseen and unpredictable causes during the period of delay are not of themselves " according to the usual course of things ". He argued that there were no facts here to bring the second part of the rule into operation, and in this I agree with him, for no special notice was given. Hence he said that damages for loss of market were not recoverable, and that these damages could only be recovered in special cases covered by the second part of the rule.

The word " probable " in *Hadley* v. *Baxendale*[1] covers both parts of the rule, and it is of vital importance in applying the rule to consider what the court meant by using this word in its context. The common use of this word is no doubt to imply that something is more likely to happen than not. In conversation, if one says to another " If you go out in this weather you will probably catch a cold ", this is, I think, equivalent to saying that one believes there is an odds on chance that the other will catch a cold. The word " probable " need not, however, bear this narrow meaning. In *Re R. and H. Hall, Ltd. and W. H. Pim (Junior) & Co.'s Arbitration*[2], VISCOUNT DUNEDIN[3], after stating his belief in a general agreement that the law as to calculation of damages, due under breach of a contract, was settled by the case of *Hadley* v. *Baxendale*[1], said that the difficulty lay in the application to the facts of each case.

The instant case furnishes an example of this difficulty. Assistance is to be gained from some of the expressions used in *Hall and Pim's* case[2] which concerned a loss of profit on resale. On failure by sellers to deliver goods to buyers, the buyers were held entitled to recover the damages which they would have to pay to a sub-purchaser. LORD DUNEDIN thought[4] that it was enough that there was an even chance of a resale happening. LORD SHAW OF DUNFERMLINE thought[5] it not unlikely that a resale would take place, and LORD PHILLIMORE[6] that the parties contemplated that a resale might take place.

In *Monarch Steamship Co., Ltd.* v. *Karlshamns Oljefabriker*[7] LORD DU PARCQ used in applying the first part of the rule in *Hadley* v. *Baxendale*[8] the words " serious possibility " and " real danger ", while LORD MORTON OF HENRYTON spoke[7] of " grave risk ".

A close study of the rule was made by the Court of Appeal in the case of *Victoria Laundry (Windsor), Ltd.* v. *Newman Industries, Ltd.*[9]. The judgment of the court, consisting of TUCKER, ASQUITH and SINGLETON, L.JJ., was delivered by Asquith, L.J., who referred to the *Monarch Steamship* case[10]

---

[1] (1854), 9 Exch. 341; [1843–60] All E. R. Rep. 461.
[2] [1928] All E.R. Rep. 763.
[3] [1928] All E.R. Rep. at p. 766.
[4] [1928] All E.R. Rep. at p. 767, letter F.
[5] [1928] All E.R. Rep. at p. 769.
[6] [1928] All E.R. Rep. at p. 771.
[7] [1949] A.C. at p. 234; [1949] 1 All E.R. at p. 20.
[8] (1854), 9 Exch. 341; [1843–60] All E.R. Rep. 461.
[9] [1949] 2 K.B. 528; [1949] 1 All E.R. 997.
[10] [1949] A.C. 196; [1949] 1 All E.R. 1.

and suggested the phrase[1] " liable to result " as appropriate to describe the degree of probability required. This may be a colourless expression, but I do not find it possible to improve on it. If the word " likelihood " is used, it may convey the impression that the chances are all in favour of the thing happening, an idea which I would reject.

I find guidance in the use of the expression " in the great multitude of cases ", which is to be found in more than one place in the judgment in *Hadley* v. *Baxendale*[2]. It indicates that the damages recoverable for breach of contract are such as flow naturally in most cases from the breach, whether under ordinary circumstances or from special circumstances due to the knowledge either in the possession of or communicated to the defendants. This expression throws light on the whole field of damages for breach of contract, and points to a different approach from that taken in tort cases. True that where the facts are the same in two cases the damages will no doubt be the same whether the claim is made in contract or in tort; compare *The Notting Hill*[3] where, although the claim was in tort, the Court of Appeal in a case like *The Parana*[4] followed the latter decision.

The approach in tort will, however, normally be different simply because the relationship of the parties is different. The claim against the tortfeasor who has inflicted tortious damage is not the same as the claim against an opposite party for breach of contract, for the latter claim depends on the contemplation of the parties to the contract and questions of remoteness as such do not arise. Consequently liability in tort may often be of a wider kind. The observations of WILLES, J., in *Horne* v. *Midland Rail. Co.*[5] state the distinction in clear language in the passage cited by my noble and learned friend LORD REID, and I agree that this passage is to be preferred to the opinion sometimes expressed that the measure of damages is the same in tort as it is in contract.

It seems that MELLISH, L.J., in *The Parana*[6] took a different view of the rule in *Hadley* v. *Baxendale*[2] when he said:

> " In order that damages may be recovered, we must come to two conclusions —first, that it was reasonably certain that the goods would not be sold until they did arrive; and, secondly, that it was reasonably certain that they would be sold immediately after they arrived, and that that was known to the carrier at the time when the bills of lading were signed."

With respect to MELLISH, L.J., this is putting the test too high. The conclusion reached on the facts of the case in *The Parana*[6] need not however be criticised, because the voyage took about twice as long as might have been expected and no reasonably accurate prediction of the length of the voyage could be expected. He did, however, make use of the general observations which have no doubt been treated as laying down a practice to be followed. In reaching the conclusion that the registrar and merchants were right in their report MELLISH, L.J., stated[7]:

> " They said that it had never been the practice in the Court of Admiralty to give such damages, and though it constantly happened that by accidents such as collisions goods were delayed in their arrival, it never had been the custom to include in the damages the loss of market; and we are of opinion that the conclusion which the registrar and merchants came to was right."

---

[1] [1949] 2 K.B. at p. 540; [1949] 1 All E.R. at p. 1003, letter B.
[2] (1854), 9 Exch. 341; [1843–60] All E. R. Rep. 461.
[3] (1884), 9 P.D. 105.
[4] (1877), 2 P.D. 118.
[5] (1872), L.R. 7 C.P. at p. 590.
[6] (1877), 2 P.D. at p. 123.
[7] (1877), 2 P.D. at p. 124.

This decision has been treated as authoritative by text writers in this country and has never been over-ruled, but the rule of practice which it purports to lay down is not followed universally and is insecurely based.

In the United States of America it seems that the courts have never followed the principle of assignment of damages laid down in *The Parana*[1]. SALMON, L.J., has pointed out[2] that in the CORPUS JURIS SECUNDUM[3], it is stated that

> " In the ordinary case of deviation or delay by a common carrier in delivering goods, the measure of damages is the difference in the market value at the time when actually delivered and when they should have been delivered . . . "

In the case of *United States* v. *Middleton*[4] and in other cases in the United States of America this position has been accepted. It would, I think, be unfortunate if the law as to the measure of damages based on the decision in *Hadley* v. *Baxendale*[5] in the two countries should be held to have developed on different lines, and I am glad that in my opinion it has not in truth done so.

I have not dealt in detail with the facts of the instant case. These have been sufficiently set out in the opinion of my noble and learned friend LORD REID. I need only say that I agree with the majority of the Court of Appeal[6] that on the correct application of the decision in *Hadley* v. *Baxendale*[5] to the facts stated in the Special Case, although no special circumstances bring the second rule in *Hadley* v. *Baxendale*[5] into operation, the shipowner is liable in damages for breach of contract in the larger sum awarded, viz., £4,188 10s. 8d., a sum which includes damages for loss of market which in this case arise " according to the ordinary course of things ".

I do not find it necessary to say that the decision in *The Parana*[1] was wrong on the facts. Somehow or other from the language used in the judgment it appears to have been elevated to a pronouncement on legal principle which is not sustainable.

Lastly there is, in my opinion, no need to enter into the difficult question whether there may be differences between cases of non-delivery by carriers and cases of delay by them. Certain decisions on this topic have been criticised and I express no opinion about them.

I would dismiss the appeal.

LORD PEARCE: My Lords, in *Hadley* v. *Baxendale*[5] the court attempted to clarify and define the boundaries of damages in contract. In *The Wagon Mound (No. 1)*, *Overseas Tankship (U.K.), Ltd.* v. *Morts Dock and Engineering Co., Ltd.*[7] the Privy Council attempted a similar task with regard to damages in tort. In the present case (as in *The Wagon Mound (No. 2)*, *Overseas Tankship (U.K.), Ltd.* v. *Miller Steamship Co. Pty., Ltd.*[8]) it was suggested in argument that there was or should be one principle of damages for both contract and tort and that guidance for one could be obtained from the other. I do not find such a comparison helpful. In the case of contract two parties, usually with some knowledge of one another, deliberately undertake mutual duties. They have the opportunity to define clearly in respect of what they shall and shall not be liable. The law has to say what shall be the boundaries

---

[1] (1877), 2 P.D. 118.
[2] [1966] 2 Q.B. at p. 745; [1966] 2 All E.R. 613, letter F.
[3] Vol. 80, p. 931, para. 124.
[4] (1924), 3 Fed. R. (2nd) 384.
[5] (1854), 9 Exch. 341; [1843–60] All E.R. Rep. 461.
[6] [1966] 2 Q.B. 695; [1966] 2 All E.R. 593.
[7] [1961] A.C. 388; [1961] 1 All E.R. 404.
[8] [1967] 1 A.C. 617; [1966] 2 All E.R. 709.

of their liability where this is not expressed, defining that boundary in relation to what has been expressed and implied. In tort two persons, usually un-known to one another, find that the acts or utterances of one have collided with the rights of the other, and the court has to define what is the liability for the ensuing damage, whether it shall be shared, and how far it extends. If one tries to find a concept of damages which will fit both these different problems there is a danger of distorting the rules to accommodate one or the other and of producing a rule that is satisfactory for neither. The problems certainly have one thing in common. In both the use of words with differing shades of meaning in the various cases makes it hard to discern with exactitude where the boundaries lie. See *The Wagon Mound (No. 2)*[1].

The underlying rule of the common law is that

" . . . where a party sustains a loss by reason of a breach of contract, he is so far as money can do it, to be placed in the same situation with regard to damages as if the contract had been performed."

(PARKE, B., in *Robinson* v. *Harman*[2]). Since, however, so wide a principle might be too harsh on a contract-breaker in making him liable for a chain of unforeseen and fortuitous circumstances, the law limited the liability in ways which crystallised in the rule in *Hadley* v. *Baxendale*[3]. This was designed as a direction to juries, but it has become an integral part of the law.

Since an Olympian cloud shrouded any doubts, difficulties and border-line troubles that might arise in the jury room and the jury could use a com-mon sense liberality in applying the rule to the facts, the rule worked admir-ably as a general guidance for deciding facts. But when the lucubrations of judges, who have to give reasons, superseded the reticence of juries, there were certain matters which needed clarification. That service was well per-formed by the judgment of the Court of Appeal in the case of *Victoria Laun-dry (Windsor), Ltd.* v. *Newman Industries, Ltd.*[4]. I do not think that there was anything startling or novel about it. In my opinion it represented (in felicitous language) the approximate view of *Hadley* v. *Baxendale*[3] taken by many judges in trying ordinary cases of breach of contract.

It is argued that it was an erroneous departure from *Hadley* v. *Baxendale*[3] in that it allowed damages where the loss was " a serious possibility " or " a real danger " instead of maintaining that the loss must be " probable ", in the sense that it was more likely to result than not. Over twenty years before, however, in *Re R. and H. Hall, Ltd. and W. H. Pim (Junior) & Co.'s Arbitra-tion*[5], VISCOUNT DUNEDIN had said that it was enough if there was an even chance of the loss happening. LORD SHAW OF DUNFERMLINE said[6] that the two parts of the rule need not be antithetically treated but might run into each other and be one; and he read[7] probable as meaning a " not unlikely " result. LORD PHILLIMORE said[8]:

" [These] are called damages in contemplation of the parties, not because the parties contemplate a breach of contract, but because they recognise that a breach or failure is possible, and they reckon that these damages may flow from that breach. I designedly use the word ' may '. There may be cases where the

---

[1] [1967] 1 A.C. at p. 634; [1966] 2 All E.R. at p. 713.
[2] (1848), 1 Exch. 850 at p. 855; [1843–60] All E.R. Rep. 383 at p. 385.
[3] (1854), 9 Exch. 341; [1843–60] All E.R. Rep. 461.
[4] [1949] 2 K.B. 528; [1949] 1 All E.R. 997.
[5] [1928] All E.R. Rep. at p. 767, letter F.
[6] [1928] All E.R. Rep. at p. 769, letter G.
[7] [1928] All E.R. Rep. at p. 770, letter D.
[8] [1928] All E.R. Rep. at p. 770, letter G.

word to be used might be ' will ', but there are also cases, and more common cases, where the word to use is ' may '."

LORD BLANESBURGH expressed agreement[1] with the others, and presumably did not dissent from the views set out above. VISCOUNT HALDANE[2] dealt with the matter as one of construction: " Whether such a re-sale was likely or not does not matter, if, as I think, the buyers stipulated for power to make it being provided."

I believe that even at that date those observations would not be regarded as novel; and the fact that the case was not included in the Law Reports may be some slight confirmation of this belief. Inevitably there is some evolution of thought in such matters, and such as there was tended in the direction of taking a wider view of probability. In 1948 in *Monarch Steamship Co., Ltd.* v. *A.B. Karlshamns Oljefabriker*[3], a case of damages for delay in carriage by sea, LORD DU PARCQ used the words " at least a serious possibility " and " a real danger which must be taken into account ". LORD UTHWATT spoke[4] of " the chance of war, not as a possibility of academic interest . . . but as furnishing matter which commercially ought to be taken into account "; and LORD MORTON OF HENRYTON spoke of " a grave risk "[5].

Accordingly in my opinion the expressions used in the *Victoria Laundry* case[6] were right. I do not however accept the colloquialism[7] " on the cards " as being a useful test, because I am not sure just what nuance it has either in my own personal vocabulary or in that of others. I suspect that it owes its attraction, like many other colloquialisms, to the fact that one may utter it without having the trouble of really thinking out with precision what one means oneself or what others will understand by it, a spurious attraction which in general makes colloquialism unsuitable for definition, though it is often useful as shorthand for a collection of definable ideas. It was in this latter convenient sense that the judgment uses the ambiguous words " liable to result ". They were not intended as a further or different test from " serious possibility " or " real danger ".

The whole rule in *Hadley* v. *Baxendale*[8] limits damages to that which may be regarded as being within the contemplation of the parties. The first part deals with those things that[9] " may fairly and reasonably be considered as arising . . . naturally, i.e., according to the usual course of things ". Those are presumed to be within the contemplation of the parties. As LORD WRIGHT said in the *Monarch Steamship* case[10]:

" As reasonable business men each must be taken to understand the ordinary practices and exigencies of the other's trade or business. That need not generally be the subject of special discussion or communication."

After referring to *Banco de Portugal* v. *Waterlow & Sons, Ltd.*[11] he continued[12]:

" Both parties were tacitly taken to be acquainted sufficiently with the general business position. The same is true in many cases of complicated conse-

---

[1] [1928] All E.R. Rep. at p. 774, letter I.
[2] [1928] All E.R. Rep. at p. 766, letter C.
[3] [1949] A.C. at pp. 233, 234; [1949] 1 All E.R. at p. 19, letter H, p. 20, letter A.
[4] [1949] A.C. at p. 232; [1949] 1 All E.R. at p. 18.
[5] [1949] A.C. at p. 235; [1949] 1 All E.R. at p. 20, letter G.
[6] [1949] 2 K.B. 528; [1949] 1 All E.R. 997.
[7] [1949] 2 K.B. at p. 540; [1949] 1 All E.R. at p. 1003, letter C.
[8] (1854), 9 Exch. 341; [1843–60] All E.R. 461.
[9] (1854), 9 Exch. at p. 354; [1843–60] All E.R. Rep. at p. 465, letter E.
[10] [1949] A.C. at p. 224; [1949] 1 All E.R. at p. 14, letter F.
[11] [1932] A.C. 452; [1932] All E.R. Rep. 181.
[12] [1949] A.C. at pp. 224, 225; [1949] 1 All E.R. at p. 14, letter H.

quences flowing from an unanticipated breach of contract, but the damages are not treated either as special or remote if they flow from the normal business position of the parties which the court assumes must be reasonably known to them. It would not be helpful to cite the familiar authorities which are numerous but depend primarily upon the facts of each case."

Even the first part of the rule however contains the necessity for the knowledge of certain basic facts, e.g., in *Hadley* v. *Baxendale*[1] the fact that it was a mill shaft to be carried. On this limited basis of knowledge the horizon of contemplation is confined to things " arising naturally, i.e., according to the usual course of things ".

Additional or " special " knowledge, however, may extend the horizon to include losses that are outside the natural course of events; and of course the extension of the horizon need not always *increase* the damages; it might introduce a knowledge of particular circumstances, e.g., a subcontract, which show that the plaintiff would in fact suffer *less* damage than a more limited view of the circumstances might lead one to expect. According to whether one categorises a fact as basic knowledge or special knowledge the case may come under the first part of the rule or the second. For that reason there is sometimes difference of opinion as to which is the part which governs a particular case, and it may be that both parts govern it.

I do not think that ALDERSON, B.[2], was directing his mind to whether something resulting in the natural course of events was an odds-on chance or not. A thing may be a natural (or even an obvious) result even though the odds are against it. Suppose a contractor was employed to repair the ceiling of one of the law courts and did it so negligently that it collapsed on the heads of those in court. I should be inclined to think that any tribunal (including ALDERSON, B., himself) would have found as a fact that the damage arose " naturally, i.e., according to the usual course of things ". Yet if one takes into account the nights, week ends, and vacations, when the ceiling might have collapsed, the odds against it collapsing on top of anybody's head are nearly ten to one. I do not believe that this aspect of the matter was fully considered and worked out in the judgment. He was thinking of causation and type of consequence rather than of odds. The language of the judgment in the *Victoria Laundry* case[3] was a justifiable and valuable clarification of the principles which *Hadley* v. *Baxendale*[1] was intending to express. Even if it went further than that, it was in my opinion right.

Nor do I consider that the *Victoria Laundry* case[3] is inconsistent with the actual decision on the facts in *Hadley* v. *Baxendale*[1]. The carriers were asked (without special directions, as the court found) to transport a broken shaft away from a mill. " In the great multitude of cases " (to quote ALDERSON, B.'s own phrase[4]) one would not expect the whole working of a mill to be stopped by a delay in transportation. The mere absence of urgent instructions spoke strongly against such a contingency. The fact that the shaft was to be used immediately by engineers for measurements (which one would have rather expected to go on paper by post) for making a new shaft would not, I think, have been in the contemplation of the carriers, on the meagre information available.

The facts of the present case lead to the view that the loss of market arose naturally, i.e., according to the usual course of things, from the ship-

---

[1] (1854), 9 Exch. 341; [1843–60] All E.R. Rep. 461.
[2] (1854), 9 Exch. at p. 355; [1843–60] All E.R. Rep. at p. 465.
[3] [1949] 2 K.B. 528; [1949] 1 All E.R. 997.
[4] (1854), 9 Exch. at p. 356; [1843–60] All E.R. Rep. at p. 466, letter C.

owner's deviation. The sugar was being exported to Basrah where, as the respondents knew, there was a sugar market. It was sold on arrival and fetched a lower price than it would have done had it arrived on time. The fall in market price was not due to any unusual or unpredictable factor.

Had this been a case of non-delivery on sale of goods whether by sea or land, it is uncontested that the defendants would be liable for the loss of market. Had it been a case of delay in sale of goods, the *prima facie* rule is that the damage is the difference between " the value of the article contracted for at the time when it ought to have been and the time when it actually was delivered " (per Blackburn, J., in *Elbinger Actien-Gesellschafft* v. *Armstrong*[1]). Nor can it really be contended that it would have been otherwise if this had been a case of delayed delivery in carriage by land. For this has been long established by such cases as *Collard* v. *South Eastern Rail. Co.*[2]; *Wilson* v. *Lancashire and Yorkshire Rail. Co.*[3] and *Horne* v. *Midland Rail. Co.*[4].

It is however argued that different considerations arise in delay in carriage at sea. The decision in *The Parana*[5], it is said, established a special principle or practice with regard to delay in carriage by sea which should apply to this case and should confine the damages to loss of interest on the value of the goods. The Court of Appeal in *The Parana*[5] appeared to decide largely on the ground that it was not " reasonably certain " that the goods would not be sold until they arrived and that they would be sold as soon as they did arrive. The estimates of the duration of the voyage appear to have varied between sixty-five days and ninety days; and in fact it took 127 days. No doubt the chief factor which influenced the court was that the uncertainties of the voyage were so great that the parties could not be said to have contracted on the footing that the goods would arrive at any particular moment. Sir Richard Henn Collins, M.R., said this when he dealt with *The Parana*[5] in *Dunn* v. *Bucknall Brothers*[6]. He pointed out that

> " It is certainly not a rule of law; it is only an inference of fact that from the circumstances of the case no reasonable assumption as to the state of the market at the time of arrival could have been a factor in the contract between the parties."

In the latter case the court did award damages for loss of market. So too in *The Ardennes (Owner of Cargo)* v. *The Ardennes (Owners)*[7].

In the United States the CORPUS JURIS SECUNDUM states[8] that

> " In the ordinary case of deviation or delay by a common carrier in delivering goods, the measure of damages is the difference in their market value at the time when actually delivered and when they should have been delivered, with interest . . . "

In 1924 in *United States* v. *Middleton*[9] His Honour JUDGE ROSE of the Federal Court of Appeals said:

> " *The Parana*[5] was decided forty-seven years ago. It is by no means certain that, even in England, it would now be unhesitatingly followed . . . Nearly half a century has elapsed since the decision of *The Parana*[5] and more than two decades since that of *Dunn* v. *Bucknall Brothers*[10]. In the meanwhile steam has

---

[1] (1874), L.R. 9 Q.B. 473 at p. 477.
[2] (1861), 7 H. & N. 79; [1861–73] All E.R. Rep. 851.
[3] (1861), 9 C.B.N.S. 632.
[4] (1872), L.R. 7 C.P. 583; *on appeal* (1873), L.R. 8 C.P. 131.
[5] (1877), 2 P.D. 118.
[6] [1902] 2 K.B. at p. 623; [1900–03] All E.R. Rep. at p. 134, letter E.
[7] [1951] 1 K.B. 55; [1950] 2 All E.R. 517.
[8] Vol. 80, p. 931, para. 124.
[9] (1924), 3 Fed. Rep. (2nd) at p. 393.
[10] [1902] 2 K.B. 614; [1900–03] All E.R. Rep. 131.

more and more taken the place of the shifting winds as the motive power upon the sea, with the result that the duration of voyages may now be calculated with at least some approach to certainty, even when they are to the ends of the earth. In these days merchants make their calculation accordingly, and it is not unreasonable to insist that shipowners shall do the like. There would seem to be little injustice in so doing, when it is remembered that they are not answerable at all when they are able to show that the delay was caused by something which due diligence on their part was powerless to prevent."

In *The Parana*[1] (and in the present case) reliance was placed on the fact that in cases of carriage by sea the goods are likely to have been sold in transit while still afloat and that therefore the shippers would not suffer by their late arrival. But, if they were so sold, under the bill of lading the buyer would stand in the shoes of the shipper, would suffer the loss, and would sue in respect of it. This fact makes the contemplation of the loss neither more nor less likely.

In my opinion the line of approach in *Dunn* v. *Bucknall Brothers*[2] and in the United States cases is correct. In most cases the loss of market will be found to be within the contemplation of the parties in carriage of goods by sea. It is however ultimately a question of fact. Moreover it may be that in some unusual cases it will be found that the situation between the parties showed that the shipper was indifferent to the time of arrival and that the parties did *not* contract on the basis that in case of deviation or delay the shipowner should be liable for loss of market; but the absence of an express clause (which could easily be inserted) to that effect will obviously make it hard to establish. I have not dealt with the various particular facts in this case by which counsel for the shipowner's able argument seeks to show that these particular parties did not contemplate damage by loss of market. For I agree with the remarks of the majority of the Court of Appeal[3] on this subject.

Accordingly if *The Parana*[1] purported to lay down any general proposition or rule of law, it was wrongly decided. Even if it was merely purporting to draw an inference of facts from the particular case, I have some doubt of its correctness even at that date, and it has no applicability today. And in my opinion *The Notting Hill*[4] which applied *The Parana*[1] to a case of tort, was wrongly decided.

I would dismiss the appeal.

Pilkington v. Wood

[1953] Ch. 770

A plaintiff is under a duty to take all reasonable steps to mitigate the loss caused by a breach of contract and may not claim compensation for any part of the damage which is due to his neglect to take such steps.

But it is for the defendant to prove that the plaintiff has failed in his duty of mitigation; and he will not discharge the burden of proof merely by showing that there were possible, but unusual or hazardous, steps which the plaintiff might have taken.

The plaintiff claimed that the defendant, when acting as his solicitor, had been guilty of negligence in advising him on the purchase of a property

---

[1] (1877), 2 P.D. 118.
[2] [1902] 2 K.B. 614; [1900–03] All E.R. Rep. 131.
[3] [1966] 2 Q.B. 695; [1966] 2 All E.R. 593.
[4] (1884), 9 P.D. 105.

known as Ewshott Corner, Ewshott, Hampshire. The negligence of the defendant was admitted after the close of pleadings in the action, and the only issue which remained for decision was the quantum of damages.

In 1950 the plaintiff, a civil engineer who had hitherto worked in Lancashire, obtained employment in Surrey, and in order to live within reach of his work, he contracted to purchase the property in question and employed the defendant to act as his solicitor in connexion with the purchase. The purchase was completed by a conveyance dated April 27, 1950, by which the vendor, one Colonel Wilks, conveying as beneficial owner, assured the property to the plaintiff in fee simple for £6,000. The plaintiff raised this sum by an overdraft at his bank on which interest was payable. He paid the defendant his scale fee of £63 for acting as his solicitor.

The plaintiff in due course went into occupation of the property. He spent £400 to £500 in improvements and repairs and purchased for a further £334 certain land surrounding his first purchase, the possession of which considerably added to the amenities and the value of the original land. In December, 1951, the plaintiff relinquished his employment in Surrey and, as he wished to be free to take employment elsewhere, he put the property into the hands of local estate agents. They found a purchaser willing to pay £7,500 for it with the additional plot, and he, in December, 1951, entered into a contract to purchase the property. The plaintiff again employed the defendant as his solicitor.

The purchaser's solicitors, on being supplied with an abstract of the plaintiff's title, pointed out that there was a defect in it, and they declined to go on with the purchase; in consequence the deposit had to be returned, and a claim arose for costs thrown away.

The defect was that it appeared on the face of the abstract of title that Colonel Wilks, the vendor to the plaintiff, had partly under a conveyance of July 22, 1937, and partly under a conveyance of February 28, 1938, purchased the property from the trustees of his father's will, of whom he was himself one. He was therefore in breach of the rule that a trustee cannot validly purchase the trust property either directly or through an intermediary.

The plaintiff, in his claim for damages, alleged that as a result of the defendant's negligence he had acquired a property with an unmarketable title, or alternatively, a property which he could only sell at a substantial loss. He also claimed as special damage the cost of a number of items, which he alleged resulted from his being unable to sell the property at the price which he gave for it, and his consequent inability to buy another house convenient for his new employment.

HARMAN, J. It was admitted before me that the class of persons claiming under the will of which the vendor Wilks was the trustee was not closed, and might embrace infants or persons unborn, and that for a number of years at any rate it would be impossible to say with certainty that no claim could arise to upset the transaction, although hitherto in fact no claim has been made. This is clearly a serious blot on the title, and not one that can be described with any propriety as a technical defect. There is a real danger that anyone acquiring this property with notice may be dispossessed of it hereafter. A beneficiary claiming to have the property restored to the trust must agree that the original purchase-money paid by Colonel Wilks and, in addition, money spent in improvements shall be repaid. The sum was assumed here to amount to £2,500. I ought to say that the defect in title does not extend to the further plot purchased by the plaintiff in 1951, but that plot by itself is of no greater value than the amount that the plaintiff paid for it. It would appear then at first sight that the measure of the defendant's liability is the diminution in value of the property; that is to say, the difference between the value in 1950, the date of the plaintiff's purchase, of the property with a good title and with the title which it in fact had.

The defendant, however, argues that it is the duty of the plaintiff before suing him in damages to seek to recover damages against his vendor Colonel Wilks under the covenant for title implied by reason of the conveyance as beneficial owner. It is said that this duty arises because of the obligation which rests on a person injured by a breach of contract to mitigate the damages. This suggestion seems to me to carry the doctrine of mitigation a stage further than it has been carried in any case to which I have been referred. The classic statement of the doctrine is that of Lord Haldane in *British Westinghouse Electric and Manufacturing Co. Ltd.* v. *Underground Electric Rail. Co. of London Ltd.*[1] The Lord Chancellor expressed it thus[2]: " The *quantum* of damage is a question of fact, and the only guidance the law can give is to lay down general principles which afford at times but scanty assistance in dealing with particular cases. The judges who give guidance to juries in these cases have necessarily to look at their special character, and to mould, for the purposes of different kinds of claim, the expression of the general principles which apply to them, and this is apt to give rise to an appearance of ambiguity. Subject to these observations I think that there are certain broad principles which are quite well settled. The first is that, as far as possible, he who has proved a breach of a bargain to supply what he contracted to get is to be placed, as far as money can do it, in as good a situation as if the contract had been performed. The fundamental basis is thus compensation for pecuniary loss naturally flowing from the breach; but this first principle is qualified by a second, which imposes on a plaintiff the duty of taking all reasonable steps to mitigate the loss consequent on the breach, and debars him from claiming any part of the damage which is due to his neglect to take such steps. In the words of James, L.J., in *Dunkirk Colliery Co.* v. *Lever*[3], ' the person who has broken the contract is not to be exposed to additional cost by reason of the plaintiffs not doing what they ought to have done as reasonable men, the plaintiffs not being under any obligation to do anything otherwise than in the ordinary course of business.' "

For the present purpose it seems to me that it is apposite to state the plaintiff's rights in the words of Scrutton, L.J., in *Payzu Ld.* v. *Saunders*[4] thus[5]: " he can recover no more than he would have suffered if he had acted reasonably, because any further damages do not reasonably follow from the defendant's breach. . . ."

Ought then the plaintiff as a reasonable man to enter on the litigation suggested? It was agreed that the defendant must offer him an indemnity against the costs, and it was suggested on the defendant's behalf that if an adequate indemnity were offered, if, secondly, the proposed defendant appeared to be solvent, and if, thirdly, there were a good *prima facie* right of action against that person, it was the duty of the injured party to embark on litigation in order to mitigate the damage suffered. This is a proposition which, in such general terms, I am not prepared to accept, nor do I think

[1] [1912] A. C. 673.   [2] *Ibid.*, 688.
[3] (1878), 9 Ch. D. 20, at p. 25.   [4] [1919] 2 K. B. 581.
                    [5] [1919] 2 K. B. 581, at p. 589.

I ought to entertain it here, because I am by no means certain that the foundations for it exist.

It may be conceded that the indemnity offered would be adequate and that Colonel Wilks is a man of substance. It was clear, however, that he would resist any claim and would in his turn claim over against his solicitors, for that was his attitude in the witness-box.

About the third condition much more doubt exists. I listened to a considerable argument based upon the extremely difficult words in which is couched the contract to be implied under section 76 of, and Sch. II to, the Law of Property Act, 1925, the defendant averring and the plaintiff denying that liability would arise in this case under these words. This is a question which I do not propose to decide. Nor need I decide whether Colonel Wilks, having regard to his position, was the " beneficial owner " of the property so as to bring the covenant into operation, it being a *sine qua non* that the covenantor must be in fact, as well as being expressed to be, the beneficial owner; compare the observations of Sir Wilfrid Greene, M.R., in *Fay* v. *Miller, Wilkins & Co.*[1], where he was discussing the covenant implied in an assurance as personal representative[2]. It appears to be the law that a breach of the covenant can be sued on at once and that there is no need to wait till a claim is made against the covenantee: see *Turner* v. *Moon*[3].

I do not propose to attempt to decide whether an action against Colonel Wilks would lie or be fruitful. I can see it would be one attended with no little difficulty. I am of opinion that the so-called duty to mitigate does not go so far as to oblige the injured party, even under an indemnity, to embark on a complicated and difficult piece of litigation against a third party. The damage to the plaintiff was done once and for all directly the voidable conveyance to him was executed. This was the direct result of the negligent advice tendered by his solicitor, the defendant, that a good title had been shown; and, in my judgment, it is no part of the plaintiff's duty to embark on the proposed litigation in order to protect his solicitor from the consequences of his own carelessness.

Next the defendant suggested that the injury might be lightened by a policy of insurance designed to cover the consequences of the defect. As to this, it is enough to say that no satisfactory evidence was adduced that any such policy could be obtained. Policies to cover defects of title are, it appears, common enough when supported by cross covenants on the part of the author of the defect, here Colonel Wilks. It is clear that he would have been entirely unwilling to enter into such a covenant, and in the absence of that there was no evidence that a policy could be obtained nor what its cost would be. In any event, though a policy might mitigate the pecuniary damage, it would not mend the title or make the purchase more attractive to a person buying the property for a home as this property would be bought.

It remains then to consider what is a proper amount of damage. This is necessarily highly speculative. The plaintiff was not bound, in my judgment, to resell in order to quantify it, particularly having regard to the fact that until quite recently the defendant denied that he was guilty of negligence. It is clear enough from the plaintiff's experience with the purchaser he found, that an ordinary purchaser finding the title defective in this respect will merely throw up the purchase, and that it would be necessary

---

[1] [1941] Ch. 360; [1941] 2 All E. R. 18.
[2] [1941] Ch. 360, at p. 363.
[3] [1901] 2 Ch. 825.

to explain in advance by way of condition of sale the existence of the defect. The result would be, I think, to bring forward a different class of purchaser, namely, the speculator willing to chance the future, but only because the property can be had cheap. The several elements to be brought into account are on the one side, first, the sum which would have to be paid before the property were returned to the trust; next, the chance that no claim will ever be made, and that the title will eventually ripen into security; and thirdly, the chance of recovering something against Colonel Wilks on his covenant for title. The sum involved under the first head may, having regard to the evidence, be put at £2,500, that under the second is not negligible after the lapse of fifteen years without a claim, and that under the third cannot be put very high as it would involve litigation with its attendant expense and delay and the uncertainty as to its result. On the other side of the account must be put the insecurity of the purchaser's tenure and the difficulties he would encounter should he wish to raise money by mortgage or to resell. On the evidence £6,000 may be taken as the true value of the property with a good title at the date of the breach in 1950.

Balancing one factor against the other as best I can after listening to the evidence, I think a fair estimate of the diminution in value of the property from its market price at the date of the breach in 1950 of £6,000 with a good title ought to be set at £2,000.

Beyond this which may be styled the general damage, the plaintiff claimed damages under a number of special heads. These were: (1) the defendant's scale fee of £63; (2) the cost of improvements done by the plaintiff and of the extra purchase; (3) the plaintiff's expenses in connexion with his new employment; (4) the cost of a valuation of the property; (5) interest on an overdraft; and (6) costs thrown away. I will deal with these in order. The first is the scale fee. It was conceded that this could not be recovered in this action. The second was cost of improvements and of the extra purchase. This claim was abandoned at the hearing. The third was the plaintiff's expenses in connexion with his new employment. In order to understand this some further facts must be stated.

The plaintiff's contract for resale of the property at £7,500 was made in December, 1951, and it appears that it was not until this event that he felt free to look for further employment. This he found in Lancashire where he had formerly been employed, and he entered on his new job on February 1, 1952. On February 18, 1952, he was obliged to return the deposit of £750 made on the contract of the previous December, the defect in his title having by then been discovered. As a result, being unable to complete the sale of the Hampshire property, he had not the financial means to purchase another property within reach of his new work, and he has ever since found himself temporary accommodation in Lancashire during the week and returned to his Hampshire home, where his wife has continued to reside, at weekends. His claim under this head is first for hotel expenses, which he puts at £175, secondly for the running expenses of his car between Hampshire and Lancashire, which he puts at £250, and thirdly for the expense of telephone calls to his wife every evening during his periods of separation from her, in respect of which he claims £50.

In my judgment, none of these sums is recoverable against the defendant. They do not fall within the second rule in *Hadley* v. *Baxendale*[1] as to remoteness of damage. This rule has recently been canvassed by Asquith,

---
[1] (1854), 9 Exch. 341.

L.J., in *Victoria Laundry (Windsor) Ltd.* v. *Newman Industries Ltd.*[1] thus[2]:
" What propositions applicable to the present case emerge from the authorities as a whole, including those analysed above ? We think they include the
following:—(1) It is well settled that the governing purpose of damages is
to put the party whose rights have been violated in the same position,
so far as money can do so, as if his rights had been observed: (*Wertheim*
v. *Chicoutimi Pulp Co.*)[3]. This purpose, if relentlessly pursued, would
provide him with a complete indemnity for all loss *de facto* resulting from a
particular breach, however improbable, however unpredictable. This, in
contract at least, is recognized as too harsh a rule. Hence, (2) in cases of
breach of contract the aggrieved party is only entitled to recover such part
of the loss actually resulting as was at the time of the contract reasonably
foreseeable as liable to result from the breach. (3) What was at that time
reasonably so foreseeable depends on the knowledge then possessed by the
parties or, at all events, by the party who later commits the breach."

These items were not, in my judgment, within the reasonable contemplation of the parties when the defendant assumed the duty of advising
the plaintiff. The change of place of the plaintiff's employment was not
one of the chances that could have been known to either of them. It was the
voluntary act of the plaintiff, not a result of any contract existing when the
bargain was made. The plaintiff chose a new job in Lancashire; he might
as well have selected one more remote in Kamschatka or less remote in
Hampshire. The defendant cannot be responsible for the expense. The
plaintiff might have bought or rented accommodation suitable to his new
employment, and there is no evidence that the defendant knew that his
financial position might render this impracticable. Still less can the defendant be called upon to pay for the telephone calls, a luxury no doubt
exemplary, yet uxorious.

The fourth head is a sum of 25 guineas paid by the plaintiff to a valuer
who, in 1950, was employed by him to value the property in order to quiet the
doubts of the plaintiff's bankers as to his financial position. He complains
that he would never have incurred this expense had he known that his title was
defective. No doubt this is true; but the defendant cannot be supposed to
know that any such step was required by the plaintiff's position or contemplated by him. This claim I reject.

The fifth claim represents the sum paid by the plaintiff to his bank
on an overdraft which he says would not have existed had he been able to
sell the property as he contracted to do as before stated. Here again it is
objected that the defendant is being asked to pay for the plaintiff's impe-
cuniosity, and it is pointed out that there is no evidence that the defendant
knew that the purchase-money had been borrowed by the plaintiff, and,
moreover, that if the plaintiff had been able to sell he would have incurred a
new liability similar to the old. In this connexion I was referred to *The
Edison*[4], and to *Trans Trust S.P.R.L.* v. *Danubian Trading Co*[5]. On the
whole, I am of the opinion that the plaintiff does not make out his case on this
point. His evidence was that it was his intention to purchase another
house with the proceeds of sale of his present one and to finance the new
purchase in the same way as before, namely, by an overdraft secured on the
new property.

[1] [1949] 2 K. B. 528; [1949] 1 All E. R. 997; see *supra*, p. 461.
[2] [1949] 2 K. B. 528, 539.   [3] [1911] A. C. 301.
[4] [1932] P. 52; [1933] All E. R. Rep. 144.
[5] [1952] 2 Q. B. 297; [1952] 1 All E. R. 970.

It appears to me, however, that, in order to put the plaintiff as far as possible in the position in which he would have been if there had been no breach, I must treat him as having sold the property at the date when the cause of action arose for what it would then fetch. This price I have assumed to be £4,000. He would then have been £2,000 out of pocket. The defendant therefore should recoup that sum with interest upon it. Under section 3 of the Law Reform (Miscellaneous Provisions) Act, 1934, the court has jurisdiction to award interest on damages from the date when the cause of action arose, and accordingly the sum of £2,000 will carry interest at 4 per cent. per annum from April 22, 1950, till the date of this judgment.

The sixth head of damages for costs thrown away was a matter of agreement at the hearing, and that agreement will be embodied in the judgment.

DUNLOP PNEUMATIC TYRE COMPANY v. NEW GARAGE AND MOTOR COMPANY, LTD.

BRIDGE v. CAMPBELL DISCOUNT CO., LTD.

A sum specified in a contract to be paid in the event of a breach may be either a penalty or liquidated damages. It is recoverable in full only if it is regarded by the court as liquidated damages. It will be regarded as liquidated damages if it may reasonably be inferred from all the circumstances of the case that the parties sought to form a genuine pre-estimate of the loss likely to be caused by the breach.

Dunlop Pneumatic Tyre Company v. New Garage and Motor Company, Ltd.

[1915] A.C. 79

LORD DUNEDIN. My Lords, the appellants, through an agent, entered into a contract with the respondents under which they supplied them with their goods, which consisted mainly of motor-tyre covers and tubes. By this contract, in respect of certain concessions as to discounts, the respondents bound themselves not to do several things, which may be shortly set forth as follows: not to tamper with the manufacturers' marks; not to sell to any private customer or co-operative society at prices less than the current price list issued by the Dunlop Company; not to supply to persons whose supplies the Dunlop Company had decided to suspend; not to exhibit or to export without the Dunlop Company's assent. Finally, the agreement concluded (clause 5), " We agree to pay to the Dunlop Pneumatic Tyre Company, Ltd. the sum of 5*l.* for each and every tyre, cover or tube sold or offered in breach of this agreement, as and by way of liquidated damages and not as a penalty."

The appellants, having discovered that the respondents had sold covers and tubes at under the current list price, raised action and demanded damages. The case was tried and the breach in fact held proved. An inquiry was directed before the Master as to damages. The Master inquired, and assessed the damages at 250*l.*, adding this explanation: " I find that it was left open to me to decide whether the 5*l.* fixed in the agreement was penalty or liquidated damages. I find that it was liquidated damages."

The respondents appealed to the Court of Appeal, when the majority of that Court, Vaughan Williams and Swinfen Eady, L.JJ., held, Kennedy, L.J., dissenting, that the said sum of 5*l.* was a penalty, and entered judgment for the plaintiffs for the sum of 2*l.* as nominal damages. Appeal from that decision is now before your Lordships' House.

My Lords, we had the benefit of a full and satisfactory argument, and a citation of the very numerous cases which have been decided on this branch of the law. The matter has been handled, and at no distant date, in the Courts of highest resort. I particularly refer to the *Clydebank* case[1] in your Lordships' House and the cases of *Public Works Commissioner* v. *Hills*[2] and *Webster* v. *Bosanquet*[3] in the Privy Council. In each of these cases many of the previous cases were considered. In view of that fact, and of the number of the authorities available, I do not think it advisable to attempt any detailed review of the various cases, but I shall content myself with stating succinctly the various propositions which I think are deducible from the decisions which rank as authoritative:—

1. Though the parties to a contract who use the words " penalty " or " liquidated damages " may *prima facie* be supposed to mean what they say, yet the expression used is not conclusive. The Court must find out whether the payment stipulated is in truth a penalty or liquidated damages. This doctrine may be said to be found *passim* in nearly every case.

2. The essence of a penalty is a payment of money stipulated as *in terrorem* of the offending party; the essence of liquidated damages is a genuine covenanted pre-estimate of damage (*Clydebank Engineering and Shipbuilding Co.* v. *Don Jose Ramos Yzquierdo y Castaneda*[1]).

3. The question whether a sum stipulated is penalty or liquidated damages is a question of construction to be decided upon the terms and inherent circumstances of each particular contract, judged of as at the time of the making of the contract, not as at the time of the breach (*Public Works Commissioner* v. *Hills*[2] and *Webster* v. *Bosanquet*[3]).

4. To assist this task of construction various tests have been suggested, which if applicable to the case under consideration may prove helpful, or even conclusive. Such are:

(*a*) It will be held to be penalty if the sum stipulated for is extravagant and unconscionable in amount in comparison with the greatest loss that could conceivably be proved to have followed from the breach. (Illustration given by Lord Halsbury in *Clydebank* case[1].)

(*b*) It will be held to be a penalty if the breach consists only in not paying a sum of money, and the sum stipulated is a sum greater than the sum which ought to have been paid (*Kemble* v. *Farren*[4]). This though one of the most ancient instances is truly a corollary to the last test. Whether it had its historical origin in the doctrine of the common law that when A. promised to pay B. a sum of money on a certain day and did not do so, B. could only recover the sum with, in certain cases, interest, but could never recover further damages for non-timeous payment, or whether it was a survival of the time when equity reformed unconscionable bargains merely because they were unconscionable—a subject which much exercised Jessel, M.R., in *Wallis* v. *Smith*[5]—is probably more interesting than material.

(*c*) There is a presumption (but no more) that it is penalty when " a single lump sum is made payable by way of compensation on the occurrence of one or more or all of several events, some of which may occasion serious and others but trifling damage " (Lord Watson in *Lord Elphinstone* v. *Monkland Iron and Coal Co.*[6]).

---

¹ [1905] A. C. 6.   ² [1906] A. C. 368.   ³ [1912] A. C. 394.
⁴ (1829), 6 Bing. 141.   ⁵ (1882), 21 Ch. D. 243.   ⁶ (1886), 11 App. Cas. 332.

On the other hand:

(*d*) It is no obstacle to the sum stipulated being a genuine pre-estimate of damage, that the consequences of the breach are such as to make precise pre-estimation almost an impossibility. On the contrary, that is just the situation when it is probable that pre-estimated damage was the true bargain between the parties (*Clydebank* case, Lord Halsbury[1]: *Webster* v. *Bosanquet*, Lord Mersey[2]).

Turning now to the facts of the case, it is evident that the damage apprehended by the appellants owing to the breaking of the agreement was an indirect and not a direct damage. So long as they got their price from the respondents for each article sold, it could not matter to them directly what the respondents did with it. Indirectly it did. Accordingly, the agreement is headed " Price Maintenance Agreement," and the way in which the appellants would be damaged if prices were cut is clearly explained in evidence by Mr. Baisley, and no successful attempt is made to controvert that evidence. But though damage as a whole from such a practice would be certain, yet damage from any one sale would be impossible to forecast. It is just, therefore, one of those cases where it seems quite reasonable for parties to contract that they should estimate that damage at a certain figure, and provided that figure is not extravagant there would seem no reason to suspect that it is not truly a bargain to assess damages, but rather a penalty to be held *in terrorem*.

The argument of the respondents was really based on two heads. They overpressed, in my judgment, the dictum of Lord Watson in *Lord Elphinstone's* case[3], reading it as if he had said that the matter was conclusive, instead of saying, as he did, that it raised a presumption, and they relied strongly on the case of *Willson* v. *Love*[4].

Now, in the first place, I have considerable doubt whether the stipulated payment here can fairly be said to deal with breaches, " some of which "— I am quoting Lord Watson's words—" may occasion serious and others but trifling damage." As a mere matter of construction, I doubt whether clause 5 applies to anything but sales below price. But I will assume that it does. None the less the mischief, as I have already pointed out, is an indirect mischief, and I see no data on which, as a matter of construction, I could settle in my own mind that the indirect damage from selling a cover would differ in magnitude from the indirect damage from selling a tube; or that the indirect damage from a cutting-price sale would differ from the indirect damage from supply at a full price to a hostile, because prohibited, agent. You cannot weigh such things in a chemical balance. The character of the agricultural land which was ruined by slag heaps in *Elphinstone's* case[5] was not all the same, but no objection was raised by Lord Watson to applying an overhead rate per acre, the sum not being in itself unconscionable.

I think *Elphinstone's* case[5], or rather the dicta in it, do go to this length, that if there are various breaches to which one indiscriminate sum to be paid in breach is applied, then the strength of the chain must be taken at its weakest link. If you can clearly see that the loss on one particular breach could never amount to the stipulated sum, then you may come to the conclusion that the sum is penalty. But further than this it does not go; so, for

---

[1] [1905] A. C. at 11.
[3] (1886), 11 App. Cas. 332, at p. 342.
[2] [1912] A. C. at p. 398.
[4] [1896] 1 Q. B. 626.
[5] (1886), 11 App. Cas. 332.

the reasons already stated, I do not think the present case forms an instance of what I have just expressed.

As regards *Willson's* case[1], I do not think it material to consider whether it was well decided on the facts. For it was decided on the view of the facts that the manurial value of straw and of hay were known ascertainable quantities as at the time of the bargain, and radically different, so that the damage resulting from the want of one could never be the same as the damage resulting from the want of the other.

Added to that, the parties there had said " penalty," and the effort was to make out that that really meant liquidated damages; and lastly, if my view of the facts in the present case is correct, then Rigby, L.J., would have agreed with me, for the last words of his judgment are as follows: " On the other hand it is stated that, when the damages caused by a breach of contract are incapable of being ascertained, the sum made by the contract payable on such a breach is to be regarded as liquidated damages. The question arises, What is meant in this statement by the expression ' incapable of being ascertained ' ? In their proper sense the words appear to refer to a case where no rule or measure of damages is available for the guidance of a jury as to the amount of the damages, and a judge would have to tell them they must fix the amount as best they can." To arrive at the indirect damage in this case, supposing no sum had been stipulated, that is just what a judge would, in my opinion, have had to do.

On the whole matter, therefore, I go with the opinion of Kennedy, L.J., and I move your Lordships that the appeal be allowed, and judgment given for the sum as brought out by the Master, the appellants to have their costs in this House and in the Courts below.

LORDS ATKINSON, PARKER OF WADDINGTON, and PARMOOR delivered judgments to the same effect.

Bridge v. Campbell Discount Co. Ltd.

[1962] 1 All E.R. 385

APPEAL by Frank Kitchener Bridge from an order of the Court of Appeal (Holroyd Pearce, Harman and Davies, L.JJ.), dated Mar. 1, 1961, and reported sub nom. *Campbell Discount Co., Ltd. v. Bridge,* [1961] 2 All E.R. 97, allowing an appeal by the respondents, Campbell Discount Co., Ltd., from an order of His Honour Judge Bassett, dated May 3, 1960, and made at Ilford County Court, whereby he dismissed the respondents' claim for money due under a hire-purchase agreement on the ground that the sum claimed was a penalty.

LORD RADCLIFFE: My Lords, it is an unfortunate circumstance that we find ourselves beginning this appeal at a very different point from that at which the Court of Appeal left it. The facts of the case, though meagre and not properly brought out in the county court proceedings, do, in my view, admit of only one conclusion on the basic question as to how the hire-purchase agreement was brought to an end; and I think it came to an end in a different way from that which was, in effect, assumed by all the members of the appeal court. In the result, the question of law which was, no doubt, the cause of their granting leave for the case to come to this House does not arise. On the other hand, the question which we do have to determine

---

[1] [1896] 1 Q. B. 626.

on the basis of fact which is, I believe, acceptable to your Lordships, is itself both important and difficult. I do not think, therefore, that either the appeal proceedings or the arguments on them have been in any way wasted.

First, then, as to the facts. We have here a hire-purchase agreement made on July 20, 1959, under which the appellant, Mr. Bridge, took from the respondents a second-hand Bedford Dormobile motor car, 1954 make, paying at once £10 in cash and receiving a credit for £95 for surrendering another motor car in part exchange and undertaking to pay thereafter thirty-six consecutive monthly sums of £10 9s. 2d. each, the first falling due on Aug. 20, 1959. At the conclusion of those payments, the appellant was to have the usual purchase option of acquiring the motor car by the payment of an additional £1. The agreement was on a printed form, which is evidently one of the regular instruments used by the respondents for transactions of this nature. It contains a somewhat voluminous set of fourteen clauses, setting out conditions, stipulations and undertakings by which the hirer is to be bound. For the purpose of deciding the issue of fact, it is enough if I note that, by cl. 6, it was provided that the hirer could at any time terminate the hiring by giving written notice of termination to the owners, whereupon the provisions of cl. 9 were to apply; that, by cl. 7, the owners had a right, if the hirer failed to pay any of the sums due under the agreement or to observe any other of the numerous stipulations contained in it, immediately to terminate the hiring and the agreement and retake possession of the motor car; that by cl. 8, it was provided that, in certain specified events, of which the death or bankruptcy of the hirer may be taken as instances, the agreement and hiring were immediately to determine, though without prejudice to (inter alia) the hirer's obligations under cl. 9; and that cl. 9, which, since it is crucial to this case, I set out in full, ran as follows:

> " If this agreement or the hiring be terminated for any reason before the vehicle becomes, under cl. 5 hereof, the property of the hirer, then the hirer shall no longer be in possession of the vehicle with the owner's consent and the hirer shall forthwith (a) at his own cost and risk deliver up the vehicle in a proper state of repair and condition together with all necessary licences, registration books or certificates, insurance policy and other documents relative to the vehicle to the owners at such address as they may direct; and (b) pay to the owners arrears of hire rent due and unpaid at the date of termination of the hiring together with interest thereon stipulated under cl. 1 hereof and by way of agreed compensation for depreciation of the vehicle such further sum as may be necessary to make the rentals paid and payable hereunder equal to two-thirds of the hire-purchase price as specified in the schedule hereto; and (c) pay to the owners such other sums due and payable hereunder including all expenses incurred by the owners in ascertaining the whereabouts of the hirer and/or in tracing and recovering possession of the vehicle and putting it into reasonable repair order and condition, fair wear and tear excepted. Provided always that if the hire-purchase price as specified in the schedule hereto does not exceed £300 (but not otherwise) such of the foregoing provisions as are inconsistent with the provisions of the statutory notice hereinafter contained shall not apply and the provisions of the statutory notice (and of the Hire-Purchase Acts) and any other statute affecting hire-purchase transactions shall prevail."

The hiring itself was not destined to have a long life. The appellant paid £10 10s. by way of his first monthly instalment on Aug. 20, 1959, but, on Sept. 3, he wrote to the respondents in the following terms:

" Agreement No. 78900
    " Dear Sir, Owing to unforeseen personal circumstances I am very sorry but

I will not be able to pay any more payments on the Bedford Dormobile. Will you please let me know when and where I will have to return the car. I am very sorry regarding this but I have no alternative."

It seems to be common ground that, on Sept. 14, he returned the vehicle to the sales room of the motor car dealers from whom he had taken it at the time when the hire-purchase transaction was entered into with the respondents. They accepted this as a return of the motor car, and in due course proceeded to sue him in the county court for the sum of £206 3s. 4d. at issue in this action. The sum was made up of £321 13s. 4d., being the two-thirds of the hire-purchase price of £482 10s. claimed as due under cl. 9 (b) of the agreement, less the £105 deposit and the £10 10s. single instalment.

It is not for me to say what exactly was the basis of fact on which the respondents launched their claim. Their particulars of claim wrapped the matter in an impenetrable obscurity and, since that was never dissipated by any amendment, it must always remain obscure what it was on which they thought that they were founding. It is obvious that there were two possible positions. One was that the appellant had decided to exercise his option under cl. 6 to terminate the hiring and thereby to bring down on his head the not insubstantial consequence of cl. 9. The other was that the appellant had fallen down on his agreement and declared his inability to perform it, with the result that the respondents were entitled under cl. 7 to treat the contract as at an end and to sue for whatever they were entitled to recover under its provisions, including those of cl. 9. The particulars of claim consisted of three paragraphs. The first merely referred to the terms of the hire-purchase agreement. The second and third were as follows:

" 2. It was a provision of the said agreement that if the [appellant] should terminate the hiring he should pay to the [respondents] by way of agreed compensation for depreciation a sum equal to two-thirds of the hire-purchase price less payments already made.
" 3. On or about Sept. 14, 1959, the [appellant] purported to terminate the hiring by returning the said vehicle to Messrs. Monarch Car Services of 625, Romford Road, Manor Park, London, E.12, from whom the [respondents] had purchased the said vehicle to let on hire with option to purchase to the [appellant]. The liability of the [appellant] on termination is calculated as follows:

	£	s.	d.	£	s.	d.
" Two-thirds of the hire-purchase price				321	13	4
" Less deposit	105	0	0			
" Instalments received	10	10	0	115	10	0
				£206	3	4

" And the [respondents] claim the sum of £206 3s. 4d."

It is to be noted that the letter of Sept. 3 is not referred to. Yet, if the hirer is to be held to have been exercising his option of determination, it can only have been exercised by the sending of this as the written notice that was required. But the letter was written on Sept. 3, and the respondents' particulars elect to say that it was on Sept. 14, the day of the return of the motor car, that the hirer " purported to terminate the hiring." I can only say that I do not know which of the two possible positions the respondents wished it to be understood that they were adopting; and I cannot think that the appellant's legal defences have been affected one way or the other by the fact that, in reply to this pleading, his solicitors merely stated in their defence that he admitted that, on or about Sept. 14, he terminated the agreement. This must refer to the return of the motor car, not to the sending of the letter; and, for the purposes of these agreements, there is a distinction between terminating a hiring (which is all that cl. 6 deals with) and terminating the agreement itself. " Terminate " is an ambiguous word, since it may refer to a termination by a right under the agreement or by a condition incorporated in it or by a deliberate breach by one party amounting to a repudiation of the whole contract. There is nothing in the learned county court judge's notes of the hearing that helps to clear up the matter. It was evidently the respondents' case by that time that the appellant had exercised the hirer's option to determine; but the judge merely dismissed the claim as involving a penalty, without any further record of his views. When the matter reached the Court of Appeal, the issue of fact was dealt with very briefly, Holroyd Pearce, L.J., who delivered the leading judgment, merely saying[1] that the letter of Sept. 3 was a notice to terminate and that it was an untenable argument to suggest that the sum claimed under cl. 9 was claimed as damages for the hirer's own breach. With great respect to the members of that court, I think, myself, that that is just what it was and that they were too summary in their disposal of this aspect of the case.

An interpretation of the facts can be derived only from what we know of the parties' acts or from the issues established by their pleadings. There is nothing else to go on. I have dealt with the latter; I think that the pleadings leave the issue too ambiguous to warrant any conclusion. There remains then the letter of Sept. 3. Is this to be treated as an exercise of the hirer's option to determine ? I cannot help saying that I can see no ground for so treating it. It makes no reference to the option; it is not expressed in the terms of a man exercising a right; its whole tenor is that of a regretful apology for unexpected inability to carry out a contract that has been undertaken. In my opinion, the natural interpretation of such a message is that the writer intended merely to state the facts of his position, that he could not carry on with his hire payments, and to ask for directions as to what he was to do with the vehicle to the possession of which he would no longer be entitled. I do not think that it would be right to proceed on any other basis of fact. The consequence is that we are dealing with a case in which the hirer declared his inability to go on with the hiring and the owners resumed possession of their vehicle and then went to court to assert their contractual rights under cl. 9 (b) of the agreement, claiming " as agreed compensation for depreciation " the balance sum of money required to make up two-thirds of the total hire-purchase price. Are they entitled to judgment for this sum, or was the learned county court judge right in dismissing their claim as being a claim for a penalty ?

My Lords, when a question arises whether a sum stipulated to be payable under a contract is liquidated damages for a breach of that contract or some part of it or is a penalty attached to the breach, I think that, by this date, there is ample guidance in the authorities how to decide between the two alternatives. The appropriate tests have been worked out in a number of leading cases and, as we know, they are conveniently brought together in the speech of Lord Dunedin in *Dunlop Pneumatic Tyre Co., Ltd.* v. *New Garage and Motor Co., Ltd.*[2] I believe that the line of demarcation is drawn in its simplest form (as Lord Dunedin himself said in *Public Works Comr.* v. *Hills*[3]) if one says that a sum cannot be legally exacted as liquidated damages unless it is found to amount to " a genuine pre-estimate of " damages (to

---

[1] [1961] 1 Q. B. at p. 454; [1961] 2 All E. R. at p. 100.
[2] [1915] A. C. 79. [3] [1906] A. C. at p. 375.

use the phrase originated by Lord Robertson in *Clydebank Engineering and Shipbuilding Co.* v. *Yzquierdo y Castaneda (Don Jose Ramos)*[1]. If it does not amount to such a pre-estimate, then it is to be regarded as a penalty, and I do not myself think that it helps to identify a penalty to describe it as in the nature of a threat " enforced in terrorem " (to use Lord Halsbury's phrase in *Lord Elphinstone* v. *Monkland Iron and Coal Co.*[2]). I do not find that that description adds anything of substance to the idea conveyed by the word " penalty " itself, and it obscures the fact that penalties may quite readily be undertaken by parties who are not in the least terrorised by the prospect of having to pay them and yet are, as I understand it, entitled to claim the protection of the court when they are called on to make good their promises. The refusal to sanction legal proceedings for penalties is, in fact, a rule of the court's own, produced and maintained for purposes of public policy (except where imposed by positive statutory enactment, as in 8 & 9 Wm. 3 c. 11; 4 & 5 Anne c. 16). The intention of the parties themselves is never conclusive, and may be overruled or ignored if the court considers that even its clear expression does not represent " the real nature of the transaction " or what " in truth " it is to be taken to be.

Is it plausible to say that we have in this " agreed compensation for depreciation " a genuine pre-estimate of damages ? The first difficulty is to know for what it is to be taken as damages, for, until one can identify the obligation and the possible consequences of its breach, one does not have anything against which to measure the stipulated sum which is claimed as liquidated damages. Now the depreciation of the vehicle is not itself a breach of contract on the part of the hirer. He has a separate obligation under cl. 9 (a) to deliver it up, if it does not become his property, in a " proper state of repair and condition "; so cl. 9 (b) does not provide any compensation for a lack of that state and condition. The depreciation referred to can only be the loss of value in the vehicle ascribable to its increasing age and the natural processes of wear and tear and there is, of course, no responsibility on the hirer to prevent this. Even if, by a less accurate use of language, depreciation is to cover the loss of market value due to the unpredictable movements of the second-hand market, the point is the same; such losses do not arise from any default of the hirer. I can say at once that, if one really tied oneself to this idea of compensation for depreciation, the case for treating the clause as a genuine pre-estimate of the damage suffered by depreciation would be almost unarguable. Since the obligation under cl. 9 (b) may mature at any time from the beginning to the end of the hiring, a week after the beginning or a week before the end, it seems to me impossible to take a single formula for measuring the damage as any true pre-estimate. It produces the result, absurd in its own terms, that the estimated amount of depreciation becomes progressively less the longer the vehicle is used under the hire. This is because the sum agreed on diminishes as the total of the cash payments increases. It is a sliding scale of compensation, but a scale that slides in the wrong direction, if the measure of anticipated depreciation is to be supposed to be the basis for the compensation agreed on. The fact that this anomalous· result is deliberately produced by the formula employed suggests, I think, that the real purpose of this clause is not to provide compensation for depreciation at all but to afford the owners a substantial guarantee against the loss of their hiring contract. The difficulty

---

[1] [1905] A. C. at p. 19.   [2] (1886), 11 App. Cas. at p. 348.

of the case, as I see it, is to decide whether an agreement of this kind falls within the legal conception of a penalty.

It is fairly easy to see what is really involved in cl. 9 (b). The purpose of an owner entering into a hire-purchase transaction is to turn goods into cash; as a moneylender, which is what he is in all but form, his purpose is to recover with interest the amount of his advance. This clause is designed to provide him with a guarantee at the expense of the hirer that, come what may, he will get out of the deal in money at any rate two-thirds of the total hire-purchase price, which is defined as being cash price plus hiring charges and option fee. The guarantee thus becomes operative whenever the hiring determines before the purchase option is exercised, provided that something less than two-thirds of the whole sum has then been paid over, and it makes no difference to the terms of the obligation whether the hiring is put an end to by the hirer under his option, or by the owner under his, or by the automatic operation of any one of the events specified in cl. 8. That is why cl. 9 (b) is not attached separately to the various preceding clauses but applies indifferently to them all. It is this aspect which has troubled several judges in the past, and has led more than one to say that such a provision is not a penalty at all or, to put the same idea in another way, to express the view that, if it is not a penalty for all purposes and in all relations, as, for instance, when the hirer brings it on himself by exercising his option to terminate, it cannot be a penalty in any one situation, as, for instance, when the owner is suing for damages for breach of the hiring obligations. I do not think that the difficulty has ever been better put than it is in the judgment delivered by Greer, L.J., in *Chester and Cole, Ltd.* v. *Wright*[1] quoted from *Jones and Proudfoot's Notes on Hire-Purchase Law* (2nd Edn.), p. 124, in *Cooden Engineering Co., Ltd.* v. *Stanford*[2].

I do not myself feel that this is a difficulty which should determine the matter. The court's jurisdiction to relieve against penalties depends on " a question, not of words or of forms of speech, but of substance and of things " (see per Lord Davey in the *Clydebank Engineering* case[3]). It cannot really depend on a point of construction, though it is often spoken of as so depending. A sum of money sued for in one set of circumstances, as on a hirer's breach, when alone the " in terrorem " idea can have any application, may be a penalty in the eyes of the law, without it being necessarily anything but the price of an option in another set of circumstances or a mere guarantee in yet a third. On this point, therefore, I agree with the views of the majority of the Court of Appeal in *Cooden's* case[4]. I know, of course, that, to travel to another branch of equity's relief jurisdiction, the precise reason why a deposit made on a sale of land is not recoverable if the bargain goes off by the purchaser's default is that it is treated as a guarantee (see *Howe* v. *Smith*[5]); but, nevertheless, every penalty, even a penal bond, is in some sense a guarantee for the due performance of the contract, and I do not see any sufficient reason why, in the right setting, a sum of money may not be treated as a penalty, even though it arises from an obligation that is essentially a guarantee. When such a sum is claimed, as it is here, as compensation for the hirer's breach of the hiring contract, I think that it bears every mark of being a penalty. The total hire-purchase price is called up to the extent of two-thirds, regardless of two considerations essential to

---

[1] (1930), unreported.   [2] [1953] 1 Q. B. at 105; [1952] 2 All E. R. at p. 925.
[3] [1905] A. C. at p. 15.   [4] [1953] 1 Q. B. 86; [1952] 2 All E. R. 915.
[5] (1884), 27 Ch. D. 89.

any measurement of the owner's loss; the price includes a considerable interest element which the owner does not in the result forgo so far as the compensation is paid immediately, and the vehicle comes back into the owner's possession with a realisable value that, in many circumstances, may exceed the one-third balance of the price which the owner has not got in. In my opinion, a clause of this kind, when founded on in consequence of a contractual branch, comes within the range of the court's jurisdiction to relieve against penalties, and the respondents should be confined to the right of claiming from the appellant any damage that they can show themselves to have actually suffered from his falling down on the contract. I think, therefore, that *Cooden* v. *Stanford*[1] was rightly decided, though I do not necessarily agree with everything that was said by the majority of the members of the court in coming to their decision. I see nothing " unconscionable " in an owner feeling that, when he goes into transactions of this nature, he should have some protection against having goods, part worn and of uncertain realisable value, thrown back on his hands, with the attendant difficulty of putting any satisfactory second-hand value on them for the purposes of proving his damage. I doubt, however, whether he could ever validly protect himself on the scale of up to two-thirds that is envisaged here, without much more elaborate provisions for adjustment according to the circumstances in which the claim falls due. Indeed, the matter may be one in which only legislation can mark the limits of what is to be treated as permissible.

Having regard to the view that your Lordships have taken as to the true facts of the case, our decision does not, I take it, conclude the question of an owner's rights under such agreements, when the hiring is determined under a hirer's option or by an event specified in the contract but not involving a breach. Such questions are closely related to what we have to consider here, but it does not follow that the legal arguments that sustain the hirer, when he is sued on breach, would be capable of sustaining him in these other situations. Indeed, although I wish to decide nothing, I appreciate that the doctrine of penalties can only be applied to those situations by the construction of almost a new set of arguments that would not arise naturally out of the arguments and considerations that have prevailed with courts, either of equity or of common law, when relieving against penalties in the past. " Unconscionable " must not be taken to be a panacea for adjusting any contract between competent persons when it shows a rough edge to one side or the other, and equity lawyers are, I notice, sometimes both surprised and discomfited by the plenitude of jurisdiction and the imprecision of rules that are attributed to " equity " by their more enthusiastic colleagues. Since the courts of equity never undertook to serve as a general adjuster of men's bargains, it was inevitable that they should, in course of time, evolve definite rules as to the circumstances in which, and the conditions under which, relief would be given, and I do not think that it would be at all an easy task, and I am not certain that it would be a desirable achievement, to try to reconcile all the rules under some simple general formula. Even such masters of equity as Lord Eldon and Sir George Jessel, M.R., it must be remembered, were highly sceptical of the court's duty to apply the epithet " unconscionable " or its consequences to contracts made between persons of full age in circumstances that did not fall within the familiar categories of fraud, surprise, accident, etc., even though such contracts

---

[1] [1953] 1 Q. B. 86; [1952] 2 All E. R. 915.

involved the payment of a larger sum of money on breach of an obligation to pay a smaller (see the latter's judgment in *Wallis* v. *Smith*[1]. But I do not speculate what principles they would have thought applicable to a hire-purchase contract, in which the hirer, I dare say willingly enough, transacts only with a dealer who is not the agent of the owner and, if he signs up at all, signs up to an elaborate fixed menu of stipulations and conditions, which he probably does not bother himself to read and very likely does not or cannot understand. I agree that the appeal should be allowed.

Judgments allowing the appeal were also delivered by Viscount SIMONDS, Lord MORTON OF HENRYTON, Lord DENNING and Lord DEVLIN.

Warner Bros. Pictures Incorporated v. Nelson

[1937] 1 K.B. 209

SPECIFIC PERFORMANCE AND INJUNCTION. Specific performance will not be decreed of a contract to perform personal services, but if the contract contains an express negative stipulation obliging one of the parties not to act inconsistently with his positive contract, an injunction may be granted against a breach of that negative stipulation.

No injunction, however, will be granted if its effect will be to make specific performance of the positive contract virtually inevitable.

BRANSON, J. The facts of this case are few and simple. The plaintiffs are a firm of film producers in the United States of America. In 1931 the defendant, then not well known as a film actress, entered into a contract with the plaintiffs. Before the expiration of that contract the present contract was entered into between the parties. Under it the defendant received a considerably enhanced salary, the other conditions being substantially the same. This contract was for fifty-two weeks and contains options to the plaintiffs to extend it for further periods of fifty-two weeks at ever-increasing amounts of salary to the defendant. No question of construction arises upon the contract, and it is not necessary to refer to it in any great detail; but in view of some of the contentions raised it is desirable to call attention quite generally to some of the provisions contained in it. It is a stringent contract, under which the defendant agrees " to render her exclusive services as a motion picture and/or legitimate stage actress " to the plaintiffs, and agrees to perform solely and exclusively for them. She also agrees, by way of negative stipulation, that " she will not, during such time "—that is to say, during the term of the contract—" render any services for or in any other phonographic, stage or motion picture production or productions or business of any other person . . . or engage in any other occupation without the written consent of the producer being first had and obtained."

With regard to the term of the contract there is a further clause, clause 23, under which, if the defendant fails, refuses or neglects to perform her services under the contract, the plaintiffs " have the right to extend the term of this agreement and all of its provisions for a period equivalent to the period during which such failure, refusal or neglect shall be continued."

In June of this year the defendant, for no discoverable reason except that she wanted more money, declined to be further bound by the agreement, left the United States and, in September, entered into an agreement in this country with a third person. This was a breach of contract on her part,

---
[1] (1882), 21 Ch. D. 243.

and the plaintiffs on September 9 commenced this action claiming a declaration that the contract was valid and binding, an injunction to restrain the defendant from acting in breach of it, and damages. The defence alleged that the plaintiffs had committed breaches of the contract which entitled the defendant to treat it as at an end ; but at the trial this contention was abandoned and the defendant admitted that the plaintiffs had not broken the contract and that she had ; but it was contended on her behalf that no injunction could as a matter of law be granted in the circumstances of the case.

At the outset of the considerations of law which arise stands the question, not raised by the pleadings but urged for the defendant in argument, that this contract is unlawful as being in restraint of trade. The ground for this contention was that the contract compelled the defendant to serve the plaintiffs exclusively, and might in certain circumstances endure for the whole of her natural life. No authority was cited to me in support of the proposition that such a contract is illegal, and I see no reason for so holding. Where, as in the present contract, the covenants are all concerned with what is to happen whilst the defendant is employed by the plaintiffs and not thereafter, there is no room for the application of the doctrine of restraint of trade.

A similar contract came before the Courts in the case of *Gaumont-British Picture Corporation, Ltd.* v. *Alexander*[1], and was upheld by Porter, J. I respectfully agree with his view.

I turn then to the consideration of the law applicable to this case on the basis that the contract is a valid and enforceable one. It is conceded that our Courts will not enforce a positive covenant of personal service ; and specific performance of the positive covenants by the defendant to serve the plaintiffs is not asked in the present case. The practice of the Court of Chancery in relation to the enforcement of negative covenants is stated on the highest authority by Lord Cairns in the House of Lords in *Doherty* v. *Allman*[2]. His Lordship says : " My Lords, if there had been a negative covenant, I apprehend, according to well-settled practice, a Court of Equity would have had no discretion to exercise. If parties, for valuable consideration, with their eyes open, contract that a particular thing shall not be done, all that a Court of Equity has to do is to say, by way of injunction, that which the parties have already said by way of covenant, that the thing shall not be done ; and in such case the injunction does nothing more than give the sanction of the process of the Court to that which already is the contract between the parties. It is not then a question of the balance of convenience or inconvenience, or of the amount of damage or of injury— it is the specific performance, by the Court, of that negative bargain which the parties have made, with their eyes open, between themselves."

That was not a case of a contract of personal service ; but the same principle had already been applied to such a contract by Lord St. Leonards in *Lumley* v. *Wagner*[3]. The Lord Chancellor used the following language : " Wherever this Court has not proper jurisdiction to enforce specific performance, it operates to bind men's consciences, as far as they can be bound, to a true and literal performance of their agreements ; and it will not suffer them to depart from their contracts at their pleasure, leaving the party with whom they have contracted to the mere chance of any damages

---

[1] [1936] 2 All. E. R. 1686. [2] (1878), 3 App. Cas. 709, at p. 719.
[3] (1852), 1 De G. M. & G. 604, at p. 619.

which a jury may give. The exercise of this jurisdiction has, I believe, had a wholesome tendency towards the maintenance of that good faith which exists in this country to a much greater degree perhaps than in any other ; and although the jurisdiction is not to be extended, yet a judge would desert his duty who did not act up to what his predecessors have handed down as the rule for his guidance in the administration of such an equity." This passage was cited as a correct statement of the law in the opinion of a strong Board of the Privy Council in the case of *Lord Strathcona Steamship Co.* v. *Dominion Coal Co.*[1], and I not only approve it, if I may respectfully say so, but am bound by it.

The defendant, having broken her positive undertakings in the contract without any cause or excuse which she was prepared to support in the witness-box, contends that she cannot be enjoined from breaking the negative covenants also. The mere fact that a covenant which the Court would not enforce, if expressed in positive form, is expressed in the negative instead, will not induce the Court to enforce it. That appears, if authority is needed for such a proposition, from *Davis* v. *Foreman*[2] ; *Kirchner* v. *Gruban*[3] ; and *Chapman* v. *Westerby*[4]. The Court will attend to the substance and not to the form of the covenant. Nor will the Court, true to the principle that specific performance of a contract of personal service will never be ordered, grant an injunction in the case of such a contract to enforce negative covenants if the effect of so doing would be to drive the defendant either to starvation or to specific performance of the positive covenants : see *Whitwood Chemical Co.* v. *Hardman*[5], where Lindley, L.J., said : " What injunction can be granted in this particular case which will not be, in substance, and effect, a decree for specific performance of this agreement ? " ; *Ehrman* v. *Bartholomew*[6], where the injunction was refused, firstly, on the ground that it was doubtful whether the covenant applied at all, and, secondly, on the ground that to grant it would compel the defendant wholly to abstain from any business whatsoever ; and *Mortimer* v. *Beckett*[7], where there was also no negative stipulation.

The case of *Rely-a-Bell Burglar and Fire Alarm Co., Ltd.* v. *Eisler*[8], which was strongly relied upon by the defendant, falls within the same category as *Ehrman* v. *Bartholomew*[6] and *Chapman* v. *Westerby*[9]. Russell, J., as he then was, said[10], after citing those two cases : " It was said on the other side that there were points of distinction. It was said that the covenants in those two cases were so framed that the servant, if the covenants were enforced, could make his living neither by serving nor by carrying on business independently ; whereas in the present case the covenant only prohibited serving. Therefore, it was said, he was still free to start in business on his own account, and it could not be said, if an injunction were granted in the terms of the covenant, that he would be forced to remain idle and starve. That distinction seems to me somewhat of a mockery. It would be idle to tell this defendant, a servant employed at a wage, that he must not serve anybody else in that capacity, but that the world was still open to him to start business as an independent man. It seems to me that if I were to restrain this man according to the terms of the covenant, he would be forced to remain idle and starve." Had it not been for that view

---

[1] [1926] A. C. 108, at p. 125.   [2] [1894] 3 Ch. 654.   [3] [1909] 1 Ch. 413.
[4] [1913] W. N. 277.   [5] [1891] 2 Ch. 416, at p. 427.   [6] [1898] 1 Ch. 671.
[7] [1920] 1 Ch. 571.   [8] [1926] Ch. 609.   [9] [1913] W. N. 277
[10] [1926] Ch. 615.

of the facts, I think that the learned Judge would have granted an injunction in that case.

The conclusion to be drawn from the authorities is that, where a contract of personal service contains negative covenants the enforcement of which will not amount either to a decree of specific performance of the positive covenants of the contract or to the giving of a decree under which the defendant must either remain idle or perform those positive covenants, the Court will enforce those negative covenants ; but this is subject to a further consideration. An injunction is a discretionary remedy, and the Court in granting it may limit it to what the Court considers reasonable in all the circumstances of the case.

This appears from the judgment of the Court of Appeal in *William Robinson & Co., Ltd.* v. *Heuer*[1]. The particular covenant in that case is set out at p. 452 and provides that " Heuer shall not during this engagement, without the previous consent in writing of the said W. Robinson & Co., Ltd.," and so forth, " carry on or be engaged either directly or indirectly, as principal, agent, servant, or otherwise, in any trade, business, or calling, either relating to goods of any description sold or manufactured by the said W. Robinson & Co., Ltd. . . . or in any other business whatsoever." There are passages in the judgment of Lindley, M.R., which bear so closely on several aspects of the present case that I shall refer to them. He begins his judgment by saying[2] that the result at which he is arriving is that justice requires that some injunction should be granted. He goes on to say : " This defendant is avowedly breaking his agreement, and the question is whether he should be at liberty to do so." There was a question raised whether that agreement was or was not illegal, and as to that the Master of the Rolls says : " There is no authority whatever to shew that that is an illegal agreement—that is to say, that it is unreasonable, and goes further than is reasonably necessary for the protection of the plaintiffs. It is confined to the period of the engagement, and means simply this—' So long as you are in our employ you shall not work for anybody else or engage in any other business.' There is nothing unreasonable in that at all." That seems to me to apply very precisely to the present case. The Master of the Rolls continues : " When, however, you come to talk about an injunction to enforce it, there is great difficulty. The real difficulty which has always to be borne in mind when you talk about specific performance of or injunctions to enforce agreements involving personal service is this—that this Court never will enforce an agreement by which one person undertakes to be the servant of another ; and if this agreement were enforced in its terms, it would compel this gentleman personally to serve the plaintiffs for the period of ten years. That the Court never does. Therefore an injunction in these terms cannot be granted, although the agreement to serve the plaintiffs and give his whole care, time, and attention to their business, and not to engage in any other business during his engagement, is valid in point of law. But the plaintiffs do not ask for an injunction in the terms of that agreement."

Before parting with that case, I should say that the Court there proceeded to sever the covenants and to grant an injunction, not to restrain the defendant from carrying on any other business whatsoever, but framed so as to give what was felt to be a reasonable protection to the plaintiffs and no more. The plaintiffs waived an option which they possessed to extend the

---

[1] [1898] 2 Ch. 451. [2] *Ibid.*, 454.

period of service for an extra five years, and the injunction then was granted for the remaining period of unextended time.

It is said that this case is no longer the law, but that *Attwood* v. *Lamont*[1] has decided that no such severance is permissible. I do not agree. *Attwood* v. *Lamont*[1] was a case where the covenants were held void as in restraint of trade. There is all the difference in the world between declining to make an illegal covenant good by neglecting that which makes it contrary to law and exercising a discretion as to how far the Court will enforce a valid covenant by injunction. The latter was done in the Court of Appeal in *William Robinson & Co.* v. *Heuer*[2], the former in *Attwood* v. *Lamont*[1].

The case before me is, therefore, one in which it would be proper to grant an injunction unless to do so would in the circumstances be tantamount to ordering the defendant to perform her contract or remain idle or unless damages would be the more appropriate remedy.

With regard to the first of these considerations, it would, of course, be impossible to grant an injunction covering all the negative covenants in the contract. That would, indeed, force the defendant to perform her contract or remain idle ; but this objection is removed by the restricted form in which the injunction is sought. It is confined to forbidding the defendant, without the consent of the plaintiffs, to render any services for or in any motion picture or stage production for any one other than the plaintiffs.

It was also urged that the difference between what the defendant can earn as a film artiste and what she might expect to earn by any other form of activity is so great that she will in effect be driven to perform her contract. That is not the criterion adopted in any of the decided cases. The defendant is stated to be a person of intelligence, capacity and means, and no evidence was adduced to show that, if enjoined from doing the specified acts otherwise than for the plaintiffs, she will not be able to employ herself both usefully and remuneratively in other spheres of activity, though not as remuneratively as in her special line. She will not be driven, although she may be tempted, to perform the contract, and the fact that she may be so tempted is no objection to the grant of an injunction. This appears from the judgment of Lord St. Leonards in *Lumley* v. *Wagner*[3], where he used the following language : " It was objected that the operation of the injunction in the present case was mischievous, excluding the defendant J. Wagner from performing at any other theatre while this Court had no power to compel her to perform at Her Majesty's Theatre. It is true that I have not the means of compelling her to sing, but she has no cause of complaint if I compel her to abstain from the commission of an act which she has bound herself not to do, and thus possibly cause her to fulfil her engagement. The jurisdiction which I now exercise is wholly within the power of the Court, and being of opinion that it is a proper case for interfering, I shall leave nothing unsatisfied by the judgment I pronounce. The effect, too, of the injunction, in restraining J. Wagner from singing elsewhere may, in the event "—that is a different matter—" of an action being brought against her by the plaintiff, prevent any such amount of vindictive damages being given against her as a jury might probably be inclined to give if she had carried her talents and exercised them at the rival theatre : the injunction

---

[1] [1920] 3 K. B. 571: *supra*, p. 288.   [2] [1898] 2 Ch. 451.
[3] (1852), 1 De G. M. & G. 604, at p. 619.

may also, as I have said, tend to the fulfilment of her engagement ; though, in continuing the injunction, I disclaim doing indirectly what I cannot do directly."

With regard to the question whether damages is not the more appropriate remedy, I have the uncontradicted evidence of the plaintiffs as to the difficulty of estimating the damages which they may suffer from the breach by the defendant of her contract. I think it is not inappropriate to refer to the fact that, in the contract between the parties, in clause 22, there is a formal admission by the defendant that her services, being " of a special, unique, extraordinary and intellectual character " gives them a particular value " the loss of which cannot be reasonably or adequately compensated in damages " and that a breach may " cost the producer great and irreparable injury and damage," and the artiste expressly agrees that the producer shall be entitled to the remedy of injunction. Of course, parties cannot contract themselves out of the law ; but it assists, at all events, on the question of evidence as to the applicability of an injunction in the present case, to find the parties formally recognizing that in cases of this kind injunction is a more appropriate remedy than damages.

Furthermore, in the case of *Grimston* v. *Cuningham*[1], which was also a case in which a theatrical manager was attempting to enforce against an actor a negative stipulation against going elsewhere, Wills, J., granted an injunction, and used the following language[2] : " This is an agreement of a kind which is pre-eminently subject to the interference of the Court by injunction, for in cases of this nature it very often happens that the injury suffered in consequence of the breach of the agreement would be out of all proportion to any pecuniary damages which could be proved or assessed by a jury. This circumstance affords a strong reason in favour of exercising the discretion of the Court by granting an injunction.

I think that that applies to the present case also, and that an injunction should be granted in regard to the specified services.

Then comes the question as to the period for which the injunction should operate. The period of the contract, now that the plaintiffs have undertaken not as from October 16, 1936, to exercise the rights of suspension conferred upon them by clause 23 thereof, will, if they exercise their options to prolong it, extend to about May, 1942. As I read the judgment of the Court of Appeal in *Robinson* v. *Heuer*[3] the Court should make the period such as to give reasonable protection and no more to the plaintiffs against the ill effects to them of the defendant's breach of contract. The evidence as to that was perhaps necessarily somewhat vague. The main difficulty that the plaintiffs apprehend is that the defendant might appear in other films whilst the films already made by them and not yet shown are in the market for sale or hire and thus depreciate their value. I think that if the injunction is in force during the continuance of the contract or for three years from now, whichever period is the shorter, that will substantially meet the case.

The other matter is as to the area within which the injunction is to operate. The contract is not an English contract and the parties are not British subjects. In my opinion all that properly concerns this Court is to prevent the defendant from committing the prohibited acts within the jurisdiction of this Court, and the injunction will be limited accordingly.

---

[1] [1894] 1 Q. B. 125.   [2] *Ibid.*, 130.   [3] [1898] 2 Ch. 451.

QUASI-CONTRACT

Metropolitan Police District Receiver
v. Croydon Corporation

Monmouthshire County Council v. Smith

[1957] 1 All E.R. 78

Money paid by the plaintiff to the defendant's use.

If the plaintiff has been compelled to pay money for which the defendant is liable, he may sue the defendant for the amount so paid. " The essence of the rule is that there must be a common liability to pay money to a particular person; that the plaintiff has been compelled to pay it by law; that the defendant is liable to pay that money; and that the defendant's debt or liability has been discharged by the plaintiff's payment ": *per* Lynskey, J. in *Monmouthshire County Council* v. *Smith*, [1956] 2 All E.R., at 809.

LORD GODDARD, C.J.: These are two appeals which raise exactly the same point. The first case is an action by the Receiver for the Metropolitan Police District against Croydon Corporation and a servant of the corporation, in which the Receiver is claiming the amount of a police constable's wages during a time when the constable was off duty on account of an accident which he met with in the course of his duty, being injured by a lorry, the property of the corporation, driven by their servant. In the second case the Monmouthshire County Council are suing for money which was paid to a police constable in the Monmouthshire Constabulary in similar circumstances, the defendant in the second case being Eric George Smith. In the first case Slade, J., held that the Receiver was entitled to maintain his action. In the second case Lynskey, J., came to the contrary decision, and in the opinion of this court Lynskey, J., was right. We do not agree with the decision of Slade, J.

It is necessary to refer briefly to the position in regard to pay, allowances and so forth of police constables, and for the present purposes there is really no difference between the two cases. In London the Metropolitan Police are under the direct control of the Home Secretary, but their wages are paid by the Receiver for the Metropolitan Police District, who, by the Metropolitan Police Act, 1829, is the person put in charge of the fund, which is derived from various sources, such as the rates and an Exchequer grant, out of which it is his duty to pay the wages of the police [s. 10 and s. 12 of the Act.] In this action the Receiver claims that, as he is the guardian of this fund, it is his duty to recover if he can any sum which is properly payable to the fund. It was contended on behalf of the Receiver that, as the police constable in question was off duty for several months, the Receiver was entitled to require the defendants to pay the wages which the Receiver had to pay to the constable during that period of incapacity.

The Monmouthshire County Council come into the matter in this way. A county police force is under the control of the standing joint committee [of the county council and of the justices at quarter sessions], and the standing joint committee see to the payment of the wages of the members of the force, requiring the county council to provide the necessary sums out of the county fund[1]. In this case Monmouthshire County Council had to provide the funds which the Monmouthshire Standing Joint Committee

---

[1] Under s. 30 (3) of the Local Government Act, 1888.

required. The county council base their claim on exactly the same ground as that on which the Receiver for the Metropolitan Police District bases his claim.

By the statutes under which the police forces, both in the metropolis and in the counties, are governed and the statutory regulations made under those statutes, the police authority are obliged to pay a constable his full wages and allowances, although he may be off duty by reason of an injury received in the course of his service. The time may come when the police constable has to retire because the injury so received has unfitted him to remain in the police force. In that case he will receive a pension, but so long as he is in the police force he is paid, whether he is fit for duty or not.

In each of the cases under appeal, the police constable was injured while he was on duty, and the injury kept him off his duties for several months. He was paid full wages during that time and received all the other emoluments to which he was entitled. He brought an action for damages in respect of the injury, but made no claim for loss of wages as part of the damage which he had sustained, because he had not sustained a loss of wages. Therefore, the damages which the police constables recovered against the respective defendants were not so large as they would have been if the constables had been entitled to claim for loss of wages. It is submitted by leading counsel for the plaintiffs (and this is the foundation of his argument) that the defendants have received a benefit by reason of the fact that, as the Receiver, in the one case, and the county council, in the other, have paid the wages during the period of incapacity, the defendants have not had to pay as large damages as they would have had to pay in the case of an injury to an ordinary person who was not paid wages while incapacitated, because in that case the defendant whose negligence had caused the injury to the workman would have to pay, as part of the special damages, the wages which the workmen had lost.

Slade, J., treated the case which was before him as one which depended on the doctrine of unjust enrichment, and held that, inasmuch as the defendants escaped paying the injured constable's wages because of the payments made by the Receiver, they must pay to the Receiver the amount of wages which they would have had to pay to the constable if he had not received his emoluments from the Receiver in the way which I have mentioned. That view seems to me to be a misconception, because I cannot see that the defendants were in any way enriched in that manner. The matter was dealt with shortly by Earl Jowett in his speech in *British Transport Commission* v. *Gourley*[1]:

> " . . . it is, I think, if I may say so with the utmost respect, fallacious to consider the problem as though a benefit were being conferred on a wrongdoer by allowing him to abate the damages for which he would otherwise be liable. The problem is rather for what damages is he liable; and, if we apply the dominant rule, we should answer, ' He is liable for such damages as, by reason of his wrongdoing, the plaintiff has sustained.' "

In that case the question was whether, in assessing the compensation payable to a man for loss of earnings, regard was to be had to his gross earnings or to the amount which would have come into his hands after deduction of income tax. The latter was held to be the right measure.

In each of the cases now before us, the police constable sustained certain damage for which he has been compensated. That damage did not include

---

[1] [1956] A. C. 185, at p. 202; [1955] 3 All E. R. 796, at p. 802.

loss of wages, because he had already been paid his wages. What is the result of that ? The Receiver, in the one case, and the county council, in the other case, have not been called on to pay anything which they would not otherwise have had to pay. Their obligation is to pay the police officers during the time they are off duty through disablement, no matter what the reason is which has caused an officer to be off duty. Therefore, the plaintiffs are no worse off than they would have been if the accidents had never taken place. It is their duty to pay the policeman so long as he is a member of the police force.

Once that point is realised, it follows that the only loss which the plaintiffs sustained is that they had to pay the police constables, although they received no service from them. That loss is exactly the loss which was recoverable, and in certain limited cases is still recoverable, in an action which is generally called an action per quod servitium amisit. Their damage consists in the fact that they were deprived of the services of the police constables. In point of fact it was never suggested, in either of the cases, that another officer had to be paid to carry out the injured constable's duty. The old action of per quod servitium amisit was an action given to a master because he was deprived of the services of his servant. In *A.-G. for New South Wales* v. *Perpetual Trustee Co. (Ltd.)*[1] the Judicial Committee held that that action would not lie in the case of a police constable, because the officer was not a servant of the police authority. He is a servant of the Crown, and may have to act independently of the police authority. In *Inland Revenue Comrs.* v. *Hambrook*[2] this court applied that judgment in the case of an injury to a civil servant and expressed the view that the action per quod servitium amisit must nowadays be confined to the case of what are generally known as menial servants. Therefore, police authorities are not entitled to claim now for loss of services of police officers against the person who injures the police officers.

In order, therefore, to maintain this action, it must be shown that the legal liability rests on some other principle. The principle which is prayed in aid here is the principle that money which constitutes unjust enrichment of a person may be recovered in an action for money had and received, or money paid to the use of the person. Both the learned judges considered with great care and very elaborately the decision of this court in *Brook's Wharf and Bull Wharf, Ltd.* v. *Goodman Bros.*[3] a case in which the plaintiffs, who were warehousemen, had taken into their bonded warehouse furs which were imported and were liable to duty. A man keeps a bonded warehouse on the terms that he will be responsible to the Commissioners of Customs and Excise for dutiable goods which are deposited in the bonded warehouse before the duties have been paid. He is responsible to the Commissioners of Customs and Excise if those goods go out of his bonded warehouse before the duties have been paid. In that case the defendants had imported skins and put them in the plaintiffs' bonded warehouse, not having paid duty, but they would have to pay duty when the goods went out. The goods were stolen from the bonded warehouse, and the Commissioners of Customs and Excise claimed the amount of the duty from the warehousemen, and recovered it from them. They had no answer; they had held the bonded goods, the bonded goods had left their warehouse and could be made avail-

---

[1] [1955] A. C. 457; [1955] 1 All E. R. 846.
[2] [1956] 3 All E. R. 338.
[3] [1937] 1 K. B. 534; [1936] 3 All E. R. 696.

able by the thieves on the home market, and the bonded warehousemen had to pay. They thereupon claimed, and were held entitled to recover, from the importers, the amount which they had paid, because it was primarily the importers' duty to have paid the import duties as soon as the goods were imported into this country, and they avoided having to pay that sum on importation only by placing the goods in the bonded warehouse. Lord Wright, M.R.[1], likened the case to one of principal and surety.

To my mind, that case and the large number of cases which were cited there and have been cited in the present cases have no bearing on the matter which we have to decide. The obligation of the defendants in this case is to compensate the injured men for the damage which they have sustained. Where a man is injured by the negligence of another, the fact that the injured man's employer had agreed to pay him his wages whether he was well or ill would, it seems to me, certainly afford a benefit in one sense to the wrongdoer, because, in an action for damages for negligence, the wrongdoer would not have to pay the damages which he would have had to pay if that agreement had not been made. That merely means that he does not have to compensate the plaintiff for an injury which he has not suffered. The obligation is, in the words of Earl Jowitt (in *British Transport Commission* v. *Gourley*[2]), merely to pay " such damages as, by reason of his wrongdoing, the plaintiff has sustained." Having paid that, his obligation seems to me to be at an end.

No doubt, if the action per quod servitium amisit had not now been held inapplicable in the case of policemen and police authorities, the police authority would have been able to recover, and probably would have recovered, damages from the wrongdoer on the ground that he had deprived the authority of the services of the servant; but that is the only claim, it seems to me, on an analysis of the matter, that the police authority can possibly put forward. Their claim is merely for the loss of services. The plaintiffs' financial position has not been altered by a sixpence in this case. Their duty is to pay the wages whether the policeman is on duty or not, so long as he remains a member of the police force.

For these reasons, I think that the judgment of Lynskey, J., was perfectly right when he held that there was no obligation on the part of the defendant to pay to Monmouthshire County Council the wages which the county council had paid to the police constable, and which they had to pay, despite the fact that the constable was injured. So long as he remained a member of the police force, the authority had to pay his wages. For these reasons I do not think that the very elaborate review of the cases which we have had, and which were before the judges, need be gone into.

My opinion is that the action of the Receiver fails, and that the appeal by Monmouthshire County Council also fails. I would, therefore, allow the appeal in the first case and dismiss it in the second. The only difference of which I know between the two cases is that in the Monmouthshire County Council case there is the question of the pension which was paid to the police constable. Leading counsel for the plaintiffs does not seek to found any argument now on that fact. As we were against him in the first case, he agrees that he cannot distinguish the Monmouthshire County Council case in any way. Indeed, as Lynskey, J., thought, the pension could in no circumstances have been recoverable from the defendant.

---

[1] [1937] 1 K. B. 534, at p. 546; [1936] 3 All E. R. 696, at p. 706.
[2] [1956] A. C. 185, at p. 202; [1955] 3 All E. R. 796, at p. 802.

For these reasons, I do not think there is any distinction between the two cases.

MORRIS, L.J. and VAISEY, J. delivered judgments to the same effect.

Morgan v. Ashcroft
[1938] 1 K.B. 49

Money paid under a mistake of fact. "Where money is paid to another under the influence of a mistake, that is, upon the supposition that a specific fact is true which would entitle the other to the money but which fact is untrue, and the money would not have been paid if it had been known to the payer that the fact was untrue, an action will lie to recover it back." (Parke, B., in *Kelly* v. *Solari* (1841), 9 M. & W. 54, at p. 58.)

In any such action it is necessary for the plaintiff to prove that he paid the money under a mistake of fact which in some aspect or another was fundamental to the transaction.

APPEAL from a decision of Judge L. C. Thomas sitting at the Abergavenny County Court.

The plaintiff was a bookmaker and he claimed to recover from the defendant, a licensed victualler, who had been in the habit of making bets with him, a sum of 24*l.* 2*s.* 1*d.*, being the amount of an alleged overpayment made by the plaintiff to the defendant in settling bets.

The claim arose in the following circumstances: According to the plaintiff's case the defendant won from the plaintiff on balance a sum of 24*l.* 2*s.* 1*d.* in respect of bets made by the defendant with the plaintiff on June 4, 1936, and this amount was credited to him for that day's transactions. On June 5 the defendant made further bets with the plaintiff, as the result of which, according to the plaintiff's case, the defendant lost 23*l.* and won 21*l.* 13*s.* 9*d.*, leaving him a loser on balance of 1*l.* 6*s.* 3*d.* By a mistake on the part of the plaintiff's clerk in making out the account, the sum of 24*l.* 2*s.* 1*d.* was carried forward into the account for June 5, with the result that this account showed the defendant to be a winner to the extent of 22*l.* 15*s.* 10*d.* instead of showing him (as it ought to have done) to be a loser to the extent of 1*l.* 6*s.* 3*d.* This sum of 22*l.* 15*s.* 10*d.* together with the sum of 24*l.* 2*s.* 1*d.*, making together 46*l.* 17*s.* 11*d.*, was paid to the defendant by the plaintiff's clerk, with the result that upon the account put forward by the plaintiff the defendant had been overpaid to the extent of 24*l.* 2*s.* 1*d.*, the sum which the plaintiff sought to recover in this action.

The defendant made a counterclaim in which he alleged that he had made other bets with the plaintiff not shown in the plaintiff's accounts, as a result of which the plaintiff owed him 9*l.* 13*s.* 4*d.* after taking into account the sum of 46*l.* 17*s.* 11*d.* paid to him by the plaintiff.

The county court judge found as a fact that the defendant had been overpaid to the extent of 24*l.* 2*s.* 1*d.*, and that the overpayment was made under a mistake of fact—namely, the mistake of the plaintiff's clerk in not noticing that the 24*l.* 2*s.* 1*d.* due on the first day's transactions had been credited twice, and he gave judgment for the plaintiff for that amount. He found as a fact that the defendant did not make the additional bets alleged in the counterclaim, with the result that the counterclaim failed.

The defendant appealed.

SIR WILFRID GREENE, M.R., delivered judgment allowing the appeal.

SCOTT, L.J. The argument for the appellant fell into two broad divisions. The first was that it was impossible for the judge to give judgment for the amount claimed without in effect enforcing claims for gaming debts and thus transgressing s. 18 of the Gaming Act, 1845.

I think the appellant was right on this first ground.

The second was that there was no such mistake of fact proved, or capable of being proved, as is necessary to found the old common law action for money had and received. This second submission was based mainly on a ground which I think insufficient by itself to entitle the appellant to our judgment; but there are in my opinion two other grounds for holding that this second submission also must succeed.

I will deal with the first submission first. The respondent is a bookmaker. The appellant is a publican who was a regular customer of the respondent for betting transactions. The nature of the mistake, which led to the alleged overpayment of 24*l*. 2*s*. 1*d*. upon which the action was brought, was proved in evidence to have been a clerical error by the respondent's clerk which led her to give the appellant credit for the sum of 24*l*. 2*s*. 1*d*. twice over; thus causing respondent to pay to the appellant 24*l*. 2*s*. 1*d*. too much. It happened in this way. That figure was the credit balance of wins by the appellant over his losses for June 4, 1936, and it was shown as a credit to the appellant at the foot of the first page of an account dated June 6, 1936, which was delivered by the respondent as bookmaker, to the appellant, as customer. The second page of the account was for the bets of June 5, but the credit balance of June 4 was carried forward from page 1, and shown on the top of page 2, and was therefore included in the final credit balance in favour of the defendant of 22*l*. 15*s*. 10*d*. shown at the bottom of page 2. The appellant called on June 6 to collect his winnings. The respondent's clerk did not notice the carry forward on page 2 of the 24*l*. 2*s*. 1*d*. from page 1, assumed that the appellant had on June 5 won 22*l*. 15*s*. 10*d*. on balance, whereas he had in fact on that day lost 1*l*. 6*s*. 3*d*. on balance of the day, and accordingly paid him 46*l*. 17*s*. 11*d*., the total of the two credit balances. The appellant in evidence alleged that he had won other bets which left the respondent his debtor to the extent of 9*l*. 13*s*. 4*d*. even after payment of the 46*l*. 17*s*. 11*d*. The action was brought by the respondent for the 24*l*. 2*s*. 1*d*. overpaid on the clerical mistake. The appellant counter-claimed for the 9*l*. 13*s*. 4*d*.

In order to establish the above facts and thereby to prove his mistake, the appellant was compelled to put the whole account before the Court and invite the Court to ascertain what was the true balance figure of bets lost and won, on each of the two days. There was, of course, no legal obstacle to the Court taking cognizance of the fact that the respondent was voluntarily giving the appellant credit for the appellant's winnings and thus paying them in account; but to ask the Court to recognize the respondent's winnings from the appellant and to set them off against his losses was in effect to ask the Court to enforce those winnings against the appellant. It was impossible for the Court to verify either the fact or the amount of the respondent's alleged mistake without going through the above process and thus in effect enforcing the respondent's claims to set off his winnings against his losses.

In the same way it was impossible to ascertain whether the sum of 24*l*. 2*s*. 1*d*., which on the above facts appeared to have been an overpayment, was in truth what it appeared to be without investigating the appellant's counterclaim and enforcing the various items *pro* and *con* which might thereby be established. Until that was done, the Court could not be satisfied as to what was the final position on the issue of overpayment by the respondent to the appellant. Both investigations by the Court, on the claim and the counterclaim, were in my view equally forbidden by s. 18 of the Act; for taking an account, whether at common law or in equity, is just as much enforcing a claim as giving judgment for a liquidated claim. Where the mistake upon which a plaintiff relies to justify a claim for money had and received to his use is one that can only be ascertained by investigating betting accounts, the Court cannot lend its aid without transgressing the statute. It follows that the Court ought to have refused to look at the accounts and to have dismissed the action on the ground that it was being asked to enforce gaming contracts contrary to s. 18 of the Act of 1845.

I now deal with the second submission, namely, that even assuming the first objection to be insufficient, there was here no such mistake of fact as is essential to the rule of the common law that money paid in mistake of fact may be recovered.

The learned county court judge relied upon a dictum of Channell, J., in *Gasson* v. *Cole*[1], a case where the plaintiff was suing for money had and received in connection with bets on horse-racing. In that case the plaintiff acting as agent for the defendant, a bookmaker, had placed a bet for the defendant on a horse which had come in second, but which, on the first horse being held by the stewards to be disqualified, was declared the winner. The plaintiff collected the amount won on the bet, 275*l*., and, believing that the defendant had really won, paid it over to him. After that the Jockey Club Committee reversed the stewards' decision, and the plaintiff sought to recover the 275*l*. from the defendant as money had and received on the ground that he had paid it in mistake of fact. There were other complications of fact in the case, but the above is a sufficient statement to explain the dictum, which is reported as follows: " During the argument he (the learned judge) had asked Mr. Colam whether the rule that money paid under a mistake of fact should be paid back applied in a betting transaction. If it was a clear mistake of fact, he thought that the person would be entitled to recover the money back."

The case was decided against the plaintiff on other grounds, and thus Channell, J.'s, opinion never became the basis of decision. But the dictum embodies the legal basis of the county court judge's decision in favour of the respondent, and we have therefore to decide whether it is right or wrong. In my opinion it is wrong.

The main ground on which Mr. Micklethwait for the appellant sought to attack the dictum was that the action for money had and received founded on mistake of fact can never lie, unless the mistake is one which induces in the plaintiff's mind a belief that he is under some legal liability to the defendant from which the payment will wholly or in part discharge him. For reasons which I will give presently I do not think that he is entitled to succeed on this particular ground. But in my opinion there are two other grounds upon which his submission ought to succeed. In the first place there is the broad ground, explained by the Master of the Rolls, that the mistake inducing the payment here had not that fundamental character which is necessary to establish a cause of action for money had and received by reason of a mistake of fact. The second is that even if the mistake was sufficiently fundamental, s. 18 of the Gaming Act, 1845, affords what may be called a special defence where the mistake is about betting transactions.

---

[1] (1910), 26 T. L. R. 468, at p. 469.

I will deal with this ground first. It is really only another aspect of the first ground of appeal.

Where the mistake relates to the amount of an honour credit for bets, the statutory veto upon the reception of evidence about gaming transactions, which I have discussed upon the first argument for the appellant, creates a special impediment, and in effect constitutes a special defence to the action for money had and received, by making it impossible to prove the mistake upon which the plaintiff is basing his claim. The position thus created is closely analogous to that which arose through the doctrine of *ultra vires* in *Sinclair* v. *Brougham*[1], where Lord Sumner[2] used the expression already quoted by the Master of the Rolls to the effect that a promise to repay will not be implied in law if an actual promise would in law be void. This special defence is in itself a sufficient reason for allowing the appeal.

Before adding what little I have to add to my Lord's discussion upon the essential nature of the action for money had and received when based on a mistake of fact, I will consider the particular argument advanced by Mr. Micklethwait. The well-known passage in Bramwell, B.'s, judgment in *Aiken* v. *Short*[3] is perhaps the strongest statement of the proposition upon which he relied, but I agree with the Master of the Rolls that the facts of that case were not such as to make what the learned Baron there said the necessary basis of decision in that case. Indeed I do not think that this limiting proposition of the law about mistake of fact as one basis of the action for money had and received has ever been the direct subject of decision, although it has been frequently stated almost as if it were an accepted rule of law. I venture to think that the mind of the Court was in all the cases where the statement has been made concentrated on the particular circumstances under discussion, and was expressing a conclusion appropriate to the facts before it rather than attempting to lay down any absolute or general rule of law. But as counsel for the appellant in the present appeal contended that there is such a rule of law, it is desirable to quote some of the leading expressions of judicial opinion upon which he relies, and all the more so as they are expressed in rather definite language.

In *Kelly* v. *Solari*[4] Parke, B., said: " I think that where money is paid to another under the influence of a mistake, that is, upon the supposition that a specific fact is true, which would entitle the other to the money, but which fact is untrue, and the money would not have been paid if it had been known to the payer that the fact was untrue, an action will lie to recover it back."

In *Aiken* v. *Short*[5], *per* Bramwell, B. (which is a rather fuller report than in 1. H. & N. at p. 215): " It seems to me that the right to recover money paid under a mistake of fact must have reference to a belief of the existence of a fact which, if true, would have given the person receiving a right against the person paying the money; and it never can be applicable to a case where the fact mistaken is a fact which would merely have made it desirable for the person paying it to pay to the person receiving it. I do not know whether that is a sufficiently comprehensive principle, but it is one which has existed throughout in my mind."

In *The Bodega Co.* case[6], Farwell, J., said of the passage last quoted: " That, I apprehend, means this. If you are claiming to have money

---

[1] [1914] A. C. 398.   [2] *Ibid.*, 452.   [3] (1856), 25 L. J. Ex. 321, at p. 324.
[4] (1841), 9 M. & W. 54, at p. 58.   [5] (1856), 25 L. J. Ex. 321.
[6] [1904] 1 Ch. 276, at p. 286.

Morgan v. Ashcroft

505

repaid on the ground of mistake, you must show the mistake is one which led you to suppose you were legally liable to pay."

In *Maskell* v. *Horner*[1], *per* Rowlatt, J.: " The plaintiff claims to recover these sums as paid under a mistake of fact, or, alternatively, as paid not voluntarily, but to prevent his goods being seized and under protest. I think it is necessary to state two principles of law to which he appeals and then to see if the circumstances bring him within either. To recover under the first principle there must be a mistake of fact and a fact going to the supposed liability. That is laid down in *Kelly* v. *Solari*[2] and *Aiken* v. *Short*[3]. An action on this ground, therefore, can only be brought by one who pays, believing in his liability, because by mistake he believes a fact upon which his liability depends." The case was decided in the Court of Appeal upon the ground that the payments were recoverable as having been made under protest to prevent seizure of the plaintiff's goods, and the above statement by Rowlatt, J., remains a dictum.

The last citation I want to make is from the case of *Steam Saw Mills Co.* v. *Baring Brothers & Co.*[4] where Lord Sterndale, M.R., said: " There seems to be ample authority for this, that if a person, under a mistake of fact, pays money, which he is not liable to pay, he may recover it back; but it makes all the difference in the world whether the fact of which he was ignorant would have discharged him from the liability to pay."

In none of the above cases, as I have already said, not even in *Aiken* v. *Short*[5], was there a decision of the Court that the action failed simply because the mistake did not induce a belief of liability. And indeed in *Kerrison* v. *Glyn, Mills, Currie & Co.*[6] it was definitely decided by Hamilton, J., and by the House of Lords that the plaintiff was entitled to recover a payment made to the defendants for the purpose of meeting an anticipated liability although he then knew that no actual liability had yet attached to him. The decision of the House of Lords seems to me conclusive that the rule as stated in *Aiken* v. *Short*[7] cannot be regarded as final and exhaustive in the sense that no mistake, which does not induce in the mind of the payer a belief that payment will discharge or reduce his liability, can ground an action for money had and received. It is, of course, obvious that such a belief must in fact have been induced in a very high percentage of mistaken payments giving rise to a dispute; in human affairs the vast majority of payments made without any fresh consideration are made to perform an obligation or discharge a liability; and I doubt not that performance of an obligation would be accounted discharge of a liability for the purpose of the *Aiken* v. *Short*[8] proposition. For this reason of human nature, that proposition is very often—and perhaps usually—a crucial test of the question whether the payment was in truth made by reason of a mistake or was merely voluntary and therefore irrecoverable. But I agree with the view of the Master of the Rolls that the final demarcation of the boundaries of the old action of money had and received has not yet been achieved, and that their final delineation can only be worked out as concrete cases arise and bring up new points for decision. And in refusing assent to the appellant's argument that the *Aiken* v. *Short*[8] proposition is of itself necessarily sufficient

---

[1] [1915] 3 K. B. 106, at p. 108.   [2] (1841), 9 M. & W. 54.
[3] (1856), 1 H. & N. 210.   [4] [1922] 1 Ch. 244, at p. 250.
[5] (1856), 1 H. & N. 210; 25 L. J. Ex. 321.
[6] (1909), 15 Com. Cas. 1; (1911), 17 Com. Cas. 41.
[7] (1856), 1 H. & N. 215; 25 L. J. Ex. 324.
[8] (1856), 1 H. & N. 210, 215; 25 L. J. Ex. 321, at p. 324.

to fix the boundary, I desire to keep clearly open the possibility of the common law treating other types of payment in mistake as falling within the scope of the action for money had and received. Without expressing any opinion, I recognize, for instance, the possibility that there may be cases of charitable payments or other gifts made under a definite mistake of person to be benefited, or of the substantial nature of the transaction, where on consideration the old principles of the action might still, in spite of limiting decisions, be held to cover such circumstances.

This whole group of common law actions known as " implied assumpsit " or " implied contract " permits the redress of so many widely different types of grievance, and thus is so useful in our jurisprudence, that it seems to me just as important not to cut them down as it is not to enlarge them beyond their true legal boundaries. And of them all the action for money had and received has the greatest variety of application and is perhaps the most useful. The name " implied contracts " is ambiguous, as it is often used of true consensual contracts which are not wholly expressed in writing or orally and have to be inferred in greater or lesser degree from the conduct of the parties. The implied contract for money had and received has no element of agreement about it; it is implied in law, the name being a misnomer. The history of implied contracts in the non-consensual sense has passed through two stages—the first during the 17th and 18th centuries, when it was being invented by the Courts and its range was ever expanding; the second from the middle of the 19th century, since when the pendulum has swung the other way and our common law Courts have tended to restrict it. It is not relevant to the present case to consider that history in detail, but the 14th Lecture by the late Professor Ames upon Implied Assumpsit printed in his Lectures on Legal History (Harvard 1913, p. 149) is full of illumination. He brings out clearly the complete absence of any consensual element. There is no doubt that the moral principle of " unjust enrichment," to which he refers and which is recognized in some systems of law as a definite legal principle, and indeed underlay Lord Mansfield's famous dictum in *Moses* v. *Macferlan*[1] in the year 1760, has now been rejected by English Courts as a universal or complete legal touchstone whereby to test this cause of action. But Professor Ames was as late as the early years of the present century still treating that principle as the underlying source of obligation upon the basis of which the action had been developed in our common law: see pp. 160 and 166. Leake devoted a long sub-division of the First Edition of his book on Contracts (published in 1867) to the title of " Contracts Implied in Law " (pp. 38 to 75) and commenced it with these two paragraphs: " Simple contracts arising independently of agreement, or contracts implied in law, include those transactions affecting the two parties, other than agreement between them, upon which the law operates by imposing a contract, that is, a liability on the one side and correlative right on the other." " The transactions between two parties, other than agreement, which give rise to contracts, may be described generally as importing that some undue pecuniary inequality exists in the one party relatively to the other, which justice and equity require should be compensated, and upon which the law operates by creating a debt to the amount of the required compensation."

The Third Edition of Bullen and Leake (1868) at p. 44 under the title

---

[1] (1760), 2 Burr. 1005.

of the "*indebitatus* count for money had and received," repeated the effect of the second of the above sentences; so did Professor Dicey in his book on Parties to an Action, published in 1870, at p. 91.

So wide a statement of the principle upon which the action for money had and received is founded, however eminent the jurists who supported it, does not at the present time afford an authoritative criterion by which the Court can decide whether a given claim discloses a cause of action for money had and received. The test is too vague; and even if it was ever a test, it has certainly been modified by recent decisions which have restricted the field of this action: see *Baylis* v. *Bishop of London*[1], *per* Hamilton, L.J.; *Sinclair* v. *Brougham*[2], *per* the same learned judge as Lord Sumner; and *Holt* v. *Markham*[3], *per* Scrutton, L.J. But my citations from jurists of such high standing as writers on the common law do emphasize the importance of trying to find some common positive principles upon which these causes of action called "implied contracts" can be said to rest, and which will not altogether exclude that of unjust enrichment embodied in those citations.

An additional reason for keeping the door open is the very heterogeneous list of causes of action which unquestionably fall within this field of implied contracts. They are so various in kind as almost irresistibly to invite the inference that there may be one or more unifying principles upon which they rest. If one takes the action for money had and received by way of illustration of this point, one finds assembled under that heading the following wholly different types of causes: (1.) money paid in mistake of fact; (2.) money paid for a consideration which has failed; (3.) money paid because it was extorted *colore officii*, or by duress, etc.; (4.) cases where the plaintiff has had an actionable wrong done him by the defendant, and "waiving the tort" sues in assumpsit—whether any of his money has actually passed from himself to the defendant or not. In this context I venture humbly and respectfully to doubt whether the criterion suggested by Viscount Haldane, L.C., in *Sinclair* v. *Brougham*[4], that "the fiction" (i.e., the common law fiction of an implied contract) "can only be set up with effect if such a contract would be valid if it really existed", is consistent with the common law history of these implied contracts; for some of them are quite incapable of formulation as real—i.e., consensual—contracts.

But I am in complete agreement with the Master of the Rolls that there is a plain principle applicable to all those cases of payments in mistake of fact, and that is that the mistake must be in some aspect or another fundamental to the transaction. On the facts of this case there was no fundamental mistake. To pay 24*l.* for a betting debt is just as much in the eye of the law a purely voluntary gift as a wedding present of 24*l.*: the law prevents the plaintiff from saying that he intended anything but a present. I agree that the appeal must be allowed.

Rowland v. Divall

[1923] 2 K.B. 500

Total failure of consideration.
If the plaintiff has paid money to the defendant in pursuance of a contract and the defendant commits a breach of such a nature as to constitute

---

[1] [1913] 1 Ch. 127, at p. 140.
[3] [1923] 1 K. B. 504, at p. 513.
[2] [1914] A. C. 398, at p. 453.
[4] [1914] A. C 398, at p. 415.

a total failure of consideration, the plaintiff may treat the contract as at an end and sue in quasi-contract for the return of the money.

APPEAL from the judgment of Bray, J. at the trial.

In April, 1922, the defendant, who lived at Brighton, bought an "Albert" motor car, and on May 19 he resold it to the plaintiff for 334*l.* The plaintiff, who was a motor-car dealer, drove the car from Brighton to Blandford, where he carried on business. When he got there he repainted it and exposed it for sale in his showroom. In July, 1922, he sold it to a Colonel Railsdon for 400*l.* In September, 1922, the police took possession of the car on the ground that it had been stolen from the owner by the person from whom the defendant had bought it, and the plaintiff refunded to Colonel Railsdon the 400*l.* that he had paid. Under these circumstances the plaintiff brought his action against the defendant to recover the price that he had paid to the defendant for the car, 334*l.*, as money paid the consideration of which had failed. Bray, J. held that as the plaintiff and his purchaser had had the use of the car from May to September there had not been a total failure of consideration, and that under those circumstances the plaintiff must be limited to his remedy in damages. He accordingly gave judgment for the defendant.

The plaintiff appealed.

BANKES and SCRUTTON, L.JJ. delivered judgment allowing the appeal.

ATKIN,L.J . I agree. It seems to me that in this case there has been a total failure of consideration, that is to say that the buyer has not got any part of that for which he paid the purchase money. He paid the money in order that he might get the property, and he has not got it. It is true that the seller delivered to him the de facto possession, but the seller had not got the right to possession and consequently could not give it to the buyer. Therefore the buyer, during the time that he had the car in his actual possession had no right to it, and was at all times liable to the true owner for its conversion. Now there is no doubt that what the buyer had a right to get was the property in the car, for the Sale of Goods Act expressly provides that in every contract of sale there is an implied condition that the seller has a right to sell; and the only difficulty that I have felt in this case arises out of the wording of s. 11, sub-s. 1 (*c*), which says that: " Where a contract of sale is not severable, and the buyer has accepted the goods . . . the breach of any condition to be fulfilled by the seller can only be treated as a breach of warranty, and not as a ground for rejecting the goods and treating the contract as repudiated, unless there be a term of the contract, express or implied, to that effect." It is said that this case falls within that provision, for the contract of sale was not severable and the buyer had accepted the car. But I think that the answer is that there can be no sale at all of goods which the seller has no right to sell. The whole object of a sale is to transfer property from one person to another. And I think that in every contract of sale of goods there is an implied term to the effect that a breach of the condition that the seller has a right to sell the goods may be treated as a ground for rejecting the goods and repudiating the contract notwithstanding the acceptance, within the meaning of the concluding words of sub-s. (*c*); or in other words that the sub-section has no application to breach of that particular condition. It seems to me that in this case there must be a right to reject, and also a right to sue for the price paid as money had and received on failure of the consideration, and further that there is no obligation on the part of the buyer to return the car, for *ex hypothesi* the seller had no right to receive it.   Under those circumstances can it make any difference that the buyer has used the car before he found out that there was a breach of the condition ?   To my mind it makes no difference at all.   The buyer accepted the car on the representation of the seller that he had a right to sell it, and inasmuch as the seller had no such right he is not entitled to say that the buyer has enjoyed a benefit under the contract.   In fact the buyer has not received any part of that which he contracted to receive—namely, the property and right to possession— and, that being so, there has been a total failure of consideration.   The plaintiff is entitled to recover the 334*l.* which he paid.

Appeal allowed[1].

Planché v. Colburn

(1831), 5 C. & P. 58 ; 1 Moo. & S. 51

Quantum Meruit.

> If a plaintiff has done work for the defendant in pursuance of a contract which has since been discharged by the defendant's breach, he may obtain reasonable remuneration for his work by suing in quasi-contract on a *quantum meruit.*

From the evidence of Mr. Jerdan, the editor of the Literary Gazette, it appeared that about September, 1830, the plaintiff, who was the author of several dramatic entertainments, was engaged by him, with the knowledge of the defendants, Messrs. Colburn & Bentley, who were the publishers of a work called " The Juvenile Library," to write for that work an article to illustrate the history of armour and costume from the earliest times, for which he was to be paid 100 guineas.   It appeared that the plaintiff went into the country to Dr. Meyrick's, a great proprietor of ancient armour, where he made various drawings ; and also, that he had prepared a consider- able portion of manuscript, when, after three volumes had been published, " The Juvenile Library " was discontinued.   The plaintiff claimed a sum of 50 guineas for the part which he had prepared, and the trouble he had taken in the business.

Spankie, Serjt., for the defendants, contended that the engagement, as set out in the declaration and also in point of fact, was an engagement to pay for the article when complete ; and this the defendants always had been and still were willing to do.

He called a witness, who proved, that in the month of November a conversation took place between the plaintiff and the defendant Bentley, in which the latter told the former that if he would finish his work he should have his money, as they were perfectly willing to publish it ; that the plaintiff said it was better for a separate publication than for the Juvenile Library, as in treating it for children he had been very much hampered, and there was great difficulty in adapting it for juvenile comprehension.

Wilde, Serjt., in reply.—The defence set up is no answer to this action. It is one thing to write an article for an Encyclopædia or a Juvenile Library, and another thing to write a separate work on the subject ; different styles of writing are required for children and grown persons.   That which was written with ingenuity, adapted to young minds, would make a man ridiculous

---

[1] The reasoning in *Rowland* v. *Divall* has been criticised by the Law Reform Committee (Twelfth Report: Cmnd. 2958, published in 1966).

if published for grown-up persons ; such, in this case, was not the contract made, and the defendants have no right to call on the plaintiff to publish on such terms. An author, also, has an interest beyond the mere payment for a particular article. The kind of work is to be taken into consideration, with reference to his reputation and the effect it will have on his future performances.

TINDAL, C.J. thus directed the jury:—The plaintiff does not seek to recover the whole sum contracted for, but only a fair remuneration for that part of the article which he had prepared, and which was rendered useless by the discontinuance of the work in which it was to appear. The object of the defendants evidently was, to have a publication adapted to persons in the younger classes of society. The question you have to consider is, what degree of credit you give to the defence ; which, it appears to me, must amount to this, or it amounts to nothing—That, after the contract was broken, an entirely new arrangement was made, to furnish the matter for publication in a separate form. It seems that in the month of November the plaintiff thought that the subject was one better suited for separate publication ; but undoubtedly, up to that time, he had been preparing it for juvenile readers ; and the form and size of the proposed new work were not settled on that occasion. It might be, that the plaintiff considered the subject matter was better adapted for a separate publication, without admitting that the MS. and drawings already prepared were suited to such a publication. It will be for you to say, whether you think that this was a separate bargain, in which the plaintiff gave up the old contract altogether ; for if you do, then you must find your verdict for the defendants. The question is, was the first agreement entirely abandoned with the consent of the plaintiff, and an entire new agreement made between the parties ?—for only in such case can the verdict be for the defendants.

Verdict for the plaintiff.—Damages 50*l.*

Mr. Serjeant *Spankie* now applied for a rule *nisi* that this verdict might be set aside, and a nonsuit entered, or a new trial had, on the ground that the plaintiff could not be entitled to recover on the special contract, as he had not tendered or delivered the whole of his work to the defendants, or even part of it, and he was not to be paid until he had completed and delivered the whole of the treatise. Although the publication of " The Juvenile Library" was suspended for a time, it does not follow that it was abandoned or given up altogether ; and the defendants recommended the plaintiff to have his treatise published as a separate and distinct work, to which he at first assented, although he afterwards refused to do so. Neither could the plaintiff recover on the *quantum meruit* count, as he was bound by his contract to complete and deliver the whole of his work, and he did not shew that the defendants had ever dispensed with his writing or completing the treatise, and he was bound to finish and deliver it in a complete state before he could call on the defendants for payment.

Lord Chief Justice TINDAL.—I agree, that, when a special contract is open and in existence, a party suing for a breach of it, cannot recede and seek to recover on a *quantum meruit* for the work and labour done. But the question here is, whether the contract remained in existence or not. That was a question purely for the consideration of the jury, and they found that the work was finally abandoned, which they were fully warranted in doing ; as it appeared, that, after three volumes of " The Juvenile Library" had been published, the work was given up and utterly abandoned. The defendants' clerk merely proved a conversation between the plaintiff and defendants as to publishing his treatise separately. I therefore left it to the jury to say whether the original contract was abandoned by the defendant, or a new contract had been entered into. They found that there was no new contract : and I think the damages found for the plaintiff are not unreasonable, and that he ought not to be deprived of the fruit of his labour in writing a great part of the treatise, which he satisfactorily proved he had done. Part of the defendants' contract was to publish the plaintiff's treatise in the work called "The Juvenile Library," which was a periodical publication : and the plaintiff might not have taken so much pains if his treatise were to be published separately, as if it were to be circulated through the medium of a popular work.

Mr. Justice GASELEE.—There is no dispute as to the law in this case, nor is there any objection to the mode in which the questions were left to the jury. If, indeed, the declaration had contained no other count than that founded on the special contract, the plaintiff could not have succeeded, as by the terms of the agreement he was not to be paid till he had delivered the whole of his treatise. The jury found that the publication of "The Juvenile Library" was wholly abandoned by the defendants. The plaintiff, therefore, is entitled to a remuneration for the part of the work he had executed, and was ready to deliver.

Mr. Justice BOSANQUET.—I am of opinion that the plaintiff is entitled to retain his verdict for the labour and attention bestowed in performing part of his work, which was to be published by the defendants, and circulated in a particular manner, namely, in a periodical work, which the jury found had been altogether abandoned by the defendants ; and if they neglected to publish the treatise in "The Juvenile Library," the plaintiff was not bound to go on and complete it ; for an author who is engaged in writing a literary work does not merely look to a pecuniary compensation, but chiefly to his reputation.

Mr. Justice ALDERSON concurred.

Rule refused.

Craven-Ellis v. Canons, Ltd.

[1936] 2 K.B. 403

Quantum Meruit.

> If a plaintiff has done work for the defendants on the assumption that a contract exists between them, but the contract is in truth a nullity, he may obtain reasonable remuneration for his work by suing in quasi-contract on a *quantum meruit*.

GREER, L.J. In the year 1927, Sir Arthur du Cros and his son Phillip became interested in the development of a building estate known as Canons Estate. They desired to have the benefit of the plaintiff's skill and experience as an estate agent in the development of the estate. For a time the estate was vested in a company called the Pard Estates, Ltd. On November 11, 1927, the plaintiff wrote to Mr. Phillip du Cros, and on November 29, to Sir Arthur du Cros, stating the terms on which he would be willing to give them the benefit of his skill and experience. On November 30, the plaintiff wrote to Sir Arthur du Cros stating revised terms on which his firm would act as managers of the Canons Park Estate. Subject to some modification to which the plaintiff agreed, Sir Arthur du Cros agreed to these terms on behalf of the Pard Estates, Ltd., the engagement to be for three years. On August 15, 1928, Canons, Ltd., was formed to purchase from the Pard Estates, Ltd., the Canons Park Estate. It then became impossible for the plaintiff to go on working for the Pard Estates, Ltd., as that company had sold the property, but the plaintiff continued to do the same work for the new company. This company for the time being did not make any contract to employ the plaintiff or his firm on the terms formerly arranged, but without any express agreement they received and accepted the services he was rendering. The signatories to the memorandum and articles, being entitled to elect the first directors, nominated Mr. Phillip du Cros, the plaintiff, and Mr. A. W. Wheeler as the first directors on August 15, 1928, and on August 23 the directors co-opted Sir Arthur du Cros as a director. Under the articles these directors could act without qualification for two months, but after that time they became incapable of acting as directors as none of them had acquired the necessary qualification. The only issued shares of the company were in the two signatories to the memorandum, but there is little room for doubt that these gentlemen were nominees of the du Cros'. Be this as it may, it is clear that on the expiration of the two months, the directors having no qualification ceased to be directors, and were unable to bind the company except as *de facto* directors by agreements with outsiders or with shareholders. But all the directors must be taken to have known the facts. They became liable to penalties for acting as directors under the provisions of section 73 of the Companies Act, 1908, then in force. On April 14, 1931, an agreement was executed under the seal of the company, purporting to be between the company and the plaintiff, stating the terms on which he was to act as managing director of the company. The seal was so affixed by resolution of the unqualified directors. The plaintiff in this action sought to recover from the defendant company the remuneration set out in the agreement, and, as an alternative, sought to recover for his services on a *quantum meruit*. Until the company purported to put an end to his engagement he continued to perform all the services mentioned in the agreement.

The company, having had the full benefit of these services, decline to pay either under the agreement or on the basis of a *quantum meruit*. Their defence to the action is a purely technical defence, and if it succeeds the Messrs. du Cros as the principal shareholders in the company, and the company, would be in the position of having received and accepted valuable services and refusing, for purely technical reasons, to pay for them.

As regards the services rendered between December 31, 1930, and April 14, 1931, there is, in my judgment, no defence to the claim. These services were rendered by the plaintiff not as managing director or as a director, but as an estate agent, and there was no contract in existence which could present any obstacle to a claim based on a *quantum meruit* for services rendered and accepted.

As regards the plaintiff's services after the date of the contract, I think the plaintiff is also entitled to succeed. The contract, having been made by directors who had no authority to make it with one of themselves who had notice of their want of authority, was not binding on either party. It was, in fact, a nullity, and presents no obstacle to the implied promise to pay on a *quantum meruit* basis which arises from the performance of the services and the implied acceptance of the same by the company.

It was contended by Mr. Croom-Johnson on behalf of the respondents that, inasmuch as the services relied on were purported to be done by the plaintiff under what he and the directors thought was a binding contract, there could be no legal obligation on the defendants on a *quantum meruit* claim. The only one of the numerous authorities cited by Mr. Croom-Johnson that appears to support his contention is the judgment of a Divisional Court in *In re Allison, Johnson and Foster, Ltd., Ex parte Birkenshaw*[1]. The Court consisted of Lord Alverstone, Wills and Kennedy, JJ., and the judgment was delivered by Kennedy, J. In giving judgment that learned judge, expressing not merely his own opinion, but that of the other two judges, said[2] : " There can be no implied contract for payment arising out of acceptance of the work done where the work was done upon an express request which turns out to be no request at all, but which down to the time when the whole of the work had been done was supposed by both parties to be valid and operative." This passage appears to involve the proposition that in all cases where parties suppose there is an agreement in existence and one of them has performed services or delivered goods in pursuance of the supposititious agreement, there cannot be any inference of any promise by the person accepting the services of the goods to pay on the basis of a *quantum meruit*. This would certainly be strictly logical if the inference of a promise to pay on a *quantum meruit* basis were an inference of fact based on the acceptance of the services or of the goods delivered under what was supposed to be an existing contract ; but in my judgment the inference is not one of fact, but is an inference which a rule of law imposes on the parties where work has been done or goods have been delivered under what purports to be a binding contract, but is not so in fact.

In *Prickett* v. *Badger*[3] the question whether an obligation to pay on a *quantum meruit* basis depended upon an inference of fact from the conduct of the parties was negatived, and such inference was stated to be one that the law imposed on the person accepting the services. In that case the services of the agent had been performed in accordance with an express contract which entitled him to $1\frac{1}{2}$ per cent., and it was impossible to infer from the evidence that by accepting those services the defendant had by conduct promised to pay for them on the basis of a *quantum meruit* ; but it was held that the contract to pay what was reasonable was a contract implied by the law, and not a question of fact to be determined by a jury. In the course of the argument Crowder, J., said[4] : " All the work done here was done under the special contract ; " but the Court held that, notwithstanding that the work was so done and accepted, there was as a matter of law an implied contract to pay a reasonable price therefor. In giving judgment, both Williams, J., and Crowder, J., speak of the obligation to pay as founded on a promise implied by law. The decisions in *Clarke* v. *Cuckfield Union Guardians*[5] and *Lawford* v. *Billericay Rural District Conncil*[6] are also authorities to the effect that the implied obligation to pay is an obligation imposed by law, and not an inference of fact, arising from the performance and acceptance of services. In the last mentioned case the work in respect of which the plaintiff sued was done in pursuance of express instructions given by the defendant council, but the contract purported to be so made was not binding on the defendants because no agreement had been executed under their seal.

---

[1] [1904] 2 K. B. 327. [2] *Ibid.*, 330.
[3] (1856), 1 C. B. N. S. 296. [4] *Ibid.*, 301. [5] (1852), 21 L. J. Q. B. 349.
[6] [1903] 1 K. B. 772.

It was impossible to say as a matter of logical inference from the facts that by accepting the advantage of the plaintiff's work they had promised to pay him a reasonable sum therefor.   Both parties assumed that there was a contract between them, and the acceptance of the work by the defendants could not in fact give rise to the inference of a promise to pay the reasonable value.   For these reasons this case seems to me to show that the obligation is one which is imposed by law in all cases where the acts are purported to be done on the faith of an agreement which is supposed to be but is not a binding contract between the parties.   Vaughan Williams, L.J., in the course of his judgment referred to *Nicholson* v. *Bradfield Union*[1], and said that the ground of the decision in that case, as he understood it, was that the law raised an implied contract by the corporate body to pay for the goods in question in that case.   In my judgment, the obligation to pay reasonable remuneration for the work done when there is no binding contract between the parties is imposed by a rule of law, and not by an inference of fact arising from the acceptance of services or goods.   It is one of the cases referred to in books on contracts as obligations arising *quasi ex contractu*, of which a well-known instance is a claim based on money had and received. Although I do not hold that the decision of the Court in *Ex parte Birkenshaw*[2] was wrong, I think that the passage I read from the judgment is not a correct statement of the law.

I accordingly think that the defendants must pay on the basis of a *quantum meruit* not only for the services rendered after December 31, 1930, and before the date of the invalid agreement, but also for the services after that date.   I think the appeal should be allowed, and judgment given for such a sum as shall be found to be due on the basis of a *quantum meruit* in respect of all services rendered by the plaintiff to the company until he was dismissed.   The defendants seem to me to be in a dilemma.   If the contract was an effective contract by the company, they would be bound to pay the remuneration provided for in the contract.   If, on the other hand, the contract was a nullity and not binding either on the plaintiff or the defendants, there would be nothing to prevent the inference which the law draws from the performance by the plaintiff of services to the company, and the company's acceptance of such services, which, if they had not been performed by the plaintiff, they would have had to get some other agent to carry out.

The appeal will be allowed, with costs here and below.   There must be, of course, some kind of reference to ascertain the amount.

GREENE, L.J., delivered judgment to the same effect, and TALBOT, J., concurred.

---

[1] (1866), L. R. 1 Q. B. 620.   [2] [1904] 2 K. B. 327.